HUMAN RIGHTS IN PRIVATE LAW

Human Rights in Private Law

Edited by

DANIEL FRIEDMANN

and

DAPHNE BARAK-EREZ

·HART·
PUBLISHING

OXFORD—PORTLAND OREGON
2001

Hart Publishing
Oxford and Portland, Oregon

Published in North America (US and Canada) by
Hart Publishing c/o
International Specialized Book Services
5804 NE Hassalo Street
Portland, Oregon
97213-3644
USA

Distributed in the Netherlands, Belgium and Luxembourg by
Intersentia, Churchillaan 108
B2900 Schoten
Antwerpen
Belgium

Hart Publishing is a specialist legal publisher based in Oxford, England.
To order further copies of this book or to request a list of other
publications please write to:

Hart Publishing, Salter's Boatyard, Folly Bridge,
Abingdon Road, Oxford OX1 4LB
Telephone: +44 (0)1865 245533 or Fax: +44 (0)1865 794882
e-mail: mail@hartpub.co.uk
WEBSITE: http//www.hartpub.co.uk

British Library Cataloguing in Publication Data
Data Available
ISBN 1–84113–213–6 (cloth)

Typeset by Hope Services (Abingdon) Ltd.
Printed and bound in Great Britain on acid-free paper by
Biddles Ltd, www.biddles.co.uk

Acknowledgments

This collection of articles by scholars from six countries (England, Germany, the United States, Canada, South Africa and Israel) originated at a conference held at the Faculty of Law of Tel-Aviv University in May 2000, under the auspices of the Minerva Center for Human Rights. We are grateful to the contributors and to those who attended the conference and chaired the sessions, as well as to the Minerva Center for its support. We are particularly grateful to our students who helped us in the editing process. Gal Levita acted as our deputy editor and offered invaluable help in the various stages of editing. Adi Aron, Nissim Gez, Hadassa Greenberg and Limor Heled were dedicated and greatly assisted us in preparing the book for publication. We would also like to thank Ms. Dana Rothman for assistance in the English editing and Ms. Yael Amitz-Lev for her administrative assistance.

DANIEL FRIEDMANN   DAPHNE BARAK-EREZ

Contents

viii   *Contents*

Contributors

Aharon Barak, President of the Supreme Court, Israel

Daphne Barak-Erez, Associate Professor and Vice Dean, Faculty of Law, Tel-Aviv University, Israel

Hugh Beale, Professor of Law, Warwick University, and Law Commissioner, England

Peter Benson, Professor of Law, University of Toronto, Canada

Roger Brownsword, Professor of Law and Head of the Department of Law, University of Sheffield, England

Reinhard Ellger, Max-Planck-Institut für Ausländisches und Internationales Privatrecht, Hamburg, Germany

Anton Fagan, Lecturer, University of Cape Town, South Africa

Daniel Friedmann, Danielle Rubinstein Professor of Comparative Private Law, Tel-Aviv University, Israel

Ofer Grosskopf, Lecturer, The College of Management, Israel

Andreas Heldrich, Professor of Law, Rector, University of Munich, Germany

Ewan McKendrick, Professor of English Private Law, University of Oxford, Fellow of Lady Margaret Hall, England

Guy Mundlak, Senior Lecturer, Tel Aviv University, Israel

Nicola Pittam, Law Commission, England

Todd D. Rakoff, Byrne Professor of Administrative Law and Dean of the J.D. Program, Harvard University Law School, USA

Gebhard M. Rehm, University of Munich, Germany

Amnon Reichman, University of Toronto, Canada

Christian Starck, Professor of Law, Chair of Public Law, Georg-August-University, Göttingen, Germany

Ernest J. Weinrib, University Professor and Cecil A. Wright Professor of Law, University of Toronto, Canada

Lorraine E. Weinrib, Professor of Law, University of Toronto, Canada

Abbreviations

AG	Amtsgericht (Magistrate's Court)
BAGE	Entscheidungen des Bundesarbeitsgerichts (Decisions of the German Federal Labour Court)
Bd	Band (Volume)
BGB	Bürgerliches Gesetzbuch (German Civil Code)
BGBl	Bundesgesetzblatt (Official Journal of Federal Statutes)
BGE	Entscheidungen des schweizerischen Bundesgericht (Decisions of the Swiss Federal Court)
BGHZ	Entscheidungen des Bundesgerichtshofes in Zivilsachen (Decisions of the German Supreme Court in civil matters)
BRAK-Mitt	*Mitteilungen der Bundesrechtsanwaltskammer* (Federal Bar Journal)
BverfG	Bundesverfassungsgericht (Federal Constitutional Court)
BverfGE	Entscheidungen des BverfG (Decisions of the Federal Constitutional Court)
Col	Column
ECHR	European Convention of Human Rights and Fundamental Freedoms
ECtHR	European Court of Human Rights
EMRK	Europäische Konvention zum Schutze der Menschenrechte und der Grundfreiheiten (ECHR)
EuGRZ	*Europäische Grundrechte-Zeitschrift*
FamRZ	*Zeitschrift für das gesamte Familienrecht*
FH	Further Hearing (Supreme Court of Israel)
GG	Grundgesetz (Basic Law—German Constitution)
HC	High Court (Israel)
JuS	Juristische Schulung
JZ	*Juristenzeitung*
LG	Landgericht (County Court)
LSI	Laws of the State of Israel
NLC	National Labour Court (Israel)
NJW	*Neue Juristische Wochenschrift*
NJW–RR	Neue Juristische Wochenschrift, Rechtsprechungsreport
OLG	Oberlandesgericht (German Court of Appeal)
PD	Decisions of the Supreme Court of Israel
PDA	Decisions of the National Labour Court (Israel)
RabelsZ	*Rabels Zeitschrift für ausländisches und internationales Privatrecht*
RGBl	Reichsgesetzblatt

Table of Cases

1

Introduction

DANIEL FRIEDMANN AND DAPHNE BARAK-EREZ

I

HUMAN RIGHTS WERE originally conceived as rights and freedoms *vis-à-vis* the State and other public authorities. Their very fundamental purpose was to protect the individual against the omnipotent State with its vast powers of detention, expropriation and censorship. The major function of human rights thus was to mitigate the imbalance between two unequal parties, the public authority and the individual. In this respect, human rights constitute an integral part of public law.

The position of private parties *vis-à-vis* each other is, of course, completely different. Private law, which regulates their legal relationship, is predicated in practically all modern societies on the theory of equality before the law.[1] The imbalance in legal power, which characterises public law, does not exist in private law. This means, for example, that if A injures B or damages his property, his liability towards B will be determined by precisely the same rules that would apply in the opposite case in which it is B who injures A or his property.[2] This equality is, of course, formal in nature. It relates merely to the legal rights and freedoms of the parties. It does not eliminate the possibility of an imbalance between the parties in other respects, such as their relative wealth, economic power or mental ability. Moreover, equality before the law does not mean that the same rules serve A and B in an equal manner. Rules aimed at protecting property against damage or misappropriation may be advantageous to A, a large property owner, whereas the same rules may be of no benefit to B who has no property. Rules imposing liability for damage caused by a certain activity

---

[1] This concept has a long tradition dating back to the Old Testament, which expressly prescribes, "Thou shall not prefer the person of the poor, nor favour the person of the mighty; but in righteousness shall thou judge thy neighbour" (Leviticus 19: 15). Over the course of history, there have, of course, been many societies that discriminated against women and have made class distinctions in terms of the various right and duties of the members of each class. But modern Western societies are committed to the ancient biblical idea of equality before the law; the Fourteenth Amendment to the US Constitution, for example, provides that no State shall deny any person "the equal protection of the laws".

[2] There may be some exceptions to this rule, for example, if one of the parties is a minor. But even this type of exception is based on the principle of equality, since it applies to both parties when they are under-age.

affect those who engage in this activity and those likely to be injured by it in dia-metrically opposed directions. Limitation on liability will benefit one group and be detrimental to the other, while expansion of liability will lead to the opposite result. There thus is a need to balance the interests of the groups involved.

Indeed, private law has always recognised that the rights and freedoms of one person must necessarily be limited by those of others and that the interests of society's members must be balanced in a way that appears fair and reasonable. The law of nuisance requires that the utility of the defendant's activity be weighed against the harm and inconvenience of that activity to others.[3] The public interest in the activity is also taken into account.[4] The law of negligence is similarly regarded as providing a balance between the actor and his potential victims. The fundamental concept developed in the nineteenth century that lia-bility ought to be based on fault and that there should be no liability in its absence was predicated on the rationale that "a man must act somehow" and "the public generally profits by individual activity".[5]

Courts and scholars have frequently exalted the specific rights and freedoms recognised under private law. Until recently, this was done without invoking human rights terminology. Referring to freedom of contract, Sir George Jessel declared that, "contracts when entered freely and voluntarily shall be held sacred and enforced by Courts of justice".[6] Today, however, freedom of con-tract can be considered a feature of the human right to dignity.[7] Sir George Jessel did not use this term. He chose another, no less powerful, image to con-vey the importance of contractual freedom: he described it as "sacred".

Some 100 years before Sir George Jessel made this statement, Lord Mansfield had to contend with the case of James Somerset,[8] a slave who had been taken from Africa to Virginia and sold there to Charles Stewart. In 1769 Stewart took Somerset, his slave, to England. Some time later, Somerset ran away. Stewart had him captured and placed on a vessel on the River Thames, intending to take him to Jamaica to be sold. An application for habeas corpus was made, and the question arose whether Stewart, who had bought the slave in accordance with the law of sale that was valid in Virginia and Jamaica, owned him and was enti-tled to transport him from England. Lord Mansfield was well aware not only of the importance of the principle involved, but also of its economic implications.[9]

---

[3] J. Fleming, *The Law of Torts* (9th edn., Sydney, LBC Information Services, 1998) 464.

[4] *Tipping* v. *St Helen's Smelting Co* (1863) B & S 608, 122 ER 588, XI HLC 642, 11 ER 1483, discussed in A. Brian Simpson, *Leading Cases in the Common Law* (Oxford, Clarendon Press, 1995) chap. 7: "Victorian Judges and the Problem of Social Cost".

[5] O.W. Holmes, *The Common Law* (Boston, Mass., Little, Brown & Co, 1881) 95.

[6] *Printing & Numerical Co* v. *Sampson* (1975) LR 19 Eq 462, 465.

[7] R. Brownsword, chap. 9 this vol.

[8] *Somerset* v. *Stewart* (1772) Lofft 1, 98 ER 499. The case is also reported in 20 St Tr 1 with addenda at 1369. See also A. Denning, *Landmarks in the Law* (London, Butterworths, 1984) 214–19.

[9] In the course of the argument, Lord Mansfield was told that there were some 14,000 to 15,000 slaves in England whose cost was £50 each, so that the total loss to the owners if the slaves were released would amount to some £700,000.

The parties to this case—as in most cases concerning slavery—were private parties, and the State was not directly involved. It was a pure case of private law.[10] Although Lord Mansfield did not refer to human rights, he did state that slavery is "odious", prohibited under the law of England, "and therefore the black must be discharged".[11] Lord Campbell attributed to Mansfield the eloquent statement that "the air of England is too pure" for a slave to breathe,[12] but these words were actually taken from the argument made by Francis Hargrave.[13]

Thus, private law has always been concerned with human rights, though without actually using this term, even in the context of such mundane topics as assault, nuisance, libel and negligence. Those specialising in this field may find themselves in a position similar to that of M. Jourdain in Molière's comedy *Le Bourgeois Gentilhomme*, who was greatly surprised to learn that he had been speaking prose all his life even when asking for his slippers or nightcap. Hence, the transformation we are witnessing may be considered merely terminological in nature and traditional issues will simply appear in the guise of human rights. However, the language we employ is not merely a tool to convey thoughts: it is a process that affects our analysis and conceptions. Hence, a change in terminology may have a more profound effect than a mere replacement of one word with another.

Moreover, while the introduction of human rights into private law does carry with it many concepts that are already well established in private law, it also brings with it values to which private law has hitherto attributed little weight. Private law will have to adapt to these values and, consequently, is likely to undergo a considerable transformation.

Another feature of this process relates to the potential transformation of human rights values within the framework of private law. Human rights were developed in the public law sphere against the background of the great imbalance that exists between the State with its vast legal powers and the individual who seeks protection against their abuse. When human rights concepts are transplanted into the private law environment, where equality before the law is the governing rule, they have to be modified and adapted.

II

The present collection of essays analyses from comparative and theoretical perspectives the application of human rights in private law and the practical implications of that application. The book is divided into five parts, with the

[10] See also T. Rakoff, chap. 12 this vol.

[11] Lofft at 19, 98 ER at 510.

[12] John Lord Campbell, *Lives of the Chief Justices of England* (London, John Murray, 1849), ii, 418–19.

[13] Lofft at 2, 98 ER at 500. See Denning, *supra* n.8, at 219. It seems that Hargrave took these words from a French source, which, not surprisingly, referred to the mere breathing of the air in France or the touching of its soil as liberating the slave. See 20 St Tr at 12–13 and 1369.

chapters arranged according to two categories: those relating to general theories and approaches regarding the application of human rights in private law and those that discuss the influence of human rights on specific branches of private law. However, it should be noted that most of the chapters deal with topics that are relevant to more than one part of the book.

Part I of the book, entitled "Constitutional Values and Private Law—The Theoretical Framework", contains chapters that discuss different models for introducing human rights into private law. Most of the constitutions and legislation that enjoy constitutional status discussed in these chapters do not include express provisions regarding their applicability to private parties. This is generally true with regard to the German Basic Law, discussed by Christian Starck, Andreas Heldrich and Gebhard Rehm; the Canadian Charter, discussed by Lorraine Weinrib and Ernest Weinrib; and the Israeli Basic Laws, discussed by Aharon Barak. Against this background, the chapters present theories on the application of human rights in private law "indirectly", especially by means of "blanket clauses" and the interpretation of values that are relevant to private law. In contrast, the new South African Constitution, discussed by Anton Fagan, explicitly recognises its binding effect on private parties.

The opening chapter, "Constitutional Human Rights and Private Law" by Aharon Barak, analyses from a comparative perspective the various models for the application of human rights in the private sphere. Barak supports the adoption of a strengthened indirect approach, which, in his view, is most consistent with the values expressed in human rights legislation. The tools facilitating the application of this model already exist in private law in the form of such general concepts as "good faith", "reasonableness" and "public policy".

This chapter also examines the mechanisms required to balance the conflicting constitutional human rights in private law, focusing mainly on examples from the law of contracts. Barak argues that such a balancing should be sensitive to the difference between the conflict of values in the realm of public law and that conflict in private law, taking into consideration that in the latter, the balance involves the rights of two private parties.

In their chapter "Constitutional Values and Private Law in Canada", Lorraine Weinrib and Ernest Weinrib describe the potential influence of the constitutional values enshrined in the Canadian Charter of Rights and Freedoms against the background of judicial denial of the direct application of human rights legislation in the private sphere. The chapter explores how constitutional values might be integrated into private law and guide its development in a manner consistent with constitutional values and thereby transform it. The authors suggest that the Canadian Supreme Court has already taken the decisive step of putting courts under the obligation to develop the common law consistently with Charter values. The consequence is that Charter values are now, in principle, admissible in any private law context. This gives rise to the apprehension of a detrimental effect on the individual freedoms cherished by private law, but this difficulty can be mitigated by sensitive application of the principle of proportionality. Moreover, the Canadian Charter of Rights and Freedoms, despite its unique features, nonetheless belongs to the family of constitutions with similar legal frameworks and which present similar challenges. It is, therefore, suggested that an inquiry into the experiences of other jurisdictions may produce useful insights into the relationship between the constitutional values and private law in Canada. Finally, the authors suggest that the idea of a free and democratic society is the broadest repository of constitutional values that must influence the development of private law in Canada.

A jurisprudential analysis of the developments in South African law is provided by Anton Fagan in his chapter "Determining the Stakes: Binding and non-Binding Bills of Rights". The chapter explains what is at stake in the choice between a bill of rights that is binding on private parties and one that is not but will nonetheless influence the development of private common law. The author suggests that this choice does not affect the private-public divide or the community's political commitments, but, rather, the justification for subjecting the development of private common law to constitutional constraints. While both binding and non-binding bills of rights equally constrain the development of private common law, each imposes a different kind of constraint. It is further argued that the answer to the question whether a community sees its bill of rights as a "framework" or a "foundation" may have implications for its choice between a binding and a non-binding bill of rights.

The next two chapters draw on the rich experience of German law in this field. In "Human Rights and Private Law in German Constitutional Development and in the Jurisdiction of the Federal Constitutional Court", Christian Starck describes the various theories regarding the application of basic rights to legal relationships between private individuals ("the third-party effect of basic rights"). He suggests that the theories of direct and indirect third-party effect in private law are not as far apart as might appear at first glance. Under both theories, there is a need to balance competing interests. Starck explores the ways in which basic rights affect rules of private law. He presents a thorough examination of German case law in various areas and shows that basic rights affect almost all branches of the law of obligations.

Andreas Heldrich and Gebhard Rehm's chapter, "Importing Constitutional Values through Blanket Clauses" presents the various views adopted by German jurists with regard to the Basic Law's impact on third parties. Heldrich and Rehm discuss the Federal Constitutional Court's decision rejecting the direct impact theory and adopting the indirect effect model. The chapter goes on to describe the mechanisms that enable the import of constitutional values into the private sphere, in particular, the interpretation of so-called "blanket clauses". The authors conclude that the case for direct applicability of basic rights in private law has, at least for now, been lost. Yet, they argue that in most cases the theory of indirect effect leads to outcomes that are quite similar to those that would be reached under the theory of direct effect, since both theories require a balancing between competing constitutional rights.

Part II of the book extends beyond the immediate boundaries of national law and explores the effect of the European Convention on Human Rights on private law. The Convention was introduced into German domestic law as early as in 1952. But for English lawyers, this is a new and provocative development, as the Convention was only recently incorporated into English law by the Human Rights Act of 1998.

In their chapter "The Impact of the Human Rights Act 1998 on English Tort and Contract Law", Hugh Beale and Nicola Pittam discuss the changes in private law which may result from the new Act. They examine the various doctrinal positions regarding the implication of the Human Rights Act in private law. The authors conclude that the Act does not have any direct horizontal effect or what has been termed "strong" indirect effect, but, rather, a "weak" indirect effect. The chapter seeks to assess the potential impact of the Convention rights on English tort law and contract law. In the field of torts, the authors address the transition from an unrestricted admission of defences like public authority immunity to their examination on a case-by-case basis in order to ensure their proportionate application. The authors argue that a similar effect of the Human Rights Act can be anticipated outside the area of public authority liability. The "weak" horizontal effect is expected to induce the courts to develop remedies against private defendants, which will lead to the development of the private equivalent of Convention rights. The Human Rights Act is also likely to affect the law of privacy and the law relating to employment contracts. However, its impact on other fields is, at present, difficult to assess.

Reinhard Ellger's chapter "The European Convention of Human Rights and Fundamental Freedoms and German Private Law", examines the effect of the European Convention of Human Rights on German private law by reference to Article 8 (protection of family life and privacy) and Article 10 (freedom of expression) of the Convention. Ellger suggests that the influence of these Articles is rather limited, though Article 8 did have an impact on a number of issues in the sphere of family law. The secondary importance of the Convention is ascribed to the fact that German private law has already been influenced by German constitutional law. The chapter also assesses the conflict between freedom of contract and human rights. It points out that human rights has the potential to limit freedom of contract and argues that such limitation may be justified in cases of market failure.

Parts III, IV and V of the book deal with the effect of human rights on specific areas of private law. Part III ("Contract and Property Law") examines the dilemmas raised by the conflict between the classical premises of freedom of contract and property rights and human rights values. Roger Brownsword's "Freedom of Contract, Human Rights and Human Dignity" explores the potential impact of the 1998 Human Rights Act on the law of contract. Brownsword suggests that the respect for human dignity should have important bearing on the way in which freedom of contract is to be understood and applied in the twenty-first century. He argues that there is need for caution in imposing limitations on freedom of contract and, in the absence of "good reasons", it ought not to be restricted. Values represented by human rights upheld by a given legal system should be incorporated into the "good reasons" that provide a legitimate basis for restricting contractual freedom. Brownsword argues that freedom of contract is a particular expression of the dignity-based human right to individual autonomy, but that there are also good dignity-based reasons for restricting contractual freedom. The chapter sketches two competing conceptions of the elusive notion of human dignity—human dignity as empowerment and human dignity as constraint—the one supporting individual autonomy and justifying the enforcement of contracts, and the other serving as a ground for limiting freedom of contract.

The other two chapters in this part of the book explore the effect of the right to equality on individual autonomy. Peter Benson's chapter "Equality of Opportunity and Private Law" discusses the power to discriminate in private law. Benson examines the question whether the juridical concept of rights and obligations in private law entails or even presupposes a notion of equality of opportunity that applies between individuals in their private transactions. He further examines the question whether private law offers a normative environment for a doctrine of formal equality of opportunity. Benson concludes that these questions should be answered in the negative. He argues, however, that the common law, in appropriate circumstances, has traditionally recognised and enforced rights that are beyond private law's juridical concept of rights and that a requirement of non-discrimination is included in this category. Consequently, courts can enforce non-discrimination requirements and yet stay within the boundaries of their competence. Such a requirement exists as an obligation owed to the public in circumstances in which property is devoted to the public or to public use. Benson also concludes that while constitutional rights might play a role in the application of the common law, they do not change the fundamental and distinct character of private law.

Amnon Reichman's chapter "Property Rights, Public Policy and the Limits of the Legal Power to Discriminate" offers another perspective on the issue of discrimination in private law. Reichman examines the nature of property rights in order to determine whether the cluster of powers and rights attributed to the concept of ownership includes the power to bar members of certain groups from entering a place of commerce. The chapter explores the possible rationale of common law's already recognised exceptions to the exercise of full ownership power in an attempt to offer a general approach regarding the limits imposed upon the exercise of property rights. The chapter further examines the doctrine of public policy and its application in cases involving property rights, suggesting that this doctrine is a necessary component of the legal structure that lies at the core of civil society. From this claim follows the argument that common law itself is the proper source of non-discrimination norms.

Part IV of the book is dedicated to labour law. Todd Rakoff's chapter "Enforcement of Employment Contracts and the Anti-Slavery Norm" explores the connection between the anti-slavery norm, the most basic of all human rights, and the treatment of employment contracts in the law of the United States. The chapter demonstrates that the anti-slavery concept continues to exert its influence on modern employment contracts, yet its application requires considerable adaptation. The broader conclusion is that a decision directly to apply a human rights norm in private law does not necessarily lead to clear results and is usually only the beginning of an inquiry as to its potential implications.

Guy Mundlak's chapter "Human Rights and the Employment Relationship: A Look through the Prism of Juridification" centres on the dynamics of the juridification of the employment relationship, namely, the growing tendency to resort to litigation and legal solutions in resolving differences in labour relationships. The chapter focuses on the Israeli experience in the field of labour law, indicating that a similar process has occurred in most developed countries. Mundlak points out that this development results from the decline of organised labour and the failure of social and economic forces to regulate management–employee relationships. He argues that although the juridification phenomenon has many problematic aspects, it is justified in so far as it seeks to protect human rights in the context of the employment relationship. In the absence of other social and economic institutions that can promote the protection of the individual worker's human rights, legal protection becomes absolutely necessary.

Part V, which concludes the book, is devoted to the effect of human rights on the law of torts. Ewan McKendrick's chapter, "Human Rights and the Law of Negligence: Re-Considering Osman", discusses the potential impact of the 1998 Human Rights Act on the English law of negligence, through a detailed analysis of the *Osman* v. *United Kingdom*[14] case. McKendrick points out that the decision weakened the prospects of defendants having negligence claims against them struck out on the ground that no duty of care is owed or on the ground of immunity. The *Osman* decision also appears to have introduced the concept of gross negligence into the English law of torts. *Osman*'s influence seems not to be confined to cases of physical injury, and its reasoning may extend to claims for recovery of economic loss. The resulting expansion of liability in torts of public authorities may have significant impact on their functioning and on public expenditure.

Ofer Grosskopf's chapter, "Horizontal Equality and the Law of Torts", explores the tension between the law of torts and the concept of equality. It discusses the non-egalitarian assumption underlying classical tort law that protects victims of certain types of accidents but disregards other victims who suffer similar damage or incapacity who have no cause of action for their misfortune. The chapter presents a distinction between "vertical equality" and "horizontal equality". Vertical equality centres on the immediate parties to a tortious event and lies at the core of classical tort law. In contrast, the concept of horizontal

---

[14] [1999] FLR 193.

equality, which is completely alien to tort law, compares the position of all those who suffer similar damage or injury. The chapter predicts that if the trend of social legislation towards horizontal equality continues, we will witness the decline of tort law in the realm of personal injuries and the flourishing of private and public causes of action that are directed at controlling tortfeasors' behaviour. The function of private tort law will thus shift from loss transfer and loss spreading to behaviour control.

The book concludes with Gebhard Rehm's "Privacy in the Digital Age: Vanishing into Cyberspace?" The chapter presents the grave risks posed to the right to privacy that derive from the rapid technological developments of the past decades. More specifically, it concentrates on one aspect of the right to privacy that has been termed by the German Federal Constitutional Court the right to informational self-determination. This right is threatened today more than ever by private actors who have the power to collect personal information on other individuals. In this respect, the field of privacy is illustrative of the importance of protecting human rights not only against public authorities but also against private parties. Examining the traditional rationales that justify the protection of privacy, the chapter evaluates their relevance and applicability to present circumstances and presents different theoretical models of regulation that can balance the competing interests involved.

Part I

Constitutional Values and Private Law— The Theoretical Framework

2

Constitutional Human Rights and Private Law

AHARON BARAK*

HUMAN RIGHTS OPERATE both vertically and horizontally. They operate vertically when applying between the State and the individual and horizontally when applying between private persons. Traditionally, common law human rights have operated in both directions, applying to both the State and private parties.[1] However, now that human rights have been constitutionalised worldwide, enshrined in constitutional bills of rights and charters, questions abound as to the scope of their application. They clearly apply vertically, restricting the power of the State *vis-à-vis* the individual. But do they also apply horizontally in the context of relations between private parties? Put another way, are legislative human rights directed towards the State only or has a "privatisation" of human rights occurred as well? Under the German tradition, the question is the *Drittwirkung der Grundrechte*[2]: do constitutional human rights apply to third parties—namely, individual persons (the second party being the State)—directly or indirectly?

Determining the applicability of constitutional human rights in the sphere of private law is an issue of central importance, which has arisen in most legal systems.[3] Though legislation in some countries explicitly addresses the possibility

---

* This chap. is based on my earlier work on constitutional human rights and private law. See A. Barak, "Constitutional Human Rights and Private Law" (1996) 3 *Rev. Const. Stud.* 218, and A. Barak, "Constitutional Human Rights and Private Law" in A.M. Rabello and P. Sarcevic (eds.), *Freedom of Contract and Constitutional Law* (Jerusalem, The Hebrew University of Jerusalem, Sacher Institute for Legislative Research and Comparative Law, 1998), 105.

[1] In Israel, for example, common law human rights have been applied to both the government and private parties.

[2] *Drittwirkung der Grundrechte* can be translated as the third-party effect of basic rights. See further text accompanying *infra* nn. 11–14.

[3] There is a great deal of literature on this topic. See, for example, M.J. Horan, "Contemporary Constitutionalism and Legal Relationships between Individuals" (1976) 25 *Int'l. & Comp. L Q* 848; A. Clapham, "The 'Drittwirkung' of the Convention" in R. St J. MacDonald, F. Matscher and H. Petzold (eds.), *The European System for the Protection of Human Rights* (Dordrecht, M. Nijhoff, 1993) 163; J.H. Garvey, "Private Power and the Constitution" (1993) 10 *Const. Comm.* 311; R.S. Kay, "The State Action Doctrine, The Public-Private Distinction, and the Independence of Constitutional Law" (1993) 10 *Const. Comm.* 331; U. Scheuner, "Fundamental Rights and the Protection of the Individual against Social Groups and Powers in the Constitutional System of the Federal Republic of Germany" in R. Cassin (ed.), *Amicorum Discipulorumque Liber* (Paris,

of horizontal application, most constitutions are silent or remain ambiguous on the issue, leaving the determination to the judiciary. This chapter explores the four most popular models of application of these rights in private law: the direct application model; the non-application model; the indirect application model; and the application to the judiciary model. The argument presented is that the adoption of a strengthened and augmented indirect approach is the most consistent with the goals supporting the human rights ideology: respect for equality, dignity and individual autonomy. Moreover, the tools for facilitating the application of this model already exist in private law in the form of general concepts such as "good faith", "reasonableness" and "public policy".

I. MODELS FOR THE APPLICATION OF CONSTITUTIONAL HUMAN RIGHTS IN
PRIVATE LAW

1. Direct application model

Under the direct application model, constitutional human rights apply directly in private law. Human rights protect the individual not only against the State, but also against private parties. Under this model, a private person is likely to obtain a result in court against another individual that would not be available otherwise. For example, if A shouts and disturbs a meeting, he infringes the constitutional human rights of B, a fellow participant, to associate freely and will be held liable to him.

(a) *Arguments in Favour of Direct Application*

Adoption of the direct application model depends on the language of the relevant constitutional provision. In some countries,[4] the formulation of the relevant provision explicitly mandates only vertical application of constitutional human rights and, consequently, the direct application model cannot be adopted. More often, however, such provisions are drafted in broad language that leaves unclear their scope of application in private law. In Israel, for example, the Basic Law: Freedom of Occupation provides that "every citizen or resident of the State is entitled to engage in every occupation, profession or business".[5] Under this formulation, direct application is linguistically possible.

Editions A Pedone, 1971), iii, 253 ; J.D.B. Mitchell, "Some Aspects of the Protection of the Individuals Against Private Power in the United Kingdom" in Cassin, *ibid.*, at 235; O. Espersen, "Human Rights and Relations between Individuals" in Cassin, *ibid.*, at 177; C.W. Summers, "The Privatization of Personal Freedoms and the Enrichment of Democracy—Some Lessons from Labor Law"[1986] *U. Ill. L. Rev.* 689.

[4] An example is provided by the First Amendment to the US Constitution, which states: "Congress shall make no law respecting an establishment of religion, or prohibiting the free exercise thereof; or abridging the freedom of speech, or of the press; or of the right of the people peaceably to assemble, and to petition the Government for a redress of grievances".

[5] Basic Law: Freedom of Occupation, 1994, 47 LSI 90, §3.

Although the textual arguments enable direct application, they do not mandate it. There are, however, substantive arguments supporting this possibility. First, the danger to human rights emanates from both the State and non-state bodies. Indeed, there are those who maintain that private parties pose a greater threat to human rights in democratic regimes than the State does.[6] Therefore, the courts need a general standard that spans the public and private sectors. Secondly, human rights are essentially "liberties" grounded in the individual's autonomy of will and in the unity of the individual and his dignity. These liberties are likely to be infringed not only by state action but also through acts of private parties. Finally, there is the pragmatic argument that the true alternative to direct application is non-application. If non-application is inappropriate, judges will invent different models based on difficult and undesirable legal distinctions. It is preferable to take the "clean" and clear path from the outset and go "all the way" by recognising the direct application model explicitly.

(b) *Adoption of Direct Application Model in Switzerland and Germany*

Switzerland has adopted the direct application model.[7] The language of the constitutions of several cantons explicitly mandates application of this model;[8] in the remaining cantons and on the federal level, direct application has been adopted by means of interpretation.[9] Accordingly, freedom of religion exists not only *vis-à-vis* the State, but also in the context of relations between private individuals. Likewise, anyone who participates in a meeting has the right not to have his freedom of association infringed through vocal disturbance by another person.[10]

As mentioned above, the *Drittwirkung* theory originated in Germany. In Germany, the human rights set forth in the Basic Law (*Grundgesetz*) apply not only to relations between an individual and the State in the sphere of public law, but also to relations between private parties in private law. Opinions differ on whether the application of these rights in private law is direct (without

---

[6] See R.A. MacDonald, "Postscript and Prelude—The Jurisprudence of the Charter: Eight Theses" (1982) 4 *Sup. Ct. Rev.* 321, 347. ("In our day, the most grievous and most frequent abuses of civil liberties occur in the exercise of private power. The occasions for discriminatory state action are both comparatively few and subject to relatively formalized procedures for their exercise, when contrasted with an employer's power to dismiss, a landlord's power to exclude the needy, or an entrepreneur's refusal to provide services".)

[7] See J.P. Muller, *Elemente einer Schweizerischen Grundrechtstheorie* (Bern, Stempfli, 1982); U. Haefelin and W. Haller, *Schweizerisches Bundesstaatsrecht* (Zürich, Schulthess Polygraphischer Verlag, 1988) 344. This is the prevailing view. For criticism of this view, see J.F. Auberet, *Traité de droit constitutionnel suisse* (Neuchatel, Editions Ides et Calendes, 1967–82) iii (Bd II, 2967) 626.

[8] See Constitution of the Canton of Jura, para. 14(2), which states that every person must use his basic rights in a manner that respects the basic rights of others.

[9] However, the 1977 Proposed Amendment to the Federal Constitution, para. 25, contains an explicit provision on the matter.

[10] See 4 BGE 434 *et seq.* and 86 II BGE 365 *et seq.*

an intermediary) or indirect (though an intermediary).[11] According to the proponents of direct application, who are in the minority, constitutional human rights influence the legal system in its entirety.[12] Human rights are intended to protect the individual against extremist powers. Though these powers were traditionally held by the State, today they may be in the hands of non-state actors as well. Of course, in relations between private parties, a conflict may arise between different human rights. For example, one person's freedom of contract may conflict with the freedom of expression of another person. Such clashes are resolved by balancing the conflicting constitutional rights directly in private law.

Several decisions handed down by German courts illustrate this approach. In one case, A had handed over to an insurance company a report on B's health. The court ruled that B was entitled to relief on the ground that A's action had breached B's constitutional right to dignity and personal development, protected under paragraphs 1 and 2 of the Basic Law.[13] In its reasoning, the court stated that the human rights set forth in the Basic Law "secure a basic right, which obtains not only regarding the State and its organizations, but also in private law relationships against every person". In another instance, the plaintiff's picture was published in connection with drugs, leading him to sue the distributor. Under German private law, in such circumstances the plaintiff is entitled to damages only if he can prove pecuniary harm. Though this type of harm was not proven, the Supreme Court (*Bundesgerichtshof*) held that the plaintiff was entitled to damages because his constitutional right to dignity and personal development had been violated.[14]

(c) *Arguments against Direct Application*

There are strong arguments against the direct application model. From a textual perspective, some constitutions contain human rights provisions that are aimed solely at the State. For example, Israel's Basic Law: Human Dignity and Freedom provides, "[t]here is to be no burdening and no limiting of a person's liberty by imprisonment, arrest and extradition or in any other manner".[15]

---

[11] Nipperdey, one of the great German jurists, and the Supreme Court of Labour which he headed, adopted the direct application model. See L. Enneccerus and H.C. Nipperdey, *Allgemeiner Teil des Bürgerlichen Rechts* (15th edn., Tübingen, Mohr, 1959) i, 93; and K.M. Lewan, "The Significance of Constitutional Rights for Private Law: Theory and Practice in West Germany" (1968) 17 *Int'l. & Comp. L Q* 571. Leisner also deals a great deal with this topic: see W. Leisner, *Grundrecht und Privatrecht* (Munich, C.H. Beck, 1960). Note, also, that Durig and the Constitutional Supreme Court (*Bundesverfassungsgericht*) adopted the indirect model. See Lewan, *ibid.*, at 576. See also P. Quint, "Free Speech and Private Law in German Constitutional Theory" (1989) 48 *Md. L Rev.* 247; and also D.P. Kommers, *The Constitutional Jurisprudence of the Federal Republic of Germany* (Durham, Duke University Press, 1989).

[12] See H. van Mangoldt and F. Klein, *Das Bonner Grundgesetz* (3rd edn., Munich, F. Vahlen, 1985) i, 132.

[13] See 24 BGHZ 72, 76.

[14] See 26 BGHZ 349.

[15] Basic Law: Human Dignity and Liberty, 1992, 45 LSI 150, §5.

"Extradition" is a government act. "Imprisonment" and "arrest" also probably refer to government acts, although unlawful arrest by a private person is conceivable. Similarly, "limitations clauses" appear alongside the recognition of "open" human rights. These "limitations clauses" apparently do not encompass relations between private individuals. Since recognition of human rights between private parties without any recognition of corresponding limitations is impossible, constitutional human rights should apply solely *vis-à-vis* the State. In the same vein, if constitutional human rights grant private parties rights *vis-à-vis* one another, they must also impose obligations on those parties. According to some views, however, only explicit legislation can limit or negate human rights.[16] Finally, some constitutions include "respect clauses" according to which "every authority" of the State is obligated to respect the basic rights set forth in them.[17] The implication of such "respect clauses" is that constitutional human rights are directed at the State and not private parties.

In addition to these textual arguments, there are numerous substantive arguments against direct application. First, constitutional treatment of human rights is always *vis-à-vis* the State.[18] Indeed, human rights were given "super-legislative" (i.e., constitutional) normative status precisely because the legislative and executive branches are likely to infringe them. Human rights in relations between private parties require no special constitutional protection, because regular legislation or common law suffices. Secondly, bills of rights and constitutional charters are designed to grant rights to individuals. Because human rights necessarily limit one another, if we apply constitutional human rights to relations between private parties, we will at the same time have to negate them. This result is untenable. Finally, because one person's right is likely to infringe that of another, direct application requires a balancing of competing human rights. Where constitutional provisions do not contain limitations clauses regarding the restriction of one person's right arising from the right of another, the obvious result is that judges will have to create judicial limitations clauses. Thus, judges will acquire enormous constitutional power without any concomitant constitutional guidance.[19]

---

[16] See HC 252/77, *Bevugnee* v. *City of Tel Aviv* 32 (1) PD 404, 415 (Hebrew); HC 337/81, *Mitrani* v. *Minister of Transportation* 37(3) PD 337 (Hebrew).

[17] See, for example, Basic Law: Freedom of Occupation, 1994, 47 LSI 90, §5; Basic Law: Human Dignity and Liberty, 1992, 45 LSI 150, §11. See also The Canadian Charter of Rights and Freedoms, §32.

[18] See K. Swinton, "Application of the Canadian Charter of Rights and Freedoms" in W. Tarnopolsky and G. Beaudoin (eds.), *The Canadian Charter of Rights and Freedoms* (Toronto, Carswell, 1982) 41.

[19] This argument is strengthened by the fact that when most legislatures sought to limit human rights against the government, they set forth "limitations clauses". The absence of a "limitations clause" in relations between private parties militates against the balancing of human rights set forth in bills of rights or charters. In the absence of such a balancing, there is no possibility of applying constitutional human rights to relations between private parties.

2. Non-application model

Under the non-application model, human rights are applicable only in public law. They are directed at the State and the State alone. In the realm of private law, the regular laws continue to apply as they did before human rights were granted constitutional status. For example, if A makes a contract with B limiting his own freedom of occupation and later breaches that contract, B has the usual remedies against A, subject only to the claim that the contract is contrary to public policy. This claim was available before human rights were granted constitutional status and remains available in its original form.

(a) *Arguments for Non-Application*

The textual and substantive arguments against direct application are the same arguments that support the non-application model,[20] the reason being that the non-application model is the complete opposite of the direct application model. The non-application model is predicated on the theory that a formal constitution is intended to protect private individuals against the State. The relationship between private parties must be regulated, as it has been from time immemorial, by private law.[21] Indeed, under this model, the end result of the application of constitutional human rights in the private sphere is the infringement of human rights. After all, what would become of the individual's autonomy of will, particularly with regard to freedom of contract, if the constitutional provisions regarding human rights were to apply to relations between private parties? Would a testator be allowed to discriminate among heirs or a seller among buyers?

Though balancing the various human rights might appear to solve the problems supporters of non-application find inherent to application models, proponents of non-application reject it on the ground that a constitution does not set forth a balancing formula for relationships between private parties. This aspect is especially problematic in light of the fact that most constitutions do provide balancing formulas where the State is concerned. Would the balancing formula in the private sphere be identical to that which applies between the State and private individuals? And if the balancing formula regarding conflicts between private parties were to be different, what would its substance be? These questions are particularly troubling for proponents of the non-application model, because in their view the argument that courts should establish a balancing formula of their own accord leads to the infringement of human rights.

Accordingly, where relations between private parties are at issue, proponents of non-application argue that private law and the accepted scales therein apply

---

[20] See *supra* text accompanying nn.15–19.
[21] See Swinton, *supra* n.18; F. Raday, " 'Privatization of Human Rights' and Abuse of Power" (1994) 23 *Mishpatim* 21 (Hebrew).

and that they must not be influenced by the constitutional provisions that govern in the public sphere. Of course, the borderline between public and private law is neither clear nor impenetrable. Indeed, reciprocal relations exist between public law and private law. Consequently, in consolidating common law private law doctrines, judges will consider public law. Such consideration, however, merely reflects the need to survey the entire structure of society, its laws and opinions and is not based on the application, direct or indirect, of constitutional provisions regarding human rights in the private law sphere.

(b) *Adoption of the Non-Application Model in Canada*

In *Dolphin Delivery*,[22] the Supreme Court of Canada adopted the non-application model. According to Justice McIntyre, human rights set forth in the Canadian Charter are directed at the State and the State alone. A decision that grants a remedy to a private party against another private party is not governed by standards of constitutional provisions. Moreover, the State's duty to respect the rights of private parties does not impose a similar obligation on the courts. Accordingly, though the court may decide that a contract that infringes human rights is contrary to public policy and therefore void, it will not do so by constitutionalising human rights. Notably, the Canadian Supreme Court's reasoning in *Dolphin* was rooted in a Charter provision that states that the Charter applies to Parliament and the Government of Canada and its provinces.[23] The rights and liberties set forth in the Charter apply to the State whether it acts in public law (as ruler) or in private law (as a private party) or whether it acts pursuant to legislation or pursuant to common law rules. In contrast, the Charter provisions do not apply to private parties in their relations with each other, whatever the source of their actions.[24]

The Supreme Court of Canada has had several occasions to reconsider *Dolphin*. Indeed, in *CBC* v. *Dagenais*,[25] the Court seemed to deviate from non-application. *Dagenais* involved a challenge to a court-ordered publication ban issued during criminal proceedings. According to the majority opinion, *Dolphin* allowed the Court to consider Charter values in the development of common law rules. In other words, the Charter was applied indirectly in *Dagenais*. However, in a subsequent case, *Hill* v. *Church of Scientology*,[26] the Court decided that it would not apply the Charter, even indirectly, to matters that were "purely private". As the case at hand involved a common law action for defamation, non-application applied. Moreover, the Court made the distinction that *Dagenais* arose in an "essentially public" context. For cases classified as

---

[22] *Retail, Wholesale and Department Store Union, Local 580* v. *Dolphin Deliver Ltd* [1986] 2 SCR 573 (hereinafter *Dolphin Deliver*). On this decision see also L. Weinrib and E. Weinrib, chap. 3 this vol.

[23] The Canadian Charter of Rights and Freedoms, §32.

[24] See P. Hogg, *Constitutional Law of Canada* (4th edn., Toronto, Carswell, 1997).

[25] *CBC* v. *Dagenais* [1994] 3 SCR 835.

[26] *Hill* v. *Church of Scientology* [1995] 2 SCR 1130.

"purely private", such as *Hill*, the Court would invoke Charter values only to influence the development of the common law. That said, the judiciary should be cautious in changing the common law and leave major changes to the legislature.[27] Accordingly, *Hill* left the common law action of defamation intact.

(c) *Arguments against Non-Application*

The arguments against non-application are the same as those raised in favour of the direct application model.[28] The danger to human rights emanates not only from the State, but also from private parties, primarily strong private parties such as big private corporations. If a small city is not allowed to discriminate because it falls within the definition of "State", why should a larger corporation be free to do so? Moreover, legislation is obviously a state action, and constitutional limitations apply to it even when its contents pertain solely to relations between private parties. But should constitutional human rights not govern the development of the common law concerning relations between private individuals and the State? Is this not, after all, "judicial legislation"?[29] Furthermore, if this is the case, why should this restriction not also apply to the courts, as it applies to the legislature, with regard to the development of the common law concerning relations between private parties? And if constitutional provisions regarding human rights are not directed at the judiciary at all, what then limits judicial development of the common law? Indeed, the perception of the court as a State body subject to constitutional provisions implies that the non-application model cannot stand. After all, even if this model prevents the infiltration of constitutional human rights into private law by means of direct application, in the end, the court will be entangled in constitutional provisions because it is a State authority. Thus, again, the direct application model proves to be preferable to non-application because it is the "cleanest" means of reaching an inevitable end.

Moreover, if constitutional provisions on human rights do not apply in relations between private parties, what law applies to the State when it operates in the private sector? Do constitutional provisions on human rights apply to the State in such instances? One possible answer is that constitutional provisions on human rights are directed at the State only when it acts in that capacity, but when it acts in the sphere of private law, it is acting in a private capacity. This response, however, is unsatisfactory. The State may not discriminate, infringe freedom of speech or freedom of movement, or otherwise violate human rights simply because it has donned another hat. Since there has been no real change of identity, constitutional human rights must be respected by the State even when it is acting in the private sphere. Moreover, the constitutional obligations

---

[27] *Hill* v. *Church of Scientology* [1995] 2 SCR 1130, at para. 95.

[28] See *supra* text accompanying nn.5–6.

[29] On judicial legislation, see A. Barak, *Judicial Discretion* (New Haven, Conn., Yale University Press, 1989) 147.

of the State towards private parties are the "personal law" of the State, and the State is subject to this law in all its activities.

In response to these arguments, proponents of non-application are likely to take the following position. Constitutional human rights apply to all state actions, whether taken in the public or private sphere. Yet this response opens the door to a variety of problems and questions. How should "State" be defined? Is a State corporation the "State" for the purposes of constitutional provisions? Moreover, how does the application of constitutional human rights *vis-à-vis* the State when it acts in the private law sphere accord with the various arguments against the application of constitutional human rights provisions in the framework of relations between private parties?

Furthermore, if constitutional human rights are not to be applied in disputes between private parties because there is no limitations clause in the country's bill of rights or charter, how can those rights be applied in the private sphere simply because the State is one of the actors? After all, the limitations clause, which applies to the State's legislative activities, does not apply to the State in private law. What limitations clause, then, will apply in the private law framework? Moreover, if courts formulate balancing formulas suitable for the relationship between the State (as a private party) and other private parties in the private sphere, why can they not develop these formulas, or similar ones, for relationships between private parties?

3. Indirect application model

Under the indirect application model, human rights apply in private law, but their application is indirect (the "cascade effect"[30]). In other words, constitutional human rights do not permeate private law "in and of themselves", but rather by means of existing or new private law doctrines. For example, if A refuses to sell his products to C, a woman, he is likely to be liable to her for lack of good faith in conducting the negotiations.

(a) *Arguments for Indirect Application*

According to its proponents, the advantage of indirect application is that it responds to some of the points of criticism levelled against direct application.[31] The point of departure for indirect application is that human rights have always played a role in private law. Indeed, at the foundation of the private law system are human rights ideals such as personhood, self-realisation and dignity. The specific private law rules—for example, protection of one's good name or property—reflect the rights of the private individual (as against the State and other

---

[30] See Rt Hon Lord Justice Sedley, *Freedom, Law and Justice* (London, Sweet & Maxwell, 1999) 25.
[31] See *supra* text accompanying nn.15–19.

private parties). At the same time, "value" concepts such as "good faith", "reasonableness" and "negligence" reflect, *inter alia*, an appropriate balance of opposing human rights.[32] Moreover, the concept of public policy essentially absorbs human rights originating in the constitution.[33] From time immemorial, confrontations between human rights—for example, freedom of contract versus freedom of occupation—have been resolved within the framework of the public policy principle,[34] which weighs conflicting rights according to their relative status in the constitutional system. Indeed, public policy is the channel through which constitutional values flow into private law.

Application of constitutional human rights indirectly in private law does not create a new system of human rights. Indeed, the advantage of the indirect application model is that it works within the old private law system, imbuing old tools with new contents or creating new tools with traditional private law techniques. In the past, common law human rights infiltrated private law by means of private law value terms. Now constitutional human rights do the same. The difference is that the constitutional status of these rights is likely to bring about a different outcome. Suppose, for example, that a private employer fires an employee because of a political opinion the employee has expressed. This termination is likely to be found unlawful. When the status of the right to free expression is not constitutional, the illegal termination may, in a given legal system, carry the "sanction" of damages but not specific performance. However, if freedom of expression is raised to a super-legislative level, the employee may be awarded specific performance. Put another way, raising the normative status of the right to free expression increases its weight in private law, thereby enabling the court to grant a remedy that would not have been previously available.

(b) *Indirect Application in Germany, Italy, Spain and Japan*

The German Constitutional Court accepted the indirect application model in the *Lüth* decision.[35] At issue in *Lüth* was the legality of a boycott initiated by Lüth, an activist, against a film produced by Harland, a film director who had directed the film *Jud Süss* during the Nazi era. According to the civil court, Lüth's boycott had violated paragraph 826 of the Civil Code ("BGB"), which provides that "everyone who intentionally causes damage to his fellow-man in

---

[32] See, e.g., CA 243/83, *City of Jerusalem* v. *Gordon* 39(1) PD 113 (Hebrew).

[33] Contract Law (General Part), 1973, 27 LSI 117, Article 30 (in English translation): "A contract the making, contents or object of which is or are illegal, immoral or contrary to public policy is void".

[34] See CA 6601/96, *AES System Inc* v. *Saar* 54(3) PD 850 (Hebrew).

[35] See 7 BVerfGE (1958); D.P. Kommers, *The Constitutional Jurisprudence of the Federal Republic of Germany* (Durham, NC, Duke University Press, 1989); P.E. Quint, "Free Speech and Private Law in German Constitutional Theory", *supra* n.11 and also D.P. Kommers, "The Jurisprudence of Free Speech in the United States and the Federal Republic of Germany", *supra* n.11. See also C. Starck, chap. 5 this vol.; A. Heldrich and G. Rehm, chap. 6 this vol.

a manner that harms good morals must compensate for the damage". On appeal, however, the Constitutional Court decided that the civil court decision had harmed Lüth's constitutional right to free expression under the Basic Law.[36] The Court reasoned that basic human rights constitute an objective value system, influencing both public and private areas of law. This objective value system is the standard for assessing every action, be it legislative, executive or judicial, and every private law arrangement must conform to this system. That said, the impact of this objective system in private law is effected by the doctrinal means of private law itself. Though private law is interpreted in accordance with the Constitution, the dispute remains a private law dispute, decided according to private law provisions. According to this rationale, Lüth's behavior did not constitute a wrongdoing. Under the indirect application model, Lüth's right to free speech outweighed the right to distribute Harland's films.

Later German decisions reinforced the *Lüth* approach. Significantly, in developing this case law, the German courts did not hesitate to create new private law tools to absorb the basic constitutional human rights. Nevertheless, in general, existing tools were relied upon. For example, the Constitutional Court considered that infringement on the freedom of expression between private parties, whether intentional or negligent, constitutes a wrong.[37] Likewise, private parties are entitled to damages for non-pecuniary injury, a remedy that previously was not available under the non-application approach.[38] By the same token, the right to privacy, derived from constitutional provisions,[39] is recognised by the BGB, protecting people against unlawful, intentional or negligent harm.[40] For example, it was decided that where the validity of dismissing a worker is limited by the requirement of "good cause" or "proper basis", a dismissal based on the fact that a worker exercised his constitutional right to free expression is unlawful.[41] Similarly, a contract between a taxi driver and his employer according to which the employee agreed not to drive for another company for three months following the date of termination of his employment was held to be void.[42] In this

---

[36] The Basic Law, Art. 5, states (in English translation):

"(1) Everyone shall have the right freely to express and disseminate his opinion by speech, writing, and pictures, and freely to inform himself from generally accessible sources. Freedom of the press and freedom of reporting by means of broadcasts and films are guaranteed. There shall be no censorship.

(2) These rights are limited by the provisions of the general laws, the provisions of law for the protection of youth, and by the right to inviolability of personal honor."

[37] 25 BVerfGE 256.

[38] See the *Syrian Princess* case: a newspaper published an entirely fabricated interview with the Princess of Syria (the former wife of the Shah of Iran), which included intimate details about her private life. Syria sued the newspaper for damages in a civil court for the non-pecuniary harm caused to it. The court held that Syria was entitled to damages; the Constitutional Court affirmed this judgment. See 34 BVerfGE 1973 269.

[39] Basic Law, §§1 and 2.

[40] BGB, §823.

[41] See 1 BAG 185.

[42] See BAG 22.11.65; (1966) VI Juristische Schulung.

case, the validity of the restraint clause was determined according to the principle of public policy. The court, having evaluated the relevant facts and attributed special weight to freedom of personhood and freedom of occupation, found that the employee's interests simply outweighed those of the employer.

Like Germany, Italy and Spain have adopted the indirect application model.[43] In Italy, for example, Civil Code provisions that had been interpreted as allowing damages only in instances where pecuniary harm was found are now interpreted as allowing damages for pain and suffering as well. The courts arrived at this conclusion by reasoning that there is a connection between constitutional provisions and the Civil Code, thus endowing the Civil Code with a constitutional dimension: in order to give content to Civil Code provisions, the courts turn to the Constitution. Likewise, in addressing a case in which an employee was dismissed for representing other employees against management, the Spanish courts held that termination of employment is unlawful where it is aimed at infringing the constitutional provision guaranteeing worker representation. Moreover, the court considered that reinstatement, not simply monetary damages, is the appropriate remedy. In other words, the civil court was called upon to create new remedies that would give expression to constitutional human rights in the private law realm.[44] Moreover, had the court failed to do so, an appeal could have been filed with the Constitutional Court on the ground that a constitutional right had been violated.[45]

Finally, Japan also has adopted the indirect application model.[46] In one case,[47] for instance, a claimant was hired as a temporary employee. After a three-month trial period, his contract was not renewed, the reason being that before he had been hired, he had intentionally refrained from disclosing the fact that he had been involved in radical political activities as a university student. The Tokyo District Court ordered reinstatement, basing its reasoning on regular civil law. The Appellate Court affirmed this decision, but on different grounds. According to the Appellate Court, the employer's questions regarding political activities violated Clauses 14 and 19 of the Japanese Constitution, which recognise the principle of equality and freedom of expression. Because the questions were unlawful, the termination was unlawful as well. On further appeal, the Supreme Court concluded that constitutional provisions apply indirectly in private law by means of private law doctrines like public policy or through specific labour laws. As a result, the conflicting values at stake in this

---

[43] See Sentenza 14 luglio 1986, 184 (Gazzella uffiale, la serie speciale, 23 lugio 1986, No 35). For a review of this decision, see Foro Italiano, 1986, I, 1, 2053 *et seq.*; Sanchis, *Estudios Sobre Derechos Fundamentales* (1990) 205.

[44] See Stc 5/1981, de 13 de febrero. See also Domenech, *Practicas De Derecho Constitucional* (1988) 167.

[45] See Moreno, *El Proceso de Amparo Constitutional* (1987).

[46] See M.J. Horan, "Contemporary Constitutionalism and Legal Relationships between Individuals" (1976) 25 *Int'l. & Comp. L Q* 848, 864.

[47] *Takano* v. *Mitsubishi Jushi KK*, 27 Minshu 1536. A summary of this decision in English appears in (1974) 7 *Law in Japan* 150.

case—namely, equality, freedom of expression, freedom of occupation and the right to privacy—had to be weighed against one another. On balance, the employer's interests won out, meaning that reinstatement was not warranted.

(c) Arguments against Indirect Application

The arguments against the indirect application model are, in principle, identical to those raised against direct application.[48] Surely, if constitutional human rights are protected solely *vis-à-vis* the State, they are not applicable, directly or indirectly, to relations between private parties. The indirect application model simply attempts to ease the "digestion" of the application of rights deriving from public law in private law. This attempt is, however, misplaced. If human dignity, liberty and property are constitutional rights that are held only *vis-à-vis* the State, how do they succeed in shaping values like public policy, which are concerned solely with relations between private parties? Why is a contract that limits freedom of occupation contrary to public policy, when freedom of occupation in principle is not directed at other private parties, but, rather, *vis-à-vis* the State?

4. Application to the judiciary model

The application to the judiciary model differs from the previous three models. While the latter are located along one continuum, the former model falls into an entirely separate category.[49] The application to the judiciary model begins with the assumption that constitutional human rights are protected only against the State. They have no application, direct or indirect, in relationships between private parties. Nonetheless, "State" includes the judiciary. Accordingly, the judiciary is prohibited from developing the common law or granting relief in a specific case in a way that violates a constitutional human right. Thus, under this model, if A is obligated to B not to sell his products to C on racial grounds and A breaches this obligation, B will not be entitled to a remedy of specific performance or damages against A. The reason for this is that if the court orders A to fulfill his obligations towards B, it will be violating C's right to equality, a right he holds against the State.

(a) Arguments in Favour of the Application to the Judiciary Model

According to its proponents, the judiciary model is the most appropriate model because the court is an organ of the State. When the court speaks, the State speaks, and when the court acts, the State acts. The judiciary is a State authority, and human rights must be protected against it as well. In a legal

[48] See *supra* text accompanying nn.15–19.
[49] See Quint, *supra* n.11.

system in which the legislative activities are limited in scope and subject to a limitations clause, there is no reason to release the common law—created by the judiciary—from all limitation. Moreover, if the common law is subject to constitutional human rights, individual judicial orders must also be subject to those rights. There should be no distinction in this regard between a general normative act of the judiciary, which develops the common law, and an individual normative act of the judiciary, which grants relief in a dispute between private parties. When a court issues an order enforcing a discriminatory contract, it places the power of the State—which acts via various means, including the rules of contempt of court—at the disposal of a private party who is infringing another private party's right to equality. The court is thus violating the State's duty not to discriminate.[50] This result should be prevented, because the principle of the rule of law also applies to the judiciary.

(b) *Application to the Judificary Model in the United States*

The United States has adopted the application to the judiciary model.[51] The US Bill of Rights is drafted in language that imposes prohibitions and obligations on the State. With the exception of the Thirteenth Amendment, which prohibits slavery, the rest of the amendments are drafted in language from which the US Supreme Court has deduced that they are directed at the State and the State alone. In determining what constitutes the "State", the Court has drawn two inferences. First, there is "state action" in the creation and development of the common law. Accordingly, in *New York Times* v. *Sullivan*,[52] the Court held that common law rules regarding defamation must be adjusted to conform with freedom of expression established in the First Amendment. Secondly, relief granted within the framework of private law should not contradict constitutional human rights. In *Shelley* v. *Kraemer*,[53] for example, A and B entered into a contract that prohibited the sale of property to African-Americans. When A sold land to C, an African-American, B turned to the Court for relief. In dismissing the suit, the Court noted that the Fourteenth Amendment, which establishes the right to equality, is directed at the State, so that it was not applicable in the case at hand. However, because judicial enforcement constitutes a "state act", the Court could not enforce the discriminatory provision.[54]

---

[50] See *Shelley* v. *Kraemer* (1948) 334 US 1 (hereinafter *Shelley*).

[51] For the situation in Canada, see *R.* v. *Rahey* [1987] 1 SCR 588; *British Columbia Government Emplolyees Union* v. *British Columbia* [1988] 2 SCR 214; Hogg, *supra* n.24, at 850. See also L. Weinrib and E. Weinrib, chap. 3 this vol.

[52] *New York Times* v. *Sullivan* 376 US 1 (1948).

[53] *Shelley*, *supra* n.50.

[54] See *Shelley*, *ibid.*, at 13 *per* Vinson, C J: "That Amendment erects no shield against merely private conduct, however discriminatory or wrongful . . . the restrictive agreements standing alone cannot be regarded as violative of any rights guaranteed to petitioners by the Fourteenth Amendment. So long as the purposes of those agreements are effectuated by voluntary adherence to their terms, it would appear clear that there has been no action by the state and the provisions of the Amendment have not been violated".

The scope of the *Shelley* rule, and of the application to the judiciary model more generally, is not at all clear. Fierce criticism has been levelled against this rule.[55] And indeed, if taken to its extreme, the decision in *Shelley* suggests that every constitutional human right directed at the State becomes, by virtue of state action, directed at private parties. American courts, however, have refrained from drawing a conclusion of this sort; extensive case law has narrowed the scope of the application of the *Shelley* rule. For example, the Court enforced the remedy of eviction against a trespasser who had entered the claimant's land, even though the claimant's sole objection was that the trespasser was an African-American.[56] Likewise, the Court has upheld the validity of wills that discriminate against African-Americans.[57]

(c) *Arguments against the Judiciary Model*

The application to the judiciary model is open to considerable criticism. To begin with, when a court grants relief in a private dispute, it is not bound by constitutional human rights. It acts as a neutral body that determines rights and obligations. If A is entitled to discriminate against B and the court enforces this entitlement—by declaratory judgment, damages or enforcement—it does not infringe upon the State's obligation not to discriminate. The court is simply recognising the non-application of the equality principle in private law.[58] Indeed, if we are to regard a judicial order as an order against which constitutional prohibitions are directed, then all of the constitutional rights that private parties hold *vis-à-vis* the State will be transformed into rights that are applicable between private parties. Thus the goal of the constitutional order will be frustrated.

To overcome this criticism, courts are likely to create distinctions between instances in which they merely recognise the freedom of action of private parties in private law (where the courts are not subject to constitutional prohibitions) and instances in which they act as an organ of the State (and are subject to constitutional prohibitions). But as soon as the courts introduce these distinctions, and comparative law points to extensive attempts in this direction, the application to the judiciary model will be open to a second point of criticism, namely, that distinctions between instances in which the court acts as a "neutral arbiter" outside the sphere of the constitutional prohibition and instances in which it acts as a State authority are artificial. Why is an order enforcing a discriminatory contract a state action that violates the constitutional duty not to

---

[55] *See* L. Henkin, "*Shelley* v. *Kraemer* Notes for a Revised Opinion" (1962) 110 *U Pa. L Rev.* 473; H. Wechsler, "Toward Neutral Principles of Constitutional Law" (1959) 73 *Harv. L Rev.* 1; H.W. Horowitz, "The Misleading Search for 'State Action' Under the Fourteenth Amendment" (1957) 30 *S C L Rev.* 208.

[56] G. Gunther and K. Sullivan, *Constitutional Law* (13th edn, Westbury, Foundation Press, 1997) 941.

[57] *See Evans* v. *Abney* 396 US 435 (1970).

[58] *Dolphin Deliver, supra* n.22, at 600.

discriminate, while an order recognising the validity of a club's discriminatory bylaws is not? To illustrate this point, suppose that a restaurant owner refuses to serve members of a certain race and that a person who is denied a meal stages a sit-in. If the court, acting as the State, grants an eviction order, is it violating its obligation not to discriminate?

Indeed, any attempt to draw reasonable distinctions between situations in which the court acts in disputes between private parties will ultimately fail. It will always be necessary to choose between one of two conclusions. One conclusion is that every judicial resolution of disputes between private parties is a state action subject to constitutional human rights. As this approach contradicts the language of the Constitution, it is inappropriate. The second conclusion, however, leads to the negation of the application to the judiciary model in its entirety. No act of the judiciary constitutes a state action at which constitutional human rights are directed. Thus, the fourth model collapses.

II. CONSIDERATIONS FOR THE PROPER SOLUTION

1. Negation of the non-application model

The approach to constitutional human rights in the private law realm that seems most appropriate to me conceives of basic human rights as a union of ideas. It is the amalgamation of human rights that grant liberty to the private individual,[59] whether *in rem* rights protected against the "entire world" or rights directed against both the government and other private parties. There can be no "double-system" of human rights, and "double-entry accounting" should not be established for those rights. There is one system of human rights, which formerly was based on regular legislation and the common law. Today, these rights are on a higher normative level. They have constitutional super-legislative status.

I do not think, therefore, that constitutional human rights apply only in public law. They merit comprehensive application to both public and private law areas, and they essentially provide the new basis for both public and private law. Indeed, if in the past basic human rights were derived from administrative and private law, then administrative and private law must now be derived from constitutional human rights. This is the meaning of the constitutional revolution in the human rights area. Viewed from this perspective, my approach clearly rejects the non-application model as the proper model.[60]

---

[59] For the Hohfeldian model, see W.N. Hohfeld, *Fundamental Legal Conceptions* (New Haven, Conn., Yale University Press, 1934). See also Crim. App. 95/51, *Pudmasky* v. *Attorney General* 6 PD 341 (Hebrew).

[60] CA 294/91, *Jerusalem Community Burial Society GHSA* v. *Kestenbaum* 46(2) PD 464, 530 (Hebrew) (hereinafter *Kestenbaum*).

The threat to human rights does, indeed, primarily emanate from the State, but this is not the sole danger. Danger to human rights also lurks in the conduct of private parties. Alongside the need to restrict the power of the State *vis-à-vis* private parties, there is also a need to limit the power of private parties in their relations with one another. The non-application model is inappropriate, because it draws too sharp a line between public and private law. Basic human rights are not directed solely at the government; they also apply to the mutual relationship between private parties.[61]

2. Direct or indirect application

(a) *Strengthened and Augmented Indirect Application*

Thus, it seems to me that basic human rights also apply in private law. Is their application direct or indirect? In my opinion, the proper model is the indirect (or "cascade") application model. Yet this is not the regular indirect application model, but, rather, a strengthened and augmented indirect application model. My approach stems from a consideration of the substance of human rights, on the one hand, and that of private law, on the other. Human rights are mutually restrictive; A's right is B's "non-right". This "non-right" detracts from B's human rights. Therefore, recognition of the human rights of one person *vis-à-vis* another inevitably involves limitation and narrowing, as a consequence of the regard for the other's rights. This limitation and narrowing must be evaluated within a particular normative framework. This framework concerns relations between private parties. This is private law. Hence, recognition of human rights necessitates restrictions and limitations set forth in private law itself. Indirect application, therefore, is required.

This conclusion derives from the very essence of private law, which is the legal regime that regulates the co-operative existence of various human rights while taking into consideration the public interest. Indeed, private law is grounded in the basic human rights directed at private individuals. In a certain sense, private law is the legal framework that determines the legal relationship between basic human rights as well as the proper balance between conflicting human rights, while considering the public interest. Private law is the expression of restrictions placed on human rights to realise human rights while safe-guarding the public interest. Private law is the framework that translates constitutional human rights into a "give and take" way of life between private individuals. Private law contains a complicated and extensive system of balances and arrangements intended to make collective life possible and enabling each of the participating individuals to enjoy basic human rights. The recognition of human rights *vis-à-vis* private individuals must, therefore, permeate via private law channels. This is the true meaning of indirect application.

---

[61] *Ibid.*

(b) *The Essence of Strengthened Indirect Application*

As mentioned, I believe that constitutional human rights apply (indirectly) in private law. This view is based on two assumptions. First, constitutional human rights are directed not only against the State but also against private parties. The right of property is the right of a private individual *vis-à-vis* both the government and other private individuals. Secondly, remedies for breaching human rights in interpersonal relations must be given a place in private law. According to this approach, private law is the "geometric location" for formulating remedies for an infringement by one private individual on the constitutional right of another individual. Under this approach, when a constitutional right of one individual is breached by another individual, the injured party must find his relief within the framework of private law. To the extent that existing private law grants an appropriate remedy—namely, one consistent with the scope of the right and the protection mandated by the constitution—it fulfills its role and does not give rise to any practical difficulty. To the extent that existing private law does not grant an appropriate remedy—namely, despite the violation of the constitutional right, no remedy is available in private law—the strengthened indirect application model mandates that private law must be revised to provide a remedy as needed. Thus, the uniqueness of the strengthened indirect application model lies in its placing a demand upon private law: it requires the formulation of appropriate tools for the absorption of constitutional human rights into private law. To the extent that these tools do not exist, it behoves private law to create them. They can be formed by means of new interpretations of existing tools (such as offering a new interpretation of the principle of good faith) or through the creation of new tools, whether by filling *lacunae* or by means of the general principle that where a right exists so does a remedy.

(c) *The Strengthened Indirect Application Model and the Direct Application Model*

In what way, then, does the strengthened indirect application model differ from the direct application model? Both models call for the application of constitutional human rights in private law. Under both models, violation of a constitutional human right is likely to constitute a breach of a constitutional obligation. The difference between the models is that the direct application model ignores private law. It calls for relief to emanate directly from the constitutional right via rules of relief that are beyond the private law sphere. It creates a type of "constitutional private law" that exists alongside regular private law. By contrast, the strengthened indirect application model regards existing private law as the appropriate normative system for providing relief for infringement of a constitutional right. Under this model, it is not necessary to ignore private law and there is no need to create constitutional private law to exist parallel to regular private law. Under the strengthened indirect application model, regular private law embodies constitutional private law, because private law is essentially an expression of the constitutional human rights of private individuals in their relationships with other individuals.

(d) *Indirect Application Model and Strengthened Indirect Application Model*

What is the difference between the classic indirect application model and the strengthened indirect application model? No difference exists between the two in situations where private law has developed appropriate tools to give expression to constitutional human rights. Therefore, when a contract is made, the general rules of public policy and good faith fill the appropriate role and permit (indirect) application of constitutional human rights in private law. The substantive difference between the two models is conspicuous in cases where private law does not contain the legal tools or institutions for the absorption of constitutional human rights. Under the classic indirect application model, in such cases, there is no alternative but to deny remedy to the injured private party. In contrast, under the strengthened indirect application model, in such a situation, it is incumbent upon private law to adapt itself and create the missing tools or institutions. Private law cannot remain indifferent to an infringement of a constitutional human right. It is obligated to absorb this violation and grant a remedy for it. "Integrated tools" must exist between public law (the creator of the right) and private law (the granter of the remedy for the right). Where the right is recognised (in public law), the remedy must also be recognised (in private law): *ubi ius, ibi remedium.*

(e) *The Strengthened Indirect Application Model and the Creation of New Legal Tools*

The strengthened indirect application model is based on the concept that private law must create tools to give relief for infringement of a constitutional human right. Where these tools do not exist, it is incumbent upon the legislature to create them. What can be done if the legislature refrains from acting? It seems to me that there are several possible avenues. First, at times, a constitutional duty (*status positivus*) is placed upon the legislature to set remedies for infringements of constitutional human rights, such as injury to human dignity. Secondly, at times, the absence of a legal arrangement is likely to be considered a *lacuna*, requiring that it be filled according to the applicable rules. Thirdly, sometimes it is possible to create new tools by renovating old ones, for example, new understandings of old concepts such as good faith, negligence and public policy. Fourthly, the general private law principle that where there is a right there is a remedy (*ubi ius, ibi remedium*) is likely to serve as a source for the creation of new tools that will be incorporated into private law.

(f) *The Strengthened Indirect Application Model and the Level of Protection Afforded to Human Rights*

Examination of human rights requires a distinction between the scope of the right and the level of protection afforded to it. The scope of the right refers to the range of actions captured within its framework. An examination of the scope of the freedom of expression requires an answer to the question whether this freedom extends to actions (and not just speech)—such as the display of a wooden dummy[62]— to the right to be silent, and to racist expression.[63] The level of protection afforded to the right considers the full range of the right and which areas within this range will be protected and which will not. Failure to protect is likely to arise for reasons of public interest alone (for example, for the purpose of protecting State secrets, speech exposing such secrets is not protected) or from private interest alone (for example, for the purpose of protecting personal privacy, speech exposing private information is not protected) or from a combined public-private interest (for example, protection of one's good name and privacy is both a public and a private interest, negating protection of speech or action that is defamatory or infringes privacy). Certainly, human rights are not protected by law to the absolute fullest extent. Protection of A's human rights to the fullest extent possible inevitably infringes B's claim for similar recognition of his human rights— hence we arrive at the concept that human rights are relative rather than absolute.

The level of protection of human rights is determined through consideration of values, interests and principles deserving protection. Some of them express a public interest (integrity of the State, its democratic nature, public order). The bulk combines public and private interests. Private law determines the level of protection to be afforded to human rights relative to other human rights. The laws of contract, property and tort determine the extent to which a person is entitled to realise his human rights without his actions violating the human rights of another. In determining the level of protection to be afforded to human rights, private law considers the other party's human rights and public interest. For example, freedom of contract is recognised under private law, but this freedom is limited by public policy, which reflects the public interest and the constitutional human rights of others. Private law recognises freedom of action, but limits it within the framework provided by the law of torts.

In formulating legislation that sets forth the limitations on the extent of protection granted to constitutional human rights in private law, the legislature must conform to the constitutional limitations clause.[64] For example, to the

---

[62] See HC 953/89, *Indor* v. *Mayor of Jerusalem* 45(4) PD 83 (Hebrew).

[63] See HC 399/85, *Kahana* v. *Havaad Hamnahel Shel Reshut Hashidur* 41(3) PD 225 (Hebrew).

[64] Basic Law: Human Dignity and Liberty, 1992, 45 LSI 150 (1991–2), Art. 8 (in English translation):

> There shall be no violation of rights under this Basic Law except by a Law fitting the values of the State of Israel, designed for proper purpose, and to an extent no greater than required or by such a law enacted with explicit authorization therein.

extent that a new property statute "infringes" a person's property—namely, it does not protect the full range of that person's property—it is necessary that the statute fulfill the requirements of the limitations clause. In determining the proper purpose of the new legislation, it is essential, of course, to consider, *inter alia*, the human rights of others. Legislation that has passed the limitations clause tests has appropriately weighed constitutional human rights. At times, this balance is formulated in value terms, such as "good faith",[65] "negligence",[66] "reasonableness"[67] and "public policy".[68] These terms reflect the basic values and concepts of the legal system. They are the expression of constitutional values. Indeed, they are the expression of constitutional human rights themselves.

Accordingly, value phrases constitute one of the important channels through which constitutional basic rights and other legal values flow into private law. To be more precise, all of private law reflects a balancing of conflicting values. It has been deemed appropriate to establish within the framework of private law value rules that permit flexibility in the operation of private law. These value provisions are particularly sensitive to constitutional considerations. They permit expression of constitutional human rights and public interests according to their state at various times, without any need to make a formal change in the private law balances. For example, public policy is a flexible principle by means of which the court balances the constitutional freedom to fashion the content of a contract against human rights and various constitutional values.[69] Similarly, good faith is an objective principle that sets a minimum level of appropriate conduct between private parties. It thereby reflects that which is deemed appropriate in society. Thus, this principle reflects and enables the proper balance to be reached between conflicting human rights.[70]

(g) *Private Law as a Balancing System*

Accordingly, private law reflects two systems of balancing. The first system determines the very content of private law itself, including the value provisos therein. The balancing is conducted according to the constitutional limitations clause. This clause is addressed to the legislature and establishes methods to determine the appropriate contents of legislation. The second system of balancing operates within the framework of private law itself, after the balancing required by the limitations clause has taken place. This balancing is mandated by the value terms themselves and is designed to give them concrete substance.

---

[65] See, for example, Contracts Law (General Part), 1973, 27 LSI 117, §§12, 39; BGB §242.

[66] See Torts (Civil Wrong) Ordinance (New Version), §§35, 36.

[67] See Contracts Law (General Part), 1973, 27 LSI 117, §§21, 41, 56; Contracts Law (Remedies for Breach of Contract), 1970, 24 LSI 16, §§6, 7, 8, 9, 14.

[68] See Contracts Law (General Part), 1973, 27 LSI 117 §30.

[69] See *Kestenbaum, supra* n.60.

[70] See HC 59/80, *Be'er Sheva Public Transportation Services* v. *National Labour Court* 35(1) PD 828 (Hebrew); CA 391/80, *Lasserson* v. *Workers Housing Inc* 38(2) PD 237 (Hebrew); CA 207/79, *Raviv* v. *Beit Yules* 37(1) PD 533 (Hebrew); FH 7/81, *Pnidar* v. *Castro* 37(4) PD 673 (Hebrew).

This balancing is conducted by the judge and occasionally constitutes an expression of judicial discretion. It also considers basic values and human rights set forth in the constitution. It is the fruit of the judicial "limitations clause", which operates within the framework of private law itself.

(h) *Adjustment of Private Law to the Application of Constitutional Human Rights*

Basic human rights apply in private law. The balancing between these rights and between them and the public interest is carried out within the framework of private law. To the extent that private law is legislated or codified, this framework reflects the status of basic rights on the eve of the enactment of the given statute. When a change in human rights occurs, the private law basic rights become constitutional rights with normative super-legislative force. What impact does this change have on private law? The answer is that it has an effect on various levels. First, with regard to the content of private law, new legislation must adjust itself to basic human rights in general and to the limitations clause in particular. Secondly, the value terms must be imbued with concrete substance by the basic rights and values at the time of their interpretation. Indeed, this is the role and power of value terms. They absorb social values, constitutional human rights and public interests according to their state at the time of their interpretation and not according to their state at the time of legislation. Therefore, current public policy is considered in light of the new constitutional system, including the super-legislative nature of human rights. To the extent that courts have formulated the contents of value terms according to the non-constitutional nature of basic rights, it is now necessary to change the common law rule and replace it with a new rule that reflects the new constitutional balance. For example, the good faith principle must reflect the proper balance between constitutional rights and basic principles as per their state at the time of interpretation. Moreover, the reasonableness restriction balances the rights of the parties and the public interest. Within the framework of this balance, the parties' rights are strengthened. In Israel, for example, the right to shape the contents of a contract—derived directly from the individual's constitutional right to autonomy of will and, in the absence of this type of explicit constitutional right, from the principle of human dignity and liberty—has been granted constitutional status, as has freedom of occupation. Concurrently, the weight of the public interest has decreased. These new relations require a renewed examination of the proper balance between conflicting values. What was conceived as "reasonable" in the past will probably no longer be conceived as "reasonable" today.

Thirdly, the need to create new norms is likely to arise in the existing private law framework, which will give expression to the new constitutional structure and new human rights. The existing private law tools will probably not suffice for the "absorption" of the new rights. This is, first and foremost, the task of the legislature.[71] If the legislature does not fulfill this task, it will then be placed upon the judiciary. The judiciary may fulfill it, first of all, by filling in the gaps in existing legislation. In Israel, there is a "late *lacuna*"[72] that resulted from the enactment of the Basic Laws. It is also possible for the judge to create new tools by developing private law.[73] Such development is likely to be required primarily in the area of remedies for infringement of constitutional human rights, wherever existing private law does not provide for adequate remedies.

3. Autonomy of the will: the conflict with other human rights in private law

(a) *The Individual's Autonomy of Will as a Constitutional Right*

The primary argument against the application of constitutional human rights in private law is that recognition of these rights in relations between private individuals will deeply harm human rights themselves, primarily the individual's autonomy of will. If a parent is required to maintain equality when distributing inheritance among his or her children and if a prospective party to a contract is obligated to maintain equality in selecting contract partners, then the principle of freedom of contract will be violated. Similarly, if a person is prohibited from making a contract that infringes freedom of occupation, or the right of property, or freedom of speech and movement, freedom of contract will be seriously curtailed. My response to this argument is that included among the entirety of basic rights that must be considered are the basic rights of human dignity and personal development, and these encompass the individual's autonomy of will, from which the principle of freedom of contract is derived.[74]

Freedom of contract, therefore, is in itself a constitutional principle and a constitutional human right.[75] When A enters into a contract with B, according to which B will refrain from exercising his freedom of expression or movement, it cannot automatically be stated that the contract is contrary to public policy because it violates B's freedom of expression or freedom of movement. In determining whether the contract is, in fact, contrary to public policy, one must consider the freedom of contract of both A and B, in addition to other liberties. The

---

[71] For example, the Civil Rights Acts in the USA, 42 USC §1971 *et seq*.

[72] A late *lacuna* is a gap created not at the time of the enactment of legislation but at a later point of time as a result of new legislative developments. On the general theory of gaps, see C.W. Canaris, *Die Festellung von Lücken in Gesetz* (Berlin, Duncker & Humblot, 1964).

[73] For the development of the law and the distinction between it and filling *lacunae*, see A. Barak, "Judicial Creativity—Interpretation, the Filling of Gaps, and the Development of the Law" (1989) 39 HaPraklit 267 (Hebrew).

[74] See G. Shalev, *The Law of Contract* (Jerusalem, Dinn, 1990) 23–35 (Hebrew).

[75] See CA 239/92, *"Eged" Aguda Shituphit* v. *Izhak Messiah* 48(2) PD 66 (Hebrew): "[c]ontractual freedom contains expression of the autonomy of the individual will, and therefore, is anchored today in the principles of Basic Law: Human Dignity and Liberty" (Justice D. Levine). See also National Labour Court 53/3–177–8–9, *Sharam Inc Spokesperson* v. *Globus Inc* 25 PDA 395, 410 (Hebrew): "[L]et us not forget, freedom of contract is a constitutional right" (Justice Goldberg).

contract will be contrary to public policy only if in the comprehensive balancing of the conflicting values, B's freedom of expression or movement is more "prominent". Similarly, in contradistinction to A's constitutional human right not to be discriminated against in the contract that B seeks to enter into stands B's right to act according to his autonomous will.

(b) *Balancing Autonomy of Will with Other Liberties*

How are the constitutional human rights balanced against one another? Most constitutions set forth a balancing formula that limits the legislature. Does this formula apply in and of itself also in relations between private parties? My answer to this question in the *Kestenbaum* case was in the negative:

> In the transference of basic principles of the legal system in general, and basic human rights in particular, from public law to private law, a change takes place. The government's duty to observe human rights is not identical in content to the private party's obligation to observe human rights.[76]

Indeed, the proper balancing of human rights and the "pure" public interest in public peace, security and prosperity differs from the proper balancing among human rights themselves. It seems, therefore, that alongside the balancing formula set forth in the limitations clause, it is necessary to establish other formulas for balancing the various human rights in their conflicts with each other. The need to create judicial balancing formulas for such conflicts gives rise to an additional argument against the application of protected human rights in private law. This argument is that the application of these rights in private law requires the creation of judicial balancing formulas, and since this was not provided for by the Basic Laws themselves, the matter becomes subject to judicial discretion. This constitutes an enormous power, which should not be placed in the hands of the judiciary.

This argument, however, is unconvincing. The need to create judicial balancing formulas in conflicts between human rights is ancient and has been faced by courts since time immemorial. Take, for example, the rules on restraint of trade. These are in essence rules that balance between the constitutional rights of freedom of contract and freedom of occupation or trade. Just as the courts performed this task of balancing in the past, they are capable of fulfilling it in the future, and just as the courts did not wrongfully exploit their power in the past, there is no reason to assume that they will abuse that power in the future. Indeed, those who fear wrongful exploitation of judicial power must be wary of the constitution itself. By its very nature, the constitution, which is accompanied by judicial review, confers upon the court broad judicial discretion.

---

[76] *Kestenbaum, supra* n.60, at 531.

(c) *Freedom to Shape Contractual Content and Protected Human Rights*

In principle, the application of protected human rights in private law need not create any conceptual difficulty where a contract is made and at issue is the extent of its validity.[77] This matter was addressed routinely in the past, before the constitutionalisation of human rights, and great experience has been accumulated in this area. Courts have dealt extensively with the question of the relationship between freedom of contract (in the sense of the freedom to shape the contents of a contract) and freedom of occupation or trade.[78] The same is true with regard to situations in which a contract is claimed to infringe a human right. For example, in the past, courts dealt with the relationship between the freedom to shape the contents of a contract and the freedom of expression, when a contract was made under which a newspaper undertook not to publish certain items.[79] Likewise, there is case law on the relationship between the freedom to shape the contents of a contract and the right to personhood and human dignity.[80] The courts have devoted much attention to the relationship between the freedom to shape the contents of a contract and the principle of equality, where a contract has created discrimination.[81]

In all these cases, a contract existed and the question that arose was whether its contents violate a human right (such as freedom of expression, freedom of occupation or human dignity). The private law principle regarding public policy considers this question, while manifesting, by its very substance, the totality of society's basic conceptions, including the weight and status of human rights. In the past, this was done with regard to human rights that "were not inscribed in a book".[82] Today, this is done with respect to "rights inscribed in a book" entitled to constitutional protection. To be more precise, just as the rights of property and freedom of occupation were elevated in normative level from a "common law" right to a "constitutional" right, so too was the freedom to shape the contents of a contract. This right is an expression of human dignity and liberty, and it too enjoys constitutional status.

---

[77] See N. Cohen, "Equality versus Freedom of Contract" (1993) 1 *HaMishpat* 131 (Hebrew).

[78] On the doctrine of restraint of trade, see G. Chesire, C. Fifoot and M. Furmston's *Law of Contracts* (13th edn., London, Butterworths, 1996) 411.

[79] See *Neville* v. *Dominion of Canada News Co* [1915] 3 KB 556.

[80] See *Horwood* v. *Millar's Timber and Trading Co* [1917] KB 305.

[81] See National Labour Court 33/25–3, *Daily Air Staff Committee* v. *Chazin* 4 PDA 365 (Hebrew); HC 410/76, *Herut* v. *National Labour Court in Jerusalem* 31(3) PD 124 (Hebrew); HC 104/87, *Nevo* v. *National Labour Court* 44 (4) PD 749 (Hebrew): "[p]aragraph 6 [of the collective agreement] creates a discriminatory arrangement, which harms the women's rights to participate equally in work affairs. Accordingly in my opinion, this paragraph is contrary to public policy, and by law, accordingly, this Court should involve itself and void its content" (Justice Bach). See also HC 6051/95, *Rekanat* v. *National Labour Court* 51(3) PD 289, FH 4191/97, 54 (5) PD 330 (hereinafter *Rekanat*) (Hebrew).

[82] *Per* Justice Landau in HC 243/62, *Ulpaney Hasrata* v. *Geri* 16(4) PD 2407 (Hebrew).

Just as courts dealt in the past, before the constitutionalisation of human rights, with the appropriate balance between the freedom to shape the contents of a contract and other human rights, so too in the future will they deal with the appropriate balance between this freedom and other constitutional human rights. Of course, the substance of the balance is likely to change. Indeed, the proper balance reflects the status and weight of one human right relative to other human rights.[83] In the past, some human rights (such as freedom of occupation) perhaps had a lower status than they enjoy today. If, in fact, a change takes place in the status of a given right, the matter will find expression in the balancing between it and other rights in the framework of the principle of public policy. To be more precise, the balance between the freedom to shape the contents of a contract and other human rights will be made according to "balancing formulas" that differ from the formulas that balance these human rights in their conflicts with the public interest. To be sure, it is necessary to distinguish the conflict of values within public law (public order against human rights) from conflicts of values in private law (the right of one person against the right of another). The difference in conflicting values brings with it a difference in balancing formulas, but this difference should not be exaggerated. The public interest will preserve the proper balance of human rights in private law. The distinction between public law, which includes, *inter alia*, consideration of private interests, and private law, which protects public interest by means of public policy, becomes blurred. This is not to be regretted. Essentially, we are dealing with "integrated tools". Public interest is not a value unto itself. It is intended to protect human rights. Human rights are not "absolute", and they are subject to one another as well as to the public interest. Human rights do not exist in the absence of order and regime. The principle of public policy, considered both in internal conflicts between human rights and in their conflicts with the general public interest, gives expression to this composite.

(d) *Freedom to Make a Contract and the Principle of Equality*

Freedom of contract has two aspects: the freedom to enter into a contract and the freedom to shape its contents. With regard to the second aspect, there is substantial legal experience in adjusting the balance between the freedom to shape the contents of a contract and other human rights. The law of restraint of trade deals with these issues. There is no legal experience, however, in setting the balance between the freedom to make a contract and other human rights.[84] The main problem arises where the freedom to make or not to make a contract conflicts with the principle of equality.[85] Is a restaurant owner entitled to refuse to serve someone on the basis of gender, race or religion? Can a private party,

---

[83] See *Rekanat, supra* n.81.

[84] On the freedom to enter into a contract and on the difference between it and the freedom to shape the contents of a contract, see Shalev, *supra* n.74.

[85] The analysis is based on the assumption that equality is a constitutional human right.

seeking to rent out a room in his apartment, refuse to rent it out on the basis of gender, race or religion? On a practical level, the problem does not arise where there is legislation dealing with the topic ("civil rights legislation"). But what is the position in the absence of relevant legislation?

My intuition tells me that the restaurant owner has an obligation to give service, that is, to make a contract, without discriminating on the basis of gender, race or religion. By contrast, the same intuition tells me that the private party renting out a room in his apartment is entitled to choose a lodger as he sees fit. This intuition is based primarily on the proper balance between the freedom to make a contract of the restaurant owner and apartment owner and the right of the persons seeking the service (food or dwelling) not to be discriminated against. I accept that the restaurant owner and apartment owner have the constitutional freedom to decide with whom to contract. Similarly, I accept that the person wishing to dine in the restaurant or rent the room is entitled not to be discriminated against (whether by the State or by private parties) and that if he is refused on the basis of gender, religion or race, this constitutes discrimination.

In balancing these rights when they conflict, the right of a person not to be discriminated against prevails in the restaurant example and the freedom to enter or not to enter into a contract prevails in the case of the apartment owner. The rationale at the base of this balance is rooted in the concept that the freedom to make a contract is stronger when it relates to a person's privacy, while it is weaker when directed against the public at large. Similarly, the right not to be discriminated against is strongest when service is offered to the general public and a person is segregated from that public on the basis of race, gender or religion. The right not to be discriminated against diminishes in strength where the service, by its very nature, is not "open" to all and is provided on a personal basis. When a restaurant owner refuses to serve a customer because of his or her race, religion or gender, the restaurant owner's freedom to enter into a contract is the weaker force, whereas the right of the customer not to be discriminated against is at its peak. In these circumstances, the customer must enjoy the advantage. By contrast, when an apartment owner refuses to rent a room on the basis of race, gender or religion, his freedom of contract is at its peak, whereas the right of the potential lodger not to be discriminated against is at its lowest point. In these circumstances, the apartment owner has the advantage.

(e) *Balancing Autonomy of Will and Equality: the Good Faith Principle*

Let us now assume that my approach is the proper one. According to my approach, a person who provides a service to the public must not discriminate among customers on the basis of gender, race or religion. Does private law include tools that permit this result? The public policy principle cannot be utilised. It can be resorted to when a contract that was formed is alleged to be contrary to public policy. The principle has an invalidating effect. It lacks creative power. Hence, when a person improperly declines to enter into a contract, the principle of public policy, as traditionally understood, cannot be applied in order to force the formation of that contract. It seems that the most appropriate principle for solving our problem is the good faith principle. The law imposes a duty on anyone who engages in negotiations towards making a contract to conduct those negotiations in good faith.[86] "Good faith" constitutes an objective criterion that reflects the proper balance between conflicting values that determine the minimum level for the proper conduct of contractual negotiations.[87] It is possible to claim, therefore, that the provider of a service is not conducting negotiations in good faith when he refuses to provide service on the basis of religion, race or gender.

In Israel, this approach is problematic because, under the case law, the good faith principle does not require equality and does not prohibit discrimination.[88] This issue was dealt with in the *Beit Yules* case,[89] in which the majority concluded that the good faith principle does not require equality, whatever the circumstances may be. Under the majority approach, the private law legal institution regarding the obligation to conduct negotiations in good faith cannot give expression to the constitutional principle of equality. The minority opinion took a different approach, noting that situations are likely to arise in which good faith will require equality, though other situations are conceivable in which good faith will not require equality.[90] Under the minority approach, the private law legal institution concerned with good faith in negotiations may provide a framework for the proper balance between freedom of contract and the equality principle. In my view, the majority opinion is erroneous, but until it is overturned, it is binding. Nonetheless, alongside the reasons for changing it, which are anchored in the minority opinion, the following reason can now be added: the equality principle is a constitutional principle by virtue of its being anchored in Basic Laws. It must find expression in private law. When inequality is expressed in negotiations towards making a contract, the main vehicle that can give effect to the equality principle is good faith in negotiations. It will, of course, have to be balanced with conflicting principles. This view acknowledges the possibility that in the appropriate circumstances—those in which the value of equality takes precedence over other values—the good faith principle requires equality. However, this interpretation raises the following difficulty: the principle that requires negotiations to be conducted in good faith applies when people negotiate the formation of a contract. It is not altogether clear whether this principle can be extended to a situation in which one party improperly declines even to start the process of negotiations. To contend with this possible argument, I shall examine in the section that follows other tools that private law provide.

---

[86]   Contracts Law (General Part) 1973, 27 LSI 117, §12.

[87]   This is the objective doctrine of *culpa in contrahendo*, which was developed in continental law. See N. Cohen, "Pre-contractual Duties: Two Freedoms and the Contract to Negotiate" in J. Beatson and D. Friedmann (eds.), *Good Faith and Fault in Contract Law* (Oxford, Clarendon Press, 1995) 25.

[88]   See FH 22/82, *Beit Yules* v. *Raviv* 43(1) PD 441 (Hebrew).

[89]   *Ibid.*

[90]   *Ibid.*, at 461.

(f) *New Tools: Negligence and Abuse of Right*

It should be acknowledged that it is necessary to develop other private law tools, by means of which it will be possible for the equality principle to permeate pre-contractual negotiations. I refer primarily to the tort of negligence and the doctrine of abuse of right. It can be argued that in balancing the principle of the freedom to make or not to make a contract against the equality principle, the equality principle prevails and a duty of care is imposed not to discriminate. Continental courts operate in this manner.[91] Responsibility for discriminatory negotiations was derived from the general tort law rule prohibiting causing damage maliciously or in an immoral manner,[92] and it is even possible to obtain an injunction in this framework.[93] Furthermore, a legal system that recognises the general principle prohibiting abuse of a right (*abuse de droit*)[94] is likely to view this rule as a source of relief in private law for an unlawful harm, namely, that which exceeds the permissible boundaries of the balancing formula, which takes the equality principle into account. To the extent that these doctrines are insufficient, the indirect application principle must develop the "Israeli-style" common law, which will give expression to constitutional rights at the pre-contractual stage. Indeed, this is the power and the impact of the indirect application principle, which enables the infiltration of constitutional human rights into private law. This process of infiltration into private law is accomplished, first and foremost, by means of existing private law tools. However, if these tools prove to be insufficient for coping with the issue of discrimination in the pre-contractual stage, it is necessary to create new private law doctrines that will give due regard to the constitutional principles of human rights and fill this *lacuna*.

(g) *The Application in Private Law and the Application to the Judiciary Model*

Recognition of the (indirect) application of constitutional human rights in private law to a great extent relieves the need to take a stand on the application to the judiciary model. Nonetheless, it appears that there is no alternative but to take a stand on this issue, for two reasons. First, it is necessary to take a stand on whether the common law is subject to restrictions similar to those placed on legislation infringing constitutional human rights. In my opinion, the judiciary

---

[91] See K. Larenz, *Lehrbuch des Schuldrechts* (11th edn., Munich, Beck, 1975) 53.

[92] See BGB, §826.

[93] See Larenz, *supra* n.91, at 53.

[94] On abuse of rights in comparative law, see H.C. Gutteridge, "Abuse of Rights" (1935) 5 *CLJ* 22; J.E. Scholtens, "Abuse of Rights" [1958] *South African LJ* 39; J. Cueto-Rua, "Abuse of Rights" (1975) 35 *La. L Rev.* 965; V. Bolgar, "Abuse of Rights in France, Germany and Switzerland: A Survey of a Recent Chapter in Legal Doctrine" (1975) 35 *La. L Rev.* 1015; K. Sono and Y. Fujioka, "The Role of the Abuse of Right Doctrine in Japan" (1975) 35 *La. L Rev.* 1037; C.J.H. Brunner, "Abuse of Rights in Dutch Law" (1977) 37 *La. L Rev.* 729.

is restricted in its development of the common law by constitutional human rights. This is certainly the case when the common law deals with relationships between private parties and the State. In my opinion, the restrictions apply to judge-made law also when it deals with relationships between private parties. The "limitation formula" is admittedly different, but, in principle, constitutional human rights restrict judicial freedom of action. Indeed, the court is an organ of the State, and it is appropriate that it be subject to the various restrictions arising from the constitutional protection given to human rights. The second reason suggests that if the private law doctrines fail to fulfill their role, assistance can be found in the creation of new tools in the application of human rights to the judiciary model. I do not in fact view this model as competing with the other models, but as a model that supplements the others, applying to them simultaneously and likely to complement them when they fail.

4. An explicit constitutional arrangement for the application of protected human rights in private law

It is universally acknowledged that constitutional human rights protect private parties against the State. Lack of clarity exists as to the application of these rights in relationships between private parties. Are private parties protected only against the State or are they perhaps also protected against other private parties? It seems to me that this ambiguity is undesirable. The issue is central for both public and private law. It is imperative to take a clear constitutional stand on this matter. It is also desirable that such a stance be taken by the constitutional legislative body rather than be left to the judiciary. This is a lesson that can be learned from the sphere of comparative law. Surely if one seeks to prevent the application of constitutional human rights in private law, it is desirable to state so explicitly. It is possible to say, for example, that "the rights set forth in this law are directed only against State authorities". Moreover, if we seek to negate the application to the judiciary model, it is desirable to use explicit language to this effect. As demonstrated, the appropriate arrangement, in my opinion, is that which recognises the indirect application of human rights to private law. It is desirable to establish an explicit arrangement on this matter. It is necessary to set forth that no use may be made of any constitutional human right except in a manner that appropriately considers the human rights of all. Indeed, A's constitutional human right is inherently limited by B's constitutional human right, even if B does not seek to suppress A's right and his only desire is to advance his own interests. Expression is thereby given to the idea that human rights are directed not only against the State, but also indirectly against other individuals.

3

Constitutional Values and Private Law in Canada

LORRAINE E. WEINRIB AND ERNEST J. WEINRIB

Strictly speaking, civil rights arise from positive law; but freedom of speech, religion and the inviolability of the person are original freedoms which are at once the necessary attributes and modes of self-expression of human beings and the primary conditions of their community life within a legal order. It is in the circumscription of these liberties by the creation of civil rights in persons who may be injured by their exercise, and by the sanctions of public law, that the positive law operates. What we realize is the residue inside that periphery.

Justice Rand in Saumur v. City of Quebec [1953] 4 DLR 641 (SCC)

I. THE RELEVANCE OF CONSTITUTIONAL VALUES IN CANADA

IN *RETAIL, WHOLESALE & Department Store Union, Local 580* v. *Dolphin Delivery*,[1] the Supreme Court of Canada articulated the relationship between the Canadian Charter of Rights and Freedoms and private law in the following terms:

> Where . . . private party "A" sues private party "B" relying on the common law and where no act of government is relied upon to support the action, the Charter will not apply . . . [T]his is a distinct issue from the question whether the judiciary ought to apply and develop the principles of the common law in a manner consistent with the fundamental values enshrined in the Constitution. The answer to this question must be in the affirmative. In this sense, then, the Charter is far from irrelevant to private litigants, whose disputes fall to be decided at common law. But this is different from the proposition that one private party owes a constitutional duty to another . . .[2]

With these words, the Court enrolled Canada in the growing family of liberal democracies that in some way connect constitutional rights to private law.[3]

---

[1] *Retail, Wholesale & Department Store Union, Local 580* v. *Dolphin Delivery* (1987) 33 DLR (4th) 174, 199 (SCC) (hereinafter *Dolphin Delivery*).

[2] *Ibid.*, at 199.

[3] For a magisterial survey and discussion see A. Barak, "Constitutional Human Rights and Private Law" (1996) 3 *Rev. Const. Stud.* 218. See also A. Barak, *supra* chap. 2. Among the significant developments since the 1996 article by the President of the Supreme Court of Israel is the adoption of the South African Constitution, which in s. 35(3) requires that "in the application and

This development, while not identical to the indirect *Drittwirkung* of constitutional rights in German law, has obvious similarities to it.[4] Both the German and Canadian systems regard the litigation as being in process and in substance a matter of private rather than constitutional law. Moreover, in both Germany and Canada, the litigation is nonetheless affected by the values encoded in the constitutional rights. In the path-breaking *Lüth* case,[5] the German Constitutional Court declared that the system of constitutional values "naturally influences private law as well; no rule of private law may conflict with it, and all such rules must be construed in accordance with its spirit".[6] This statement would be perfectly at home in the Canadian jurisprudence after the *Dolphin Delivery* case.[7] The Canadian and German approaches differ only in the source of the obligation to consider the constitutional values. Under the German approach that obligation arises out of the constitution itself; whereas under the Canadian approach it arises from the inherent jurisdiction of common law courts to develop private law. Even this difference may reflect not divergence concerning the significance of constitutional values but merely contrasting conceptions of judicial creativity within code-based and common law systems.

Despite these similarities, the Supreme Court's formulation in the *Dolphin Delivery* case seemed to come from nowhere. In Canada the debate about the impact on private law of the Charter's adoption had centred on the possibility of direct application. The extensive and profound German debate about direct and indirect application had no Canadian parallel and was ignored. Nor was any notice taken of German developments in the decades since the *Lüth* case.[8] As in other areas of Charter jurisprudence, the Supreme Court contributed to the mystification of its own decisions by failing to advert to foreign influences

development of the common law and customary law, a court shall have due regard for the spirit, purport and objects" of the fundamental rights provisions. See *Du Plessis* v. *De Klerk* 1996 (3) SA 850 (CC) and A. Fagan, chap. 4 this vol. Another significant development is the enactment in Britain of the Human Rights Act 1998, which makes it unlawful for a public authority (defined to include a court) to act in a way that is incompatible with specified rights and freedoms under the European Convention of Human Rights and Fundamental Freedoms. For further exploration of the impact of the Human Rights Act on public authorities see H. Beale and N. Pittam, chap. 7 this vol.

[4] For descriptions of the *Drittwirkung* in English, see K. Lewan, "The Significance of Constitutional Rights for Private Law: Theory and Practice in West Germany" (1968) 17 *Int'l. & Comp. L Q* 571; P. Quint, "Free Speech and Private Law in German Constitutional Theory" (1989) 48 *Md. L Rev.* 247; S. Oeter, "Fundamental Rights and their Impact on Private Law—Doctrine and Practice under the German Constitution" (1994) 12 *Tel Aviv Stud. L* 7; E. Eberle, "Public Discourse in Contemporary Germany" (1997) 47 *Case. W. Res. L Rev.* 797; B.S. Markesinis, "Privacy, Freedom of Expression, and the Horizontal Effect of the Human Rights Bill: Lessons from Germany" (1999) 115 *LQR* 47.

[5] (1958) 7 BVerfGE 198 (hereinafter *Lüth*). An English version of the case can be found in B.S. Markesinis, *The German Law of Obligations* (3rd edn., Oxford, Clarendon Press, 1997), ii, 352. For a more complete text, see *Decisions of the Bundesverfassungsgericht—Federal Constitutional Court—Federal Republic of Germany, Freedom of Speech*, Vol II/2 (Karlsruhe, Nomos Verlagsgesellschaft, 1998) 1–20. See also C. Starck, chap. 5 this vol.

[6] Markesinis, *supra* n.5, at 355.

[7] *Supra* n.1.

[8] *Supra* n.5.

and parallels.[9] Accordingly, the Court's holding that Charter values were relevant to private law even though the Charter itself did not apply to private law appeared to be an idiosyncratic and contradictory pronouncement.[10]

Nor, having articulated this connection between Charter values and private law, has the Court's handling of its implications been particularly illuminating. The Court explicitly dealt with this connection in only two cases. The first, *Dolphin Delivery*[11] itself, upheld the granting of an interlocutory injunction against secondary picketing, on the ground that the picketers' purpose was to induce a breach of contract. Having affirmed that the common law should be developed in a manner consistent with Charter values, the Court gave no indication of how these values were to be elucidated in the dispute at hand. Moreover, despite its conclusion that the Charter did not apply to a dispute between private parties, the majority of the Court, in a detailed Charter analysis, held that the injunction was justified as a reasonable limitation on Charter rights. It is as if the Court, by holding that there would be no Charter violation if the Charter applied directly, felt itself absolved from addressing what, in its own view, was the different task of determining the relevance of constitutional values to a tort remedy that restricted freedom of expression.

In the second case, *Hill* v. *Church of Scientology*,[12] the Court held that defamatory statements made about the plaintiff lawyer's conduct of a prosecution exceeded the scope of the defendant's qualified privilege. In examining the impact of constitutionally guaranteed freedom of expression on defamation rules, the Court restated its view that in purely private civil litigation only Charter values and not Charter rights are relevant. This, it said, required balancing the interest in reputation—which the Court elevated to a quasi-constitutional value[13]—against the equally important right of freedom of expression. But invited to replace the qualified privilege with the American rule that only malicious criticism of a public official triggers liability for defamation, the Court canvassed general criticisms of the American rule and then upheld the narrowness of the qualified privilege.[14] The Court's focus was broadly on

---

[9] L.E. Weinrib, "Canada's Rights Revolution: Paradigm Lost?", forthcoming in *Rev. Const. Stud.*

[10] For example, see B. Slattery, "The *Charter*'s Relevance to Private Litigation: Does *Dolphin Deliver*?" (1987) 32 *McGill LJ* 905, 921. More recently, *Dolphin Delivery* has been described as "a decision . . . famous for its incoherent approach to the application of the *Charter* to the private sphere": see P. Macklem, "Secondary Picketing, Consumer Boycotts, and the *Charter*" (2000) 8 *Cana. Labour and Employment LJ* 1, 9.

[11] *Supra* n.1.

[12] (1995) 126 DLR (4th) 129 (SCC) (hereinafter *Hill*).

[13] "Although it is not specifically mentioned in the Charter, the good reputation of the individual represents and reflects the innate dignity of the individual, a concept which underlies all the Charter rights": *ibid.*, at 163.

[14] On the validity of these criticisms see J. Ross, "The Common Law of Defamation Fails to Enter the Age of the Charter" (1996) 35 *Alberta L Rev.* 117, 133–5. Prof. Ross points out that some of these criticisms were offered not because the malice defence was too unfavourable to interests in reputation, as one would think from the court's judgment, but because it was too restrictive of freedom of expression.

the desirability of a malice standard, rather than specifically on the balance between reputation and freedom of expression. Accordingly, the judgment yields little clarification of the process by which to assess the relevance of a Charter value to private law litigation.

The consequence is that the significance of the relationship between constitutional values and private law has yet to be elucidated at the highest level in Canada. In neither case before the Court to date has the presence of constitutional values made much difference to the result or the analysis. In both cases the prior doctrine remained unchanged in the face of the Charter's reference to freedom of expression. Moreover, while pointing to the need to balance freedom of expression against the plaintiff's protected interest in contractual relationships or reputation, the Court has provided sparse guidance on how this balancing is to be carried out or even what it means.

Nonetheless, *Dolphin Delivery*[15] has the potential to transform private law in Canada. The effects on legal doctrine may be as far-reaching as that produced by any of the great landmark cases of private law. The minimal impact and sketchy elucidation accorded to Charter values so far might lead one to suspect that the Court's references to them are rhetorical rather than substantive. Our analysis here attempts to take these references seriously and explore how constitutional values might explicitly be integrated into private law.

II. THE RECEPTIVITY OF PRIVATE LAW TO CONSTITUTIONAL VALUES

Taking for granted that Charter values are relevant to private law, we first consider the theoretical place of constitutional values within private law. What is it about the nature of private law that allows it to be affected by constitutional values?

Of course, the nature of private law is itself a matter of considerable controversy. Among contemporary scholars, the main line is that drawn between those who see private law non-instrumentally as the juridical realisation of corrective justice and those who see it instrumentally as the vehicle for promoting economic efficiency. Our point of departure is the corrective justice approach, not merely because we believe it to be superior,[16] but also because it is more germane to considering the influence of constitutional rights. Under the economic approach rights carry no independent normative content but are merely labels attached to the results of calculations about the economic desirability of given legal arrangements. In contrast, the corrective justice approach presupposes the normative significance of rights as embodiments of the freedom of the interacting parties. Corrective justice thus points to the orientation common to private law and constitutional rights.

Under the corrective justice approach, private law is the operation of public reason on the bipolar relationship of plaintiff and defendant. The distinguishing

[15] *Supra* n.1.
[16] E.J. Weinrib, *The Idea of Private Law* (Cambridge, Mass., Harvard University Press, 1995).

feature of private law is that the liability of the defendant is simultaneously a liability to the plaintiff. For private law to be an exercise of public reason, there must be a publicly available justification not merely of why the law takes something from the defeated defendant or gives something to the victorious plaintiff, but why in every case liability consists in the law's giving to one party what it takes from the other. Moreover, this publicly available justification must be consistent with the institutional framework of private law: since courts administer private law, the justifications they deploy must draw on facts and embody reasons that are within their limited institutional competence. Complex calculations and assumptions of omniscience are excluded.

Corrective justice locates the requisite framework of justification in the correlativity of the plaintiff's right and the defendant's duty. Because the parties' normative positions are correlative, a justification for liability that applies to one of them also applies to the other. This correlativity of right and duty is then articulated into the principles that figure in private law and are evident in such truisms as the requirement of causation in tort law and contract law and of the defendant's enrichment at the plaintiff's expense in the law of restitution. A court's reasons elaborate these bipolar concepts in the context of specific occurrences and determine whether the defendant has something or has done something inconsistent with the plaintiff's right. Since the court's attention is limited to the normative implications of a bipolar interaction and since the participants in that interaction can produce the relevant facts and the arguments, the issues are within the court's institutional competence. The process is public through and through, from the law's construction of the categories to the court's adjudication of particular instances of litigation. Indeed, opacity at any point in the process is a legitimate ground for criticism.

One can distinguish three conceptual stages or moments (as Kant called them) to the elucidation of private law as an enterprise in public reason.[17] The first moment is the conception of the person presupposed in the relationship of the parties. The person in private law is a self-determining agent characterised solely by the capacity for purposive action without being obligated to act for any purpose in particular. This capacity for purposiveness is the basis for ascribing dignity to every self-determining agent and is presupposed in the law's notions of imputability and entitlement. By virtue of one's self-determining agency, a person has the normative status to assert one's dignity in relation to others and therefore to be an end and not merely a means for them. Rights are the juridical embodiments of the dignity inherent in self-determining agency. Correlatively, a duty is the restraint that the existence of another's right imposes on the exercise of one's freedom.

The second moment is the ensemble of juridical categories that express these rights and duties in the interaction of one person with another. Because persons

---

[17] For a fuller statement of the Kantian position adumbrated here, see E.J. Weinrib, "Publicness and Private Law" in H. Robinson (ed.), *Proceedings of the Eighth International Kant Conference* (Milwaukee, NJ, Marquette University Press, 1995) i, 191; Weinrib, *supra* n.16, at 100–9.

are conceived as having a capacity for purposiveness without regard to particular purposes, the relationships of private law are defined in terms of non-interference with the rights of others. These rights arise in so far as the capacity for purposive agency is not merely an inward attribute but achieves external existence in social interactions through its exercise by or embodiment in an agent. Among these rights are the right to the integrity of one's body as the organ of purposive activity, the right to property in things appropriately connected to an external manifestation of the proprietor's volition, and the right to contractual performance in accordance with the mutually consensual exercises of the parties' purposiveness. The existence of these rights gives rise to correlative duties of non-interference whose content and application vary with the nature of the right.

The third moment is the operation of these categories through a set of legal institutions. Private law requires a system of public law not only coercively to guarantee the security of everyone's rights, but also authoritatively to determine the meaning of the various rights in the context of specific interactions. Reflection on the implications of self-determining agency may lead to the conclusion under the second aspect that one has a right to physical integrity or to property or to contractual performance. Nonetheless, authoritative institutions of public reason must work out the specific rules that apply to particular transactions. Does physical integrity, for instance, include protection against an apprehended contact or merely an actual one (that is, is there a tort of assault)? Does it include security against mental suffering? Does it include the interest in one's reputation?[18] Without institutions that determine the content of the rights to which self-determining agents are entitled, these rights cannot really function as juridical expressions of the dignity of self-determining agents.

To determine the content of private law rights, the court as an institution of public reason views the litigants as participants in a social relationship within a world of shared social meanings. The working out of the juridical significance of the parties' conduct is historically variable and relative to societal contexts and understandings. The court's task is to draw on the public culture (which of course includes the court's own prior determinations) in order to give concrete meaning to the legal categories expressive of the parties' self-determining capacity as normatively equal participants in the transaction. The court must also present a public justification of its conclusion by appealing to considerations that others, as self-determining beings engaged in interactions with one another, can reasonably acknowledge. As the development of liability for mental suffering shows, these considerations can change over time as new forms of knowledge

---

[18] For example, Kant seems to have considered reputation as the same kind of right as bodily integrity. "[A] *good reputation* is an innate external belonging . . . that clings to the subject as a person": see "The Doctrine of Right", Section 35 in *The Metaphysics of Morals* (Gregor (trans.), Cambridge, Cambridge University Press, 1991) 111 [295]. Kant defines an innate right as "that which belongs to everyone by nature, independently of any act that would establish a right": *ibid.*, at 63 [237]. Compare the statement in the *Hill* case, *supra* n.13, that good reputation "represents and reflects the innate dignity of the individual".

and new appreciations of the social implications of different behaviours arise. In this way the specific content of the rights is derived, not through philosophical speculation, but through reference to beliefs, values, and modes of reasoning that have public plausibility.[19]

Accordingly, public law requires judicial and political institutions to perform the functions of guaranteeing security and determining rights. Even when operating in contexts not indigenous to private law, these institutions affect the judicial project of determining the content of private law's categories.

The relevance of statutes to private law provides an example of this. The behaviour that private law addresses is also regulated by a variety of statutes that are designed to promote safety and to penalise those who endanger others. These statutes may not only be enforced in their own terms but may also, where appropriate, be treated as relevant to the setting of private law standards. In Canada, such statutes are regarded not as formulating a *per se* standard or as grounding a distinct tort of statutory breach, but as providing evidence for determining whether the defendant should be considered negligent under the general principles of tort law.[20] Accordingly, even where they do not directly apply to the facts being litigated, statutory norms can be regarded "as crystallizing a relevant fact situation which, because of its authoritative source, the Court [is] entitled to consider in determining, on common law principles, whether a duty of care should be raised".[21] In such a case the statute assists in specifying the content of private law categories in contexts beyond its scope as a legislative command.

Constitutional protections of human rights can play a similar role. A constitutional democracy guarantees certain basic liberties as a way of obligating itself to respect the dignity and self-determining capacity of those who are subject to its power. Inscribed in the constitution are rights that enumerate the specific features of self-determining agency that a particular society regards as pertinent to the relations of government and governed. These rights may be held not to be directly applicable to private law. Nonetheless, because the constitution commits the legal order to the priority of human dignity and enumerates the constituents of dignity for political purposes, constitutional values are available for specifying the incidents of dignity included within private law. Even if the constitutional document was created to restrain government, it shares with private law a concern for dignity. The constitution, as society's authoritative repository of legally supreme and publicly accessible values concerning human dignity, is a pre-eminent source on which public reason can draw as it gives concrete meaning to the categories that comprise private law. Indeed, from the standpoint of public reason, the constitution crystallises in a uniquely conspicuous way the

---

[19] See especially J. Rawls, "The Idea of Public Reason Revisited" (1997) 64 *U Chi. L Rev.* 765, 766–73. On the significance for private law of Rawls's idea of public reason see P. Benson, "The Idea of a Public Basis of Justification for Contract" (1995) 33 *Osgoode Hall LJ* 273.

[20] *The Queen in the Right of Canada* v. *Saskatchewan Wheat Pool* (1983) 143 DLR (3d) 9 (SCC).

[21] *Jordan House* v. *Menow* (1973) 38 DLR (3d) 105, 109 (SCC, *per* Justice Laskin).

values to be recognised in the process of ascribing specific meanings to the rights and correlative duties of private law.

Constitutional values, then, can become relevant to private law at the stage of specifying the content of the private law categories. Private law's use of the constitution resembles its use of statutes. Neither the constitution nor the statute directly governs the situations for which private law invokes them. Nonetheless, the constitution and the statute serve to flesh out the meaning of private law categories and standards.

Yet the specifying functions of a statute and of the constitution are importantly different, as is evident in the way the Supreme Court of Canada refers to them. Under *Dolphin Delivery*,[22] the judiciary is required to develop the principles of the common law in a manner consistent with Charter values. By contrast, the use of a statutory provision reflects no parallel requirement. The existence of a statutory safety standard relevant to determining whether the defendant breached a common law duty of care cannot be said to create a judicial obligation to develop the common law consistently with that particular statute or even with the entire ensemble of statutes. The statutory provision is merely incidental to the development of the common law. Because it provides evidence of the standard in a particular case, its availability is a happy fortuity that a plaintiff can exploit and that a court can find helpful. But it does not present a norm to be incorporated for its own sake.

Charter values are different. If the principles of the common law must be developed in a manner consistent with Charter values, it must be that those values as a set have an affirmative and non-incidental significance for private law. The very fact that these values refer to legally cognisable aspects of dignity endows them with systemic normative significance within private law. They are therefore apposite for specifying the content of the categories of bodily integrity, property and contract—themselves the juridical embodiments of the dignity inherent in self-determining agency—that arise at the second moment in the conceptualisation of private law. It is as if, in the social contract that marks the transition from the second moment of legal categories to the third moment of judicial and political institutions, citizens subscribe to the State and its institutions only on terms that make the respect for human dignity through Charter values an interpretive principle in the elucidation of private law. The assumption underlying the requirement that private law be consistent with Charter values is that self-determining agents contracting to enter a constitutional democracy could not reasonably acknowledge a specification of private rights that is inconsistent with the indicia of dignity to which citizens have accorded constitutional recognition. In this sense, constitutional values are constitutive of the juridical relationships of private law, even though constitutional rights as such are not applicable to them.

The constitution thus serves a double function. On the one hand, it sets out the limits to which the idea of human dignity constrains government action. On

---

[22] *Supra* n.1.

the other hand, it provides a catalogue of values that can guide courts in the elaboration of the principles and standards that govern the private law relationships.[23] In this respect, the Charter is more than a statute writ large that itemises particular restrictions on the jurisdiction of particular governmental authorities. It is a repository of the principles animating the polity as a whole. Consequently, it affects the legal order not only through its explicit provisions and its mechanisms of enforcement, but also through the values implicit in its conception of a free and democratic society.[24] Linking these functions is the exercise of public reason by the courts in constitutional cases, for in elucidating the constitutional limits on government action, courts inevitably explicate constitutional values. Constitutional jurisprudence thereby even further enriches the resources on which public reason can draw in the private law context.

On this basis, the constitution does not merely contain rights that a citizen can assert against governmental power. It also establishes (in the words of the German Constitutional Court) "an objective system of values in its section on basic rights . . . This system of values, centring on the freedom of the human being to develop in society . . . must direct and inform legislation, administration, and judicial decision. It naturally influences private law as well".[25] The statement from *Dolphin Delivery*[26] with which we began is the official Canadian recognition of this role for constitutional values.

III. ENTITLEMENT AND RELATIONSHIP

This role is facilitated by the fact that structural features are common to the working of rights in the private law and in the constitutional law contexts. The first of these, which we term the "entitlement" element, concerns the content of the right or of any other ingredient in the claim. The second, which we term the "relationship" element, goes to the relationship between that entitlement and the other legal components of the controversy. In a coherent legal system these two elements are mutually entailed: because all the components in any controversy form a unified whole, the content of any entitlement and the relationship between that entitlement and the other components can be defined only by reference to each other. Nonetheless, it is convenient as a matter of exposition to hold the two elements apart and to examine the considerations that are initially

[23] In the language of German constitutional theory, the constitution contains both "subjective rights" of individuals that the State must respect and "objective principles" governing the entire legal order, including relationships of citizens to each other: see B. Schlink, "German Constitutional Culture in Transition" in M. Rosenfeld (ed.), *Constitutionalism, Identity, Difference, and Legitimacy: Theoretical Perspectives* (Durham, NC, and London, Duke University Press, 1994) 197.

[24] *Reference re Remuneration of Judges of the Provincial Court of Prince Edward Island* [1997] 3 SCR 3; *Reference re Secession of Quebec* (1998) 161 DLR (4th) 385 (SCC).

[25] Markesinis, *supra* n.5, at 355.

[26] *Supra* n.1.

pertinent to each.[27] In this section, we outline these two elements in both private and constitutional law. The two elements will then form the organising ideas for the remaining sections of this chapter.

Consider private law first. Private law is a regime of rights and their correlative duties of non-interference. The content of these rights consists in such matters as one's physical integrity, one's property, and the contractual performances that one might be owed. The nature and extent of the obligations of others not to interfere goes to the element of relationship. Accordingly, what constitutes an interference cannot be settled merely by adverting to the plaintiff's right, but is a relational issue that must take account of both parties. For example, tort law rejects strict liability, that is, liability incurred merely by injuring another's physical integrity, on the assumption that although such injury damages the content of the plaintiff's right, it does not in itself give the right-holder a claim to the injurer's liability. Instead, tort law insists that the relationship between the defendant's behaviour and the plaintiff's right be constituted by fault consisting either in the intentional execution of the injury or in the materialisation of a negligently created risk.

The relational element reflects the private law's fundamental moral impulse to maintain the equality of the parties in considering the injustice that one of them is alleged to have done to the other. This transactional equality is rooted in the parties' equal normative status as self-determining agents. It is inconsistent with this equality for the considerations pertaining to one of the parties to determine the legal position of the entire relationship. For instance, by focussing solely on the plaintiff's right, strict liability would in effect allow plaintiffs to set the terms on which others interact with them. Conversely, negligence law sets an objective standard of due care rather than a subjective one, which would unilaterally favour the defendant by defining the plaintiff's area of immunity from injury in terms of the defendant's particular capacities.[28] These doctrines are merely instances of the general imperative that governs private law from within: to work out norms of liability that treat the interacting parties as equals and are therefore fair to both of them.

The constitutional guarantees of the Canadian Charter also have elements of entitlement and of relationship. The element of entitlement consists in the guaranteed rights that are familiar features of modern constitutional democracies. It is a commonplace in the jurisprudence of such democracies that rights are not absolute. This means that a further relational element comes into play—either implicitly through constitutional interpretation or explicitly through piecemeal textual qualifications—to deal with the extent of the State's obligation with respect to these rights. Canada's constitution, however, is distinctive in providing

---

[27] The two elements reflect the two great abstractions that underlie private law generally: correlativity and personality. For a description of these abstractions and a discussion of the relationship between them see E.J. Weinrib, "Correlativity, Personality, and the Emerging Consensus on Corrective Justice" (2001) 2 *Theoretical Inquiries in Law* 107.

[28] Weinrib, *supra* n.16, at 172–83.

for the relational element through a general textual provision applicable to all rights. The opening provision of the Charter reads: "[t]he *Canadian Charter of Rights and Freedoms* guarantees the rights and freedoms set out in it subject only to such reasonable limits prescribed by law as can be demonstrably justified in a free and democratic society".[29] This section qualifies the circumstances under which the State is duty bound to respect the enumerated guarantees. Impugned legislation that can be brought within the ambit of the section's description will be sustained despite its inconsistency with an enumerated right.

Of course, although the rights of both private and constitutional law have a relational element, that element is not the same for both. In private law, persons are at liberty to act as they wish provided they do not interfere with another's rights. The relationship in private law is between the plaintiff's right and the correlative duty not to interfere with the right. Here the law's task is to connect the two parties through a set of principles, categories and standards that treat them as equals, so that one person's actions can fairly be combined with another person's rights.

In contrast, the relational element in the constitutional context goes to the connection between the enumerated right and state action. Constitutional law conceives of the State not as a private party free to act as it wishes, but as a body politic acting within its constitutional authority for the common good. The system of rights does not merely restrict the State's actions, but indicates the State's constitutional nature. Accordingly, actions that trench on the enumerated rights may nonetheless be consonant with the underlying constitutional values that those rights instantiate. In working out the relationship between the rights-holder and the State, constitutional jurisprudence needs to elaborate the circumstances in which an enumerated right cedes to the constitutional values inherent in the system of rights.[30] Thus, in the constitutional context the element of relationship is concerned not with maintaining the transactional equality between the doer and the sufferer of a harm, but with negotiating the tension between specific rights and general values within the constitutional scheme. Section 1 of the Charter does this by setting out exclusive criteria for justifying limitations upon enumerated rights.[31]

The relevance of Charter values affects both elements of private law. So far as the entitlement element is concerned, a new set of interests—those associated with the values inherent in the constitutionally guaranteed rights—becomes eligible for legal protection. So far as the relational element is concerned, the law has to work out the effects that protecting those interests in one party has on the

---

[29] The Canadian Charter of Rights and Freedoms, s. 1.

[30] L.E. Weinrib, "The Supreme Court of Canada and Section 1 of the Charter" (1988) 10 *Sup. Ct. L Rev.* 469.

[31] S. 33 of the Charter allows for the overriding of a Charter right. This s. does not set out justificatory criteria. Moreover, it deals with the denial rather than the limiting of an enumerated right. It is therefore not directly relevant to the consideration the relational element triggered by the existence of a right. On the connection between s. 1 and s. 33 see L.E. Weinrib, "Learning to Live with the Override" (1990) 35 *McGill LJ* 541.

position of the other. This involves determining the relationship between the constitutional value and all the other legal components in the controversy between the parties. The new relevance to private law of constitutional values triggers an expansion of legally protected interests, necessitating adjustments within the conceptual ecology of private law.

The possible impact of Charter values on the law of defamation illustrates both kinds of effect. On the entitlement side, the law can now recognise and explicitly protect the defendant's freedom of expression as a constitutional value. That value needs no longer to be treated, at best, as merely implicit in the traditional set of haphazardly developed privileges and defences. The relevance of constitutional values is thereby capable of imparting a new content to the defendant's liberty. On the relationship side, the law would then have to work out the impact of the defendant's freedom of expression on the plaintiff's legally protected interest in reputation.

IV. RELATING CHARTER VALUES TO OTHER PRIVATE LAW INTERESTS

In this section we consider the relational element. What is involved in the interplay of Charter values with other components of private law? A complicating feature of this question is that the constitutional rights that embody these values in their indigenous context have a relational element that is expressed in section 1 of the Charter and has received extensive judicial elaboration. Accordingly, one wants to know to what extent the relational element of Charter rights in constitutional law carries over to the relational element of Charter values in private law.

On this issue the Supreme Court of Canada has offered helpful but very general remarks. It recognises a similarity between the relational elements inspired by the Charter in the two domains. Section 1 is the justificatory framework for reconciling encroachments on an enumerated right with the underlying values of the constitutional regime. Similarly, the private law context involves reconciling specific constitutional values with the whole range of interests that private law protects. Both the constitutional and the private law contexts provide occasions for balancing, though of different kinds. The difference is described as follows:

> When the common law is in conflict with Charter values, how should the competing principles be balanced? . . . [A] traditional s. 1 framework for justification is not appropriate. It must be remembered that the Charter "challenge" in a case involving private litigants does not allege the violation of a Charter right. It addresses a conflict between principles. Therefore the balancing must be more flexible than the traditional section 1 analysis undertaken in cases involving government action . . . Charter values, framed in general terms, should be weighed against the principles which underlie the common law. The Charter values will then provide the guidelines for any modification to the common law which the court feels necessary.[32]

---

[32] *Hill, supra* n.12, at 157.

Can one flesh out the references to the contrast with section 1, the greater flexibility, and the nature of the balancing exercise?

Section 1 reflects the idea that Canadians are to enjoy not merely a collection of discrete rights, but a coherent set of constitutional arrangements. As noted above, section 1 of the Charter guarantees rights "subject only to such reasonable limits prescribed by law as can be demonstrably justified in a free and democratic society". Absent this section, the constitution would provide no guidance for situations in which these rights conflict with each other or fail to represent exhaustively the constitutional values that animate a free and democratic society. The presence of section 1, together with the main lines of the Court's interpretation of it, allows the Charter to function as a coherent scheme of constitutional protections in which the enumerated rights are adjusted to one another and to the broader constitutional values that underlie the constitution as a whole.[33] Section 1 sets out a series of conditions that must be satisfied if an encroachment on an enumerated right is to stand. The requirement that the encroachment be prescribed by law affords all the protections of the rule of law and of a public process of enactment. The standard of demonstrable justification casts upon the State the onus of showing that the limit expresses the values of freedom and democracy that underlie the rights themselves. This involves recourse to a test of proportionality in which the government shows that the law's objective is pressing and substantial in a free and democratic society, that the means are rationally connected to the objective and impair the right as little as possible, and that the beneficial effects aimed at outweigh the adverse effects on the encroached right.

The functioning of this limitation belongs to the world of government action rather than private law. Section 1 assumes that the enumerated rights are controlling until displaced, and then imposes on the government the heavy onus of demonstrably justifying what would otherwise be an encroachment. The rationale for this onus has particular application to government and reflects the citizen's entitlement to constitutional behaviour by those who govern. When legislation is impugned, the government is present as the litigant responsible for the entire ensemble of the exercises of governmental power over time. Section 1 gives the government the opportunity under stringent conditions to show that, despite the encroachment on an enumerated right, this responsibility has been constitutionally discharged. The government does this by demonstrating the importance of the legislative objective and the reasonableness of the chosen means to achieve it. The objective, in turn, cannot merely be asserted or manufactured for the occasion of the constitutional hearing but must refer to the historical reason for the legislature's action. The discharge of its responsibility for what has been enacted can be relative only to the actual reason for enacting it. Justification therefore consists in the adducing of legislative facts in a legislative

---

[33] L.E. Weinrib, "Canada's Constitutional Revolution: From Legislative to Constitutional State" (1999) 33 *Israel L Rev*. 13, 26–37.

process for which government is responsible. The organising of these facts into a presentable file is peculiarly within the resources of government as the entity responsible for the legislative product. Thus, the requirement of demonstrable justification mirrors the government's responsibility for any exercise of state power, the particular availability to it of the material relevant to support any such exercise, and the necessity for state power to be consonant with constitutional strictures. Section 1 is the ultimate expression in the Canadian constitution of the idea that with governmental power comes governmental responsibility.

Private litigation differs in that neither of the parties is responsible for the rules being invoked. These rules are merely available to them in the controversy in which they find themselves. It is open to them to argue about the facts and what the rule should be in a particular case. But responsibility for the whole system over time belongs to neither of them. (If it belongs to anyone, it belongs to the judge.) Nor does either of them have an advantage over the other in the availability of evidence to support the impugned rule. And since they are not responsible for the creation of the rule, there is no reason for them to be committed to the particular historical objective that produced it. Thus, from the standpoint of private litigation, no reason exists for imposing on one of the litigants the heavy burden of demonstrable justification of the constitutionality of a rule.

Moreover, from the standpoint of private law, no reason exists for regarding the Charter values as controlling until displaced in a second stage of legal argument. Whereas constitutional law gives individual rights priority against government action by treating those rights as norms whose infringement the government must demonstrably justify, private law regards the plaintiff and the defendant as parties whose legitimate interests the law must consider on terms of equality. The doctrine that private law should be developed in a manner consistent with Charter values does not transform private law into constitutional law. Rather, Charter values enter private law as considerations that interplay with other private law considerations in a way that is fair to both parties. It would be odd to think of the tort of defamation, for instance, as devoted to protecting the defendant's freedom of expression except where the plaintiff could demonstrably justify the need to protect reputation. Defamation's organising concern is the interest in reputation; the constitutional value inherent in freedom of expression is merely an interest against which the interest in reputation must be fairly balanced. Neither interest starts with a priority with respect to the other.

Accordingly, the Court rightly thinks that the balancing of constitutional values against other considerations does not involve recourse to section 1. That section is peculiarly suited to the assessment of government encroachments on guaranteed rights rather than of the interaction between private law litigants.

Nonetheless, although not applicable to private law, section 1 is suggestive. Consistent with the operation of other post-war rights-protecting instruments, the Court has interpreted section 1 as entailing a test of proportionality between the effects on the enumerated right and the importance of the legislative objective. Under this test, even an encroachment that is rationally connected to a pressing legislative objective must impair the right only to the minimal extent possible. Moreover, such an encroachment may fail if the deleterious effect on the right is disproportionate to the salutary effects of the encroaching legislation. This test of proportionality functions to preserve the difference between justifiably limiting a right, which is permitted by section 1, and nullifying that right, which falls outside section 1 and requires recourse to the legislative override in section 33 of the Charter. The implication is that a justified limitation needs to preserve intact, so far as possible, the central range of application of the right on which it encroaches.[34] In this way, the Canadian jurisprudence runs parallel to the German constitutional provision that allows a basic right to be restricted so long as there is no encroachment on its "essential content".[35]

The idea of preserving intact this central range of application is relevant to the invocation of Charter values in private law. For purposes of private law two modifications are necessary. First, the test of proportionality has to be stripped of its connection to a legislative objective, since such objectives are absent in private law. Secondly, the central range of application matters not only for constitutional rights and the values inherent in them but also for every normative component in the parties' legal relationship. This is because Charter values have relevance but not priority within private law. The consequence of the Court's jurisprudence about Charter values is to include those values on terms of equality within the ensemble of considerations that matter to private law. Therefore, an idea applicable to Charter values is also applicable to every member of the ensemble. Charter values are thus integrated into private law through the mutual adjustment of Charter values and other normative components in a way that preserves intact, so far as possible, the central range of application of each of them. One may recall the Court's cryptic observation that balancing in the private law's treatment of Charter values is more flexible than in traditional section 1 analysis. The loosening of the test of proportionality from its moorings in legislative objective and the extension of the idea of the central range from Charter values to other normative features of the parties' relationship perhaps suitably illuminate this reference to increased flexibility.

Thus, in the case of a conflict between Charter values and other principles, a version of proportionality geared to private law is available.[36] This version

---

[34] The formulation in terms of preserving intact the central range of application comes from J. Rawls, *Political Liberalism* (New York, Columbia University Press, 1993) 295–6.

[35] Basic Law of the Federal Republic of Germany, Art. 19.

[36] Compare the treatment in *Dagenais* v. *Canadian Broadcasting Corporation* (1994) 120 DLR (4th) 12 (SCC) of a publication ban imposed by a court under its common law authority. In articulating a standard for assessing such bans that "clearly reflects the substance of the *Oakes* test applicable for assessing legislation under Section 1 of the Charter" Chief Justice Lamer said (at 37):

"It is open to this court to "develop the principles of the common law in a manner consistent with the fundamental values enshrined in the Constitution": *Dolphin Delivery* . . . I am, therefore, of

involves a balancing process in which a central aspect of one normative principle is granted priority over a comparatively more marginal aspect of another. Relevant to this exercise would be a comparison of the principles that favour the two parties, in which one asks whether the triumph of the plaintiff's principle would impact more heavily on the defendant's than the triumph of the defendant's principle would impact on the plaintiff's. This process of mutual adjustment also entails softening the hard edges of traditional private law concepts, so that the marginal aspects of one concept can yield to the more central aspects of another.

The purpose of this version of proportionality is not to give the law a utilitarian cast. That would be foreign to a system of rights regarded as embodiments of self-determining agency. The marginality or centrality of the aspects being compared does not depend on their role within a calculus of the overall utility of the resulting doctrine. Nor is the aim to achieve a "utilitarianism of rights"[37] by minimising the total weighted amount of all the rights violations in the legal order. These utilitarianisms could properly draw the charge that the individual is being sacrificed to the production of some desirable end state. The balancing in this conception of proportionality occurs entirely within a transaction, with each of the principles in play being examined from its own normative standpoint in order to determine what applications are more or less central to it. The marginality and centrality of the aspects being compared reflect their internal significance for their respective principles, and their practical effect on the interests that the principles protect. There is no summing across transactions, and thus no sacrifice of the individual in one transaction to the aggregated advantages of others. Although the litigation produces a winner and a loser, the law does not sacrifice the latter to the former. As long as the principles are balanced in a fair way, so that neither litigant can complain that the other is being unfairly preferred, the decision merely determines the entitlements that any right-holder (including the loser) has in an interaction with others.

Proportionality expresses the form of transactional equality relevant to the presence of constitutional values. Transactional equality is the most deeply ingrained and pervasive relational principle of private law. The principle affirms that, since the plaintiff and the defendant have equal status in their relationship, the decision between them cannot be made on the basis of considerations that reflect the normative position of only one of them. The idea of proportionality maintains the transactional equality of the two parties by treating their relationship as informed by an ensemble of normative concepts, no one of which is absolute. Through a comparison of the reciprocal effects of the concepts in play

the view that it is necessary to reformulate the common law rule governing the issuance of publication bans in a manner that reflects the principles of the *Charter*. Given that publication bans, by their very definition, curtail the freedom of expression of third parties, I believe that the common law rule must be adapted so as to require a consideration both of the objectives of a publication ban, and the proportionality of the ban to its effect on protected *Charter* rights".

[37] R. Nozick, *Anarchy, State, and Utopia* (New York, Basic Books, 1974) 28.

on both sides, proportionality preserves intact, so far as possible, the central range of application of all of them. In this way proportionality reconfigures the idea of transactional equality to include constitutional values.

The similarity of this notion of private law proportionality to section 1 analysis has the following advantage. Private law is often intimately related to legislation: private law concepts appear in legislation; areas of private law may be codified; under Canada's federal system, what is private law in one province may be the subject of legislation in another. Thus, the judicial development of the common law with its recognition of Charter values has to coexist with the constitutional assessment of legislation that is subject to section 1 analysis. It would be undesirable if the common law development and the constitutional assessment of the same kind of transactions were widely divergent. Recourse to related versions of proportionality in the private and constitutional law contexts can be expected to keep the two streams of development roughly compatible. This is because in their different ways both versions aim at preserving intact the central range of application for constitutional rights and for the values that these rights contain.

So far, our discussion of the balancing process for Charter values in private law has been fairly abstract. We conclude this section with two illustrations.

The first is the famous *Mephisto* case in Germany.[38] That case concerned the publication of a *roman à clef* by the writer Klaus Mann based on the life of a well-known and easily recognisable theatre personage (in fact, Mann's one-time brother-in-law), who had advanced his career by opportunistically currying favour with the Nazi authorities. The book was intended, as the author put it, "to expose and analyse the abject type of the treacherous intellectual who prostitutes his talent for the sake of some tawdry fame and transitory wealth".[39] The author, however, wove into the novel discreditable episodes that had not occurred in the life of the person on whom the book was based. Would such a publication be defamatory under Canadian law?

These facts afford a sharp contrast between pre-Charter and post-Charter approaches. Before the Charter, the case for liability would have been overwhelming. A reasonable person could be in no doubt that the book referred to the plaintiff. The episodes were such as to lower the plaintiff in the estimation of others. They could not be justified as being true. No privilege attached to them. As a fictionalised portrayal rather than a comment on facts, they did not qualify as fair comment. Aside from the incidental protection afforded by the established categories of defences, freedom of expression had no pertinence.

The requirement that the common law develop in a manner consistent with Charter values opens up new possibilities for invoking freedom of expression. The question now becomes one of balancing the defendant's freedom of expression

---

[38] (1971) 30 BVerfGE 173. A translation of parts of the case can be found in Markesinis, *supra* n.5, at 360. For a more complete text, see *Decisions of the Bundesverfassungsgericht, supra* n. 5, at 147.

[39] Markesinis, *supra* n.5, at 361.

against the plaintiff's protected interest in reputation. On the proportionality approach, the balance inclines in favour of the defendant. Central to the artist's freedom of expression is the power to create an imaginative picture based on the artist's life experience. The artist's creativity and imagination cannot be constrained to reproduce the precise historical reality of the person on whom the artist's portrait is based. The plaintiff, to be sure, is entitled to the protection of his reputation. But in this case the damage to his reputation is marginal, since the defamatory episodes were merely exaggerations of conduct that was discreditable.[40]

The second illustration is the pre-Charter Canadian case of *Harrison* v. *Carswell*,[41] which dealt with the right of the owner of a shopping centre to exclude an employee who was picketing one of the businesses in the course of a labour dispute. Justice Dickson, on behalf of the majority, held that the employee, by continuing to picket in the face of a demand by the owner to leave the property, had committed a trespass. He rejected the contention that the Court "should weigh and determine the respective values to society of the right to property and the right to picket". That contention "raises important and difficult political and socio-economic issues, the resolution of which must, by their very nature, be arbitrary and embody personal economic and social beliefs".[42] Chief Justice Laskin dissented. In his view, the case called not for a strict application of "an ancient legal concept, trespass, . . . in all its pristine force", but for "a balancing of rights, a consideration of the relativity of rights involving advertence to social activity as well as personal advantage".[43] He emphasised the importance of public access to the owner himself and the absence of any challenge by the picketer to the owner's title, possession or privacy.

It goes without saying that such a dispute now would require precisely the judicial exercise that Justice Dickson repudiated. Unanchored in a constitutional document, the assessment of the competing claims could in pre-Charter days arguably be described as the "arbitrary" recourse to "personal economic and social beliefs". Now the significance of the Charter value inherent in freedom of expression cannot be avoided in considering the use of trespass to suppress picketing.

In contrast, Justice Laskin's judgment foreshadows the post-Charter analysis suggested above. The proportionality approach would proceed roughly as follows. The presence of a competing constitutional value entails a softening of the hard edges of the classic property right to exclude.[44] The central range

---

[40] In the actual case, the civil court decided in favour of the claim, and the Constitutional court declined to interfere with the civil court's balancing. We ignore here the complication that the person on whose life the novel was based was dead at the time of the action.

[41] (1976) 62 DLR (3d) 68 (SCC) (hereinafter *Harrison*).

[42] *Ibid.*, at 82.

[43] *Ibid.*, at 73, 75.

[44] Justice Laskin himself seemed to be concerned not with freedom of expression but with the role of picketing in the equilibrium between the parties to a labour dispute. Hence he describes the case as one in which "trespass is invoked to suppress a lawful activity supported both by legislation and by a well-understood legislative policy" (*ibid.*, at 69). Complicating the case was the fact that in a previous judgment, *R.* v. *Peters* (1971) 17 DLR (3d) 128 (hereinafter *Peters*), the court, with Justice

of application of the owner's property right in this case has to be considered in the light of the dependence of a shopping centre on public accessibility. An owner's interest in title, possession and privacy remains within that central range, but, as Justice Laskin pointed out, these are not under threat. Indeed, in these circumstances the proprietor, by setting up a shopping centre, has put the property to a use that signals the relative insignificance of this privacy interest. On the other hand, the picketer's exercise of her freedom of expression to draw attention to her employment demands cannot be effective unless carried out in the proximity of her employer's business. Granting the owner the power to proscribe picketing in the shopping centre would cut more deeply into the picketer's freedom of expression than would the permissibility of picketing cut into the owner's proprietary rights.

So far, we have been treating *Harrison* for illustrative purposes as a private law case about the tort of trespass. In fact, the case involved charges under a penal trespass statute. If that statute were challenged today, the issue would be whether legislation that had the effect of curtailing a picketer's speech could be saved under section 1 of the Charter. The general lines of the analysis, however, would remain. Even if the protection of the proprietor's right to exclude was considered an important legislative objective and the exercise of penal power was regarded as having a rational and necessary connection to that objective, a court would then be required to compare the salutary effects of protecting the shopping centre owner's right to exclude with the adverse effects on the encroached right. Presumably the factors that Justice Laskin mentioned and that were incorporated into the private law proportionality just outlined would be equally significant for the analysis under section 1. As noted above, the use of proportionality in the private and constitutional contexts would be compatible. While the exact form of the analysis would differ, the content of the picketer's rights would not significantly vary at common law and under the legislation.

V. THE INFLUENCE OF CHARTER VALUES ON ENTITLEMENTS

Having situated Charter values in the ensemble of components that make up the relationship between the parties, we now turn to the influence of Charter values on the content of the parties' entitlements. How does the idea that the development of the common law ought to be consistent with constitutional values affect the rights, freedoms and powers that a private litigant can invoke?

The most obvious and least problematic effect is the elimination of settled doctrines that are inconsistent with Charter values. For example, at common law a husband can claim damages for loss of consortium if, as a result of a tort

Laskin concurring, had upheld the invocation of trespass in a non-labour context to suppress pick-eting on behalf of a boycott on California grapes. Justice Laskin's concurrence in *Peters* would have made it awkward for him to base the picketer's right in *Harrison* on freedom of expression. For further exploration of the classic property right to exclude, see A. Reichman, chap. 11 this vol.

suffered by his wife, he is deprived of her society. No parallel action exists on behalf of the wife.[45] Even before *Dolphin Delivery*,[46] trial courts began to invoke the Charter to eliminate this anomaly, either by giving the wife an equivalent claim[47] or by abolishing the husband's claim.[48] The latter alternative, based as it was on the rejection of the notion that the husband has a quasi-proprietary interest in the wife, can itself be regarded as developing the common law in a manner consistent with Charter values.[49] This kind of effect, one hopes, is not very significant. One can perhaps assume that private law, which in its own way treats the parties as having rights that embody dignity, is not rife with settled doctrines that contradict Charter values.

Another possible effect involves the filling in of gaps and indeterminacies in doctrine that is as yet unsettled. Consider the calculation of the future income component of tort damages for a girl who is injured at birth or in childhood. What is the court to make of the argument that employment inequities have resulted in women earning less than men? Should a court base its calculation on the projected earning power of women, reflecting the possibility that wage parity might not be achieved? Or should it base its calculation on male earning tables? The Supreme Court of Canada has adverted to this problem, but has not yet been presented with a case where the evidentiary foundation for dealing with it has been properly laid.[50] One might argue that compensation for the plaintiff entails merely calculating, to the best of the judge's powers, what the plaintiff in fact would have earned in a world still beset by wage inequity. On the other hand, consistency with Charter values might justify adopting a method of calculation that does not replicate the gender stereotyping that the Charter's equality provisions are designed to uproot.

Related to this function is the use of Charter values to give content to amorphous ideas such as just cause, illegal means and public policy. The conceptions like dignity and autonomy that underlie today's constitutional rights have often, even in the absence of a constitutional document, found judicial expression through reference to public policy. For example, in *Horwood* v. *Millar's Timber and Trading Company*[51] a borrower assigned to his creditor his present and future earnings. He also promised that he would not change his employment or his residence, put himself further into debt, or sell or pledge his household effects. The Court of Appeal of England struck the contract down as being against public policy because it effectively created an obligation of servitude.[52]

[45] *Best* v. *Samuel Fox Ltd.* [1952] AC 716 (HL).
[46] *Supra* n.1.
[47] *Power* v. *Moss* (1987) 61 Nfld & PEI Rep. 5.
[48] *Shkwarchuk* v. *Hansen* (1984) 34 Sask. Rep. 211; *Baker* v. *Pleasant* (1989) 89 NSR (2d) 301.
[49] Compare the American case of *Kline* v. *Ansell* 414 A 2d. 929 (Md SC, 1980), abolishing the tort of criminal conversation on the basis of the state's Equal Rights Amendment.
[50] *Toneguzzo-Norvell* v. *Savein* (1994) 110 DLR (4th) 289 (SCC).
[51] [1917] 1 KB 305.
[52] For an example of a similar analysis in a pre-Charter constitutional context, see the dissenting judgment of Justice Idington in *Quong Wing* v. *The King* (1914) 49 Sup. Ct. Rep. 440 (racist provincial labour law does not apply to a British subject).

The Charter has expanded the scope for infusing public policy with the values enshrined in the constitution, at least at judicial levels below that of the Supreme Court of Canada. Illustrative of this is the massive shift in doctrine concerning discriminatory restrictions on the disposition of property. Shortly after the conclusion of the Second World War, an Ontario trial judgment struck down as against public policy a restrictive covenant that barred land from being sold to "Jews or persons of objectionable nationality".[53] After noting that Ontario was a province of minorities and referring to Canada's recent international commitments to respect human rights, the judge observed that "nothing could be more calculated to create or deepen divisions between existing religious or ethnic groups in the Province, or in this Country, than the sanction of a method of land transfer which would permit the segregation or confinement of particular groups to particular business or residential areas, or conversely, would exclude particular groups from particular business or residential areas".[54] Unfortunately, this enlightened view did not enjoy a long currency. A few years later in a case concerning a similar restrictive covenant, the Ontario Court of Appeal upheld the covenant and rejected this ruling about public policy.[55] In a further appeal, the Supreme Court of Canada struck down the covenant for uncertainty and for failing to touch and concern the land. The Court said nothing about the public policy argument, leaving in place its rejection by the Ontario Court of Appeal.[56]

In the aftermath of the adoption of the Charter, however, the idea that a racially discriminatory term in a property instrument can be struck down as against public policy has returned. In *Canada Trust v. Ontario Human Rights Commission*,[57] the Ontario Court of Appeal held that discriminatory restrictions on eligibility for scholarships under a charitable trust were contrary to public policy. Alluding to the equality and multiculturalism provisions of the Charter, Justice Robins explained:

> To say that a trust premised on these notions of racism and religious superiority contravenes contemporary public policy is to expatiate the obvious. The concept that any one race or any one religion is intrinsically better than any other is patently at variance with the democratic principles governing our pluralistic society in which equality rights are constitutionally guaranteed and in which the multicultural heritage of Canadians is to be preserved and enhanced . . . The settlor's freedom to create a

---

[53] *Re Drummond Wren* [1945] 4 DLR 674 (Ont HC). For an exposition of this and related cases, see J. Walker, *"Race", Rights and the Law in the Supreme Court of Canada: Historical Case Studies* (Toronto, Wilfrid Laurier University Press, 1997) 182–245.

[54] *Ibid.*, at 678 (Justice Keillor McKay).

[55] *Re Noble and Wolfe* [1949] 4 DLR 375 (Ont CA).

[56] *Noble and Wolfe v. Alley* [1951] 1 DLR 321 (SCC). Cf. *Board of Governors of Seneca College of Applied Arts and Technology v. Bhadauria* (1981) 124 DLR (3d) 193, 202 (SCC).

[57] (1990) 69 DLR (4th) 321 (Ont. CA) (hereinafter *Canada Trust*). For a detailed and illuminating comment see J. Phillips, "Anti-Discrimination, Freedom of Property Disposition, and the Public Policy of Charitable Educational Trusts: A Comment on Re Canada Trust Company and Ontario Human Rights Commission" (1990) 9 *Philanthropist* 3. See also B. Ziff, *Unforeseen Legacies: Reuben Wells Leonard and the Leonard Foundation Trust* (Toronto, The Osgoode Society for Canadian Legal History, 2000).

charitable trust fashioned along these lines must give way to current principles of public policy under which all races and religions are to be treated on a footing of equality and accorded equal regard and equal respect.[58]

Public policy has been called "the channel through which constitutional values flow into private law".[59] The availability of this channel allows constitutional values to give content to a general norm in the same way that, in Canadian law, safety legislation can provide standards for the law of negligence. It is the same technique as that used in *Drittwirkung* jurisdictions where constitutional values give content to general provisions of the civil code. But in view of the supposedly less constrained possibilities for judicial innovation in the common law and the consequent fear of free-wheeling judges, the question arises whether this concretisation of public policy marks an outer boundary for the influence of Charter values.

The problem can be put this way. One invokes public policy to counteract some claim or right or power that would otherwise be available to the party asserting the validity of some legal act. As the examples so far referred to show, it is deployed to strike down a contract or a contractual term, to invalidate a restrictive covenant, or to avoid a condition of a trust. Its use is essentially defensive. It therefore cannot serve as the basis for new causes of action in private law. The incompatibility between public policy and the racially discriminatory exercise of a settlor's power does not in itself entail making racially discriminatory behaviour an actionable wrong. But if public policy and similarly defensive references to Charter values[60] represent the most extreme use of those values, new torts dealing with actions that violate Charter values are precluded. Is there a principled basis for such preclusion?

An initially appealing positive answer to this question rests on the defensive nature of public policy. As the embodiments of human autonomy, the rights of private law are based on the conception of dignity that is autonomy's inseparable companion. Accordingly, the assertion of a right or the exercise of a power must be compatible with the presuppositions of all private law rights and powers as legal vehicles for respecting dignity. Rights and powers that violate dignity manifest the contradiction of being incompatible with their own presuppositions. The claimant is insisting on respect for dignity, as represented by the impugned term of the contract or deed while, through the content of that term, denying dignity's normative significance. It is as if public policy operates as a massive estoppel on all claims of private law. On this view of public policy, the flaw in the money-lender's contract in the *Horwood* case was that the lender was asserting that the law, as the guarantor of freedom, should recognise

---

[58]   *Canada Trust ibid.*, at 334.

[59]   Barak, *supra* n.3, at 237.

[60]   By this we mean to include cases like *Hill, supra* n.12, where the Charter value was proffered to defeat a defamation claim, and was considered by the court on that basis. This was not a case of public policy, but of a possible modification of the previously well settled defence of privilege.

the validity of the debtor's having contracted himself into a condition of non-freedom.[61] This estoppel argument can then be extended to the Charter. By pointing to certain values, the Charter functions to specify the dignitary pre-suppositions of private law in a more concrete form. Therefore, the significance of these values for private law is triggered only by the assertion of a claim that they are enlisted to deny.

This estoppel argument may well supply a plausible view of the nature of public policy, but it does not provide an entirely satisfactory account of the role of Charter values. Once Charter values are taken to be specifications of the dig-nity presupposed in the categories of private law, there is no reason to assign these values a purely defensive role. As a presupposition of private law, dignity is also a presupposition of causes of action. This is shown by the use of inten-tional torts, such as battery, to protect the plaintiff's dignitary interests. In this vein, the Supreme Court of Canada itself in the *Hill* case[62] has declared that the interest in reputation, which forms the basis for an action for defamation, "reflects and represents the innate dignity of the individual, a concept which underlies all Charter rights". The restriction of Charter values to the estoppel argument assumes, wrongly, that one avails oneself of private law only when making a claim, so that Charter values can be invoked as a shield only to defeat a claim that is inconsistent with its own presuppositions about dignity. The truth is that private law is a framework for interaction, and that persons avail themselves of private law simply by enjoying the protections to which it entitles them. If the function of private law is to safeguard embodiments of self-determining agency from wrongful interference, any plaintiff who can identify such an interference should be allowed to base a cause of action on it. Once the principle is established that Charter values serve to specify an interest that the private law should respect, those values should not be disqualified as bases of causes of action. To do so would involve the oddity that law could create causes of action for non-constitutional interests,[63] but would find its creativity cur-tailed in the face of the very values that are important enough to have constitu-tional significance.

If they can serve as the basis of causes of action, Charter values open up inter-esting possibilities. One is a new tort of discrimination. In pre-Charter decisions the Supreme Court of Canada denied the existence of a tort of racial discrimin-ation[64] and then denied that the values inherent in human rights legislation could serve as the basis for such a tort.[65] These decisions were much criticised

---

[61] This argument replicates G. Hegel's analysis of inalienability in *Hegel's Philosophy of Right* (Oxford, Clarendon Press, 1945) sections 66–67. For a recent discussion of contract in these terms see H. Stewart, "Where is the Freedom in Freedom of Contract?" (1995) 33 *Osgoode Hall LJ* 258.

[62] *Supra* n.12.

[63] An example is the creation of the tort of intentional infliction of mental suffering in *Wilkinson* v. *Downton* [1897] 2 QB 57.

[64] *Christie* v. *York Corporation* (1940) 1 DLR 81 (SCC).

[65] *Board of Governors of Seneca College of Applied Arts and Technology* v. *Bhadauria* (1981) 124 DLR (3d) 193 (SCC).

at the time, and there has been some debate recently about whether the Court's views on racial discrimination were correct as a matter of common law reasoning.[66] One can now question the status of these pre-Charter decisions in the light of the Court's present insistence that private law be developed in a manner consistent with Charter values. The Charter may now be viewed as fortifying the conclusion that discriminatory action, because it has the social meaning of insult to one's human dignity, should be regarded as a tortious infringement of one's protected sphere of integrity.

A second possibility is the explicit recognition of a common law tort of invasion of privacy. In describing the right against unreasonable search and seizure, the Court has remarked that "[g]rounded in man's physical and moral autonomy, privacy is essential for the well-being of the individual".[67] Sentiments like this, when combined with the relevance of Charter values to private law, have led to the plausible suggestion that privacy should be regarded as protected by the law of torts.[68] Indeed, the Court has already invoked privacy as a Charter value in determining whether the records of the plaintiff's psychiatric treatment have to be produced in a civil action for damages based on the defendant's alleged sexual conduct.[69] Similar reasoning supports recognising a cause of action for the invasion of privacy. Charter values would then serve the function of specifying privacy as a legally recognised incident of one's personal integrity and of allowing the law to affirm that the individual's self-construction in the world is bound up with that integrity.

Perhaps the ramifications are even wider than the possibility of these new nominate torts. To be sure, recognition of torts of discrimination and the invasion of privacy would be remarkably innovative in the Canadian context. But the fact that discrimination has been pressed on courts before, that the invasion of privacy is recognised as a tort in other common law jurisdictions and in Quebec's civil law, and that the courts often find oblique means of protecting against discrimination and invasion of privacy[70] means that these two potential torts at least have a familiar feel to them. One must keep in mind, however, that the kind of thinking that would create these torts may be available for the creation of new torts out of the value inherent in *any* of the constitutional human rights. Constitutional litigation continues to flesh out the meaning of these rights in particular cases, generating jurisprudence that articulates the values

---

[66] For a recent contribution see A. Reichman, "Professional Status and the Freedom to Contract: Toward a Common Law Duty of Non-Discrimination" (2001) 14 *Can. J Law & Juris.* 79.

[67] *R* v. *Dyment* [1988] 2 SCR 417, 427.

[68] J. Craig, "Invasion of Privacy and Charter Values: The Common Law Tort Awakens" (1997) 42 *McGill LJ* 355.

[69] *A.M.* v. *Ryan* [1997] 1 SCR 157.

[70] For a recent description of the treatment of discrimination claims under the rubrics of wrongful dismissal and intentional infliction of mental suffering, as well as other means of redress, see T. Witelson, "Retort: Revisiting Bhadauria and the Supreme Court's Rejection of a Tort of Discrimination" (1998) 10 *Nat'l. J Const. L* 149.

inherent in them. For any such value the question now arises: does this have any implications for private law?[71]

VI. TRANSACTIONAL EQUALITY

The incorporation of Charter values into private law is subject, however, to an important caveat. The judgments and the reasoning supporting them must be kept consistent with the parties' transactional equality. Transactional equality is the most deeply ingrained and pervasive relational principle of private law. The principle affirms that, since the plaintiff and the defendant have equal status in their relationship, the decision between them cannot be made on the basis of considerations that reflect the normative position of only one of them. If private law reasoning referred only to what was normatively relevant to one of the parties, it would provide no basis for regarding a decision about liability as fair to both of them.

The idea of proportionality outlined in section IV of this chapter reconfigures transactional equality to allow for the inclusion of constitutional values. To maintain a balance between the entitlements of the two parties, proportionality treats their relationship as informed by an ensemble of normative concepts, no one of which is absolute. The balancing exercise mandates a comparison of the reciprocal effects of the concepts in play on both sides, so as to preserve intact, so far as possible, the central range of application of all of them. This balancing precludes either litigant from complaining that the other has been unfairly preferred.

Let us now look at two situations where judges have invoked Charter values without giving due weight to the maintenance of transactional equality.

The first situation involves trusts whose terms mandate or allow discrimination. We noted above in section V that in *Canada Trust*[72] the Ontario Court of Appeal struck down the discriminatory terms of eligibility for scholarships under a charitable trust. Justice Robins, speaking for the majority of the Court, formulated his judgment in broad terms applying Charter values to trusts generally. In a concurring opinion, Justice Tarnopolsky (probably Canada's leading expert on human rights law) gave narrower grounds. Charter values were decisive here because the trust was a charitable one. The law treats a charitable trust more favourably than other trusts because it is dedicated to the benefit of the community and therefore has a public nature. This public nature attracts the requirement that it conform to the public policy against discrimination. He

---

[71] For instance, in *Dobson* v. *Dobson* (1999) 174 DLR (4th) 1 (SCC), Justice McLachlin referred to the pregnant woman's fundamental right to control her own body, based on s. 7 of the Charter, as relevant to a determination of liability for injuries the woman negligently causes to her own foetus. This case is discussed in s. VI below.

[72] *Supra* n.57.

specifically observed that that his decision did not affect what he termed "private, family trusts".[73]

From the standpoint of transactional equality, the concurring opinion makes better sense than the majority one. In contrasting charitable and other trusts, Justice Tarnopolsky was expressly concerned to avoid a decision that would drastically affect testamentary freedom.[74] The charitable trust is an oddity within the universe of trusts in that the law relaxes the usual trust criteria in order to allow a public benefit. Testamentary freedom expresses itself here only through the public benefit, in the absence of which testamentary freedom counts for nothing. Because public benefit constitutes the entire range of application for testamentary freedom in charitable trusts, that freedom has no application inconsistent with Charter values. Accordingly, in the case of a charitable trust, no tension exists between Charter values and the only form of testamentary freedom that the law of trusts allows. For this reason, striking down the discriminatory aspects of a charitable trust creates no transactional inequality.

A "private, family trust" is different. Here the testator uses the trust mechanism to bestow a benefaction on a particular or ascertainable beneficiary. Testamentary freedom is precisely the freedom to choose that beneficiary and to set the conditions for the benefaction. As with any gift, the grounds of this choice are entirely personal to the benefactor and subject to whatever conditions the benefactor imposes. To invoke Charter values to upset what the testator has done strikes at the core of testamentary freedom in circumstances so personal that Charter values are peripheral. As Lord Wilberforce observed when invited to invalidate as against public policy a clause under which a benefit was forfeited on the beneficiary's becoming a Roman Catholic:

> To do so would bring about a substantial reduction in another freedom, firmly rooted in our law, namely that of testamentary disposition. Discrimination is not the same thing as choice: it operates over a larger and less personal area, and neither by express provision nor by implication has private selection yet become a matter of public policy.[75]

The majority opinion in the *Canada Trust* case indicated that the Court would be willing to invalidate a discriminatory clause even in a non-charitable trust. This, we suggest, would upset the parties' transactional equality by granting Charter values an unwarranted preference over testamentary freedom.[76]

---

[73] *Supra* n.57, at 353.

[74] *Ibid.*

[75] *Blathwayt* v. *Lord Cawley* [1975] 3 All ER 625, 636 (HL).

[76] The overriding of testamentary freedom implicit in the majority's opinion in *Canada Trust* was followed by Justice Galligan in *Fox* v. *Fox Estate* (1996) 28 Ont. Rep. 496 (CA). There the will had given the testator's widow and his son a life interest in shares of the estate, with the widow having the power to encroach for the benefit of the son's children. The widow exercised that power to encroach when the son married a non-Jewish woman. Citing the *Canada Trust* case, Justice Galligan held that this exercise of discretion was improper:

> "It is abhorrent to contemporary community standards that disapproval of a marriage outside one's religious faith could justify the exercise of a trustee's discretion. It is now settled that it

The second situation in which Charter values were invoked was the case of
Dobson v. *Dobson*.[77] The case dealt with a mother's tort liability to her child for
injuries suffered in the womb as a result of a collision caused her negligent driving when she was pregnant. The Court dismissed the action, on the ground that
any liability attaching to a woman's behaviour during pregnancy for injuries
suffered in the womb was incompatible with the woman's right to privacy and
autonomy. For the majority, this reasoning was not based on Charter values. A
concurring judgment by Justice McLachlin added observations about the constitutional values underpinning the pregnant woman's autonomy interest.
Referring to the constitutional decision that struck down the abortion provisions of the Criminal Code,[78] Justice McLachlin pointed out that because legal
action against the pregnant woman could place under legal scrutiny the whole
of her conduct—her diet, her work habits, her hours of sleep—it could jeopardise her fundamental right to control her own body.

Although the woman's autonomy is relevant in this situation, it is not the
whole story. Even if this were a constitutional case, protection of the woman's
constitutional right would have to be assessed in the light of allowable limits to
it under section 1. Similarly in a private law case the reasoning must maintain
the parties' transactional equality. Whether the woman ought to be liable for
her negligence in injuring her child cannot depend entirely on her autonomy
right.

The principle of transactional equality excludes two solutions. The first is
that the woman be liable for any actions that foreseeably might injure the foetus. Given the physical unity of the foetus and pregnant woman, this would in
effect hold the woman completely hostage to the interests of her future child.
Considerations unilaterally pertinent to the child would then determine the
legal relationship with the pregnant woman. The other excluded solution is the
one the Court adopted, that the importance of the woman's autonomy (rightly
considered a Charter value by Justice McLachlin) precludes any liability to the
child. This solution also makes considerations pertinent only to one of the parties decisive for the whole relationship. The only difference between these two
solutions is in the identity of the party that each unilaterally favours. The solutions share a disregard for the transactional equality of the parties. That shared
feature should have been fatal to both.

Instead the Court should have worked through the standard tort analysis in a
form that was relevant to the physical unity of pregnant woman and foetus. A
tort duty to the plaintiff exists if the plaintiff is within the class foreseeably put

is against public policy to discriminate on grounds of race or religion . . . In [*Canada Trust*]
Robins J.A. was discussing the restraint which public policy puts on the freedom of the settlor
to dispose of his property as he saw fit. If a settlor cannot dispose of his property in a fashion
which discriminates upon racial or religious grounds, it seems to me to follow that public policy also prohibits a trustee from exercising her discretion for racial or religious reasons": *ibid.*,
at 501.

[77] (1999) 174 DLR (4th) 1 (SCC).
[78] *R* v. *Morgentaler* [1988] 1 SCR 30.

at risk by the defendant's unreasonable act. Duty is always relative to a class of persons whose potential injury constitutes the reason for thinking of the defendant's act as wrongful. The definition of the class is a normative construct that reflects what it is that renders the defendant's act wrongful. The duty is owed to the plaintiff only inasmuch as the plaintiff is within that class.[79] If that class is such that it can include others beside the foetus *in utero* who is the eventual plaintiff, then there is no reason for the law to treat the plaintiff differently from anyone else who might have been in it. If on the other hand the nature of the class is such that only the foetus could be in it, then the foetus' injury is the result of a risk confined to the physical unity of woman and foetus during the pregnancy. To grant liability on the materialisation of such a risk would be inconsistent with the woman's autonomy. The careless driving of the defendant in the *Dobson* case was wrongful because of its potential effect on anyone who might be injured through the automobile's impact. The plaintiff, who was within this class, had as much right to recover in tort as anyone else who might have been within it. On this distinction, a pregnant woman would not be liable to her eventual child for the excessive consumption of alcohol, but she would be liable for injury suffered by the foetus in an accident due to her drunk driving.

This disposition of the claim in *Dobson* would have been consistent with the transactional equality between the woman's constitutionally fortified interest in autonomy and the child's interest in physical integrity. To preserve intact the central range of application for the value inherent in the woman's autonomy, she should not be held liable for injury that is peculiar to her physical unity with the foetus. Such injury is in any case not central to the range of application of the plaintiff's right to physical integrity. Being by its nature particular to the plaintiff rather than shareable with other potential plaintiffs, the injury would be merely the consequence of an exceptional susceptibility and therefore outside the defendant's tort duty.[80] In contrast, the injury that occurred was centrally within the range of application of the right in physical integrity that can be vindicated by those injured through another's careless driving. Granting the woman an immunity from liability would extend her autonomy interest beyond what is necessary to secure it.[81]

In both the trust and the prenatal injury situation, judges were concerned to protect the Charter value that these differing facts implicated, but were less

---

[79] For an accurate formulation, see *McCarthy* v. *Wellington City* [1966] NZLR 481, 521 (CA):

> "The injury which happened to the respondent was of a general character which a reasonable person would have foreseen as being likely to happen to the class of which the respondent was one, and that class was so closely and directly affected by the appellants act that the appellant owed a duty of care to those in it".

For an explanation of the necessity to think of the negligence duty of care in terms of a class, see Weinrib, *supra* n.16, at 164–7.

[80] Compare *Rogers* v. *Elliott* 15 NE 768 (Mass. SJC, 1888).

[81] For other problems with the Dobson case and the method used by the Supreme Court of Canada to determine the duty of care in negligence see E.J. Weinrib, "Does Tort Law Have a Future?" (2000) 34 *Val. U L Rev.* 561, 567.

sensitive to the transactional equality of the parties. Of course, one would not be justified in thinking that these few cases establish a long-term pattern. Nor can comments of the various judges in these cases be regarded as definitively authoritative. Their comments are mere straws in the wind. The wind, however, seems to be blowing in the wrong direction.

VII. CONCLUSION

In this chapter we have attempted to describe the implications in the Canadian context of taking seriously the mandate to develop private law in a manner consistent with constitutional values. This mandate opens up new grounds of liability and requires a new application of proportionality. These developments would give substance to the Supreme Court's hitherto shadowy references to Charter values and would bring its jurisprudence closer to that of related constitutional jurisdictions. Will the Canadian courts actually proceed down these uncharted avenues?

In the *Hill* case[82] the Supreme Court of Canada noted that the "obligation [to consider Charter values] is simply a manifestation of the inherent jurisdiction of the court to modify or extend the common law to comply with prevailing social conditions and values".[83] It then sounded a cautionary note:

> Courts have traditionally been cautious concerning the extent to which they will amend the common law. Similarly, they must not go further than is necessary when taking Charter values into account. Far-reaching changes to the common law must be left to the legislature.[84]

It also went on to observe that parties should be able to rely on "law which may have a long history of acceptance within the community".[85]

Of course, no one could disagree with caution in principle. But three considerations might be worth keeping in mind if caution is not to slide into timorousness.

First, although certainty in the law is a virtue, the Court has already taken the decisive step toward undermining previous certainties by putting courts under the obligation to develop the common law consistently with Charter values. The common law in Canada can now never be the same as it was. Charter values are now in principle admissible in any private law context. Every properly advised litigant must now understand that even rules with a long history must accommodate the significance of Charter values. The only thing that matters now is that the courts perform the legal analysis properly. A proper analysis cannot be undermined by the fact that it changes a legal rule (even if the change is far-reaching) any more than an improper analysis can be strengthened by the fact that it does not change a legal rule.

[82] *Supra* n. 12.
[83] *Ibid.*, at 156.
[84] *Ibid.*, at 157.
[85] *Ibid.*, at 158.

Secondly, from the first discussion in Germany of the impact of constitutional rights on private law to subsequent discussion in Canada, a constant theme has been the apprehension of a disastrous effect upon the individual freedom that the private law manifests. The idea of proportionality addresses this apprehension. By maintaining a balance between the entitlements on both sides, proportionality vindicates the parties' transactional equality. If sensitively done, this exercise prevents one party from using Charter values to intrude into the central range of application of the other's freedom.

Thirdly, the relationship between the constitution and private law is a comparatively new problem in Canada but not a new problem in the rest of the world.[86] Other jurisdictions have extensive experience in applying constitutional norms to private law. In this respect, as in others, one should be mindful of the new cosmopolitanism of constitutional law. Canada's constitution, while distinctive in its own way, is nonetheless one member in a family of constitutions that set up similar legal frameworks and present similar challenges.[87] By looking into past experiences of others we can perhaps glimpse our own future, or at least learn both the good and the bad from their examples.

Years ago the Supreme Court of Canada, in explicating the final words of section 1,[88] noted that the purpose for which the Charter was entrenched was that Canadian society was to be free and democratic. The Court therefore had to be guided by the values essential to a free and democratic society, including respect for the inherent dignity of the human person. These values, it said, were the "genesis of the rights and freedoms guaranteed by the Charter". In view of these words, one may perhaps add that the idea of a free and democratic society is also the most general repository of the constitutional values that must influence the development of private law in Canada. Private law too will have to play its part in fulfilling the constitutionally enshrined aspiration that Canadian society be free and democratic.

---

[86] Justice Barak rightly emphasises the significance of this point: *supra* n.3, at 242–4.

[87] L.E. Weinrib, "The Supreme Court in the Age of Rights: Constitutional Democracy, the Rule of Law and Fundamental Rights under Canada's Constitution" (2000) 80 *Can. Bar Rev.* 730.

[88] R. v. *Oakes* (1986) 26 DLR (4th) 200, 225.

4

Determining the Stakes: Binding and Non-Binding Bills of Rights

ANTON FAGAN

I. INTRODUCTION

THE AIM OF this chapter is to explain what is at stake in the choice between a Bill of Rights that is binding (i.e. imposes duties) on private parties and a Bill of Rights that is not binding (i.e. does not impose duties) on private parties but is nonetheless to influence the development of private common law (i.e. judge-made law regulating relations between private parties). For the sake of simplicity, I will throughout this chapter refer to a Bill of Rights of the first kind simply as a "binding" Bill of Rights and to a Bill of Rights of the second kind simply as a "non-binding" one.

For South African lawyers, the determination of what is at stake in the choice between the two kinds of Bills of Rights is important. Under its interim Constitution (from 1994 to 1996) South Africa had a non-binding Bill of Rights. Under its new Constitution (in force since 1997) South Africa has a binding one. For some time after the enactment of the interim Constitution, there existed a dispute among South African lawyers as to whether its Bill of Rights was binding or non-binding. In the case of *Du Plessis and others* v. *De Klerk and another*,[1] the South African Constitutional Court settled the dispute in favour of the latter view. The Court, *per* Kentridge AJ, chiefly relied on two provisions in the interim Constitution: Section 7(1), which states that the Bill of Rights "shall bind all legislative and executive organs of State at all levels of government" and section 35(3), which states that in "the application and development of the common law . . . a court shall have due regard to the spirit, purport and objects" of the Bill of Rights. While section 7(1) was taken to establish that the interim Constitution's Bill of Rights does not bind private parties,[2] section 35(3) was held to establish that the Bill of Rights should influence the development of private common law.[3] As far as the new Constitution is concerned, there is as yet no Constitutional Court pronouncement to the effect that its Bill of Rights

---

[1] [1996] 3 SA 850 (CC) (hereinafter *Du Plessis*).
[2] *Ibid.*, at 877B–E.
[3] *Ibid.*, at 885E–F.

is binding rather than non-binding. However, section 8(2) of the new Constitution plainly establishes that this is so. The subsection reads as follows: "[a] provision of the Bill of Rights binds a natural or a juristic person if, and to the extent that, it is applicable, taking into account the nature of the right and the nature of any duty imposed by the right".

The determination of what is at stake in the choice between binding and non-binding Bills of Rights should also be of interest to certain non-South African lawyers. Canada, Germany and the United Kingdom all have Bills of Rights that are non-binding, just like South Africa had under its interim Constitution. Differences in terminology should not blind one to this fact. The Canadian Supreme Court has expressly held that "[p]rivate parties owe each other no constitutional duties", but that private common law is nonetheless to be "interpreted", "developed", "modified", "extended" or "revised" so as to make it "consistent" or "compliant" with Charter "values" or "principles".[4] In Germany, the view that the basic rights in the German Basic Law do not bind private parties but should nevertheless influence the development of private common law has been expressed by the rejection of direct horizontal application (*unmittelbare Drittwirkung*) in favour of indirect horizontal application (*mittelbare Drittwirkung*). More specifically, the German Constitutional Court in the *Lüth* case stated that, though the Basic Law confers (defensive) rights only against the State, it establishes an objective order of values which should guide the development of private common law.[5] As regards the United Kingdom, the key provision is section 6 of the Human Rights Act 1998. Section 6 imposes a duty on courts in the United Kingdom to act consistently with certain rights in the European Convention on Human Rights. The precise implications of this duty are at present a matter of some debate. However, there appears to be an emerging consensus that "*direct* horizontal application is not intended": that is, the Convention rights do not bind private parties.[6] There also appears to be agreement that, though direct horizontality is precluded, some form of horizontal application is required: that is, the Convention rights must influence the development of private common law in some manner.[7]

---

[4] See *Retail, Wholesale & Department Store Union, Local 580* v. *Dolphin Delivery* [1986] 2 SCR 573 (hereinafter *Dolphin Delivery*), per McIntyre J at 603; *Hill* v. *Church of Scientology of Toronto* [1995] 2 SCR 1130 (hereinafter *Hill*), per Cory J at 1169–71, per L'Heureux-Dubé J at 1214.

[5] 7 BverfGE 198 (1958). See also D.P. Kommers, *The Constitutional Jurisprudence of the Federal Republic of Germany* (Durham, NC, Duke University Press, 2nd edn., 1997).

[6] M. Hunt, "The 'Horizontal Effect' of the Human Rights Act" (1998) *PL* 423, 438. See also B.S. Markesinis, "Privacy, Freedom of Expression, and the Horizontal Effect of the Human Rights Bill: Lessons from Germany" (1999) 115 *LQR* 47, 72; R. Buxton, "The Human Rights Act and Private Law" (2000) 116 *LQR* 48, 56–7; A. Lester and D. Pannick, "The Impact of the Human Rights Act on Private Law: the Knight's Move" (2000) 116 *LQR* 380; J. Beatson and S. Grosz, "Horizontality: a Footnote" (2000) 116 *LQR* 385. For a dissentient view, see H.W.R. Wade, "Horizons of Horizontality" (2000) 116 *LQR* 217.

[7] Hunt, *supra* n.6, at 439–41; Markesinis, *supra* n.6, at 73; Lester and Pannick, *supra* n.6; Beatson and Grosz, *supra* n.6; N. Bamforth, "The Application of the Human Rights Act 1998 to Public Authorities and Private Bodies" (1999) 58 *CLJ* 159. See also H. Beale and N. Pittam, chap. 7 this vol.

The main thesis of this chapter is as follows: at stake in the choice between a binding and a non-binding Bill of Rights is the justification of subjecting the development of private common law to constitutional constraint. Regardless of whether a community has a binding or a non-binding Bill of Rights, the development of its private common law will be constitutionally constrained. For both binding and non-binding Bills of Rights will at times provide reasons for a judge to change private common law, and the reasons that are so provided will at times defeat whatever reasons the judge may have for maintaining private common law as it is. Yet, while it is so that binding and non-binding Bills of Rights equally constrain the development of private common law, it is also so that each imposes a different kind of constraint. That is, the reasons for changing private common law that each provides are distinct in nature.

What is the difference? It is that, whereas a right in a binding Bill of Rights may constitute an "operative" reason for changing private common law, a right in a non-binding Bill of Rights can serve only as an "auxiliary" one. In the case of a non-binding Bill of Rights, the operative reason for changing private common law must be the value of legal coherence: the rights in the Bill of Rights at best serve to identify the changes that legal coherence requires. This description of the different ways in which binding and non-binding Bills of Rights constrain the development of private common law requires both explanation and justification. These are to be found in section II of the chapter. Section II starts by explaining the distinction (and relationship) between operative and auxiliary reasons. Thereafter it attempts to justify the claim that the rights in a binding Bill of Rights provide operative reasons for changing private common law. Finally it tries to demonstrate that the rights in a non-binding Bill of Rights cannot do the same.

The fact that the constraint imposed by a binding Bill of Rights differs from that imposed by a non-binding one means that each requires its own justification. It is possible for a community's private common law to be developed altogether free from constitutional constraint. For it is possible that a community have no Bill of Rights at all, or that it have a Bill of Rights that is neither binding nor non-binding. Indeed, this was the situation in South Africa until 1994, and in the United Kingdom until even more recently. As is explained in section III of this chapter, it is not obviously unjustified or illegitimate for a community's private common law to be developed in such a constitutionally unconstrained fashion. In fact, if there is a problem of justification here, it appears to be the opposite one. How could it be justified for judges to develop private common law subject to constitutional constraint? Why should judges not rather change private common law only for moral reasons and reasons that the common law itself provides? Section III shows that the answer to these questions depends, crucially, on the nature of the constitutional constraint to which the development of private common law is subjected. Thus the development of private common law on the basis of the operative reasons in a binding Bill of Rights can be justified in three ways. The first invokes the superior moral expertise of the constitution-makers. The second relies on the consent of an historically significant majority. The third appeals to the importance of preserving moral consensus around mid-level principles, despite pluralism about fundamental values. In section III, it is argued that none of these justifications is available when private common law is developed on the basis of the auxiliary reasons in a non-binding Bill of Rights. In that case, the justification has to be that legal coherence is intrinsically valuable.

Having shown in sections II and III that what is really at stake in the choice between binding and non-binding Bills of Rights is the justification of constitutionally constraining the development of private common law, the chapter in section IV deals with three mistaken ideas about what is at stake. These are ideas that have surfaced in the writings of South African legal academics and in certain judgments of the South African courts. The first idea is that what is at stake is the survival of private common law: that, if one recognises the importance of that survival, one must favour a non-binding Bill of Rights. The second idea is that what is at stake is the private-public divide: that, if one recognises the need to restrain not only public but also private power, one must favour a binding Bill of Rights. The third idea is that what is at stake is a community's political commitments: that there is a connection between non-binding Bills of Rights and political conservatism, on the one hand, and binding Bills of Rights and political transformation, on the other. Although widely held in South Africa, all three of these ideas are mistaken. The aim of section IV is to explain why.

Finally, in its conclusion, this chapter looks at how the distinction between binding and non-binding Bills of Rights intersects with another important distinction. That is the distinction between a "framework" and a "foundational" conception of a Bill of Rights. Roughly, whereas the foundational conception requires every rule of private common law to be (in some sense) justified by the Bill of Rights, the framework conception demands only that every rule of private common law be (in some sense) consistent with the Bill of Rights. The conclusion shows that the choice between the two conceptions has not been settled in South Africa, neither regarding the non-binding Bill of Rights created by the interim South African Constitution nor regarding the binding one created by the new South African Constitution. The conclusion further suggests that whether a community sees its Bill of Rights as a framework or a foundation may have implications for its choice between a binding and a non-binding Bill of Rights.

II. TWO KINDS OF CONSTRAINT

The aim of this section is to demonstrate that, although both binding and non-binding Bills of Rights constrain the development of private common law, they do so in different ways. More specifically, the aim is to explain and justify the claim that, whereas the rights in a binding Bill of Rights may serve as operative reasons for changing private common law, the rights in a non-binding Bill of Rights can at best serve as auxiliary reasons for such change. If we are to understand this claim, we must first understand the distinction between operative and auxiliary reasons. The distinction is not my own. It is made by Joseph Raz, in his *Practical Reasons and Norms*, in order to draw attention to two different roles or functions that reasons can have in a justification.[8] The best way to explain the distinction is by way of an example.

Consider therefore the following argument: it is good to facilitate the happiness of those one loves; A loves B and B loves roses; therefore, A has a reason to buy B a rose. Now, each of the premises in this argument states a reason. So does the argument's conclusion. The reason in the conclusion is justified by the combination of the reasons in the premises. But, as Raz has observed, though the reasons in the premises together justify the reason in the conclusion, they have distinct roles (or functions) in that justification. The reason in the first premise provides the "motivating" or "normative" force for the reason in the conclusion. It does so by "point[ing] to the need for action in pursuit of a certain goal".[9] Here the goal is the happiness of one's loved ones. The reason in the second premise, by contrast, is itself devoid of normative force. Its function is merely an identifying one. As Raz puts it, it merely serves to "connect a certain course of action to that goal by showing it to be a route to its achievement".[10] In the given example, the reason in the second premise identifies A's buying B a rose as a route to achieving the happiness of A's loved ones. It is in order to mark this difference in role or function that Raz introduces the distinction between operative and auxiliary reasons. The reason in the first premise is an operative reason: it is a reason that motivates or has normative force. The reason in the second premise is an auxiliary reason: it is a reason that "transmits, as it were, the force of [an] operative reason to [a] particular act".[11]

Now that the distinction between operative and auxiliary reasons has been explained, it is possible to provide a less technical description of the different ways in which binding and non-binding Bills of Rights constrain the development of private common law. In the case of a binding Bill of Rights, the rights themselves motivate changes to private common law. In the case of a non-binding Bill of Rights, the motivation for change does not come from the rights, but from some other value or goal. The rights merely identify the changes that will serve that other value or achieve that other goal. What could that other value or goal be? What is it that drives changes to private common law where the Bill of Rights is non-binding? It is, as we shall see, the value of legal coherence.

---

[8] J. Raz, *Practical Reason and Norms* (Oxford, Oxford University Press, 1999), 33–5; J. Raz, *Ethics in the Public Domain* (Oxford, Clarendon Press, 1994), 241.

[9] Raz, *Ethics in the Public Domain, ibid.*, at 241.

[10] *Ibid.*

[11] Raz, *Practical Reason and Norms, supra* n.8, at 34–5.

1. Binding bills of rights: operative reasons for change

In this subsection I explain why it is that the rights in a binding Bill of Rights may provide operative legal reasons for changing private common law. The explanation relies on a hopefully uncontroversial thesis about rights and their relationship to duties. It also relies on two theses about the limits of law, one of which undoubtedly is controversial. I set out these three theses at the start of this subsection. Thereafter, I proceed to show that it follows from these three theses that legal rights in certain circumstances constitute operative legal reasons for changing law. Finally, I apply this to the rights in binding Bills of Rights.

Rights impose or justify duties. That much is commonplace. Less commonplace, perhaps, is the fact that the duties imposed or justified by rights are of two kinds. To distinguish them, I will call the one kind "corresponding" duties and the other kind "derivative" ones. A duty corresponds to a right if its content can be inferred from the content of the right without reliance on additional premises. Thus, for example, where A has a right to freedom of expression, the corresponding duty is the duty to secure A in his freedom of expression. Similarly, where A has a right to property against B, the corresponding duty is B's duty to secure A in his property. There are of course a number of ways in which one person can secure another in something: by giving it to him, by helping him to have or do it, or by refraining from interfering with his having or doing it.[12] What then are a right's derivative duties? They are duties the content whereof can be inferred from the content of the right only with reliance on additional premises. Thus B's duty to restrain himself from shouting A down while A is making an anti-royalist speech on a street corner may be derived from A's right to freedom of expression, but does not correspond to it. For such a duty could be inferred from the right only with the aid of additional premises concerning, amongst other things, the nature of expression and its value.

I said that I would also be relying on two theses about the limits of law. One is Joseph Raz's so-called "sources thesis". Raz's sources thesis holds that all of a community's law is "source-based", by which it means that all of a community's law "can be identified by reference to social facts alone, without resort to any evaluative argument".[13] Although Raz's sources thesis is a positivist thesis of law, not all positivists endorse it. Thus a distinction is commonly drawn between two kinds of positivism: exclusive positivism, which accepts the sources thesis, and inclusive or soft positivism, which rejects it.[14] It is not only

---

[12] See A. Gewirth, "Why Rights are Indispensable" (1986) 95 *Mind* 329, 330; J. Raz, *The Morality of Freedom* (Oxford, Clarendon Press, 1986), 171.

[13] Raz, *Ethics in the Public Domain, supra* n.8, at 211.

[14] See J. Coleman, "Negative and Positive Positivism" in M. Cohen (ed.), *Ronald Dworkin and Contemporary Jurisprudence* (London, Duckworth, 1983); P. Soper, "Legal Theory and the Obligation of a Judge: The Hart/Dworkin Dispute" in *ibid.*; D. Lyons, "Principles, Positivism, and Legal Theory" (1977) 87 *Yale LJ* 415; H.L.A. Hart, *The Concept of Law* (2nd edn., Oxford, Clarendon Press, 1994), in the postscript; W.J. Waluchow, *Inclusive Legal Positivism* (Oxford, Clarendon Press, 1994).

soft positivists who deny the sources thesis. Ronald Dworkin, one of positivism's most celebrated critics, has attacked it time and again.[15] Notwithstanding the controversial nature of Raz's sources thesis, I cannot in this chapter attempt a defence thereof. I have however attempted a defence thereof elsewhere,[16] and so, on numerous occasions, has Raz.[17] The other thesis about law's limits upon which I will be relying is what I will call the "implied content" thesis. The implied content thesis holds that the law of a community is not exhausted by the explicit content of its source-based law, but includes some of its implications. This thesis is not contradicted by the sources thesis, but is limited by it. For the sources thesis determines which implications are included, namely those that are determinable by social facts without resort to moral reasoning.

Having presented my thesis about corresponding and derivative duties, as well as the sources and implied content theses, I am now in a position to explain how legal rights can in certain circumstances constitute operative legal reasons for changing law. I should point out that, while the explanation's details are mine, its general contours are Raz's.[18]

The first point to grasp is that, if the three theses are sound, then the duties that correspond to a legal right necessarily are themselves legal duties. That is, the duties are legally valid: they have legal force. The same is not true, however, of a legal right's derivative duties. While a legal right's derivative duties may themselves be legal duties, they need not be. That is, they could but need not be legally valid: they could but need not have legal force. What accounts for this difference? Well, a legal right's corresponding duties are legal duties (they are legally valid), because they are implied by the right and the implication does not rely on moral reasoning. In other words, a legal right's corresponding duties satisfy both the implied content and the sources thesis. The position is significantly different as regards a legal right's derivative duties. To be sure, a legal right's derivative duties are implied by the right. They do therefore satisfy the implied content thesis. However, by definition, a right's derivative duties are implied only with the aid of additional premises. By and large, these additional premises will be moral ones. This means that a legal right's derivative duties do not necessarily satisfy the sources thesis and are therefore not necessarily legal duties (i.e. they are not necessarily legally valid). Of course, while the sources thesis has the result that a legal right's derivative duties need not be legal duties, it does not have the result that they cannot be so. A duty that is derived from a legal right

---

[15] See R. Dworkin, *Taking Rights Seriously* (London, Duckworth, 1977) and R. Dworkin, *Law's Empire* (London, Fontana, 1986).

[16] A. Fagan, "Delivering Positivism from Evil" in D. Dyzenhaus (ed.), *Recrafting the Rule of Law: The Limits of Legal Order* (Oxford, Hart Publishing, 1999), 88–97.

[17] See J. Raz, *The Authority of Law* (Oxford, Clarendon Press, 1979), 41–5, 48–52; J. Raz, *The Concept of a Legal System* (2nd edn., Oxford, Clarendon Press, 1980), 216; J. Raz , *Ethics in the Public Domain*, supra n.8, at 210–37, 296–301; J. Raz, "Intention in Interpretation" in R. George (ed.), *The Autonomy of Law* (Oxford, Clarendon Press, 1996), 256–62; J. Raz, "On the Nature of Law" (1996) 82 *Archiv für Rechts- und Sozialphilosophie* 1, 17–18.

[18] See Raz, *Ethics in the Public Domain*, supra n.8 at 238–76.

will be a legal duty, according to the sources thesis, provided it is source-based. That is, provided it can be identified without moral reasoning. It is possible that a duty that is derived from a legal right can be so identified: all that is required is that the duty be recognised in a judicial precedent or a statute. In that event, the duty will be a legal duty. But it will not be a legal duty because it is derived from a legal right. To summarise, a legal right's corresponding duties necessarily are themselves legal duties, since they are both implied and source-based. By contrast, a duty that is derived from a legal right may or may not be a legal duty. For, though a derivative duty is implied, it could but need not be source-based.

Derivative duties that are not legal duties (i.e. do not have legal force) hold the key to the explanation of how legal rights in general can provide operative legal reasons for changing law. As Joseph Raz has explained, in so far as a legal right's derivative duties are not already legal duties (i.e. do not already have legal force), the right constitutes a legal reason for making the derivative duties legal ones (i.e. for giving the derivative duties legal force).[19] Why so? Because, by definition, a derivative duty is justified by the right from which it is derived. If the right is a legal right, the justification is a legal justification. Thus a legal right necessarily provides a legal justification for all its derivative duties, whether they be legal duties (have legal force) or not. But, if a legal right's derivative duties are legally justified by the right, then the right constitutes a legal reason for making those duties legal ones (i.e. for giving those duties legal force). For, if a duty is justified, there is a reason to make it a legal duty (to give it legal force). If, moreover, the justification for the duty is a legal one, the reason for making the duty a legal one (for giving the duty legal force) is a legal reason.

I have explained how legal rights can constitute legal reasons for changing law. But I have yet to explain why those reasons are operative rather than auxiliary. As indicated in my discussion of corresponding and derivative duties, one cannot identify the duties that are derived from a right by looking at the right alone. One will have to rely on additional premises. It is the combination of the right and the additional premises that justifies the derivative duties. However, as in the example used to explain the distinction between operative and auxiliary reasons, the right and the additional premises have different roles in that justification. The right is responsible for the derivative duties' normative force. The right, therefore, is the operative reason. The additional premises, by contrast, have no more than an identifying function: they identify the acts that will serve the right, and thus serve to transfer the right's normative force to those acts. The additional premises, therefore, are auxiliary reasons.

I have been dealing generally with legal rights and their ability to provide operative legal reasons for changing law. It is time now to look specifically at binding Bills of Rights and private common law, and at the ability of the former

[19] See Raz, *Ethics in the Public Domain, supra* n.8 at 238–76. Note that Raz does not speak of "corresponding" and "derivative" duties.

to provide operative legal reasons for changing the latter. My contention, to recall, is that operative legal reasons for changing private common law can be provided by the rights in a binding Bill of Rights. This follows from three premises. The first has been established by the argument so far: a legal right is an operative legal reason for giving legal force to derivative duties that do not already have legal force. The second premise arises from the definition of binding Bills of Rights and the distinction between corresponding and derivative duties: the rights in a binding Bill of Rights impose or justify corresponding and derivative duties on private parties. The third premise concerns the nature of private common law: private common law consists of judge-made duties on private parties, so that, whenever a judge gives legal force to a duty on a private party, he changes private common law.

How do the above three premises establish that the rights in a binding Bill of Rights can constitute operative legal reasons for changing private common law? Well, taken together, the first and second premises yield the conclusion that the rights in a binding Bill of Rights may constitute operative legal reasons for giving legal force to duties on private parties. The duties in question will be duties on private parties that are derived from the Bill of Rights, but do not yet have the force of law. When this conclusion is combined with the third premise, we get the further conclusion that the rights in a binding Bill of Rights may constitute operative legal reasons for changing private common law.

2. Non-binding bills of rights: coherence as operative reason

In the previous subsection, I explained why binding Bills of Rights can provide operative legal reasons for changing private common law. In this subsection, I explain why non-binding Bills of Rights cannot do likewise. The rights in non-binding Bills of Rights, as we shall see, at best provide auxiliary reasons for changing private common law: the operative reason has to be the value of legal coherence.

The explanation starts with a puzzle. By definition, non-binding Bills of Rights have the following two features: they do not impose or justify duties that have private parties as their subjects; they do influence the development of private common law. Now, a Bill of Rights can influence the development of private common law only if it provides reasons for changing private common law. Private common law, by definition, consists of duties that have private parties as their subjects. Thus, a Bill of Rights can influence the development of private common law only if it provides reasons for changing duties that have private parties as their subjects. Here then is the puzzle: how can a Bill of Rights that does not impose or justify duties that have private parties as their subjects provide reasons for changing duties that do have private parties as their subjects? Or, more briefly, how can a Bill of Rights simultaneously not bind private parties and influence the development of private common law?

The solution to this puzzle lies in the well-known distinction, made in Canadian and South African constitutional jurisprudence, between the rights in a Bill of Rights and the values or principles that underlie those rights.[20] According to this solution, the rights in a Bill of Rights are not ultimate values, but can themselves be justified by more fundamental ones. Moreover, it is possible that a right does not justify any duties on private parties, but that the values underlying the right do so (i.e. justify duties on private parties). The duties justified by the underlying values may or may not be part of private common law: that depends on whether they have a source. If a duty that is justified by the underlying values is not part of private common law, so the solution goes, a court has a reason to change private common law so as to make the duty part thereof.

I do not intend to challenge the solution just outlined. It is a genuine solution to the puzzle of non-binding Bills of Rights. For it does explain how a Bill of Rights that does not bind private parties may nonetheless influence the development of private common law. However, the solution has certain implications for the role (or function) that rights in non-binding Bills of Rights have in justifying changes to private common law. It is these implications that I wish to focus on now.

The solution just outlined is incomplete. It contains two premises. The first is that the rights in a Bill of Rights are justified by more fundamental values. The second is that the values in turn justify duties on private parties that are not yet recognised in private common law. By themselves, these two premises are incapable of supporting the desired conclusion, namely that a court therefore has reason to change private common law so that it does recognise the mentioned duties. Let us assume, for example, that the right to freedom of expression is justified by the more fundamental value of equal concern and respect. Let us further assume that the value of equal concern and respect in turn justifies a duty on private parties not to discriminate unfairly. According to the proposed solution it follows that, if the right to freedom of expression is contained in a non-binding Bill of Rights but the duty not to discriminate unfairly is not contained in private common law, a court has reason to change private common law by creating the duty. But this does not follow unless a further premise is added. What is the additional premise? It is that legal coherence is a goal that has to be pursued in adjudication.

This is not the occasion for a detailed analysis of legal coherence. The following remarks will, I hope, serve to capture its essence. For the law of a community to be coherent it is not enough that the community's legal rules are consistent. That is, it is not enough that no legal rule contradicts another.[21] The legal rules also have to be, in Ronald Dworkin's words, "consistent *in*

---

[20] See *Dolphin Delivery*, *supra* n.4, at 603 and L. Weinrib and E. Weinrib, chap. 3 this vol.; See also *Hill*, *supra* n.4, at 1170–1, 1214; *Du Plessis*, *supra* n.1, at 887.

[21] See N. MacCormick, "Coherence in Legal Justification" in A. Peczenik *et al.* (eds.), *Theory of Legal Science* (Dordrecht, D. Reidel, 1984), 235.

principle".[22] How is consistency in principle different from consistency *sans phrase*? Well, a community's legal rules are consistent in principle, according to Dworkin, if they "express a single and comprehensive vision of justice".[23] In other words, for a community's law to be coherent, it must be possible to justify all its rules by a set of moral principles that display a degree of unity. The greater the degree of unity, the more coherent the law is. Of course, this explanation leaves many questions unanswered. What makes for a unified set of principles: is mere consistency enough, or must they be in some way interdependent or ranked?[24] Moral principles cannot here mean morally sound principles, but must mean principles that are moral "in form",[25] principles that are morally intelligible: but what are the limits of moral intelligibility or form?

If legal coherence is a goal of adjudication, then judges have reason to change law in so far as it lacks coherence. Of course, a judge's ability to change law is always severely constrained. On the one hand, a judge cannot change law that is not pertinent to the case before him. On the other hand, there may be law that a judge cannot change, even if it is pertinent to the case before him. Thus, from a judge's point of view, the goal of coherence is always to be pursued within a context of immutable law: some of it absolutely so, some of it relative to the matter at hand. This has the important consequence that, from a judge's perspective, the way in which coherence is to be pursued invariably depends on immutable law. To put it another way, while it is the goal of legal coherence that motivates changing the law, it is the content of immutable law that determines the change to be made.

It should now be clear why, if legal coherence is a goal of adjudication, a judge has reason to change private common law in the circumstances described earlier. Those circumstances were, first, that a right in a Bill of Rights is justified by some more fundamental value and, secondly, that the fundamental value in turn justifies a duty on private parties that is not yet recognised by private common law. In these circumstances, legal coherence would be as well served by changing the Bill of Rights as it would be by changing private common law. However, the former is normally not possible for a judge: Bills of Rights tend to be absolutely immutable. Thus, if a judge is to serve coherence in these circumstances, he can normally do so only by changing private common law. The judge can only remedy the incoherence, in other words, by creating the duty on private parties that is justified by the fundamental value that underlies the right in the Bill of Rights.

It remains only to make the point that, in the solution as it has now been fully developed, coherence serves as the operative reason for changing private common law, while the rights in the Bill of Rights serve merely as auxiliary reasons. In the fully developed solution, the motivation for changing private common

---

[22] R. Dworkin, *Law's Empire, supra* n.15, at 134, 167, 184, emphasis added.
[23] *Ibid.*, at 134.
[24] See Raz, *Ethics in the Public Domain, supra* n.8, at 290.
[25] R. Dworkin, *Taking Rights Seriously, supra* n.15, at 343.

law clearly is the goal of coherence. Coherence therefore is the operative reason. The rights in the Bill of Rights merely determine how private common law is to be changed in order to achieve that goal. Thus, though the rights in the Bill of Rights are reasons for changing private common law, they are only auxiliary ones.

III.   JUSTIFYING CONSTITUTIONAL CONSTRAINT

The previous section described the different constraints that binding and non-binding Bills of Rights impose on the development of private common law. This section explains that, because of that difference, it is impossible to provide a single justification both for the constraint that binding Bills of Rights impose and for the constraint imposed by non-binding Bills of Rights. The section starts by explaining why there is a need to justify the imposition of constitutional constraints upon the development of private common law. Thereafter, it discusses three ways in which the constraint imposed by a binding Bill of Rights could be justified and shows that these justifications are not available when the Bill of Rights is non-binding.

Some lawyers may be surprised by the contention that one needs to justify the imposition of constitutional constraints upon the development of private common law. They may feel that, far from presenting a problem of justification, the imposition of constitutional constraint on the development of private common law in fact solves such a problem. This seems to be the view of David Beatty.[26] According to Beatty, judges' ability to change private common law is potentially "anti-democratic".[27] For, on the one hand, private common law is "coercive" in character. On the other hand, judges are "a group of unelected individuals".[28] In Beatty's view, the anti-democratic potential of judges' ability to change private common law will be contained only if judges accept that, also when they develop private common law, they should not "elevate themselves above the Constitution".[29] In other words, in Beatty's view, for the development of private common law to be democratic, it must be subjected to constitutional constraint.

I do not find Beatty's view compelling. The fact that judges are unelected (and unrepresentative and unaccountable) matters a great deal when the law they are changing is statutory. For not only does a statute represent the decision of an elected (and representative and accountable) legislative majority, but it is usually also impossible for a legislative majority to undo a judicial change to statute law. It thus is counter-majoritarian and, on the face of it, anti-democratic for an unelected judge to change statute law. It is not clear, however, that it is similarly

---

[26] D. Beatty, "Constitutional Conceits: The Coercive Authority of the Courts" (1987) 37 *U Toronto LJ* 183.

[27] *Ibid.*, at 190.

[28] *Ibid.* See also at 189.

[29] *Ibid.*, at 190.

counter-majoritarian and thus anti-democratic for an unelected judge to change private common law. First of all, private common law does not represent the decisions of elected legislative majorities, but rather of other (unelected) judges. In the second place, a judicial change to private common law can at any time be undone by a legislative majority.

I do not share Beatty's dislike of the idea that judges should develop private common law free from constitutional constraint. This was, of course, precisely how private common law was developed, until recently, in the United Kingdom, in Canada and in South Africa. Many people, myself included, believe that the bodies of private common law that were developed in these countries are, while certainly not perfect, nonetheless of great value. In fact, some might even go so far as to view them as remarkable human achievements. But if these bodies of private common law really are of great value, then so, for instrumental reasons, is the judicial practice that generated them. An essential feature of that practice was the fact that judges changed law for reasons that were not constitutionally constrained.

So, for judges to develop private common law free from constitutional constraint is both compatible with democracy and instrumentally valuable. This suggests, on the one hand, that it is in fact justified for judges to develop private common law free from constitutional constraint. It suggests, on the other hand, that the real difficulty is to justify the removal of that freedom. That is, it suggests that the real difficulty is to explain why judges should change private common law for reasons (operative or auxiliary) provided by a Bill of Rights (binding or non-binding), rather than for moral reasons and reasons provided by private common law itself.

In my view, how the imposition of a constitutional constraint upon the development of private common law is justified must depend on the nature of that constraint. Ultimately, therefore, it must depend on whether the constraint is imposed by a binding or a non-binding Bill of Rights. Let me start my explanation of this with an example from ordinary life. Say a friend asks me to go out and buy her an excellent novel. Assume, as I think one must, that my friend's request reflects a judgement on her part as to what is good for her. Say further that, in response to the request, I go out and purchase Jane Austen's *Emma*, in the belief that it is an excellent novel. Moreover, say that I reached this belief by considering several premises not provided by the request alone: premises about the criteria for literary excellence and their satisfaction by *Emma*. It seems to me that my action here is best described by saying that I have gone beyond my friend's judgement, but have done so only in order to give effect to it. It also seems to me that, if *Emma* really is an excellent novel, I have in fact succeeded in giving effect to my friend's judgement. It follows that, provided that *Emma* is an excellent novel, I can justify my action (the purchasing of *Emma*) by appealing to my friend's judgement.

Imagine now a somewhat different response. Instead of purchasing *Emma*, or indeed any novel at all, I purchase a ticket to a retrospective on the work of

David Hockney. Moreover, I do so for the following reasons. One: underlying my friend's request that I buy her an excellent novel is a concern on her part to do what is good for her. Two: attending a Hockney retrospective will be good for her: in fact, it will be better for her than reading *Emma*. Now, my friend may be very pleased to receive a ticket to the retrospective rather than a copy of *Emma*. But if she is not, I could hardly hope to placate her by saying: "But I was only carrying out your request. I was only giving effect to your judgement". The judgement that is reflected in her request is the judgement that an excellent novel will be good for her. Far from giving effect to this judgement, I have in fact bypassed it.

When a judge changes private common law on the basis of a right in a binding Bill of Rights, his action is comparable to the first response that I have described. But when a change is based on the values underlying a non-binding Bill of Rights, then we have an action comparable to the second response. The rights in a Bill of Rights (be it binding or non-binding) represent a judgement by the constitution-makers as to how certain fundamental values or goals are to be achieved. If a judge (with additional premises) correctly determines that a certain duty can be derived from a right in a binding Bill of Rights and changes private law accordingly, he gives effect to the constitution-makers' judgement, even though (and in fact by) exceeding it. The judge can therefore justify the change by invoking the constitution-makers' judgement. But if a judge (with additional premises) correctly determines that certain values underlie the rights in a non-binding Bill of Rights and changes private common law so as to conform to those values, he exceeds the constitution-makers' judgement without giving it effect. In this case, therefore, there is no possibility of an appeal to the constitution-makers' judgement.

This has important implications for the justification of constitutional constraint. One way of justifying the idea that a judge should change private common law for reasons (operative or auxiliary) provided by a Bill of Rights (binding or non-binding) is by invoking the superior moral expertise of the constitution-makers. Such an appeal inevitably relies on the following argument. One, the constitution-makers' moral judgement is more reliable than that of the average judge. Two, the Bill of Rights reflects the constitution-makers' (superior) moral judgement. Three, private common law is therefore likely to turn out morally better, in the long run, if judges change it for reasons provided by the Bill of Rights rather than in accordance with their own moral convictions.[30] This argument is basically a sound one, though the truth of its first premise is of course contingent. However—and this is the important point—the argument can justify changes to private common law for reasons provided by a Bill of Rights only if the Bill of Rights is binding, and not if it is non-binding. Why? Because the argument applies only in so far as changes to private common law for reasons provided by the Bill of Rights actually give effect to the judgement

---

[30] See Raz, *Ethics in the Public Domain*, *supra* n.8, at 210–37.

of the constitution-makers. As we have seen, that is not the case when changes are made on the basis of the values that underlie a non-binding Bill of Rights.

I have identified one possible justification for changing private common law for reasons provided by a Bill of Rights, namely to invoke the superior moral expertise of the constitution-makers. I have also shown that this justification is unavailable if the Bill of Rights is non-binding. This can be generalised. It is not only the described justification that is unavailable to non-binding Bills of Rights, but also any other justification that relies on or presupposes the idea that the judgement of the constitution-makers deserves special respect. The described justification gives one reason for such respect, namely that the constitution-makers have moral expertise greater than that of judges. But there could be other reasons for respecting the constitution-makers' judgement, such as the fact that it was a judgement approved of, or consented to, by an historically significant majority.

Of course, it may be possible to justify the practice of changing private common law for reasons provided by a Bill of Rights, without relying on or presupposing the idea that the constitution-makers' judgement merits special respect. One such justification is suggested by Cass Sunstein's work on "incompletely theorised agreements" and Michael Bayles's work on "mid-level principles".[31] It is important for any community that its members share practices and values: that there be, in other words, a degree of moral consensus. At the same time, many communities display a high degree of pluralism about fundamental values. How, then, is the necessary moral consensus to be achieved? The answer, say Sunstein and Bayles, is to be found in incompletely theorised agreements or mid-level principles. What they mean by this is that people may diverge about morality at the highest and most abstract theoretical level, yet their moral judgements may converge at a lower and more concrete one. So, for example, utilitarians and Kantians may agree that freedom of speech is a value, but disagree about the reasons for its value. So too a socialist and a capitalist may agree that workers should be allowed to unionise, but again for different reasons. The importance of incompletely theorised agreements provides a justification for law, since law provides a means of entrenching such agreements. For the same reason, it might provide a justification for a Bill of Rights and for changing private common law for reasons provided by a Bill of Rights.

Once again it seems to me that this is a justification that applies only when private common law is changed to accord with a binding Bill of Rights, and not a non-binding one. For, so it seems to me, this justification extends only to law-making acts that preserve the moral consensus achieved by the entrenchment of incompletely theorised agreements in a Bill of Rights. That moral consensus is,

---

[31] See C.R. Sunstein, *Legal Reasoning and Political Conflict* (New York, Oxford University Press, 1996), 35–61 and C.R. Sunstein, "Constitutional Agreements Without Constitutional Theories" (2000) 13 *Ratio Juris* 117; M.D. Bayles, "Mid-Level Principles and Justification" in J.R. Pennock and J.W. Chapman (eds.), *Justification: Nomos XXVIII* (New York, NYU, 1986), 61–2. See also Raz, *supra* n.12, at 58, 181.

however, fractured rather than preserved when judges change private common law so as to accord with the values that underlie a Bill of Rights.

In the previous section, I explained that a non-binding Bill of Rights could provide reasons for changing private common law only on the assumption that legal coherence is a value. In this section, I have identified a range of justifications that do not apply when changes to private common law are made in accordance with the values underlying a non-binding Bill of Rights. What this means is that, if indeed coherence is a value, it is not valuable because it serves any of the justifications that I have identified. I suspect, though I have not proved it, that this conclusion can be generalised. That is, I suspect that, if legal coherence is a value, it must be an intrinsic rather than an instrumental one.

IV.   THREE FALLACIES

There is general agreement amongst South African lawyers that something significant is at stake in the choice between a binding and a non-binding Bill of Rights. However, no South African lawyer has endorsed the thesis proposed and defended in the previous two sections of this chapter, namely that what is at stake in that choice is how we justify the imposition of constitutional constraints upon the development of private common law. Instead, some South African lawyers have supposed that what is at stake in the choice between a binding and a non-binding Bill of Rights is the survival of private common law. Some have thought that it is the private-public divide. And some have suggested that it is a community's political commitments. The aim of this section is to show that these three views are mistaken. In order best to explain the error of these views, the section starts by making a preliminary point. This is that whether a community has a binding or a non-binding Bill of Rights, or indeed whether it has a Bill of Rights at all, has no necessary implications for the power of the community's judges to change private common law. Thereafter, the section tries to refute each of the three views in turn.

1. The power to change private common law

My account of what is at stake in the choice between a binding and a non-binding Bill of Rights depicts both as imposing a constraint upon the development of private common law. According to my account, Bills of Rights of both kinds impose that constraint because they provide judges with reasons for changing private common law that judges would otherwise not have had. It may be thought that binding and non-binding Bills of Rights not only constrain but also "liberate" the development of private common law. For, it may be felt, binding and non-binding Bills of Rights not only provide judges with new reasons for changing private common law, but also increase their power to do so. Do binding and non-binding Bills of Rights really have this liberating effect? Do they really increase judges' power to change private common law? I believe not, and the aim of this subsection is to explain why.

Consider for a moment the power of the South African courts to change private common law, before South Africa had a Bill of Rights. There can be no doubt that the South African courts had this power. Equally uncontroversial is the fact that this power was subject to the following two limitations. One, an inferior court could not change private common law by overruling a precedent of a superior court. Two, a court was not supposed to change private common law by overruling a precedent of its own, unless it believed the precedent to be clearly mistaken.[32] The effect of these limitations was that, even where a judge believed a rule of private common law to be legally or morally unjustified, he may have been constrained from changing it, either because he was unable to overrule the precedent that established the rule (the first limitation) or because he was under an obligation not to overrule it (the second limitation). In short, the effect of the limitations was that it was sometimes impossible, at other times inappropriate, for a judge to shape private common law according to his own legal or moral judgement.

Now ask the question: did the enactment of either the non-binding Bill of Rights in the interim South African Constitution or the binding Bill of Rights in the new one alter the power of South African courts to change private common law? It has never been suggested that the enactment of either Bill of Rights reduced the power of South African judges to change private common law. It has also never been suggested that the power of South African judges to change private common law has been altered in respect of "post-Constitutional" private common law (i.e. private common law created subsequent to the enactment of the Bills of Rights). We can thus narrow the focus of our question: did the enactment of either Bill of Rights expand the power of South African courts to change "pre-Constitutional" private common law (i.e. private common law that antedates the Bills of Rights)? It seems to me that, if the enactment of either Bill of Rights did expand that power, it could only have been by relaxing one or both of the limitations described above. We can thus rephrase our question as follows: did the enactment of either Bill of Rights have the consequence that South African judges can now overrule pre-Constitutional precedents of superior courts and/or may now overrule pre-Constitutional precedents of their own that they do not believe to be clearly mistaken?

Several South African judges seem to have assumed an affirmative answer to this question. In the case of *Holomisa* v. *Argus Newspapers Ltd*,[33] for example, Cameron J introduced a completely novel principle to South African defamation law, on the ground that it was required by the values underlying the interim Constitution. In laying down this new principle, Cameron J expressly overruled

---

[32] On these limitations, see H.R. Hahlo and E. Kahn, *The South African Legal System and its Background* (Cape Town, Juta, 1968), 237–60.
[33] [1996] 2 SA 588 (W).

two pre-Constitutional precedents of the South African Appellate Division, a superior court.[34] Although Cameron J seemed to be unaware of this, he in all likelihood overruled a third precedent, also of the Appellate Division.[35] Clearly, Cameron J's overruling of these precedents was valid (i.e. actually succeeded in changing the South African law of defamation), only if the first limitation no longer applied: or, at least, only if it no longer applied to (certain) pre-Constitutional precedents.[36]

Cameron J is not altogether clear about why the first limitation should be relaxed in this way. There is some suggestion in his judgment, however, that he believes it necessarily to follow from, or to be entailed by, the fact that the interim Constitution's Bill of Rights provides reasons for changing private common law.[37] If this is Cameron J's belief, it is erroneous. The point of the first (and the second) limitation is to constrain judges from changing private common law that they believe to be morally or legally unjustified. This constraint reflects the fact that it is sometimes justified—for second-order reasons—for a court not to change private common law that is unjustified—for first-order reasons. The second-order reasons (constituting the justification for not changing unjustified private common law) have to do with the importance of legal certainty, predictability, uniformity and efficiency.[38] Now, the enactment of a binding or a non-binding Bill of Rights certainly changes the first-order reasons by which the justification of private common law is to be judged. It may even have the result that private common law previously justified is no longer so, and the converse. But it does not alter the second-order reasons for a court not to change unjustified private common law. To assume that it does is to confuse the two orders of justification.

2. The survival of private common law

So, neither the enactment of a binding Bill of Rights nor that of a non-binding one entails that judges' power to change private common law has been in any way augmented. Binding and non-binding Bills of Rights only constrain the

[34] The precedents had been established by Hoexter JA in *Neethling* v. *Du Preez and others*; *Neethling* v. *The Weekly Mail and others* [1994] 1 SA 708 (A).

[35] The third precedent is that of Rumpff C J in *Pakendorf* v. *De Flamingh* [1982] 3 SA 146 (A) (hereinafter *Pakendorf*).

[36] Other judgments in which an affirmative answer to the question was assumed are that of Froneman J in *Gardener* v. *Whitaker* [1995] 2 SA 672 (E), 684F–G, 686A–B; that of Davis AJ in *Rivett-Carnac* v. *Wiggins* [1997] 3 SA 80 (C), 86E–F, 87D–G; and that of Du Plessis J in *McNally* v. *M&G Media (Pty) Ltd and others* [1997] 4 SA 267 (W), 275.

[37] See at 598A–B, 603D–E, G–H, 606B–C.

[38] See Hahlo and Kahn, *supra* n.32, at 215. For a detailed discussion of such second-order reasons, see E.H. Caminker, "Why Must Inferior Courts Obey Superior Court Precedents?" (1994) 46 *Stanford L R* 817. See also Z. Bankowski, D.N. MacCormick, L. Morawski and A. Ruiz, "Rationales for Precedent" in D.N. MacCormick and R.S. Summers (eds.), *Interpreting Precedents: A Comparative Study* (Dartmouth, Ashgate, 1997).

development of private common law: they do not liberate it. This has implications for the view that what is at stake in the choice between a binding and a non-binding Bill of Rights is the survival of private common law. More specifically, it has implications for the view that private common law is under greater threat from the former kind of Bill of Rights than it is from the latter.[39]

As I see it, there are two ways that the survival of private common law might be undermined by the enactment of a Bill of Rights. The first is if, as a result of that enactment, private common law were to lose its resistance to change. How could the enactment of a Bill of Rights, binding or non-binding, cause private common law to lose its resistance to change? Only, I believe, by relaxing one or both of the limitations (discussed above) on courts' power to change private common law. But, as we saw, the enactment of a Bill of Rights, be it binding or non-binding, does not entail the relaxation of either limitation. Thus it does not threaten the survival of private common law in this way.

There is, however, a second way that the survival of private common law might be undermined by the enactment of a Bill of Rights. This is if a court adjudicating a dispute between private parties could ignore, or bypass, private common law, and reach its decision on the basis of reasons provided by the Bill of Rights alone. Some of the South African opposition to binding Bills of Rights seems to have been motivated by the belief that binding Bills of Rights inevitably have this result.[40] The argument is roughly as follows: "If a community has a binding Bill of Rights, private parties can found their causes of action on the rights therein. In a defamation case, for example, the plaintiff could claim damages for an infringement of his constitutional right to dignity. The defendant could respond that he had been exercising his constitutional right to freedom of expression. A court having to decide this dispute would do so by striking the balance it believes appropriate between the competing constitutional rights. It would not, or at any rate need not, have recourse to the whole gamut of common law doctrines regulating defamation. The common law of defamation would, or could, therefore be ignored or bypassed".

I do not believe that the enactment of a binding Bill of Rights necessarily has the consequence that private parties can bypass private common law in the way just described. Legal doctrines are often (even typically) stacked in justificatory hierarchies. For example, the South African law of defamation, at its highest and most abstract doctrinal level, states that a plaintiff can recover damages for a defamatory publication that is wrongful and culpable. At a lower level, there are doctrines explaining what counts as a publication (communication between spouses does not), when it is defamatory (if the publication, given its ordinary meaning, would lead a right-thinking member of the community to think less of the plaintiff), when it is wrongful (if it is neither true and in the public interest, nor fair comment, nor privileged), and when it

---

[39] For this view, see Ackermann J in *Du Plessis, supra* n.1, at 903C.
[40] See for example Ackermann J in *Du Plessis, supra* n.1, at 900F–G, 902A–B, 906G.

is culpable. Below these doctrines are still further ones, characterising the right-thinking member of the community, stating the criteria for a comment to be fair or a statement to be privileged, and so on. A typical, possibly even a necessary, feature of a justificatory hierarchy of the kind just described is that the doctrines at the lower levels are not fully transparent to the doctrines at the higher levels that justify (or purport to justify) them. This lack of transparency can be either partial or complete. It is complete if a lower-order doctrine constitutes an indefeasible guide to a higher-order one. It is partial if the guidance provided by a lower-order doctrine is exceptionally defeasible: that is, if the lower-order doctrine operates as a "rule of thumb".

The existence and nature of these justificatory hierarchies has an important consequence for the way litigants plead, argue and win cases. This is that, though a litigant may frame his cause of action in terms of a doctrine at the pinnacle of a justificatory hierarchy, he will have to argue and win it in terms of the doctrines at its base. This is illustrated by the South African law of defamation. A plaintiff's cause of action may well be that a publication by the defendant has wrongfully and culpably defamed him. The defendant may well respond by denying wrongfulness. But the dispute will be thrashed out and decided in terms of lower-order doctrines: was the publication a reasonable inference from true facts; did the defendant have a legitimate interest in making it and the audience a legitimate interest in receiving it; did the defendant act with malice?

How does this show that the enactment of a binding Bill of Rights does not necessarily have the result that private parties will be able to bypass private common law? Well, nothing in the nature of a binding Bill of Rights precludes the possibility of a single justificatory hierarchy, with the rights in the Bill of Rights at the top and the various doctrines of private common law at the bottom. By the same token, nothing in the nature of a binding Bill of Rights precludes the possibility that this hierarchy be less than fully transparent. Thus, while it will be possible (because of the single hierarchy) for the parties in a defamation suit to frame their causes of action in terms of the constitutional rights to dignity and freedom of expression, they will (because of the hierarchy's lack of transparency) nonetheless have to argue and win their cases in terms of the usual doctrines of private common law. The enactment of a binding Bill of Rights does not, therefore, entail that private common law will be ignored or bypassed.

3. The public-private divide and the political commitments of a community

I have shown that it is wrong to think that what is at stake in the choice between a binding and a non-binding Bill of Rights is the survival of private common law. For the enactment of a Bill of Rights, be it binding or non-binding, entails neither that private common law must lose its resistance to change nor that it may be bypassed or ignored. I now wish to consider, somewhat more briefly, the other two views about what is at stake in the choice between a binding and a non-binding Bill of Rights: that it is the private-public divide and that it is a community's political commitments.

In South Africa, the view that the choice of Bill of Rights has implications for the private-public divide has received both academic and judicial endorsement.[41] While those implications are nowhere clearly stated, they are, I think, believed to be as follows. One: in South Africa, private common law will check private power if and only if its development is subjected to constitutional constraint; and it will check private power to a greater degree if the constraint is provided by a binding Bill of Rights rather than a non-binding one. Some judges and academics combine one with two: in South Africa, private power should be checked (particularly as the distribution of private power in South Africa reflects the country's apartheid past). This yields three: in South Africa, the development of private common law should be constrained by a Bill of Rights, and preferably by a binding rather than a non-binding one.

I do not intend to refute any of the three claims just outlined. For all I know, all three may be true. The point I want to make is a more limited one. This is that, if the first claim is true, it is contingently rather than necessarily so. That is, if the first claim is true, it is not because of the nature of private common law, or of binding and non-binding Bills of Rights. It is rather because of factors particular to the South African judiciary and to the South African interim and final Constitutions. Of course, if the first claim is at best contingently true, so is the third.

The explanation for this is as follows. As was demonstrated earlier in this section, the power of judges to change private common law is not necessarily affected by whether a community has a Bill of Rights or not, nor by whether, if a community has a Bill of Rights, it is binding or non-binding. As was shown in section II of this chapter, what is necessarily affected is the nature of the reasons judges have for changing private common law. But whether private common law changes so as to check private power and, if so, to what degree, depends not on the *nature* of judges' reasons for changing it, but rather on the *content* of those reasons. Moreover, and this is the crucial point, neither the fact that a community has a Bill of Rights, nor the kind of Bill of Rights it has, has any necessary implications for the *content* of judges' reasons to change private common law. The content of those reasons is contingent, in the absence of a Bill of Rights, on the moral convictions of judges (present and past). It is contingent, in the presence of a binding or a non-binding Bill of Rights, on the content of the Bill of Rights, and thus ultimately on the moral convictions of

---

[41] See H. Cheadle and D. Davis, "The Application of the 1996 Constitution in the Private Sphere" (1997) 13 *S African J on Human Rights* 44, 50, 54, 56, 66; A. Cockrell, "Private Law and the Bill of Rights: A Threshold Issue of 'Horizontality' " in *The Bill of Rights Compendium* (Durban, Butterworths, looseleaf), 3A–3–3A–5; Mahomed DP in *Du Plessis, supra* n.1, at 892F–I, 896F–897G; Madala J in *Du Plessis, supra* n.1, at 922E–F, 926A–B, 927A–C; Davis J in *McCarthy* v. *Constantia Property Owners' Association* [1999] 4 SA 847 (C), 855C–E.

the constitution-makers. This means that, for it to be a necessary truth that private common law will check private power if and only if it is to be changed for reasons provided by a Bill of Rights (and more so if the Bill of Rights is binding rather than non-binding), it must be a necessary truth that judges are less likely to endorse such checks than are constitution-makers. That is clearly not the case.

A similar response can be made to the idea that what is at stake in the choice between a binding and a non-binding Bill of Rights is a community's political commitments. In South Africa, this idea has been put forward by Dennis Davis (now a judge of the High Court) and Stuart Woolman.[42] They suppose, first, that South Africa's private common law will reflect communitarian rather than libertarian liberalism, if and only if it is constrained by a Bill of Rights, and that it will better reflect communitarian liberalism if it is constrained by a binding rather than a non-binding Bill of Rights. They believe, secondly, that communitarian liberalism is better than libertarian liberalism. Hence they believe, thirdly, that South Africa's private common law should be constrained by a Bill of Rights, and preferably by a binding rather than a non-binding one.

Again, I am not concerned here to refute any of these three beliefs (though I must confess to not sharing any of them). The point I wish to make is again the more limited one that, if the first, and thus also third, beliefs are true, they are true for contingent reasons (the moral convictions of South African judges, on the one hand, and of the South African constitution-makers, on the other) rather than necessary ones (the nature of private common law, and of binding and non-binding Bills of Rights). The explanation of this is essentially the same as the one presented a moment ago, when discussing the private-public divide. So I will not repeat it here.

V. CONCLUSION

I have established my main thesis, namely that what is at stake in the choice between a binding and a non-binding Bill of Rights, is how we justify the imposition of a constitutional constraint on the development of private common law. I have also tried to dispel three misconceptions about what is at stake in this choice. To conclude this chapter, I would like to make a few remarks about the way that the distinction between binding and non-binding Bills of Rights relates to another important distinction, that between "framework" and "foundational" conceptions of Bills of Rights. A Bill of Rights is foundational if a rule of private common law is justified only if the Bill of Rights provides a reason for it. A Bill of Rights constitutes a framework if a rule of private common law could be justified even though the Bill of Rights

---

[42] S. Woolman and D. Davis, "The Last Laugh: *Du Plessis* v. *De Klerk*, Classical Liberalism, Creole Liberalism and the Application of Fundamental Rights under the Interim and the Final Constitutions" (1996) 12 *S African J on Human Rights* 361, especially at 380–404.

provides no reason for it, but lacks justification if the Bill of Rights provides a reason against it.

It is unclear whether the Bills of Rights created by the interim and new South African Constitutions have been conceived as frameworks or foundations. The South African Supreme Court of Appeal, in two recent cases, appears to have adopted the framework conception. So, for example, in the case of *National Media Ltd and others* v. *Bogoshi*,[43] the Supreme Court of Appeal overruled a precedent of its own that had established strict liability for the press in defamation.[44] The court's basis for doing so was that the precedent was clearly wrong, because it struck the wrong balance between the moral (and not the constitutional) rights of freedom of expression and reputation that underlie the South African law of defamation. Only once it had determined that the precedent should be overruled, for these moral reasons, did the court look at the Bill of Rights (in the interim Constitution). However, the court looked at the Bill of Rights only to see whether it provided any reasons against the proposed change. As the court explained:

> In the present case I have not sought to revise the common law conformably to the values of the interim Constitution; I have done no more than to hold that this Court stated a common-law principle wrongly in *Pakendorf*. It is plain, nevertheless, that Section 35(3) requires an examination of the constitutional compatibility of my conclusion.[45]

There is reason to believe that the South African Constitutional Court may have a different view. In the recent case of *Pharmaceutical Manufacturers Association of SA and another: in re ex parte President of the RSA and others*,[46] the Constitutional Court may well have aligned itself with the foundational conception. In its judgment, the court makes the following two claims:

> There is only one system of law. It is shaped by the Constitution which is the supreme law, and all law, including the common law, derives its force from the Constitution and is subject to constitutional control.[47]
> The common law supplements the provisions of the written Constitution but derives its force from it. It must be developed to fulfil the purposes of the Constitution and the legal order that it proclaims . . .[48]

Admittedly, the import of these passages is not entirely clear. If what the court meant to say was only that the common law now owes its legal validity to the Constitution, then it cannot be seen (on the strength of saying that) to be taking sides on the foundations-framework question. However, there is some suggestion

[43] [1998] 4 SA 1196 (SCA). The other case in which the Supreme Court of Appeal took a framework view is *Amod* v. *Multilateral Vehicle Accidents Fund* [1999] 4 SA 1319 (SCA).
[44] The precedent had been established in the *Pakendorf* case, *supra* n.35.
[45] *Ibid.*, at 1216E–F.
[46] [2000] 2 SA 674 (CC).
[47] *Ibid.*, at 696B–C.
[48] *Ibid.*, at 698B–C.

in these passages that the court may have had something more in mind, namely that the common law owes its justification to, or can only be justified in terms of, the Constitution. That entails, of course, that private common law may be changed only if the Bill of Rights provides a reason for the change. It entails, in other words, a foundational rather than a framework conception of the Bill of Rights.

It should be obvious that, irrespective of whether a Bill of Rights is binding or non-binding, it will place fewer restrictions on the content of private common law if it functions as a framework than if it functions as a foundation. Partly because of this, I prefer the framework conception, but that is not a preference that will be defended here. Instead, I want to draw attention to an interesting implication that a community's choice between the framework and foundational conceptions has for its choice between a binding and a non-binding Bill of Rights. This is that, if a community adopts the framework conception, the content of its private common law will be restricted less by a binding Bill of Rights than a non-binding one. However, if the community adopts the foundational conception, the opposite will be the case: the content of its private common law will be restricted to a greater degree by a binding Bill of Rights than a non-binding one.

The explanation is as follows. If a community has a foundational Bill of Rights, the duties that comprise its private common law will be justified only in so far as the Bill of Rights provides reasons for their recognition. This means that the content of the community's private common law will be restricted to a greater degree by a binding Bill of Rights than a non-binding one, if a binding Bill of Rights provides reasons for the recognition of fewer duties than does a non-binding Bill of Rights. Precisely that is the case. While a binding Bill of Rights provides reasons to recognise only the duties that can be derived from it, a non-binding Bill of Rights provides reasons to recognise all the duties that cohere with it. Clearly, far fewer duties can be derived from a Bill of Rights than cohere with it. For the duties that cohere with a Bill of Rights include all the duties that can be derived from it, as well as many others. A similar line of reasoning shows that, if a community has a framework Bill of Rights, the content of its private common law will be restricted to a lesser extent by a binding than a non-binding Bill of Rights.

The foregoing observations, concerning the way that the framework-foundations distinction relates to the distinction between binding and non-binding Bills of Rights, are tentative and inconclusive. The observations do, however, serve to identify an issue that requires further investigation, particularly in South Africa, where a clear choice between the framework and foundational conceptions will at some stage have to be made by the courts.

5

Human Rights and Private Law in German Constitutional Development and in the Jurisdiction of the Federal Constitutional Court

CHRISTIAN STARCK

I. VARIOUS THEORIES OF THE THIRD-PARTY EFFECT OF BASIC RIGHTS

IN GERMANY, THE issue of whether basic rights affect legal relationships between private individuals is known as the "third-party effect of basic rights". Theories of third-party effect attempt to justify the contention that basic rights bind individuals to greater or lesser degrees. Any exploration of the issues raised by this topic must consider not only legal relationships between private individuals, but also the positions of the legislature, which is the source of private law, and the judge who decides civil cases. Whatever their individual differences, however, all theories of third-party effect have two things in common: they all posit that private individuals are to some extent bound by basic rights, and they view that binding effect as being transmitted either by the enactment of private law norms that are consistent with basic rights or by the judgments of the civil courts, which must also be consistent with the basic rights. One of the preliminary difficulties involved in tackling the problem of third-party effect is evident from the names of the theories proposed to solve the problem. The terms "direct" and "indirect" do not describe different types of effects particularly accurately, yet they are commonly used in the literature on third-party effect.

In the opinion of the Federal Labour Court, certain individual basic rights directly affect legal relationships between private individuals. This view has found some support in the literature.[1] Its proponents derive the direct third-party effect from the function of basic rights as fundamental objective norms

---

[1] L. Enneccerus and H.C. Nipperdey, *Allgemeiner Teil des Bürgerlichen Rechts* (15th edn., Tübingen, Mohr-Siebeck, 1959), i/1, 92 *et seq.*; H.C. Nipperdey, *Grundrechte und Privatrecht* (Krefeld, Scherpe, 1961), 13 *et seq.*; *Entscheidungen des Bundesarbeitsgerichts* (*Reports of the Federal Labour Court*) (Hereinafter BAGE) 1, 185, 193 *et seq.*; 4, 274, 276 *et seq.*; 7, 256, 260; 13, 168, 174 *et seq.*; 16, 95, 100 *et seq.*; K. Stern, *Staatsrecht* (Munich, Beck, 1988), iii/1, 1531 *et seq.*, 1538, lists further writers who support this view.

for the whole of the legal order. Others[2] derive this effect from the state guarantee of private autonomy.[3] Under the latter approach, the State has a duty to respect basic rights when acting as regulator, judge or enforcer with regard to private law. Clearly, this entails a third-party effect by means of legislation and adjudication. Theories of direct third-party effect avoid the dilemma posed by the basic right to equality by subordinating it to the principle of private autonomy. Private law is deemed as falling outside the ambit of the principle of equality on the ground that a duty to give effect to equality would distort the basis of private law.[4] The great strength of theories of direct third-party effect is that basic rights affect the enactment and the application of private law in equal measure.

Theories of an indirect third-party effect of basic rights allow the values incorporated in basic rights to affect private law through open-textured norms that require judicial interpretation.[5] These theories uphold the principle of private autonomy, which the German Constitution guarantees, refusing to sacrifice it to the principle of equality or any other basic right. This view, which is supported by decisions of the Federal Constitutional Court,[6] is based on the principle that the Constitution and private law are not mutually independent components of the legal order. Rather, basic rights are understood as an objective system of values that permeate every field of law. Theories of indirect third-party effect do not address the question of whether and to what extent basic rights affect private law where no open texture norms can serve as the appropriate portals for their entry into this sphere.

Theories of direct and indirect third-party effect are not as far apart as it might appear at first glance. *Nipperdey*, the father of the doctrine of direct third-party effect, notes that the meaning of basic rights in the modern constitutional framework is not entirely identical with the meaning these rights bore earlier on. However, he believes that any change in meaning is necessarily restricted, since only some (!) basic-rights norms have the important role of basic principles that are directly binding on the entire legal order and, hence,

---

[2] J. Schwabe, *Die sogenannte Drittwirkung der Grundrechte* (Munich, Goldmann, 1971), 16 *et seq.*, 67 *et seq.*; idem, *Probleme der Grundrechtsdogmatik* (Darmstadt, Schadel, 1977), 213.

[3] See Stern's extensive treatment of theories of third-party effect: Stern, *supra* n.1, at 1518 *et seq.*; A. Bleckmann, *Staatsrecht* (3rd edn., Cologne, Heymanns, 1989), ii, 175 *et seq.*, both with further references; S. Oeter, " 'Drittwirkung' der Grundrechte und die Autonomie des Privatrechts" (1994) 119 *Archiv des öffentlichen Rechts* 529.

[4] For example, 13 BAGE 103, 105.

[5] G. Dürig, "Grundrechte und Zivilrechtsprechung" in T. Maunz (ed.), *Vom Bonner Grundgesetz zur gesamtdeutschen Verfassung (Festschrift zum 75. Geburtstag von Hans Nawiasky)* (Munich, Isar-Verlag, 1956), 157 *et seq.*; idem, "Zum 'Lüth-Urteil' des Bundesverfassungsgerichts vom 15.1.1958" in *Die öffentliche Verwaltung* (1958), xi, no. 8, 9, 194 *et seq.*; 3 BAGE 296, 301; for further literature see Stern, *supra* n.1, 1532.

[6] 7 *Entscheidungen des Bundesverfassungsgerichts (Reports of the Federal Constitutional Court)* (hereinafter BVerfGE) 198, 205; 25 BVerfGE 256, 263; 34 BVerfGE 269, 280; 42 BVerfGE 143, 148; 49 BVerfGE 89, 142 m. w. N.; 52 BVerfGE 131, 165 *et seq.*; 73 BVerfGE 261, 269; see also C.D. Classen, "Die Drittwirkung der Grundrechte in der Rechtsprechung des Bundesverfassungsgerichts" (1997) 122 *Archiv des öffentlichen Rechts* 65 *et seq.*

also on private law.[7] Here, Nipperdey is clearly referring to the particular influence exercised by basic rights on civil legislation and on the interpretation of open norms (*Generalklauseln*). In Nipperdey's earlier writings,[8] he makes it clear that the effect of the basic rights guaranteed under the German Basic Law cannot be decided one way or another on the basis of a particular historically determined perspective. Rather, Nipperdey asserts, the appropriate starting point is the function, nature and specific content of the basic right in question and the individual norms that derive from that right in the modern context.[9] From the standpoint of legal theory, this approach may be somewhat rough and ready.[10] It does, however, make a reasonable decision possible in each case that arises.[11]

The Federal Labour Court has not formally abandoned its approach in favour of direct third-party effect. Nonetheless, its decisions reflect a change in perspective: basic rights are understood to give expression to a general value system that influences private law and exercises that influence via open-textured norms.[12] This is clear from the structure of the court's judgments. The court first reviews the legal issues on the basis of private law and then, in a second step, considers whether the solution it has reached is consistent with the value system expressed by the basic rights.[13] Dürig's theory of the indirect third-party effect of basic rights does not address the influence of those rights on the enactment of legislation—a lacuna, since basic rights must affect the enactment of legislation if they influence its interpretation. In defence of the autonomy of private law, which he derives from basic rights, Dürig criticises Nipperdey's doctrine. He does not, however, deal in any depth with its theoretical flexibility or with the distinctions that that flexibility allows the interpreter to draw. Even if Dürig's view that traditional private law represents a significant guarantee of freedom and equality is correct, it is by no means the case that that guarantee permeates every aspect of private law.

---

[7] H.C. Nipperdey, "Freie Entfaltung der Persönlichkeit" in K.A. Bettermann and H.C. Nipperdey (eds.), *Die Grundrechte: Handbuch der Theorie und Praxis der Grundrechte* (Berlin, Duncker & Humblot, 1962), iv/2, 748 *et seq.*

[8] H.C. Nipperdey, "Die Würde des Menschen", *supra* n.7 (Berlin, Duncker & Humblot, 1954), ii, 18.

[9] Similar positions have been taken in countries other than Germany in the context of constitutional reform. On the Netherlands, see D. Simons, "Bestand und Bedeutung der Grundrechte in den Niederlanden" in *Europäische Grundrechte-Zeitschrift* (1978) v, 19–22, 450, 454; on Switzerland, see the *Report of the Commission of Experts for the Preparation of a Complete Revision of the Federal Constitution* (1977), 55; for an overview, see C. Starck, *Der demokratische Verfassungsstaat* (Tübingen, Mohr-Siebeck, 1995), 212 *et seq.*; Stern, *supra* n.1, at 1533 *et seq.*

[10] For criticism, see Oeter, *supra* n.3, at 542 *et seq.*

[11] See also W. Leisner, *Grundrechte und Privatrecht* (Munich, Beck, 1960), 358; see also W. Rüfner in J. Isensee and P. Kirchhof (eds.), *Handbuch des Staatsrechts der Bundesrepublik Deutschland* (Heidelberg, C.F. Müller, 1992), v, § 117 n.58.

[12] 7 BAGE 256, 260; 13 BAGE 168, 176; emphatically 48 BAGE 122, 138–9: "In answering the question 'what does good faith require?' the value system given expression in the Basic Law's catalogue of rights should also be borne in mind".

[13] In 24 BAGE 438, 441, the Federal Labour Court declined to deal with issues of third-party effect.

II.   THE MULTI-LAYERED PROBLEM OF FREEDOM AND BASIC RIGHTS AS
GUARANTEES AGAINST THE STATE

Whether basic rights are understood simply as defences against the State or, in an earlier conception of rights, as relating to the whole of the law, including private law, depends on how far one is willing to trace their historical roots. For Kant, private law is founded on the principle that one person's freedom should be reconciled with another's.[14] The Prussian General Law (*Preußisches Allgemeines Landrecht*) grants protection to the freedom that a human being naturally enjoys "to pursue and increase his own well-being without harming the rights of another".[15] Carl von Rotteck also recognises that the issue of freedom is multi-layered.[16] In his view, the State, as a legal institution, must "respect and protect the freedom which its subjects enjoy in every sphere of activity simply by virtue of being human beings". Even if the State "has itself refrained from infringing its subjects' rights of freedom, it must still protect its subjects against those who might threaten them in the course of their interaction". The State, von Rotteck explains, may not tolerate slavery or serfdom (*Leibeigenschaft*) and may not allow anything of that kind to develop. Moreover, by enacting wisely chosen laws and by administering them carefully, the State should channel other threats to freedom away from its citizens, wherever those threats may arise. Of particular relevance in this context are abuses of private power in house and home.[17]

Von Rotteck's understanding of basic rights did find expression in the 1789 French Declaration of Human and Civil Rights.[18] As time progressed, however, the discussion of legal relationships between private individuals began to distance itself from the general discussion of civil rights and civil liberties. This can be attributed to the rise of positivism and to the successful codifications of private law, which secured contemporary ideals of freedom and equality.[19] The European States' declarations of rights had their origins in the effort to give

---

[14] I. Kant, *Metaphysik der Sitten, Rechtslehre* (Leipzig, Meiner, 1797, edition 1922), §§ 5, 10, 18.

[15] § 83 Einleitung zum Preußischen Allgemeinen Landrecht (1794).

[16] C. von Rotteck, "Freiheit" in C. von Rotteck and C. Welcker, *Staats-Lexikon* (2nd edn., Altona, Hammerich, 1847), v, 184, 186; see also *idem, Lehrbuch des Vernunftrechts* (2nd edn., Stuttgart, Franckh, 1840), ii, 78.

[17] See also L. von Rönne, *Staatsrecht der preußischen Monarchie* (4th edn., Leipzig, 1882), ii, 38. Third-party effect of basic rights was mentioned in the Paulskirche in connection with the privacy of mail: H. Schöller, "Einleitung" in H. Schöller (ed.), *Die Grundrechtsdiskussion in der Paulskirche* (Darmstadt, Wissenschaftliche Buchgesellschaft, 1973), 20.

[18] See Art. 2(4). American declarations of human rights treat the problem of freedom only from the perspective of the relationship between citizens and the State. The common law, which the American states inherited, allows the problem of freedom among individual citizens to be resolved without reference to external catalogues of rights.

[19] See R. Scheyhing, "Zur Geschichte des Persönlichkeitsrechts im 19. Jahrhundert" (1959–60) 158 *Archiv für die civilistische Praxis* 503, 521 *et seq.*; O. von Gierke advances a dual construction of liberty (freedom among private individuals; freedom against the depredations of the State; in the latter instance, the position of subjective rights is weak): *Die Grundbegriffe des Staatsrechts* (1874), quoted according to the edition of 1915 (Tübingen, Mohr), 106 *et seq.*, 109.

legislative effect to the anti-absolutist doctrines of natural law, according to which state power was limited and individual rights of freedom and equality were inalienable.[20] In this context, then, the classical understanding of basic human rights was that these were negative rights that inhered in the individual and could be brought to bear against the exercise of state power, thus securing the right of the individual to a sphere devoid of State influence and limiting the State's right to interfere in the individual's legal relationships.

The norms that found expression in basic rights, then, were not intended to function as a yardstick, or a limit, to legal relationships among private individuals. They were not universal guarantees of freedom and equality; they were not directed at third parties, but were directed at the State, guaranteeing that the State will respect freedom and equality. This is clear, today, from the formulation of the basic rights in the German Basic Law. Article 1(3) of the Basic Law states that only state power is *directly* bound by basic rights.

The basic rights in the Weimar Constitution also provided protection against the State. There were, however, two notable exceptions to this principle, namely Article 118(1)(2) and Article 159(2), which protected freedom of expression and association and which explicitly granted protection against "social forces" other than the State. Clearly, the formulation of these two rights as exceptions lends weight to the view that rights were, in general, directed against the State. The equality of men and women, for example, was restricted to their rights and duties as citizens; it did not affect the law of marriage and the family. It is, incidentally, clear from that particular example that some basic rights are potentially very relevant to private law and, given their status as higher law (Article 1(3); Article 20(3)), may influence private law. When Article 3(2), sentence 1, of the Basic Law is read in conjunction with Article 117(1), it is clear that the Basic Law reflects a clear decision to deviate from the Weimar Constitution and the law of marriage and the family in force under that constitution. In relationships between men and women, private law is subject to the influence of basic rights.

III. BASIC RIGHTS OF EXPLICIT RELEVANCE TO PRIVATE LAW

As the above examples make clear, some basic rights not only guarantee or grant protection against the State, but also enable individuals to protect themselves against other private persons. One example is the right to unionise (Article 9(3), sentence 3, of the Basic Law). Alternatively, basic rights may impose duties of protection on the State,[21] as with the guarantee of human dignity (Article 1(1),

---

[20] R. Thoma, "Die juristische Bedeutung der grundrechtlichen Sätze der deutschen Reichsverfassung im allgemeinen" in H.C. Nipperdey (ed.), *Die Grundrechte und Grundpflichten der Reichsverfassung* (Berlin, Hobbing, 1929), i, 15.

[21] G. Dürig was one of the first to draw attention to this: "Der Grundrechtssatz von der Menschenwürde" (1956) 81 *Archiv des öffentlichen Rechts* 117, 118 *et seq.*; *idem*, in T. Maunz and G. Dürig, *Grundgesetz* (Basic Law), Article 1, n.131; W. Canaris, "Grundrechte und Privatrecht" (1984) 184 *Archiv für die civilistische Praxis* 201, 225 *et seq.*

sentence 1, of the Basic Law) and the protection of marriage, the family and mothers (Article 6(1) and Article 4). Similarly, the State is required to guarantee property and succession (Article 14(1)) and the undisturbed exercise of religion (Article 4(2)). Two of the basic rights require the State to ensure equality (Article 3(2), sentence 1, in conjunction with Article 117(1) and Article 6(5)). These duties exert a direct effect on private law, where the relevant norms are contained.[22] Notably, these basic rights are not—or not only—negative rights in the classical sense. Rather, they are rights of equality or rights that cannot be realised in practice unless the norms of private law are modified in order to give them effect. This is also true of the guarantee of a parent's right to bring up his or her child, which is contained in Article 6 and has clear implications for family law.[23] Clearly then, some of the problems associated with the issue of third-party effect can be solved without a blanket extension of basic rights to civil law, frequently accompanied by arbitrary exceptions.[24]

IV. PRIVATE LAW CONSIDERATION OF THE OBJECTIVELY NORMATIVE EFFECT OF BASIC RIGHTS

The constitutionally anchored norms mentioned above have an explicit effect on private law. There is, however, another way to derive the influence that constitutional norms exercise on private law. First, we should recall that the catalogue of rights contained in the Basic Law affects the relationship between the State and its citizens,[25] for basic rights are a constitutional response to the lesson that state power tends to infringe individual liberty. As discussed above, however, freedom is not only an issue between citizens and the State: it is also a relevant consideration in the context of individuals interacting with each other, especially with regard to gender differences and the imbalance of power in society. Since these issues had been discussed during the Weimar Republic,[26] the framers of the Basic Law were certainly aware of them in 1948–9. With the

---

[22] 3 BVerfGE 225, 242 *et seq.*; 25 BVerfGE 167, 196 *et seq.*; considered in 49 BVerfGE 304, 319 *et seq.*; see V. Götz, "Die Verwirklichung der Grundrechte durch die Gerichte im Zivilrecht" in W. Heyde and C. Starck (eds.), *Vierzig Jahre Grundrechte in ihrer Verwirklichung durch die Gerichte* (Munich, Beck, 1990), 51 *et seq.* On protection under criminal law see 39 BVerfGE 1, 41 *et seq.*

[23] 24 BVerfGE 119, 143 *et seq.*; 56 BVerfGE 363, 381 *et seq.*; 64 BVerfGE 180, 187 *et seq.*; 84 BVerfGE 168, 179; 92 BVerfGE 158, 176 *et seq.*

[24] Alternatively, artificial legal constructs must be used. The Federal Labour Court's method of subjecting union tariff agreements to Art. 3(2) of the Basic Law is one example (1 BAGE 258, 262; 4, 240, 252).

[25] This view recently has been vigorously affirmed by the Federal Constitutional Court: 52 BVerfGE 131, 165 *et seq.*

[26] See the references in H.V. Mangoldt and F. Klein, *Das Bonner Grundgesetz* (2nd edn., Berlin/Frankfurt a. M., Vahlen, 1957), i, 62. Civil liberties are thus not indicative of distance between the citizen and the State. U. Scheuner takes a different view, however: "Die rechtliche Tragweite der Grundrechte in der deutschen Verfassungsentwicklung des 19. Jahrhunderts" in E. Forsthoff, W. Weber and F. Wieacker (eds.), *Festschrift für Ernst Rudolf Huber zum 70 Geburtstag* (Göttingen, Otto Schwartz, 1973), 139, 147.

exception of Article 3(2), sentence 1, and Article 9(3), however, the Basic Law does not address them, instead placing its trust in contemporary and future private law. This decision should be respected; it should form the linchpin of any interpretation of basic rights. The magic formula "constitutional change" is out of place here: nothing has changed significantly since the Weimar Republic, the yardstick for those who compiled the catalogue of basic rights in the Basic Law.

With all due respect to the above considerations, however, we should bear in mind that the Constitution and private law do not exist independently, in isolation from one another.[27] It is quite true that life, health, freedom, honour and property must be respected during the course of our daily dealings, but the reason for this is not that citizens are bound directly by basic rights anchored in law. Rather, the norms and cultural customs that govern our social interactions impel us to act as we do; they are also the foundation on which the basic rights rest.[28] The understanding of human beings that underpins the Basic Law thus does not only provide the foundation for the basic rights in the relationship between citizens and the State; it is also the basis upon which norms of private law rest.[29] For example, the guarantee of human dignity in Article 1(1) of the Basic Law not only requires the State to refrain from violating human dignity, but also imposes a duty on the State to protect that dignity. This duty requires the State to make sure that private individuals do not place dignity in jeopardy in the course of their dealings with one another.

It is clear from the above reasoning that those basic rights that lack any obvious reference to private law cannot be applied by way of analogy to legal relationships that fall wholly within the scope of civil law. Private law must respect the understanding of human beings to which the Basic Law gives expression, and nothing more. The Federal Constitutional Court derives this consideration from what is known as the objectively normative effect of basic rights (*objektiv-rechtliche Wirkung der Grundrechte*).[30] This approach does provide a solution to the problem addressed by theories of third-party effect. Its theoretical basis is clear and appropriate: it does not distort fundamental rights concerning the relationship between citizens and the State. It is also eminently practicable:

---

[27] G. Dürig, in T. Maunz and G. Dürig, *Grundgesetz*, Article 1 n.127 *et seq.*; T. Maunz and R. Zippelius, *Deutsches Staatsrecht* (29th edn., Munich, Beck, 1994), 134; R. Zippelius in R. Dolzer (ed.), *Bonner Kommentar zum Grundgesetz*, Article 1, n.34 *et seq.*; in general see P. Kirchhof, *Verwalten durch mittelbares Einwirken* (Cologne, Heymanns, 1977), 329, n.49; J. Schmidt-Salzer, "Vertragsfreiheit und Verfassungsrecht" (1970) 23 no 1/2 *Neue Juristische Wochenschrift* 8, 10 *et seq.*; K. Hesse, *Verfassungsrecht und Privatrecht* (Heidelberg, C.F. Müller, 1988); Stern, *supra* n.3, at 1563 *et seq.*; Rüfner, *supra* n.11, § 117, n.62 *et seq.*

[28] Rupp's view that the objectively normative aspect of the basic rights is the reason for their influence on private law goes too far; its consequences are not addressed with sufficient precision. See H.H. Rupp, "Vom Wandel der Grundrechte" (1976) 101 *Archiv des öffentlichen Rechts* 161, 170.

[29] The Federal Constitutional Court refers to a hierarchical value system (Wertordnung): 52 BVerfGE 131, 165 *et seq.*

[30] 7 BVerfGE 198, 205.

adopting the understanding of humans to which the Basic Law gives expression means that uniform, cookie-cutter solutions can be avoided. Wherever an ordinary court of law or constitutional court identifies any influence of basic rights on private law beyond the State's responsibility to protect its citizens and secure their equality, explicit justification is required.

It is essentially up to the legislature to give effect to the influence that basic rights have on private law, whether in respect of the duty to protect citizens and secure equality among them, the understanding of human beings to which the Basic Law gives effect, or the objectively normative effect of basic rights.[31] It is up to judges, on the other hand, to give contour to open-textured norms.[32] It is they who decide disputes, fulfilling the duty to secure justice in individual cases. The Federal Constitutional Court may only determine whether the decision of an ordinary law court, when generalised and viewed as a norm, can be reconciled with a given basic right, to the extent that that right is relevant to private law.[33]

Clearly, the judge has a duty to balance competing legal interests. Here it suffices to note that the depth or intensity of an infringement of a basic right must be thoroughly investigated[34]; the end result must represent the best possible balance between competing interests.[35] Examples include:

1. Freedom of contract and the ban on discrimination (Article 3(3) of the Basic Law) and on activity that is contrary to custom[36];
2. The right to refuse to act, derived from the guarantee of human dignity, in the context of a continuous obligation;
3. Freedom of opinion and the duty to avoid harm[37];
4. Freedom of the press and personality rights[38];

---

[31] For example, 14 BVerfGE 263 *et seq.*; 39, 1 *et seq.*; 73 BVerfGE 261, 270; Götz, *supra* n.22, at 46 *et seq.*; P. Badura, "Kodifikatorische und rechtsgestaltende Wirkung von Grundrechten" in R. Büttcher, G. Hueck and B. Jähnke (eds.), *Festschrift für Walter Odersky zum 65. Geburtstag* (Berlin/New York, Walter de Gruyter, 1996), 159, 172 *et seq.*

[32] For example, 7 BVerfGE 198 *et seq.*; 35 BVerfGE 202 *et seq.*; Götz, *supra* n.22, at 58 *et seq.*

[33] See C. Starck, "Verfassungsgerichtsbarkeit und Fachgerichte" (1996) *Juristenzeitung*, Vol 51, no. 21 1033, 1039 *et seq.*

[34] W. Rüfner, "Grundrechtskonflikte" in C. Starck (ed.), *Bundesverfassungsgericht und Grundgesetz (Festgabe aus Anlaß des 25 jährigen Bestehens des Bundesverfassungsgerichts)* (Tübingen, Mohr-Siebeck, 1976), ii, 453, 465 *et seq.*; similarly H. Bethge, *Zur Problematik der Grundrechtskollisionen* (Munich, Vahlen, 1977), 323; J. Schwabe, *Probleme der Grundrechtsdogmatik* (Darmstadt, Schadel, 1977), 317 *et seq.*

[35] K. Hesse, *Grundzüge des Verfassungsrechts* (20th edn., Heidelberg, C.F. Müller, 1995), 354 *et seq.*; F. Müller, *Normstruktur und Normativität* (Berlin, Duncker & Humblot, 1966), 213; 35 BVerfGE 202, 219–44.

[36] 89 BVerfGE 214, 230; see G Spieß, "Inhaltskontrolle von Verträgen—das Ende privatautonomer Vertragsgestaltung" (1994) *Deutsches Verwaltungsblatt*, Vol 109, no. 21 1222 *et seq.*; J. Gernhuber, "Ruinöse Bürgschaften als Folge familiärer Verbundenheit" (1995) *Juristenzeitung*, Vol 50, no. 22 1086; P. Derleder, "Unterlegenenschutz im Vertragsrecht" (1995) 28 *Kritische Justiz* 320, 325 *et seq.*; R. Singer, "Vertragsfreiheit, Grundrechte und Schutz des Menschen vor sich selbst" (1995) *Juristenzeitung*, Vol 50, no. 23 1133, 1136.

[37] 7 BVerfGE 198, 203 *et seq.*; 62 BVerfGE 230, 243 *et seq.*

[38] 35 BVerfGE 202, 219.

5. Freedom of artistic expression and human dignity[39];
6. Property interests of small shareholders and property interests of large shareholders[40]; and
7. Freedom of contract and power imbalances in contract.[41]

As these examples show, private law has its own rules for balancing competing interests. To analyse these rules and to investigate the mechanisms by which that balance is achieved, we must turn to case law and judicial decisions.

V. GERMAN CASE LAW

1. Law of contracts

German trade law allows the owner of a business to impose contractual restrictions on the extent to which his or her agent may engage in a particular trade for up to two years after the expiry of the contract of agency. Non-competition clauses of this kind are designed to protect principals from competition from former agents; the agents are, of course, appropriately compensated for refraining from engaging in trade. If, however, the principal has rescinded the contract because of a breach by the agent, he need not pay compensation.

The Federal Constitutional Court found this rule incompatible with the basic right to freedom of profession (Article 12(1) of the Basic Law).[42] In the case of an agent's breach, the legislature, so the Court ruled, must modify the non-competition clauses in a way that still respects the principal's interests, but also takes account of the agent's weaker bargaining position. Both parties' interests set limits to legislative discretion, since the interests of both principals and agents are derived from basic rights. Neither the restriction of freedom nor its protection may, according to the Court, be given undue weight in determining the limits of the interplay of competing interests.

This reasoning shows, with perfect clarity, how far basic rights have infiltrated private law. Under the interpretation of the Federal Constitutional Court, basic rights delineate the process by which competing interests are weighed up, and they determine the extent of the parties' freedom of contract.

In the view of the Federal Constitutional Court, compensation for restraint of competition is a particularly suitable instrument for reconciling competing interests without interfering unduly with freedom of contract. It respects the fact that since the agent requires freedom of profession in order to secure the economic basis of his or her existence, far-reaching restrictions on his or her freedom of profession require financial compensation. The principal is free to

---

[39] 30 BVerfGE 173, 195 *et seq.*
[40] 14 BVerfGE 263, 282.
[41] 89 BVerfGE 214, 232 *et seq.* (with reference to guarantees); 97 BVerfGE 169, 175 (with reference to freedom of contract and protection from dismissal in labour law).
[42] 81 BVerfGE 242, 260 *et seq.*

choose whether to pay compensation or refrain from inserting a non-competition clause in the contract. The Federal Constitutional Court considered the existing law in this area unconstitutional because the two-year time frame and the refusal to pay any compensation whatsoever lacked an objective basis in the specific circumstances attending the termination of a contract where the agent is in breach. It was not necessary, the court found, to impose such severe sanctions in order to counterbalance the competitive disadvantage suffered by the principal who rescinded the contract. Agents could not reasonably be expected to suffer the drastic consequences of such a step.

2. The law of torts

In 1950, Erich Lüth, the president of the Hamburg Press Club, repeatedly publicly criticised Veit Harlan, who had made the anti-Semitic film "Jud Süß" during the Third Reich. Lüth called upon distributors, cinema owners, and the public to boycott Harlan's new film, "Immortal Beloved" ("*Unsterbliche Geliebte*"). Lüth was ordered to refrain from calling for such a boycott in the future or else face a fine or imprisonment. The court based its decision on section 826 of the German Civil Code ("BGB"). Section 826 requires someone who has harmed another in a way that is contrary to public morals to compensate that person for the damage that results; read in conjunction with section 1004 of the BGB, it grants the person who has suffered harm the right to have the tortfeasor ordered to refrain from the conduct in question.

The Federal Constitutional Court found the judgment of the civil court unconstitutional on the basis that it could not be reconciled with the basic right to freedom of expression contained in Article 5(1), sentence 1, of the Basic Law.[43] Admittedly, the court reasoned, basic rights are to be understood first and foremost as defences against the State. Nonetheless, the Basic Law is not intended as a value-neutral structure. Its basic rights catalogue, the court said, has established an objective system of values, strengthening the validity and application of the rights themselves. The value system thus established is to be seen as a basic constitutional premise, underpinning the entirety of the legal order and, hence, also private law. No private law norm may contradict this value order; each norm is to be interpreted in a way that gives effect to the system of values. Therefore, when applying one of the substantive provisions of private law, judges are to determine whether basic rights might affect it. If this happens to be the case, the judge is to interpret and apply the provision with appropriate modifications. Judges should be especially careful to assess the impact of basic rights when applying "open clauses" like section 826 of the BGB, which assess human behaviour using extra-legal yardsticks like public morals.

[43]   7 BVerfGE 198.

Therefore, in assessing whether any given behaviour can be reconciled with public morals, the court said, the judge has to respect the basic value judgements and principles of social order contained in the Constitution's basic rights catalogue. Within this system of values, which, the court said, must necessarily also be a *hierarchical* value system, the basic right to freedom of expression in Article 5(1), sentence 1, of the Basic Law must be weighed against the rights and legal interests that might restrict its exercise.

Accordingly, the Federal Constitutional Court found, the civil court had failed to recognise the particular emphasis to be given, in judging Lüth's behaviour, to the basic right to freedom of expression. This right is also to be respected where it conflicts with the private interests of others. The judgment of the civil court was therefore set aside, and Lüth met with success in his constitutional complaint.

3. The law of associations

According to the German Law of Associations, an association acquires legal personality when it is entered in the register of associations kept by the local district court. An association will be registered only where it satisfies the criteria listed in section 21 of the BGB and its constitution does not conflict with the principle of the autonomy of associations (*Vereinsautonomie*), which means that the association must be independent and must manage itself.

In Germany, the Bahá'í religious community is represented by the National Spiritual Council, which consists of local spiritual councils elected at the parish level. One of these local spiritual councils had been refused registration as an association. The local court's decision justified the refusal to grant registration on the ground that the local council's constitution gave the National Spiritual Council the right to decide questions involving the exclusion of members, constitutional changes, the dissolution of the local council and other matters involving the local council. This degree of external influence on the local council was, in the Court's view, a bar to registration, since it could not be reconciled with the principle of the autonomy of associations. A constitutional complaint was brought on the ground that since the institutional structure of the global Bahá'í community was based on an act of divine foundation, it could not be altered. This, it was submitted, had not been taken sufficiently into consideration when the Civil Code's law of associations had been applied.

The Federal Constitutional Court found that the basic rights contained in Articles 4(1) and 2 of the Basic Law in conjunction with Articles 140 of the Basic Law and 137(2) and (4) of the Weimar Constitution, which guarantee freedom of religious association, had not been adequately protected by the judicial decisions that have interpreted and applied the Civil Code's law of associations thus far. The constitutional complaint was successful.[44]

---

[44] 83 BVerfGE 341.

According to the Federal Constitutional Court, the right to freedom of religious association meant that the way in which a religious community conceived of itself was—to the extent that that conception was protected by Article 4(1) and (2) of the Basic Law—to be respected when any relevant provisions of private law (here, the Civil Code's law of associations) were interpreted or applied. Where a decision-maker has discretion in the interpretation of a private norm, that discretion should be exercised in favour of the religious community. This, the court said, should not be applied in a way that jeopardises legal certainty or the rights of others. In any case, an interpretation that, on the basis of a religious community's internal organisation, prevents it from forming legal relationships at all or imposes undue restrictions on its ability to form legal relationships is inadmissible.

The ordinary courts, the Federal Constitutional Court found, had not properly respected freedom of religious association. First, the Court found, the interpretation of the law relating to associations must respect the fact that an association's restriction, in its constitution, of its right to organise itself is an autonomous decision. Given that for reasons integral to their faith, many religious societies are organised hierarchically, the Court also found it probable that an association that was a component of a larger religious society might want to integrate itself into the society's hierarchy. There was no need, the Court held, to equate that with a surrender of autonomy, since it was an expression of religious self-determination for a religious association to submit itself to a superior authority as an expression of common faith. If, however, the hierarchically determined limits placed upon the association were to go so far beyond those required for religious reasons that the association could no longer be said to represent the will of its members, a limit would be reached.

Thus, where a religious association is structured as one component of a larger association with attendant restrictions upon its power to dissolve itself, exclude members or determine its own activities, the court will not find that the association is subject to external influence to a degree that cannot be reconciled with the principle of the autonomy of associations. This will only hold, however, where the restrictions placed upon the association are intended to secure its place in the structure of the religious movement to which it belongs and are no more severe than those necessary for achieving that aim, thus ensuring that religious associations retain sufficient residual autonomy. The ordinary court's refusal to enter the Bahá'í Local Spiritual Council in the register of associations had therefore violated the Council's basic right to religious association.

4. Property law

According to section 564 b of the BGB, a lessor may terminate a lease only where he or she has a justifiable interest in its termination. A justifiable interest exists when the lessor needs the rooms in question as living space for him or herself, for the members of his or her household, or for the members of his or her family. In one case, a lessee had been given notice because of the lessor's personal need and had been required by court order to leave his apartment. The lessor successfully established personal need on the ground that she needed the apartment for her son, whom she needed to have near her because of her poor health. The lessee had argued that since the lessor's son already lived in a neighbouring house, he was already able to reach his mother's side, so that it had been unjustified to give him notice. The court rejected this argument, and the lessee brought a constitutional complaint, arguing that his basic right to property, as guaranteed under Article 14 of the Basic Law, had been infringed.

The Federal Constitutional Court considered the question whether the rights of possession granted by a lease constitute property within the meaning of Article 14.[45] It responded in the affirmative, noting that a person's dwelling-place is the centre of his or her existence: it is a prerequisite for meeting the most basic human needs, a bulwark of individual freedom, and a *sine qua non* for an individual to develop his or her personality adequately. Since a large proportion of the German population cannot own a home and, hence, has to rent, a lessee's rights of possession fulfills the function typically fulfilled by ownership simpliciter. The legal possession created by a lease, the court found, is analogous to that created by outright ownership.

The law of landlord and tenant needs to be regulated by statute, since both lessor and lessee enjoy rights of property deriving from Article 14. The court found that the legislature, required by Article 14(1), sentence 2, to determine the substance and limits of property rights, must give the competing interests shape and form. It must demarcate them, ensuring that the property rights reflected in both legal positions are adequately protected; it must protect those interests of each side deserving protection, making sure that the relationship between them is appropriately proportionate.

With regard to standard termination, the court found that section 564 b did represent a successful attempt by the legislature to balance the competing interests. Both the lessee's interests in continuing the tenancy and the lessor's interest in making use of his or her property had been taken into consideration. Neither side had been unduly advantaged or disadvantaged.

When interpreting and applying section 564 b of the BGB, ordinary courts must respect the constitutionally based protection given to lessors and lessees. They must, the Federal Constitutional Court stated, give effect to the balance of interests incorporated by the statute in a way that respects the protection of both parties' property rights and avoids disproportionate restrictions on the extent or enjoyment of those rights. Consequently, the court held that the judge must investigate a lessee's objections to termination on the basis of the lessor's personal need in a way that respects the extent and import of the lessee's property rights. For example, the judge must assess whether a lessor claiming personal

---

[45] 89 BVerfGE 1 *et seq.*

need seriously intends to make use of the property in question, or whether he or she has exaggerated the extent of his or her need, or, indeed, whether it is possible to meet the lessor's personal need without rescinding the contract of lease (for example, if another similarly appropriate property belonging to the lessor is available). Finding that the lower court had correctly applied these tests, the Federal Constitutional Court refused to uphold the lessee's constitutional complaint.

5. Labour law

The German Protection against Termination of Employment Contracts Act (*Kündigungsschutzgesetz*) provides that an employer may only give an employee notice only where it would be socially just to do so. Section 1(2) of the Act provides that the termination of an employment contract is just when it is for reasons relating to the employee's personality or behaviour or there are urgent reasons arising from the state of the employer's business that make it necessary to terminate the contract of employment. Section 23(1), sentence 2, of the Act provides that these provisions do not constrain small businesses. (A small business is a business that generally employs five or fewer employees.) Required to decide whether this "small business clause" is constitutional, the Federal Constitutional Court used the basic right to choose and exercise one's profession freely (Article 12(1) of the Basic Law) as the yardstick.[46] That right, it said, constitutes neither a right to a job nor a right to be able to continue in employment. It could not, then, provide *direct* protection against the loss of employment attendant upon the termination of a contract of employment by an employer. Nonetheless, the right did impose a duty of protection on the State: it required the State to protect employees against termination.

When assessing the constitutionality of the small business clause, one norm among the many that mould the law of contracts, the Federal Constitutional Court took into consideration the fact that the norm protects competing constitutionally protected interests. The employee's interest in the protection of his job, which derives from Article 12(1), may conflict with the employer's interest in employing only those who fit the particular profile he or she has in mind and in determining the number of his or her employees without outside interference. These interests also fall under freedom of profession in the meaning of Article 12(1), which encompasses economic activity in general. Reconciling these competing interests is the task of the legislature. The Court held that Parliament, in so doing, is required to consider the ways in which the interests of employer and employee exercise influence on each other; it has to delineate them in such a way that both employer and employee enjoy their rights under Article 12 to the fullest possible extent. Here, the court found, the legislature has broad discretion to act

---

[46]   97 BVerfGE 169.

as it sees fit. However, it must not subordinate the rights of one party to those of another to such an extent that the rights at issue can no longer be said to be suitably balanced.

The situation is quite different for small businesses, the court held. Protection against termination addresses significant needs: employment is the basis of the employee's economic existence, as well as that of his or her family. Nonetheless, the employer's right to terminate an employment contract also deserves considerable protection: in a small business, the relationship of trust between employer and employee is of particular importance. A small business' success, the court said, depends much more on the performance of individual employees than is the case in larger firms. Given the small business employer's significant, constitutionally protected rights, it is not unreasonable to expect his or her employees to assume a greater risk of termination.

In any case, the Court said, small business employees are not left completely unprotected just because statutory protection does not apply to them: Private law's open norms protect them against the termination of a contract of employment in bad faith or in a way contrary to public morals. Private law's open norms must, of course, be interpreted in the light of the basic rights. The minimum standards of protection against the employer's unrestrained exercise of his or her rights, the Court considered, was clearly present.

VI. CONCLUSION

As the cases outlined illustrate, according to the jurisprudence of the Federal Constitutional Court, basic rights affect almost all areas of the law of obligations. This, in turn, means that private law and the law of the jurisdiction in civil matters fall within the scope of the Federal Constitutional Court's bailiwick. In countries lacking a constitutional court with jurisdiction to decide individual constitutional complaints, the last word in these matters is that of the Supreme Court. The reconciliation of competing interests does not need to take place, as it does in Germany, within a framework influenced by basic rights. In Germany, however, those rights are the only yardstick that may be used by the Federal Constitutional Court.

6

Importing Constitutional Values through Blanket Clauses

ANDREAS HELDRICH AND GEBHARD M. REHM*

I. INTRODUCTION

IN LATE 1944, during the last months of World War II, many German fugitives arrived from East Prussia in the western part of Germany. A woman who had sought refuge in the town of Göttingen paid a visit to a couple she had met on a previous occasion. After describing the awful living conditions and the rapid advance of the Red Army, she concluded that the German forces were defeated and that nobody in East Prussia believed in Adolf Hitler anymore. In those days, this was a very dangerous remark that could result in a death sentence. Her host, an ardent supporter of the Nazi regime, reported her comment to the German secret police, the infamous Gestapo. The woman was arrested and remained imprisoned until the American army arrived in the spring of 1945. During her imprisonment, the woman's health suffered badly. After the War, she sued her denunciator for damages. Her claim was based on section 826 of the German Civil Code ("BGB"), which provides for compensation for damage intentionally caused in a manner violating good moral standards.[1]

This provision is one of the so-called general clauses of the German Civil Code, which are framed in such unspecific terms that they provide courts with a considerable degree of discretion. Their scope of application is so broad that they can be used to adapt a 100-year old Code to the changing needs of society and the economy. Other such general clauses are section 138, which provides for the nullity of legal acts violating good moral standards, and section 242, which establishes the principle of good faith as a guideline for legal relationships between individuals.[2] What exactly is meant by good moral standards or good

---

* Professor Heldrich presented this paper at a conference in Tel Aviv; Mr. Rehm participated in drafting this written version.

[1] The text of this provision, translated in S Goren, *The German Civil Code* (Littleton & Rothman, 1994), at 153, is as follows: "§ 826. A person who willfully causes damage to another in a manner contrary to public policy is bound to compensate the other for the damage". All subsequent translations of provisions from the German Civil Code are taken from this source.

[2] The text of these provisions is as follows: "§ 138. (1) A legal transaction which is against public policy is void. § 242. The debtor is bound to effect performance according to the requirements of good faith, giving consideration to common usage".

faith in a specific case must be decided by the judge. His personal attitude and experience play an important role in the decision-making process. On principle, he or she is free to imbue those terms with a meaning that the legislator would never have thought of or that a judge at the time at which the relevant facts occurred would never have attributed to them. Thus it is clear that a German judge in late 1944 would never have found the denunciator guilty of violating good moral standards. The defendant had done precisely what the judiciary in those awful times would have expected him to do. Nevertheless, this did not stop the German court three years later from awarding the victim compensation for having been intentionally harmed in an immoral manner.

In this case, the Court of Appeal of Celle held that the denunciator, in reporting the plaintiff's comment to the police, had violated common decency in an outrageous manner. He knew the arbitrariness and brutality with which the Gestapo and the Nazi judiciary reacted to even trivial political remarks. Taking this into consideration, the defendant had wilfully taken part in a violation of human rights. Although the court did not state this expressly, it was precisely this that had constituted the violation of basic moral principles and led to the conclusion that the plaintiff's action was well-founded under section 826 of the German Civil Code.

The above-described case offers an interesting example of the relevance of human rights in private law matters. Human rights in German law are enshrined in the catalogue of so-called Basic Rights in the first part of the Constitution, the Basic Law. In addition, Germany has adopted the European Convention on Human Rights, framed under the auspices of the Council of Europe, as well as the UN Universal Declaration of Human Rights. However, the relationship between human rights and private law in Germany is currently being discussed primarily under the heading of the enforcement of constitutional basic rights in the framework of private law relations.

II. THE RELATIONSHIP BETWEEN THE BASIC LAW AND PRIVATE LAW FROM A DOCTRINAL POINT OF VIEW

In the late 1950s, shortly after the Basic Law's entry into force, a lively discussion flared up as to whether and, if so, how the Basic Law affects party obligations under private law. Then president of the Federal Labour Court Nipperdey, foremost among many prominent scholars, led those arguing that fundamental rights do not bind only the government with respect to its citizens, but also bind parties in private law relationships.[3] With Nipperdey at the helm, the Federal

---

[3] See L. Enneccerus and H.C. Nipperdey, *Allgemeiner Teil des Bürgerlichen Gesetzbuchs* (15th edn., Tübingen, Mohr, 1959), § 15 IV 4; other proponents of this theory are W. Leisner, *Grundrechte und Privatrecht* (Munich, C.H. Beck, 1960) 356 *et seq.*; F. Gamillscheg, "Die Grundrechte im Arbeitsrecht" (1964) 164 *Archiv für die civilistische Praxis* 386, 419 *et seq.*; E. Steindorff, *Persönlichkeitsschutz im Zivilrecht* (Heidelberg, Müller, 1983) 12.

Labour Court applied this concept, the so-called theory of direct impact on third parties (*Theorie der unmittelbaren Drittwirkung*), in several of its decisions.[4]

However, the text, structure and history of the Basic Law suggest rather that the fundamental rights contained therein shall—with a few express exceptions such as Article 9(3)—only protect individuals against public authorities, not against private parties. Hence, the Federal Constitutional Court rejected relatively early on the theory of direct impact.[5] Invoking mainly historical reasons, the court held that basic rights are defensive rights of citizens against the government, not rights against other individuals.[6] However, the court did not assume the Basic Law's irrelevancy for the private law system. Even though fundamental rights do not directly bind individuals with respect to one another, they do have an indirect effect on private law relations. In the view of the Federal Constitutional Court and under the now-prevailing German doctrine, the Basic Law not only provides for legally binding obligations, but also establishes an order of values that judges have to respect in private law adjudication. The German Civil Code, as mentioned, contains a number of blanket clauses, such as section 242 (the duty of good faith), section 138(1) (nullity of agreements infringing public policy) and section 826 (willful damage contrary to public policy), all of which the courts must construe in light of general values and rules not explicitly defined by legislation. These general clauses are considered the entrance gates through which constitutional values may gain access to the private law sphere. Thus, from the perspective of private law, the Basic Law and the basic rights contained therein serve as tools for putting these blanket clauses into more concrete terms. But the Federal Constitutional Court's doctrine is not limited to these blanket clauses. The German Basic Law exerts a pervasive influence on private law in the sense that judges have to interpret statutes limiting basic rights "in the light of the constitution", i.e., they have to give them the most constitution-friendly understanding possible. Thus, provisions of the Civil Code may not contradict the order of values as contained in the Basic Law.[7]

This understanding of the constitutional impact on private law attaches to basic rights only an attenuated effect compared to the effect under a theory of direct impact. In order to find an agreement void on grounds of a violation of basic rights, judges still have to rely on the provisions of the Civil Code. Nullity under section 138 is a relatively extreme sanction, and it requires not only an

---

[4] See, for example, Bundesarbeitsgericht (Federal Labour Court) (hereinafter BAG), 10 May 1957, Entscheidungen des Bundesarbeitsgerichts (Reports of the Federal Labour Court) (hereinafter BAGE). 4, 274 and the decisions cited therein. In more recent decisions, however, the Federal Labour Court has distanced itself from this theory or else simply not applied it; see, for example, BAG, 20 Dec. 1984 [1986] *Neue Juristische Wochenschrift* (hereinafter NJW) 85, 86; BAG, 23 June 1994 [1994] *Neue Zeitschrift für Arbeitsrecht* (hereinafter NZA) 1080.

[5] Bundesverfassungsgericht (Federal Constitutional Court) (hereinafter BVerfG), 15 January 1958, 7 Entscheidungen des BVerfG (Reports of the Federal Constitutional Court) (hereinafter BVerfGE) 198, 204—*Lüth* (hereinafter *Lüth*).

[6] *Ibid.*

[7] See again the landmark *Lüth* decision, *supra* n.5, at 205.

objective violation of public policy, but also the perpetrator's subjective awareness of the facts causing this violation.[8]

III.   THE APPLICATION OF THIS CONCEPT IN PRACTICE

How does the prevailing opinion's theoretical concept work in practice? A discussion of a few more German cases in which this problem has arisen can
demonstrate this. The first two cases relate to the law of succession. They lead
us into a Disneyworld that, for certain privileged strata of German society, sur-
vives to this day.

1. The succession cases

In 1991, following the death of his first wife, the German Prince of Leiningen
married a woman who, by all standards, seemed to be a good match that most
fathers-in-law would welcome in the family: a beautiful woman from a wealthy
family, with a perfect educational background, and a trained lawyer with a doc-
torate in law from the University of Cologne. Unfortunately, these qualifications did not seem to have been good enough, and the newlywed couple's
happiness did not last very long. The house rules of the princes of Leiningen,
passed in 1897 and incorporated by reference in a contract of inheritance
concluded in 1925, require the pretender to the position of ruling prince, usually
the eldest son, to seek the approval of his marriage from the current ruling
prince. Offspring living in an unapproved marriage are automatically disqualified from being a substitute heir. The unfortunate pretender had failed to seek
this consent beforehand, and his father, the ruling prince, was not amused and
unwilling to give his approval to the marriage. Given that the family assets
amount to approximately 100 million DM (roughly US $50 million), one is
inclined to understand the pretender's determination to contest the validity of
this disqualification in court.

A similar case arose in the Hohenzollern family of the late and last German
Emperor Wilhelm II, in 1995. Under the house rules of the Hohenzollern family,
the pretender to the position of ruling prince, unlike his counterpart in the
Leiningen family, does not even have the chance of seeking the ruling prince's
approval. He automatically loses his heritage if he marries a woman of less than
equal birth. The legal problems, though, are obviously quite similar to those in
the Leiningen case. To our republican minds, all these problems may seem quite
odd and evidence of the headaches of a fortunately bygone era of nobility privileges that should not overly concern us. But these seemingly outdated problems

---

[8] See, for example, H. Heinrichs "§ 138 BGB" in O. Palandt (ed.), *BGB* (59th edn., Munich,
C.H. Beck, 2000), n.8.

are far from irrelevant, as the size of the assets to be passed on indicates. And constitutional rights apply to everybody, even to those whose families may not have excelled in their promotion in the past.

These two cases involved a number of constitutional rights of the respective parties, which the courts had to balance against each other. The testators relied mainly on their freedom of testamentary disposition, limited only by the heirs' right to a compulsory share.[9] Article 14 of the Basic Law[10] constitutionally protects this right.[11] On the other hand, the pretender to the position of ruling prince can also invoke a number of constitutional rights. The requirement to marry a woman of equal birth undoubtedly affects the individual's right to free marriage guaranteed in Article 6(1) of the Basic Law.[12] Moreover, the choice of one's spouse is a choice protected under one's general right to personhood, a right that the Federal Constitutional Court derives from the provisions in Article 1(1) and Article 2(1) of the Basic Law.[13] This right primarily protects the right to make important decisions, freely to develop one's personality, and to be left unhindered in one's private sphere. In addition, contracts of inheritance raise a number of equal protection and discrimination problems. They generally exclude female descendants from the position of ruling prince, something that seems difficult to reconcile with Article 3(2) of the Basic Law,[14] even though female descendants receive certain compensation in the form of guaranteed regular allowances in return for their willingness to forgo their right to a compulsory share. Furthermore, these agreements—in requiring future heirs to be the offspring of unions of equal blood—violate at least the spirit of the anti-discrimination provision in Article 3(3) of the Basic Law.[15] It is also not difficult to imagine that the

[9] According to ss. 2303 *et seq.* of the German Civil Code ("BGB"), offspring, parents and spouses of the deceased who are disinherited by the deceased's will are entitled to half of the statutory shares that they would have received absent any testamentary disposition.

[10] The text of Art. 14(1) of the Basic Law is as follows: "[p]roperty and the right of inheritance are guaranteed. Their content and limits are determined by statute". An English translation of the Basic Law can be found at www.uni-wuerzburg.de/law/gm00000. All subsequent citations to the Basic Law are taken from this source unless otherwise indicated.

[11] Even though the text of Art. 14 of the Basic Law does not state this explicitly, the Federal Constitutional Court has frequently held that this provision protects the testator's right freely to dispose his property. See, for example, BVerfG, 16 Oct. 1984, 67 BVerfGE 329, 341; BVerfG, 11 Nov. 1981, 58 BVerfGE 377, 398.

[12] Art. 6(1) Basic Law reads as follows: "[m]arriage and family are under the special protection of the State".

[13] The Federal Constitutional Court has recognised this general right to personhood in numerous decisions. See, for example, BVerfG, 31 Jan. 1973, 34 BVerfGE 238, 245; BVerfG, 5 June 1973, 35 BVerfGE 202, 219 *et seq.*; BVerfG, 3 June 1980, 54 BVerfGE 148, 152 *et seq.*; BVerfG, 15 Dec. 1983, 65 BVerfGE 1, 41 *et seq.* The text of these provisions is as follows: Art. 1(1) provides, "[h]uman dignity is inviolable. To respect and protect it is the duty of all State authority". Art. 2(1) provides, "[e]veryone has the right to free development of his personality insofar as he does not violate the rights of others or offend against the constitutional order or against morality".

[14] The text of Art. 3(2) is as follows: "[m]en and women are equal. The State supports the effective realization of equality of women and men and works towards abolishing present disadvantages".

[15] The text of Art. 3(3) is as follows: "[n]o one may be disadvantaged or favoured because of his sex, his parentage, his race, his language, his homeland and origin, his faith, or his religious or political opinions. No one may be disadvantaged because of his handicap".

candidate for the position of ruling prince undergoes a particularly tough education and has to meet rigorous standards in order to be considered worthy of leading the principal family. The Leiningen pretender's lawyers argued that these sacrifices confer a constitutionally protected position in the form of a property right in the heritage.[16] A further aspect to the Leiningen case was the requirement that the ruling prince be of the Protestant denomination. Religious requirements of this type could be considered a violation of Article 4 of the Basic Law.[17] The courts have been able to set this matter aside because all pretenders to the position of ruling prince have actually met this requirement.

How does one reconcile these contrary constitutional rights? Four prominent German courts—the Court of Appeal of Stuttgart, the rather conservative Bavarian Supreme Court in Munich, the German Federal Supreme Court and, eventually, a chamber of the Federal Constitutional Court—had the opportunity to express their opinions on this matter. The Bavarian Supreme Court was the first high court to issue an opinion in the Leiningen case.[18] The Bavarian Justices found that the house statutes had been repealed by the Weimar Imperial Constitution, but that the members of the Leiningen House had been free to agree on identical rules in inheritance contracts. Until the entry into force of the Weimar Imperial Constitution, the noble families in Germany had been entitled to arrange the transfer of the family property without regard for the general rules of the German Civil Code, which generally do not permit arrangements for the transfer of property in case of death outside the rules of succession law. These special rules for aristocratic families were intended to allow them to maintain their assets as a single unit of property instead of having to split them with each devolution of an inheritance. But since the transitory rules for the dissolution of these units of property allowed them to be held for a certain period of time, this type of transferral of property could, in the opinion of the Bavarian Supreme Court, hardly be in violation of the Weimar Imperial Constitution.

The Bavarian Supreme Court confirmed the view that a primogeniture clause, i.e., a clause giving preference to the eldest child (usually the eldest son), does not violate section 138 of the German Civil Code. Under the prevailing opinion, the contemporary views at the time of the contract's conclusion determine whether a contractual provision violates public policy—or, as I would prefer to call it, common decency—not the prevailing views at the time at which the contract takes effect. Obviously, certain contractual provisions that seemed completely out of place in 1996 could have passed muster in 1925 without problem. The Court concluded that applying current standards would violate the justified reliance interests of the other parties to the contract.

---

[16] Property rights are protected under Art. 14 of the Basic Law; see *supra* n.10.

[17] The text of Art. 4 of the Basic Law is as follows: "(1) [f]reedom of creed, of conscience, and freedom to profess a religious or non-religious faith are inviolable. (2) The undisturbed practice of religion is guaranteed".

[18] See [1996] Entscheidungen des Bayerischen Obersten Landesgerichts (Reports of the Bavarian Supreme Court) (hereinafter BayObLGZ) 204 *et seq*.

More importantly, though, the Bavarian Supreme Court had no objection to the testator's decision to disinherit the plaintiff for not marrying the "right" person. Generally in line with Federal Constitutional Court case law,[19] the Court held that the right to dispose freely of one's assets is the main factor in deciding the validity of wills and inheritance contracts.[20] Only a clear value judgement in the legislation or a clear general opinion to this effect—even though it is unclear how the court would find out about the latter or define it—could justify limitation on this freedom.[21] The freedom allows the testator to make highly subjective decisions. In testifying, he or she is generally not obliged to respect general views on how to testify.

The Court did not object to the limitations on the freedom of marriage either. Apart from the fact that the Weimar Imperial Constitution did not explicitly guarantee this freedom at the time when the parties concluded the contract of inheritance, the Justices did not find the contractual clause to be a substantive limitation on this freedom. The clause placing a sanction on a marriage with a person of unequal blood supposedly does not directly compel anybody to marry a particular person or to abstain from marrying someone, but only triggers certain indirect financial consequences. This distinction between direct and indirect sanctions is not very convincing. Did the court seriously think that the freedom of marriage would have been violated only if the pretender had been forced physically—what else would be direct compulsion as opposed to "merely" indirect financial sanctions?—(not) to get married? How can someone in a modern democratic country be influenced in his or her marriage decision other than by financial sanctions, which, after all, amounted to roughly 100 million DM? On the other hand, in its second decision in the matter,[22] the court pointed out that the pretender could have avoided disinheritance by signing an agreement regarding the administration of the family property that would protect the property against being passed to his wife's family in the event of his death. He could thus have avoided even those adverse indirect financial consequences.

The main argument for the validity of the contested provision, however, was the court's recognition of a valid motive for the clause. An offence against common decency leading to nullity would require that the testator acted intentionally, without any possible motive for his decision. However, the intention to hold the family assets together and to do everything to perpetuate the family tradition justifies this type of clause. A number of family members had renounced their rights to a compulsory share of the heritage in return for flat-rate

---

[19] See *supra* n.11.

[20] See [1996] BayObLGZ 204, 225.

[21] *Ibid.*, citing the Federal Supreme Court, 20 Oct. 1993 in 123 Entscheidungen des Bundesgerichtshofs in Zivilsachen (Reports of the Federal Supreme Court in civil law matters) (hereinafter BGHZ) 368, 378.

[22] See BayObLG, 4 Aug. 1999 [2000] *Zeitschrift für das gesamte Familienrecht* (hereinafter FamRZ) 380, 385 *et seq.*

allowances. The motive of holding the family assets together protects the family's vital interests in securing the financial basis of these allowances.

An important constructive difference between this case and the Hohenzollern case was that the Leiningen pretender did not lose his heritage automatically upon marrying a woman of unequal birth, but the ruling prince had the right to approve of this marriage. In the court's opinion, it was less the clause in the contract of inheritance and more this decision that was subject to constitutional scrutiny. Since nothing indicated improper motives on the part of the ruling prince in not granting his approval, the court upheld his decision and ruled that the pretender was to be disinherited.

In the Hohenzollern case, the Court of Appeal of Stuttgart came to the opposite conclusion.[23] At the outset and in principle, it agreed with the prevailing interpretation of section 138 of the BGB: whether a legal transaction violates common decency depends upon the contemporary standards at the time of the conclusion of the transaction, not on those prevailing when it takes effect. The rationale underlying this interpretation is the protection of the legitimate interests of those who, for many years, relied on the validity of the transaction. Since the standards of common decency change slowly over long periods of time, it would be very difficult for the parties to judge at what time the clause would have to be considered void with the consequence that their reliance on it would cease to be justified. The court also confirmed the principle that testators enjoy a wide latitude of discretion in deciding on their heritage. However, the court then employed a trick that is quite questionable, as it clearly served as a tool for justifying a result that is hard to reach from the court's starting point of not applying section 138 of the BGB. Stating that the good faith clause of section 242 of the BGB[24] is universally applicable to all types of private law relations and that it obligates the parties not to exercise existing rights improperly,[25] the court held that relying on the contract of inheritance would be an improper exercise of a right. In its view, the freedom to make a will does not justify infringements of the freedom freely to choose one's spouse or discrimination against possible heirs because of their descent from a marriage of unequal partners. This latter aspect particularly raised the court's ire because it considered this type of clause to conflict seriously with the principles of a legal order founded upon the democratic equality of all.[26] The court therefore declared the claimant barred by the principle of good faith from invoking this clause. Even though the result seems perfectly justifiable under constitutional standards, the court's interpretation— i.e., reliance on section 242 of the BGB—is highly questionable. As one commentator has rightly remarked, the legal consequence derived from this

---

[23] See Oberlandesgericht (Court of Appeal) (hereinafter OLG) Stuttgart, 19 Aug. 1997 [1998] *FamRZ* 260.

[24] For the text of this s., see *supra* n.2.

[25] One traditional situation in which s. 242 of the BGB applies is somewhat similar to the common law concept of equitable estoppel.

[26] See OLG Stuttgart, *supra* n.23, at 261 *et seq*.

provision in this case does not really follow from the provision.[27] Raising the objection of improper exercise of a right requires—as the term says—*exercising an existing right*. Under German law, however, the heir automatically becomes owner of the heritage; he does not have to exercise any right to this effect.[28] Section 242, therefore, cannot block the heir from becoming the owner of the inheritance. The Stuttgart Court of Appeal's judgment is understandable, but its reasoning is not. The doctrinally viable way would have been—as another commentator has noted—to contest the prevailing opinion with respect to the interpretation of section 138 of the BGB. If one were to judge the compliance of a legal transaction with common decency from the perspective of the time at which the transaction takes effect, the contract of inheritance, or at least the controversial clause, could have been declared void. To be sure, there are difficult questions to answer with respect to the reliance interests involved, and it cannot be ruled out that these constitutionally protected interests[29] should eventually be allowed to govern the interpretation of section 138 of the BGB, which would lead to the validity of the controversial clauses. On the other hand, German restitution law might provide mechanisms that could offer the necessary protection for reliance interests while declaring the clauses void. But courts need openly to address and discuss these concerns instead of deliberately ignoring them and applying the law arbitrarily.

The Federal Supreme Court had to decide the Hohenzollern case because the Bavarian Supreme Court's ruling in the Leiningen case had blocked the Stuttgart Court of Appeal's intended decision.[30] The Federal Supreme Court's ruling[31] did not follow the beaten path these two decisions had taken, even though the result was in line with the Bavarian Supreme Court ruling. It decided that the inheritance contract did not violate common decency either when it was concluded in 1938 or when it took effect.[32] The Justices based their decision mainly on the paramount importance of the freedom of testamentary disposition. Even though this freedom is limited by the standards of common decency codified in section 138 of the BGB, judges may assume wills and contracts of inheritance to be void only in extreme cases. Presumably talking to the Court of Appeal of Stuttgart, the Federal Supreme Court emphasised that a judge may not apply his own concepts of justice to a will or a contract of inheritance in lieu of the testator's will. The constitutionally protected freedom of testamentary disposition would be violated by such an intensity of control. The Court also held that the

---

[27] See Otte [1998] *Zeitschrift für Erbrecht und Vermögensnachfolge* 187.

[28] See s. 1922 of the German Civil Code: "(1) [o]n the death of a person (accrual of the inheritance), his property (estate) passes in its entirety to one or several other heirs". This means that no further act of the heir is required to acquire the property; see W. Edenhofer "§ 1922" in O. Palandt (ed.), *supra* n.8, n.6; D. Leipold in K. Rebmann and F.J. Säcker (eds.), *Münchener Kommentar zum BGB* (3rd edn., Munich, C.H. Beck, 1997), § 1938, n.62.

[29] The protection of legitimate reliance interests is a fundamental constitutional rule in Germany.

[30] See § 28(2) Gesetz über die Angelegenheiten der freiwilligen Gerichtsbarkeit.

[31] BGH, 2 Dec. 1998, 140 BGHZ 118.

[32] Both Courts of Appeal had found that the contracts of inheritance were valid according to 1925 and 1938 standards, but did not make any explicit pronouncement on current standards.

prohibitions on discrimination in Articles 3(2) and 3(3) of the Basic Law do not apply to the testator making out his will. His freedom of testamentary disposition allows him to discriminate against his heirs if he is pursuing a legitimate goal in doing so. Like the Bavarian Supreme Court, the Court held that the intention to perpetuate the tradition of nobility in one's family and to preserve the family assets in a single unit met this requirement.

This, however, was not the last decision in the matter. That privilege was reserved for the Federal Constitutional Court. This court increasingly groans under the burden of the flood of disputes of all kinds in which the parties are dissatisfied with the outcomes before the specialised supreme courts and therefore—often improperly—claim unconstitutionality of the decision in order to gain access to the Federal Constitutional Court. The tendency not to resolve disputes in the institutions provided for that purpose (such as the respective specialised courts) but to try to have them resolved "in Karlsruhe" (the seat of the Federal Constitutional Court) unfortunately has gained ground in the German political arena as well. Often, minority parties or the parliamentary opposition, having been outvoted on a political matter, resort to the Federal Constitutional Court in order to overturn undesirable political decisions by claiming them to be unconstitutional. In the succession cases, however, the constitutional ramifications were strong enough to warrant a Federal Constitutional Court ruling, and it was not improper to bring a constitutional complaint. The Leiningen pretender, the protagonist in the case before the Bavarian Supreme Court, brought this complaint, arguing that the decision by the Bavarian Supreme Court had violated his basic rights. To his likely great disappointment and quite surprisingly, a chamber of the Federal Constitutional Court refused to take the case.[33] Relying on a provision in the Statute on the Constitutional Court that allows it to reject a case that does not have fundamental constitutional importance or in which the complainant will most likely not succeed,[34] the court did not even reach the merits of the case. In a short judgment meant to explain its assessment that basic rights had probably not been infringed, the court held that the Bavarian Supreme Court, in construing the civil law statutes, had sufficiently balanced the constitutional value of the freedom to testify with the values of the right freely to choose one's spouse, the right to be generally free from discrimination because of one's sex or parentage, and possible property rights.

There is longstanding case law to the effect that the Constitutional Court is not entitled to dictate the specific interpretation of statutory law because this function is reserved for the specialised courts. There is no violation of the Constitution if the contested court decision balances the competing constitutional values in detail in a different way from that in which the Federal Constitutional Court would have done.[35] Rather, a violation requires errors of

---

[33] BVerfG, 21 Feb. 2000 [2000] *NJW* 2495.
[34] See § 93a Bundesverfassungsgerichtsgesetz.
[35] BVerfG, 19 Oct. 1993, 89 BVerfGE 214, 230.

interpretation that are based on a fundamentally incorrect concept of a basic right's importance, particularly the scope of the right, and that are materially relevant for the case at hand.[36] In its decision, the Federal Constitutional Court, as the Bavarian and the Federal Supreme Courts before it had done, emphasised the importance of the freedom of testamentary disposition as the fundamental element of the right of inheritance guaranteed in Article 14 of the Basic Law. It held that a testator may discriminate against his offspring and that the concept he follows in making his will does not need to conform with general convictions in society or the views of the majority. The Court also accepted the Bavarian Supreme Court's emphasis on the ruling prince's right not to approve a marriage of unequal blood and its finding that there was no evidence that this decision was made in bad faith. And since the pretender could have saved his heritage by agreeing to contractual provisions that would have excluded his wife from obtaining a substantial stake in the family property in the event of his death, he did not sustain any serious injury to his constitutional right to freely choose his spouse. Finally, the Federal Constitutional Court roundly rejected any property right in the future right to succession because of sacrifices in upbringing and preparation for the position of ruling prince. The pretender's right was always subject to the fulfillment of the requirements of succession at the time of the accrual of the inheritance. He had never acquired a right to the heritage without meeting these requirements.

What is the essence of all this? Basic rights do play a considerable role in these factual constellations. Even though they do not apply directly, they have an important bearing on whether a legal transaction, in this case a contract of inheritance, is void or not. Since the decision largely depends on balancing two competing constitutional entitlements, the fact that basic rights apply only in an attenuated manner has no direct effect, because this is true for both parties. The hypothetical causation argument, i.e., the fact that the testator could have made his will without giving any reason for his decision, however, is not a prominent reason. On the contrary: the Federal Supreme Court and the Bavarian Supreme Court both reasoned extensively that the testator's motives are supremely important for judging the controversial clause's validity. The testator's legitimate alternative of hiding his real reasons is never discussed explicitly, although—at least at first glance—the argument seems quite convincing that one should be able to reach a result that one could reach legally even if one has improper motives under the particular circumstances. This argument might have influenced the judges in deciding this case, but they did not refer to it explicitly. Be that as it may, officially, the testator's motive is a decisive factor in determining the validity of contractual clauses.

[36] BVerfG, 11 May 1976, 42 BVerfGE 143, 148 *et seq.*

2. The labour law cases

The German labour courts also have had to decide several cases involving the application of basic rights.

In 1954, a student nurse was forced to leave her job after getting married. Her employment contract contained a clause that the contract would come to an end upon her marriage. Invoking her right to marriage and to found a family under Article 6 of the Basic Law,[37] she claimed that this condition was null. The Federal Labour Court had to decide in this matter.

In 1991, an employer fired one of his workers after employing him for just seven weeks. This in and of itself should hardly be worthy of mention. In Germany, employees enjoy quite extensive protection, by international standards, against dismissal. But this protection usually comes into force only after six months of employment, the so-called trial period. During this period, employees can be fired without cause, the employer otherwise being generally required to justify dismissal.[38] How then could the employee attack his dismissal in court? He had found out—apparently correctly—that his employer had dismissed him merely for his homosexual orientation. Arguing that dismissal motivated by his employer's distaste for homosexuality violates his constitutional rights to personhood, he took his case to court, and the Federal Labour Court again had the final say in the matter.

With respect to the celibacy clause, the Federal Labour Court held the clause not to be void as a violation of section 138 of the BGB. Section 138 requires not only an objective violation of common decency, but also proof of fault on the part of the person who allegedly violated common decency. The court did not find any evidence of fault in this case. The employer had merely followed a ministerial ordinance that required the inclusion of this clause in employment contracts with nurses, and he supposedly genuinely believed that this provision was necessary to keep his business going. Following the theory of direct impact, the court held that certain basic rights apply directly to the behaviour of private parties[39] and therefore can directly invalidate contractual provisions that are in violation of those rights. Article 6 of the Basic Law, which guarantees the right to get married and found a family, and the right to personhood guaranteed in Articles 1 and 2 of the Basic Law do not allow contractual provisions of this type. Article 6 does not even tolerate indirect obstacles to getting married. Articles 1 and 2 of the Basic Law guarantee every individual the right to decide how to manage his or her life, including whether and whom to marry.

---

[37] For the text of Art. 6 of the Basic Law, see *supra* n.12.

[38] See § 1 of the Statute Against Dismissal (Kündigungsschutzgesetz). This s. permits the dismissal of an employee for only a limited number of reasons (behaviour, personality, business requirements).

[39] BAG, see *supra* n.4, 4 BAGE 276.

Prohibiting somebody from getting married is one of the most extreme violations of the right to personhood.[40]

The thrust of this decision is still certainly valid. Even though the Federal Labour Court no longer applies the theory of direct impact, the same result could and would be reached on the basis of section 138 of the BGB. The subjective requirement in this provision that prompted the Federal Labour Court in 1957 to find no violation of common decency has since been relaxed. In today's circumstances, hardly anyone could justify his actions by contending—as some scholars cited in the judgment seriously did—that this type of celibacy clause is necessary to guarantee a woman's full performance as wife and mother. We have fortunately progressed beyond this type of paternalism. Furthermore, we do not think that any contradiction exists between the courts allowing a clause limiting the right to marriage in an inheritance contract and prohibiting it in employment contracts. This distinction is based on the requirement of legitimate motives for such clauses. Whereas the courts found such motives in the succession cases, none existed in the employment cases. Whether an employee is married or not is immaterial to his or her job performance and should, therefore, not be a criterion in his employment.

What about the supposedly homosexual employee then? In its decision, the Federal Labour Court held that the dismissal of an employee only for his homosexual orientation violates the duty of good faith under section 242 of the BGB.[41] This reasoning indicates that the court has abandoned the theory of direct impact and instead follows the Federal Constitutional Court's conception of the basic rights as values that serve to concretise blanket clauses rather than being directly applicable legal provisions.

The Federal Labour Court expressly left open the question whether the dismissal might infringe common decency and therefore be void under section 138 of the BGB. The court considers a dismissal void if it violates section 242 of the BGB, an outcome that the text of this provision does not support. The broad formulation of this section makes it a very convenient and malleable—and, therefore, dangerous—tool in the hand of judges, as we saw with the Stuttgart Court of Appeal's decision in the Hohenzollern case. But the labour courts have long applied section 242 of the BGB in a different way from its application by the general civil courts. However, unlike the Court of Appeal of Stuttgart, the Federal Labour Court at least had to decide on the exercise of a right, i.e., the right to dismiss an employee. The court correctly assumed that the right to personhood and the right freely to develop one's personality under Articles 1 and 2 of the Basic Law guarantee the right to lead one's private life and, particularly, one's sexual life as one sees fit as long as this does not interfere with the employer's legitimate interest in the undisturbed organisation of his business.[42] The employer, however, had not been able to prove that his employee's sexual

---

[40] *Ibid.*, 282.
[41] See BAG, *supra* n.4 [1994] NZA 1080, 1082.
[42] *Ibid.*

orientation had had any negative effect on his job performance, which, quite to the contrary, had been spotless. It is still somewhat unclear why the court did not apply section 138 of the Civil Code. The conditions of this provision are a little harder to prove, which may have made the decisive difference between proving the requirements of section 138 and those of section 242. But if the employer dismissed his employee solely for his sexual orientation—and this condition would have to be met with respect to section 242 as well—there is no reason to assume that he did not act in bad faith.

In general, we see that the labour case law largely follows the same principles as the general civil case law, even though there are some differences in detail, particularly the importance and function of section 242 of the Civil Code. Basic rights do not apply directly in private law cases but, rather, acquire weight through blanket clauses such as sections 138 and 242 of the Code, which allow the incorporation of constitutional values.

3. Denunciation cases

The case decided by the Court of Appeal of Celle in late 1947 has already been mentioned. It concerned the denunciation of a woman who had made a provocative remark during the final months of the Nazi regime. Without expressly invoking any constitutional right, the Celle Court of Appeal found that the Nazi denunciator, in reporting the woman's comment to the police, had violated public policy and was thus liable to pay damages to his victim.[43] This case has long been forgotten by the German legal literature, although it is cited in an American law textbook.[44] In recent years, similar problems have arisen in the aftermath of German reunification.

One example of such a case involved a law lecturer who had planned to flee the German Democratic Republic ("GDR") in 1985. The lecturer told his nephew, whom he trusted fully, of his intentions. The latter immediately informed the Ministry of State Security, the notorious Stasi. The secret police asked the nephew not to disclose his denunciation to his uncle and to participate in his uncle's venture and report to the police about the plan and further potential participants. The nephew agreed to this and subsequently informed the police continually about the escape plan's progress. In the end, the lecturer was arrested and spent about two years in prison, at times in solitary confinement. After the German reunification, the lecturer sued his nephew for damages based on injuries suffered as a result of the denunciation.

The Federal Supreme Court, in deciding the case, had to apply the law of the GDR, since the denunciation had occurred on GDR territory when its legal system was still in force.[45] The defendant in fact raised the objection that the GDR

---

[43] See OLG Celle, 5 Dec. 1947 [1948] *Monatsschrift für Deutsches Recht* 174.

[44] R. Schlesinger *et al.*, *Comparative Law* (6th edn., New York, Foundation Press, 1998) 803.

[45] See BGH, 11 Oct. 1994, 127 BGHZ 195.

criminal code had obliged him to report any escape plans of which he became aware and had provided for a penalty of up to five years' imprisonment if he failed to do so. He argued that he thus could not be held liable under a GDR tort provision for conduct that the GDR criminal code had mandated. The Federal Supreme Court held that this criminal provision violated the International Covenant on Civil and Political Rights, a convention ratified by the GDR, particularly the provision guaranteeing freedom of movement. However, the resulting nullity of the criminal code provision did not automatically bar the defendant from raising his objection, because it would be too great a burden to expect a layperson to recognise the nullity of a legal norm that the GDR government and courts frequently applied. The Court did, however, include a caveat to this holding, which somewhat resembles the Court of Appeal of Celle's decision. If through his willingness to spy on his uncle the defendant had contributed to particularly grave violations of human rights through obviously arbitrary governmental acts, he could be held liable. The Federal Supreme Court remanded this case for determination of whether these conditions had been met.

The denunciation cases can be regarded as another example of the importance of human rights in private law. A person who denounces another person and leaves him at the mercy of arbitrary judicial institutions that do not offer the slightest respect for the rule of law—an important constitutional principle in all Western democracies—is liable in torts.

IV. CONCLUSION

The discussion has shown that the case for the direct applicability of basic rights in private law has—at least for the time being—been lost. But we do not think that the difference between the theories of direct and indirect impact leads to different results in practice. Both theories have to balance competing constitutional rights. This is particularly clear in the succession cases, but equally true in the labour law cases. An employer can legitimately invoke his or her right to the free exercise of his profession guaranteed under Article 12 of the Basic Law[46] or his property rights, which also extend to a going concern. The basic right freely to exercise one's occupation encompasses the right to dismiss employees under certain conditions.[47] Regardless of whether one accords direct or indirect effect to countervailing basic rights, the decision always involves a balancing of these rights. The cases described here serve only as examples to illustrate how basic rights influence this fundamental balancing process in civil law adjudication.

---

[46] The text of the provision is as follows: "Article 12 (1) All Germans have the right to freely choose their occupation, their place of work, and their place of study or training. The practice of an occupation can be regulated by or pursuant to a statute".

[47] See R. Scholz, "Art. 12 GG" in T Maunz and G Dürig (eds.), *Kommentar zum Grundgesetz* (Munich, C.H. Beck, 2000), n.86.

It is quite remarkable that German courts attach such great importance to the motives of the actor. It is of great significance whether a person intended to abrogate somebody's civil rights (as in the case of the dismissed homosexual employee) or whether the person had legitimate motives in acting in the way he or she did (as in the succession cases). But is this a valid distinction? With respect to public authorities, basic rights apply regardless of whether the public authority intended to violate a basic right. In this sense, a distinction can be made between the theories of direct and indirect impact. The celibacy clause case demonstrates that the theory of direct impact does not require any malicious intent, which is a necessary condition under the theory of indirect impact.

There are many arguments in favour of giving greater discretion to private parties in framing their legal rights *vis-à-vis* one another than to the structurally more powerful State in its dealings with individuals. Other than in relation to powerful public authorities, freedom of contract allows private parties to do whatever serves their interests best. In this respect, the distinction between a willful abrogation of basic rights and an abrogation of rights that is incidental to pursuing legitimate goals makes sense. It indicates a dangerous imbalance of power between the parties if one party is able to impose contractual duties that do not serve any legitimate goal, but, rather, aim only at infringing basic rights. This is inconsistent with the fundamental prerequisite on which contractual freedom is based: an at least theoretical balance of power between the parties involved.[48] Willful violation of one party's basic rights, which does not serve any legitimate purpose, indicates the absence of contractual freedom in making the contract and, therefore, justifies judicial intervention with regard to the relevant clause. This concept, based on contractual freedom, also justifies subjecting wills to less stringent judicial review than inheritance contracts or other contracts are subject to. In the case of a will, unlike that of a contract, the heir has no enforceable rights in the heritage prior to the testator's death. Therefore, wills are generally not subject to a general duty of good faith, and the importance of the freedom of testamentary disposition is greater than in the context of inheritance contracts. This notwithstanding, a certain degree of judicial scrutiny of wills nevertheless seems warranted. Wills often serve to motivate the beneficiaries to behave in a certain way and thus create relations between the parties involved similar to contractual relations, but without being enforceable as contractual obligations: a benefit accrues to a party in return for specific behaviour. This similarity in structure and purpose justifies at least rudimentary scrutiny of the contents of a will and whether the testator in fact abused his or her freedom of testamentary disposition. The German law of succession thus far has not recognised such limitations to the freedom of the testator. It will have to undergo a somewhat revolutionary change in the years to come. But this would be the subject for another paper.

---

[48] See BVerfG 19 Oct. 1993, 89 BVerfGE 214, 232.

Part II
The Impact of the European Convention on Human Rights

7

The Impact of the Human Rights Act 1998 on English Tort and Contract Law

HUGH BEALE AND NICOLA PITTAM

THIS CHAPTER IS in two parts. The first part (Section I) outlines the effect of the Human Rights Act 1998 (HRA) in general terms, in particular the question of the extent to which the Act will affect relationships between private parties. The second part (Sections II–III) attempts to predict what substantive impact the HRA may have on English tort and contract law.

I. APPLICABILITY OF THE HRA

The HRA, which came fully into force on 2 October 2000, prohibits public authorities from acting incompatibly with Convention rights.[1] This raises two questions: what counts as a public authority for this purpose, and will the HRA have any effect as between private parties?

1. Public authorities

The Act defines "public authority" quite widely, in that it includes "any person certain of whose functions are of a public nature".[2] Thus if a private company such as Railtrack (which operates the track and signalling systems on which other companies run their trains) has regulatory functions, for example in relation to safety, it counts as a public authority while exercising this public function, though it is not a public authority for this purpose if the nature of the act is private.[3] In other words, a "mixed function" body counts as a public authority when exercising its public functions.

---

[1] S. 6(1).
[2] S. 6(3)(b).
[3] S. 6(5). This example was given by the Lord Chancellor, HL Debs., 24 Nov. 1997, col. 784.

From this it seems to follow that a body which has only public functions[4] is subject to the Act in all its activities, even in those relationships which are otherwise governed by private law, for example when contracting with suppliers or employees. Such activities have not hitherto been subject to the "public law control" of judicial review.[5]

2. Horizontal effects

It also appears to follow that a person or body with no public functions is quite outside the HRA. But in fact whether the HRA has a "horizontal effect" has been very controversial. The discussion is well-known and this chapter will not attempt more than a summary. At some risk of over-simplification there seem to be three positions: "direct horizontal effect", strong "indirect" horizontal effect and weak indirect horizontal effect.

The principal protagonist of direct horizontal effect is Sir William Wade.[6] He argues that the HRA will affect relationships between private parties on the basis of a literal reading of the Act, on the basis of Parliamentary intention as expressed in debates and on the basis of the "Spirit of the Act".

As to the literal meaning, he points out that by section 6(3) "public authority" includes "a court or tribunal" and that therefore a court must decide in accordance with Convention rights whatever the status of the parties. In response to the argument (see below) that the European Convnetion on Human Rights (ECHR) itself is enforceable only against States, he replies that it does not follow logically that the HRA is similarly limited. Further, the European Court of Human Rights (ECtHR) has held that the State may have not just an obligation to refrain from infringing Convention rights but a positive obligation to protect citizens from infringement of their Convention rights even by other individuals. "Incorporation" of the Convention must mean that there should now be a direct right as against that other individual and a UK court is unable to do "otherwise than enforce the Convention rights".[7]

At the other extreme Buxton LJ argues[8] that the ECHR itself applies only as against the State and that, while the HRA creates Convention rights enforceable in English law, the content of the rights cannot have changed. They still apply only as against the State.[9] This is not just a question of against whom the right may be asserted but of the content of the right itself.[10] The obligation to provide protection is one on the State; "[t]hat cannot be translated into a direct right

---

[4] S. Grosz, J. Beatson and P. Duffy, *Human Rights: the 1998 Act and the European Convention* (London, Sweet & Maxwell, 2000) refer to these as "obvious" public authorities.

[5] *Ibid.*, at § 4–09.

[6] Sir William Wade, "Horizons of Horizontality" (2000) 116 *LQR* 217.

[7] *Ibid.*, at 220.

[8] Wade, *supra* n.6, at 48.

[9] *Ibid.*, at 50.

[10] *Ibid.*, at 51–2.

held by the applicant against . . . other subjects".[11] In any event many of these "positive obligation" cases were based on Article 1 of the Convention, which is not incorporated.[12] Though for HRA purposes courts are treated as public authorities, this means no more than that they should not enforce orders, such as injunctions, which infringe a person's Convention rights.[13] Section 6 does not create any new rights as between individuals; and in any event the only remedy against a judicial act is normally by way of appeal.[14]

3. Direct horizontal effect?

There are a number of issues on which there are differences of opinion. The first is whether, as Buxton LJ says, under the ECHR itself Convention rights are only rights against the State; or whether they are broader rights which the Strasbourg Court has power to enforce only against the State but which may exist as against other citizens. Certainly many of the Convention rights are stated in broad terms which are then qualified. Thus Article 8 provides:

> Everyone has the right to respect for his private and family life, his home and his correspondence.
>   There shall be no interference by a public authority with the exercise of this right except..".

It is possible to interpret this as merely giving rights against the State or as stating a more general right which the State may not interfere with save in the stated circumstances.[15]

The question arises in particular when the case is one in which the court holds that a State has an obligation to take positive steps to protect a citizen against another citizen. In exceptional cases the State may owe an obligation to provide physical protection: for example a person who is known to be at particular risk of an attack by another individual may have to be provided with a guard.[16] More usually the obligation is to provide the victim with a remedy against the attacker after the event.[17] The language used by the ECtHR is sometimes cast in terms of positive obligations against the State, not in terms of Convention rights against other individuals which the State has a duty to protect.[18] But at other times the position is more ambiguous. In some cases the court has founded the obligation of positive protection on the duty of States under Article 1 to "secure" the

---

[11] *Ibid.*, at 53.
[12] *Ibid.*, at 54.
[13] *Ibid.*, at 55.
[14] *Ibid.*, at 57; see S. 9(1).
[15] Wade, *supra* n.6, at 219.
[16] See the discussion in *Osman* v. *UK* (1998) 5 BHRC 293.
[17] For example, *X and Y* v. *Netherlands* (1986) 8 EHRR 235.
[18] For example, *Marckx* v. *Belgium* (1979) 2 EHRR 330 (hereinafter *Marckx*).

Convention rights of individuals.[19] It is hard to interpret this otherwise than as recognition than Convention rights apply as between the individuals concerned.[20]

However, even if Convention rights under the ECHR exist as between individuals, it is far from clear that such rights have been incorporated into English law by the HRA. As Phillipson points out,[21] the Act nowhere states that citizens should have Convention rights. It merely provides that public authorities must not act incompatibly with Convention rights, and the Lord Chancellor stated that Convention rights will not become part of our substantive law.

Nor does it seem that the inclusion of courts within the definition of public authorities necessarily changes this: it is explicable in that a court may not impose an order (for example a seizure order[22]) which would infringe an individual's Convention rights. This may have an effect as between private parties as the court may have to refuse an order which might otherwise have been given, but this is no more than an indirect effect.

The argument based on the cases in which the ECtHR has held that a State has a "positive obligation to protect" an individual's Convention rights against another private party may at first sight seem more promising as the basis for direct horizontal effect. This is at least closer to saying that there are Convention rights as between individuals. But, as Phillipson points out, the Act does not allow for direct actions by one individual against another.

If it were the case that an individual whose Convention rights had been infringed by another individual could force the State to provide positive protection in the form of a remedy against the infringer, it might be argued that the Act has more or less direct effect, though in two stages—first get your action, then sue your infringer. However, although the HRA is intended to "bring rights home" by creating remedies in domestic law, the remedies available under the Act in this type of case are very limited. The remedy would have to be against either the State for failing to legislate or the court for failure to protect the individual. But the definition of unlawful act which is sanctioned under section 6 excludes failure to legislate[23] (and Parliament in its legislative capacity is not a public authority[24]). Secondly, remedies against the court may be sought only by way of appeal.[25] If the appellate courts consider themselves unable, or simply refuse, to provide a remedy, nothing more can be done in the domestic forum. This does not create any direct horizontal rights. The claimant will have, as at present, to take the long road to Strasbourg.

---

[19] For example, *A v. UK* (1998) 27 EHRR 611.

[20] A. Drzemczewski, *The EHRC in Domestic Law* (Oxford, Clarendon, 1997) 221 (quoted in G. Phillipson, "The Human Rights Act, Horizontal Effect and the Common Law: a Bang or a Whimper?" (1999) 62 MLR 824, 836).

[21] Phillipson, *supra* n.20, at 834–5.

[22] Formerly known as an *Anton Piller* order.

[23] S. 6(6).

[24] S. 6(3).

[25] S. 9(1). Damages may not be awarded in respect of any judicial act done in good faith except as required by Art. 5(5) of the Convention (arrest or detention).

4. "Weak" horizontal effect

We have noted already one indirect horizontal effect of the HRA: a court will be prohibited from making an order which would infringe a party's Convention rights even in litigation between private parties.[26] However, it seems likely that there will be a further indirect horizontal effect in the "weak" sense that the law as between private individuals will be influenced by Convention rights.

First, even if rights under the ECHR itself, and *a fortiori* those under the HRA, are interpreted as rights against the State or its emanations, a strict divide between rights as against the State and rights against private individuals is unlikely to be attractive. It will produce what may be seen as anomalies, for example if an employee of a mixed body who is working in its regulatory office is subject to a different regime from a fellow employee in the commercial side of the business. Moreover we have the tradition that public bodies are subject to the normal law of the land, and to some it seems as unnatural to treat them as subject to special responsibilities as it does to treat them as having special privileges.[27]

Secondly, we have seen already that commentators on the ECHR have frequently interpreted Convention rights as being general rights; and when in cases between individuals the English courts have considered the influence that the ECHR should have on English law, they have not treated Convention rights as applying only as between private individuals and the State.[28] (It must be said that many of the references to the Convention in cases between individuals involve either freedom of expression[29] or freedom of assembly,[30] and raise the question whether an order the court might otherwise make would unduly infringe that freedom. They therefore may seem to fall within the category of cases in which the courts' order might infringe a litigant's Convention rights.[31]

Thus it is submitted that when the courts are obliged to construe legislation, so far as possible, consistently with Convention rights, they are unlikely to confine this interpretation to matters of rights against public authorities. No doubt

---

[26] See *supra*, text accompanying n.22. The impact of the HRA on interim orders is discussed by N. Bratza [2000] *Eur. Hum. Rts. LR* 1.

[27] For example, A. Clapham, *Human Rights in the Private Sphere* (Oxford, Clarendon, 1993), 93 *et seq.*

[28] For example, *Blaythwayt* v. *Baron Cawley* [1976] AC 397 (though the Convention value was not applied in that case); *Ahmad* v. *ILEA* [1978] QB 36 (employer was a local authority but nothing made of point by majority which found rule not inconsistent with ECHR); *Panesar* v. *Nestlé* [1980] ICR 144; *Cheall* v. *APEX* [1982] 3 All ER 855, rev'd. [1983] QB 126, judgment restored [1983] 2 AC 180. But compare *Metropolitan Property Realizations Ltd* v. *Cosgrove* (CA, 27 Jan. 1992, unreported: ECHR not applicable to rights against individuals). This note is based on the list of cases to 1996 in M. Hunt, *Using Human Rights Law in English Courts* (Oxford, Hart, 1997), App. 1.

[29] For example, *Associated Newspapers Group* v. *Wade* [1979] 1 WLR 697, 708–9; *Rantzen* v. *Mirror Group Newspapers* [1994] QB 670; *John* v. *Mirror Group Newspapers* [1996] 2 All ER 35, 51, 58, *Douglas* v. *Hello! Ltd* [2001] 2 WLR 992.

[30] For example, *Express Newspapers* v. *Keys* [1980] IRLR 247.

[31] See *supra* text accompanying n.13.

they will equally be influenced by human rights thinking in developing the common law. It is submitted that this must be what the Lord Chancellor had in mind when he said, on the one hand, that:

> [Section 6 of the Act] should apply to public authorities, however defined, and not to private individuals. That reflects the arrangements for taking cases to the Convention institutions in Strasbourg. The Convention had its origins in a desire to protect people from the misuse of power by the State, rather than from the actions of private individuals.[32]

Yet, on the other, that:

> In my opinion, the court is not obliged to remedy the failure by legislating via the common law either where a Convention Right is infringed by incompatible legislation or where, because of the absence of legislation—say, privacy legislation—a Convention right is left unprotected. In my view, the courts may not act as legislators and grant new remedies for infringement of Convention rights unless the common law itself enables them to develop new rights or remedies . . . They may have regard to the Convention in developing the common law, as they do today and . . . it is right that they should.[33]

5. "Strong" horizontal effect?

The Lord Chancellor may have had more than persuasive authority in mind. He also said:

> We believe that it is right as a matter of principle for the courts to have the duty of acting compatibly with the Convention not only in cases involving other public authorities but also in developing the common law in deciding cases between individuals.[34]

Some have argued that, even though the HRA has no direct horizontal effect, the courts have a duty in cases between individuals to interpret, apply and develop that law consistently with Convention rights.[35] We do not understand the Lord

---

[32] HL Debs., 3 Nov. 1997, vol. 582, cols. 1231–2.

[33] *Ibid.*, at col. 785.

[34] HL Debs., 24 Nov. 1997, vol. 583, col. 783.

[35] M. Hunt, "The Horizontal Effect of the Human Rights Act" [1998] *PL* 423, 441. Phillipson interprets Hunt's argument more narrowly, as adopting the position taken by Kreigler J in his dissent in the South African case of *Du Plessis* v. *De Klerk* (1996) 3 (3) SA 850. This is that private parties may conduct their affairs as they please unless it is necessary for them to resort to law to protect their "freedom"—at which point the State, as maker, administrator, interpreter and applier of the law governing the relationship, comes under a duty to act in a way that upholds fundamental rights. But though Hunt explains and refers to Kreigler's dissent several times, he does not limit his concluding remarks (at 441) in this way unless this is intended to be the point of his example (at 442) of a woman ejected from an all-male golf club. He argues that the Act will mean that "the common law of trespass cannot be interpreted and applied in such a way as to provide the club with a defence to lawful ejection to the assault claim, because . . . [o]nce the club puts forward its defence, it is seeking to enlist the assistance of the State in the form of the courts) in preserving its present freedom to discriminate, and that is something which Section 6 of the Act arguably does not permit the courts to do". However it is difficult to see how the example fits Kreigler J's analysis.

Chancellor as endorsing that position. It might mean that existing rules of common law would have to be abandoned in favour of Convention rights, so that, for example, the defence to an action for battery that reasonable force was used in self-defence might have to be replaced by a rule allowing force only if absolutely necessary.[36] Of course Convention rights are themselves flexible and the *prima facie* rights stated in the Articles may be heavily qualified where there are countervailing justifications, which would permit the survival of many common law principles (such as freedom of contract) which are not mentioned in the Convention.[37] Even so, the Lord Chancellor cannot have intended that the common law should give way to Convention rights in such a dramatic fashion, for that would be incompatible with what he had said earlier in the first passage quoted in paragraph 19 and with another statement he made on the same day when discussing the question of a right to privacy:

> I would not agree with any proposition that the courts as public authorities will be obliged to fashion a law on privacy because of the terms of the Bill. That is simply not so. If it were so, whenever a law cannot be found either in the statute book or as a rule of common law to protect a convention right, the courts would in effect be obliged to legislate by way of judicial decision and make one. That is not the true position.[38]

6. Conclusion

The position is thus not completely clear, but it seems that the HRA does not have any direct horizontal effect nor what we have termed a "strong" indirect effect, in the sense that the courts are required to supplant common law rules by Convention rights. But a "weak" indirect effect seems almost inevitable. At the least it is hard to resist Grosz's conclusion that, even if there is no duty on the courts to apply Convention rights as between private individuals, the courts "are likely to accept this invitation" to have regard to the Convention in developing the common law.[39]

II. THE POSSIBLE SUBSTANTIVE IMPACT

In this part of the chapter we make one of two assumptions: either the simple one that the defendant is a public authority, or a "mixed authority" which is exercising its public functions; or the heroic one that the HRA will have horizontal effect in some form. The question is: on which areas of the substantive law of tort and contract will Convention rights actually have some impact?

---

[36] M. Brazier (ed.), *Clerk & Lindsell on Tort* (4th Supp. to 17th edn., London, Sweet & Maxwell, 1999), § 1–05C.

[37] I. Leigh, "Horizontal Rights, the Human Rights Act and Privacy: Lessons from the Commonwealth" (1999) 48 *Int'l. & Comp. LQ* 57, 73.

[38] *Supra* n.34, at col. 784.

[39] Grotz, *supra* n.4, at 4–24.

This involves two questions. The first is whether the Convention rights apply to the topic at all; the second whether the law is likely to be changed, given that the ECHR contains many checks and balances which in fact allow a considerable latitude both to the law of a State and to its public authorities.

1. A supplementary remedy or parallel jurisprudence?

There is also the preliminary question of the relationship between the HRA and the existing law. The ECtHR will not accept an application if the applicant has domestic remedies which appear to be effective to achieve her aim and which she has not exhausted. Does a similar principle apply under the HRA? In other words, does the HRA have only a supplementary role, as equity did, or can it create a separate (but unequal?) system of rights?

Suppose a claimant alleges that she has been illegally detained by the police. She clearly has a claim for false imprisonment. Does this mean that she has no claim—or at least will be refused a remedy—under the HRA? The notion that the Act is simply, as the Government White Paper suggested, "bringing rights home", suggests that an applicant would have no more rights under the HRA than she would have under the ECHR at present. But the answer is not obvious.

In practice in such a case the claimant will normally prefer the claim in tort, since damages will then be as of right and may include punitive damages which the Strasbourg jurisprudence does not recognise and which will therefore not be available under the HRA.[40] But one can imagine a litigant who is more interested in making a point than in obtaining compensation instructing her lawyers to press the HRA claim and perhaps even not to include a claim for false imprisonment.

No requirement of exhaustion of other remedies has been included in the HRA. This suggests that the HRA action is not intended to be an action of "last resort" in the same way as an application to the ECtHR. This seems to be confirmed by consideration of section 7(5) of the HRA which provides that proceedings under the HRA must be brought within 12 months of the date on which the act complained of took place (though it should be noted that the court has a discretion to permit proceedings "within such longer period as the court considers equitable having regard to all the circumstances"). It seems likely that an application under the HRA must be pursued first, or at any rate together with an action in, for example, negligence (assuming that the applicant is in a position to bring such an action within 12 months of the relevant act), rather than after all other remedies have been exhausted.

---

[40] S. 8(4). The English and Scottish Law Commissions have recently published a Report (Law Com No 266, Scot Law Com No 180, 2000) on *Damages under the Human Rights Act 1998*. The text is available from the English Commission's website, which is at: www.lawcom.gov.uk.

Section 8 of the Act provides:

> In relation to any act (or proposed act) of a public authority which the court finds is (or would be) unlawful, it may grant such relief or remedy, or make such order, within its powers as it considers just and appropriate.
>
> . . .
>
> (3) No award of damages is to be made unless, taking account of all the circumstances of the case, including—
>
> (a) any other relief or remedy granted, or order made, in relation to the act in question (by that or any other court), and
>
> (b) the consequences of any decision (by that or any other court) in respect of that act, the court is satisfied that the award is necessary to afford just satisfaction to the person in whose favour it is made . . .

It will be seen that section 8(3) directs the court, in deciding whether to grant a remedy, to take into account remedies which have been granted; it does not refer to remedies which are available but which the claimant has not sought or which are being sought in the same proceedings.

One possibility is that the courts will use their general discretion under the test of whether the award is necessary to afford just satisfaction to the claimant to refuse a remedy under the HRA when there is already a remedy under common law or statute. But it is not clear that all judges would take this approach.

If HRA claims are permitted when there is already a remedy by common law or statute, we may see the development of parallel streams of jurisprudence. For example, we have seen it argued that ultimately the State's obligation to provide "adequate" health care might lead to the replacement of the standard test of professional negligence[41] by a test of whether the standard of care was "adequate".[42] This initially struck us as wildly implausible, but we assume the speaker was thinking along the lines of a parallel jurisprudence.

This would in fact be possible only in cases in which the claimant alleges direct interference with her Convention rights by a public authority, or in cases in which the State had a positive obligation to take physical steps to protect an individual from attack by another.[43] In cases where the positive obligation is merely to ensure that the claimant has a remedy in domestic law,[44] the obligation is of course satisfied if domestic law does provide one and thus there will be no infringement of Convention rights.

However, for the purposes of this chapter we am going largely to ignore the idea of a parallel jurisprudence. The question then becomes: what acts or omissions, in the areas of tort or contract, will the HRA reach that our existing law does not reach?

---

[41] The "*Bolam*" test, see *Bolam* v. *Friern Hospital Management Committee* [1957] 1 WLR 582.

[42] Owen, "The Impact of the ECHR on Medical Negligence and Personal Injury Claims', seminar paper for London Common Law and Commercial Law Bar Association, 27 March 2000 (unpublished).

[43] See the discussion in *Osman* v. *UK, supra* n.16.

[44] For example, *Marckx, supra* n.18 or *X & Y* v. *Netherlands, supra* n.17.

2. Tort[45]

(a) *Intentional Torts*

It has been suggested that a number of rules of intentional tort may not conform to the ECHR. One has already been the subject of litigation in Strasbourg: the right of a parent to chastise a child was challenged in *A v. UK*[46] and the English law was found inadequate to fulfil the State's obligation to ensure that individuals are not subjected to inhuman or degrading treatment. Other rules which may be at risk include the right to use reasonable force in self-defence or to prevent a crime or effect an arrest. The decision that detention in intolerable conditions does not amount to false imprisonment is also suspect; such conditions may contravene Article 3.[48]

Probably the most discussed topic within intentional torts is whether the HRA will encourage the courts to develop fuller protection against invasions of privacy and abuse of confidential information.[49] It is well known that English law does not protect privacy on any coherent basis; the claimant will have a remedy only if he or she can shoe-horn his or her claim into one of the existing categories such as trespass, nuisance or breach of confidence.[50] This was the example of an indirect effect of the HRA used by the Lord Chancellor in Parliament:

> The judges are pen-poised regardless of the incorporation of the Convention to develop a right to privacy to be protected by the common law. This is not me saying so; they have said so. What I say positively is that it will be a better law if the judges develop it after incorporation because they will have regard to arts 8 and 10, giving art.10 its due high value.[51]

It has to be said that as yet the lack of remedies for "invasions of privacy" or harassment at common law has not led to a finding by the Strasbourg bodies that the UK is in breach of the ECHR.[52] However the principle seems to have been accepted by the Commission that Article 8 requires the State to provide

[45] This section relies heavily on *Clerk & Lindsell on Tort*, (18th edn., London, Sweet & Maxwell 2000) § 1–67 *et seq.*

[46] *A v. UK, supra* n.19.

[48] *Clerk & Lindsell on Tort, supra* n.45, at 1–74.

[49] See for example, T. Bingham [1996] *Eur. Hum. Rts. LR* 450; Grosz, *supra* n.4, at C8–49 *et seq.*; R. Singh, "Privacy and the Media: the Impact of the Human Rights Bill" in B. Markesinis (ed.) *Protecting Privacy* (Oxford, Oxford University Press, 1998); Leigh, *supra* n.37, at 57; N. Bratza [2000] *Eur. Hum. Rts. LR* 1; and the items in a select bibliography in B. Markesinis and S. Deakin, *Tort Law* (4th edn., Oxford, Clarendon, 1999) 661–2.

[50] A very useful discussion will be found in Markesinis and Deakin, *supra* n.49, at 647–61.

[51] *Supra* n.34, at col. 784. s. 12(4), which requires the court to have particular regard to the right to freedom of expression, was included in anticipation of the development of a tort of infringement of privacy.

[52] See *Winer v. UK*, App. no 10871/84 (1986) 48 DR 154; *JS v. UK*, App. no 191173/91, 3 Jan. 1973, see Leigh, *supra* n.37, at 57.

protection against both harrassment[53] and publication of private information.[54] Some of the cases have failed on the ground that domestic remedies had not been exhausted.[55]

(b) *Unintentional Torts*

"Immunities" of public authorities[56]

The most obvious impact of the ECHR on unintentional torts to date has been in relation to actions for negligence against public authorities.

To be able to recover damages in negligence, the claimant must be able to show that the public authority was in breach of a duty of care owed to him. The courts have been reluctant to accept that public authorities are under a duty of care to all those who could be affected by a negligent exercise of their statutory powers. It has always been recognised that there is an area in which decisions by public authorities should be immune from questioning by the courts. These decisions have in the past been characterised as "policy" decisions, as opposed to operational decisions taken in the implementation of the policy.[57] In *X* v. *Bedfordshire County Council* it was explained that[58]:

> Most statutes which impose a statutory duty on local authorities confer on the authority a discretion as to the extent to which, and the methods by which, such statutory duty is to be performed. It is clear both in principle and from the decided cases that the local authority cannot be liable in damages for doing that which Parliament has authorised. Therefore if the decisions complained of fall within the ambit of such statutory discretion they cannot be actionable in common law.

Factors which will indicate that a decision is not for this reason justiciable by the courts include the fact that the decision concerns the allocation of scarce resources or the distribution of risks,[59] or the weighing of competing public interests (and particularly financial or economic interests).[60] The divide between "policy" or "discretionary" decisions and operational decisions which do not benefit from the immunity may be a very fine one, creating considerable uncertainty about whether the claimant has a cause of action for negligence or not,[61] and it has recently been recognised by the courts that this distinction can provide only limited guidance.

---

[53]   *Whiteside* v. *UK* (1994) 18 EHRR CD 126 (hereinafter *Whiteside*).
[54]   *Spencer* v. *UK* (1998) 25 EHRR CD 105 (hereinafter *Spencer*).
[55]   As in both *Whiteside*, *supra* n.53, and *Spencer*, *supra* n.54.
[56]   This section was prepared by Nicola Pittam.
[57]   See, for example, *Anns* v. *London Borough of Merton* [1978] AC 728 (Lord Wilberforce).
[58]   [1995] 3 All ER 353, 368.
[59]   See *Rowling* v. *Takaro* [1988] AC 473, 500 (PC).
[60]   See *Lonrho* v. *Tebbit* [1991] 4 All ER 972, 981 (aff' [1992] 4 All ER 280).
[61]   See in particular *Rowling* v. *Takaro* [1988] AC 473.

Even where it is accepted that the decision under attack may be reviewed by the courts, the courts have been reluctant to subject public authorities to a duty of care. With the retreat from the two stage test proposed by the House of Lords in *Anns* v. *London Borough of Merton* has come increased emphasis on the need to develop the law of negligence incrementally and by analogy with decided cases.[62] However, there are few instances where the courts have accepted that public authorities are subject to a duty of care, particularly where the claimant is seeking damages for economic loss.

One area of administrative action which has been examined in detail by the courts is that of banking regulation. In *Yuen Kun-yeu* v. *Attorney General of Hong Kong*,[63] the claimant alleged that the Commissioner of Deposit Taking Organisations (the bank regulatory body in Hong Kong) was under a duty of care to would-be depositors. The court considered the purpose for which the Banking Ordinance was enacted, noting that the Commissioner was obliged to consider not only would-be but existing depositors in the exercise of his powers, and that the Commissioner had little power to control the day-to-day affairs of the company. The court decided that there was no intention on the part of the legislature that in considering whether to register or de-register a company the commissioner should owe any statutory duty of care to potential depositors and noted that it would be strange if a common law duty of care were to be super-imposed on a statutory framework. The Privy Council was influenced by the argument that if the regulators were held liable, the principles leading to such liability "would surely be equally applicable to a wide range of regulatory agencies, not only in the financial field, but also, for example, to the factory inspectorate and social workers, to name only a few".[64]

By contrast, in *Lonrho* v. *Tebbit*,[65] the Court of Appeal acknowledged the possibility that the Secretary of State for Trade and Industry might owe a duty of care to release a company from its undertaking not to bid for the share capital of House of Fraser when the undertaking ceased to be in the public interest (though as the matter arose on a striking out application, the Court of Appeal did not need to decide the point). It upheld the decision of the court of first instance, where the Vice Chancellor, though aware of the risk of "overkill" (that the risk of liability would led regulators to adopt an unduly cautious and defensive approach to decision-making) was influenced by the fact that it was a one-off case, having no impact outside its own facts.

[62] See, for example, *Sutherland Shire Council* v. *Heyman* (1985) 60 ALR 1, 43–4.

[63] [1988] AC 175 (PC).

[64] A similar conclusion was reached in the case of *Davis* v. *Radcliffe* [1990] 1 WLR 821. Again, the Privy Council was examining whether a banking regulator (this time the Treasurer and Finance Board of the Isle of Man) owed a duty of care to depositors of a failed bank. The Privy Council drew attention to the following factors as suggesting that there should be no duty of care: (a) that the functions of the regulator were typical functions of modern government, to be exercised in the general public interest; (b) that it was being sought to make the agency liable for damage caused by the default of a third party; (c) that the duty of care argued for would be owed to an unlimited class of persons.

[65] See [1991] 4 All ER 973, 984.

The courts have also taken a restrictive view in relation to the liability of the police for failing to prevent harm to a claimant. The question whether the police should be under any duty of care in negligence has been extensively examined, and in most cases, from the decision in *Hill* v. *Chief Constable of West Yorkshire*,[66] it has been held no duty of care should be imposed on the police in relation to their function in the investigation and suppression of crime. *Hill* itself concerned a claim by the mother of the last victim of the Yorkshire Ripper for damages on behalf of her estate for negligence in the conduct of the enquiry which led to his apprehension. The House of Lords found on the facts that, although likelihood of harm to future victims of the Ripper was reasonably fore-seeable, there was no special relationship between the police and Miss Hill suf-ficient to subject the police to a duty of care to Miss Hill. This, as Lord Keith noted, was sufficient to dispose of the case. However, he then went on to discuss the policy reasons why no action should lie against the police in negligence. In particular, he noted that imposition of liability could have no benefits as "the general sense of public duty which motivates police forces is unlikely to be appreciably reinforced by the imposition of such liability so far as concerns their function in the investigation and suppression of crime". On the contrary, Lord Keith felt that it could lead to a "detrimentally defensive" frame of mind which would impair the efficiency of the police. He also noted that if potential liabil-ity was imposed, many actions might be brought against the police. Such actions would require a detailed examination of the police investigation. Many of the decisions taken in that investigation would involve questions of policy and dis-cretion which the courts would not consider to be justiciable—but elaborate investigation of the facts would be required to see if this was so. The prepara-tion of a defence would place a significant burden on police resources. Closed investigations would be required to be reopened. Lord Templeman, who based his judgment solely on policy grounds, also agreed that the police should not be subject to a duty of care in negligence. The House of Lords therefore held that the police should be held to be immune from an action of this kind.

Alexandrou v. *Oxford*[67] was a case where the police were alleged to have been negligent in their response to a burglar alarm (which therefore fell within the function of controlling and keeping down the incidence of crime in the same way as *Hill*). Here the Court of Appeal, which also refused to subject the police to a duty of care, noted that the observations of Lords Keith and Templeman with respect to the need for an immunity for the police were of general relevance in relation to suits against the police, rather than limited to the facts of the par-ticular case. In *Ancell* v. *McDermott*,[68] the police were alleged to have been neg-ligent in their response to a potentially hazardous traffic situation, with the result that the claimant suffered serious personal injury. The Court of Appeal held that the reasons which led the House of Lords to reject the existence of a

---

[66] *Hill* v. *Chief Constable of West Yorkshire* [1988] 2 All ER 238 (hereinafter *Hill*).
[67] [1993] 4 All ER 328.
[68] [1993] 4 All ER 355.

duty of care in *Hill* also applied in this case. In *Osman* v. *Ferguson*[69] the Court of Appeal went further. In this case, an unbalanced schoolteacher who was obsessed with one of his pupils killed the boy's father and seriously injured the boy himself. Despite a number of warnings from the boy's parents, his school, and the education authority the police did not take any action in time to protect the family. The Court of Appeal, though accepting that it was arguable that there was sufficient proximity between the family and the police to support a duty of care, held that the case was indistinguishable from *Hill* on policy grounds. The police were therefore immune. An argument by the claimant that the immunity applied only to policy decisions, but not to operational decisions, was rejected.

In contrast, *Swinney* v. *Chief Constable of Northumbria*[70] rejected the suggestion that the police benefit from a "blanket immunity" in relation to their activities in the investigation and suppression of crime. In this case the claimant had provided information to the police about the identity of an alleged criminal. She alleged that the police had negligently allowed information about her identity to be stolen, which placed her at considerable risk and was the direct cause of an arson attack she suffered. Hirst LJ noted:

> The *Hill* case is, of course, one of cardinal importance. As held in the *Alexandrou* case and in the *Osman* case, it lays down a principle of general application which is not specifically limited to the facts of that particular case, and nothing I say should be interpreted as in any shape or form seeking to undermine that principle. However, in my judgment, that principle cannot be completely divorced from the circumstances highlighted by Lord Keith of Kinkel in his judgment, which recurred mutatis mutandis in the *Osman* case and in the *Elguzouli-Daf* case. It follows that I cannot accept Mr Gompertz's submission that the police have a blanket immunity which gives them a complete answer in the present case.

He noted that there were other considerations of public policy which needed to be given weight, and in particular the need to protect informers and to encourage them to come forward without an undue fear of the risk that their identity will subsequently become known. Because of the need to weigh these factors against the policy arguments which were highlighted in *Hill* and its successors, Hirst LJ found that he could not hold that the claimant was bound to lose at trial. He therefore refused to strike out the claimant's action.[71]

---

[69] [1993] 4 All ER 344.

[70] [1996] 3 WLR 968 (hereinafter *Swinney*).

[71] The courts have also considered the position of the Crown Prosecution Service. In *Elguzouli-Daf* v. *Commissioner of Police* [1995] 2 WLR 173 both the claimants had been arrested (in one case for an explosives offence, and in the other for rape) and held in custody for 85 days and 22 days respectively before the CPS decided that no prosecution should be brought against them. They alleged that the CPS had been negligent in failing earlier to obtain the forensic evidence which would have demonstrated that the prosecutions had no hope of success. Steyn LJ noted that there were a number of other remedies and protections available to the claimant, both public and private, namely the accountability of the Attorney General to Parliament, the possibility of judicial review, the tort of malicious prosecution and the tort of misfeasance in public office. Imposing a duty of care would inhibit the CPS in prosecuting crime, lead to a defensive approach by prosecutors and waste the

In *X* v. *Bedfordshire County Council*,[72] the House of Lords rejected the argument that local authorities should be subject to a duty of care in respect of decisions taken in the field of child protection, and provision of education for children with special needs. The Law Lords expressed concern that imposing a common law duty of care would cut across the statutory system set up for the protection of children at risk (notably, the existence of an alternative remedy under the statutory scheme has frequently been treated as a strong counter-indication to there being a common law duty of care, whether or not that remedy provides for monetary compensation for the claimant's loss: see *Jones* v. *Secretary of State for Employment*).[73] They were also influenced by the "extraordinarily delicate" nature of the local authority's task, and concern lest the local authority would adopt a more cautious and defensive approach to their duties if they feared liability, in an area where that would be particularly inappropriate.

The approach in *X* v. *Bedfordshire County Council* should however be contrasted with that the more liberal approach in *Barrett* v. *Enfield London Borough Council*[74] where at least two members of the House of Lords were prepared to subject a local authority to a duty of care in some cases, and *Gower* v. *London Borough of Barnet*.[75]

The European Court of Human Rights

The extent of the immunity afforded by the English courts to public bodies in relation to negligence claims has been examined by the European Court of Human Rights in *Osman* v. *United Kingdom*,[76] *Z* v. *United Kingdom*[77] and *TP and KM* v. *United Kingdom*.[78]

The claimants in *Osman* alleged, inter alia, that they had a right under domestic law to seek a ruling on their claim that the police owed them a duty of care in negligence and that the police were in breach of that duty. In consequence they alleged that the action of the courts in striking out their claim on the ground that there was an exclusionary rule preventing civil actions against the police was in breach of Article 6(1) of the Convention.

The applicants argued that the exclusionary rule operated as an absolute immunity to negligence actions. This argument was rejected by the court, which noted the submission of the Government that "the rule does not automatically

resources of the CPS in defending suits for negligence. Following the decision in *Hill*, he decided that the interests of the whole community were better served by not imposing a duty of care on the CPS. See *Hill*, *supra* n.66.

[72] *Supra* n.58 .
[73] [1989] QB 1.
[74] [1999] 3 WLR 79 (hereinafter *Barrett*).
[75] [1999] ELR 356 (hereinafter *Gower*). This case and the *Barrett* case are discussed *infra*, text accompanying nn.87–94.
[76] (1998) 5 BHRC 293.
[77] Application no 29392/95, 10 May 2001.
[78] Application no 28945/95, 10 May 2001.

doom to failure such a civil action from the outset but in principle allows a domestic court to make a considered assessment on the basis of the arguments before it as to whether a particular case is or is not suitable for the application of the rule". This view was supported by reference to *Swinney*—where it was accepted that the police could in certain circumstances be under a duty of care in negligence—and *Kirkham* v. *the Chief Constable of Manchester*,[79] *Rigby* v. *the Chief Constable of Northamptonshire*,[80] and *Knightley* v. *Johns*,[81] all cases where it had been found that the police were under a duty of care to the claimant, that they had breached that duty and in consequence were liable in negligence.

The court concluded that there was a substantive right under English law for the claimants "to seek an adjudication on the admissibility and merits of an arguable claim that they were in a relationship of proximity to the police, that the harm caused was foreseeable and that in the circumstances it was fair, just and reasonable not to apply the exclusionary rule outlined in the *Hill* case". Article 6(1) was therefore applicable.

The court then examined whether the exclusionary rule (which prevented the claimants receiving a full trial on the merits) could be justified on the grounds that it pursued a legitimate aim and did not offend against the principle of pro-portionality. The court accepted that the aim pursued—which was presented as ensuring that the efficiency and effectiveness of the police service in the battle against crime are not jeopardised by the risk of constant exposure to tortious lia-bility for policy and operational decisions—was legitimate. However, it drew attention to the disparity between the arguments of the Government that the immunity afforded to the police was not an absolute rule applying in all cases, and the approach of the Court of Appeal in the instant case, which appeared to have proceeded on the basis that the exclusionary rule did provide a watertight defence for the police in all cases.[82] The court noted that

> "The application of the rule in this manner without further enquiry into the existence of the competing public-interest considerations only serves to confer a blanket immu-nity on the police for their acts and omissions during the investigation and suppression of crime and amounts to an unjustifiable restriction on an applicant's right to have a determination on the merits of his or her claim against the police in deserving cases".

It drew attention to a number of policy considerations which might have been felt to counter the public policy arguments in favour of the immunity in this case, and held that the absolute immunity which was applied by the Court of Appeal was disproportionate. The argument that there were alternative reme-dies available to the parties was also rejected. The court recognised that an action against the police would perform an important function in giving the

---

[79] [1989] 2 QB 283.
[80] [1985] 2 All ER 986.
[81] [1982] 1 All ER 301.
[82] (1998) 5 BHRC 293. See para. 150 of the judgment.

claimants information not otherwise available to them. Neither an action against the teacher who had killed Ali Osman, or against the ILEA psychiatrist who certified that he was still fit to teach would have enabled the claimants "to secure answers to the basic question which underpinned their civil action, namely why did the police not take action sooner to prevent Paget-Lewis from exacting a deadly retribution against Ali and Ahmet Osman". In consequence, the court held that there had been a breach of Article 6.

In *Z* v. *United Kingdom* and *TP and KM* v. *United Kingdom,* the European Court of Human Rights departed significantly from its decision in *Osman* v. *United Kingdom.* The complaint in *Z* v. *United Kingdom* came from the claimants in *X* v. *Bedfordshire County Council*.[83] The complaint in *TP and KM* came from the claimants in *M* v. *Newham London Borough Council*.[84] In each case, the claimants alleged, inter alia, that the immunity which was bestowed on the local authority was in the circumstances disproportionate and inflexible and deprived the applicants of the essence of their right of access to court under Article 6 of the ECHR to argue the justice of their case. The European Commission on Human Rights noted the similarity between these cases and *Osman* v. *United Kingdom*[85] and decided that there was no basis on which to apply a different rule. It held therefore that the English courts had imposed a restriction on the applicants' access to court by applying a bar to their claims which operated "to protect a particular defendant from negligence actions for damage caused in a particular sphere of their competence". Though the Commission accepted that the restriction pursued a legitimate aim, it found that in neither case was it proportionate to that aim.

However, the European Court rejected the decision of the Commission. It held that, although Article 6 was applicable to the proceedings alleging negligence by the local authority, the requirements of the Article had been satisfied by that litigation. The Court found that the striking out procedure did not necessarily offend the principle of access to court. It rejected the applicants' argument (which relied on *Osman* v. *United Kingdom)* that the exclusion of liability in negligence acted as a restriction on access to the court and reiterated the principle that Article 6 does not itself guarantee any particular content for civil rights and obligations in national law. The Court also accepted that the fair, just and reasonable criteria was an essential element of the duty of care (noting that the "reasoning in the Osman judgment was based on an understanding of the law of negligence . . . which has to be reviewed in the light of the clarifications subsequently made by the domestic courts and notably the House of Lords"). However, noting that the applicants' case had been struck out by the House of Lords, and that (as the Human Rights Act 1998 was not in force at that time) the applicants had had no other remedy under the law as it then stood for a serious

---

[83] *Supra* n.58.
[84] This was a case heard by the House of Lords with the *X* v. *Bedfordshire* case.
[85] *Supra* n.16

violation of their rights under Article 3 of the Convention, the Court found that there had also been a violation of Article 13 of the Convention.

The effect of the European Court of Human Rights decisions

The decision of the European Court of Human Rights in *Osman* v. *United Kingdom* was followed by a number of cases in our courts on the liability of public authorities which have reflected the influence of that decision. In the first case, *Barrett,*[86] the claimant had been placed in the care of the defendant following a care order made when he was 10 months old, and remained in care until the age of 17. He alleged, inter alia, that the authority had been negligent in failing to arrange his adoption, or provide him with properly monitored placements, and in failing to obtain appropriate psychiatric treatment for him and mismanaging the reintroduction to his mother. He claimed that this negligence had caused his psychological and psychiatric problems. The claim was struck out on an appeal from a district judge, a decision upheld by the Court of Appeal. The House of Lords overturned this decision.

Lord Browne-Wilkinson noted that it is impossible to say that all careless acts or omissions of a local authority in relation to a child in its care are not actionable. He suggested that "it becomes necessary to divide the decisions of the local authority between those which are 'policy' and those which are 'operational'". Although admitting that it is not clear precisely what is meant by 'policy' and 'operational' decisions, he continued to apply the distinction, suggesting that "unless it can be said . . . that operational carelessness could not have caused the damage alleged in the present case it would be impossible to strike out any part of the claim". He then reiterated the rule that "in an area of the law which was uncertain and developing (such as the circumstances in which a person can be held liable in negligence for the exercise of a statutory duty or power) it is not normally appropriate to strike out" to ensure that developments in the law are made on the basis of actual facts found at trial.

However, Lord Browne-Wilkinson then went on to examine, and heavily criticise, the judgment of the European Court of Human Rights in *Osman* noting that "I find the decision of the Strasbourg Court extremely difficult to understand". He suggested that the court had held that the claimants had a right to go to court for a declaration that apart from the public policy preventing suits against the police they would have had a claim in negligence against the police and further, that it was not fair, just and reasonable in the circumstances of that case to apply the "exclusionary rule", and that the application of a blanket exclusionary rule which excludes all claims against the police for negligent failure to investigate or protect from crime was in breach of Article 6. He noted that there were problems in reconciling the decision with English law on negligence and in particular the ability of the courts to strike out a claim where it appears

---

[86] *Supra* n.74.

on the basis of past authority that one of the pre-requisites for liability for negligence cannot be made out by the claimant (as noted above, these concerns have now been met by the judgment of the European Court in *Z* v. *United Kingdom* and *TP and KM* v. *United Kingdom*).

Lord Browne-Wilkinson noted that in view of the decision in *Osman* it was likely that if the House of Lords upheld the strike out order, the Strasbourg court would hold that the decision was a breach of Article 6. In the light of that fact he found that there was no clear and obvious case calling for striking out, and held that the action should proceed to trial. He added: "In the meantime one can only hope that the law applicable under Article 6 is further interpreted". The judgments of Lord Slynn of Hadley and Lord Hutton (the only other law lords who gave an opinion) were substantially different. Both found it unnecessary to consider *Osman* v. *United Kingdom*. Instead, each recognised the need to limit, or at least to examine carefully, the extent of the immunity which public authorities can assert, and held the local authority to be subject to a duty of care on the facts of the case.

Other decisions on the liability of public authorities in negligence since *Osman* v. *United Kingdom* illustrate the influence of that decision, and in some cases the more liberal approach to liability which appears to have been adopted by Lords Slynn and Hutton in *Barrett*. In the first case, *Brindle* v. *Commissioner of Police for the Metropolis*[87] the claimant had been shot and seriously wounded by a gunman whom police officers knew to be dangerous, probably armed, and seeking to kill the claimant. He was under close police observation for two months, but was allowed to get close enough to the claimant to shoot him. The police could have arrested the man at any time within that period, but chose not to do so. The claimant had not been warned of the danger. The Court of Appeal took the view that given the unusual facts, it was arguable that a duty of care could be established.

In *Palmer* v. *Tees Health Authority*,[88] the claimant's daughter had been abducted, sexually assaulted and murdered by a patient of a hospital run by the defendant. The claimant suffered severe post-traumatic stress disorder and pathological grief reaction. It was alleged that the defendant had failed to diagnose that there was a real substantial and foreseeable risk of the patient sexually assaulting and injuring children, and that in consequence they failed to provide any adequate treatment to reduce the risk of this happening or to prevent him being released from the hospital or another appropriate institution whilst he was at risk of committing such offences.

The Court of Appeal noted that following the case of *Osman* v. *United Kingdom*,[89] and its interpretation in *Barrett*, a decision striking out a negligence claim out on the grounds that it is not fair, just and reasonable to impose a duty

---

[87] Unreported (29 March 1999).

[88] *Palmer* v. *Tees Health Authority* (2000) 2 LGLR 69[hereinafter *Palmer*].

[89] In relation to which he agreed with Lord Browne-Wilkinson that the decision was "not easy to understand . . . in the context of the English law of negligence".

of care, could not be sustained. This can only be decided once the facts are established. Both Lord Justice Stuart-Smith and Lord Justice Pill found the position unsatisfactory. Instead, they each focussed on the question whether the claimant had demonstrated the necessary degree of proximity. Lord Justice Stuart-Smith noted that "it is implicit in the judgment of the Strasbourg court in *Osman* that it is appropriate to strike out actions on the grounds that in law proximity is not established". Each noted that the question of 'proximity' does not stand on its own, but must be resolved by reference to considerations of fairness, justice and reasonableness. Lord Justice Pill noted that foreseeability, proximity and policy can be regarded as facets of the same thing, but stressed that there is a distinction between

> assessing in accordance with principles of fairness and reasonableness whether a special relationship exists, and assessing the more general public policy requirements identified in *Hill* and expressed by Lord Browne-Wilkinson as the balance between the 'hardship suffered by [the claimant] and the damage to be done to the public interest'.

On the facts he found that there was no proximity between the defendant and the claimant's daughter. Lord Justice Stuart-Smith reached the same conclusion.

The judgments prior to *Z* v. *United Kingdom* and *TP and KM* v. *United Kingdom* show a clear tendency to assimilate the 'fair just and reasonable' criteria was the question of 'proximity', to avoid the perceived problems with striking a claim out on the first criteria after *Osman*. It is unlikely that this approach will continue, given the express acceptance in *Z* and *TP and KM* v. *United Kingdom* that the striking out procedure does not *per se* offend the principle of equal access to the court in Article 6, and in *Z* v. *United Kingdom* that, where there is no precedent for liability, the 'fair just and reasonable' criteria is an integral part of the test for the existence of a duty of care under the law of negligence.

Gower[90] suggests a slightly more liberal approach. Here, the claimant, who had been a disabled pupil at a special school run by the local authority, claimed that the teaching staff of the school had failed, in breach of their duty of care to him, to take reasonable care for his health and safety and to provide teaching and special educational provision at an appropriate standard to meet his needs. In consequence he was alleged to have suffered social deprivation, clinical depression and financial loss. The claim had been struck out at first instance on the ground that a local authority is not under a duty of care in relation to the quality of the education provision which is made for children attending its schools. Auld LJ noted that the claim did not concern the discretionary exercise by the authority of its statutory duty under the Education Acts, or raise any questions as to the limits of the authority's responsibilities. He commented that the law in relation to the responsibility of a school authority for negligent acts or omissions of its staff was now clear. He suggested that a number of

---

[90] *Supra* n.75.

propositions emerged from the authorities. A head teacher and teachers have a duty to take such care of pupils in their charge as a careful parent would have in the same circumstances. Equally, they have a duty to exercise the skill and care of a reasonable head teacher or teacher in teaching and otherwise responding to the educational needs of their pupils. Their failure to do so may lead to vicarious liability on the part of those responsible for them. The justiciability of such a claim is the same whether or not the teachers are operating under a statutory scheme and whether or not the school is in the public or private sector. He found that there was clear proximity between the teachers and the claimant "which, notwithstanding some overlapping of the notions of proximity and 'fair, just and reasonable' . . . it is likely that the plaintiff could establish at trial".

In relation to the question whether it was fair, just and reasonable for a duty of care to be imposed in these circumstances, Auld LJ commented that "it was evident, even before the recent decision of the ECHR in *Osman* v. *UK*, that such an assessment could normally only properly be made after full consideration of the evidence and circumstances at trial". He noted that *Osman* (as interpreted by *Barrett* and *Palmer*) confirmed this, so that where an application was made to strike out a claim on the basis that it is not fair, just and reasonable to impose a duty of care, it should be denied and the question left for the judge on a full trial of the matter.

In *Gallagher* v. *Berrow Wood School Ltd*,[91] the claimant was applying for leave to appeal against a strike out decision. The claimant alleged that he had suffered serious abuse while attending a school run by the local authority, and that it had had a marked effect on his psychological development. The judge at first instance had struck out the claim against the local authority on the grounds that there was no proximity between the claimant and the defendant authority, that all the defendant authority had done was in the exercise of their statutory discretion, and it was not just, fair and reasonable to impose a duty of care on the defendant. Lord Justice Stuart-Smith held that the requirements that the claimant show proximity and the justice, fairness and reasonableness of making a claim are distinct "although in some cases they come very close to each other and it may not be necessary to consider them separately". He upheld the judge's finding that there was no proximity between the claimant and the defendant, and that the defendant had been acting within the ambit of his discretion.

The decision of the ECHR in *Osman* at first seemed likely to have a significant effect on the approach adopted by English courts when considering the liability of public authorities, by making it impossible to strike out a claim solely on the ground that it would not be 'fair, just and reasonable' to impose a duty of care. However, even before the later decisions of *Z* and *TP and KM* v. *United Kingdom* had corrected that perception, there were few signs that the previous reluctance of the courts to impose a duty of care on public authorities acting within their statutory functions was being reconsidered. On the contrary, it

[91] Unreported CA 7 October 1999.

seemed that the concept of 'proximity' might be developed by the courts to fulfill, as far as possible, the function of the 'fair, just and reasonable' test for imposing a duty of care.[92] A slightly more liberal approach can be seen in the opinions of Lord Slynn, and Lord Hutton in *Barrett* (an approach which does not appear to have been influenced by the decision in *Osman* and which may therefore survive the reconsideration of that decision) and in *Gower*. However, though the fact that the law of negligence did not provide the claimants with a remedy in *X* v. *Bedfordshire County Council* and *M* v. *Newham London Borough Council* led to the ECtHR finding in *Z* and *TP and KM* v. *United Kingdom* that there had been a violation of Article 13 of the Convention, the ECtHR appears to have accepted in those cases that the remedy provided by the Human Rights Act 1998 would in future be sufficient to redress this. This is likely to limit the influence of the ECtHR jurisprudence on the development of the law of negligence.

Other Immunities

English law also conferred immunity on judges and arbitrators, witnesses and on lawyers for negligence "in the courtroom".[95] Lord Bingham (at the time, Lord Chief Justice) suggested in a recent case that the last would be reviewed in the light of the HRA.[96] The case has now been heard by the House of Lords, before the coming into force of the Act.[97] The immunity of lawyers has been removed. What is interesting is that the majority speeches do not rely on the Act or the Convention, Lord Hoffmann (who gives the fullest speech) explicitly so,[98] merely Lord Hobhouse remarking that if the immunity were to be kept it would undoubtedly be challenged again when the HRA comes into force.[99] It was the minority, who believed that the immunity should be kept for criminal proceedings though not for civil proceedings, who dealt in detail with the Convention, principally to argue that their conclusion was not inconsistent with it.[100] So it may be that the influence of the HRA on private law will be even less direct than we argue above, and that some English judges will develop the law in ways that are consistent with the Convention without relying on it.

It also seems likely that witness immunity at least will be subject to challenge. Needless to say, the courts may well find that both rules are in fact justifiable— though, as with public authorities, it may be that the courts will no longer be able to strike out claims without some examination of the merits to ensure that the immunity is not disproportionate.

---

[92] See in particular *Palmer* v. *Tees Health Authority* (2000) 2 LGLR 69.
[95] *Rondel* v. *Worsley* [1969] 1 AC 191; *Saif Ali* v. *Sydney Mitchell & Co.* [1980] AC 198.
[96] *Arthur J.S. Hall & Co (a firm)* v. *Simons* [1999] Lloyd's Rep. Professional Negligence 47.
[97] *Arthur J.S. Hall & Co (a firm)* v. *Simons* [2000] 3 All ER 673.
[98] *Ibid.*, at 707.
[99] *Ibid.*, at 751.
[100] *Ibid.*, Lord Hope at 711, 717; Lord Hutton at 733.

Omissions

It is well known that English law is very reluctant to impose a duty to act, for example to assist in rescue, even where there would be little or no danger to the rescuer. In *Hughes* v. *UK*[101] the Commission was asked to rule that the State should place a general obligation on private persons (on the facts, a private school which until very recently had employed the applicant's husband, who suffered a heart attack on the premises) to call promptly for medical assistance. Though the case failed utterly on causation (the victim could not possibly have been saved even by prompt medical attention) the possibility that Article 2 might impose such an obligation on the State was not altogether ruled out.

Defences

There may also be a question mark over the rule that the court will not assist a claimant who in making his claim relies on his own criminal act, and knew or should be presumed to have known that it was wrong. This also seems likely to offend the proportionality principle if it is applied mechanically, as seems to be suggested in the latest tort case.[102] However other tort cases have applied a more flexible rule,[103] sometimes explained as dependent on whether the illegality shocks the conscience of the court[104] (despite the rejection of this principle in trust and contract cases by the House of Lords in *Tinsley* v. *Milligan*[105]). This, we suspect, would mean that any HRA claim would fall at the second hurdle, in that the courts consider the justification for applying the *ex turpi causa* defence on a case-by-case basis.[106]

Environmental Torts

The Strasbourg jurisprudence covers some aspects of environmental damage. In *Baggs* v. *UK*[107] the Commission held admissible a complaint from a farmer whose farm lay at the end of a runway at Heathrow but who was not protected by legislation which covered only developments subsequent to 1969. However another application from someone who lived further away and who had "come

---

[101] App. no 11590/85 (1986) 48 DR 258.

[102] *Clunis* v. *Camden and Islington HA* [1998] 3 All ER 180.

[103] For example, *Saunders* v. *Edwards* [1987] 2 All ER 651.

[104] The judge in *Thackwell* v. *Barclays Bank* [1986] 1 All ER 676 seems to have approved a submission by the defendant in these terms, and this in turn was approved by Nicholls LJ in *Saunders* [1987] 2 All ER 651.

[105] [1994] 1 AC 340.

[106] The Law Commission's Consultation Paper, *Illegal Transactions: the Effect of Illegality on Contracts and Trusts* (No. 154, 1999) hazarded the view that the discretionary approach provisionally proposed was, if anything, less likely to infringe the ECHR than the present regime in contract and trusts, which provides no opportunity to assess the prortionality of allowing an illegality defence to defeat the plaintiff's claim: para. 1.23. See also Law Commission Consultation Paper, *The Illegality Defence: Tort* (No. 160, 2001).

[107] App. no 9310/81 (1985) 44 DR 13.

to the nuisance" was rejected; although the level of noise amounted to interference with his Article 8 rights, the steps taken (including the provision of grants for noise insulation) meant that there was no unreasonable burden on the applicant.[108] Some of the Strasbourg cases seem to add nothing in terms of substantive coverage to what would be available under English law,[109] but the case of *Guerra* v. *Italy*[110] is suggestive. Here the State was held to have failed to fulfil its obligation to secure respect for the applicant's private life in that it failed to ensure the provision of information about the environmental risks of a chemical plant so that the applicants lacked essential information about the risks of continuing to live near the plant. One can imagine that a court might decide that information must be given even if it cannot be shown that to operate the plant was a nuisance or negligent.

Nuisance

In *Hunter* v. *Canary Wharf*[111] the House of Lords ruled that only the owner or tenant of land can claim in nuisance for interference with the enjoyment of land, in the relevant case by dust created by a road-building project. Other persons, for example the owners' families, could recover for personal injury through the tort of negligence but had no remedy for other interference. It is clearly arguable that the State has a positive duty to protect the right to family life under Article 8, and when another case arising from the same facts reached the Commission, the latter stated, first, that Article 8(1) applied to both owners and occupiers living on the property; and, secondly, that the interference impaired their right to enjoy their family lives.[112]

However, the same case shows some of the difficulty which would be involved in moving beyond an argument that a situation involves a potential infringement of Convention rights to showing that it in fact does infringe them. The Commission stated that under Article 8 a balance must be struck between the competing interests of the individual and of the community as a whole. As the building of the road was an essential part of the regeneration of Docklands, which itself was a legitimate and important aim, and as the applicants had not suffered any injury, merely temporary inconvenience, there was no infringement.

In this decision the Commission was doing no more than following an established line in the jurisprudence of the Strasbourg Court, which accepts that general arguments may weigh against a duty to create a remedy. Article 8 provides the clearest example. First, Article 8(2) allows a State to justify interference with

---

[108] *Rayner* v. *UK*, App. no 9310/81 (1986) 47 DR 5.

[109] For example, *Lopez-Ostra* v. *Spain* (1994) 20 EHRR 277 (severe interference from waste treatment plant allowed by State to operate without a licence).

[110] (1998) 26 EHRR 357. It was also claimed that a "disaster plan" as to what steps should be taken in the event of a major accident had not been produced as required by law.

[111] [1997] 2 All ER 426.

[112] *Katun* v. *UK* (1998) 26 EHRR CD 212.

this right on the grounds of necessity "in the interest of national security, public safety or the economic well being of the country". Secondly, the ECtHR has said that in cases where it is claimed that the State had a positive obligation to protect the invasion of one party's Convention rights by the activities of another, broadly similar principles apply in that a fair balance must be struck between the interests of individuals affected and of the community as a whole.[113] Indeed the factors listed in Article 8(2) have "a certain relevance" in cases where the interference is not by the State but by another private body.[114] Applying this to the situation of dust created by road-building affecting non-owners, the court would almost certainly be convinced that the law in fact struck a fair balance. Moreover, it could probably take into account the same practical argument as swayed the House of Lords. This was that a company wanting to carry out an activity which may result in a nuisance may wish to negotiate with those who will be affected, and it will be very difficult to do so if they have to deal with all occupiers, not just with owners and tenants.

Another example of the ECtHR reluctance to interfere with domestic law where there seem good reasons for the domestic rule is its approach to limitation periods. Clearly a very short limitation period may mean that the applicant is deprived of any effective remedy for what, in the absence of a remedy, might well be an infringement. In *Stubbings* v. *UK*[115] it was argued that the absence of any discretion on the court to extend the time for bringing an action for intentional child abuse, whereas there was a discretion in negligence cases, infringed the applicant's rights. The Court held that there was no justification for the difference in treatment, yet it held that as the aim of the rule was legitimate, it was proportionate and it did not impair the essence of the remedy, there was no infringement.

III. CONTRACT LAW

We have heard it said that the HRA will be of very little relevance to contract except perhaps to contracts of employment.[116]

1. Employment

The most likely one to be affected is the contract of employment.[117] Here the ECtHR has already decided that secret monitoring by a public employer of an employee's private telephone conversations infringed her rights under

---

[113] See A. Lester and D. Pannick, *Human Rights Law & Practice* (London, Butterworths, 1999) 4.88.

[114] *Lopez-Ostra* v. *Spain* (1994) 20 EHRR 277.

[115] (1993) 23 EHRR 213.

[116] Booth, *Introduction to Common Law Claims and the HRA 1998*, seminar paper for London Common Law and Commercial Law Bar Association, 27 March 2000 (unpublished).

[117] See S. Palmer, "Human Rights: Implications for Labour Law" [2000] *CLJ* 168.

Article 8.[118] Equally other forms of secret monitoring, at least without warning, must be at risk.

We would also expect some impact on discrimination cases. In 1996 it was held by the Court of Appeal that personnel who had been discharged from the armed forces on the grounds of their homosexuality had no claim under English law.[119] Discrimination on such grounds is not *per se* a contravention of Convention rights,[120] but Article 14 requires that enjoyment of other Convention rights shall be without discrimination on any ground. This is interpreted not as meaning that there must be some other infringement of Convention rights—that would make Article 14 redundant—but that once the applicant shows that the matter is within the potential area of operation of a Convention right, there must be no discrimination.[121] The Convention does not refer to employment as a right protected in itself, but it must be arguable that being barred from their chosen careers brings the ex-service personnel within the ambit of Article 8, so that Article 14 would then bite.[122] In fact in its judgment the ECtHR held that the investigation into the applicants' sexual orientation and their subsequent discharge solely on the ground of homosexuality was a violation of Article 8 and there was no separate issue under Article 14.[123]

There may also be infringements through restrictions on appearance and dress, in so far as these are seen to restrict individuals' freedom to express their personality.[124]

However, it has been pointed out that in some respects the Strasbourg jurisprudence has been less protective of employees than one might expect. There have been two cases in which employees complained that their right to religious freedom under Article 9 was infringed when, in one case, the applicant was refused time off on Fridays for prayer and, in the other, when the applicant was required by her employer to work on Sunday. An author describes the recognition of human rights in the employment context as piecemeal and so far lacking in any unifying conception.[125]

2. General contract law

As far as general contract law is concerned, the principal difficulty is to get the case within the ambit of Convention rights, given that these do not include economic rights. There seem to be two possibilities: (1) where a rule of law

---

[118] *Halford* v. *UK* (1997) 24 EHRR 523.
[119] R. v. *Ministry of Defence, ex p. Smith* [1996] QB 517.
[120] See Lester and Pannick, *supra* n.113, at 1.14.1.
[121] *Ibid.*, at 4.14.4.
[122] The Court of Appeal left the question of Convention rights to be decided by the Strasbourg Court.
[123] *Smith & Grady* v. *UK* (1999) 29 EHRR 493.
[124] See Palmer, *supra* n.89, at 185 *et seq.*
[125] *Ibid.*, at 169.

allows a result which might interfere with respect for family life and (2) where it might result in a person being deprived of his possessions within Article 1 of the First Protocol.

Under Article 8, not only must the State itself respect citizens' family life and home, but it may have positive obligations to protect these at least by providing adequate legal protection. In *Marckx*[126] it was held that the failure of Belgian law to grant normal inheritance rights to those born out of wedlock was a failure to provide such protection. Could any rule of contract law result in either direct infringement by the State or a failure to protect? We have thought of two possibilities, both involving loss of the family home. Both seem within the ambit of the Convention right but neither seems a strong case.

The first is if the law entitles a purchaser to specific enforcement of a contract to sell the home although that would leave the vendor's family homeless and without the possibility of acquiring another home. But this is precisely the kind of case in which the court will normally refuse specific performance under its general discretion.[127]

The second is the type of case exemplified by *Barclays' Bank* v. *O'Brien*,[128] in which a wife charged the matrimonial home to secure her husband's business debts. In that case the bank was prevented from enforcing the charge on the ground that it had constructive notice of a misrepresentation by the husband. The bank knew that the debtor and the surety were in the kind of relationship in which misrepresentation, undue influence or duress was likely and also knew that the transaction was not to the wife's advantage. Unless it had advised the wife to take independent advice, the bank would be fixed with constructive notice of any wrong by the husband. Due to an oversight this had not been done and, as the husband had misrepresented the effect of the charge as being for a limited amount when in fact it was unlimited, the charge was unenforceable. On the other hand, the House of Lords rejected a doctrine suggested by the Court of Appeal[129] which would have required the bank to ensure that the wife understood the transaction. Might it be argued that to allow the bank to take the family home of a surety who has not been the victim of a wrong by the husband but who has not understood the risks of the charge, or who has been the victim of duress by the husband but in circumstances where the bank has no constructive notice,[130] is contrary to the surety' right to respect for the family home?

This might seem a weak argument, one which is bound to fail at the second hurdle—the question of balance between the rights of the bank and those of the

---

[126] *Marckx, supra* n.18.
[127] *Patel* v. *Ali* [1984] Ch. 283.
[128] [1994] 1 AC 180.
[129] [1993] QB 109.
[130] For example if the bank has been misled into believing that the charge is for the benefit of the wife as well as the husband, as in *CIBC Mortgages plc* v. *Pitt* [1994] 1 AC 200.

surety are surely a matter of ensuring that the victim does not suffer dispropor-
tionately, and the particular rules of English law must be within the margin of
appreciation. The counter-arguments might be that the Court in Strasbourg has
shown itself willing to challenge the substantive law of States if it thinks that
that law does not provide adequate protection,[131] and that continental-trained
judges may start off with a hostile reaction to the English law, since they may be
used to a system under which (a) there are broad duties of disclosure [132] and (b)
duress by a third person entitles the victim to avoid a contract whether or not
the duress was known to the party against whom avoidance is sought.[133]
However, one has the sense of clutching at straws.

Turning to rules which might be seen as within the ambit of the First
Protocol, a possible area relates to forfeiture. English contract law sometimes
permits the victim of a breach of contract who has justifiably terminated the
contract to retain money which has been paid to him even though it exceeds the
loss which he has suffered. This seems to be the case with a deposit: save in cases
relating to the sale of land,[134] it seems that the deposit paid by a buyer may
be retained by a seller after the buyers' default.[135] It can also result from the
operation of a forfeiture clause, for example if land is sold under instalment
payments with a proviso that, in the event of default, the purchaser will lose
both the land and any payments made. Such clauses will sometimes be subject
to judicial control anyway, for example if they occur in a consumer contract.[136]
But in other cases they are not controlled.[137] But whether any court would be
prepared to find that such rules infringe the defaulting party's Convention rights
seems speculative, particularly when both parties are private. There has been no
clear decision that the State has any positive obligation to protect citizens' rights
under the First Protocol against other individuals, though the case law does not
seem to rule this out.[138]

Even more so is the converse case in which the innocent party is permitted to
retain benefits received under the contract without having to pay for them. This
is the result of the rule that, in a contract for work in exchange for a single pay-
ment the obligation to do the work is entire and nothing is due, neither any part
of the contract price nor by way of restitution, for work which amounts to less

---

[131] For example the English law on parental chastisement. See *supra*, text accompanying nn.46–8.

[132] Such as exist in, for example, German or French law. For a valuable summary see H. Kötz,
European Contract Law (Oxford, Clarendon, 1997), 181 *et seq.*, 198 *et seq.*

[133] *Ibid.*, at 213. See French Civil Code, Art. 1111.

[134] Which will fall under either the Law of Property Act 1925, s. 49 or the rule developed by the
PC that any deposit greater than the customary 10% used in land transactions must be shown to be
justified on the facts of the case: *Workers Trust & Merchant Bank Ltd* v. *Dojap Investments Ltd*
[1993] AC 573.

[135] See H. Beale, "Unreasonable Deposits" (1993) 109 *LQR* 524.

[136] Under the Unfair Terms in Consumer Contracts Regulations 1999.

[137] It seems that relief is limited to giving the defaulting party extra time in which to make good the
payments: see H. Beale, *Remedies for Breach of Contract* (London, Sweet & Maxwell, 1980), 15–113.

[138] See *James* v. *UK* (1986) 8 EHRR 123 (leasehold enfranchisement scheme held not to infringe
Convention rights, but not on this ground).

than substantial performance of the contract.[139] The Law Commission recommended changing this rule so that the guilty party should be reimbursed for any net benefit to the victim after the latter's losses have been taken into account; but the government did not accept the recommendation. Apparently it was persuaded by the dissenting view of Mr Commissioner Davenport that to change the rule would take away the one hold that householders have over jobbing builders who do not finish the work.[140] This seems to be precisely the kind of economic counter-argument which States may use to justify an apparent infringement of Convention rights.

IV. CONCLUSION

After such a long chapter we will keep our conclusions very short. It is not easy to assess the likely impact of the Human Rights Act 1998 on the law of contract and tort in England and Wales. Where it can be shown that a public authority has infringed the claimant's Convention rights, the claimant will now have a potential claim, whereas in the past the liability of public authorities has been rather carefully circumscribed. However, it must be recalled that the Strasbourg Court accepts that there may be good reasons justifying what might otherwise be a violation of the Convention, and we must expect the UK courts to take a similar line. The factors which in the past have been seen as justifying immunity may now have to be examined on a case-by-case basis to ensure that the application of them is proportionate to the end to be achieved and the harm suffered, but the policies are unlikely to be abandoned.

Even outside the area of public authority liability, it seems likely that there will be some "weak horizontal" effect, in that the courts are likely to develop remedies against "private" defendants which will protect the private equivalent of Convention rights. The "lawyers' immunity" case[141] suggests that the courts may in fact develop the law without explicit reliance on the Convention. Now that the Act is in force we may expect more arguments based on the Convention to be made by advocates, and this may mean that the judges are more likely at least to deal with them, but some judges may still prefer to rest their judgments principally on non-Convention grounds. We suggest, however, that this does not mean that the HRA will not have had indirect influence. We expect it to act as at least a hidden catalyst for change, and often we think it will be overt. We may expect developments in privacy and in employment contracts. Whether there will be very much impact in other fields is, frankly, anyone's guess.

---

[139] For example, *Sumpter* v. *Hedges* [1898] 1 QB 673; *Bolton* v. *Mahadeva* [1972] 1 WLR 1009.

[140] See H. Beale, W. Bishop and M. Furmston, *Contract Cases and Materials* (3rd edn., London, Butterworths, 1995) 494,

[141] See *supra* text accompanying n.95.

8

The European Convention of Human Rights and Fundamental Freedoms and German Private Law

REINHARD ELLGER*

I. INTRODUCTION: FUNDAMENTAL RIGHTS AND PRIVATE LAW—
A GLIMPSE AT THE GERMAN DISCUSSION

IN THIS CHAPTER, I seek to demonstrate the effect of the European Convention of Human Rights ("ECHR") in the sphere of German private law by referring to Article 8 of the Convention (protection of family life and privacy) and Article 10 (freedom of expression). In section IV, I comment on the clash between the principle of freedom of contract and human rights, an issue not specifically related to the Convention but nonetheless a focal point in any discussion on the role human rights play in the sphere of private law.

Fundamental rights have been traditionally understood as claims the individual has *vis-à-vis* the State.[1] Such rights delineate the areas in which the individual is able to live without government intervention. Beyond the intrinsic extensions of their traditional role, these rights have gained inestimable influence in the context of the private legal relationships among individuals. This new approach clearly crosses the boundaries of the traditional role of fundamental rights.

---

* Sections I to III of this chap. are a short version of an article published in German in (1999) 63 *Rabels Zeitschrift für ausländisches und internationales Privatrecht* (hereinafter RabelsZ) 625 *et seq.*, under the title Europäische Menschenrechtskonvention und deutsches Privatrecht- Die Einwirkung von Art. 8 und 10 Europäische Konvention zum Schutze der Menschenrechte und der Grundfreiheiten auf die deutsche Privatrechtsordnung. Section IV of this chap. is not included in the German article.

[1] Bundesverfassungsgericht (Federal Constitutional Court) (hereinafter BVerfG) 15 Jan. 1958, 7 Entscheidungen des BVerfG (Reports of the Federal Constitutional Court) (hereinafter BVerfGE) 198, 204 (hereinafter *Lüth*); 8 July 1982, 61 BVerfGE 82, 101; 31 Oct. 1984, 68 BVerfGE 193, 205; Grundgesetz (Basic Law) (hereinafter GG)-*Kommentar* (Tübingen, Mohr Siebeck 1996) (H. Dreier) i, Vorbem. Randzahl (number at the margin of page) (hereinafter Rz) 45; J. Isensee and P. Kirchhof (W. Rüfner) (Heidelberg, C.F. Müller, 1992), Handbuch (manual) StaatsR V, § 117, Rz 55 *et seq.*; K. Stern and M. Sachs, *Das Staatsrecht der Bundesrepublik Deutschland* (Munich, Beck, 1988), III/1, § 76.

In Germany, the Federal Constitutional Court, the highest court of the land and with constitutional jurisdiction, has proved to be a determinative element in the development of the theoretical groundwork for this new approach to fundamental rights. The Court has interpreted the fundamental rights guaranteed under the German Constitution as not only defensive rights of the individual *vis-à-vis* the State (and having force only in the context of that relationship), but also forming an objective system of values that bind all branches of government—the legislature, judiciary and executive—even when acting in the sphere of private law. This expansion of the role of human rights is particularly relevant for those courts charged with adjudicating conflicts between private parties.[2]

Fundamental rights can influence the sphere of private law only in an indirect manner, because fully direct application of fundamental rights would severely curtail freedom of contract, which constitutes one of the basic elements of a free society. As part of the objective legal system, fundamental rights are binding on the judiciary also in civil proceedings. The courts in civil matters have to interpret the numerous blanket clauses contained in the Civil Code ("BGB") and other parts of private law in a way that corresponds with the fundamental rights in the Constitution.[3] These blanket clauses form a gateway for the entry of constitutional law into private law. This approach is referred to as the indirect horizontal effects of fundamental rights in private law (*"mittelbare Drittwirkung"*).

It should be noted, however, that the Constitution is not the only source of fundamental rights in the German legal system. The Federal Republic has adopted the International Covenant on Civil and Political Rights[4] as well as the European Convention on Human Rights and Fundamental Freedoms (ECHR).

The fact that the ECHR celebrates its fiftieth birthday this year is only one reason for inquiring into the significance of the Convention's fundamental rights in the German legal system. To demonstrate the effect of the ECHR, I examine the application of Article 8 (family life and privacy) and Article 10 (freedom of expression) in German private law. The rights to family life and privacy as well as freedom of expression are protected under the German Constitution (Articles 2I, 13, and 6—privacy and family life; Article 5—freedom of expression), just as they are under the ECHR. The fundamental rights guaranteed under the Constitution have assumed extraordinary importance in the private law sphere, just as they have in public law. This holds true especially for

[2] BVerfG 15 Jan. 1958, 7 BVerfG 205; 19 June 1979, 51 BVerfG 304, 323; 4 May 1982, 60 BVerfGE 348, 357 *et seq.*; 12 Jan. 1983, 63 BVerfGE 45, 67 *et seq.*; 19 Oct. 1983, 65 BVerfGE 196, 215; 8 Oct. 1985, 70 BVerfGE 297, 317; BVerfG 7 Feb. 1990, [1990] JZ, 691, 692 *et seq.*; *GG—Komm* (H. Dreier) Vorbem. Rz 57; *Alternativ-Kommentar GG* (2nd edn., Neuwied, Luchterhandt, 1989) (E. Denninger) Art. 1 Rz 29.

[3] See, for example, BVerfG 12 Jan. 1958, 7 BVerfGE 205; 22 Aug. 1979, 73 BVerfGE 261, 269; 11 June 1991, 84 BVerfGE 192, 195.

[4] [1973] II , Bundesgesetzblatt (Official Journal of Federal Statutes) (hereinafter BGBl) 1543; the treaty entered into force in Germany on 23 March 1976: see notice 14 June 1976 [1976] BGBl II 1068. The Federal Republic of Germany has also signed the Universal Declaration of Human Rights of 10 Dec. 1948, Res 217 (III), UNGA Official Records Third Session (Part I), Resolutions (Doc A/810).

the constitutionally protected general right of personhood, which encompasses the right to privacy, on the one hand, and freedom of expression, on the other. One leading case decided by the Federal Constitutional Court concerned the impact and importance of freedom of expression in the private law sphere. In the 1950s, a private individual publicly called for the boycott of a film made by a director renowned for producing propaganda films for the National Socialist Regime during the Third Reich. The production company of this (post-war) film began an action requesting that this individual be enjoined from repeating his appeal to boycott the film. The Federal Constitutional Court refused to grant the requested injunction, holding that the appeal to boycott the film was within the scope of the individual's constitutionally guaranteed freedom of expression. Therefore, his public call was not actionable under the relevant provisions of tort law, and he could not be enjoined from making it.[5]

The question that will be addressed in this chapter is whether and to what extent these provisions in the ECHR have influenced German private law as compared with the impact German constitutional law has had in that sphere. This question has both a normative and a factual element, with the normative dimension relating to the status and position of the ECHR within the German legal system.

In order to shed light on the importance of the ECHR for German private law, the discussion examines decisions made by German courts and the European Court of Human Rights when applying Articles 8 and 10 of the ECHR in cases involving German private law.

II. THE INFLUENCE OF THE ECHR ON GERMAN PRIVATE LAW: THE THEORETICAL FRAMEWORK

1. Integration of the ECHR in the German legal system

(a) *Incorporation into German Law*

The German legislature incorporated the ECHR into German law by statute on 5 December 1952,[6] whereunder the Convention became an integral part of the German legal system. The Convention's implementation mechanism was changed fundamentally by the Eleventh Protocol: private individuals, non-governmental organisations, and groups of individuals can now bring complaints with regard to a Member State's infringement of their rights under the Convention and the Protocols directly to the European Court of Human Rights.[7] In contrast to the previous version of the ECHR, there was no longer

---

[5] *Lüth* case, *supra* n.1, 198 *et seq.*

[6] [1952] BGBl II 686. The Convention entered into force on 9 Sept. 1953, see notice of 15 Dec. 1953 [1954] II BGBl 14.

[7] Art. 34 of the ECHR.

an intermediate judicial authority in the form of a Commission.[8] These changes also were integrated into German law.

(b) *The Status of the ECHR within the German Legal System*

The scope and extent of the influence that the ECHR would exert on German private law was to depend on the normative status of the Convention within the German legal system.

This matter was fiercely debated among legal scholars. Some posited that the Convention supersedes the Constitution[9]; others held that they share equal status.[10] A third opinion considered that the Convention was at a lower normative rung than the Constitution, but that it superseded regular federal statutes.[11] This last opinion relied on Article 25 of the Constitution, which provides that the general rules of public international law take precedence over German statutory law. These general rules do not require incorporation into German law. However, the European Convention on Human Rights is not included amongst these general rules of public international law.[12]

The Federal Constitutional Court[13] and the majority of legal scholars[14] agree that the Convention is a legal instrument of the same normative status as a German federal statute. This seems to be accurate, since the incorporating act was a federal statute and the incorporated Convention cannot differ in status from the actual transforming act itself. Thus, the Convention takes precedence

---

[8] Cf Art. 25 ECHR, previous version.

[9] See the references in M. Wenserski, *Geheimnisschutz nach Art 8 MRK und die Einwirkungen auf das deutsche und englische Recht* (Munich, Florentz,1988) 133.

[10] R. Echterhölter, "Die Europäische Menschenrechtskonvention im Rahmen der verfassungsmäßigen Ordnung" (1955) 10 *JZ* 689, 692; R. Echterhölter, "Die Europäische Menschenrechtskonvention in der juristischen Praxis' (1956) 11 *JZ* 142 at 142; H. Guradze, Anm zu BVerfG 14 Jan. 1960 (1960) *Neue Juristische Wochenschrift* (hereinafter *NJW*) 1243.

[11] R. Herzog, "Nochmals: Verfassungsbeschwerde gegen Verletzungen der Menschenrechtskonvention?" (1960) 13 *DÖV* 775; N. Erdsiek, "Umwelt und Recht" (1959) 12 *NJW* 1215, at 1216; M. Wenserski, "Geheimnisschutz nach Art. 8" *MRK*, 134.

[12] See H. von Mangoldt, F. Klein and C. Starck (eds.), *Bonner Grundgesetz. Kommentar* (4th edn., Munich, Beck, 2000) (C. Koenig), Art. 25 Rz 18; T. Maunz, G. Dürig and R. Herzog (eds.), *Grundgesetzkommentar* (looseleaf) (T. Maunz) (Munich, Beck), Art. 25 Rz 19, 20.

[13] BVerfG 15 Dec. 1965 19 BVerfGE 342, 347; 19 July 1967 22 BVerfGE 254, 265; 15 Apr. 1969 25 BVerfGE 327, 331; 16 May 1973 35 BVerfGE 311; 26 Mar. 1987 74 BVerfGE 358, 370; 29 May 1990 82 BVerfGE 106; [1990] NJW 2741.

[14] R. Bernhardt, "Verfassungsrecht und völkerrechtliche Verträge" in Manual StaatsR VII (Heidelberg, C.F. Müller,1992) § 174 Rz 29; J.A. Frowein, "Übernationale Menschenrechtsgewährleistungen", in Manual StaatsR VII (Heidelberg, C.F. Müller,1992) § 180 Rz 6; J.A. Frowein and W. Peukert, *Europäische Menschenrechtskonvention: Europäische Konvention zum Schutze der Menschenrechte-Kommentar* (2nd edn., Kehl, Engel, 1996) (hereinafter Frowein and Peukert), Einf Rz 6; M. Hilf, "Der Rang der Europäischen Menschenrechtskonvention im deutschen Recht" in E. Mahrenholtz, M. Hilf and F. Klein, *Entwicklung der Menschenrechte innerhalb der Staaten des Europarats* (Heidelberg, C.F. Müller,1987) 19 *et seq.*, 39; G. Ulsamer, "Europäische Menschenrechtskonvention als innerstaatlich geltendes Recht der Bundesrepublik Deutschland" in J.A. Frowein and G. Ulsamer, *Europäische Menschenrechtskonvention und nationaler Rechtsschutz* (Heidelberg, C.F. Müller,1985), 39.

over sub-statutory legal instruments and over federal statutes adopted prior to the Convention's incorporation into German law.

Remarkably, however, the Federal Constitutional Court elevated the Convention's ranking in the hierarchy of legal rules in Germany. The Court held that:

> Also statutes . . . have to be interpreted and applied in harmony with the duties of the Federal Republic of Germany under public international law, even if they have been adopted later in time than the international treaty; for it cannot be assumed that the legislature intends to neglect such obligations of the Federal Republic of Germany or intends to enable the addressees of the statute to violate such obligations.[15]

Thus, even statutes that entered into force after the ECHR was incorporated into German law must be interpreted to conform with the requirements of the Convention.

2. The impact of the ECHR on private law

(a) *The ECHR and the Problem of Horizontal Effect*

Like the fundamental rights guaranteed under the German Constitution, the human rights under the Convention are primarily directed at the State. This function of the Convention is supported by its legislative history as well as by its wording. The text of the Convention was influenced by the UN Universal Declaration of Human Rights. The drafters of the Convention clearly had in mind the memory of the total lack of justice in Nazi Germany and the Soviet Union and the atrocities committed against individuals by the public authorities in those countries.[16]

The formulation of Article 1 of the Convention suggests that it is directed principally at state action[17]:

> The High Contracting Parties shall secure to everyone within their jurisdiction the rights and freedoms defined in Section I of this Convention.

While the ECHR undoubtedly has binding force *vis-à-vis* the Member States and their actions against private parties, the question whether and to what extent the Convention's provisions are relevant to the behaviour of private

---

[15] BVerfG 26 Mar. 1987 74 BVerfGE 370.

[16] Cf H. Glatzel, *Die Einwirkung der Rechte und Freiheiten der Europäischen Menschenrechtskonvention auf private Rechtsbeziehungen. Ein Beitrag zum Problem der sog. Drittwirkung* (Diss, Bonn, 1968) 58 (hereinafter Glatzel); M.A. Eissen, "La Convention et les devoirs de l'individu" in *La protection internationale des droits de l'homme dans le cadre européen—Travaux du colloque organisé par la Faculté de droit et des sciences politiques et économiques de Strasbourg en liaison avec la Direction des droits de l'Homme du Conseil d'Europe*, 14–15 Nov. 1960 (Paris, 1961), 169 *et seq.*, both with further hints at relevant material.

[17] See also Frowein and Peukert, *supra* n.14, Art. 1 Rz 9.

parties *inter se* was subject to intense controversy.[18] Some legal scholars took the view that the Convention was directly applicable to the legal relations among private citizens (*"direkte Drittwirkung"*).[19] This approach, however, was not shared by the judicial authorities authorised under the Convention or by the majority of the legal community. The arguments in favour of direct applicability were not convincing.

Today, the judicial authorities authorised under the Convention and academics concur that at least some of the Convention's fundamental rights have an indirect horizontal effect on private law. In the early cases, the European Court of Human Rights stressed the function of the Convention to control state action against the individual. With regard to Article 8, the Court stated in the 1968 *Belgian Linguistic Case*[20]:

> This provision itself in no way guarantees either a right to education or a personal right of parents relating to the education of their children: its object is essentially that of protecting the individual against arbitrary interference by the public authorities in his private family life.

However, 11 years later, in the famous *Marckx* case from 1979, the Court extended the narrow boundaries of the functions of the Convention[21]:

> As the court stated in the "Belgian Linguistic" case, the object of the Article is "essentially" that of protecting the individual against arbitrary interference by the public authorities. Nevertheless it does not merely compel the State to abstain from such interference: in addition to this primarily negative undertaking, there may be positive obligations inherent in an effective "respect" for family life. This means, amongst other things, that when the State determines in its domestic legal system the regime applicable to certain family ties such as those between an unmarried mother and her child, it must act in a manner calculated to allow those concerned to lead a normal family life.

This decision proved to be the starting point for the development of such positive obligations for the signatory states to the Convention with regard to guaranteeing these rights in the framework of the legal relations between private individuals.

The following are examples of different duties placed on the State to protect the interests of its citizens in the sphere of private law:

---

[18] For a survey of this debate, see E. Alkema, "The Third-party Applicability or 'Drittwirkung' of the European Convention on Human Rights" in F. Matscher and H. Petzold (eds.), *Protecting Human Rights, The European Dimension, FS Wiarda II* (Cologne, Carl Heymanns, 1990) 33 at 36 *et seq.*; P. van Dijk and G. van Hoof, *Theory and Practice of the European Convention of Human Rights* (Antwerp, Kluwer, 1984) 13 *et seq.*; Glatzel, *supra* n.16, 50 *et seq.*

[19] See, for example, H.C. Nipperdey, "Die Würde des Menschen" in K.A. Bettermann, F.L. Neumann, H.C. Nipperdey and U. Scheuner, *Die Grundrechte, Handbuch der Theorie und Praxis der Grundrechte* (Berlin, Duncker & Humblot, 1954), II *et seq.* (21, Anm 44); R. Herzog, *Grundrechtsbeschränkung nach dem Grundgesetz und Europäischer Menschenrechtskonvention* (Diss, Munich 1958) 25 *et seq.*

[20] European Court of Human Rights (hereinafter ECtHR) 23 July 1968, Series A Nr 6; [1975] Europäische Grundrechte-Zeitschrift (hereinafter EuGRZ) 298, 300.

[21] ECtHR 13 June 1979 (*Marckx*), Series A Nr 31; [1979] EuGRZ 454, 455.

(1) Article 8 calls on the Member States to provide the legal means in their domestic legal systems for marital separation, to be available to all irrespective of one's financial state.[22]

(2) Article 8 requires the Member States to protect the family life of illegitimate children by respecting the principle of equal treatment under the law.[23]

(3) Article 8 requires Member States to enact criminal sanctions against sexual abuse of minors.[24]

Article 8 is not the only provision in the Convention to have this type of indirect horizontal effect on private law provisions. Other fundamental rights under the Convention, including those guaranteed in Article 10, also have such an indirect horizontal effect. Direct application of fundamental rights in the framework of private legal relationships cannot be allowed because it would be inconsistent with basic principles of private law.

(b) *The Mode of Operation of Indirect Horizontal Effects of ECHR Provisions in German Private Law*

As noted, upon its incorporation, the ECHR became immediately applicable in the German legal system.[25] It has binding force with regard to the actions of all branches of government, including the legislature when enacting private law provisions and the courts when deliberating civil proceedings. The Federal Constitutional Court recognised the indirect horizontal effect of the ECHR by obliging lower courts "to interpret and apply" statutes—namely, private law provisions—in conformity with the public international law obligations of the Federal Republic of Germany.[26] The vague and broad clauses of private law provisions (blanket clauses), which require interpretation, are the gateway for the infiltration of human rights into German private law.

III. THE ACTUAL IMPACT OF ARTICLES 8 AND 10 OF THE ECHR ON GERMAN PRIVATE LAW

The ECHR can affect German private law in two ways: (1) the Convention may influence German private law inasmuch as the domestic courts refer in civil proceedings to ECHR provisions in order to interpret rules of German

[22] ECtHR 9 Oct. 1979 (*Airey*), Series A Nr 32; [1979] EuGRZ 626, 629.

[23] *Ibid.*

[24] ECtHR 26 Mar. 1985 (*X & Y v. Niederlande*), Series A Nr 91; [1985] EuGRZ 297, 298.

[25] See J. Frowein, "Der Europäische Menschenrechtsschutz als Beginn einer europäischen Verfassungsrechtsprechung" [1986] *Juristische Schulung* (hereinafter *JuS*) 845, at 847; J. Frowein, "Übernationale Menschenrechtsgewährleistungen" in Manual StaatsR VII (Heidelberg, C.F. Müller,1992), § 180 Rz 6; U. Häde and M. Jachmann, *Anm zum Beschluß des Amtsgerichts* (Magistrate's Court) (hereinafter AG) Kamen 13 Apr. 1995, [1996] (43) Zeitschrift für das gesamte Familienrecht (hereinafter FamRZ) 632 at 633.

[26] BVerfG 26 Mar. 1987 74 BVerfGE 370.

private law. (2) The German legal system may be influenced by the case law of the European Court of Human Rights. This Court occasionally decides cases in which provisions of German private law are at issue.

1. The protection of private life and family life under Article 8 of the ECHR and its influence on German private law

Article 8 of the Convention guarantees every individual respect for his or her private and family life, home and correspondence. The Article encompasses four different elements. It differs from other provisions of the Convention in that it does not contain a prohibition or grant any freedom.[27] It mandates "respect" for the matters enumerated in Article 8, namely, private life, family life, home and correspondence.

The only one of these four elements that has had any influence on German private law is respect for family life. The other three elements have not had any apparent effect in this sphere.

Below, I briefly set out the instances in which German courts have referred to Article 8 of the ECHR.

(a) *Preclusion of Joint Custody for Children of Unmarried Parents*

Until the recently adopted reform of the German law relating to children, effective from 1 July 1998,[28] German law discriminated against children born out of wedlock in several respects.

Under section 1626 of the BGB, the parents of a legitimate child are his or her joint legal guardians. This law did not provide for the possibility of granting the father and mother of an illegitimate child joint custody. The former section 1705 of the BGB provided that the mother of an illegitimate child is his or her custodian. In 1981, the Federal Constitutional Court held that this legal situation was not in violation of Article 6 of the Constitution, which protects family life.[29] However, in a decision rendered in 1991, the Court voiced doubts about the constitutionality of such discriminatory regulations for illegitimate children in the area of custody, but did not annul section 1705, because this question was not at issue in the case at hand.[30]

This was the legal background when the father of an illegitimate child filed an application for joint custody at the Magistrate's Court of Kamen in the Land of North Rhine-Westphalia. The Court upheld the application and issued an order

---

[27] Cf Frowein and Peukert, *supra* n.14, Art. 8 Rz 1.
[28] Gesetz zur Reform des Kindschaftsrechts, 16 Dec. 1997 [1997] I BGBl 2942.
[29] BVerfG 24 Mar. 1981 [1981] FamRZ 429.
[30] BVerfGE 7 May 1991 [1991] FamRZ 913, 915.

for joint custody.[31] As the legal basis for the claim of joint custody, the Court directly applied Article 8 of the ECHR. The Court alluded to the *Keegan* v. *Ireland* case decided by the European Court of Human Rights[32] and held that the right to respect for family life encompasses not only the married family unit; a family unit of cohabiting non-married parents is also entitled to the protection of Article 8. The Court held that Article 8 requires the Member States to make provisions to enable the integration of an illegitimate child into his or her natural family. The court was of the opinion that the preclusion of joint custody by section 1705 of the BGB constituted a violation of Article 8 of the Convention.

From the perspective of constitutional law and legal policy, the decision handed down by the Magistrate's Court in this case has to be viewed favourably. However, the Court did not follow the accepted methods of legal reasoning in reaching the decision. It did not provide an interpretation of section 1705 of the BGB, but, rather, declared it void under the Convention and refused to apply it. Under the German legal system, the Federal Constitutional Court has exclusive jurisdiction to declare void statutes, which are the product of the democratic political process, on grounds of unconstitutionality. No other court has such authority. Therefore, the Magistrate's Court did not have competence to make this decision.

Moreover, the violation of a human right guaranteed under the ECHR by a legal provision of a Member State does not render the provision void. The competent authorities of the Member State concerned, especially the legislative bodies, are obligated to remove the infringing provision in order to reconcile their legal system with the ECHR.[33] But until such time as those bodies fulfill this duty, the infringing provision of domestic law remains in force.

However, the question became moot with the entry into force of the new German law relating to parent–children relations on 1 July 1998. This legislation expressly provides for the possibility of joint custody for non-married parents.[34]

(b) *Paternal Right of Access to Children Born out of Wedlock*

Article 8 of the Convention has occasionally been referred to by German courts in cases involving paternal right of access to an illegitimate child. Under section 1711(1) of the BGB, a child's legal guardian determines whether a third party can have access to the child. Under the previous family law, the guardian of an illegitimate child was his or her mother. Accordingly, she was in a position to

---

[31] AG Kamen 13 Apr. 1995, 1077 with note by U. Häde and M. Jachmann [1996] *Fam RZ* 632 *et seq*. The court reached the same decision in a similar case; see AG Kamen 4 Aug. 1995 [1996] Neue Juristische Wochenschrift, Rechtsprechungsreport (hereinafter NJW-RR) 199.

[32] ECtHR 26 May 1994, *Keegan* v. *Irland*, Series A Nr 290; [1995] EuGRZ 113 (hereinafter *Keegan*).

[33] Frowein and Peukert, *supra* n.14, Art. 53 Rz 6–10.

[34] § 1626a of the BGB. Parents who are not married to each other can secure joint custody by agreement or by marriage.

prevent the father from having contact with his child even if this was not in the child's best interest. In cases of conflict over access, the family court has jurisdiction to determine right of access. It can grant the father of an illegitimate child access to the child if this promotes the child's welfare. The German courts have held that it is inconsistent with Article 8 of the Convention for the question of access to be wholly contingent on the wishes of the mother; Article 8 protects the "natural" family born out of wedlock, of which the father is also a part, no less than it protects the married family unit.[35] Such conflicts have been resolved by the German courts by interpreting the welfare clause of the BGB in such a way that the father's claim to access can be denied only if the child's physical health will be jeopardised by contact with the father.

(c) *The Weak Legal Position of Fathers of Illegitimate Children in Respect of Adoption*

In the *Keegan* case, the European Court of Human Rights held that provisions of Irish law were in violation of Article 8 of the Convention in allowing adoption of an illegitimate child by a third party without the father's knowledge or consent.[36] In *Keegan*, the Court recognised the existence of a family unit even when the parents had lived together for only a short period of time prior to the birth of the child, but only if producing the child had been the joint wish of both partners.

The previous German law on adoption did not meet these requirements. Under that law, adoption of an illegitimate child was possible without the father's consent.[37] Nor did the father have any standing in the adoption proceedings. The German Federal Constitutional Court, taking note of the *Keegan* case, decided that the German adoption law violated the right to family life under Article 6 of the German Constitution.[38]

Under the new German adoption law, the adoption of an illegitimate child requires the consent of both parents.[39]

(d) *Protection of Privacy*

The German case law with regard to the protection of privacy makes no reference to Article 8 of the ECHR. The right to privacy is an acknowledged element of German private law.[40] It has been grounded not by reference to Article 8 of

---

[35] Landgericht (Regional Court) (hereinafter LG), Zweibrücken 3 June 1996 [1997] FamRZ 633.

[36] *Supra* n.31, at 113.

[37] S. 1747 II of the BGB (previous version) required only maternal consent to hand over an illegitimate child for adoption.

[38] BVerfG 7 Mar. 1995, 92 BVerfGE 158, 176 *et seq.*; [1995] FamRZ 789, 792.

[39] § 1747 I BGB.

[40] See H. Stoll, "The General Right of Personality in German Law: An Outline of its Development and Present Significance" in B. Markesinis (ed.), *Protecting Privacy* (Oxford, Oxford University Press, 1999), with further references.

the ECHR but through the application of Article 1 (inviolability of human dignity) and Article 2 (right of personality) of the German Constitution. Article 8 of the Convention, therefore, has not played any apparent role in the interpretation of this sphere of German private law.

2. Freedom of expression under Article 10 of the ECHR and German private law

To a certain extent, Article 10 of the ECHR constitutes the counterpoint to Article 8 of the Convention: whereas the latter protects different elements of privacy, Article 10 safeguards the participation of the individual in the social process of communication.

(a) *The Application of Article 10 of the ECHR by German Courts in Civil Proceedings*

Article 10 of the ECHR plays a less significant role than Article 8 in German private law.

Article 10 and the German law of landlord and tenant: the Magistrate's Court (*Amtsgericht*) of Tauberbischofsheim in the State of Bavaria was required to decide whether the tenant of an apartment can demand that his landlord allow him to install a satellite dish on property belonging to the landlord.[41] Under German law, a landlord is required to allow the installation of a satellite dish only if there is no other adequate possibility—for example, through cable—of receiving the normal variety of television programmes.[42] In this case, the tenant was of Turkish origin and wanted to receive Turkish television broadcasts by satellite, which he could not receive by cable or the airwaves. The court found as an important reason to allow the tenant to install the dish the fact that it would provide him with an appropriate source of information.[43] This was based on the tenant's freedom of expression and information under Article 10 of the ECHR.

We can assume that the court applied Article 8 of the Convention rather than Article 5 of the German Constitution, which also guarantees freedom of information, because there was a transnational dimension to the case's set of facts. A Turkish citizen living in Germany wanted to receive television broadcasts from Turkey.

Article 10 of the ECHR and restrictions on attorneys advertising: Article 10 of the ECHR became relevant in connection with cases involving restrictions on advertising for certain professions on the basis of professional codes of conduct.

---

[41] AG Tauberbischofsheim, 8 May 1992 [1992] NJW-RR 1089.

[42] LG Koblenz, 24 June 1991 [1991] NJW-RR 1162; LG Karlsruhe, 11 Apr. 1991 [1991] NJW-RR 1163; LG Arnsberg, 15 Apr. 1991 [1992] NJW-RR 9.

[43] Cf ECtHR, 26 Apr. 1979, *Sunday Times*, Series A 30 [1979] EuGRZ 386.

The Court of Appeal (*Oberlandesgericht*) in Karlsruhe took Article 10 as the yardstick for the admissibility of restrictions on advertising by practising lawyers.[44] Under German law, attorneys are forbidden to advertise. In this case, an attorney had written to certain individuals informing them that he had opened a subsidiary office in a foreign country. Not all of the addressees of the letter were already clients of the attorney. The court held that the restriction on advertising in German law did not violate Article 10 of the ECHR, because paragraph (2) allows certain limitations on the exercise of the freedom of expression. Such limitations are admissible if they are aimed at protecting one of the wide variety of interests listed in Article 10(2) of the Convention.

In the case at hand, the court held that the prohibition on attorneys advertising infringes the attorney's freedom of expression. However, this restriction, in the court's opinion, was justified under Article 10(2) of the Convention. The prohibition on attorneys advertising was supposed to serve an "urgent social need". This "urgent social need" was outweighed neither by the interests of the attorneys immediately subject to the prohibition nor by the interests of society at large.[45]

This decision can be criticised with regard to both the legal reasoning and the result. The court failed to make clear what was the "urgent social need" that mandated the restriction of this fundamental right of attorneys. Moreover, the prohibition on attorneys advertising leads to far-reaching non-transparency for consumers in the market for legal services. Such a prohibition makes it more difficult for potential clients to make an informed choice between attorneys who offer their services, because they lack the necessary information for such a choice. Therefore, like most limitations on the freedom of expression and information, such a prohibition on advertising is more damaging than beneficial.

(b)   *Decisions of the European Court of Human Rights with Respect to German Private Law*

In two cases, the European Court of Human Rights was required to address the relationship between Article 10 of the ECHR and section 1 of the German Act against Unfair Competition. The latter provision makes a person subject to a restraining order and a claim for damages if, in the course of his or her business dealings, he or she commits acts contrary to honest business practices (*gute Sitten*) for the purposes of competition.[46]

In the *Barthold* case,[47] the applicant was a veterinary surgeon in Hamburg, Germany, who ran a veterinary clinic which, like some other clinics but only a

---

[44] Oberlandesgericht (Court of Appeal) (hereinafter OLG) Karlsruhe, 24 June 1992 [1992] Mitteilungen der Bundesrechtsanwaltskammer (Federal Bar Journal) (hereinafter BRAK-Mitt) 226.

[45] *Ibid.*, at 227.

[46] Gesetz gegen unlauteren Wettbewerb of 7 June 1909 [1909] Reichsgesetzblatt (Imperial Gazette) (hereinafter RGBl) 499, as amended.

[47] ECtHR, 25 Mar. 1985, *Barthold*, Series A Nr 90 [1985] GRUR Int 468.

minority of all Hamburg veterinary clinics, offered round-the-clock emergency services. In a newspaper interview, the President of the Hamburg Veterinary Surgeons' Association expressed strong support for the idea of establishing a night emergency service in which all veterinary clinics would take part on a rotational basis. Along with the interview, the newspaper published a photograph of the applicant with his name and the names of the other clinics providing a night service and their telephone numbers for potential clients.

Under the professional rules for veterinary surgeons, members of the profession are not allowed to publish advertisements.

On the basis of a complaint by an agency against unfair competition, the applicant was enjoined from again publishing his photograph and telephone number in connection with the services offered by his clinic. The applicant filed a complaint with the Federal Constitutional Court against the decision of the Hamburg Court of Appeal, which had issued the injunction. The complaint did not meet with success. He then turned to the Commission and the European Court of Human Rights. The Court of Human Rights concluded that the injunction issued against the applicant on the basis of section 1 of the Act against Unfair Competition was in violation of Article 10 of the ECHR.

The infringement by the restraining order of the applicant's freedom of expression went further than necessary for the aims pursued by the restraining provisions. The court acknowledged that the newspaper article had provided the applicant with some publicity, which could contribute to the success of his veterinary clinic. However, the court stressed that the newspaper article had touched upon a subject of interest to the general public. The applicant had presented his viewpoint in a public debate. Such participation in the public discussion of socially relevant topics lies at the very core of Article 10. In the opinion of the court, the fact that he had received some publicity was of only secondary importance. In light of the eminent importance of freedom of expression in a democratic society, the court held that the government bore the burden of providing convincing justification for the necessity to limit this freedom.[48]

The court, however, reached the opposite result in the case of *Markt Intern & Beermann*.[49] In this case, an injunction issued under the German Act against Unfair Competition was under review. The injunction prohibited a commercial news service from publishing certain critical statements about a mail-order company in cosmetics. The unfavourable statements had been true. A client in Germany had ordered cosmetic articles from an English mail-order firm that had guaranteed reimbursement to dissatisfied customers. The client had, indeed, been dissatisfied with the goods and returned them to the mail-order firm, but she was not reimbursed. Markt Intern published the story, raising the question whether this was merely a single incident or part of the general business policy of the mail-order firm. Markt Intern had informed the manager of

---

[48] *Ibid.*, at 471.
[49] ECtHR, 20 Nov. 1989, *Markt Intern Verlag GmbH & Klaus Beermann*, Series A Nr 165.

the mail-order firm of the incident, and the latter had promised to investigate the case. The mail-order firm applied for an order to restrain Markt Intern from repeating the statements. This order was granted on the basis of section 1 of the Act on Unfair Competition. Although the statements made by Markt Intern had not been false, the European Court of Human Rights, in a split decision with the President's vote tipping the balance, held that under certain circumstances the publication of true statements can be prohibited without constituting a violation of Article 10 of the ECHR.[50] The Court held that the facts in the *Markt Intern* case amounted to such circumstances, which justified the limitation. The European Commission of Human Rights, which deliberated the case before it reached the Court, voted 12 to one that Article 10 had been violated.[51]

The Court reasoned that the German restraining order was justified under Article 10(2) of the Convention, because in a democratic society such an order was necessary for protecting the rights of others, in this case the mail-order firm. The Court stated:

> However, even the publication of items which are true and describe real events may under certain circumstances be prohibited: the obligation to respect the privacy of others or the duty to respect the confidentiality of certain commercial information are examples. In addition, a correct statement can be and often is qualified by additional remarks, by value judgments, by suppositions and even insinuations. It must also be recognized that an isolated incident may deserve closer scrutiny before being made public: otherwise an accurate description can give the false impression that the incident is evidence of a general practice . . . The article itself undoubtedly contained some true statements, but it also expressed doubts about the reliability of the Club, and it asked readers to report "similar experiences" at a time when the Club had promised to carry out a prompt investigation of the one reported case.[52]

The Court held that it was within the discretion of Member State courts to decide on the conduct of Markt Intern in the framework of interpreting Article 10 of the ECHR.[53]

In this case the Court's ruling and the outcome are unacceptable. Suppression of the dissemination of true statements is clearly in violation of Article 10 of the ECHR. Furthermore, the manner in which the information was published did not infringe the commercial interests of the criticised firm to the point of justifying a ban on the statements. At several points in its decision, the Court intimated that the statements at issue were made in a commercial context. This reasoning gives the impression that this type of information enjoys a lesser degree of protection under Article 10 than do other types of information. Such a distinction, however, cannot be derived from the wording of Article 10.

---

[50] ECtHR, 20 Nov. 1989, *Markt Intern Verlag GmbH & Klaus Beermann*, Series A Nr 165, at 22.
[51] *Ibid.*, at 43.
[52] *Ibid.*, at 21.
[53] *Ibid.*, at 20 *et seq.*

IV. SOME THOUGHTS ON THE IMPACT OF HUMAN RIGHTS ON PRIVATE
CONTRACTUAL RELATIONS

The areas of German private law that are affected by the ECHR, especially Articles 8 and 10, do not include the branch in which the application of human rights is presumably the most problematic: contract law.[54] It is difficult to determine the exact extent to which human rights can legitimately affect private contractual relations. This problem is created by the obvious tension between the basic principle of freedom of contract, which governs the entire field of contract law, and the obligations that would be rendered by the application of human rights with respect to private parties—for example, equal treatment. The majority of contributions to this conference deal with the problem from the standpoint of common law. It seems to me that there is a considerable amount of support for and willingness to accept the application of human rights in private contractual relations.[55]

There are nonetheless valid reasons against excessively extending the impact of human rights in the framework of contract law. In the German legal system, the problem of the role of the human rights guaranteed under the German Constitution has been the subject of discussion since the 1950s. The courts as well as legal scholars have argued in favour of a certain degree of restraint in applying human rights in contract law. Under the German legal doctrine, the effect of human rights on private law is indirect: it operates through the acts of the legislature and the interpretation of private law statutes by the judiciary. Formally, parties to private legal agreements are not directly bound by the provisions of the Constitution.[56] Moreover, freedom of contract is protected under Article 21 of the Constitution. This right extends in two directions. First, it gives private parties the choice to decide for themselves with whom they want to enter into contractual relations (the freedom to conclude contracts, known as *Vertragsabschlußfreiheit*). Secondly, the parties to a contract are free to determine the contents of their contract (the freedom as to the contents of a contract, known as *Vertragsinhaltsfreiheit*). It certainly does not make any sense to grant individuals free choice under the freedom of contract, yet simultaneously deprive them of that choice by binding them strictly to other constitutional provisions, such as equal treatment, which limit the scope of their choice in concluding contracts. Furthermore, making contracts between private parties strictly bound to uphold human rights would lead to the elimination of freedom of contract as the main functional element of a market economy based on the principle of competition.

---

[54] Cf GG-Komm (H. Dreier), Art. 2 Rz 47; W. Rüfner, *Manual StaatsR* v, § 117 Rz 68 *et seq.*; K. Stern and M. Sachs, *Staatsrecht der Bundesrepublik Deutschland*, III/1, 1595.

[55] See, for example, the discussion of the issue of discrimination and freedom of contract at common law in A. Reichman, *The Common Law of Anti-Discrimination*.

[56] BVerfG, 25 July 1979, 52 BVerfGE 131, 173; W. Rüfner, Manual StaatsR V, § 117 Rz 59.

One also has to take into consideration the fact that basic legal values are not only protected by constitutional law, but are also addressed at the private law level.

Traditionally and functionally, the human rights guaranteed in the constitutions of Western countries are directives to the State in its dealings with the individual. The ascent of and regard for these rights can be traced to the fact that the individual is always the weaker party *vis-à-vis* the State. Accordingly, the function of human rights is to limit the powers of the State in its relations with individuals by granting the latter legal rights that cannot be infringed upon by the State.

However, the problem of asymmetry in the balance of power exists not only in the relationship between the individual and the State, but also in the relationship between private individuals. Freedom of contract enables private individuals to organise their affairs in accordance with their personal wishes and preferences by entering into contractual relations with other individuals. In so far as these relationships are aimed at the transfer of scarce resources, contracts lead to a Pareto-superior allocation of goods. However, contracts can lead to such an allocative improvement only if the preferences of the parties regarding the resources concerned are properly reflected in the contract. If one party to the contract is in the position to force the other (for example, by means of superior economic strength) to enter into the contract even though the latter's interests are not properly represented, the contract does not necessarily lead to a more efficient allocation of resources.

In a system of effective competition, the competitive forces prevent private parties from abusing their power by coercing other parties into entering into contracts and contract terms they do not want or by refusing to conclude contracts with them. Competition works to neutralise the economic power of market actors by preventing individual market participants from influencing the prices of the resources. The only way for market participants to react to a change in prices is to adjust the quantities of supply and demand.

However, the positive effects of competition with regard to allocative efficiency are not achieved if competition fails. The proper functioning of the competitive process is impeded in cases of market failure. Market failure can be caused by monopolistic or market-dominant firms, by external effects, or by asymmetric information between the contracting parties.

This, for instance, is why the German Act against the Restraint of Trade[57] provides in section 20 that market-dominant firms are prohibited from discriminating against potential and actual suppliers and purchasers of goods and services without valid reason. This prohibition on discrimination can lead to a duty being imposed on a market-dominant firm to conclude a contract with a client if the firm has contracted with other clients and there is no reason to treat the client in question any differently from the other contracting parties. Section 22

---

[57] Gesetz gegen Wettbewerbsbeschränkungen, as amended on 26 Aug. 1998 [1998] I BGBl 2546.

of the Act against Restraint of Trade can thus lead to a legal duty to conclude a contract (*Kontrahierungszwang*), thereby extremely limiting freedom of contract. Yet it must be borne in mind that section 20 applies only to market-dominant enterprises. Firms lacking this quality will not be forced to treat their suppliers and customers indiscriminately because it is assumed that the invisible hand of competition will induce them not to discriminate against contracting parties.

The existence of structural imbalances of economic power between potential contracting parties led the Federal Constitutional Court to declare unconstitutional and void a provision of the German Commercial Code allowing principals of commercial agents under certain circumstances to contract for non-competition agreements after the termination of the contract without compensation to the commercial agent.[58] In its reasoning, the Court alluded to the basic precondition of freedom of contract: freedom of contract leads to fair and just results only if there is an "approximate equilibrium of bargaining power" between the contracting parties.[59] If there is a sustained lack of such parity and one of the parties disposes of its constitutionally guaranteed interests, it is the task of the legislature to devise regulations to protect such interests also at the level of contract law. Such an argument, appealing as it may sound, is not without risks. In a dynamic market economy, favourable economic positions of market participants rise and fall as part of the normal process of competition. Judicial or legislative intervention in the market forces on the ground of protecting human rights seems to be justified from the viewpoint of freedom of contract only if a market failure can be shown.

Hence, given the effect of competition in neutralising economic power and the existing protection of human-rights values at the level of statutory private law (for example, civil codes), it seems that the application of human rights in the context of contract law is warranted only in exceptional circumstances. A situation justifying the application of human rights guarantees in contract law arises in the case of market failure. In such a case, the process of competition does not succeed in neutralising economic power.

Apart from market-failure situations, the application of human rights in the framework of contract law necessarily curtails the freedom of choice of the contracting parties. This is why there should be clear, stringent and narrowly tailored prerequisites for the application of human rights in contracts. Under the conditions of free competition, attempts to discriminate will be punished by the market, because potential clients are free to conclude their contracts with competitors of the discriminating party.

---

[58] BVerfG, 7 Feb. 1990 [1990] JZ 691.

[59] *Ibid.* at 692: "*Wo es an einem annähernden Gleichgewicht der Beteiligten fehlt, ist mit den Mitteln des Vertragsrechts allein kein sachgerechter Ausgleich der Interessen zu gewährleisten*". ("Where there is no approximate equilibrium of bargaining power between the parties, the means of contract law alone cannot guarantee an appropriate settlement of the interests involved"— author's translation).

V. CONCLUSIONS

In sum, the influence of Articles 8 and 10 of the ECHR on German private law is rather limited and modest. The main reason for the minor importance of the ECHR for the interpretation and application of German private law is that the German Constitution provides a catalogue of fundamental rights, which are at least equivalent to, if not wider in range than, the rights provided for under the Convention. The Constitution enjoys a higher normative status in the German legal hierarchy than the ECHR and has a more efficient implementation mechanism than the ECHR does. German courts, therefore, normally will determine the constitutionality of private law provisions with respect to fundamental rights by referring to the German Constitution. Only in exceptional cases will they find it necessary to turn to the ECHR.

Situations in which German courts might find it useful to apply Articles 8 and 10 of the ECHR may arise when changes occur in social values that are not yet appropriately reflected in the interpretation of the German Constitution by the Federal Constitutional Court. In the sphere of family law, the judicial organs of the ECHR were, in some respects, faster than the German Federal Constitutional Court to react to the changes in the social values underlying the legal concept of the family, which were the result of the increasing number of unmarried parents living together.

In addition, German courts occasionally apply the ECHR in private law cases involving some foreign element, as in the case of the Turkish citizen living in Germany who sought to install a satellite dish on his landlord's property in order to receive Turkish television broadcasts.

The ECHR has no apparent ascertainable influence in the area of contracts in Germany. In general, the long-established and constitutionally protected freedom of contract implies that the parties to a potential contract have—within the limits of the law—free choice with regard to with whom to conclude a contract and what the contents of that contract will be. The application of human rights in the framework of the law of contracts limits the parties' freedom of contract. Legislative or judicial restrictions on freedom of contract should be allowed only if the neutralising effect of competition with regard to economic power fails. In such a situation, the approximate equilibrium of bargaining powers between the potential contracting partners does not exist. Hence in cases of market failure, judicial or legislative restriction on freedom of contract is justified for protecting human rights.

Part III

Contract and Property Law

9

Freedom of Contract, Human Rights and Human Dignity

ROGER BROWNSWORD

I. INTRODUCTION

IF THE INTENTION underlying the Human Rights Act 1998 (which, broadly speaking, incorporates the European Convention on Human Rights into domestic English law) was to draw a bright line between the public and the private, between public implementation of the Convention rights and private reliance upon them, then the legislation has conspicuously failed to do so.[1] For, there is already a considerable literature debating, not so much whether the Act will have some kind of horizontal application, but just how far the Act will impinge on private proceedings.[2] Generally, it is agreed that the Act will not have a direct horizontal application (so that it will not be possible, for example, to found a tortious action for infringement of privacy by appealing to the Convention right to the protection of private life); hence, on this view, the Convention rights are not to be treated as free-standing private law pegs on which new causes of action can be hung.[3] Rather, the emerging consensus seems to be that the Act will have some degree of indirect horizontal application. What this means is that private law claims will continue to need to be founded on recognised causes of action; however, once a claim is up and running, it must be handled in a way that is compatible with the Act or, giving this a bit more interpretive leeway, in a manner that is compatible with the *values* represented by the

---

[1] See K. Ewing, "The Human Rights Act and Parliamentary Democracy" (1999) 62 *MLR* 79.

[2] See, for example, G. Phillipson, "The Human Rights Act, "Horizontal Effect" and the Common Law: a Bang or a Whimper?" (1999) 62 *MLR* 824; M. Hunt, "The Horizontal Effect of the Human Rights Act" [1998] *PL* 423; A. Lester and D. Pannick, "The Impact of the Human Rights Act on Private Law: the Knight's Move" (2000) 116 *LQR* 380. Lester and Pannick suggest that the application of the Act should be thought of as "more diagonal than directly horizontal. In terms of chess, the judge moves the unwritten law more in the manner of the Knight, that is forward and diagonally, but not directly sideways and horizontally, unlike the Queen or the castle" (*ibid.*, at 383).

[3] But, *contra*, see the position famously taken by Sir William Wade. For Sir William's fourth, and most recent, assertion of strong horizontality, see "Horizons of Horizontality" (2000) 116 *LQR* 217, this being in response to a very restrictive reading of the Act contended for by the Rt. Hon Sir Richard Buxton in "The Human Rights Act and Private Law" (2000) 116 *LQR* 48.

Convention rights.[4] It is in this qualified sense that the Convention rights will have their indirect application.[5]

If we assume that the Act will have such an indirect horizontal application, then it remains moot whether its impact on private law will be marginal or central.[6] In so far as we anticipate that there will be a significant impact, it is probably in the area of torts[7] and perhaps employment contracts,[8] rather than with regard to the general law of contract. However, the thrust of this chapter is that the value of respect for human dignity, which is closely related to the notion of respect for human rights, could have an important (although far from unproblematic) bearing on the way in which we come to understand and apply the principle of freedom of contract in the twenty-first century.[9]

If this proposition sounds somewhat implausible, at any rate to English contract lawyers, the decision of the Supreme Court of Israel in *"Jerusalem Community" Funeral Society* v. *Lionel Aryeh Kestenbaum*[10] should give pause for thought. There, the respondent contracted with the funeral society for his wife's funeral arrangements. According to the respondent, it was his deceased wife's wish that her tombstone should show her name, Gregorian date of birth and Gregorian date of death in Latin characters. However, the funeral society refused to so engrave the tombstone, relying on a term in its standard form of contract to the effect that no letters other than those of the Hebrew alphabet should be engraved on its tombstones. The majority of the Supreme Court held that this term was void on the ground (*inter alia*) that it violated the respondent's right to freedom of expression, conscience *and human dignity*. Whilst the majority saw the preservation of human dignity as a reason for restricting the funeral society's freedom of contract, the minority opinion treated the preservation of the dignity of the cemetery (in the sense of maintaining its traditional character) as an argument in favour of upholding the funeral society's freedom of contract.

---

[4] Following the example of *Retail Wholesale and Department Store Union Local 580* et al. v. *Dolphin Delivery Ltd* (1987) 33 DLR (4th) 174 (a case concerning freedom of expression and association in the context of a secondary picketing dispute). For further details see L. Weinrib and E. Weinrib, chap. 3 this vol. And, generally, on the Canadian experience, see A. Clapham, *Human Rights in the Private Sphere* (Oxford, Clarendon Press, 1993), 164–74.

[5] For the way in which indirect application can operate, see further Justice A. Barak, "Constitutional Human Rights and Private Law" (1996) 3 *Rev. of Const. Stud.* 218. See also A. Barak, chap. 2 this vol.

[6] See Phillipson, *supra* n.2.

[7] Quite apart from the much-debated issue of privacy, there is the question of how deeply Art. 6 will cut into the handling of negligence actions: see L.C.H. Hoyano, "Policing Flawed Police Investigations: Unravelling the Blanket" (1999) 62 *MLR* 912 (for commentary on the *Osman* case at the ECtHR) and, subsequently, *Barrett* v. *London Borough of Enfield* [1999] 3 WLR 79. See also H. Beale and N. Pittam, chap. 7 this vol. and E. McKendrick, chap. 14 this vol.

[8] For a nice example, see Lester and Pannick, *supra* n.2, at 384, where they discuss a French case involving a challenge to a mobility clause in an employment contract.

[9] Cf Clapham, *supra* n.4, for the suggestion that the complementary values of democracy and dignity "are the tools with which to analyse human rights in the private sphere", at 145.

[10] CA 294/91, 46 (2) PD 464 (Hebrew).

The argument in this chapter is in four parts. In the first section of the chapter, it is suggested that the principle of freedom of contract (as embedded in the institution of contract law) should not be thought of as a licence to contract with whomsoever one wishes on whatever terms one wills. Rather, it is a principle enjoining regulatory restraint in relation to transactional freedom. So interpreted, the principle holds that, in the absence of "good reasons", contractual freedom should not be restricted. And, where a legal system is committed to respect for human rights, as we must assume is now the case with the English legal system, it follows that the values represented by those rights must be incorporated into the body of "good reasons" on the basis of which contractual freedom may be legitimately restricted.

The second section of the chapter opens with two questions: first, whether liberty of contract must itself be understood as a species of human right; and, secondly, whether the particular Convention rights incorporated by the Human Rights Act will have much scope for restricting freedom of contract. It is suggested that either or both questions might prompt the thought that the broader implications of the Act can be drawn out by focusing on the principle of respect for human dignity (which, it would be widely accepted, is immanent in any human rights instrument). With human dignity explicitly in play, it is arguable that freedom of contract is a particular expression of the (dignity-based) human right to individual autonomy but equally that there are good reasons (i.e., dignity-driven reasons) for restricting contractual freedom—for example, many see human dignity as being compromised if the law recognises commerce in human body parts and human tissue (particularly where this is coupled with a liberal law of intellectual property that permits the patenting of human gene sequences);[11] and, in a similar way, some might argue that there is a lack of respect for human dignity if the law permits genetic profiles to be used by contractors (especially by insurers and employers) to select their co-contractors.

The third section of the chapter sketches two conceptions of human dignity, human dignity as empowerment and human dignity as constraint. According to the first conception, it is because humans have a distinctive value (their intrinsic dignity) that they have rights *qua* humans. Commonly, it is the capacity for autonomous action that is equated with human dignity and this, in turn, generates a regime of human rights organised around the protection of individual autonomy. In this way, respect for human dignity empowers individuals by protecting their choices against the unwilled interferences of others (rather in the way that the majority responded to the appeal in the *"Jerusalem Community" Funeral Society* case). By contrast, the second conception presents human dignity as a value that stands over and above individual choice and consent (somewhat

---

[11] See, further, D. Beyleveld, R. Brownsword and M. Llewelyn, "The Morality Clauses of the Directive on the Legal Protection of Biotechnological Inventions: Conflict, Compromise, and the Patent Community" in J. Lonbay and R. Goldberg (eds.), *European Health Care: Intellectual Property, Product Liability, Regulatory and Professional Dimensions* (Cambridge, Cambridge University Press, 2000), 157.

akin to the minority approach in the same case, at least, if we read the minority as implying that respect for dignity itself restricted the funeral society's freedom to agree to the non-Hebrew inscription on the tombstone). Individual (and joint) autonomy is thus constrained—actions, no matter how free, that compromise human dignity (whether the dignity of the acting individual or dignity as recognised by the community at large) are simply off limits.

In the fourth section of the chapter, the logic of these rival conceptions of human dignity is applied to the regulation of contracts. Whereas human dignity as empowerment serves to reinforce the idea that freedom of contract is itself a fundamental right (but which must be operated in a way that is consistent with respect for the human rights of others), human dignity as constraint adds to the list of "good reasons" (by reference to which contractual freedom may be restricted) a certain vision of respect for human dignity that goes beyond restraining unwilled interferences by others. It is suggested that, even if (exceptionally) these two conceptions might run along parallel tracks to condemn genetic discrimination, by and large they are on a collision course with one another relative to the freedom of contractors to pursue their own plans and projects, and to determine their own risks.

What conclusion should we draw from this discussion? It is that, sooner or later, contract lawyers will surely discover that a principle of respect for human dignity can plausibly be read into the Human Rights Act; that, when they do so, it will not be long before the rival conceptions of the principle find their articulation in the common law; and that a move that might have been made with a view to strengthening respect for human rights might invite a reaction that limits the autonomy of contractors. Tension is not new to contract law, but whether we welcome the prospect of this new friction depends largely on whether we are on the side of empowerment or that of constraint.

II. FREEDOM OF CONTRACT [12]

According to the standard account,[13] it was axiomatic within the classical law of contract that parties should enjoy freedom of contract—that, as Sir George Jessel MR famously put it in *Printing and Numerical Registering Co* v. *Sampson*,[14] "men of full age and competent understanding [should] have the utmost liberty of contracting, and . . . their contracts when entered into freely and voluntarily [should] be held sacred and [should] be enforced by Courts of justice". However, with the development of mass consumer markets, standard form dealing, and carefully crafted exclusion clauses, freedom of contract was virtually written out of the modern script (or so it is commonly said).

---

[12] The analysis in this section draws on R Brownsword, "Freedom of Contract" in the American Bar Association's *Common Law, Common Values, Common Rights* (ABA and West Group, St. Paul, Minn., 2000), 135.

[13] P.S. Atiyah, *The Rise and Fall of Freedom of Contract* (Oxford, Clarendon Press, 1979).

[14] (1879) LR 19 Eq. 462, 465.

Yet, is it true that the principle of freedom of contract has been consigned to history? In Sir George Jessel's articulation of the idea, freedom of contract is best understood as calling for a two-pronged form of legislative and judicial restraint. First, if parties are to have "the utmost liberty of contracting", it follows that legislatures and courts should be slow to limit the kinds of transactions, or the kinds of terms, that the parties can agree upon within the domain of contract. (Similarly, it might be said that "the utmost liberty of contracting" implies a freedom *not* to contract, and a freedom to choose one's contracting partners). Secondly, where agreements have been freely made, the temptation to release parties from hard bargains should be resisted; excusing conditions should be given only limited recognition and applied sparingly, for even well-meaning paternalism betrays a lack of respect for the ideal of "sanctity of contract". So understood, these cornerstones of the classical law seem to be well-inspired.[15] After all, if contract is to function as a vehicle through which autonomy and rational planning can be simultaneously promoted, through which private ordering and risk-allocation can be facilitated, then freedom of contract coupled with sanctity of contract is surely an enduring regulatory ideal.

It would be implausible to read the idea that parties should be protected against legislative and judicial intervention in setting their contractual terms as a prescription for licence. The activities of contractors must be subject to whatever restrictions are necessary for the protection of the legitimate interests of third parties or the public interest. More plausibly, then, freedom of contract holds that parties should be permitted to make their own bargains, to set their own terms, unless there is "a good reason" for non-enforcement or even prohibition. In principle, such alleged good reasons might be based on one or more of the following three grounds: (i) that the terms (or the general purpose of the contract) are harmful to the protected interests of third parties; (ii) that the terms (or the general purpose of the contract) are harmful to the public interest;[16] and (iii) that the transaction is harmful to the interests of one or both of the contracting parties.

Clearly, the background philosophy of the particular legal order in which freedom of contract is so recognised matters a great deal to the way in which the category of good reasons is understood and applied. Historically, freedom of contract tends to be associated with an ideology of robust individualism coupled with Benthamite utilitarianism.[17] Where such a background philosophy obtains, the *raison d'être* of allowing the parties freedom to set their own terms will be that such an approach (favouring private ordering over public allocation) is expected to maximise utility (or wealth); and, where freedom is restricted, the good reasons supporting the restriction will involve calculations

---

[15] Cf, for example, Lord Diplock, echoing Sir George Jessel's remarks, in *Federal Commerce and Navigation Co Ltd* v. *Tradax Export SA (The Maratha Envoy)* [1978] AC 1, 8.

[16] Cf Lord Atkin in *Fender* v. *St John Mildmay* [1938] AC 1, 12.

[17] Although, for a more complex history, see H.N. Scheiber (ed.), *The State and Freedom of Contract* (Stanford, Cal., Stanford University Press, 1998).

of disutilities (or wealth losses) occasioned by freedom of contract. Where, however, a legal system takes human rights seriously then freedom of contract will need to be operated in a way that is compatible with respect for the rights of both the contractors and third parties. On the one side, if the contractors' freedom is itself seen as an aspect of a protected right to individual autonomy, then it should not be abridged for simple utilitarian considerations (which will entail a restricted reading of public interest limiting reasons); on the other side, if the contractors' actions threaten the human rights of third parties, this will be a good reason for restricting freedom of contract.

Allowing that it will rarely be the case that we can neatly package a community's background morality within an established school of thinking (whether of a utilitarian or rights kind), we can at least say that, *where freedom of contract is taken seriously*, it will certainly not count as a *sufficient* reason for intervention that the transaction is judged to be harmful to the interests of either or both of the contracting parties and, at strongest (where the contractors' autonomy rights trump other considerations), harm to such interests will not count as a good reason at all. Thus, where commitment to freedom of contract is at its strongest (as in mainstream liberal-rights thinking), it is not a good reason for (negative) interference that others would prefer the contractors not so to transact—as it has been said on countless occasions, the price of liberty (and liberty of contract is like any other life-style liberty in this respect) is that the mere preferences of the majority must give way to the preferences of the contracting parties.[18]

Turning to the linked idea of sanctity of contract, the modern law of contract (in contrast with the classical law) has taken a harder look at the all-important predicate that the agreement has been freely made. Certainly, parties should be held to their agreements; contracts should be enforced; no one doubts the wisdom of *pacta sunt servanda*, but only where the agreement was freely made, only where the parties dealt on an informed consent basis.

Looking back at the supposed decline of freedom of contract in the modern law, we can see that the strategy of much modern regulation is to ensure that contractors understand the terms of the agreement and have a degree of choice about whether to proceed, rather than to declare terms void and unenforceable. In other words, one of the tendencies of the modern law has been to regulate the bargaining process without directly regulating the bargain itself. Even in the case of the Unfair Contract Terms Act 1977 which many commentators would point to as the best evidence of the decline of freedom of contract in the modern English law whilst some types of exclusionary provisions are declared to be (in effect) void, much of the Act is concerned with subjecting questionable provisions to a test of reasonableness which, in turn, is largely a matter of confirming (or disconfirming) the integrity of the particular bargaining situation. A good

---

[18] See, for example, R. Dworkin, *Taking Rights Seriously* (London, Duckworth, 1978); M.J. Trebilcock, *The Limits of Freedom of Contract* (Cambridge, Mass., Harvard University Press, 1993).

deal of the modern law, then, does not involve any kind of challenge to freedom of contract; rather it is concerned with ensuring that terms are transparent and the product of' genuine negotiation—in short, its concern is with whether the parties came to terms on a free and informed basis.

In a similar way, modern legislation restricting a contractor's right to discriminate on racial or sexual grounds can be seen as compatible with freedom of contract. Indeed, in the neatest case, it is eminently arguable that the deep rights theory on which freedom of contract itself rests actually *requires* such legislative restrictions because the discrimination otherwise permitted violates rights protected by the same deep theory.

Just as the idea of a "good reason" (as a limit on freedom of contract) will draw its substance from a particular background politico-moral theory, so the idea that contracting should be free and informed is open to interpretation. The expansion of the idea of economic duress in English law coupled with an unwillingness to adopt a general doctrine of inequality of bargaining power tells us something about the difficulties of deciding where coercion and unfair pressure ends and freedom begins.[19] Similarly, the idea of an *informed* consent is problematic. The tightening up of the classical reasonable notice test draws no clear line between terms that are perceived to be usual and those that are judged unusual; in the context of non-disclosure, the line between material and immaterial facts cannot be drawn in a clear-cut way; and, in all cases, how far must one party go to bring the terms home to the other side?

With the enactment of the Human Rights Act, we can certainly say that the background morality against which the English law of contract operates has taken an explicit tilt towards acceptance of human rights. At minimum, the courts must ensure that the common law is compatible with the Convention rights, and this must surely mean that any infringement of these rights counts as a good reason for restricting freedom of contract. Whether this adjustment to the background morality requires a reconceptualisation of the basis on which contractual freedom itself rests, as whether the Convention rights will have a significant purchase on contractual freedom, are questions to which we turn in the next section.

III. INTENSIFYING THE IMPACT OF HUMAN RIGHTS

Following the implementation of the Human Rights Act, it will be arguable that contractual provisions should be interpreted in a way that renders them compatible with the Convention rights[20] and that contracts that cannot be so interpreted will be unenforceable as contrary to public policy. Nevertheless, we may

---

[19] Seminally, see D. Kennedy, "Distributive and Paternalist Motives in Contract and Tort Law, with Special Reference to Compulsory Terms and Unequal Bargaining Power" (1982) 41 *MLR* 563.

[20] For a helpful discussion, see A. van Aswegen, "The Implications of a Bill of Rights for the Law of Contract and Delict" (1995) 11 *S Afr. J Hum. Rts.* 50.

speculate that contracts will only occasionally fall foul of the Convention rights and that, by and large, contractual business will continue much as usual. If we think such thoughts, then we may ponder whether we are drawing down the full value of the legislation. In particular, we may wonder whether the spirit, if not the letter, of the newly incorporated human rights supports the idea that liberty of contract is itself a fundamental human right and whether we can give the rights a stronger purchase on (for want of a better term) those several forms of "biocommerce" that now trouble many Europeans. In both cases, we may come to think that human dignity is the resource that we need in order to intensify and broaden the impact of the Act in relation to freedom of contract.

Before we press ahead with this thought, however, we should pause: after all, neither the European Convention on Human Rights nor the Human Rights Act explicitly mentions human dignity, so what basis is there for treating human dignity as an unstated element in the new code? Whilst we may accept that a number of the Convention rights, particularly the right not to suffer torture, inhuman, or degrading treatment, and the right not to be held in servitude, imply that there is a right not to be demeaned, degraded or denied one's dignity, we may still wonder whether human dignity has a deeper or more general connection with human rights. The short answer is that the Convention copies across for Europe the principles agreed in the Universal Declaration of Human Rights 1948 (which, together with the International Covenant on Economic, Social and Cultural Rights 1966, and the International Covenant on Civil and Political Rights 1966, comprises the so-called "International Bill of Rights"), in which human dignity is explicitly declared to be one of the foundational ideas. Thus, the Preamble to each instrument provides that "recognition of the inherent dignity and of the equal and inalienable rights of all members of the human family is the foundation of freedom, justice and peace in the world"; and Article 1 of the Universal Declaration famously proclaims that "[a]ll human beings are born free and equal in dignity and rights". What this seminal cluster of preambular ideas amounts to is this: that each and every human being has inherent dignity; that it is this *inherent* dignity that grounds (or accounts for) the possession of *inalienable* human rights; and that, because all humans have dignity, they hold rights equally. So understood, human dignity is much more than a background implication that we can tease out of a number of particular rights, it is the infrastructure on which the entire superstructure of human rights is constructed. Accordingly, unless one stands on an extreme literalism, it is difficult to resist the proposition that respect for human dignity is the implicit foundation of the Human Rights Act.[21]

Having so linked human rights and human dignity, the next question is whether the latter can assist us in characterising liberty of contract as an example of the former. This invites another short answer because there is a relatively

---

[21] See Clapham, *supra* n.4, at 143, n.22, for examples of the recurrent use of human dignity in international human rights declarations, covenants, conventions and resolutions.

familiar and widely accepted chain of thinking, linking human dignity with a right to individual autonomy that, in turn, expresses itself through the exercise of contractual freedom. Indeed, we can trace this idea in nineteenth-century America where the proponents of the "free labour" ideology in the northern states were fond of contrasting "the dignity and vitality of the free white workers" with "the laboring man's poverty, degradation, and lack of opportunity for advancement in the South".[22] On this view, respect for human dignity and freedom of contract forms a virtuous circle: without at least the right to make our own contracts, we lack dignity (being reduced to a mere status); with such a right, we recover our human dignity.

If we accept that contractors, in choosing their partners and agreeing their terms, are exercising a human right (an aspect of the right to autonomy), then two matters invite further consideration. First, as a human right, liberty of contract must have at least some exclusionary force which, of course, harks back to the classic articulation of freedom of contract as a liberty with which we should not lightly interfere. Quite how much exclusionary force this right has remains moot. Nevertheless, if we are to take the right at all seriously, then we must give it priority over the mere preferences of others and the opinion of others that the right is exercised in ways that are judged (by others) to be immoral. Secondly, if we presuppose a will theory, rather than an interest theory, of human rights, then it must be open to contractors to waive the benefit of their right to freedom of contract. This seems perfectly plausible—that is, it seems plausible that contractors should be entitled to agree to restrict both their liberty to contract with others and their liberty to contract on particular terms. What emerges indirectly from this point, however, is the more important general matter of whether the Convention rights should be read under a will theory or an interest theory. For, if they were to be read under a will theory, there would be at least three important consequences. First, in principle, the benefit of otherwise protected rights could be freely waived. Secondly, by virtue of exercising a contractual right, a contractor could agree to give up the benefit of a right (although not the right itself) that would otherwise be protected. For example, by contract, one might waive the benefit of what would otherwise be a protected right to family life or freedom of expression. Thirdly, where argument centred on whether a particular right should yield, the initial inquiry would be into whether or not the benefit of the right at issue had been waived, not into balancing competing interests. For example, in a dispute between contractors about the effect of a confidentiality clause, the initial inquiry would be into whether the benefit of the right of freedom of expression had been waived rather than into weighing the competing interests of the parties and, if the benefit had been waived, that would be the end of the matter.[23] Whether this is the correct reading of the Convention rights

[22] See C.W. McCurdy, "The 'Liberty of Contract' Regime" in H.N. Scheiber (ed.), *The State and Freedom of Contract* (Stanford, Cal., Stanford University Press, 1998), 161, 168.

[23] Compare *Attorney General* v. *Barker* [1990] 3 All ER 257, especially Lord Donaldson MR's emphasis on the importance of sanctity of contract at 261.

is a large issue which cannot be pursued here. However, to avoid any mis-understanding, it should be emphasised that, if citizens are free to contract away the benefit of their Convention rights, it is not so much because they have free-dom of contract or that liberty of contract is itself a human right but that the Convention rights fall under a will theory of rights.[24]

So far, so good. However, we may see another way of importing human dig-nity into the Human Rights Act. For, even if the Council of Europe drafted the European Convention on Human Rights without explicitly relying on the notion of human dignity, it has conspicuously changed its practice in the recent Convention on Human Rights and Biomedicine 1996.[25] There, in the Preamble, we find the signatories resolving "to take such measures as are necessary to safe-guard human dignity and the fundamental rights and freedoms of the individual with regard to the application of biology and medicine"; Article 1 provides that the parties "shall protect the dignity and identity of all human beings"; and the Explanatory Report accompanying the Convention emphasises that "human dignity . . . constitutes the essential value to be upheld . . . [and] is at the basis of most of the values emphasized in the Convention".[26] For present purposes, it is Article 21 of the Convention that is of most direct interest. According to this Article:

> The human body and its parts shall not, as such, give rise to financial gain.

In so prohibiting such commerce, the intention is that "body parts" should apply to "organs and tissues proper, including blood"[27] but not to products such as "hair and nails, which are discarded tissues, and the sale of which is not an affront to human dignity".[28] If the idea of respect for human dignity can be read into the Human Rights Act, it is at least arguable that it constitutes a "good rea-son" for restraining certain forms of biocommerce and the Convention on Human Rights and Biomedicine clearly signals a European view that freedom of contract should be so limited.

If we open up the Human Rights Act to the influence of respect for human dig-nity, there is one other question that we may anticipate. Just as legislation was introduced in England to regulate contractual discrimination on the grounds of race or sex, so too we may duly expect legislation to regulate the possibility of genetic discrimination in contractual practice. Pending the introduction of

---

[24] For an excellent general discussion, see A. McHarg, "Reconciling Human Rights and the Public Interest: Conceptual Problems and Doctrinal Uncertainty in the Jurisprudence of the European Court of Human Rights' (1999) 62 *MLR* 671.

[25] Council of Europe, *Convention for the Protection of Human Rights and Dignity of the Human Being with regard to the Application of Biology and Medicine: Convention on Human Rights and Biomedicine* (DIR/JUR (96) 14) (Strasbourg, Directorate of Legal Affairs, Nov. 1996).

[26] Council of Europe, *Explanatory Report to the Convention for the Protection of Human Rights and Dignity of the Human Being with regard to the Application of Biology and Medicine: Convention on Human Rights and Biomedicine* (DIR/JUR (97) 1) (Strasbourg, Directorate of Legal Affairs, Jan. 1997) para. 9.

[27] *Ibid.*, at para. 132.

[28] *Ibid.*, at para. 133.

dedicated legislation, however, may the common law respond to abuse of the freedom not to contract by developing a protective strategy based on the notion of respect for human dignity? This is a question to which we will return shortly. Before doing so, though, we need to sharpen our appreciation of the two principal conceptions of human dignity that are already implicit in our discussion.

Two conceptions of human dignity

Human dignity is an elusive concept, used in many senses by moral and political philosophers.[29] In modern debates, however, it regularly appears in two very different roles, in one case acting in support of individual autonomy (human dignity as empowerment) and, in the other case, acting as a constraint on autonomy (human dignity as constraint). Human dignity, as David Feldman has rightly observed, can thus cut both ways:

> [W]e must not assume that the idea of dignity is inextricably linked to a liberal-individualist view of human beings as people whose life-choices deserve respect. If the State takes a particular view on what is required for people to live dignified lives, it may introduce regulations to restrict the freedom which people have to make choices which, in the State's view, interfere with the dignity of the individual, a social group or the human race as a whole . . . The quest for human dignity may subvert rather than enhance choice . . . Once it becomes a tool in the hands of lawmakers and judges, the concept of human dignity is a two-edged sword.[30]

Both interpretations—human dignity as empowerment and human dignity as constraint—can claim to be anchored in the seminal writing of Immanuel Kant. For, in Kant's work, we find not only the idea that humans have intrinsic dignity (which suggests a conception of human dignity as empowerment, albeit duty-driven rather than rights-driven[31]) but also that human dignity has no price and that humans owe themselves a duty of self-esteem (which may suggest a conception of human dignity as constraint). In *The Metaphysics of Morals*, Kant collects together the strands of his thinking as follows:

> Every human being has a legitimate claim to respect from his fellow human beings and is *in turn* bound to respect every other. Humanity itself is a dignity; for a human being cannot be used merely as a means by any human being . . . but must always be used at the same time as an end. It is just in this that his dignity (personality) consists, by which he raises himself above all other beings in the world that are not human beings and yet can be used, and so over all *things*. But just as he cannot give himself away for

---

[29] See R. Dworkin, *Life's Dominion* (London, Harper Collins, 1993), especially at 233–7.

[30] D. Feldman, "Human Dignity as a Legal Value: Part I" [1999] *PL* 682, 685.

[31] For the significance of this distinction, see D. Beyleveld and R. Brownsword, "Human Dignity, Human Rights, and Human Genetics' in R. Brownsword, W.R. Cornish and M. Llewelyn (eds.), *Human Genetics and the Law: Regulating a Revolution* (Oxford, Hart Publishing, 1998), 69. Cf. also the two aspects of public policy, the one based on freedom of contract which thus justifies the enforcement of contracts and the other which serves as grounds for limiting freedom of contract. See G. Williams, "Language and the Law" (1946) 62 *LQR* 387, 399.

any price (this would conflict with his duty of self-esteem), so neither can he act contrary to the equally necessary self-esteem of others, as human beings, that is, he is under obligation to acknowledge, in a practical way, the dignity of humanity in every other human being. Hence there rests on him a duty regarding the respect that must be shown to every other human being.[32]

In these much-quoted remarks, modern writers can (and do purport to) find support for a variety of supposed applications of Kantian morality, not just in practical matters generally but specifically within the field of biocommerce.[33] For Kant's remarks, if taken literally, are an open invitation to claim that commercialisation of the human body is an affront to dignity (by putting a price on something that is beyond price). Thus, for example, we find distinct echoes of Kantian thinking in the famous French dwarf-throwing (*"lancer de nain"*) case,[34] which provides a vivid illustration of the tension between human dignity as empowerment and human dignity as constraint.

In this case, the Conseil d'Etat, having affirmed that respect for human dignity was one of the constituents of *ordre public*, confirmed a municipal police power to prohibit any spectacle that represented a threat to such respect. Accordingly, it was held that, where police powers had been exercised in Morsang-sur-Orge and Aix-en-Provence to ban the attraction of dwarf-throwing in local clubs, such steps were lawfully taken in order to secure respect for human dignity and *ordre public*. However, the legality of the bans was challenged by, among others, one of the dwarfs, who argued that he freely participated in the activity, that the work brought him a monthly wage (as well as allowing him to move in professional circles) and that, if dwarf-throwing was banned, he would find himself unemployed again. To this, the Conseil d'Etat responded that the dwarf compromised his own dignity by allowing himself to be used as a projectile, as a mere thing, and that no such concession could be allowed.[35]

On the one side, the dwarfs were relying on the conception of human dignity as empowerment. For the dwarfs, the central issue was whether others were acting against their (the dwarfs') dignity. Their argument was that they were *not* being treated as mere things; others were not disregarding their capacity to control the situation. It was only to the extent that the dwarfs freely chose to participate that the activities took place. Moreover, from the dwarfs' viewpoint, to be deprived of their status as employed persons was to undermine the

[32] I. Kant, *The Metaphysics of Morals* (M. Gregor trans. and ed., Cambridge, Cambridge University Press, 1996) (first published 1797), 209.

[33] See, for example, W. Wolbert, "The Kantian Formula of Human Dignity and its Implications for Bioethics" (1998) 4 *Hum. Reproduction & Genetic Ethics* 18.

[34] Conseil d'Etat (27 Oct. 1995) req. nos. 136–727 (Commune de Morsang-sur-Orge) and 143–578 (Ville d'Aix-en-Provence).

[35] See M.C. Roualt's note on the two decisions, *Les Petites Affiches* (24 Jan. 1996, No. 11) 30, 32. And, for reflections on the case, with dignity being interpreted as the essence of humanity, see B. Edelman, "La Dignité de la Personne Humaine, un Concept Nouveau" [1997] *Recueil Dalloz* 23e Cahier, Chronique, 185, 187–8.

conditions in which they experienced a sense of their own dignity. So interpreted, it was the well-meaning paternalism of the Conseil, rather than the actions of the dwarf-throwers, that represented a threat to the dignity of the dwarfs.[36]

On the other side, the Conseil d'Etat was operating with a conception of human dignity as constraint. Central to this conception is the idea that the dwarfs might compromise *their own* dignity and/or, with that, the dignity of fellow humans as understood in contemporary France. This is the idea of human dignity as an overriding value (whether grounded in individual humans or in groups of humans), a value to be respected by all members of human society. On this view, the fact that the dwarf-throwers did not intend to demean or degrade the dwarfs, or that the dwarfs freely consented to their participation, is immaterial: *ordre public* (including respect for human dignity) sets limits to autonomy—certain expressions of free choice are, quite simply, out of bounds. As for undermining the conditions in which the dwarfs recovered a sense of self-esteem, presumably the Conseil judged that this must be a case of false consciousness; for, surely, no genuine sense of self-esteem could be derived from participation in dwarf-throwing when the activity could not stand alongside respect for human dignity.

With these two conceptions of human dignity in competition with one another, we can return to the question of how the principle of freedom of contract may be affected by the Human Rights Act when the legislation is read through the lens of human dignity.

IV. HUMAN DIGNITY AND FREEDOM OF CONTRACT

The emphasis of freedom of contract, we have suggested, is on the necessity of having "good reasons" for interference. If we practise what we preach, contractors will enjoy freedom in two spheres, in relation to their choice of purposes and terms (term freedom) and in relation to their choice of co-contractors (partner freedom). In this section, we can, first, follow through the logic of the two conceptions of human dignity in relation to term freedom and then we can consider how they bear on genetic discrimination as an issue within the sphere of partner freedom.

Term freedom

With regard to term freedom, the logic of human dignity as empowerment is fairly straightforward. Contractors, evincing their human dignity, are to make

---

[36] For a rather different concern with the conditions in which human dignity may be realised (in the context of housing provision), see the decision of the Conseil Constitutionnel No 94–359 (19 Jan. 1995) [1995] JORF 1166.

their own free choices and (other things being equal) those choices must be respected, otherwise there is a failure to respect human dignity. In the field of biocommerce, some might disapprove of surrogacy contracts, or of contracts for the sale of organs and human tissue,[37] but human dignity as empowerment argues in favour of enforcing these transactions provided that they are freely made. Clearly, the prerequisite of informed consent is an important proviso: human dignity as empowerment is a licence for the exercise of autonomy, not for exploitation or abuse of human rights.[38]

By contrast, the logic of human dignity as constraint is that even free transactions must be checked for compatibility with respect for human dignity. In other words, informed consent is a necessary but not a sufficient condition for contractual enforcement. As we have seen, Article 21 of the Convention on Human Rights and Biomedicine relies on respect for human dignity in order to prohibit financial gain from commerce in the human body or body parts. And, a decade prior to this, the Warnock Committee in England noted that some opposition to surrogacy was based on the ground that "it is inconsistent with human dignity that a woman should use her uterus for financial profit and treat it as an incubator for someone else's child".[39] Such constraints may be traced back to the Kantian duty of self-esteem or to the idea that human dignity has no price; or, the constraint may rest simply on the vision of human dignity that is taken to define one's community as the particular community that it is. As we have said, human dignity as constraint is seriously at odds with human dignity as empowerment, not least because its communitarian reading implies that it is culture rather than commerce, common values rather than common markets, that bind societies together.

Returning once more to the *"Jerusalem Community" Funeral Society* case,[40] we may see the minority opinion as relying on dignity in order to support the stance taken by the society, not so much as a matter of free choice, but more in the way of a constrained respect for Jewish culture, the Hebrew language, and

[37] In the famous case of *Moore* v. *Regents of the University of California* (1990) 271 Cal. Rptr. 146, (1990) 793 P. 2d 479; cert. denied (1991) 111 S Ct. 1388, John Moore was unaware of the commercial intentions of the doctors. However, had he known what was proposed by the doctors, and had he then contracted for the sale of his tissue, or for a share of the profits flowing from the commercial exploitation of the cell-line, would some want to condemn such an agreement as compromising human dignity? For an excellent discussion and critique of the Moore case, see J. Boyle, *Shamans, Software, and Spleens* (Cambridge, Mass., Harvard University Press, 1996), especially at 21–4, 99–107.
[38] In the context of a surrogacy contract, the majority judgment of Panelli J in *Johnson* v. *Calvert* (1993) 851 P 2d 776 (Cal SC) nicely illustrates a concern that the parties should enter such an agreement on an informed and free basis.
[39] *Report of the Committee of Inquiry into Human Fertilisation and Embryology* (London, HMSO, 1984), para 8, 10. In the UK, no surrogacy arrangement is enforceable as a contract by or against any of the parties, see s. 1A of the Surrogacy Arrangements Act 1985 (inserted by s. 36 of the Human Fertilisation and Embryology Act 1990). Generally, for discussion of the legal position, see, for example, J.K. Mason and R.A. McCall Smith, *Law and Medical Ethics* (5th edn., London, Butterworths, 1999), 77–85.
[40] *Supra* n.10.

the identifying characteristics of the local community. On the other side, the majority clearly relies on human dignity to prioritise freedom of choice over the cultural context (or, possibly, to redefine that context so as to privilege individual choice on this matter). Thus, had the contractors agreed that the tombstone should be engraved in accordance with the wishes of the deceased, it seems clear that the majority would have supported that agreement, the dignity of the cemetery notwithstanding. In the absence of such agreement, however, what remains to be explained is why, in the name of human dignity, the respondent should be empowered at the expense of the appellant.

Before we move on to partner freedom, it is as well to underline just how deeply human dignity as constraint threatens to cut into the principle of freedom of contract. Potentially, our understanding of a "good reason" for restricting contractual freedom is modified in two ways. First, contracts that are judged to involve a compromise with the contractor's own dignity may be regulated; and, secondly, contracts that are judged to compromise the community's vision of respect for human dignity may also be regulated. Contractors are no longer free to assess what is in their own interest; and, by adding respect for human dignity to the category of public policy, the community takes control of what is good for contractors and for society at large. For those who think that recognition of human dignity leads directly to a fortified respect for contractual autonomy, there is reason to think again.[41]

Genetic discrimination and partner freedom

Article 11 of the Convention on Human Rights and Biomedicine, reflecting widespread concern about the potentially exclusionary effects of genetic discrimination, prohibits "any form of discrimination against a person on grounds of his or her genetic heritage". As is well known, particular concern has been expressed about the possibility of one's genetic profile being a required part of one's curriculum vitae which will then lead to bad genetic risks being excluded from contracts, particularly by insurers and employers.[42] Last year, for instance, it was reported that President Clinton had barred American Federal government agencies from discriminating against employees on the basis of genetic tests.[43] Moreover, the President gave his backing to a Senate Bill designed to extend similar protection to the private sector and

---

[41] For instance, for those who think that an appeal to human dignity may strengthen the right to make enforceable surrogacy agreements, it may actually have the opposite effect (by strengthening the public policy restrictions on freedom of contract).

[42] See, for example, *Nuffield Council on Bioethics, Genetic Screening: Ethical Issues* (London, Nuffield Council on Bioethics, 1993), chaps. 6, 7; P. Gannon and C. Villiers, "Genetic Testing and Employee Protection" (1999) 4 *Med. L. Int.* 39; and the issue has been revisited by the UK Human Genetics Commission in section 9 of its discussion document, *Whose Hands on your Genes?* (London, Nov. 2000).

[43] See report in *The Guardian*, 9 Feb. 2000, 14.

insurance purchasers. If such a scenario of adverse selection were to material-ise, the practice of declining bad risks might be defended under the rubric of freedom of contract. The question is whether the Human Rights Act, with or without the aid of human dignity, would have any purchase on such exercises in partner freedom.

A natural starting point seems to be the provision in Article 14 of the Convention that the Convention rights and freedoms are to be secured without discrimination on any ground, including the standard grounds of sex, race, colour, language, religion, political opinion or the like. Although the Convention does not specifically identify genetic discrimination as a prohibited ground, it is eminently arguable that such a ground could be read as within the ambit of Article 14. For instance (and in addition to Article 11 of the Convention on Human Rights and Biomedicine), one might cite in support of this view Article 2 of the Universal Declaration of Human Rights, which articulates a broad principle of non-discrimination. This may then be tied to Article 2 of the UNESCO Universal Declaration on the Human Genome and Human Rights,[44] according to which:

(a) Everyone has a right to respect for their dignity and for their rights regardless of their genetic characteristics.

(b) That dignity makes it imperative not to reduce individuals to their genetic char-acteristics and to respect their uniqueness and diversity.

Commenting on this Article, Hectór Gros Espiell, the Chairman of the Legal Commission of UNESCO's International Bioethics Committee, has said:

Article 2 of the Declaration asserts that the genetic characteristics of the person can in no way justify limits on the recognition of his or her dignity or the exercise of his or her rights. This is a fundamental principle whose corollary is the prohibition of all dis-crimination based on genetic characteristics [see Article 6 which prohibits "discrimi-nation based on genetic characteristics" such as would infringe human dignity]. This article is derived from Article 2 of the Universal Declaration of Human Rights . . . and adds the genetic criterion to it.

Many other instruments adopted by UNESCO also refer to this principle of non-discrimination . . . In taking the dignity of the human person as its reference, the Declaration seeks above all to condemn any attempt to draw political or social inferences from a purported distinction between "good" genes and "bad" genes.[45]

At the very least, then, it is arguable that a principle of non-discrimination (including genetic discrimination) protects the implementation of the Convention rights.

Now, if one of the Convention rights provided that there was a right to insist upon a contract of employment, or a contract of insurance, or whatever, there

---

[44] This Declaration was adopted in Nov. 1997 and, on 9 Dec. 1998, the UNGA adopted Resolution A/RES/53/152 endorsing the Declaration.

[45] H.G. Espiell, "Introduction" to *Birth of the Universal Declaration on the Human Genome and Human Rights* (Paris, Division of the Ethics of Science and Technology of UNESCO, 1999), 1, 3.

would clearly be a "good reason" in the Human Rights Act to limit the freedom *not* to contract. However, there is no such right and, thus, no such direct route to a legitimate restriction on freedom of contract. Is there, then, an indirect route?

The most promising indirect argument is to view the specific principle of non-discrimination in the Human Rights Act as a particular application of a general principle of non-discrimination. In England, where there is a considerable jurisprudence relating to racial and sexual discrimination (and, more recently, recognition and regulation of disability discrimination), it seems perfectly plausible to argue from a general principle of non-discrimination (including genetic discrimination). Moreover, it seems perfectly plausible to argue that such a principle applies to the field of contract (as is already the case in respect of racial and sexual discrimination). Plausible though this all may seem, we need to be clearer about why genetic discrimination should be thought to be as unacceptable as racial or sexual discrimination. Why, precisely, is this?

For those who think the Rawlsian[46] thought that racial or sexual discrimination is *prima facie* unjust, genetic discrimination will seem to be a similar case. Behind a Rawlsian veil of ignorance, contractors will have no more knowledge of their actual genetic profile than of their race or sex. In consequence, their risk-averse approach will dictate that the basic principles of fair dealing in society should not allow for one's genetic characteristics to be used against one. This may be another way of saying, as the UNESCO Universal Declaration on the Human Genome and Human Rights says, that respect for human dignity condemns any attempt to discriminate on genetic grounds. If we were to adopt such an approach, would this be to presuppose human dignity as empowerment or human dignity as constraint? Interestingly, this may be one case where the condemnation of genetic discrimination could be supported (at least up to a point) on either conception.

From the perspective of human dignity as empowerment, it is true that the tide runs strongly in favour of individual choice—the right to say yes but equally the right to say no—but only so long as this is compatible with human rights, including the right to be protected against actions that represent an affront to one's dignity as a human.[47] If discrimination on genetic grounds involves regarding bad risk humans as incapable of exercising choice, or as inferior, or something of that kind, then this is certainly something to be targeted. Similarly, if genetic discrimination has the effect of excluding persons from the enjoyment of conditions in which one can maintain a sense of one's own value, or if it consigns persons to circumstances that are demeaning or degrading, then respect for human dignity is also violated. However, where selection (and non-selection) is illegitimate only if specific discriminatory reasons or attitudes or effects are in play, this weakens the regulatory control.

[46] J. Rawls, *A Theory of Justice* (London, Oxford University Press, 1972).

[47] See further Gannon and Villiers, *supra* n.42, for comments on the significance of autonomy where genetic tests are proposed for employees who are already in employment.

If, instead, we consider genetic discrimination from the standpoint of human dignity as constraint, we may also judge that genetic discrimination should be prohibited. To allow for discrimination on genetic grounds is to make a certain sort of statement about the kind of community that this is. If this is not the community vision that we share, if this is not our idea of a civilised society, then a limit must be placed on partner freedom. Again, this particular vision may be refined so that only certain specific discriminatory reasons or attitudes are controlled. On the other hand, a more robust view may be taken, prohibiting all forms of genetic discrimination (in other words, there would be a prohibition on the use of genetic information for the purposes of selection or non-selection, irrespective of the particular reason for which that information would be employed). Such a precautionary approach might make very good sense where the protection of the culture is judged to be more important than the preservation of the maximum amount of freedom and choice. It would be ironic, indeed, if human dignity as constraint proved the more effective basis for regulating genetic discrimination in a freedom-loving society.

Although the indirect argument against genetic discrimination looks sound enough, and although it may be relied on where the Human Rights Act has a vertical application, it must be said that there is a difficulty about implementing the principle in private law. It will be recalled that the consensus forming in England is that the Act will have only an indirect horizontal application, in which case it will not be possible to allege unlawful (genetic) discrimination unless such a claim can be grounded on a recognised cause of action. Perhaps the longstanding recognition of good faith in insurance contracts and its more recent reception in consumer contracts might coalesce to support a duty to negotiate in good faith which would then act as a conduit leading from contract negotiation to a general principle of non-discrimination.[48] Failing this, where the boundary between the public and private is hazy, there may be opportunities to plead abuse of contractual right by way of judicial review.[49] Generally, though, in the absence of considerable common law engineering, the Human Rights Act (even backed by the principle of respect for human dignity) does not seem to be the answer to this particular problem.

V. CONCLUSION

For those who fear that the Human Rights Act, at any rate so far as the law of contract is concerned, may prove to be more of a whimper than a bang,[50] there

---

[48] Generally, see R. Brownsword, "Positive, Negative, Neutral: the Reception of Good Faith in English Contract Law" in N.J. Hird and G. Howells (eds.), *Good Faith in Contract: Concept and Context* (Aldershot, Ashgate, 1999), 13. For some signs that the tide of opinion may be turning in favour of a general principle of good faith in contracts, see several of the papers in A.D.M. Forte (ed.), *Good Faith in Contract and Property Law* (Oxford, Hart Publishing, 1999).

[49] See R. Brownsword, "General Considerations' in M. Furmston (ed.), *The Law of Contract* (London, Butterworths, 1999), 137–45.

[50] Cf Phillipson, *supra* n.2.

is a temptation to uncover the idea of human dignity lying behind (or alongside) that of human rights. Even if this is little more than a passing thought at the moment, it is likely to become a pressing thought in due course because so many of the perceived abuses of freedom of contract arise in the context of bio-commerce where respect for human dignity is seen as central. When this happens, the culture of human rights (backed by human dignity as empowerment) is liable to run into the culture of human dignity as constraint. Of course, it is no novelty to find cross-currents in contract law [51] but, if the Human Rights Act ushers in a debate about human dignity and freedom of contract, then we can expect to run into some extremely choppy waters.

---

[51] See J.N. Adams and R. Brownsword, *Understanding Contract Law* (3rd edn., London, Sweet and Maxwell, 2000).

10

Equality of Opportunity and Private Law

PETER BENSON*

I. INTRODUCTION

T HIS CHAPTER IS a theoretical inquiry into the relation between private law
and the liberal principle of formal equality of opportunity. This principle
holds that the positions, opportunities and institutions of society must be
equally open to all who are willing and able to strive for them. A social system
that respects this principle is one in which careers are open to talents.[1] With
greater or lesser success, modern liberal democracies have given this principle
legal force and effect. In Canada, for example, it is enshrined in the constitution
in a provision that guarantees equality before and under the law. Beyond
this, there are human rights codes that establish comprehensive, though non-
constitutional, legislative schemes which ensure that the principle of formal
equality of opportunity is respected across a range of transactions and
opportunities—transactions and opportunities that otherwise come under private law in general and the law of contract in particular.

In this chapter, I wish to consider whether private law does, or should reasonably be made to, incorporate the idea of formal equality of opportunity consistently with its fundamental and distinctive normative character. It would seem
offhand that if there is any fundamental right that could be so incorporated, it
must be the principle of formal equality of opportunity. After all, private law, it

* I wish to thank Amnon Reichman, who first persuaded me of the pertinence of the common
calling cases, for valuable discussions about a number of important aspects of my argument. Above
all, I am grateful to my wife, Ann, without whose encouragement and many suggestions I could not
have written this piece.

[1] This formulation of formal equality of opportunity is taken from J. Rawls, *A Theory of Justice*
(Cambridge, Mass., Harvard University Press, 1971), 66. Note that, in contrast to *formal* equality
of opportunity, *fair* equality of opportunity requires that individuals with the same abilities and
willingness have the same chances of success in occupying the positions in the basic social, economic
and political institutions of society. Fair equality of opportunity requires, then, that measures be
taken across generations to ensure that individuals' starting points—in terms of their resources, educational opportunities, and so on—are fair. Formal equality of opportunity, however, simply
requires that positions be open to everyone. It does nothing to regulate or mitigate differences in
starting-points, however morally undeserved these may be. In this chapter I am concerned only with
the relation between private law and formal equality of opportunity.

is said, treats parties to transactions as formally equal. In this respect at least, there seems, *prima facie*, to be a fit between private law and formal equality of opportunity. I wish to see whether this is indeed the case. If we may suppose, as seems clearly reasonable, that the freedom and equality of citizens require that transactions and positions be open to all on a basis of formal equality of opportunity, the question still remains *where* in the legal system this requirement ought to be appropriately recognised. It is not satisfactory merely to collect instances where norms of non-discrimination have been applied to private transactions or where individuals have successfully brought claims against others for breach of such norms. The crucial issue is conceptual: how are such claims to be conceived? Do they display the fundamental and distinctive character of rights and obligations in private law or are they something else? Only a theoretical inquiry can clarify this question. And as I will now explain, I shall undertake this investigation from the standpoint of a "public basis of justification".[2]

It is often assumed that, in providing legal and political justification, it is necessary to seek a grounding in some foundational principle such as utility, Kantian freedom, natural law, and so forth. However, given the fact that citizens reasonably hold—and are entitled to hold—different, and indeed conflicting, conceptions of ultimate value, justification carried on in such terms cannot purport to be generally acceptable to all on a basis that all may reasonably be expected to endorse. It does not provide a shared basis of justification that comports with the essential character of democratic citizenship. But a democratic regime requires the latter sort of justification, at least where what is at stake is the possible application of coercive law. Only such a justification can be democratically legitimate. A public basis of justification takes this requirement to heart and formulates the needed shared basis by drawing upon the norms, values and principles that are latent in the public legal and political culture of a democratic society—that is, in the publicly recognised principles, doctrines and interpretations of its private and public law as realised in its legal and political institutions. With respect to a given legal or political question, a public basis of justification tries to show how a public legal and political culture contains, even if only latently, the normative resources to provide an intelligible and reasonable answer. While a public justification goes one step further than the public legal and political culture by articulating its values and principles at a higher

---

[2] The idea of a public basis of justification is taken from the work of John Rawls. See J. Rawls, *Political Liberalism* (New York, Columbia University Press, 1993) and J. Rawls, "The Idea of Public Reason Revisited" (1997) 64 *U. Chi. L Rev.* 765. The notion of "public" in this sort of justification does not refer to public law as opposed to private law—there can be a public basis of justification for both private and public law and these justifications will differ in ways that reflect the distinctive character of each. A basis of justification is public in so far as it articulates a shared and reasoned standpoint from which those who participate in practices and institutions involving the possibility of state coercion can reasonably settle their conflicting claims. I discuss the idea of a public basis of justification for contract law in P. Benson, "The Idea of a Public Basis of Justification for Contract" (1995) 33 *Osgoode Hall LJ* 273 and I work out such a justification in detail in P. Benson, "The Unity of Contract Law" in P. Benson (ed.), *The Theory of Contract Law: New Essays* (New York, Cambridge University Press, 2001), 118–205.

level of abstraction and with greater explicit unity than the way they are presented in the public culture, it does not seek to root them in, or to show them to be an expression of, some ultimate principle or idea. Whether the latter is necessary or even possible and how it may be accomplished are matters that it leaves to philosophy. A public basis of justification, it must be emphasised, is normative throughout: it articulates conceptions of how, in justice, transactions or distributions ought to be ordered and it contends that these conceptions can and ought reasonably to be endorsed by all citizens.

So far as the common law of Canada is concerned, the natural starting point for inquiry into the relation between the principle of formal equality of opportunity and private law is the seminal decision of the Supreme Court of Canada in *Board of Governors of Seneca College of Applied Arts and Technology* v. *Bhadauria*.[3]

In *Bhadauria*, the plaintiff, a highly educated woman of East Indian origin with a Ph.D degree in mathematics as well as a valid Ontario teaching certificate and seven years' teaching experience in mathematics, responded to newspaper advertisements placed by the defendant college regarding a number of teaching positions. In fact, the plaintiff made some 10 separate applications for teaching positions over a period of four years. Although the defendant sent her letters telling her that she would be contacted for an interview, this was never done nor was any reason given for the rejection of her applications. The plaintiff claimed that she had been discriminated against because of her national origin, alleging that the positions for which she had applied were filled by others without her high qualifications but who were not of East Indian origin. While the plaintiff contended that the defendant was in breach of section 4 of the Ontario Human Rights Code as amended,[4] she also claimed—and it is this claim that is of central relevance for our purposes—that the defendant had violated a common law tort duty not to discriminate against her. The contention was that this duty is founded upon the public policy of equality of respect and of opportunity that is expressed in but not limited to the Code. For the alleged breach of this duty, the plaintiff sought damages for being deprived of the teaching opportunities at the college, for the lost opportunity of earning a teaching salary, and for mental distress and loss of self-esteem and dignity.

---

[3] (1981) 124 DLR (3d) 193 (hereinafter *Bhadauria*). While the matter is not clear-cut, it accurately summarises the law since *Bhadauria* to say that the cases do not reveal any significant trend away from that decision. Courts still uphold the principle that breach of a human rights statute is not a civilly actionable wrong at common law. There is a move toward applying *Bhadauria* more leniently where the issue is a motion to strike out the plaintiff's claim rather than to decide the merits of the case. In *Frame* v. *Smith* (1987) 42 DLR (4th), the Supreme Court of Canada applied *Bhadauria*, holding that there was no such thing as a common law right of access to one's children, that no existing tort action covered the circumstances of the case, and that the Court was precluded by the existence of a comprehensive statutory scheme from extending existing principles into this area. I thank Katie Sykes for researching this point.

[4] S. 4(1) specifies the prohibition against discrimination on enumerated grounds in relation to employment: "[n]o person shall (a) refuse to refer or to recruit any person for employment; (b) dismiss or refuse to employ or to continue to employ any person".

Peter Benson

204   *Peter Benson*

In an unanimous opinion written by Chief Justice Bora Laskin, the Supreme Court of Canada dismissed the plaintiff's claim.[5] A tort of discrimination, Chief Justice Laskin held, would create a new species of economic tort not analogous to any recognised instance of tort duty. Moreover, a refusal to enter into, or even to consider the prospect of, contract relations has not, he wrote, been recognised as giving rise to any liability in tort. In those cases where plaintiffs have succeeded in claims for damages for denial of services or accommodation on the ground of race or other arbitrary disqualifications, recovery has been based on innkeepers' liability. But the long recognised obligation of innkeepers and others engaged in common callings to receive members of the public without arbitrary discrimination cannot be relied upon to found a general tort duty not to discriminate. According to Laskin, the same is true of decisions such as *Ashby* v. *White*[6] where Holt CJ held that if a plaintiff has a right, whatever may be its source, he or she must of necessity have a means to vindicate and maintain it: right and remedy being reciprocal, the common law must provide a remedy where Parliament has not done so, or reasonably need not do so. Both the common calling cases and *Ashby*, Laskin noted, presuppose that the plaintiff has a legally protected interest, whereas the question in the present case is precisely whether there is a right at all; that is, an interest which the law will recognise as deserving protection. While a common law tort of discrimination cannot readily be conceptualised within the existing understanding of tort law, the Code establishes a comprehensive legal regime that embodies and vindicates the public policy of equality of opportunity, one that makes the courts part of the enforcement machinery under the Code. This legislative initiative, Laskin concluded, forecloses the possibility of creating a common law tort of discrimination.

The reasoning in *Bhadauria* rests upon the following interconnected propositions. First, tort law—and more generally private law—does not itself have the normative resources to found a duty not to discriminate that would express the value of equality of opportunity as embodied in the Code. Secondly, unless this duty can be established or, in other words, unless a corresponding right in the plaintiff to be free from such discrimination can be established, tort law—and more generally private law—does not itself necessitate a remedy. Thirdly, while

[5] In so doing, the Supreme Court of Canada allowed the defendant's appeal from a judgment of the Ontario Court of Appeal ((1980) 105 DLR (3d) 707) which held the defendant liable in damages on the basis of a general tort of discrimination founded upon the public policy of the Ontario Human Rights Code.

[6] (1703) 2 Ld. Raym. 938, 92 ER 126 (hereinafter *Ashby*). In *Ashby*, the plaintiff sought a private law remedy against the defendant, an elections officer, for having intentionally prevented the plaintiff from exercising his right to vote. Holt CJ concluded that the plaintiff did have a right to vote—a right, it should be emphasised, which Holt did not view as arising from contract but rather from custom and statute—and that, in the absence of the provision by Parliament of a remedy for breach of this right, a court of common law was competent and indeed obliged to provide the appropriate remedy. Holt CJ held that for breach of this right, the plaintiff was entitled to receive nominal damages even in the absence of any pecuniary or other loss. While his opinion was dissenting, the House of Lords affirmed it upon appeal by the plaintiff. I discuss *Ashby* further *infra* in the text accompanying n.40.

the Code itself *does* give the plaintiff a legally protected interest or right against discrimination, the possibility of a civil cause of action has been superseded by the comprehensiveness of the Code which both establishes the right and provides an elaborate enforcement scheme to vindicate it. Are these propositions compatible with a reasonable conception of private law in a modern liberal democracy—that is, in a society which views *all* law, *both* private and public, as expressing respect for individuals as free and equal and which, more specifically, takes equality of opportunity as a fundamental, indeed constitutional, principle of justice? To assist us in organising our thoughts about this question, I shall refer to the classification of the different ways of conceiving the relation between private law and basic human rights which has been proposed by Justice Aharon Barak.[7] Justice Barak's classification is elaborated from a legal point of view and is richly illustrated by references to a wide range of different legal jurisdictions.[8] As such, it may be used for the purpose of working out a public basis of justification.

Barak distinguishes the following four approaches. First, there is the "direct application" model according to which constitutional human rights hold not only against the government but also against private parties. Such rights, just as they are defined and enshrined in basic laws and constitutions, are to be applied directly both to government-individual relations and to relations between private individuals. The definition and vindication of these rights are fully independent of the doctrines and operation of private law. By contrast, the second approach, the "non-application" model, denies that constitutional human rights apply directly or indirectly to relations between private individuals. Such rights, this model holds, apply *only* to government-individual relations. The "indirect-application" model is the third approach. Like the direct-application approach, this model affirms that constitutional human rights *do* apply to private law transactions; but, in contrast to the first model, it holds that this application is accomplished via private law itself. More particularly, the application of human rights to private transactions between individuals is channelled through the doctrines, methodology and procedures of private law. Far from being irrelevant to the actualisation of the promise of human rights, private law, on this approach, is essential. The fourth approach, "the judiciary application" model, concurs with the non-application model in holding that constitutional human rights are protected only as against the government. It qualifies as a distinct approach, however, because it views the judiciary as an arm of government and therefore as itself subject to this constraint. On this fourth model, adjudication is itself an instance of governmental action. Thus, to some extent at least, a court is barred from enforcing private law claims that are deemed to impair constitutional rights. As in the direct-application model, the characteristic doctrines, procedures and methodology of private law play no positive role here in realising a regime of human rights.

---

[7] See A. Barak, "Constitutional Human Rights and Private Law" (1996) 3 *Rev. Const. Stud.* 218. See also A. Barak, chap. 2 this vol.

[8] See his discussion *ibid.*, at 241–57.

Because, as we will shortly see, it is the third model—the indirect-application approach—that is most pertinent to our present inquiry,[9] I should explain in a little more detail its essential premises as reflected in Justice Barak's account. It is these premises, in Barak's view, that commend some version of the third model over the others.

First, the indirect application model presupposes that both private and public law share the same foundation, namely, respect for the basic human rights of personhood, self-realisation and dignity. There is but one system of human rights.[10] Human rights are intrinsic to private law. Now protection of these rights must take into proper consideration the public interest. But more than this, since, according to Barak, the assertion of one person's rights necessarily detracts from or at least narrows and limits the rights of others, a balance must be struck between such conflicting human rights.[11] Barak contends that it is the private law—and it alone—that can provide the appropriate framework within which to balance conflicting human rights between private individuals. This function defines the very essence of private law.[12] And it is this fact that is the second fundamental premise of the indirect application model.

Taking the two premises together, namely, first, that one system of human rights underpins both private and public law and, secondly, that it is private law which can achieve the necessary balancing between conflicting human rights, we reach the conclusion that the "recognition of human rights against private parties *must*, therefore, 'permeate' via private law 'channels'".[13] This, Barak states, is the true meaning of the indirect application.

It should be emphasised that the realisation of human rights via private law channels does not mean merely that private law provides a remedy for breach of a right that is worked out independently of and apart from it.[14] To the contrary, "[p]rotected human rights do not directly permeate private law 'in and of themselves'".[15] Rather, the indirect application model supposes that the human right which is given protection through a civil action and remedy is specified and given place from within private law itself. According to the indirect application model, this is accomplished either through doctrines that are necessary to establish liability or through considerations that are invoked to qualify, limit, or negate liability. In contract law, for instance, this is done through the principles of contract formation, requirements of good faith, or the invocation of public policy as a limiting consideration. In tort, it is accomplished through the conception of duty and protected interests, the notion of reasonableness or the idea of abuse of right. It is also within the framework established by these

---

[9] This being said, I shall refer to the other models from time to time where pertinent to the argument that I am making.

[10] Barak, *supra* n.7, at 236 and 257.

[11] *Ibid.*, at 258–9.

[12] *Ibid.*, at 259.

[13] *Ibid.* (emphasis added).

[14] This, I will suggest, is what the common calling cases and *Ashby* entail.

[15] Barak, *supra* n.7, at 226.

principles and considerations as they are characteristically combined in private law analysis that the parties' conflicting human rights are to be balanced.

The previously stated propositions of law in the *Bhadauria*[16] decision seem to be in tension with the indirect application model at a fundamental level. *Bhadauria* challenges the indirect actualisation of human rights, and, more precisely, the vindication of the principle of equality of opportunity, via private law. It does so in two basic respects.

First, *Bhadauria* appears to deny that tort law and contract law have the normative resources to sustain rights and duties that reflect the value of even formal equality of opportunity. This seems clearly to be its view with respect to such fundamental doctrines as offer and acceptance, consideration, and unconscionability in contract law or the idea of duty and protected interests in the law of tort. But more than this, *Bhadauria* appears to deny that the value of formal equality of opportunity, as a general principle of justice applicable to private transactions, can be incorporated into private law via the invocation of public policy that is characteristic of private law adjudication. At least, considerations of public policy do not provide the plaintiff with the basis for a remedy in the particular circumstances of the defendant's alleged failure to accord her equal treatment. While the principle of equality of opportunity can and does apply to the sort of private transactions that come under private law, the rights and duties which this presupposes are not rooted in private law itself. They belong to a different domain of the legal system.

Secondly, *Bhadauria* supposes that the appropriate balancing between "conflicting rights" need not take place within the framework of private law. To the contrary, the framework that balances must be the one that determines the definition and scope of the right to equal opportunity, and this is neither contract nor tort law but the legislative scheme set up by the human rights code. *Bhadauria* seems to reflect the idea that any attempt to accomplish the balancing function outside this legislative framework is both unnecessary and potentially prejudicial to the full and integrated accomplishment of that function.

I wish to focus my remarks on the first tension between *Bhadauria* and the indirect application model. This is for two reasons. First, if in fact it is the case, as *Bhadauria* supposes, that private law does *not* contain the intrinsic normative resources to ground, define or even incorporate by way of considerations of public policy a right to formal equality of opportunity, we must question the idea that there is one and the same system of rights at the basis of private and public law. At the same time, if private law is to be compatible with the fundamental character of modern liberal democracy, we must specify how this conception of private law nevertheless embodies respect for the equality and freedom of citizens. This goes to the very legitimacy of private law as such. Secondly, if indeed the first tension is resolved along the lines suggested in *Bhadauria*, it seems to follow that private law cannot be the locus for balancing

---

[16] *Supra* n.3.

conflicts between this right and others, even under the rubric of public policy. The appropriate framework for balancing must be found elsewhere. So even if we do not directly address the second tension, the discussion of the first tension nevertheless clears the way by determining that such balancing *must* be done under some part of the legal system *other* than private law. Whether this should be done under the sort of legislative scheme established by the Code or somewhere else is an important question for further inquiry.

The indirect application model and *Bhadauria* disagree at a fundamental level in their respective understandings of the appropriate relation between private law and the human right of equality of opportunity. Both sides suppose, however, that the proper appreciation of that relation depends upon how one conceives the essential character of private law. Thus while Justice Barak argues for a "strengthened indirect application" approach that envisages the channelling of human rights via new interpretations of existing doctrine or even altogether new doctrines if the existing doctrines prove inadequate to that purpose, the creation of such new tools must be consistent with the fundamental and essential character of private law—or else the indirect application model collapses as an approach that is distinct from the other models. Accordingly, the first and most pressing question is: what is the fundamental character of private law and does it imply the idea of formal equality of opportunity?

My analysis of private law will be under two aspects.[17] I do this so that, within the parameters of a discussion that, of necessity, can be painted only in broad strokes, the treatment of private law is as comprehensive as possible. The first aspect concerns the basic intrinsic character of right and obligation in private law. This basic character consists in "the juridical conception of rights", as I shall call it. Viewed in terms of this conception, private law is understood as a set of doctrines, principles, and values that specify fair and reasonable terms for voluntary and involuntary interactions between individuals. Under this first aspect, private law is elucidated in terms of its inherent normative idiom. Under the second aspect, however, we take into account the form that the determination of private law rights and duties must have to meet the additional criteria of public knowability and certainty as required by a court of law. With these two aspects in mind, we may reformulate our central question as follows: does private law, viewed in terms of both the juridical conception of rights and the further requirements that are necessary to make it knowable and certain, incorporate a notion of formal equality of opportunity that applies between individuals in their private transactions, such as might give rise to a duty not to discriminate with respect to those transactions?

The remainder of the chapter is divided into two main sections. In the next and longer section, I discuss whether private law offers a normative home for a

---

[17] The distinction between these two aspects is, I believe, immanent in the public legal culture. It is reflected in the oft-made distinction between the requirements of fairness and justice on the one hand and the need for predictability and certainty on the other. It is also present in philosophical accounts of law. In particular, both Kant and Hegel take pains to mark it and to explain the underlying normative premises that make it possible. See *infra* n.32.

requirement of formal equality of opportunity. I begin by identifying the essential character of the juridical conception of rights which, I argue, represents the intrinsic and distinctive normative character of private law. I try to show that although this conception entails an idea of equality—and more precisely an idea of formal or abstract equality—this does not, and cannot, include a notion of formal equality of opportunity. I then briefly discuss the considerations and values that are added when private law rights and duties are given institutional expression by a court. Here also, I conclude that there is no basis for a principle of formal equality of opportunity.

In the third and final section, I outline what I believe is a plausible basis for a justiciable common law action for non-discrimination with respect to private transactions. To prevent misunderstanding, a crucial premise of my argument is that the common law traditionally has recognised and enforced—and presently continues to do so—rights that do not come under private law's juridical conception of rights. Yet in doing this, courts do not go beyond their judicial function. My thesis is that a requirement of non-discrimination is arguably a right of this kind: not part of the juridical conception yet fully within the competence of a common law court to recognise and enforce in its capacity *as a court*. In keeping with the idea of a public justification, I arrive at this requirement through an analysis of the common calling cases and of the notion of "property affected with a public interest". To my knowledge, these cases represent the one continuous and continuing line of purely common law decisions that expressly enforce an actionable requirement of non-discrimination against individuals in their exercise of what are, *prima facie*, private entitlements. However, with respect to their character and basis, the rights and duties that are recognised in these decisions are distinct from those of private law. Moreover, I am at pains to underline the limits of this requirement of non-discrimination, at least in so far as it can be imposed by a court acting *as a court* apart from legislative requirement. My conclusion is that the sort of justiciable common law claim to non-discrimination that can be justified on this basis would not assist, for example, the plaintiff in *Bhadauria*. And while the proposed analysis of such a claim shows how constitutional rights can play a role (albeit circumscribed) in the application of the common law, it does not imply any change in the fundamental and distinctive normative character of private law.

II. PRIVATE LAW AND FORMAL EQUALITY OF OPPORTUNITY

1. The relation between formal equality of opportunity and the juridical conception of rights in private law

(a) *Right and Obligation in Private Law*

Does the conception of right and obligation in private law have the normative resources to ground a right to formal equality of opportunity as against other individuals in private transactions? To answer this question, we must first set out the essential character of right and duty in private law.

Private law, as I understand it, is characterised by a specific, and indeed a distinctive, conception of rights that I shall call "juridical". I present this conception at the start of this section in order to orient the discussion that follows. It is not to be taken as an *a priori* foundation or explanatory principle for what follows. Rather the conception is intended to express at a high level of generality pervasive features and requirements that, even if implicitly, are supposed by the most basic doctrines of the different parts of private law, as these have been largely settled across most common law jurisdictions and when we approach the doctrines on their own terms.[18] My analysis is guided throughout by the idea of a public basis of justification. For purposes of this preliminary statement, I identify three essential features of the juridical conception of rights.

First, this juridical conception presupposes that, in order to establish a valid claim *vis-à-vis* the defendant, the plaintiff must have, independently of and prior to the defendant's wrong, something that comes under his or her right exclusively as against the defendant. We abstract this feature from the fact that in tort or contract, for example, the law views an award of damages or specific relief for breach of a plaintiff's rights as a matter of compensation that is owed by the defendant to the plaintiff and that is intended to place the plaintiff in the position that he or she was in prior to the defendant's wrong. Because in legal contemplation, the remedy is not understood as bestowing upon the plaintiff something new, it must suppose that prior to and independently of the wrong, the plaintiff *already has something* that is by rights his or her own (*suum*), with which the defendant is duty-bound not to interfere. Moreover, since the remedy is owed by the defendant to the plaintiff, the latter must have something that comes under his or her rights exclusively *as against the defendant*: an ownership interest of some kind. (We shall see that the objects of this interest include bodily integrity and external things.) So far as the juridical conception is concerned, an individual's "protected interests" are, and must be, characterised just in this way. Unless and until one has an ownership interest, one lacks a basis, within the juridical conception of rights, to make a valid claim against others. The fact that one may want or need something does not, as such, give one any valid claim against others. In this respect, the notion of protected interest in the juridical conception of rights differs sharply from the parallel idea in, say, a political conception which typically takes legitimate needs to be an appropriate basis for making claims *vis-à-vis* others. Absent the requisite ownership interest,

---

[18] I stress that the presentation of the juridical conception in this section is a mere sketch, incomplete and in summary form. I have discussed elsewhere and in more detail how this conception informs different parts of private law. In particular, see P. Benson "The Basis for Excluding Liability for Economic Loss in Tort Law" in D. Owen (ed.), *The Philosophical Foundations of Tort Law: A Collection of Essays* (Oxford, Oxford University Press, 1995), 427–58; P. Benson, "The Unity of Contract Law", *supra* n.2; and P. Benson "The Idea of Property in Private Law" in J. Coleman and S. Shapiro (eds.), *The Oxford Handbook of Jurisprudence* (Oxford, Oxford University Press, forthcoming 2001).

the juridical conception does not recognise any relation of right and duty between individuals and so no possibility of liability or wrong. It follows that a defendant is subject only to a *prohibition against injuring what already comes under the plaintiff's right of ownership.*

Secondly, the juridical conception supposes that this protected ownership interest, and hence the plaintiff's right, is of such a kind that the *only* way it can be injured is just through an *external interaction* between the parties. And this supposes in turn that what the plaintiff has is something that can be affected externally by the defendant's externally manifested choice. The sole relevant question is whether the defendant's choice (act or omission), as exercised in relation to the plaintiff, can count as a voluntary interference with the latter's protected interest, irrespective of the defendant's particular purposes or inward intention and independent of the impact the choice may have on the plaintiff's needs, wishes or advantage. This quite radical indifference to need is, I have already said, a hallmark of the juridical conception, in contrast to a political conception of rights. It also fits with the common law principle of no liability for non-feasance. There cannot be a general duty of rescue, for this would suppose that, even where a defendant has not done anything to affect or endanger the plaintiff's protected interests, the latter's needs count as such as against the former. But this would be incompatible with the irrelevance of need in the juridical conception.

Thirdly and finally, the juridical conception of rights supposes that, from within its own standpoint, determinations of liability can be complete and self-sufficient when made just on the basis of the abovementioned normative considerations, that is, when limited to considerations that are intrinsic to external interactions between parties that affect their protected (ownership) interests, without assessing what the general welfare or common good may require. In so restricting its purview, the law purports to articulate terms that are fair and reasonable *as between the parties*, in light of their particular interaction and recognising them throughout as free and equal persons.

I now wish to discuss the specific juridical conditions that are necessary and sufficient for persons to have the sort of protected interests that give them claims against others under the juridical conception of rights. As well, I will try to specify the idea of freedom and equality that is attributed to persons under the juridical conception. The purpose of the following remarks is to provide an outline of the rights under the juridical conception that is sufficient to enable us to see whether or not private law does, or reasonably should, incorporate the principle of formal equality of opportunity.

There are two sorts of entities that can be externally affected by others within the meaning of the juridical conception of rights: bodily integrity and external things. We begin with the right in one's body, since protected interests in external things presuppose that one is alive and that, being alive, one is untouchable by others. In contrast to rights in external things, the right of bodily integrity (which includes a psychological as well as physiological dimension) is innate;

that is, persons are in rightful exclusive possession of their bodies simply in virtue of being alive. One need not *do* anything to have such possession. So far as others are concerned, I, *qua* alive, am already in actual juridically protected possession of my body. Put slightly differently, the fact that I am alive is a sign to others—it reasonably makes manifest to them the fact—that I am in possession of my body. And since this sign of my having possession is manifest to others in general, *any* other person must so view me. The fact that I need not do anything (other than be alive) to have legally protected possession of my body has the important implication—which is just the other side of the coin—that I cannot do anything to divest myself of this possession. In other words, the right in one's body does not include, as one of its incidents, a right to alienate it. In this respect, we will see, there is a basic difference between the right of bodily integrity and rights in external things.

Here it is crucial to note the parameters of the right of bodily integrity. The immediate correlative of my right is the imposition of a *disability* upon everyone else in general: others cannot rightfully bring my body under their purposes, thereby making it their own; nor can they do anything at all that can alter my rightful possession of my body. The fact that I am in rightful possession of my body necessarily implies that it is not available to others for their possession and use. But the right does not imply more than this. Thus, it does not require that others assist me or do anything to preserve my life or wellbeing. My protected interest in my body is simply and solely exclusive as against others: the fundamental import of my right is that I—in my body—should be left alone. My right does not encompass the conditions and circumstances in which I am situated and which determine how I fare. Such conditions and circumstances are not me (that is, my body) and so do not come under my exclusive right. In short, my right in my body does not as such give me any right to the continuance or creation of certain external conditions and circumstances. The limited scope of the right is reflected in the common law principle that there is no liability for nonfeasance. One does not violate another's right in his or her body merely by not rescuing him or her from circumstances of peril to which one has not oneself contributed. Nor does one infringe this right just by failing to provide others with the resources necessary for their maintenance or improvement.

Beyond possession of one's body, there is possession of external things, that is, of things that may be reasonably distinguished from one's (or another's) body. The analysis of the modes of having external things is itself divisible into two kinds, depending upon the condition of the object at the time property is acquired in it: either the thing may be unowned or it may already be the property of another. In contrast to the right of bodily integrity which is innate, property in external things both unowned and owned must be acquired through acts of choice. One gains rightful possession of unowned things by exercising one's choice in accordance with the idea of first occupancy, and the resulting right is characterised as a right *in rem*; where something already belongs to another, one can acquire it only by acts that are in conformity with the idea of "derivative acquisition", that is, through a voluntary transfer of ownership from one person to another, and the resulting right is a right *in personam*. I will discuss each in turn.

By the principle of first occupancy,[19] in accordance with which one acquires an unowned thing, a person obtains rightful possession by doing something to or with the thing that may be reasonably viewed by others as effectively and presently bringing it under his or her control and power. It is not enough, therefore, for the person to have, or even to express, a wish to do this. There must be the requisite externalisation of intention in an act. Now something external to me is initially independent of me. To establish the requisite external relation between person and thing as is required by the juridical conception of rights, the act must be such that, from the standpoint of others, it reasonably appears to deprive the thing of its independence *vis-à-vis* the agent and effectively to subordinate it to his or her control and purposes. The physical act must signal to others the voluntary, that is, purposive, bringing of the thing under the agent's control. The act must manifest an *animus possidendi*. In the case of external physical things, cancelling the thing's independence requires that the person physically affect it in some externally discernible way. It may be necessary for the person physically to subdue or to change it. Sometimes merely marking it symbolically will suffice. Everything depends upon the particular character and condition of the thing. Note that what is crucial here is just whether others can reasonably ascertain the existence of the requisite act; the particular motivation, purposes, interests, or intention which the agent may have in so acting are in and of themselves irrelevant. The operative fact here is simply the act, not the agent's actual or even apparent reasons for acting.

It is therefore as a result of what a party *does* that he or she obtains property in the thing.[20] Moreover, in the case of acquisition by first occupancy, it is by his or her unilateral act *alone* that this is accomplished. And in so far as the subordination of the thing is in principle reasonably manifest to anyone who comes

[19] The following discussion draws on the law as settled in such leading cases as *Pierson* v. *Post* (1805) 3 Caines (NY) 175 and as interpreted in such writings as Holmes' account of possession in M. DeWolfe Howe (ed.) *The Common Law* (Boston, Mass., Little, Brown & Co, 1963), Lecture VI. I wish to underline that a number of the points that I make here are presented in the form of summary conclusions—for instance, the brief mention of the three incidents of the right of property. Certainly a fuller discussion of these matters is necessary. I try to provide this in "The Idea of Property in Private Law", *supra* n.18.

[20] Although I will not discuss the idea of liability in any detail in this chap., I wish to point out the parallels between the analysis of property acquisition and that of liability. Just as one must do something to gain legally protected possession of something external, so it is only by an external act that such possession can be injured. Moreover, the external act must be one that, reasonably viewed by others, affects the thing in a way that only the owner has a right to do: it must amount, even if implicitly, to taking possession, making use of or alienating the thing. And just as the act that is requisite to gaining rightful possession must be an expression of choice, so the external act that infringes possession must manifest choice. The sole operative fact that is relevant to the existence of a wrong is just such an act; the wrongdoer's needs, interests, purposes or advantage play as such no role whatsoever. There is, as it were, an equivalence between the right-creating act and the right-infringing act.

after, the act establishes a right of property against (indifferently) anyone who comes after: a right *in rem*. This right may be specified further as the right to possess, use and alienate the external thing. In the face of one person's manifest and effective subordination of an external thing to his or her power, others, who come after, are excluded from taking possession of, using, or alienating it without his or her consent. They are under a disability which did not exist before; namely, that they can no longer rightfully treat the thing as available to them for appropriation.

While acquisition in accordance with the principle of first occupancy requires that there be an initial act of taking physical possession of the thing, even if in the form of marking it, the continuance of the right, once established, does *not* necessarily depend upon one's having it in one's continuous physical possession.[21] In relation to others, one continues to occupy the thing as long as the fact that one has brought it under one's purposes is reasonably apparent to them, whether or not one has actual physical possession of it. In certain modes of taking possession, such as grasping the thing, occupancy must reasonably appear to others as coeval with physical possession. However, where occupancy consists in forming, changing or marking the thing, this need not be so. Indeed, unless first occupancy allows for the possibility of individuals being in possession of things even when they do not have physical possession, a proprietary right over external things becomes categorically ambiguous relative to the right of bodily integrity. For if one takes the view that the continuance of a right of property necessitates continuous physical possession, then, on this understanding, interference with property always entails interference with bodily integrity and can take place only via the latter. A right of property in external things that is demonstrably independent of the right of bodily integrity supposes that it must be possible for someone to have legally effective possession of something without having physical possession of it. Acquisition of property by first occupancy implies the possibility of non-physical, though complete and fully effective, possession of external things.

Unless and until a person has subordinated something to his power in the requisite manner, he cannot complain, as a matter of right, if someone else affects it in any way whatsoever. It follows that no one is under a duty to ensure that an external thing remains available to others for appropriation. Nor is the operation of the principle of first occupancy conditional upon others having the same access in fact to the thing. All that people have is an equal *permission* to exercise their will with respect to something that has not yet been brought under another's power and control. The absence of any duty or constraint here holds irrespective of another's needs, purposes, interests or any other personal feature and circumstance. The validity of one's acquisition is not dependent upon there being as good and enough left for others. The greatest inequality in holdings is

---

[21] The argument in this para. was first made by Kant. See I. Kant, *The Metaphysics of Morals*, Part I, Metaphysical First Principles of the Doctrine of Right (M. Gregor trans. and ed., Cambridge, Cambridge University Press, 1996), 401–4 (6:245–50).

in principle compatible with the operation of first occupancy. Within the parameters of the principle of first occupancy, considerations of distributive justice are irrelevant and give rise to no claims.

The right acquired by first occupancy, I have just indicated, presupposes that all persons have an equal permission to bring unowned things under their control. Each has, in short, an equal capacity for rights. In the operation and application of first occupancy with respect to any given external thing, however, one side—and one side only—has a right and everyone else is under a duty of non-interference. The equal capacity for rights—and thus the fundamental postulate of equality that one has duties only in so far as one also has rights and vice versa—remains merely presupposed by and implicit in the right of first possession. What is needed is a category of acquisition in which the other's equal capacity for rights is not merely presupposed but is the explicit condition of one's gaining legally protected possession. "Derivative acquisition" represents this further step.

In derivative acquisition, I obtain legally protected possession of something that is already the property of another: more precisely, I acquire it *in the condition of being rightfully possessed by the other*. There is a categorical difference between first occupancy and derivative acquisition. In first occupancy, the thing is acquired in the condition of being unowned (*res nullius*) by anyone else. Derivative acquisition is not reducible to a sequence initiated by the owner's abandonment of his or her thing and completed by another's appropriation of it. *Qua* abandoned, the thing is acquired in the condition of being unowned and so, in accordance with the principle of first occupancy. If it is to be a distinct mode of acquisition, derivative acquisition must be such that at no point in the procedure of appropriation is the thing ownerless. The very possibility of derivative acquisition rests upon the following presuppositions which together constitute the logic of acquisition by one person from another.[22]

First, I can acquire the other's thing only with the latter's consent. More specifically, the other must come to a decision which, reasonably construed, entails the alienation of his or her thing. In keeping with what is necessary to acquire possession in the first place, there must be an external manifestation of will or choice. The decision to alienate must, further, be *for* and *to* me. But the other's decision is not by itself enough. This one-sided alienation can at most effect an abandonment of the thing, not a transfer of the property to me. A second decision or external act is necessary: my act of appropriating the thing. And since appropriation via derivative acquisition must not be reducible to a sequence in which there is a first act of abandonment followed by appropriation of the thing in the condition of being unowned, the two acts must be unified in such a way that there is no gap between them. There must be a *unity* of expressions of choice, with the relation of will to will being the irreducibly fundamental unit of analysis Each side can be

---

[22] The following summary discussion of derivative acquisition and of contract is developed and elaborated in detail in my piece "The Unity of Contract Law", *supra* n.2.

analysed only in its relation with the other. Unless and until there is this unity of wills, I can acquire no right from and through you. In its very concept, then, derivative acquisition is necessarily and originally two-sided. In contrast to original acquisition which can be brought about by a single person's act alone, derivative acquisition is effected only in and through interaction between two.

Thus far I have discussed the idea of derivative acquisition, not the different legal instantiations of that idea. Contract, I will now explain, may reasonably be conceived as an instance of derivative acquisition. For, according to the common law (as well as the civil law), the normal remedy for breach of contract is either an award of expectation damages or a decree of specific performance. This is a fundamental and settled principle which the law takes to be a principle of compensation. Now if either remedy is to count as *compensation* for wrong done, it must be the case that parties acquire entitlements at formation, that is, prior to and independently of performance. For if damages or specific performance are to be viewed as repairing loss caused rather than as conferring a new benefit upon the plaintiff, it is necessary that the breach represents an injury to something that, prior to and independently of performance, *already* belongs to the plaintiff. To satisfy this condition, the plaintiff must acquire this entitlement from the other party at contract formation. This is the only possible source of the entitlement. Accordingly, it must be possible to view contract formation as a mode of derivative acquisition whereby the rights of one party are acquired through voluntary interaction with the other.

To show that contract can be so conceived requires that we explain how the central doctrines of contract law together articulate a conception of the contractual relation that reflects the logic of derivative acquisition. I will not attempt to do this here, even in summary fashion. Rather, I wish to point out certain basic features and implications of this view of contract that are pertinent to our main question concerning the relation between private law and formal equality of opportunity.

First, the conception of contract as derivative acquisition presupposes that at contract formation one party can acquire something that qualifies as his or her own (*suum*) exclusive as against the other party. Since the acquisition must be prior to and independent of actual performance, the party obtains non-physical but legally effective possession at contract formation. Performance complies with or respects this non-physical acquisition by giving the party physical possession of what is already his or hers by rights. The conception of contract as derivative acquisition makes explicit the distinction between legal and physical possession which, I indicated earlier, is also presupposed by, but not necessarily expressed in, first occupancy.

Secondly, the interaction that brings about contract formation consists of two mutually related expressions of assent which, in and of themselves, effect an alienation and appropriation that do not require any change in either party's physical relation to the object of acquisition. All that is necessary is that each party's decision be reasonably manifest to the other. Indeed, whether the requisite expression of assent has been given by one party is decided by how that party's words and actions reasonably appear to the other. And once again, the legally operative fact that brings about formation is just this combination of externally manifested assents reasonably construed from within the standpoint of the parties' inter-action. These assents count just in their externality, not because they may be evidence of the actual inner intentions of the parties. Contract formation is construed from the standpoint of the so-called objective test. Here again, the parties' particular purposes, needs and interests are in and of themselves irrelevant to the legal analysis of contract formation, in this way showing that contract embodies the juridical conception of rights. And because the relevant standpoint is how my words and actions reasonably appear to the other party in the circumstances of our interaction, the right I gain at contract formation must, and can only be, a right against that other party: a right *in personam*.

Thirdly, unless and until there is a combination of mutually related assents, no right is acquired. Supposing for the purposes of this chapter that the common law doctrines of offer and acceptance and of consideration articulate, respectively, the form and content of the kind of interaction that brings about derivative acquisition, it follows that unless or until an offer is met by acceptance or a promise is supported by consideration, no right is acquired by one party from the other.

The doctrine of offer and acceptance, to focus upon it, clearly reflects this conclusion. Standing alone, an offer gives the offeree no right but merely a power of acceptance. At common law, prior to acceptance, there can be no contractual relation of right and duty between the parties. While the offeree is at liberty to accept the offer, he or she has no right that it be given in the first place and no right to its continuance after it has been made. Unless or until the offer has been accepted, the offeror may retract it at will without violating any entitlement in the offeree coming under contract.[23] Since duty and right are correlative, there cannot be a duty in contract law to make an offer to anyone. And since intention, purpose, interest and advantage are, in and of themselves, irrelevant to the analysis of the obligation, a person's reason for deciding to offer or alternatively for declining to do so is simply irrelevant. The reason may be legitimate or arbitrary and even malicious. The irrelevance of reasons is content-neutral and general. What counts—and the only thing that counts—is whether a person has done something which, from the standpoint of another, reasonably appears to be an offer or an acceptance. Just as there is a perfect liberty to decide to accept or not, so there is a complete liberty to decide to offer or not.

---

[23] Note that I have qualified the entitlement as one coming under contract. The possibility of a claim arising from the offeree's reasonable detrimental reliance upon the offeror's representations is not thereby excluded. I have argued elsewhere, however, that such an action is best viewed as sounding in tort law. See Benson, "The Unity of Contract Law", *supra* n.2 at 174–7. I should add that the understanding of offer and acceptance set out here is found in the work of the natural law writers in the civilian tradition. See, for example, H. Grotius, *The Law of War and Peace* (F.W. Kelsey, trans., Oxford, Clarendon Press, 1925), Book II, chap. X.

In connection with this third set of remarks, we should make explicit the notion of contractual liberty that informs the law of contract. Contractual liberty is rooted in the fact that no one is obliged to enter into contractual relations with anyone else. Individuals do not have a pre-existing duty toward others to contract with them. In other words, others do not have a right against me that I make them offers or even that I take them into consideration when deciding whether to offer or not; nor do they have a right against me that I maintain an offer once I have made it. The crucial point here is that it is not unless and until I have—for whatever reason—decided to offer and the offeree has—again for whatever reason—decided to accept that either of us has any contractual rights against each other. Contract law's complete indifference toward reasons for acting—in contrast to the acts themselves—means, by implication, that arbitrariness is given free rein in determining whether or not to posit the acts that can bring about contract formation. Nevertheless, parties cannot determine the kind of operative facts that are necessary conditions of contract formation. There must be offer and acceptance, promise and consideration, and so forth. Interaction that fails to satisfy these requirements produces no contractual effects. Contractual freedom is simply the unfettered liberty to choose to posit or not the kind of act, which in conjunction with the act of another, is necessary to bring about contract formation.

Fourthly, the law of contract is informed by a certain conception of equality. As authors of offer and acceptance, the parties figure as persons undifferentiated by reference to any of their particular features, purposes, interests or needs. They count simply and identically as persons with a juridical capacity to appropriate or alienate through external manifestations of choice in interaction with each other. In contract, both parties are exhibited identically as endowed with the very same capacity that is attributed to the single person acting alone under the principle of first occupancy. Moreover, since legally effective offer and acceptance must each state the same terms of a whole transaction, each side of the contractual relation is identical to the other. This identity between the two sides achieves fullest expression, however, in the principle of unconscionability. For here contract law takes as its baseline each party's right to receive the quantitative equivalent in value of what he or she gives.[24] In virtue of this principle, parties are no longer differentiated by the fact that they alienate and appropriate different things. From the standpoint of contractual analysis, each counts as an owner of the same thing—quantitatively equal value. In treating the parties via the baseline of equivalence as owners of quantitatively equal value, the law presents both the subjects and objects of the transaction in terms that abstract

---

[24] In "The Unity of Contract Law", *supra* n.2 at 184–201, I have tried to provide a detailed presentation and defence of this interpretation of unconscionability in conjunction with the other main doctrines of contract law. As I explain in that piece, the right to receive equal value is a normative (juridical) baseline inasmuch as persons are at liberty to accept less than equal value either by expressing donative intent or by assuming the risk of the difference. To my mind, the best judicial formulation of the principle is still that of Lord Denning MR in *Lloyds Bank* v. *Bundy* [1975] 1 QB 326.

from their particular qualitative differences and therefore as the same. The contractual relation postulates interaction between two parties who figure simply
as abstractly equal owners of the same things.

Taking the discussion of freedom and equality one step further, we may say
that the juridical conception of rights supposes a certain normative conception
of the person. Individuals are recognised as being free in the sense of having a
capacity to set their own ends but in such a way that they are not inevitably tied
to them. Private law views them as having the capacity to take responsibility for
their ends and to pursue them in a way that respects the equal standing of others. It is just in virtue of their capacity to set and to pursue ends in this manner
that they must be accorded respect and can establish claims *vis-à-vis* others
through their mere existence (the right of bodily integrity) as well as through
their acts, whether unilateral (first occupancy) or mutually-related (contract).
To use Rawls's term, individuals are viewed as "self-authenticating sources of
valid claims".[25] They are the opposite of slaves, who are not recognised at all as
having the power to make any claims on their own behalf—claims that have a
weight of their own independently of being derived from the interests of, or
duties owed to, others or society as a whole. Moreover, the status of individuals as self-authenticating sources of claims does not depend upon the particular
content of their ends. Finally, individuals are viewed as having the capacity to
take responsibility for their ends precisely in so far as they are not regarded as
at one with their needs, desires, purposes, external circumstances, and so forth.
They have the capacity to stand above all these, to judge and evaluate them in
the light of what is reasonable and fair, and to act on this assessment. It is
this capacity for taking responsibility that is directly reflected in the juridical
conception when it exhibits indifference toward persons' needs, preferences,
particular purposes and satisfaction. The crucial moment of the *non-identity*
between persons on the one hand and their needs, interests and desires on the
other is enshrined as the essential character of the juridical conception of rights.
The distinctiveness of the latter, as contrasted, say, with political conceptions of
rights and justice, lies just in the fact that it does not go further than this.[26]

This completes our sketch of private law's juridical conception of rights.
Indeed, so far as this conception of rights goes, the rights of bodily integrity, first
occupancy and contract exhaust the elementary modes of establishing primary
claims against others. Under the juridical conception, an object of rights must
be either one's body or something other than it, and within the latter category,
external things must be either unowned or already owned. If private law embodies the principle of formal equality of opportunity, it must be present in or
implied by the rights that make up the juridical conception. We will now determine whether this is the case.

---

[25] Rawls, *Political Liberalism, supra* n.2 at 32–3.

[26] In Rawls's conception of political and social justice, for example, the idea of "legitimate needs"
plays an essential role, via the specification of social primary goods, in the argument for the appropriate principles of justice.

(b) *Is a Right to Formal Equality of Opportunity Intrinsic in Private Law?*

To begin, let us return to *Bhadauria*[27] and fix precisely the character of the alleged discrimination by the defendant. The plaintiff's complaint was not that the defendant interfered with her liberty to enter contractual relations. Her liberty, her capacity to do this, remained perfectly intact and untouched. Rather the *gravamen* of her complaint must be that whereas the defendant was willing to offer others an opportunity to contract, it decided not to do so in her case for reasons having nothing to do with her competence or qualifications and everything to with her ethnicity and place of national origin. What the defendant denied the plaintiff for discriminatory reasons was therefore an occasion to exercise her capacity to acquire rights via a contractual relation. It did not interfere with the exercise of her liberty but rather refused to provide the occasion for exercising it. Can this be a wrong under private law?

Unless the defendant was under a duty to provide this opportunity and the plaintiff had a corresponding right to its provision, the defendant's refusal, even if deliberate, cannot be a wrong in private law. What the plaintiff must establish is that the opportunity to contract is something that came under her exclusive right as against the defendant. But the opportunity to contract essentially requires reference to the action of another—the defendant. It depends upon the defendant's decision to make an offer or at least to consider the plaintiff as a potential offeree. It involves the determination of the defendant's conduct and the imposition of a constraint upon the defendant's liberty. Such determination of, and constraint upon, the action of another can be acquired only with and through the other's assent: no one is naturally or originally subject to another's determination. Absent the defendant's assent, the plaintiff cannot acquire a right to it. In other words, the plaintiff can have such a right only if it is given to her by a contract with the defendant. But this is precisely what the defendant refuses.

To avoid this conclusion, it is necessary to show that the protected interest alleged by the plaintiff is not in the provision of the opportunity as such but is in something else that already belongs to her independently of the wrongful acts or omissions of the defendant. Offhand, it seems difficult to conceive of anything that fits within one of the categories of rightful possession—that is, within the right of bodily integrity, first occupancy or contract. The deeper difficulty is that whatever interest may be suggested must be construed consistently within the limited parameters of right and duty in private law. The interest must be conceived in terms of a right to be left alone, in keeping with the exclusionary character of right in private law.

Perhaps, one may object, the plaintiff has a "dignitary interest" which is injured by the defendant's intentionally discriminatory refusal to contract. The defendant's refusal to make an offer to the plaintiff, or even to consider the plaintiff as a potential offeree, amounts to a denial of her equal capacity for

---

[27] *Supra* n.3.

rights: she counts for nothing in the defendant's eyes and the defendant has manifested this contempt for her in the clearest way. The affront to her dignitary interest is wrought through the defendant's willful refusal even to contemplate the possibility of a contractual relation with her because of the defendant's intolerance and prejudice.

The difficulty with this suggestion, however, is that dignity as such does not constitute a protected interest. Human beings have dignity in so far as they have the capacity to set ends for themselves in accordance with a conception of themselves as responsible for those ends. This capacity is the inward property of the person and as such is inherently invulnerable to imposition and injury. It is beyond the reach of others. To constitute a protected interest, the idea of dignity must be embodied in something that can be affected by others and that ought not to be touched by them. More particularly, in private law, dignity is embodied as legally protected interests in one's body and in external things. Persons have dignity but they can be touched and injured only with respect to their protected interests. It is only in so far as persons claim their bodies and the external world as their own that they can be injured. "Dignitary interest" can mean in private law nothing other than rightful possession of one's body or of external things.

There is a final argument that should be considered. It might be thought that while it is *prima facie* difficult to explain the plaintiff having a protected interest that fits with one of the categories of right in private law, nevertheless the defendant's willful denial of the plaintiff's equal standing *makes* it so. We are to view the defendant's contempt as an attempt to dispossess the plaintiff of her sense of self and equal worth and therefore as implicitly treating her dignity as something that can be appropriated by others at will—in other words as something that can be rightly or wrongly possessed. Even though dignity does not in and of itself constitute a protected interest, the defendant's intentional refusal to contract with the plaintiff because of racial intolerance must be characterised and rectified as an assault upon the plaintiff's rightful possession; otherwise, the defendant's implicit assertion of its liberty to take away the plaintiff's equal standing remains unchallenged and to all appearances valid.

In my view, this argument cannot succeed. The fact that the defendant desires, and expresses the desire, to deprive the plaintiff of her equal standing and worth is in and of itself irrelevant to the analysis of right and duty in private law—as is any purpose, interest or need, whether inwardly felt or outwardly manifested. Intention of whatever kind is pertinent only in so far as it animates external action and external action, in turn, is relevant only in so far as it affects protected interests. And protected interests must be determinable as such *independently of and prior to* the defendant's wrongful action, intentional or not. This requirement reflects the logic of the fundamental idea at common law that there can be no liability for non-feasance.[28]

---

[28] My argument is that this is how intention is treated in private law as part of our public legal culture. A leading illustration of this view is the decision of the House of Lords in *Mayor of Bradford* v. *Pickles* [1895] AC 587. As for the idea of no liability for mere non-feasance, recall that it means

The conclusion that I have reached—namely, that formal equality of opportunity is not, and cannot be, part of the conception of rights in private law—may seem paradoxical, given that this conception supposes the formal or abstract equality of persons. How can private law not include formal equality of opportunity without repudiating its own essential conception of equality? The paradox may be restated as follows: how can private law not incorporate the principle of formal equality of opportunity when its fundamental premise is the equal capacity for rights and the equal permission to acquire external things as property?

There is, however, no paradox in my view if we keep clearly in mind the import of formal equality and of equal permission in the juridical conception of rights. Individuals are formally equal in the sense of being identical, because of the irrelevance of any particular factors that may distinguish them. More specifically, they count identically, that is, indifferently, as persons who have equal standing as self-authenticating sources of claims to produce juridical effects through being alive and by positing certain external acts that conform with the requirements of first occupancy and contract. The fact that they can produce juridical effects depends upon their having the capacity to set ends for themselves in accordance with a conception of themselves as responsible for those ends. The one and only general imperative in private law is the prohibition against acting in a manner that is inconsistent with the equal capacity of others to produce juridical effects. But this capacity can be denied only through non-recognition of the juridical effects it produces.

For example, enslavement is the subordination of another's life, that is, the totality of his or her powers, to the purposes of another. It is the subjection of *this real embodiment* of the person that constitutes the injury to his or her dignity and capacity for rights. To repeat, the source of dignity, which is the capacity to set ends in accordance with a conception of oneself as responsible, is purely inward and can *never* as such be touched by another: even in chains, one can still be free. It is this invulnerability that is the foundation of all rights, including those of private law. Similarly, it is only if another intentionally or foreseeably imposes effects on an external thing that one has *already* acquired by first occupancy or by contract that there can possibly be injury to one's capacity for rights. There is, of course, a general permission to appropriate. But it is *only* a permission. It means just that there is no general duty to leave external things in a condition of being ownerless and that no one can reasonably com-

that there is no injury in private law unless the defendant interferes with something that belongs to the plaintiff as his or her own (*suum*) exclusive as against the defendant. I should clarify that, so understood, the distinction between non-feasance and misfeasance is *not* merely the difference between omissions and acts, as is sometimes stated. Misfeasance can consist in an omission (for example, failure to perform one's agreement) and non-feasance can consist in an act (for example, causing financial loss to a business rival by drawing its custom and business away). Clear judicial statements of this idea are found in Lord Diplock's speech in *Dorset Yacht* v. *Home Office* [1970] AC 1004, 1060 (HL) and Justice Cardozo's judgment in *H.R. Moch Co* v. *Rensselaer Water Co* (1928) 159 NE 896, 899 (NY). I discuss this in "The Basis for Excluding Liability for Economic Loss in Tort Law", *supra* n.18, at 444–50.

plain if and when someone chooses to appropriate to the exclusion of others. This permission is *not* as such a right, in the sense of entailing a claim as against others who are under a corresponding duty. And if one wishes to view the permission as granting people access to things, the meaning of this access is simply the fact that they are under no general prohibition against appropriating things and that no one of them has standing to complain just because another has appropriated something, thereby making it unavailable to everyone else.

The normative import of the plaintiff's complaint in *Bhadauria*[29] is categorically different. At bottom, her claim must be that she, no differently from others, should have the formally same opportunity to acquire something, although her chances of success can be affected by her resources, abilities, circumstances, and so forth. This claim would, however, place constraints upon what others may do—constraints that are not required by the juridical conception itself. For example, if we take equality of opportunity seriously in relation to the acquisition of ownerless things, it seems problematic to allow the principle of first possession to operate without qualification. At the very least, it would seem essential that those excluded either knew or reasonably were able to know that something was available, as a precondition of giving it to the first in possession. Otherwise, it would be illusory to speak of an even formal equality of opportunity with respect to its acquisition. The point can be made more clearly with contractual acquisition. Here it would be essential that, if the plaintiff were able to provide what the defendant sought by way of acceptance, the defendant not exclude the plaintiff from the set of potential offerees for reasons that denied the fundamental identity between persons. In both instances, the claim would constrain the operation of the elementary principles of first occupancy and of offer and acceptance, reflecting the fact that the normative import of the claim goes beyond the recognition of formal equality in private law. The idea of formal equality in private law, it must always be emphasised, is specified in terms of the fundamental distinction between misfeasance and non-feasance: unless and until rightful possession is gained, there can be no duty because there is no right. The plaintiff's claim in *Bhadauria* does not remain within these parameters.

Thus far I have argued that the juridical conception of rights that animates private law does not entail a right to formal equality of opportunity. The main contention of the indirect application model, discussed earlier, cannot be sustained. In this connection, it should be emphasised that even the more "open-ended" concepts in private law, such as the idea of reasonableness in the interpretation of contracts or in the determination of tort liability, must be specified in a way that fits with the juridical conception of rights. And the same is true of an attempt to bridge the gap by fashioning "new tools" of private law doctrine. If it is to live up to its claims, the indirect application model must understand private law in its own terms and in accordance with its own distinctive normative character.

---

[29] *Supra* n.3.

To conclude this discussion of the relation between formal equality of opportunity and the conception of rights in private law, I wish to consider one further
contention of the indirect application model: human rights (here equal opportunity), it says, can be incorporated into private law via reference to considerations of public policy. To clarify, the question is not whether private law in
general or contract law in particular can be constrained by public policy or
whether legislation may authorise and indeed bind courts to do so. It is uncontroversial that private law is and should be regulated by, and indeed be subordinated to, requirements of public policy. The point at issue here is different.
The question is whether there is a form of public policy that is native to private
law—one that can be invoked *from within and from the standpoint of* private
law itself—and, if so, whether this policy incorporates a right to formal equality of opportunity. It is only a conception of policy which is intrinsic to private
law that fits with the point of view and the fundamental claims of the indirect
application model.

The juridical conception of rights suggests only one kind of consideration of
policy that is intrinsic to private law. This consideration reflects the most fundamental premise of a liberal conception of private law, namely, the difference
between persons and things. A person, in contrast to a thing, can never be subordinated to another's will. Only things, not persons, can be owned. Persons can
own things but cannot themselves be owned. Since persons are not things and
cannot be owned, whatever constitutes my personhood—whatever capacities,
powers and rights define my being a person—cannot be the subject of ownership.
From a juridical point of view, not only can these characteristics not be acquired
by others, they are not even owned by me. For the same reason, they are, quite
literally, inalienable. This distinction between person and thing is not so much a
right as the very basis and presupposition of the possibility of any rights. It may
accordingly be invoked as a policy that must be respected in the analysis of rights
and duties. So, for example, while the principle of first possession can formalis-
tically apply to the capture and subordination of human beings, the policy of private law forbids it.[30] Similarly, a contract of self-enslavement or one that severely
limits my ability to participate in economic and social life or to fulfill familial or
political responsibilities is void *ab initio* by policy, not because the requirements
of formation are not met—on the contrary, they can be.[31]

To count as a consideration of policy that is intrinsic to private law, a principle, value, or other normative requirement must reflect the idea of policy just
discussed. For instance, my moral responsibility for my acts and omissions, my
right of conscience, and my fundamental obligations and rights as a citizen are
all constitutive of my personhood and are therefore outside the sphere of things
that can be owned or alienated. The same is true, or at least may reasonably be
supposed, of my responsibility to recognise the equal standing of others and, in

---

[30] See *Smith* v. *Gould* (1707) 2 L Ld. Raym. 1275; 92 ER 338.
[31] See *Horwood* v. *Millar's Timber and Trading Co, Ltd* [1917] 1 KB 305.

turn, my right to such recognition by them. One cannot bind oneself contractually to discriminate against others or impose such an obligation upon another. An agreement of this kind could reasonably be avoided on the basis of public policy. At least this is the sort of argument that would have to made.

My point is that the invocation of public policy must fit this form if it is to be internal to private law. On the facts of *Bhadauria*, however, this form of policy consideration cannot play any role precisely for the reason that no contract—let alone one purporting to limit, affect or appropriate something that is inalienable—is ever formed. And this will typically be the difficulty in the very sorts of circumstances which most flagrantly violate the principle of equality of opportunity. The public policy that is intrinsic to private law can be invoked only to void what might otherwise amount to an illegitimate appropriation whether by first occupancy or by contract, not to establish it.

(c) *The Regime of Private Law and Equality of Opportunity*

To complete the analysis of the relation between private law and equality of opportunity, it is necessary to take a final step and view private law under a second aspect; namely, as it is given institutional expression by a court of law in the quest of making it certain and publicly knowable. Does private law, viewed in these terms, incorporate the principle of formal equality of opportunity?

At first blush, it may seem unlikely that the answer could be different from our previous conclusion concerning the relation between the juridical conception of rights and equality of opportunity. After all, the private law that is embodied in the decisions of a court of common law or the provisions of a civil code consists of the basic private law doctrines that reflect the juridical conception of rights discussed in the previous section. If the content of private law remains essentially the same when a court gives it institutional form as positive law, what difference does this form make?[32]

Let us say, provisionally, that what a court accomplishes, and seeks to accomplish, is just to make the private law *publicly knowable and readily applicable or certain*. Indeed, the knowability and applicability of the law are preconditions of its legitimacy and authority. The doctrines of private law must be made knowable to any person in general, irrespective of his or her purposes and moral character. This is the condition *sine qua non* of the presumption that everyone knows the law. This is accomplished in part through the systematic articulation

---

[32] My brief remarks draw on the accounts of the administration of justice and the rule of law in the work of I. Kant, G. Hegel and M. Oakeshott, among others. For Kant's discussion, see in particular Kant, *supra* n.21, at Part I, chap. III, The Doctrine of Right ("On Acquisition that is Dependent Subjectively upon the Decision of a Public Court of Justice"); for Hegel's account, see G.W.F. Hegel, *The Philosophy of Right* (T.M. Knox, trans. London, Oxford University Press, 1952), paras. 209–29 ("The Administration of Justice"); and for Oakeshott, see M. Oakeshott, *On History* (Oxford, Basil Blackwell, 1983), the chapter "The Rule of Law" at pp. 119–64. However, we need only consult the public legal culture to see that the knowability and applicability of law are fundamental values and indeed necessary conditions of the law's legitimacy and authority.

of legal doctrines, principles and policies in the form of abstract universal categories and through their being made publicly available as such. The doctrines
are made applicable by a court of justice to particular instances and single cases,
all in accordance with definite requirements of publicity. Title to property and
contractual agreements must be provable before a court. Legal formalities, such
as the common law seal, and proofs of title become the foundation of rights. In
this way, individuals can know the boundaries which they must not transgress
and the legally effective ways of accomplishing their purposes. They are able
to rely on the public validity, certainty and finality of transactions that have
been conducted in conformity with legal formalities and generally known
procedures.

But while the effort to bring certainty and transparency to the law in its
application to particular cases can sometimes make a difference in the determination of who has the right to something or whether one has subjected oneself to
a contractual obligation,[33] it does not alter the fundamental conception of rights
at work in private law. To acquire something, one must perform a publicly
ascertainable act of some kind; for there to be legal injury, one must affect something that is already in another's rightful possession and so forth. The organising idea of no liability for non-feasance must still be respected. Because the
concerns of certainty, reliability, ease of determination and public knowability
do not change the basic conception of rights and duties or the categories and
contents of protected interests, they do not provide the needed basis for a right
to equality of opportunity.

It is true that a court must always act from a standpoint that honours the
equality of persons. It does this by upholding the equal standing of parties to be
protected in their rights. Parties are equal under and before the law and they
receive the equal benefit of the law, so far as their rights are determined and vindicated.[34] If the court is itself but the embodiment of the parties' equality, must
this not constrain the kinds of private transactions it can enforce, on pain of acting inconsistently with this its basic character?

We have already seen that immanent in private law is the policy distinction
between persons and things. Reflecting this, a court does not enforce obligations
that treat what is inalienable as something that can be disposed of, appropriated
or limited. The content of the inalienable can incorporate values, capacities, and
powers that are not directly operative in private law: for example, freedoms and
responsibilities pertaining to family life, civil association and political participation. There are other cases where courts, pursuant to their interest in basing
judgment on what is certain, are justified in striking down provisions between

---

[33] Kant famously discusses four examples in which this is true: *supra* n.21, at 444–50.

[34] I should add that, as participants in the legal process of determining and vindicating rights
before a court of justice, the parties themselves do not come under a new category of rights or duties
except the right *in judicio stare* (there is no outlawry) and the concomitant duty, when their rights
are in dispute, of acknowledging the courts' jurisdiction and authority as well as submitting to its
decision as final.

private parties that create difficulties and uncertainties in defining or ascertaining the rights and duties between them. For example, restrictive covenants that limit an owner's freedom to use or dispose of his or her in ways tied to race or religion can be struck down as uncertain in application or as contradictory with the right of ownership.[35] And there are legal forms and transactions that, strictly speaking, do not belong to private law but rather are creatures of the positive law itself. It was Hegel's view, for example, that testamentary dispositions are not contracts in the strict sense (because they presuppose that the disposition is effected at the moment of death and therefore by one who, not being alive, cannot produce juridical effects).[36] Or the transaction may be defined by the positive law with reference to public values, such as a charitable trust.[37] In such instances where it is the social and legal order that breathes life into and determines the character of a transaction, a court is justified in ensuring that, both in purpose and effect, the transaction is non-discriminatory.

The same cannot be said, however, about a court's alleged power to refuse to enforce an accepted offer on the ground that the offer was *not* made to someone else for reasons of race and to judge the refusal to deal a tort. A court does not betray its character by enforcing the offer and by holding that the claim is not actionable in tort. It can enforce the offer because an offeror's reasons of *any* kind for deciding to offer or not are as such categorically irrelevant to the analysis of offer and acceptance and therefore to the question of whether a right is vested in the plaintiff or is violated by the defendant. In other words, the court has a *general* basis for its action and, far from being essentially linked to inequality, this basis—the irrelevance of the parties' particular purposes, motives, needs and reasons—is just what makes possible, and in turn is required by, the parties' abstract equality in private law. To avoid this conclusion, one must set aside the central distinction between misfeasance and non-feasance and, with it, the distinctive conception of rights in private law.

III.   THE BASIS FOR A COMMON LAW RIGHT TO EQUAL OPPORTUNITY

The preceding analysis of private law places severe limitations on the possibility of incorporating the human right of formal equality of opportunity in it, thereby bring into question the indirect application model. On the contrary, it seems to vindicate Chief Justice Laskin's rejection of a tort of discrimination in *Bhadauria*.[38] While the principle of formal equality of opportunity is essential

---

[35] A case which strikes down for uncertainty is the decision of the Supreme Court of Canada in *Noble and Wolf* v. *Alley et al*. [1951] SCR 54 (SCC). One may plausibly view the important decision of the US Supreme Court in *Shelley* v. *Kraemer* 334 US 1 (1948) as striking down a restrictive covenant because it was contradictory with the right of ownership.

[36] Hegel, *supra* n.32, para 80.

[37] As in *Re Canada Trust Co* v. *Ontario Human Rights Commission* (1990) 69 DLR (4th) 321 (Ont. CA).

[38] *Supra* n.3.

and fundamental to the justice of a liberal democracy, it is not part of the juridical conception of rights or of the enforcement of this conception by a court of law. It plays no role in the analysis of private transactions from the standpoint of private right as such. But this does *not* mean that a right to formally equal treatment is therefore unenforceable and not justiciable before a court of law. Not all the individual rights that a court enforces are rooted in the juridical conception. Once we suppose a positive system of private law that is administered by a court of justice, there is further material for its content in rights and duties that have their source in the administration of justice, in civil society, in the State and constitution, and so forth.[39] An obvious example is the fact that individuals may have individual enforceable rights directly established by or derived from legislative provisions.

In my view, *Ashby*,[40] which I discussed briefly in connection with *Bhadauria*, is clearly such an instance. According to Holt CJ, so long as a court can conclude that the plaintiff *qua* individual is vested with a right and that the defendant has interfered with it, an action can and must lie: "it is a vain thing to imagine a right without a remedy; for want of right and want of remedy are reciprocal".[41] This is true irrespective of the source of the right. In *Ashby*, the plaintiff's right was a right to vote that could originate in statute, custom or the political incidents attaching to estates. While the "inheritance of this right, or the right of election itself, is in the whole body politic . . .", "the exercise and enjoyment of this right is in the particular members".[42] The defendant "having hindered [plaintiff] of it, it is an injury to the plaintiff".[43] It is important to note here that the court does not construe the plaintiff's right in its very origin and conception as exclusive against the defendant and therefore as correlative to a duty in the defendant. This contrasts with the basic character of right and duty in the juridical conception which *does* suppose their correlativity—the very notion of a right in property is that it is exclusive as against another. So while the plaintiff's right in *Ashby* does not have the basic character of rights in the juridical conception, it is ascertainable and enforceable as a right before a common law court.

We see then that the fact that a court of justice recognises and enforces by way of damages or specific implement a right does not make that right or the remedy part of private right, understood as embodying the juridical conception. What is fundamentally at stake here is a conceptual point concerning the normative character of the right and corresponding duty. What makes a right part of the juridical conception and therefore part of private right (or law) is its intrinsic character. The form of legal relation that comes under the juridical conception is not merely a two-sided plaintiff–defendant relation in which each side has equal standing, with values on both of the sides being given appropriate weight.

---

[39] Hegel makes this point explicitly in *supra* n.32, para 213.
[40] *Supra* n.6.
[41] *Per* Holt CJ, *supra* n.6, at 136.
[42] *Ibid.*
[43] *Ibid.*

This is to frame the nature of the legal relation at a level of abstraction that is too high to reflect the specific and distinctive character of the legal relation in private law. The sort of two-sidedness that is characteristic of private law is that which pertains to the kind of rights that come under the juridical conception. And this, as I tried to outline in the previous sections, is the sort of two-sidedness that is specifically entailed by the rights of property and contract.

Guided by the idea of a public basis of justification, we ask whether there are instances where the common law has recognised requirements of non-discrimination which, although they do not come under the juridical conception or directly flow from legislative provisions, are nevertheless justiciable and enforceable before a court exercising its inherent jurisdiction and authority to vindicate individual rights. Now in fact there *is* such a body of law, dating from the Middle Ages and continuing to the present day, that recognises just this sort of requirement. I am referring to the cases involving common or public callings and property affected with a public interest. For centuries, individuals engaged in public callings or claiming the rights of property with respect to something deemed affected with a public interest have been held subject to a variety of requirements that, on their face, go beyond the duties and liabilities of the juridical conception. Among these requirements is the firmly established and fundamental duty to deal with all members of the public without invidious discrimination.

Now some commentators and courts have viewed this requirement as an early instance of the State's exercise of its police power to regulate private transactions and property in furtherance of the common good and therefore as the exercise of a legislative function.[44] Indeed, it is uncontroversial that the State can regulate the use of property via the exercise of its police powers. And it is not implausible to view the cases setting requirements for common callings and property affected by a public interest as incipient instances of this essentially legislative function. In fact, much of this law that has survived until now has been incorporated in statutory provisions.[45] But there is a second view which holds that these cases are not reducible just to an exercise of the legislative power. On this second view, the imposition of requirements for the benefit of members of the public is a genuinely judicial response which does not so much pit values of the common good against the right of property as spell out the reasonable and fair implications of putting one's property to a use that brings into play a normative (legal) idea of the public, thereby vesting rights in individuals against those

[44] This is the view taken by such writers as B. Wyman, "The Law of Public Callings as a Solution of the Trust Problem" (1904) 17 *Harv. L Rev.* 156 and N. Arterburn, "The Origin and First Test of Public Callings' (1927) 75 *U Pa. L Rev.* 411 and by courts in *Munn* v. *Illinois* 94 US 113 (1876) (US Sup. Ct.) (hereinafter *Munn*) (*per* Waite, CJ) and *People* v. *Budd* (1889) 117 NY 1 (NY CA) (hereinafter *Budd*) (*per* Andrews, J), to name two particularly clear and thoughtful judicial statements of this view.

[45] For example, in Great Britain (excluding Northern Ireland) the common law governing common inns is now superseded by the Hotel Proprietors Act 1956.

who do so. This was certainly the traditional English common law view.[46] Judging from past efforts, however, it appears to be very difficult, if not impossible, to explain all these cases on a single unified basis. It is quite plausible that a number of different considerations are at play. Nevertheless, I want briefly to explore the second view and try to bring out its fundamental premises. I do so because, in this way, I hope to show how certain recent cases, which at first glance may seem unrelated to the older precedents, can in fact be understood as continuing them in a different context, thereby establishing the possibility—as well as the parameters of—a justiciable purely common law right to formally equal treatment.

Where a private individual, natural or corporate, is vested with rights, privileges or powers that are granted by the public authority and that ordinarily can be exercised only by such authority, that individual must exercise the right, etc. in a manner that benefits and respects the public. Instances of rights and powers of this kind include the power to take property by eminent domain and the privileges of possessing a legal monopoly or of receiving aid through taxation. To elaborate a little, such rights, powers or privileges can be granted only if the grantee's purpose is not merely private but also public: it must be of potential benefit either directly to individual members of the community or indirectly to the community as a whole. The provision of electrical power is an instance of direct benefit whereas the development of mining is an example of indirect benefit. The fundamental point is that no one should have powers that ordinarily belong to the public authority if the exercise of such powers is for a purely private purpose: this would be incompatible with the equality of all members of the public. But further, in exercising the right or power, the individual must accomplish the public purpose in a way that actually benefits the public. The acceptance of the grant of right, power or privilege carries with it the obligation to use it reasonably and impartially for the benefit of all relevant members of the public.[47] And this entails, minimally, that the right-holder "must be equal in its dealings with all".[48] This requirement of non-discrimination is a reasonable

---

[46] This view is reflected in such cases as *Lane* v. *Cotton* (1701) 12 Mod. 472 (hereinafter *Lane*) (*per* Holt CJ) and is explored and defended in the particularly instructive set of articles by C. Burdick, "The Origin of the Peculiar Duties of Public Service Companies' (1911) 11 *Columbia L Rev* 514–31, 616–38, and 743–64. For a thorough presentation of the different rationales that have been proposed for the common calling cases, see A. Reichman, "Professional Status and the Freedom to Contract: Towards a Common Law Duty of Non-Discrimination" (2001) 19 *Can. J L Juris*. 1. In this interesting piece, Reichman argues, among other things, that none of the usual rationales explains the whole body of cases. He proposes instead that the common calling requirement of non-discrimination is best viewed as making explicit the normative import of transactions that are intrinsically impersonal and non-individualised in character and purpose. Essentially any exchange of commodities comes under this category. In relation to such transactions, discrimination on the basis of a party's particular characteristics is foreign to the very purport of the transaction. This rationalisation of the cases seems, however, to deny any fundamental juridical difference between most contracts and the common callings. My own view is different. See *infra*, text accompanying n.63.

[47] For a generous sampling of judicial statements of this idea, see Burdick, *supra* n.46, at 620–38.

[48] *State of Missouri* v. *Bell Telephone Co* (1885) 23 Fed. 539.

implication, drawn by a court independently of statutory mandate, of the grant of public powers to private individuals.

Certain of the old precedents clearly fall within this line of reasoning—for instance, the peculiar public responsibilities of those who own and operate "ancient ferries",[49] "public wharves",[50] and (in many circumstances) common carriers.[51] What is striking about these and other examples of individuals being held subject to public obligations is that often the power or privilege granted limits, or places a burden upon, pre-existing rights of members of the public to benefit from the use of certain facilities that are of common interest to anyone and everyone in general. The paradigm of such facilities is the public highway over which there exists a "public" or "common" right of passage; that is, a right that inheres in each and every subject to pass without let or hindrance at any time freely and at will. In the English cases, each individual is said to have this right of passage just in virtue of being one of Her Majesty's subjects. One who limits or burdens this public right in any way must do so in a manner that ensures that each and every member of the public is benefited thereby. Thus a public ferry transports members of the public over waters that in law are deemed to be a public highway. By enjoying a legal monopoly on such service and having the privilege of imposing a toll for it, the owner places a common charge on the public. But this can be done only if the owner assumes and discharges certain obligations to the public so affected.[52] This is simply another way of inferring the public obligation, which in the preceding paragraph was derived solely from the grant of a power, right or privilege that ordinarily resides with the public authority. Even in the absence of an express grant from the public authority, we may say that no private individual can limit or burden a public or common right except on the presumption of an implied grant from that authority.[53]

In the discussion thus far, I have identified two distinct considerations that, often in combination, are at play in the public calling cases: first, the grant of some

[49] See D. Storey, "Origin and Monopoly Rights of Ancient Ferries' (1915) 76 *U Pa. L Rev.* 718.

[50] See Lord Hale's characterisation of public wharves in Lord Hale, *"De Portibus Maris"*, 1 *Harg Law Tracts* 78 excerpted and translated in *Munn, supra* n.44, at 127. *De Portibus Maris* was written in the mid-seventeenth century.

[51] See cases referred to and discussed by Burdick, *supra* n.46, at 621–4.

[52] In the English case of *Letton* v. *Godden* (1866) LR 2 Eq. 122, the court stated that the ancient ferry franchise was in derogation of common right but that the assumption by the owner of public obligations was "compensation for that derogation of common right" that gives the public "this great advantage . . . that they have at all times at hand, by reason of the ferry, the means of travelling on the king's highway, of which the ferry forms a part . . ." The same sort of analysis applies to public wharves. As for the right of eminent domain, it seems clearly to be the case that this analysis holds for takings of property already dedicated to the public's use, such as streets, highways, and so forth. In the case of takings of private property, one may be able to bring it into line with the analysis by saying that it is a taking of property that affects the right of the public inasmuch as the property could have been dedicated by the public for common use.

[53] I note that in the case of public ferries, the proprietor either must establish that it was granted a franchise from the Crown or Parliament to operate the ferry or that it acquired one by prescription on the presumption of a lost grant. See Halsbury's Laws of England *Ferries* (4th edn., London, Butterworths, 1993), vol. 21, para. 877, and Storey, *supra* n.49, at 722–5.

right, privilege, or power, such as legal monopoly, eminent domain or assistance through taxation, which is not ordinarily exercised by individuals and, secondly, a pre-existing common right in members of the public which is limited or burdened by the exercise of the right so granted. An important question is whether, even in the absence of any grant by the public authority, a public obligation can be imposed by a court upon one who uses his or her property in a way that adversely affects a common right. It is clear that the State can permissibly regulate such use of property via appropriate legislation.[54] But can a court impose this obligation as a matter of its inherent jurisdiction and authority?

While the matter is not clear-cut, it is arguable that the common law governing common or public inns illustrates precisely this possibility.[55] At common law, the keeping of an inn was not a franchise and anyone might operate an inn without a licence permitting him or her to do so. By holding out one's inn as available to members of the public in general, without express limitation, for the provision of accommodation, including food, drink and rooms for sleeping, one makes one's inn a common inn. By contrast, where one invites individuals to enter into special contracts, each distinct and different, for the provision of accommodation, the inn, to this extent, is *not* common or public. One who operates a common inn is under an obligation to receive *without discrimination any traveller* (but *only* travellers), supposing that the inn is objectively in a position to accommodate the traveller and the traveller is both willing and able to pay for the accommodation and is in a fit state to be received. Whether an owner has explicitly or implicitly invited the public in general and whether a member of the public is a traveller are questions of fact to be decided in accordance with the objective test. The most oft-quoted rationale for the obligation owed to travellers is that they "shall not, while upon their journeys, be deprived of necessary food and lodging".[56] The obligation, it is said, is rooted in a kind of public necessity.[57]

To modern eyes, the requirement of holding out one's inn as available to the general public may suggest that the innkeeper's duty to accept everyone without distinction is rooted in a tort obligation arising from induced reasonable reliance by travellers upon the innkeeper's invitation, express or implied. But a traveller's right to reasonable accommodation does not depend upon the existence of any

---

[54] An excellent judicial discussion of this point is by Andrews J in *Budd, supra* n.44, at 19.

[55] The following remarks draw on Halsbury's *Laws of England, supra* n.53, vol 24 ("Inns and Innkeepers"); Lord Anderson's comprehensive analysis in *Rothfield* v. *North British Railway Co* [1920] SC 805 (hereinafter *Rothfield*) and *Lamond* v. *Richard and the Gordon Hotels, Ltd* [1897] 1 QB 541 (Eng CA).

[56] *Burgess* v. *Clements* (1815) 4 M & S 306. In *Rothfield, ibid.,* at 817, Lord Anderson put it this way:

> "I have no doubt, however, that the considerations on which the decisions are based are just these: travellers ought not to be compelled to sleep on the highways or in the fields. Private hospitality might fail them. There might be no private house available, or the occupier might be churlish. The monastery might be fully occupied. There remained the inn—the public house— which originated in a purpose of entertaining travellers. This was obviously the institution in which a traveller should have the power of demanding necessary accommodation".

[57] Burdick, *supra* n.46, at 528.

interaction between the parties.[58] The traveller may not have changed position to his or her detriment. Some may think, then, that what is at work here is a notion of "general reliance"[59] that refers to general expectations in the community which a given individual may or may not have shared. But general reliance by travellers cannot assist a particular traveller who is expressly refused, so long as the innkeeper has done nothing to induce the traveller to change position to his or her detriment. Reliance-based liability does not seem to fit since an innkeeper's refusal to accommodate can give rise to nominal damages even though the plaintiff is able to find suitable accommodation elsewhere at no extra expense.[60] What has to be explained is just why the innkeeper is not permitted to withdraw the invitation in the absence of any detrimental reliance by the plaintiff.

I would like to suggest a different rationale, one that brings into play the idea of necessity noted above. We start from the premise that, as a member of the public, every individual is vested with the common right to make use of public highways, passes and so forth, and that, while *in itinere*, travelling members of the public may need accommodation. In the absence of possible accommodation, the value of the common right may be seriously reduced, if not eliminated. Anything that derogates from or impairs the value of such a right is of public, that is common, concern. Like a common ferry, a common inn is deemed in law to be a use of private property that affects a public highway. When an innkeeper opens his or her inn to the general public, the public that is so invited in *must not exclude travellers*. There cannot be an inn that is public and that being such is the only facility which, by the character of the use it is put to, can appear available to travellers, yet that distinguishes travellers from the rest of the general public, thereby burdening their common right to use highways. In legal contemplation, the owner of a common inn has dedicated his or her property to a public use, making it "no longer bare private interest, but . . . affected by the public interest".[61]

---

[58] The requirement of interaction between the parties is emphasised, rightly in my view, by Lord Mustill as a prerequisite to liability for negligent misrepresentation in his dissenting speech in *White v. Jones* [1995] 1 All ER 691, 729–30.

[59] In English and Commonwealth cases, the idea of general reliance was first suggested by Mason J in *Sutherland Shire Council v. Heyman* (1985) 157 CLR 424, 464 and has been more recently discussed at the House of Lords in *Stovin v. Wise* [1996] AC 923, 937 (*per* Lord Nicholls) and 953–4 (*per* Lord Hoffmann).

[60] This is the conclusion reached in *Constantine v. Imperial London Hotels, Ltd* [1944] 2 All ER 171.

[61] *Per* Lord Hale, *supra* n.50. The more complete quotation is:

"A man, for his own private advantage, may, in a port or town, set up a wharf or crane, and may take what rates he and his customers can agree for cranage . . . for he doth no more than is lawful for any man to do, viz. makes the most of his own . . . If the king or subject have a public wharf, unto which all persons that come to that port must come and unlade or lade their goods as for the purpose, because they are the wharfs only licensed by the queen, . . . or because there is no other wharf in that port, as it may fall out where a port is newly erected; in that case there cannot be taken arbitrary and excessive duties for cranage . . . &c., . . . but the duties must be reasonable and moderate . . . For now the wharf and crane and other conveniences are affected with a public interest, and they cease to be *jus privati* only; as if a man set out a street in new building on his own land, it is now no longer bare private interest, but is affected by a public interest.

Moreover, the inclusion of travellers in the definition of "the general public" is fully consistent with the use which the innkeeper has chosen for his or her property. By requiring travellers to be included within the public invitation, the law does not give the travelling public a proprietary interest of any kind, such as an easement, in the use of the inn. The determination of use still lies with the owner. The law must respect the reasonable import of the proprietor's decision. However, the notion of the reasonable here incorporates the normative idea of the public and with it the common right that must be taken as established in each member of the public to make use of the ways of passage. The idea of public is specified here in terms of common or public rights vested in individuals just as members of the public. By making the inn available to the public in general, the owner is deemed to bring it under this idea of the public. For this reason, the operation of a common inn is rightly called a "public employment" or "public office and trust".[62] In deciding whether to make his or her inn available to the general public as a whole, the innkeeper must view the choice in light of this idea, which he or she must take as at once valid and beyond the reach of any private individual.

The obligations imposed upon common innkeepers are not reducible to those that ordinarily come under the juridical conception of rights. This was emphasised by the great writers of modern private law.[63] We can see why. The common right that is vested in members of the public is not innate to each individual *qua* separate and distinct person (as is the right of bodily integrity) or acquired by them through unilateral or bilateral acts of will (as are the rights of first occupancy and contract). It is neither an innate nor an acquired right within the meaning of the juridical conception of rights. *From the standpoint of private law*, requiring a common innkeeper to accommodate any member of the public is to compel him or her to confer a benefit upon the latter, thereby making the breach of this obligation a non-feasance. There is an idea of the public supposed here that goes beyond the parameters of private law. That is why, in what is perhaps the single most influential characterisation of the sort of rights and obligations at issue here, Lord Hale referred to the common ferry, though an object of private ownership, as "affected with a public interest, and [not] juris privati only".[64] Each individual, as a member of the public, has a formally equal right of access to the facility which is of common advantage. It is, we may say, as members of civil society, that individuals are recognised as vested with this equal right. The obligation is owed toward individuals who count, not merely as distinct and separate persons with their own ends, but as members of the public who, as such, have been vested with certain rights of access for the

---

[62] See, for example, *Lane, supra* n.46, at 484–5 (per Holt CJ) and Bacon's *Abridgment*, tit Inns and Innkeepers, chap. 1: "For, he, who takes upon himself a public employment, must serve the public as far as employment goes . . .".

[63] See, for example, S. Williston, *Treatise on the Law of Contracts* (3rd edn., Mount Kisco Baker, Voorhis & Co Ltd, 1957), i, section 32A ("Duties Imposed by Law Without Assent Distinguished") and Holmes, *supra* n.19 at 160.

[64] *Supra* n.50.

accomplishment of their ends. From this standpoint, breach of the public obligation is not merely a failure to confer benefits on them but an actual injury to what is "their own" as members of the public. While not misfeasance within the parameters of private law, the breach is in and of itself a legally cognisable injury for which damages ought to be, and are, given.

Yet the recognition and enforcement of the common innkeeper's obligation may reasonably be viewed as consonant with the exercise of the judicial function of a court. It is true that the court must refer to a common right that is vested in individuals as members of the public—a right, therefore, which a court may lack the competence to establish or validate on its own authority. But in the common calling cases, the courts do not generate this right. On the contrary, they take it as already established and valid on the basis of customary law or legislative provisions.[65] It is true that the courts do not permit the private use of property to impair the value of, or unreasonably to burden, the common rights. However, in doing so, they do not go beyond their traditional function of ensuring that private rights are not construed in a way that subordinates what is inalienable—here, the common rights that inhere in individuals just as members of the public.[66] Moreover, it is the common innkeeper's own act that makes the use of his or her property affected with a public interest. The owner retains the right to determine the use to which his or her property is to be put. The Court does not, and need not, weigh, balance or harmonise the (competing) values of property and common right. It does not engage in this sort of analysis, which would certainly be appropriately and necessarily undertaken from a legislative or a constitutional point of view. Finally, the public obligations imposed on common innkeepers, as on the other common callings, such as the duties to serve all without arbitrary distinction, to charge a reasonable price, and to provide service of a reasonable standard, are all justiciable before, and readily determinable by, a court in the traditional context of two-party litigation.

The foregoing analysis of the common callings cases illumines more recent decisions that concern the relation between private entitlements on the one hand and constitutional or statutory rights on the other, in a variety of situations. I shall consider here two such situations. In my view, they suggest the limits of the reach of formal equality of opportunity in relation to the claims of property so far as this is determinable by a common law court acting on the basis of its inherent jurisdiction and authority.

The first situation is illustrated by the US case of *Doe* v. *Bridgeton Hospital Association*.[67] In *Bridgeton Hospital*, the plaintiffs, two women, instituted an action to compel the defendant, a non-sectarian, non-profit hospital, to make its

---

[65] For instance, in English law the basis was largely customary whereas in Scots law it was statutory. On the source of the common right, see *Rothfield*, *supra* n.55, at 809–11.

[66] In section II 1 (B), I suggested that this function of the law is fully consistent with an idea of policy intrinsic to private law. That common rights are inalienable follows necessarily from the fact that they are not, and cannot be, acquired by individual acts of will.

[67] (1976) 366 A 2d 641 (SCNJ) (hereinafter *Bridgeton Hospital*).

facilities available to the plaintiffs and their physicians, who were members of the hospital staff, for elective abortion procedures during the first trimester of pregnancy. Objectively speaking, the hospital was fully able to accommodate the plaintiffs—there were adequate facilities, rooms, staff, and so forth—but the hospital's board of directors had previously adopted a policy of permitting only therapeutic abortions. The basis of the board's decision was conscientious moral opposition to elective abortions, notwithstanding that such abortions were legally permissible since *Roe* v. *Wade*.[68] The defendant contended that this policy reflected the community's conscience and that to overrule that sentiment would cause the loss of substantial support. The Supreme Court of New Jersey rejected the defendant's arguments and held that the hospital's policy against elective abortions was in breach of a public obligation owed by it toward individual members of the public to provide medical care and services without distinction or discrimination.

The basis of the decision is the court's conclusion that the defendant hospital is a "quasi-public" institution within the meaning of the common callings and Lord Hale's characterisation of private property as affected with a public interest. A number of factors lead the court so to conclude: the hospital is a non-sectarian institution that makes its medical facilities available to the general public; it is the beneficiary of tax exemptions; and it receives substantial financial support from federal and local governments. As a quasi-public institution, the defendant cannot pick and choose its patients or the services it provides to them on any basis other than a purely medical one, related to the hospital's purposes and operational needs. Accordingly, "moral concepts cannot be the basis of a non-sectarian non-profit . . . hospital's regulations where that hospital is holding out the use of its facilities to the general public".[69] As the court observes, this conclusion perfectly parallels the old law governing common inns which held that moral objections, unrelated to the fitness of a traveller to be admitted to an inn, could not be a reasonable basis for refusing to accommodate him or her. What is striking is that at *no* point in the court's reasoning does the fact that the plaintiffs have a *constitutional* right to an abortion play any role as such. The only thing relevant and sufficient is just that an abortion is a lawful medical procedure like any other.

The court's characterisation of the defendant as a quasi-public institution subject to public obligations is arguable on either of the two bases discussed above. Being the recipient of public funding and tax benefits, the hospital is the grantee of privileges that are justifiable only if it operates for a public purpose in a way that serves the members of the public impartially and reasonably. Hence its obligation to provide medical service and care to members of the public without making distinctions on non-medical and non-operational grounds. In the alternative, assuming that individuals, as members of the public, have a

---

[68]   410 US 113 (1973).
[69]   *Bridgeton Hospital, supra* n.67, at 647.

common right to make use of facilities that provide medical care and service in the same way that they have such a right with respect to public highways,[70] and supposing that the hospital, in virtue of its holding out to the general public, has made itself affected with a public interest, the defendant has impaired the common right of the plaintiffs by denying them access for medical purposes on non-medical grounds. On neither approach, however, is the constitutional character of the plaintiffs' interest specifically relevant: the exact same conclusion would be reached if the plaintiffs had instead needed routine medical check-ups or tests and were denied access for irrelevant reasons.

The second situation that I wish to discuss brings out not only the basis but also the limits of a justiciable common law claim to formally equal treatment in relation to the exercise of private rights by others. I am referring to the "shopping centre cases". While there are a number of important decisions of the United States Supreme Court in this area,[71] I want to focus on the great dissenting opinion of Chief Justice Laskin in the case of *Harrison* v. *Carswell*.[72] By ending with the author of Bhadauria,[73] we come full circle.

In *Harrison*, the accused, Mrs Carswell, who was involved in a labour dispute, sought to picket peacefully her employer, a tenant in a shopping centre, in support of a lawful strike. The shopping centre had the usual public amenities, such as access roads, car parks and pavements, which were open for use to members of the public who might or might not be buyers at the time they came to the shopping centre. Carswell picketed her employer peacefully on the pavement in front of its premises. Although the picketing neither obstructed use of the pavement nor inconvenienced others, the owner of the plaza introduced himself into the situation and warned Carswell that if she did not leave she would be charged with trespass. As a matter of its own policy, the centre had prohibited the distribution of pamphlets or leaflets anywhere on its premises and did not permit any person to walk in the mall carrying placards. When Carswell continued to picket on the shopping centre pavement, she was charged with trespass. The majority of the Supreme Court upheld her conviction at the trial level.

It is possible to read the Laskin dissent as centring upon the need to strike a balance between the conflicting values of property and labour rights. Indeed,

---

[70] This is arguably the main thrust of the court's discussion of New Jersey public policy and legislation at *ibid.*, at 646. I acknowledge, however, that the idea of such a common right is not free from difficulties and that it has to be further clarified and more fully explained. That is why, for the present purposes of illustration, I have merely assumed it.

[71] The leading decisions of the US Supreme Court are *Marsh* v. *Alabama* 326 US 501 (1945) (hereinafter *Marsh*); *Amalgamated Food Employees Union Local 590* v. *Logan Valley Plaza, Inc*, 391 US 308 (1968); *Lloyd Corp, Ltd* v. *Tanner* 407 US 551 (1972) (hereinafter *Lloyd Corp*); and *Pruneyard Shopping Center* v. *Robins* 447 US 74 (1980).

[72] (1975) 62 DLR (3d) 68 (hereinafter *Harrison*). I note that Justices Beetz and Spence joined Laskin CJC in the dissenting opinion. I am grateful to my wife, Ann, for making clear to me that the Laskin dissent is not about balancing property and statutory rights but rather about the reasonable implications that follow from an owner's decision to make his or her property accessible to the public in general.

[73] *Supra* n.3.

this is how the majority opinion of Justice Dickson views the dissent's approach. But if this is right, then, as the majority emphasises, correctly in my view as I shall explain shortly, the question is not one that a court can appropriately answer, at least not in the absence of applicable legislative provisions. I want to offer a different view of the dissent—one that captures better what Laskin wrote and that construes the issue in a way that places it squarely within a court's competence. The disagreement between the dissent and majority is not concerning the proper role and limits of the judicial function. They differ only in so far as Laskin, I will now suggest, correctly sees that, in the words of Lord Hale, the plaza owner's use of his property is not a matter of *juris privati* merely but is affected with a public interest. There is no need to balance competing values or to subordinate property to the rights of labour.

Right from the start, Chief Justice Laskin emphasises that Carswell is making use of a facility to which the plaza owner has invited the general public and which is freely accessible to that public. It is "in respect of areas of the shopping centre which have been opened up by him to public use, and necessarily so because of the commercial character of the enterprise" that the court must judge whether Carswell is committing a trespass. Here is the nerve of Laskin's proposed analysis[74]:

> The considerations which underlie the protection of private residences cannot apply to the same degree to a shopping centre in respect of its parking areas, roads and sidewalks. Those amenities are closer in character to public roads and sidewalks than to a private dwelling. All that can be urged from a theoretical point of view to assimilate them to private dwellings is to urge that if property is privately owned, *no matter the use to which it is put*, trespass is as appropriate in the one case as in the other and it does not matter that possession . . . is recognizable in the one case but not in the other . . . What does a shopping centre owner protect, for what invaded interest of his does he seek vindication in ousting members of the public from sidewalks and roadways and parking areas in the shopping centre? . . . Should he be allowed to choose what members of the public come into those areas when they have been opened to all without discrimination? . . . Disapproval of the owner, in assertion of a remote control over the "public" areas of the shopping centre, whether it be disapproval of picketing or disapproval of the wearing of hats or anything equally innocent, may be converted (so it is argued) into a basis of ouster of members of the public. Can the common law be so devoid of reason as to tolerate this kind of whimsy where public areas of a shopping centre are concerned? . . . A more appropriate approach . . . is to recognize a continuing privilege in using the areas of the shopping centre *provided for public passage* subject to limitations arising out of the nature of the activity thereon and to the object pursued thereby, and subject as well to a limitation against material damage.

This analysis is fundamentally the same as that which the common law traditionally applied by the common law in the case of common inns. Indeed, it is perhaps an even more straightforward application of the underlying idea. To begin, we should recall Lord Hale's statement that "if a man set out a street in

---

[74] *Harrison, supra* n.72, at 73–6 (emphasis added).

new building on his own land, it is now no longer bare private interest, but is affected by a public interest".[75] In effect, the Laskin opinion says, the plaza owner has decided to put certain parts of its private property to a use that gives it the character of a public street or highway. Recall here that whether an owner has so dedicated his or her property is a question of fact to be decided in accordance with an objective test: by how, given the factual context, the owner's intention would reasonably appear to others. Having dedicated his property, and continuing to do so, the owner cannot unreasonably deny access to any member of the public who makes use of it in a manner that is consistent with the reasonable character and import of the owner's invitation. While, in the absence of legislation, it is open to the owner to determine the use to which his property shall be put—hence, open to the owner *not* to invite the public in general but to limit the invitation to only certain classes of public entrants[76]—he cannot unreasonably burden the common right of members of the public to make use of a public way of passage once he has dedicated his property to such use. But an individual's common right is burdened if she cannot be present and move on the public areas simply by reason of the fact that she is exercising a legal right (as is the case here) that is consonant with the character of the owner's property and the activities that ordinarily take place thereon.

The proposed analysis does not subtract from the owner's exclusive right to possess, use or alienate his or her property. It does not give members of the public a proprietary interest of any kind in the public parts of the plaza. The owner is not to any extent obliged to continue to use the plaza in any particular way, except as he chooses. Moreover, members of the public can claim the privilege to use the public areas only if they are doing so in a way that is compatible with the character and purposes which the owner has chosen for his property. Here, the accused was exercising her statutory right to picket on the pavement immediately adjacent to her employer's premises in the shopping centre. Had she been demonstrating for some cause unrelated to her legal rights as against a tenant in the plaza, the outcome, Laskin noted, might be different.[77]

Moreover, on the Laskin approach, the fact that the accused is exercising what is otherwise a statutory or even a constitutional right plays, as such, no essential role. The wrong by the plaza owner or the common innkeeper is not that he or she impairs the value and enjoyment of the excluded individual's right to picket or to demonstrate. It is rather that the owner burdens the latter's common right as a member of the public. For it is only the common right that is engaged by the owner's dedication of his or her property to a public use. The point is that Mrs Carswell's common right should not be burdened just because

---

[75] For the full passage from which this sentence is taken, see *supra* n.61.

[76] Laskin CJC notes this possibility at *supra* n.72, at 74.

[77] *Ibid.*, at 77. It is interesting to note that Laskin CJ distinguishes the factual context in *Harrison* from that in a prior decision of the Court in R v. *Peters* (1971) 17 DLR (3d) 128 on precisely this point: in *Peters*: "the picketing arose not out of a labour dispute with an employer tenant of premises in the shopping centre, but was by way of a boycott appeal against the selling of grapes"; *ibid.*, at 70.

she is engaged in this particular kind of lawful activity. But, as already noted, if the activity is *not* consonant with the character of the owner's property and the reasonable import of his or her public invitation, denying the individual access will not be deemed a burden upon the individual's common right, even where the activity entails what, for other purposes, is an exercise of a legal, statutory or even a constitutional right. We must emphasise that the baseline or starting-point for analysis is that, in the absence of valid legislative enactment to this effect, no one has a right to exercise his or her rights (of whatever character) on the private property of another.

These considerations and limits are articulated in the US cases, some of which the Laskin dissent refers to with approval. The upshot of these decisions is to root firmly the proprietor's duty to members of the public in the character of the use to which he or she puts the property. This is brought out clearly in the more recent and very interesting case of *State of New Jersey* v. *Schmid*.[78]

In *Schmid*, the Supreme Court of New Jersey had to determine whether the defendant, who had been convicted of trespass for distributing political litera-ture on the campus of Princeton University without its prior authorisation, could rely on his federal or state constitutional rights to set aside the conviction and whether, in evicting him, it was in fact the university that had violated his rights. What is striking is that the court makes the very possibility of a violation of the defendant's constitutional rights[79] depend upon the nature, purposes and primary use of the university's property as well as upon the extent and nature of the public invitation to use that property: the character and extent of the owner's holding out of his property for public use determine what, if any,

---

[78]   (1980) 423 A 2d 615 (hereinafter *Schmid*).

[79]   By way of background, it should be noted that, in the absence of state action, American jurisprudence does not countenance the possibility of a private individual violating another's con-stitutional rights under the *federal* US Constitution. By contrast, state constitutions have been inter-preted as providing individuals with rights that are enforceable against other individuals in limited circumstances—essentially where the latter "have otherwise assumed a constitutional obligation not to abridge the individual exercise of such freedoms *because of the public use of their property*": *ibid.*, at 628 (emphasis added). The US courts thus view State constitutions, in contrast to the fed-eral constitution, as allowing the *direct* application of constitutional rights in circumstances where property is affected with a public interest. According to the view that I have proposed, what is owed by the owner to those who make use of the premises as a result of an invitation to the public in gen-eral is a public obligation not to burden their common rights. In cases such as *Schmid*, the individ-ual's common right to use public places is burdened if he is excluded simply because he is engaged in the expressive activity of handing out pamphlets, etc. As the court in *Schmid* emphasises, this activity, even if it involves the exercise of a right under the constitution, must be consonant with the character of "the nature, purposes, and primary use of such private property [and] the extent and nature of the public's invitation to use that property"; *ibid.*, at 630. In fact, therefore, the analysis proposed by the court need not be viewed as endorsing the direct application of state constitutional rights. It vindicates the common rights of all members of the public in circumstances where private property has been dedicated to a public use. This line of argument should therefore applicable even where an individual member of the public is making use of dedicated property in a way that involves the exercise of his or her *federal* constitutional rights. And this, I suggest, is how the decision of the US Supreme Court in *Marsh*, *supra* n.71, which held that an individual's exercise of a federal con-stitutional right could not be a reasonable basis for the owner revoking the public invitation, is best understood.

public function has been undertaken, and the scope of the constitutional restraints in that public function can then be ascertained.[80] Where the parties are purely private and there is no applicable legislation or state action, courts can subject the exercise of private entitlements to constitutional requirements or, more correctly, can bring such requirements to bear *only* in so far as and because the owner has made the object of his right affected with a public interest, and even then only within the scope of the reasonable import of the dedication.[81] It must be emphasised that where the invitation to the public is not open-ended,[82] there must always be a qualitative determination of whether the exercise of a constitutional freedom or legal right is consonant with the reasonable import of the invitation, viewed in light of the character and normal operation of the property.[83]

The fact that the courts view constitutional rights as coming into play only if this is consonant with the use that an owner happens to make of his or her property shows that what is at stake cannot be the balancing of property and constitutional freedoms or the placing of limitations upon property in favour of such freedoms. For basic constitutional freedoms are inalienable; as such, they are, in their very nature, rights that cannot be subordinated to the determinations of property owners. It is not at all a matter of vindicating fundamental freedoms in the face of the right of property. Rather, as I have tried to argue, in these situations, like that of the common inn, the question is whether, by putting his property to a certain use, the owner has brought into play a common right that is vested in everyone as a member of the public and whether the owner has unreasonably burdened this right by excluding an individual, *qua* member of the public, on a particular ground—whether it is the fact that the individual is a traveller, is exercising a statutory or constitutional right, or, to use Chief Justice Laskin's example, is simply wearing a hat. Despite the diversity of grounds for exclusion, the wrong remains the same.

Within these parameters, the decisions remain judicial rather than legislative. Or at least I have tried to suggest an argument why they may reasonably be viewed as such. Once, however, the analysis is not constrained by the idea of

---

[80] *Ibid.*, at 639–40, *per* Schreiber J, concurring.

[81] "*Since* Schmid's political expression is consistent with the achievement of Princeton's goals [in virtue of which it has held out its property for a public use], he is entitled to the protection of the right of free speech guaranteed by the New Jersey Constitution"; *ibid.*, at 639 (emphasis added).

[82] Arguably the owner's dedication of its property to public use in *Marsh*, *supra* n.71, was open-ended, or virtually so, where it was a whole town that was privately owned by a company and the appellant, a Jehovah's Witness, was charged with trespass for distributing religious literature on one of its pavements. Given the comprehensive character of the property—a municipality by ordinary standards—any activity that would ordinarily take place on the public places of a town would be consonant with the company's invitation to the public.

[83] In *Schmid*, the court underlined the fit between the defendant's activity of distributing political literature in the furtherance of political debate and exposure to different ideas and the distinctive character and function of the university as well as the purpose of its dedication of certain places to a public use—which is to make its campus available as a forum for open and robust exchanges of political views by both the university community and the public generally. See *supra* n.78, at 630–3 and 640.

dedication to public use—once, in other words, it is a question of balancing or reconciling property and fundamental freedoms outside this context—a court must inevitably be engaged in what is conceptually a legislative enterprise. In keeping with its judicial character, a court must take up each side—property and fundamental rights—in its own terms. It is as such that the court must then seek to balance or reconcile them. How it can do so is not clear for the right of property is either respected or it is not: from the standpoint of the law of property itself, there is not, and cannot be, any distinction between a "central range" or "essential core meaning" of property rights on the one hand and a "peripheral" or "less central" dimension on the other hand. Such a distinction may be intelligible and reasonable from the standpoint of the common good and the state's police power to regulate the use of property—including the power to determine what (alienable) items may be subject to private ownership[84]—in furtherance of the common good. But then the relevant normative framework is legislative and constitutional, not that of the common law enforceable by a court acting on its inherent authority and competence as a court.

To be more concrete, suppose we try to reconcile property and freedom of expression in a shopping mall case where, we shall suppose, the expressive activity, though perfectly lawful, falls outside the scope of the reasonable import of the owner's dedication to public use.[85] The inquiry must then take the following form: we have to decide whether it is reasonable and fair to subordinate a particular property, which a non-owner happens to choose as the site for exercising his or her constitutional freedom, to the exercise of that freedom. This can only be a legislative decision which assesses a whole range of social, political and institutional facts and considerations, including the need to uphold a certain range of liberties and rights associated with a particular regime of private property and the equal, if not more fundamental, necessity of securing the fair value of fundamental (constitutional) rights and freedoms. So, in the case of a shopping centre dispute, it would be a matter of deciding whether, as against the values associated with the possession and enjoyment of private property, it is reasonable to require plazas to be used for the exercise of, say, political speech in order to ensure that there is ample space and occasion for the exercise of this freedom, not just in this particular instance, but for citizens more generally, viewed across society and over time. Conceptually speaking, this sort of inquiry is the same as that which must be undertaken in deciding questions of zoning. It is quintessentially a legislative determination.

---

[84] Thus Rawls argues that while a right to personal property is a basic liberty of free and equal citizens in a constitutional liberal democracy, private ownership of the natural resources, the means of production, and so forth is not a basic liberty. It is a legislative decision, made in light of a given society's history, traditions, and social conditions, whether or not, and to what extent, such things should be subject to private ownership. See Rawls, *Political Liberalism*, *supra* n.2, Lecture VIII.

[85] For example, the US Supreme Court determined that this was the case on the facts in *Lloyd Corp*, *supra* n.71.

To bring this discussion to a close, it is appropriate to return to *Bhaudauria*[86] and ask whether the argument that I have presented for a justiciable claim to formally equal treatment would support the plaintiff's common law action in that case. I think the answer must be not, unless the defendant college can be regarded as a quasi-public institution by virtue of its being granted certain otherwise public powers, rights and privileges by the State or, alternatively, unless it can be reasonably viewed as having dedicated its property to a public use (in the sense discussed in this section) simply by advertising for teachers and pursuing its search for them. But, so far as the second ground goes, it seems implausible to equate a decision to search for potential parties to a special, individualised contract with the kind of public invitation to make use of one's property that must exist for there to be a public dedication. This does not seem reasonably to make the defendant's property or exercise of private entitlement (in this case the liberty to decide whether to enter into contractual relations with others) affected with a public interest. Here we see the limits of the possibility of a justiciable right to non-discrimination. Nor can one avoid this difficulty by saying that while the exercise of private entitlements is not directly subject to a duty to respect constitutional rights and freedoms, it is permissible to constrain that exercise to comport with constitutional "values", as distinct from constitutional rights: in both cases, the limitation is legislative in character unless the property or private entitlement may reasonably be viewed as affected with a public interest.

The fundamental question here is not whether a limitation on property or other private entitlements in favour of non-discrimination can be legitimate—I have supposed throughout this chapter that it can be and is. Rather, what is at stake is the conceptual issue of the normative character and basis of such a limitation and of its place within the legal system as a whole. My conclusion is that a limitation of this kind cannot be rooted in private law, understood as the institutional expression of the juridical conception of rights; and that while there is a basis for a requirement of formal equality of opportunity in common law, this requirement can function only as an aspect of a public obligation that is owed to members of the public in circumstances of a dedication of property to the public. It is via this route that the constitutionalisation of rights can play a role, albeit circumscribed, in the application of the common law. But this does not imply any change in the distinctive and fundamental character of private law.

[86] *Supra* n.3.

11

Property Rights, Public Policy and the Limits of the Legal Power to Discriminate

AMNON REICHMAN*

I. OVERVIEW

CAN A RESTAURANT owner rely on his property rights to establish a rule prohibiting blacks, Jews, gays, women or members of other similarly constructed groups from entering his restaurant?[1]

In Canada, the answer to this question was settled in a handful of cases decided in the first half of the twentieth century.[2] The courts determined that, generally, the property rights of an owner of a commercial establishment include the legal power to bar any and all members of a certain group from entering the place of business solely because of their membership in that group. The courts found that property rights entitle the owner to institute whatever rule regarding the use of the property the owner saw fit, save for rules that were otherwise illegal or that contradicted public policy.[3] The courts viewed the exercise of one's property rights to establish a rule excluding blacks from

* This chap. is based on a chapter of my SJD dissertation entitled *Taking Constitutional Structures Seriously: A Canadian Case Study* (Faculty of Law, University of Toronto, 2000, written under the supervision of Professor Lorraine Weinrib). I would like to thank Peter Benson, Alan Brudner, Denise Réaume and Ernest Weinrib for their helpful comments, and Alison Warner and Vanessa Yolles for their editorial assistance. The responsibility for any error is mine.

[1] The question at the core of this chap. should not be confused with a similar question regarding the freedom of the restaurateur to refuse to serve, based on his freedom of contract (or more specifically, his freedom not to contract). For a discussion of the freedom not to contract and the duty to provide equal service placed upon members of non-associational professions see A. Reichman, "Professional Status and the Freedom to Contract: Toward a Common Law Duty of Non-Discrimination" (2001) 19 *Can. J L & Juris.* 79. See also *infra* n.43.

[2] *Christie* v. *York Corp.* [1940] SCR 139 (hereinafter *Christie*); *Loew's Theatres* v. *Reynolds* (1921) 30 Que. KB 459 (hereinafter *Loew's*); *Franklin* v. *Evans* (1924) 55 OLR 349 (KB) (hereinafter *Franklin*).

[3] "Every proprietor is master of his own domain; he may, as he pleases, establish any rule that does not conflict with standards of good behaviour or public order. Thus, a theatre manager could admit only persons dressed in evening attire. The rule might appear arbitrary, but it would be neither illegal nor prohibited": *Loew's, supra* n.2, at 460–1 (and later referred to in *Christie, supra* n.2); translated from French original.

a restaurant or a theatre for no other reason but their race as raising no public policy concerns.[4]

Were these cases correctly decided? Did the courts fully ascertain the powers and obligations that flow from the underlying premise of property rights, when applied to property used for commercial purposes? Did the courts thoroughly engage the analytical structure of the public policy doctrine?

The first part of this chapter will examine some aspects of property rights in order to determine whether the cluster of rights and powers bundled into the ownership of property includes the power to institute a legally enforceable rule which bars members of a certain group from entering a place of commerce, that is, a rule which deems such members trespassers should they enter the property, solely because of their group membership. More specifically, this chapter will point to case law that suggests a different outcome. A skeletal argument from theory will follow, contending that the *in rem* nature of property places a constraint on the use of property rights so that one may not rely on *in rem* property rights to deny members of groups constructed around immutable or nearly immutable characteristics access to property used for commercial, rather than associational, purposes.

The chapter will then examine the courts' conclusion that public policy is not implicated when property rights are used to restrict access of members of certain immutable groups solely on the basis of membership in the group. Two Canadian cases where the doctrine of public policy played a prominent part either explicitly, in the courts' reasoning, or implicitly, in counsel's arguments, will be reviewed. The chapter will suggest that, properly conceived, the doctrine of public policy is not a "policy-based" addendum to the common law, but rather a necessary component of the legal structure at the core of civil society, consistent with the premise of property rights.

Contained in the analysis above is the submission that the common law itself is the proper normative source whence non-discrimination norms should be sought. Rather than skipping over the underlying structure of the common law and turning to external normative sources, such as human rights codes or the constitutional bill of rights, this chapter suggests that the common law itself

---

[4] *Loew's, supra* n.2, at 460–1; *Franklin, supra* n.2. In response, Canadian legislatures enacted human rights codes which outlaw such discrimination (W.S. Tarnopolsky and W.F. Pentney, *Discrimination and the Law* (Scarborough, Carswell, 1994), chaps. 1, 2). Consequently, courts now view public policy as rejecting some forms of discrimination (see for example, *Canada Trust* v. *Ontario Human Rights Commission* (1991) 74 OR 481 (CA) (hereinafter *Canada Trust*)). However, the presence of the codes does not render the analysis of common law property rights and public policy moot. Theoretically, the codes focus on the duty to provide equal service, which is a freedom of contract claim, rather than a property claim. Practically, as *Canada Trust* reveals, common law analysis (in that case, of public policy regarding a charitable trust) cannot be avoided. Moreover, some codes do not protect against discrimination on all relevant grounds. In *Vriend* v. *Alberta* [1998] 1 SCR 493, the Supreme Court of Canada was forced constitutionally to review the Individual's Rights Protection Act, RSA 1980, c I-2, am SA 1985, c 33, SA 1990, c 23, for its failure to protect against discrimination on the grounds of sexual orientation. For a critique of such constitutional approach see A. Reichman, *Taking Constitutional Structures Seriously* (SJD Thesis, University of Toronto, 2000) chap. 3 and references therein.

should be the first legal tier engaged in the search for the contours and limits of common law property rights, including the limits on the use of property rights to discriminate.

It should be stated at the outset that, methodologically, this chapter approaches the common law as a system of rules and principles organised around the idea of reason, at the core of which lie the concepts of moral agency and human dignity of all community members. Put differently, this chapter assumes the following: that the content of common law norms, as part of the common law legal regime, draws its ultimate legitimacy from reason rather than from political decisions of elected or non-elected representatives; that the institutional guardian of the common law, namely the common law court of general jurisdiction, is obligated to strive for coherence and consistency among the common law principles derived from reason; and that the theory of justice at the core of the common law governing private entities is corrective rather than distributive. Corrective justice stipulates that rights and correlative duties owed by one individual to another flow from an imperative to respect the embodiment of human dignity and the expression of autonomy of all community members, and the breach of such imperative warrants a remedy at law. Thus, the primary function of a court under the common law is to settle disputes according to the litigants' rights and obligations; in so doing, the court effectuates the litigants' membership in the community of moral agents.[5]

This, of course, is not to suggest that the body of law thus far developed by common law courts is the best articulation of reason-based principles. Courts often "get it wrong", and establish doctrines that are in tension with the principles derived from reason, as some of the case law discussed in this chapter demonstrates. Yet the fact that courts on some occasions have reached troubling conclusions and have failed fully to grasp the scope and limits inherent to the concept of property rights are just that: judicial mistakes. Such errors should not prompt us to cease our attempts to elucidate a clearer understanding of common law principles and doctrines in favour of other normative sources, at least until we are convinced that the common law has reached its conceptual limits, and the answer we seek lies in a different theoretical approach to justice and law.

The aim of this chapter, then, is to reintroduce the common law as the relevant legal regime with which to combat discrimination. By presenting possible bases from which to conceptualise the limits on the exercise of property rights,

---

[5] This "19th century view" of the common law (so labelled unpejoratively in J.W. Singer, "No Right To Exclude: Public Accommodations And Private Property" (1996) 90 *Nw U L Rev.* 1283, 1304) is formalistic (E. Weinrib, *The Idea of Private Law* (Cambridge, Mass., Harvard University Press, 1995); A. Brudner, *The Unity of the Common Law* (Berkeley, Cal., University of California Press, 1995)). Under this approach the common law is not seen as a reflection of organic community norms which differ among the various communities (R. Post, "Cultural Heterogeneity and the Law: Pornography, Blasphemy, and the First Amendment" (1988) 76 *Cal. L Rev.* 297) or an expression of a political decision made by judges, in essence no different from a political decision made by the legislature (R. Dworkin, *Law's Empire* (Cambridge, Mass., Belknap Press, 1986). Rather, this approach puts forward a justification for the common law which views the creative judicial craft as an attempt to articulate and apply universal reason-based principles.

this chapter invites further discussion of the case law and theory governing private law and the administration of justice in civil society.

At first blush, it appears that a person can do whatever she pleases with her own property; after all, that is the meaning of ownership.[6] Ownership of property includes, it seems, the ultimate power to destroy the property, and certainly the lesser power to put in place rules regarding the disposition of the property which should apply to all those who wish to use the property, whether they agree to them or not. In that respect, full ownership is equated with sovereignty. Such full powers could include, one would think,[7] the right to refuse the entry of people of a certain race, gender, religion, hair colour or sexual orientation to one's commercial property.

However, further analysis reveals that common law courts have recognised exceptions to that rule. Four possible articulations of the rationale behind these exceptions will be presented, in an attempt to generalise a principled approach to the limits of the exercise of property rights: undertaking a common calling, property affected with a public interest, the necessity doctrine, and the *in rem* nature of property rights.

1. The undertaking of a common calling

Perhaps the most notable articulation of the limits placed on the exercise of one's property rights is related to the law governing professions deemed "common callings". The common law does not allow an innkeeper—a vocation classified as a common calling—to deny a traveller lodging in his inn without good reason,[8] the race of the guest not being one of them.[9] In other words, the

---

[6] For theoretical and contextual discussions of the concept of property see J. Tully, *A Discourse on Property: John Locke and His Adversaries* (Cambridge, New York, Cambridge University Press, 1980); J.W. Singer, *Entitlement: The Paradoxes of Property* (New Haven, Conn., Yale University Press, 2000); J. Waldron, *The Right to Private Property* (Oxford, Clarendon Press, 1988); J.R. Pennock and J.W. Chapman (eds.), *Nomos XXII: Property* (New York, New York University Press, 1980); L. Becker, *Property Rights: Philosophical Foundations* (London, Routledge & Kegan Paul, 1977); A. Carter *The Philosophical Foundations of Property Rights* (Toronto, Harvester Wheatsheaf, 1989); See also the collection of articles in (1993) 6 *Can. J L & Juris.* and P. Benson, chap. 10 this vol.

[7] Courts certainly thought so: see *supra* n.2.

[8] See generally *Halsbury's Laws of England* (4th edn., London, Butterworths, 1980) (hereinafter *Halsbury's Laws of England*) vol. 34, "Innkeepers". An innkeeper is a proprietor of an establishment held out as offering food, drink and, if so required, sleeping accommodation, without special contract, to any traveller presenting himself who appears to be able and willing to pay a reasonable sum for the services and facilities and who is in a fit condition to be received.

[9] *Constantine* v. *Imperial Hotels* [1944] 1 KB 693.

innkeeper may not establish a rule barring black guests from the inn, even though the inn is, technically speaking, private property; once he has designated his lodging to serve as an inn and once he has undertaken to act in his professional capacity as an innkeeper, he may not exercise his property rights in a manner inconsistent with the purpose of an innkeeper. The same presently applies to common carriers[10] and ferrymen[11]; it also applied to a long list of other common callings in the past.[12]

Since the common callings, past and present, are organised around non-individual or non-associational commerce, that is, the provision of goods and services irrespective of the group-based characteristics of the provider or the customer, allowing the provider to exercise his property rights so as to exclude a customer (or a prospective customer) based on such group-based characteristics is inconsistent with the provider's undertaking.

Conceptually, the common calling cases can be seen as focusing on the exercise of property rights by the rights-holder. The limit on the exercise of property rights stems from the rights-holder's undertaking to designate his property for the purpose of carrying out his vocation, in light of the nature of the vocation as common, i.e., open to all. Since an innkeeper requires an inn for carrying out his calling (or profession), a ferryman a ferry and a common carrier a designated vehicle, and since members of these callings undertake to provide the services at the core of their profession by holding themselves out as acting in their professional capacity, the professional is, in a sense, estopped from establishing rules over his inn, ferry or vehicle that are inconsistent with his undertaking to exercise his property rights in accordance with his professional role. Since the common callings are organised around an impersonal commercial transaction open to the public at large—that is, the profession constructs a customer stripped of any characteristics irrelevant to the transaction—the professional role-obligation, by which the professional is bound, is not to exercise his property rights (when acting in his professional capacity) so as to institute access rules based on irrelevant group-based characteristics.

The law of common callings should not necessarily be thought of, conceptually or historically, as restricted to the three callings still recognised by contemporary

[10] See generally *Halsbury's Laws of England, supra* n.8, at "Common Carries" (in *Carriers*) vol. 5(1), especially paras. 402, 441, 498: A common carrier is one who exercises the public profession of carrying the goods of all persons wishing to use his services or of carrying passengers whoever they may be.

[11] See generally *Halsbury's Laws of England, supra* n.8, at "Ferries" (in *Highways, Streets and Bridges*) vol. 21 paras. 877, 886. A ferryman is the holder of a franchise to operate a ferry. Such a franchise is granted by the Crown or Parliament, or acquired by prescription (continuing use) which assumes a lost grant. A ferry line is considered to be a "highway of a special description": *Huzzey* v. *Field* (1835) 2 Cr M&R 432; a highway in turn, is defined as a "way over which there exists a public right of passage, that is to say a right of all Her Majesty's subjects at all seasons of the year freely and at their will to pass and repass without let or hindrance": *ibid.*, at para. 1. The right to charge tolls is usually incident to a ferry operation: *ibid.*, at para. 877.

[12] C.K. Burdick, "The Origin of the Peculiar Duties of Public Service Companies" (1911) 11 *Colum. L Rev.* 514; E.A. Adler, "Business Jurisprudence" (1914) 28 *Harv. L Rev.* 135; N.F. Arterburn, "The Origin and First Test of Public Calling" (1926) 74 *U Pa. L Rev.* 411.

doctrine. Rather, except for associational commerce (such as identity-sensitive clubs or other associations that require meaningful membership[13]), all business is "common", and thus it is not surprising that most callings were recognised as common by courts at some point in time.[14] It follows, then, that there is support in the case law for the proposition that property rights over commercial property, i.e., property designated for conducting such commerce, cannot be used to exclude members of the public based on irrelevant group-based characteristics.

2. Property affected with a public interest

A different approach to the limits on the scope of property rights shifts the focus from the rights-holder to the nature of the property itself. Some types of land (and other property) were deemed at one point or another as "public", and thus could not be privately owned. The ancient theatre,[15] the market-place and high-way are examples; no one could own a theatre, although other proprietary rights were available, such as a lease from the sovereign or a right of access. Property rights vested in such property were limited and did not include the power to institute rules over the property that were deemed detrimental to the public's interest in that property. Other types of property, while capable of accepting private ownership, were deemed "public" so as to qualify the breadth of legal powers generally[16] associated with ownership. More specifically, such property would not accept the owner's legal power to bar access of members of the public who sought to use the property for its public purpose. For example, even if one owned a crane on a public wharf, one could not rely on property rights to deny the use of the crane to unload a boat when such an action was necessary.[17]

---

[13] The term "associational commerce" is contrasted with "general commerce". The latter captures all commerce that is premised on an interaction between the provider of goods and services and the impersonal customer as such. Associational commerce is premised on a form of meaningful relationship between the two contracting parties, where the exact identity and characteristcs of the parties intrinsically matters, as would be the case with operating an associational club. For the distinction see Reichman, *supra* n.1.

[14] Adler, *supra* n.12.

[15] Bracton, *The Laws and Customs of England* (S.E. Thorne trans., (Cambridge, Mass., Harvard University Press, 1968) states that ultimate ownership over some property, "by its nature" (at 41) cannot be owned by another person, and some ownership of some property is vested in God the community, or the *universitas*. Curiously enough, for the purposes of *Loew's*, among these things are "theatres, stadia and the like; if there are any [such] they are the common property of the citizenry. Theatres are so called from 'theorando', that is watching as a spectator. . . . Such are said to be the property of the *universitas* in dominion and use": *ibid.*, at 28, 41.

[16] Without delving into the intricacies of property law, it is established that even full ownership is limited: it does not include, for example, the power to control air traffic above the property or the passage of electromagnetic waves through the property, even though ownership extends to the surrounding air as well as above and below the land. Air traffic and telecommunication, in a sense, were deemed "public", and hence unsusceptible to the "exclusive" powers of the landowner. In the same vein, when a property owner builds a road on his property, the regulation of the manner of driving—left or right—escapes the powers of the landlord even though theoretically a landlord may put in place rules regarding the manner in which his property is to be used.

[17] *Bolt* v. *Stennet* (1800) 8 Term. Rep. 606, 101 ER 1572.

The categorisation of property affected with a public interest so as to place it beyond the unrestricted control of its owner (or possessor of lesser proprietary rights) requires the determination of which property falls into this category, and what legal powers are outside the reach of the rights-holder *vis-à-vis* the property. As for the first question, US jurisprudence[18] suggests that eventually all commercial property is invested, to some extent, with a public interest, since as soon as general commerce is engaged, the public at large, and thus the public interest, is engaged. As for the second question, i.e., the contours of legal powers that cannot be applied to commercial property, the examples in the case law suggest that the property may not be disposed of in a manner which undermines the features of the property in which the public is "interested". Ownership of a warehouse designated to serve as a duty-free space does not allow the owner to institute a rule that will result in damage to the goods or in otherwise subjecting their owner to substantial and unnecessary expense (an expense which the warehouse was created to avert).[19] The warehouse is affected with a public interest precisely because of the public interest in avoiding such harms; this is what the warehouse is there for.

Extrapolating from the public interest cases, it is possible to articulate a general public interest affecting property used for commercial purposes in assuring that such property will not be used to harm general commerce itself. When the commerce is premised on interaction with the public at large, i.e., when the commerce is non-associational and not premised on meaningful (as opposed to technical) membership in an identity-sensitive club, society may seek to ensure that access to the property for the purposes of engaging in commerce is not restricted based on irrelevant group-based characteristics of prospective customers.

The affinity between such an articulation and the status-based duties attached to members of common callings is clear. It is conceivable that the case law could, by analogy, be read to suggest that once a landowner has designated part of her land as a place of general commerce, or once certain types of property have been deemed essential for general commerce by virtue of their public nature (such as certain areas of the waterfront, or the market itself), these properties are placed in a public domain of sorts, under a legal regime that applies to lands used for business purposes. Since commerce in such places is by definition common in the sense that the community at large is engaged in the commercial activity, the community has a kind of proprietary interest in the commercial or otherwise public property. Thus, the legal regime governing such places of business cannot permit the property owner (or the holder of lesser proprietary rights) to exclude would-be patrons on the basis of

---

[18] M. Taggart, "Public Utilities and Public Law" in P.A. Joseph (ed.), *Essays on the Constitution* (Wellington, NZ, Brooker's, 1995).

[19] *Allnut* v. *Inglis* (1810) 12 East 527, 104 ER 206.

group-based personal characteristics that are irrelevant to the *raison d'être* of the commerce.[20] In a manner of speaking, by zoning[21] part of the land to be used for non-individual business purposes—be it a restaurant, a theatre or a supermarket—the landlord has placed that part under a legal regime applicable to land invested with a specific public use. Such placement, it could be argued, removes whatever vast powers of exclusion the landlord might otherwise claim, until the land is returned to uses other than for non-individual business. Of course, recognising that the owner is not all-powerful does not mean that her interests should be ignored, or that her property should be treated as public property for all purposes.[22] However, the case law considering land imbued with a public interest could be interpreted to say that the decision to refuse access to persons seeking to purchase goods or services offered on the premises cannot be based on considerations irrelevant to the nature of the commercial enterprise. A different conclusion would be incongruent with the public nature of the property or the commercial use that the owner herself has chosen for the property.

3. The necessity doctrine

Another articulation of the limits of (the exercise of) property rights focuses on the underlying premise of property rights by situating those rights and their exercise in civil society. At the crux of this approach is the contention that property rights are a manifestation of moral agency, and thus must cohere with other

---

[20] "[W]hen property owners open their premises to the general public in the pursuit of their own property interests, they have no right to exclude people unreasonably. On the contrary, they have a duty not to act in a . . . discriminatory manner toward persons who come on their premises. That duty applies not only to common carriers, *Messenger* v. *Pennsylvania Railroad Co* 37 NJL 531 (E & A 1874), innkeepers [*Garifine* v. *Monmouth Park Jockey Club*, 29 NJ 47, 148 A 2d 1 (1959)], owners of gasoline service stations, *Streeter* v. *Brogan*, 113 NJ Super 486 (Ch Div 1971), or to private hospitals, *Doe* v. *Bridgeton Hospital Ass'n, Inc*, 71 NJ 478 (1976), cert den, 433 US 914, 97 S Ct 2987, 53 L Ed 2d 1100 (1977), but to all property owners who open their premises to the public. Property owners have no legitimate interest in unreasonably excluding particular members of the public when they open their premises for public use": *Uston* v. *Resorts Int'l Hotel*, 89 NJ 163, 173 (1982). See also "Note: The Antidiscrimination Principle in the Common Law" (1991) 102 *Harv. L Rev.* 1993.

[21] It could be argued that the very act of designating some property for commercial use displaces the classic property law regime in favour of a quasi-public law analysis. While ownership may entail robust legal powers, such powers do not include powers that belong to "the public". When owners decide to zone, either through their elected representatives in the municipality or by signing a covenant restricting future ownership or use of the land, they in fact exercise a public function. In functionally trespassing into the public domain, the owners may no longer rely on the infinite powers embodied in the concept of ownership. Compare: *Shelley* v. *Kraemer* 334 US 1 (1948) (hereinafter *Shelly*).

[22] For example, it is not clear that a property owner is under a duty to allow access for expressive purposes, or even equal access for such purposes. She may choose to allow those with whom she agrees to demonstrate, or not allow demonstrations and picketing at all. Such access, it is argued, does not necessarily flow from the commercial use designated to the land by its owner.

demands that flow from moral agency.[23] For example, property rights of one moral agent cannot be used in such a way that destroys a more valuable property of another, since such use disrespects the idea of property (or property rights). This principle was captured in the Latin maxim *sic utere tuo ut alienum non laedas*—use your own (property) so that you do not harm another's (property). The manifestation of this principle is found in the case law governing the "necessity doctrine", where courts declared that property rights cannot be used to prevent the rescue of more valuable property that otherwise would be lost. Thus, the owner of a private dock is responsible in damages if he unmoors a boat docked without permission and thereby permits it to run ashore.[24] Similarly, one may not use property rights to deprive another moral agent of her life. In asserting property rights one expresses one's moral agency as a human being. Since moral agency requires life, and since an assertion of moral agency by one moral agent (through the assertion of property rights) entails the recognition of agency of the person towards which the right is asserted, the assertion of property rights cannot, consistently, deprive the latter of life. Thus, if A refuses to allow B, a physically unwell guest with no alternative place to stay, to spend the night at A's property for consideration, and if as a consequence B, the evicted guest, is harmed, A would be liable in law.[25]

The underlying premise of the necessity doctrine is relevant beyond situations of necessity. If indeed property rights are an expression of autonomy, and if indeed autonomy is an aspect, an expression or a derivative of the capacity to see right from wrong, then it could be argued that property rights may not be exercised so as to injure other aspects or consequences of this capacity, namely the embodiment of human dignity of the person towards which the property rights are asserted.[26] In other words, one branch of moral agency—autonomy—may not be used to cut another derivative of moral agency—human dignity. Accepting that the law prohibits the exercise of autonomy so as to injure the embodiment of another person's human dignity would entail, by extension, the conclusion that one may not use property rights to exclude another from access to one's commercial property solely on account of group-based characteristics.

---

[23] The concept of property could be defined, using Bractonian (and Lockean) terms, as the infusion of human action over material (or non-material) things. Therefore the law governing the human action and the law governing the material thing must cohere. Thus, in assessing the scope of property rights in concrete cases, we must ascertain what it is that the owner wishes to do (her volition), and with respect to what kind of property she wishes to do it. It is submitted that property used for business organised around non-individual transactions is not amenable to an act of rejecting a trespasser, if the only classification that makes the customer a trespasser is his or her race (or analogous grounds).

[24] *Ploof* v. *Putnam* 81 Vt 471, 71 Atl 188 (1908); see also *Vincent* v. *Lake Erie Transportation Co* 124 NW 222 (Minn. SC 1910).

[25] *Depue* v. *Flatau* 100 Minn. 299, 111 NW 1 (1907).

[26] Locke, to whom we usually attribute the strong justification of a right to property, treats property as emanating from the same normative source as liberty, indeed, as life itself (J. Locke, *Two Treatises of Government* (ed.) P. Laslett (Cambridge, Cambridge University Press, 1988)) Accordingly, we may seek to reconcile the concept of property with other aspects of that which makes human life morally unique.

Excluding a segment of the community from property used for commercial purposes with the community of moral agents at large on grounds irrelevant to the commerce itself must mean that members of the excluded group are not treated as full (or equal) members in the community of moral agents. Such exclusion, particularly where the group is constructed around immutable or nearly immutable characteristics, injures the embodiment of human dignity of the excluded group (in a manner similar to the injury one suffers when one is defamed), and thereby dilutes the embodiment of human dignity of all members of the community.

4. The *in rem* nature of property rights (as applied to commercial grounds)

Yet another way to approach the limits of property rights is to examine their *in rem* nature.[27] As mentioned above, ownership (or a secondary proprietary right, such as that of a lessee toward all but the landowner) presents, in essence, a claim against the community at large to respect a member's property right over the land by refraining from trespass. The claim is greater than an *in personam* demand *vis-à-vis* each named living individual to refrain from trespass. It is a demand against the world, the community of moral agents as a whole; it is a claim against "the public" or civic society as such. Thus, the property right claim views the rights-holder as possessing a kernel of sovereignty over her property, sovereignty that must be respected by the *rem*, that is, the community *qua* community.[28]

It seems that this *in rem* feature, in and of itself, gives rise to a reciprocal duty to respect the community as such, including *all* its members. Or, more specifically, should an owner demand from the community respect for her choices regarding the use of her property, she should respond in kind by respecting the community's definition of who belongs to the community (i.e., respect minorities as a part of the community). The use of (immutable or nearly immutable) group-based characteristics disrespects the integrity of the community as a whole. It fractures the community into groups from which members cannot (realistically) extricate themselves. In other words, the community is placed in a position of self-contradiction: it demands respect from itself by requiring all not to trespass onto members' property, and at the same time it allows disrespect to itself by accepting its dismemberment through legally enforceable classifications along immutable group-based lines.

---

[27] See, for example, J. Austin, *Lectures in Jurisprudence* (Lecture XLVII), who refers to the right of ownership, or *dominium*, as a right availing against the world over a determinate thing, indefinite in point of user, unrestricted in point of disposition. For a critique of such a conception of an *in rem* right in law see W.N. Hohfeld, "Fundamental Legal Conceptions as Applied in Judicial Reasoning" (1917) 26 *Yale L J* 710, arguing that an *in rem* right will always materialise *vis-à-vis* a concrete person, thus amounting to an aggregation of *in personam* rights.

[28] The sovereign element associated with *in rem* rights is revealed once its non-contractual premise is acknowledged: the property owner does not need anyone's assent to impose a rule which applies to anyone who wishes to use the property.

This line of argument is compatible with the previous articulation of property rights as part of civil society. As mentioned, property rights are premised on our capacity to see right from wrong (or, put theologically, on having been created in God's image). From this capacity flows our autonomy as moral agents and our inalienable human dignity. Civil society provides for the legal form through which the autonomy and human dignity are expressed and protected. The community, defined through law, rests on the inalienability of the human dignity of *all* its members. Thus, property rights cannot, coherently, allow for legal ownership of another human being, or for a legal rule which bars certain groups from owning property. Similarly, property rights cannot include the legal power to invoke nearly immutable group-characteristics in order to exclude some groups from the enjoyment of one's property. Otherwise, an *in rem* right—ownership—shows disrespect to the very community from which it demands respect.

As a matter of case law, the notion of *in rem* rights is reflected in cases dealing with restrictive covenants[29] or wills[30] that placed group-based restrictions upon future transferability of land or future access to land. Conditions such as "this land should not be sold to Jews", or "should only be sold to Caucasians", or "this park is bequeathed to the public provided the trustees ensure its enjoyment only by whites" raise concerns regarding the scope of legally enforceable property rights.[31] The Supreme Court of Canada chose to analyse one such condition as a conceptual matter in terms of whether such a condition by its nature "runs with the land". The Court held that it did not.[32] In other words, the Supreme Court found that the use of such conditions is, on some level, incompatible with the concept of full-fledged property rights.

This line of argument leads to the conclusion that instead of providing the owner with greater power, the *in rem* nature of property rights actually restricts the owner's powers. In putting forward a claim against the entire community, the owner has to respect the community in its entirety.

[29] *Re Drummond Wren* [1945] OR 778; *Noble and Wolf* v. *Alley* [1951] SCR 64 (hereinafter *Noble and Wolf*). See in the US *Shelley, supra* n.21.

[30] See *e.g. Evans* v. *Newton*, 382 US 296 (1966).

[31] Since the cases involve covenants and wills, they could be analysed also under the contractual paradigm, and tenancy, or access to parks, could be conceived of as instances of goods and services available to the general public. Under the paradigm suggested above, the relevant common law rules would require the landlord to provide equal service upon request, but at the same time permit the landlord to decline to rent for cause, such as distrust of the applicant, as long as the landlord does not institute a policy of rejecting applicants on the basis of any group-based affiliation. In other words, although a contract might not yet have been signed, a landlord may be seen as owing a duty to an applicant to ignore group-based prejudice in her decision. Compare: *Gooding* v. *Edlow* [1966] Que. SC 436 (hereinafter *Gooding*), where an offer to Mme Gooding to rent an apartment was rescinded by the landlord upon learning that the applicant was black. The Court found enough support for the claim that the offer had already been accepted, and thus a contract was entered into, but stated also that the landlord's behaviour was against public order and good faith (at 442) and therefore illegal, suggesting that had racial considerations been behind rescinding an offer prior to acceptance, such behaviour would not have been valid at law.

[32] *Noble and Wolf, supra* n.29.

Such a conceptualisation does not confer upon any individual the right to access any private property. All it does is remove the legal power from the owner to institute a classification, based upon nearly immutable characteristics, that determines trespass to his property. Should the property owner nonetheless attempt to institute such a classification, courts will have to decide whether its legal effect is that all are allowed access, or that no one is allowed access. It should further be noted that such conceptualisation does not address the owner's *in personam* powers to permit any specific individual to enter the property or prohibit any specific individual from entering the property.

Having set out the argument, its weaknesses should be recognised. Removing the owner's legal ability to institute classifications as to who may enter her property runs afoul of the rights-holder's liberty. Since the harm described above is the conceptual harm to the community, and since no particular individual necessarily has the right to vindicate that harm, one could argue that ethics, rather than adversarial common law adjudication, is the proper forum through which to address a discriminatory use of property rights. Moreover, it is not clear that the community, through its laws, can impose on a landowner a binary choice of either refraining from using such group characteristics in her disposition of land or losing the protection that ownership offers altogether. It could be argued that such an imposition itself amounts to disrespect for the human dignity of the landowner.[33] The community is under an obligation to respect property rights, if agency matters.

The demand, placed on the community, to recognise legally the human dignity of all, including those who dispute the integrity of the community, may be seen as a tension within the concept of community itself. On the one hand, the community of moral agents assumes a rather thin relationship among the members—each concerned with his or her own autonomy—but on the other hand, each agent requires that all fully recognise her agency, which suggests a richer notion of community. It could similarly be argued that a tension exists between our visions of the self.[34] On the one hand each individual is viewed as a single unit of agency, which may retreat to an isolated space where it can perform the act of moral judgement and set its own ends, distinguish between good and bad, just and evil and right and wrong. At the same time, experience teaches us that

---

[33] See *supra* n.26. Locke himself wrote that "though the Earth, and all inferior Creatures, be common to all Men, yet every Man has a Property in his own Person, This no Body has any Right to but himself. The Labour of his body; and the Work of his Hands, we may say, are properly his" (*supra* n.26, at chap. 5, para. 27, The Second Treatise of Civil Government). It seems that Locke identifies that which sets a person as a rights bearer as related to matters which are held in close proximity to the person: his body, and the labour of his body. With respect to these, Locke seems to suggest absolute sovereignty. Locke, then, might differentiate between the claim a person has regarding his body and the direct labour of his body, and things that are more remote from the core of personhood. In other words, Locke's idea of ownership, if it is to be read consistently, may in fact distinguish between the immediate circle of things one owns—one's home, for example—and property less proximate, such as land used for non-individual, non-associational commerce.

[34] C. Taylor, *Sources of the Self: The Making of the Modern Identity* (Cambridge, Mass., Harvard University Press, 1989).

we cannot ignore the role that concrete communities play in shaping our values and identity, values without which moral judgement is impossible. We often, if not always, exercise our moral agency within relationships and associational spaces. Can the law impose upon us with whom to associate? Can the law deny us the private space in which to form our judgement by imposing on us the requirement to accept into our associational space those with whom we do not wish to associate? Arguably, one's home is not only deeply constitutive of one's identity[35] but also forms a constructed space from which one may evaluate the community. Providing the community with the power to force access to the home, or to similar familial or associational space, would amount to the destruction of a private sphere from which an individual may critically evaluate the community. Without such space, the community may no longer present itself as being governed by judgements of its autonomous members, but rather would simply be reaffirming itself.[36] It therefore seems difficult to deny a landowner the decision of who shall enter her house, including the decision that no males are allowed. Communal intervention in such a decision could itself be seen as a form of trespass, raising the prospect of self-contradiction yet again.

A stalemate, it seems, is reached. A landowner must respect the community, hence must not discriminate against groups which comprise the community, and the community must respect the landowner, hence cannot intervene in the landowner's decision regarding to whom she grants access. We see that the *in rem* nature of property does not fortify the claim of the landowner.

Such an impasse is considerably less acute when a landowner decides to use her property for the purposes of conducting impersonal business with non-specific members of the community without requiring initial membership. Land used for commercial activity escapes the dilemma. Arguably, such land is less meaningful to one's identity than one's domicile and perhaps the claim for a private space is satisfied by one's powers to control access to one's domicile rather than to one's place of business. More importantly, however, land used for commercial activity escapes the dilemma primarily as a consequence of the very idea of non-individual commerce and the decision to allocate a portion of one's land for such use. As mentioned under subsections 1 and 2 above, by exercising *in rem* property powers to interact with the community *in rem*, as is inherent in the provision of goods and services available to the general public on a non-individual basis, a landowner may not force *her* definition of who belongs to the community. If the landowner decides to use her property for business purposes with the community at large, it is difficult to deny a reciprocal duty of respect to the community. When the landowner chooses to use her land for

---

[35] The argument for the centrality of some property to the idea of self is not new. See recently D. Cohen, "On Property as Self" (1998) 26 *J Psychiatry & Law* 3.

[36] A similar argument can be put forward in support of not applying a constitutional bill of rights to the common law governing private entities. See J.D. Whyte, "Is the Private Sector Affected by the Charter?" in L. Smith *et al.* (eds.), *Righting The Balance: Canada's New Equality Rights* (Saskatoon, Canadian Human Rights Reporter, 1986) at 145; Reichman, *Constitutional Structures, supra* n.4, chap. 2.

non-associational commerce—commerce which by its functional nature is based on a relationship with the community as a whole—she can be seen as having waived her claim against engaging with, or experiencing intervention from, the community as a whole. By choosing to make available one's property for commerce with non-individual clientele, the owner can be held to her choice; commerce with non-individual clientele does not entail the legal power to segregate the community along group-based characteristics.

Because this argument rests on the *in rem* nature of ownership, it is concerned with the relationship between the landowner and the community, and the inability of the landowner to use her rights over land where non-associational commerce is conducted in a manner which forces the community to fracture itself. Therefore, under this articulation of the limits of property rights, a merchant might *arbitrarily* exclude individual members from her business-related property but would not be entitled to use group characteristics as a proxy for her right of exclusion. Otherwise, the property right contradicts the foundation on which it rests. Put differently, since the community at large is fully engaged when property is designated for non-associational commerce, and since the community at large is implicated when a person invokes her property rights, and since the community is organised around the preservation of the embodiment of human dignity of all its members, it is difficult to support the exercise of property rights so as to injure the human dignity of community members by excluding them from commercial property because of their immutable, or nearly immutable group-based characteristics. Such a discriminatory use of property rights over commercial land thus injures the integrity of the community as a whole and the protection afforded to the embodiment of human dignity of its members.

5. Interim conclusion: property rights and the private/public divide

Four approaches were identified to challenge the widely-held view that property rights can be used to institute a rule restricting access to commercial property to members of certain groups sharing immutable or nearly immutable characteristics. Other approaches may also be available. For example, support could be found for the argument that group-based characteristics are intrinsically indefinite and thus conditions invoking them should not be legally enforced.[37] Yet

---

[37] See *Noble and Wolf, supra* n.29, where Rand J suggests that the use of racial, ethnic or religious lineage is uncertain *per se*, and therefore unenforceable in law: "it is impossible to set such limits to the lines of race or blood as would enable a court to say in all cases whether a proposed purchaser is or is not within the ban" (at 70). In other words, Rand J does not deny the paradigmatic cases; rather, he suggests that the law (or the courts) lack a legitimate methodology with which to ascertain the objective condition. Interestingly, Lon Fuller, in his famous debate with H.L.A. Hart, advocated a similar idea as one of the eight conditions a law must fulfill in order to be worthy of the term "law" (see L. Fuller, *The Morality of Law* (New Haven, Conn., Yale University Press, 1964)). But see Tarnopolsky and Pentney, *supra* n.4, at chap. 1, 25–6 for critiques.

after consideration it appears that the error in Canadian case law lies in the Supreme Court's conclusion that *"chaque propriétaire est maitre chez lui"*[38] without distinguishing owners of land used for commerce. Philosophically, all four articulations, or approaches, could be read as requiring the redrawing of a segment of the private-public divide. All lead to the conclusion that the community may not be entitled to prevent an individual from discriminating in her own domicile—inviting only Jews, or only non-Jews, for dinner. However, the community may be entitled to require an individual in her interactions with the community at large, as is the case with non-individual commerce, to adhere to the community's self-definition as a community of *all* moral agents. Conceptually, interacting with the community at large by opening a non-individual business on one's property is a public activity, as opposed to engaging in "private" activities in one's domicile, such as organising a dinner. It would follow that a different set of norms should apply to these two activities. A person may decide to allow only members of her family, or tribe, to park their cars in her driveway. But a car dealer may not decree that Christians, or gays, may not enter the property in order to conduct business. It should be noted, however, that such a public-private divide is internal to the common law and does not invite the application of a constitutional bill of rights, since government or its agencies are not involved.[39]

All four approaches suggest that either by focusing on the agent who designated her land to be used for non-associational commercial activity, or by focusing on the essence of the property (and of commerce in general), or both, the purely private law notion of property rights is not exhaustive of the legal landscape. In civic society, other features of the common law that are designed to address the public feature of the transactions come into play. This categorisation is not intended to threaten the integrity of private law, or to suggest that the distinction between private law and public law is meaningless. On the contrary, it is meant to highlight that the common law is greater than private law: it contains private law governing non-governmental entities engaged in private transactions, the common law of common callings and businesses affected with a public interest, and administrative law regulating the activities and transactions

---

[38] Every proprietor is master of his own domain: *supra* n.3.

[39] The private-public divide is contextual. In Britain, the debate has thus far centred around the application of judicial review under Order 53, and the source of judicial review as *ultra vires* jurisdiction (see P.P. Craig, *"Ultra Vires* and the Foundations of Judicial Review" (1998) 57 *CLJ* 63; C. Forsyth, "Of Fig Leaves and Fairy Tales: The *Ultra Vires* Doctrine, The Sovereignty of Parliament and Judicial Review" (1996) 55 *CLJ* 122; D. Oliver, "Is the *Ultra Vires* Rule the Basis of Judicial Review?" [1987] *PL* 543). Of course, the Human Rights Act, 1998 will raise new questions as papers in this vol. suggest. In the USA and Canada, the debate is organised around state action for the purposes of applying constitutional judicial review (see State Action Symposium in (1993) 10 *Const. Comm.* at 309–441; *Eldridge* v. *British Columbia (AG)* [1997] 3 SCR 624; P. Hogg, "The Application of the Charter to Private Action" (1986) 51 *Sask. L R* 273). This paper suggests that a "public" aspect is integral to the common law governing market activities of private bodies *without* annexing that body of law to the administrative domain. Contrast: M. Taggart (ed.), *The Province of Administrative Law* (Oxford, Hart Publishing, 1987); D. Oliver, *Common Values and the Public-Private Divide* (London, Butterworths, 1999).

of governmental agencies. Each of these sections of the common law is reason-based, in the sense that the legitimacy of the content of the norms ultimately rests on reason. Therefore, each section must cohere with the others, and must adhere to the form of the common law. Each is premised on a concept of corrective justice, correlative rights and duties and a legal obligation to remedy breaches of these duties. Because the subject matter of the law is different in each segment, and because the source of the relevant correlative rights and duties is different, the content of the norms need not be identical. Paying attention to the constitutive elements of the common law is helpful in our quest to maintain the integrity of that regime. It also proves to be a helpful tool in preserving the embodiment of human dignity of all community members.

III. FURTHER LIMITS ON THE DISPOSITION OF PROPERTY— THE PUBLIC POLICY DOCTRINE

1. Introducing public policy

Public policy, one would think, is a matter for the legislature, or the Crown in Parliament, to address. Matters of policy appear as matters of choice (or even preference): the community decides what is important to it, what ailments it seeks to cure, and the best societal tools to achieve this objective. The common law, and common law courts, it appears, should refuse to undertake such an exercise. However, as is apparent from the four arguments presented above, the notion of a community, or a public, is central to the common law. It is therefore not surprising that the common law includes the doctrine of public policy. The public policy doctrine is designed in part to allow the application of private law to non-governmental entities engaged in non-associational commerce; it is to ensure that the private law form accommodates the public element in general commerce. In that respect, public policy is no more a matter for legislative policy than any other common law doctrine.

Rather than fully canvassing the case law governing public policy, this section will focus on two specific Canadian cases: *Franklin*[40] and *Canada Trust*.[41] These two cases are relevant since both involve aspects of the doctrine. Each reveals the aforementioned accommodation of the "public" element, which is required to avoid contradiction between the legal protection accorded to property rights and the relevant common law segment of which these rights are a part. Thus, these cases will illustrate that public policy arguments, whether generally labelled as such or whether cast in the language of "the limits on one's legal power to dispose of one's property as one sees fit", are not foreign to the common law, but an integral part of the law governing non-governmental entities engaged in non-associational commerce.

[40] *Supra* n.2.
[41] *Supra* n.4.

Beyond illustrating the above argument, the two cases relate to the secondary claim of this chapter: that the common law, rather than the statutory or the constitutional regime, should be the starting point for delineating the limits of property rights. Both *Franklin* and *Canada Trust* are examples of how that exercise should *not* be conducted. *Franklin* avoids the doctrine of public policy altogether, without providing any reasons (and, not surprisingly, without reaching the right conclusion). The court in *Franklin* failed to address precedent presented to the court as well as statutory developments that should have sparked further discussion of the common law's position on point. Thus, the precedential value of this case is dubious. *Canada Trust* errs in the other direction by mimicking policies adopted by the legislature as if the statutory regime directly altered the content of the common law. Fortunately, the relevant legislative policies are just, in the sense that the distributive theory they are based upon is fair, and thus the conclusion of *Canada Trust* is laudable. Yet both these approaches, it will be argued, are legally problematic since they are inconsistent with the common law as a cohesive legal regime.

This section will sketch an alternative way to approach public policy when applied to dispositions[42] regarding one's commercial property. In particular, this section will focus on public policy as applied to dispositions that include the institution of a group-based condition (or rule) on the use of the property. The suggested approach neither ignores the statutory regime, as did *Franklin*, nor embraces it as determinative, as did *Canada Trust*. Rather, it advocates taking notice of the statutory position as part of the common law methodology that requires the court to reason with arguments put before it.

2. An exercise in reconstruction: the public policy arguments in *Franklin*

Franklin involved an action brought by a black resident of Kitchener, Ontario against owners of a restaurant who refused to serve him lunch because of his race and used humiliating language to eject him from the restaurant. Mr Franklin sued for damages. As is apparent from the court's reasoning, Mr Franklin did not suggest that this was a breach of contract case, even though, conceivably, the case involved a general offer to the public, an offer accepted by Mr Franklin through his behaviour when he sat down and ordered lunch. Rather, Mr Franklin appeared to have questioned Mr Evans' property right to remove customers from the premises on account of their race, and suggested that not only did Mr Evans lack the legal power to evict him, but he was under a duty to provide equal service (a claim discussed at length elsewhere).[43]

---

[42] By disposition it is meant a transfer of ownership, possession, or a conferral of any other right or privilege, including a right of access, temporary or permanent, conditional or non-conditional.

[43] Reichman, *supra* n.1. See also H. Molot, "The Duty of Business to Serve the Public: Analogy to the Innkeepers Obligations" (1968) 46 *Can. Bar Rev.* 613. See in the USA, Singer, *supra* n.5; C.M. Haar and D. Wm. Fessler, *The Wrong Side of the Tracks* (New York, Simon & Schuster, 1986); "Note: The Antidiscrimination Principle", *supra* n.20. See in the UK, D. Oliver, "Common Values in Public and Private Law" [1997] *PL* 630.

Mr Franklin's counsel submitted authorities which suggest that he argued that such use of a property right—that is, the institution of access rules along racial lines to property used for impersonal commerce—would be contrary to public policy.

The court began, and in effect ended, its property law analysis by a reference to *Sealey* v. *Tandy*[44] for the proposition that a licensee or occupier of licensed premises has "a right to request a person to leave, if he does not wish him to remain on the premises".[45] This proposition, according to the court in *Franklin*, supported Mr Evans' legal power to eject Mr Franklin from his premises for whatever reason he saw fit. However, such use of *Sealey* is far from trivial. An *ad hoc* request to leave, even if based on an irrational impulse, as was arguably[46] the case in *Sealey*, is quite different from the institution of a general rule regarding the use of the premises such as "no blacks allowed". The court in *Franklin* did not seem to find that distinction relevant, or at least did not direct its attention to the possible difference. In so doing, it is submitted, the court failed to notice the full scope of the *in rem* power exercised by Mr Evans.

The court's failure to approach seriously the public policy angle of the case is revealed in the final paragraphs of the judgment, which are worth quoting in full:

> Mr. Buchner [counsel for Mr. Franklin] referred me to *Egerton* v. *Earl Brownlow*,[47] Broom's Legal Maxims;[48] Broom's Common Law.[49] The *Brownlow* case—about a will—covers 256 pages. I have not time to read it carefully. However, all these references, I take it, are in support of the same point, namely the discussion of certain well recognized legal maxims, such as *sic utere tuo ut alienum non laedas* [use your own (property) so that you do not harm another]; *Nihil quod est inconveniens est licitum* [Nothing which is disagreeable/inappropriate is legal]; and *Salus republicae suprema lex* [The welfare (well-being) of the people is the best law]—all of them epigrammatically useful at times, but I find myself quite unable to apply them to the question in litigation here.
>
> I have read the judgment of Lord Mansfield in *Sommersett's Case* (1772).[50] This does not help me to the conclusion that the plaintiff has a right of action, and the same may be said of *Smith* v. *Gould* (1707).[51]

[44] *Sealey* v. *Tandy* [1902] 1 KB 296 (hereinafter *Sealey*).

[45] *Franklin*, *supra* n.2, at 351.

[46] *Sealey* concerned an assault charge against a person who refused to leave a public house, and apparently used force against the owner who tried to eject him. The court found that the owner was not under an innkeeper obligation, meaning he was not barred from refusing service or denying access. However, the court saw it as necessary, although not as a basis for the decision, to state that "there was nothing unjustifiable in any sense in the conduct of the owner, because the man who was requested to leave was one of a gang of men who had been disorderly and had given trouble" (at 299). Thus, the *Sealey* case in fact is not so irrational: the owner of a bar ejected a known troublemaker, but the court was careful to state that it was not prepared to scrutinise the motive of the proprietor.

[47] (1853) 4 HLC 1, 195–6; 10 ER 359, 436–7 (HL).

[48] H. Broom, *A Collection of Legal Maxims Classified and Illustrated* (9th edn., London, Sweet & Maxwell, 1924), 151–3.

[49] W. Archibald and H. Colefax, *H. Broom, Commentaries on the Common Law* (9th edn., London, Sweet & Maxwell, 1896), 674, 681.

[50] (1772) 20 St Tr 1 79–80 (hereinafter *Sommersett*).

[51] (1707) 2 Ld. Raym. 1274, 92 ER 338 (hereinafter *Smith*).

I must dismiss the action, but the unnecessary harsh, humiliating, and offensive attitude of the defendant and his wife toward the plaintiff induces me to dismiss it without costs.

These paragraphs are illuminating for several reasons, among which is the insight it provides into the case made by counsel for the plaintiff ("who, as I would expect", wrote Lennox J, "made an excellent argument", and was later referred to as "painstaking and experienced", albeit to the detriment of his arguments).[52] More specifically, the authorities cited allow us to reconstruct, hypothetically, counsel's arguments, and evaluate the court's response.

The authorities suggest that counsel argued the following: that property rights are not absolute;[53] that *in rem* property rights have to be understood as operating within a community (public) and therefore have to cohere with other aspects that constitute the community (call this a public policy consideration);[54] that such public policy considerations have to be informed by developments in our understanding of that which constitutes the public (or who belongs to the community), and that these developments[55] include the realisation that blacks are equal members of the community.[56]

Counsel may then have submitted that the disposition of property rights—a cluster of rights that demands respect from the community as such—must be exercised in the manner least inconsistent with the concept of a community as an integral unit. Allowing owners of land used for commercial purposes, who by such use interact with the community at large, to exclude members of the community on the basis of innate group characteristics, without showing any relevance of such use to the *raison d'être* of the commerce, disrespects the

---

[52] "The fact that a counsel so painstaking and experienced as Mr. Buchner could find no decided case in support of his contention, coupled with the obvious dividing line between a case of this character and one which brings into question the duties imposed upon an inn-keeper . . ., confirms to me . . . that [the appeal should be dismissed]": *Franklin, supra* n.2, at 350.

[53] Setting the discussion of the limits of property rights in context, Mr Buchner must have argued that a person cannot fully own another. See *Smith, supra* n.51, at 338, where a Trover claim over a black slave was rejected, since "the common law takes no notice of negroes being different from other men. By the common law no man can have a property in another . . .".

[54] *Egerton, supra* n.47, is one of the leading cases on public policy, suggesting that counsel had this concept in mind when he referred the court to the specific page dealing with that concept.

[55] Counsel creatively referred the court to the then recent developments in statutory law with respect to women's legal powers (*Broom's Common Law, supra* n.49). Broom notes that the common law has been transformed by statutory intervention to recognise that women have equal juridical personalities, and have been freed from misperceptions barring them from marital ownership, for example. Such statutory interventions, Mr Buchner must have suggested, should inform our concept of a community of equals, based upon principles of "justice" (at 681, quoting the preamble to the Married Women's Property Act 1870).

[56] In *Sommersett's Case, supra* n.50, referred to by counsel, Lord Mansfield decided that public policy considerations demanded that ownership of a black slave established abroad could not be enforced in Britain itself: Public policy considerations disallow enforcement of property rights that are contrary to essential concepts of a community, central to which is the irreducible equal moral worth of a human being as such. Mr Buchner may well have argued that taking the concepts of personhood, property and public policy seriously must entail that property rights cannot be used further to exclude blacks from full membership by barring access to commercial land/services based on such membership.

integrity of the community. It severs the community into hierarchical sub-communities or, worse still, it casts certain groups outside the community altogether. Moreover, on a substantive level, a thread that unites the common law into a community is the equal respect for the human dignity of all members *qua* members. Therefore, allowing the prejudicial use of property rights by commercial landowners against defined sub-groups of the community, suggesting that such sub-groups are less deserving of respect, violates the latter's exercise of human dignity and threatens to unravel the common law quilt. Substantively then, before any group characteristic is used as a proxy by a property owner with respect to property that is used for non-individual commerce, she must show a direct connection between such a classification and the purpose of the business, lest the common law run into self-contradiction. If public policy is to have any meaning at all, such self-contradiction cannot be tolerated as it is repugnant to the law.

The final point supported by the authorities that Mr Buchner presented goes to the remedy required by law[57] in light of the harm associated with an unjustifiable exclusion incurred both by the community and by the member, who is treated as a non-member. The cases suggest that the person harmed is entitled to sue for at least nominal damages, if not for humiliation.[58] Such a tort, it seems, is akin to a tort of defamation, or to nuisance, when one is prevented from fully enjoying one's own—be it property or meaningful membership in the community—on account of someone else's misuse of her legal powers.

It is perhaps of interest that throughout the judgment, Lennox J and arguably counsel did not explicitly refer to the concept of public policy. This reluctance may be attributable to then recent developments in the common law that called for a cautious approach to the wild horse of public policy.[59] However, even if *Franklin* did not refer to public policy, the authorities cited certainly did.

The remainder of this section will consider the authorities invoked by counsel in detail, so as to demonstrate that had the court taken the time fully to discern the law on the point it could not have dispensed with the public policy doctrine offhand, as it did. Rather, the court would have been confronted with the shared underlying principles at the core of the argument against the limitless use of private property when such use conflicts with foundational elements around which the very concept of the public is organised. The trail of cited authorities covers conditions in wills and bonds (including marriage brokerage bonds), restraint of trade, sale of offices and the legal maxims; all demonstrate

---

[57] Counsel relied on the maxim *ubi jus ibi remedium*, as is apparent from the reference of the court. In Reichman *supra* n.1, I develop the source of a tort of anti-discrimination as flowing from a breach of one's status-based obligation to be faithful to the constitutive elements of one's profession, when that profession is premised on non-associational interactions. In that respect, the tort is not technically part of private law, but akin to *Ashby* v. *White* (1703) 2 Ld. Raym. 938, 92 ER 126.

[58] Lennox J specifically noted the harsh and humiliating manner in which Mr Evans treated Mr Franklin, as quoted above.

[59] *Egerton, supra* n.47, notes that as a general matter new heads of public policy will not be invented by the court. See generally *Halsbury's Laws of England, supra* n.8, at vol. 9, para. 390.

that the conclusion in *Franklin* is in tension with the concept of a civil society (public).

Our first stop on the route laid out by Mr Buchner is the leading case analysing public policy—*Egerton*[60] (which the court in *Franklin* unfortunately had no time to read carefully). *Egerton* stands, among other things, for the proposition that should one wish to place a condition on transferring one's land to another, that condition may not be enforced if its enforcement is repugnant to basic principles of the legal order. One may not use one's property rights, at least one view in *Egerton* suggests, in such a manner as to undermine the legal fabric that unites the community, or as to harm social institutions constitutive of the community.

In his analysis of a condition in a will which withdrew a gift should the recipient not be given the title of a Marquis, Lord Truro concluded that such a condition was invalid.[61] As his reasoning reveals, Lord Truro saw an overarching principle governing the power to dispose of property: conditions on disposition must not prejudice legal concepts (or institutions) as important as property. In the case before the court, Lord Truro found that allowing the aforementioned condition in a will to stand might lead to the corruption of the institution of noble titles since people and government would be induced to trade in such titles, instead of following the fundamental concept around which the legal edifice of nobility is organised—duty.

The analogy to *Franklin* is clear: the trade in noble titles is antithetical to the concept of nobility because it undermines the core idea of duty without which nobility is meaningless; similarly, the use of property rights over land used for non-individual commerce so as to exclude a prospective customer solely on the basis of race (or other such group characteristic) undermines the concept both of a community and of non-individual commerce. Property rights are meaningful only *vis-à-vis* a community. Ejecting a prospective customer from commercial premises on the basis of her race severs the community that identifies itself as based upon such principles as equal moral worth, moral agency and human dignity; it fractures the community into hierarchical communities, some deserving respect and some less deserving.

Examining Lord Truro's examples of the principle governing the limits of property rights is illuminating as well. Lord Truro cited Lord Coke[62] for the proposition that some conditions could be against the law as being repugnant to the State.[63] Also cited is Sheppard's Touchstone, where among a list of

---

[60] *Supra* n.47.

[61] Lord Truro stated in *Egerton, supra* n.47, at 437, that "it cannot be denied that ... dispositions [of property] are subject to some limits and restraints, and that the law will not uphold such as have a tendency prejudicial to the public weal: every man is restricted against using his property to the prejudice of others ... The principle I conceive to be universal, as governing as well transfers by deed as the validity of contracts and dispositions by will".

[62] (1629) 1 Inst. 206 b.

[63] Lord Coke was referring to the prohibition against barring a tenant from enjoying the fruits of the land, when the nature of the transaction as it was understood then was that the tenant would enjoy such fruits. Ignoring such function, or nature, was repugnant or self-contradictory.

prohibited conditions (those tending "to provoke or further the doing of some unlawful act or restrain or forbid a man from doing his duty") it is stated that "conditions as are against the liberty of law"[64] are against "public good". The term liberty of law could suggest that not only is the liberty of the contracting parties involved, but also the law, as the guardian of liberty, must take into account the meaningful enjoyment of liberty by all members of the community.[65] Put differently, it is the liberty of the law, or the common law itself, which is challenged when common law rights over non-associational commercial property are used in order to institute group-based access rules that dismember the community.[66] In the same vein, the liberty to remain authentic and genuine to one's identity, including one's race or ethnicity, cannot be subjected under a coherent analysis of the common law to a prejudicial (if not superstitious[67]) use of property powers in the commercial context when such powers are used by non-associational businesses. The public, as a concept, would be harmed.[68]

The next stop in the trail of authorities leads us to the marriage brokerage cases where a bond or a contract was used to procure marriage or to restrain it. Party X contacted a broker—usually a person who had influence over a rich prospective bride or groom—in order that the broker would convince such a man or woman to marry party X. In order to secure the success of such influence a bond would be issued under which money would be paid to the broker upon marriage. The Chancery was quite hostile to such a bond. Although the bond was valid at law, since the technical requirements were met, marriage advice, the court thought, should be true and honest, not motivated by irrelevant

---

[64] W. Sheppard, *The Touch-Stone of Common Assurances* (London, printed for W. Lee, 1651), 132.

[65] The idea of meaningful enjoyment of liberties by all is emphasised in J. Rawls, *Political Liberalism* (New York, Columbia University Press, 1993).

[66] Compare: R. Epstein, "In Defence of the Contract at Will" (1984) 51 *U Chi. L Rev.* 947. Yet Epstein's comments should be confined to associational relationships, where the identity of the parties matter. There, ignoring the property boundaries of the owner who chooses to discriminate ignores her personhood. However, where the owner is no longer associated directly with the property, as is the case with a charitable trust, or as is the case with land operated by a corporation or a non-associational business geared towards the provision of services to the general public, the human dignity of the owner is arguably not threatened to the same degree, whereas the dignity of the excluded groups is threatened and so is the integrity of the community.

[67] Similarly, as Sheppard, *supra* n.64, informs us, a condition mandating the transfer of profits to superstitious uses is unsupportable in law. The term "superstitious uses" does not cover, of course, support of religious activities. It should, however, cover uses of property rights where one's prejudice, bias or "superstition" conflicts with the nature of the property right or with one's undertaking regarding the manner in which the right is to be exercised, as is the case with rights over property used of commerce with the general public. In such context the common law right, as a reason-based instrument, is incompatible with bias and superstition.

[68] Avoiding harm to the public is echoed in another concept of equity referred to in *Egerton*: "fraudulent to the public". This doctrine allows the court, "for the sake of the publick" to protect people (such as heirs and benefactors) against the enforcement of bonds signed under pressure or inflicted with misrepresentation of third parties (*Chesterfield* v. *Janssen* (1750) 1 Atk. 339, 26 ER 191, 225). The "sake of the public" could arguably include the demand to respect the integrity of the public against a divisive use of rights over commercial property contrary to the idea of impersonal commerce.

personal gains.[69] Even where the transaction was direct, between the prospective husband and the prospective wife to secure future marriage by issuing a bond, the Chancery found that the bond must be cancelled, since "marriage ought to be free and without compulsion".[70] Similarly, bonds restraining marriage received a cold shoulder.[71]

It could be said that these cases not only stand for interfering with the freedom of contract for public policy reasons related to protecting the institution of marriage; they also stand for the proposition that the decision whom to marry should not be influenced through a coercive legal tool such as a bond. The use of bonds for these purposes introduces an element (a consideration) irrelevant to the nature and foundation of marriage.

In the same vein (skipping 300 years ahead), it could be argued that if indeed it is agreed that non-associational commerce is a social institution, broadly defined, then allowing the law governing property rights and transactions to permit the provider of such goods and services to consider the racial identity of a customer amounts to introducing an irrelevant element, consideration or legal tool, contrary to the welfare of the community at large.[72] Therefore, one's legal power to dispose of one's property may, in that respect, be limited.

The next step in our journey, the early restraint of trade cases, reveals sensitivity on the part of the courts to the necessary relationship between a liberty claim, including the liberty to dispose of one's property as one sees fit, and the underlying foundation of that claim as the expression of autonomy. For example, in *Mitchel* v. *Reynolds*,[73] the court stated that general restrictions on trade are void: a person cannot promise, by way of covenant (contract) or bond, with or without consideration, to abstain from a certain trade without a time limit or a place limit.[74] Beyond harms to the economy,[75] allowing such restrictive bonds to stand would conceptually amount to using one's autonomy (in the present) to place too great a restriction on one's autonomy (in the future). Using agency substantially to curtail one's own agency is difficult to support in law; similarly, using one's agency in a manner disrespectful of another's agency is problematic.

Turning back to *Franklin*, when Lennox J was confronted with the question whether an owner of a restaurant can evict solely on the basis of race, he could

---

[69] *Arundel* v. *Trevillian* (1635) 1 Rep. Ch. 87, 21 ER 515; *Hall* v. *Potter* (1695) Shaw Parl. Cas. 76; 1 ER 52 (HL).

[70] *Key* v. *Bradshaw* (1689) 2 Vern. 102, 23 ER 675.

[71] *Anon* (1589) Owen 34, 74 ER 880. See also *Baker* v. *White* (1690) 2 Vern. 215, 23 ER 740, where the court cancelled a bond, the condition of which was that the wife would not marry anybody, and upon her death money would be paid to her heirs.

[72] Compare to Lord Hardwicke C in *Cole* v. *Gibson* (1750) 1 Vern. Sen. 503, 27 ER 1169.

[73] (1711) 24 ER 347. The defendant agreed to a condition, part of a bond, barring him, on a penalty of £50, from exercising his trade (a baker) in the parish of St. Andrews Holborn for five years.

[74] *Ibid.*, at 349; See also *Rogers* v. *Parrey* (1613) Bulst 136, 80 ER 1012 ; *Prugnell* v. *Gosse* (1648) Allen 67, 82 ER 919.

[75] For a discussion of restraint of trade and other market failures see M. Trebilcock, *The Limits of Freedom of Contract* (Cambridge, Mass., Harvard University Press, 1993).

have learned from restraint of trade cases that the integrity of agency matters. Consequently, he should have assessed whether instituting race-based rules is compatible with respect for equal agency. Furthermore, as the guardian of the common law, the court in *Franklin* had to consider the consequences if *all* restaurant owners denied access to blacks. Ignoring systemic considerations, that is, ignoring the legal state of affairs established if all were to rely on their legally available powers as elucidated by the court, is difficult to accept as a commendable discharge of the judicial obligation.[76]

The final set of authorities relates to the sale of offices. This body of law highlights the importance of recognising the public element that might be present in some private transactions. For example, there might be a public element involved in the manner people acquire some positions, even if these positions are within private companies. The reason, again, has to do with the "nature" or "function" of the company. If the company provides services to the general public in a common calling-like fashion, it is not clear that a person holding a position in such a company can accept a fee for selling his position to another.[77] With holding offices in a company comes a host of duties, or restrictions on the use of one's property, assuming one owns one's office, or at least has a proprietary interest in it. Alternatively, the court could be read as challenging the notion that people fully own their offices, and thus the subject matter of the contract, that is, the discretion bought and sold (the discretion to extend pension benefits, to recommend who should replace whom) is not a commodity the individuals "own" for such sale.

Along these lines, it could be argued that there is a distinction between Mr Evans as a private person and Mr Evans as an owner of a restaurant. As articulated above, when one holds oneself out as a member of a profession organised around non-associational transactions with the public, one can be seen as undertaking to act so as to respect the professional position and the public at large. Similarly, it could be asked whether the restaurant owner, even if allowed to "act arbitrarily" nonetheless "owns" the discretion whether to

[76] In *Davenant v. Hurdis* (1598) Moore 576, 72 ER 769, the court rejected as a restraint of trade a bylaw of the Company of the Merchants and Tailors of England. The bylaw ordered members who contracted for outside labour to set aside half the work to be done in-house or pay 10s fine per cloth sewn by a non-member, in order to support the poor members of the company. The court accepted the argument that if the bylaw could order half, it could have ordered all work to be done in-house, and hence other cloth-workers would suffer (i.e., be denied *their* liberty to pursue their livelihood).

[77] *Blachford v. Preston* (1799) 8 TR 89, 101 ER 1282; *Parsons v. Thompson* (1790) 1 HBl 322, 126 ER 190 (hereinafter *Parsons*). At issue was the sale of positions such as ship commanders or a master of a dockyard. For example, the transaction regarding the master of the dockyard involved the master retiring so as to vacate the position, and, expecting the foreman to assume it, the latter, once appointed master, would exercise his discretion to allow the retired former to keep some superannuation (extra-pension). Such an exchange was deemed unlawful because "public policy required that there should be no money consideration for the appointment to an office in which the public are interested; the public will be better served by having the person best qualified to fill offices appointed to them; but if money may be given to those who appoint, it may be a temptation to them to appoint improper persons" (*Blachford*, at 1284).

apply racial or other group-based characteristics, or whether such a discretion is outside his competence as a restaurant owner.

The notion that one may not own all aspects of one's business, job or position—i.e., may not dispose of them as one sees fit—is most evident in *Hanington*,[78] quoted by Lord Truro in *Egerton*. In that case, Thurlow LC, after admitting that the sale of a job recommendation by the Groom of the Stole to his Majesty did not fall under the statute prohibiting sale of offices, and after conceding that this household position was part of the King's private, rather than public, character, nevertheless accepted the argument that the Groom of the Stole abused the confidence placed in him by the King, and that such an abuse is a public matter: "treating it as a matter of public policy of the law, and similar to marriage brokage bonds, where, though the parties are private persons, the practice is publicly detrimental".[79] The Lord Chancellor ordered an injunction restraining the sale. Again, the analogy is clear. While owning a restaurant is a private matter, its operation nonetheless enters the public domain, since as a business it is organised around service to the general public. Therefore, the enactment of a policy excluding members of the community on the basis of group characteristics may be publicly detrimental, i.e., detrimental to the concept of a public organised around the concept of equal membership in the community.

It is in that context that counsel for the plaintiff in *Franklin* brought to the attention of the court the Latin maxim *sic utere tuo ut alienum non laedas* (use your own (property) so that you do not harm another's (property)). Indeed, this maxim is generally used to justify restrictions placed on a property owner regarding the wellbeing of adjacent lots.[80] However, its logic arguably extends beyond protecting the neighbour's lot, or beyond protecting merely the neighbour (or his property), to protecting the community within which commercial property operates, as was done in *Egerton*. Therefore, under the maxim, property rights cannot be used to justify nuisance to others: "[e]very man is restricted against using his property to the detriment of others", wrote Lord Truro.[81] In our context, this principle could support the conclusion that a business that is open to the public without requiring membership cannot be used to fracture the public by denying service solely on the basis of group characteristics.

The study of *Franklin* and the authorities presented to Lennox J was intended to suggest several things. At the most basic level is the observation that there

---

[78] *Hanington v. Du-Chatel* (1781) 1 Bro. CC 125, 28 ER 1028 (also known as *Hannington*; *Haneington*).

[79] *Ibid.*

[80] See generally E. Marshal, *General Principles of Scots Law* (5th edn., Edinburgh, W. Green, Sweet & Maxwell, 1991) 14–19.

[81] *Egerton, supra* n.47, at 473. This principle should be read not as dismantling the entire concept of private property; such a conclusion would place this principle in self-contradiction since it relies on the concept of private property. In other words, allowing autonomy over private property could be seen, as mentioned before, as an example of fulfilling one's human dignity. It should be restrained, however, much like other aspects of autonomy are, when its use encroaches upon the core of another person's human dignity.

exists a robust body of law dealing with the concept of public policy which suggests that uses of property rights cannot ignore the concept of the public. Community and its social institutions are presupposed by rights. Because the common law is a system of principles organised around reason, the common law cannot accept the self-contradiction entailed by respecting property rights but rejecting a concept of a community of rights-holders. Therefore taking property seriously demands that one core element, liberty rights, cannot be used to self-destruct another core element, the integrity of the public. More specifically, as revealed by the excursion into the authorities cited in the judgment, the legitimate use of property rights does not unequivocally include the power of an owner of a non-associational commercial enterprise to put in place a rule barring entrance of community members solely on the basis of group characteristics which bear no relevance to the *raison d'étre* of the commerce. Consequently, the law should allow for compensation where the public and its institutions are ignored by a rights-holder.[82]

Methodologically, had Lennox J stepped back and studied the aforementioned cases, as Lord Truro did in *Egerton*, perhaps he would have seen the relevance of the legal maxims counsel was submitting, and would have been able to distinguish cases standing for the proposition that no limits were placed on keepers of establishments which did not qualify as inns.[83] Since the court failed to do so, the precedential value of *Franklin* is doubtful at best. Moreover, the premise under which Lennox J was acting, namely that the law of property is intelligible without determining whether blacks (or other minorities) are truly equal members of the community (and therefore equal at common law), was misguided. Either black persons are equal, deserving of equal respect and consideration as members of the general community with which commerce is conducted, or not. Denying the relevance of the question is legally problematic.

At the very least, Lennox J's insistence on a search for a binding precedent is difficult to defend. His refusal to engage in a fuller analysis of the common law is in tension with the interpretative approach which requires the interpreter to seek the rationale, or the principle, that justifies previous cases.[84]

Lastly, *Franklin* and the authorities contained therein were put forward to show that the common law is not subsumed in the statutory regime—the statutes prohibiting sales of offices, although not covering all offices, were not seen by the courts as negating a common law prohibition[85]—but nor does the

---

[82] S.C. Coval and J.C. Smith, "Compensation for Discrimination" (1982) 16 *U B C L Rev.* 71.

[83] *Sealey, supra* n.44.

[84] Lord Mansfield stated in *Jones* v. *Randall* (1774) 98 ER 954, 955 that a contractual behaviour, while "not adjudged illegal by precedents, . . . may be decided to be so upon principles; and the law of England would be a strange science indeed if it were decided upon precedents only. Precedents serve to illustrate principles, and to give them a fixed certainty. But the law of England . . . depends upon principles; and these principles run through all the cases according as the particular circumstances of each have been found to fall within one or other of them".

[85] While the court saw the regulation of the sale of offices as the domain of the legislature, it nonetheless realised the common law cannot stay inert and by default allow such sale. See *Parsons, supra* n.77. The relevant governing statute was 5&6 Edw 6 at chap. 16 (1552).

common law stand in isolation from the statutory regime. The statutes prohibiting sales of offices were taken by the courts as a manifestation of the legislative conclusion that such a sale is unlawful, and consequently the presence of such statutes require that the common law determine whether the legislative rationale embodied in the legislation—the rationale that led the legislature to conclude that certain behaviours are not permitted—applies to the common law as well. In the same vein, Mr Buchner called upon the court to take notice of the statutory expansion of franchise for blacks and the recognition of women as equal moral agents under the family law acts. These developments should have prompted a common law court to re-examine its doctrine, in order to ensure that it is consistent and coherent. Unfortunately, the court ignored the statutory regime altogether. This chapter suggests that such an approach is problematic because it is in tension with the reason-based methodology of the common law.

3. *Canada Trust*—more heritage from the 1920s

Conceptually the analysis presented above examined case law that recognised, in some instances, the limits of the power to dispose of one's property as one sees fit. The doctrinal tool used to delineate these limits was termed "public policy". In advocating the use of this legal tool, its drawbacks have to be recognised and addressed. Perhaps the most obvious objection centres on the indeterminate scope of public policy. It can mean whatever the judge says it means. Indeed, public policy was referred to as an unruly horse, which threatened to empower judges to pursue "idiosyncratic inferences of a few judicial minds".[86] It is therefore not surprising that the bench has been reluctant to expand the doctrine of public policy, stressing that public policy considerations fall within the legislative, rather than the judicial, sphere.[87] Yet these concerns are justified only if public policy is taken as external, rather than internal, to the common law.

Public policy, this chapter argues, is about the *public*, as a concept, rather than about distributive or utilitarian policy. It is about (or should be about) ensuring that private law doctrine recognises the public element when applied to sections of the common law where the public is engaged. Having understood that the common law demands, analytically, a concept of a community, and having accepted that commercial, non-associational commerce operates on a communal level (i.e., takes place in a community of abstract rights-holders), public policy becomes a legal tool that safeguards against a clash between rights and community. The content of legal rights cannot include the power to disintegrate the community against which, within which and with which rights

---

[86] *Re Miller* [1938] SCR 1 (*per* Crocket J), quoting (at 13) Lord Aitkin in *Fender* v. *Mildmay* [1937] 3 All ER 403.

[87] "Judges are more to be trusted as interpreters of the law than as expounders of public policy": *Halsbury's Laws of England, supra* n.8, at vol. 9, para. 392, "Contracts".

meaningfully operate. Viewed as such, the suggested concept of public policy is integral to the rights themselves. It is presupposed by the rights, so the exercise of the rights has to take it into account. At the same time, because the justification for the doctrine of public policy lies in the very existence of the common law community, the invocation of the doctrine cannot be used to abrogate liberty without demonstrating that without such abrogation, the community and/or its social institutions will disintegrate. Put differently, since the common law community, as it has emerged through a thousand years of adjudication, is organised around the concept of moral agency (from which autonomy and human dignity flow), public policy cannot be used to dismantle either autonomy or human dignity in the name of the community of moral agents. Such internal constraints alleviate at least to some degree the indeterminacy critique. Judges may not ride the horse of public policy to their own destination, nor may they allow the horse to take them for a ride to the unknown.

Furthermore, the concept suggested here does not attempt to trespass into policy issues properly left to the deliberation of the party-political arena. The legislature is free to debate what the content of statutory law should be, and what institutions should administer that body of law. The legislature is indeed in charge of ascertaining the common good and the best means to achieve it. Again, under the relatively tight concept of public policy argued for here, the court would have to demonstrate that the concept of a community—a concept without which the concept of rights is meaningless—requires placing limits on the exercise of rights. It would not suffice for courts to say that a certain use of private property is offensive, or does not, in their opinion, promote the welfare of the polity in the best way possible. The court would have to present convincing arguments why allowing such an offensive or ineffective use contradicts the concept of a community or why such use otherwise contradicts the underlying foundation of the right invoked. Put differently, judges will have to demonstrate that the common law itself, as a structure of argument, calls for a certain public policy, in the legal sense of the term. The statutory regime governing the regulation of matters of social policy is not usurped by such an exercise.

It is in this context that *Canada Trust* will be analysed. More specifically, like *Franklin*, *Canada Trust* is presented to demonstrate how public policy analysis should *not* be conducted. At the centre of *Canada Trust* was a charitable trust, established in 1923. The trust was dedicated to educational and clerical scholarship, and was open to white Protestants only. As if to add insult to injury, a cap of one-fourth was put on the money that could be granted to female recipients. After the Human Rights Commission filed a complaint against the trust, the trustee sought the advice and direction of the court.[88]

---

[88] It is interesting to point out that the trustee, the trial court and the Court of Appeal all agreed that the common law court had jurisdiction to address the issue, even though the Human Rights Commission had initiated an investigation. Compare *Bhadauria* v. *Board of Governors of Seneca College* [1981] 2 SCR 181 (hereinafter *Bhadauria*). See analysis in Reichman, *supra* n.1.

The Court of Appeal for Ontario invalidated the restriction and used its *cy-près* powers[89] to reinstate the trust as open to all, notwithstanding the settlor's power to dispose of his property as he saw fit.[90] The reasoning provided by the majority relied heavily on the recitals of the trust, which stated that the settlor believed that the "white race" is, as a whole, best qualified by nature to be entrusted with the development of civilisation, and that the progress of the world depends on the maintenance of the Christian religion. Clearly, it is difficult to imagine a world view as offensive as this. In the court's words, "to say that a trust premised on these notions of racism and religious superiority contravenes contemporary public policy is to expatiate the obvious".[91]

However, the judicial justification for disallowing a trust to fund solely white and predominantly male Protestants is somewhat odd. The majority held that "the concept that any one race or any one religion is intrinsically better than any other is patently at variance with the democratic principles governing our pluralistic society in which equality rights are constitutionally guaranteed and in which the multicultural heritage of Canadians is to be preserved and enhanced".[92] But this assertion is not free from difficulties. First, monotheistic religion, almost by its definition, includes some claim, even if modified, of religious superiority; this is integral to its *raison d'être*; this is why it argues believers should follow its dogmas and not convert to another religion.[93] Secondly, if pluralism matters it becomes difficult to exclude those who do not believe in pluralism, as arguably they are part of the plurality as well. At the very least, it has to be shown that those who reject pluralism *actually* threaten pluralism. That is, actual evidence must demonstrate that the multi-cultural heritage of Canada is in fact threatened by allowing the settlor to restrict the trust along religious, ethnic, racial, gender or other lines. The threat has to be real. It should be noted that Robins JA, writing for the majority, did not comment on the gender cap, although the court's disposition invalidates all conditions. Thirdly, the fact that equality rights are constitutionalised does not necessarily mean that equality has displaced autonomy, or at least not in the private sphere. Arguments must be provided as to how the constitutionalisation of some rights affects the common law, since there are theoretical and doctrinal arguments to suggest that constitutional rights should not apply directly to the common law.[94]

An additional argument provided by the court is problematic as well: "[t]he widespread criticism of the Foundation by human rights bodies, the press, the

---

[89] For evaluation of the court's reasoning on that point see L.A. Turnbull, "Case Comment" (1990) 38 ETR 47.

[90] For the limits of such powers in the area of trust and for an analysis of the trial court decision see J.C. Shepherd, "When The Common Law Fails" (1988) 9 *ETJ* 117, arguing at 128–30 for a more restricted idea of "property powers".

[91] *Canada Trust, supra* n.4, at 495.

[92] *Ibid.*

[93] Recently, Pope John Paul made this exact statement. See P. Pullella, "Vatican Says No Religion Equals Roman Catholicism", *Reuters (Vatican City)* 5 Sept. 2000.

[94] *Supra* n.36. Compare L. Weinrib and E. Weinrib, chap. 3 this vol.

clergy, the university community and the general community serves to demonstrate how far out of keeping the trust now is with prevailing ideas and standards of racial and religious tolerance and equality and, indeed, how offensive its terms are to fair minded citizens".[95] If this reasoning is taken seriously, the line between the political process and the judicial one becomes ever more blurred. Should the court administer public opinion polls to determine what fair-minded citizens believe? And should a situation arise when such public sentiment shifts back toward a segregative mood, would courts be bound to bow?[96] Indeed, scholars have pointed to the problematic nature of such reasoning.[97]

The concurring opinion of Tarnopolsky JA is disquieting as well. He identifies the three conditions that a trust must satisfy in order to achieve charitable status: it must have as its object one of four purposes, among which is education; its purpose must be wholly and exclusively charitable; and it must promote a public benefit. In order to pass the latter requirement a trust must be available to a cross-section of the public, rather than only to those bearing a personal nexus to the settlor, and it *must not be harmful to the public*.[98] Tarnopolsky JA, steering his opinion quickly towards public policy waters, dispensed with this requirement in a brief sentence: "[e]ducation is clearly to the benefit of the public".[99] Such an assertion, while indisputable, renders either the first prong of the test—the purpose element—or the "no-public-harm" segment of the public benefit prong superfluous. More specifically, since education is explicitly mentioned as a legitimate purpose under the first prong, it seems analytically redundant to state that any educational purpose satisfies the third prong, that is, promotes a public benefit. There must be more to the requirement of public benefit, and its ingredients, such as "no public harm". If indeed the no public harm requirement is taken seriously, its analysis is tantalisingly similar to what public policy analysis should yield: a trust must not be used to the detriment of the concept of a public, or a community, as such.[100] Such an analysis would have

---

[95] *Canada Trust, supra* n.4, at 495.

[96] In discussing the *cy-près* issue, Robins JA noted that in 1923, when the funds were invested, "the terms of the indenture would have been held to be certain, valid and not contrary to any public policy which rendered the trust void or illegal or which detracted from the settlor's general intention to devote property to charitable purposes. However, *with changing social attitudes, public policy has changed*. The public policy of the 1920s is not the public policy of 1990s. As a result, it is no longer in the interest of the community to continue the trust on the basis predicated by the settlor" (*Canada Trust, supra* n.4, at 496–7, emphasis added). Such an analysis opens a window to a backlash argument, should social attitude change. Furthermore, it is not clear whether indeed it is just the change of attitude that changed public policy. It could very well be that such objectives were wrong in 1923, and should have been found so had they been contested in a common law court which adopted the approach of *Egerton, supra* n.47.

[97] B. Vizkelety, "Discrimination, the Right to Seek Redress and the Common Law: A Century Old Debate" (1992) 15 *Dalhousie LJ* 304, 311–12.

[98] *Halsbury's Laws of England, supra* n.8, at vol. 5, "Charities", 309, para. 505; *Canada Trust, supra* n.4, at 507.

[99] *Canada Trust, supra* n.4, at 508.

[100] Compare *Ateliers d'ingénirie Dominion Ltée* v. *Commission des droits de la personne du Québec* [1980] RP 209, stating at 216 that the subject matter of human rights is greater than "work conditions"—it is the conditions of "life in a society".

required the court to show why a charitable trust, one of the objects of which is to promote racial superiority, is harmful to the concept of public.

A further difficulty with Tarnopolsky JA's approach is its ambiguity with respect to the normative status of statutory law, parliamentary debates, the Charter and international conventions *vis-à-vis* the common law doctrine of public policy. The foray into these bodies of law begins with: "further evidence of the public policy against discrimination can be found in . . .".[101] It is unclear whether such normative sources are capable of serving as "evidence" of that which constitutes public policy, properly understood. It seems that further analysis is required to demonstrate not only who, institutionally, should argue public policy[102] and decide it, but, substantively, why an international convention or even a constitution should directly influence arguments regarding public policy or other common law instruments.[103] After all, the normative source of the common law is distinct from the source of the legislative process, as well as from the source of international obligations.[104] This is not to say that the stand taken by provincial legislatures, the federal parliament, the constitutional assembly or the world community is irrelevant. Its relevance, however, is not as evidence, since these communities acting in their political capacity are not binding on the common law self-rationalisation, unless explicitly regulating a legal matter.

The relevance of these normative sources is, it is submitted, that they contain arguments, and thus the common law as a body of law based on reason must confront them.[105] The public policy embodied in these normative sources is not relevant because these laws represent the will of the people, as Tarnopolsky JA might be read to suggest, but because such laws represent a view with which the common law, as a deliberative arena constructed around reason, has to take issue. The relationship between the common law and statutory law can, in that respect, be thought of as similar to the dialogue between the common law and the civil law, a dialogue hailed by commentators and judges.[106]

The relevance of neighbouring legal regimes, and the statutory one in particular, is heightened when what is at issue are the contours of the community itself, or who belongs to "us". The common law, for better or worse, has a slower updating mechanism, which results in delays before

---

[101] *Canada Trust, supra* n.4, at 512.

[102] Shepherd, *supra* n.90, at 121, pointing to deficiencies in the arguments before the trial court, but in fact taking issue with the adequacy of the adversarial system to decide public policy as if it were the legislature. See L. Fuller, "The Forms and Limits of Adjudication" (1978) 92 *Harv. L R* 353.

[103] P. Atiyah, "Common Law—Statute Law" (1985) 48 *MLR* 1; J.M. Landis, "Statutes and the Sources of Law" (1965) 2 *Harv. J on Legis.* 7.

[104] See generally M. Damaska, *The Faces of Justice and State Authority* (New Haven, Conn., Yale University Press, 1986). The different normative sources of the different legal regimes that comprise "the law" in a given jurisdiction are sketched in Reichman, *supra* n.4.

[105] For a similar idea in a different context see S. Choudhry, "Globalization in Search of Justification: Toward a Theory of Comparative Constitutional Interpretation" (1999) 74 *Indiana L J* 819.

[106] T. Rinfret, "Reminiscences from the Supreme Court of Canada" (1956) 3 *McGill L J* 1, 2.

precedents are reconsidered. Moreover, the legal process may suffer from access barriers that preclude judges from properly realising who belongs to "us". Therefore, when the legislature, through emancipatory laws such as human rights codes, has realised that the community includes members of different group characteristics, the common law may not stay inert. It should take notice of such statutory developments, and evaluate its own position *vis-à-vis* its underlying principles in light of the reasoning at the core of such statutory developments. In so doing, the common law is not subsumed by the statutory regime, nor does it act to displace the means stipulated by statute to effectuate such policy. Rather, its focus is to root out inner inconsistencies.[107]

How, then, should we proceed to analyse the restrictive trust? It could be argued that the restrictive trust should be analogised to a restrictive or a conditional covenant (where the condition involves a public element). It is suggested here that charitable trusts contain a unique public element, in the same way as non-individual commerce, wills conditional upon the grant of a noble title, or the institution of marriage do. Charitable trusts by their very nature are legally created institutions that enable a donor to bestow a benefit *to the community* according to the donor's understanding of the best way of improving an aspect of communal life. In turn, such a charity receives preferential treatment from the community in the form of a favourable tax regime. In other words, the reciprocal transaction occurs on a communal level. This insight is reinforced by the evaluation of the legal requirements that a trust must fulfill in order to be deemed charitable that were analysed in *Canada Trust*. For example, insisting that the trust be available to a cross-section of the public suggests that the "function" or "nature" of the institution does not merely engage testamentary freedom, but also the public. The charitable trust as a legal construct presupposes interaction with the community on a non-individual basis, for the purpose of benefiting the community, and for this purpose alone.

The public feature is most visible in the requirement that the trust must not be harmful to the public. The community cannot be expected to honour the status of a trust as charitable when the objectives of the trust challenge the community's very definition of itself, and of who belongs to the community.[108]

---

[107] Such an approach is in less tension with Laskin CJ's opinion in *Bhadauria, supra* n.88, an opinion ignored by Tarnopolsky JA. Indeed, it seems that such an omission by a member of the Ontario Court of Appeal bench comes close to defying a Supreme Court *ratio decidendi*. Clearly Tarnopolsky JA was aware that Wilson JA's opinion in *Bhadauria*, upon which he relied for the relevance of human rights legislation to the common law (*Canada Trust, supra* n.4, at 510–11), had been specifically overruled by the Supreme Court. Not only is such judicial behaviour curious, but it hinders reliance on Tarnopolsky JA's judgment. Tarnopolsky JA ought to have at least attempted to distinguish *Bhadauria* for his opinion to withstand the test of critical analysis.

[108] When the objectives of a trust clash with the glue that bonds community members together, namely their human dignity, the community faces, yet again, a definitional inner tension. If the community honours the charitable status of a trust the objects of which require the denial of equal human dignity, as was the case with the trust at issue in *Canada Trust*, it uses its communal space (or powers), which belongs to all members, to acknowledge that such an objective is in fact beneficial to the community, hence valid. In so doing the community uses its powers to dismantle itself, thus inflicting "harm to the public".

The public is harmed not only because a trust that involves the violation of equal human dignity is not the best means to promote the common good. The public is primarily harmed precisely because a violation of equal human dignity denies the very idea of a community of equal membership, that is, the public as such is harmed. When addressing the public harm requirement, Tarnopolsky JA's reliance on Mackay J in *Re Drummond Wren* is helpful. The public harm, wrote Mackay J, is the "fissiparous tendencies which would imperil national unity".[109] This sentence should not be read as suggesting that the common law has a stand *vis-à-vis* the separatist movement of Quebec, but as suggesting that the conceptual community constructed by the common law could not consistently uphold the use of a common law tool—a charitable trust—in a manner which threatens to destroy the common law community from which this tool draws its operative power. It cannot obey the demand of respect advanced by the settlor when the objective at the core of that demand is the unravelling of the bond that ties the community together. Such an analysis is closer to the majority's view in *Canada Trust*, since it focuses on the objectives of the trust in order to determine whether the associational interests of the settlor could be reconciled with the greater association within which they are meaningful, namely the common law community.

It is perhaps important to draw a distinction between a trust and a charitable trust in this context. All trusts, and particularly a non-charitable trust, may be seen as involving autonomy claims akin to associational ones. A person chooses to restrict the use of her funds to causes with which she identifies, or to people with whom she associates. Similarly, a person may choose whom to invite to her home, or to whom to bequeath her property. More specifically, if there is no law prohibiting a person from setting up a private religious programme only for Protestants, and/or only for men, and even only for whites, it is not clear why such a person may not choose to bestow her money to scholarships which would advance only these groups.

Yet the status of a *charitable* trust, like the status of non-individual commerce, involves a reciprocal interaction with the general public. A charitable trust is distinct from a "private, family trust".[110] Since a charitable trust accepts preferential tax treatment from the public, it cannot reciprocate by challenging the integrity of the public. In some respects, *Canada Trust* was an easy case because not only the invocation of the group-based characteristics but the explicit objectives clearly fell afoul of the very idea of "a common", underlying the common law community. As the majority alluded to,[111] had the objectives of the trust been

---

[109] *Re Drummond Wren, supra* n.29, at 783, as cited in *Canada Trust, supra* n.4, at 511.

[110] Tarnopolsky JA draws this distinction in *Canada Trust, supra* n.4. While contesting other aspects of the thesis of this chap., Weinrib and Weinrib subscribe to this distinction, see *supra* n.94, especially their reference to *Blathwayt* v. *Lord Cawley* [1975] 3 All ER 625, 636 (HL) dealing with a private will. But see *Fox* v. *Fox Estate* (1996) 28 OR (3d) 496 (CA) for the opposite conclusion.

[111] *Canada Trust, supra* n.4, at 496.

different,[112] yet the same restrictions used, the problem the court would have had to face might have been more complex given the associational interests involved. Future analysis is required in order to determine whether we can justify under the common law remedial use of group-based characteristics by individuals in charitable trusts—where the groups preferred have been suffering from systemic harm in the sphere of life towards which the trust is directed—in a manner akin to remedial affirmative action by government entities.[113]

4. Public policy and prejudicial considerations—conclusion

The Quebec Court of Appeal in *Loew's*, the Supreme Court in *Christie*, followed by the British Columbia Court of Appeal in *Rogers* v. *Clarence Hotel*[114] and the Alberta Court of Appeal in *King* v. *Barclay and Barclay's Motel*,[115] have all refused to find that considering race or analogous grounds in the exercise of one's (commercial) property rights amounts to a violation of public policy. At least in one case and in a different context, a court has gone so far as to suggest that admitting women to the bar would be nothing short of a direct infringement upon public order.[116] On the other hand, the Quebec Superior Court in *Johnson* v. *Sparrow*,[117] the Ontario High Court in *Re Drummond*

---

[112] It is difficult to conceive of benign objectives behind the restrictions used. However, had the world-view guiding the trust been different, perhaps some of its objectives could have been saved. Preserving the Protestant cultural heritage, encouraging males to pursue higher education, and in particular religious education, and encouraging those who define themselves as Caucasians to discern their responsibilities in society, might affront the community less, compared to the objectives of the Foundation.

[113] Lord Truro in *Egerton, supra* n.47, suggests that in some cases a concrete objective could be benign, yet the systemic effect of the tools used for its promotion be malignant. While this argument seems to reinforce the objection to the use of group characteristics regardless of their objectives, if nonetheless the effect matters, perhaps remedial effect is acceptable. Upon showing a concrete harm to a specific group within the community in the past, perhaps the use of charitable trusts could be seen as beneficial and healing, rather than fissiparous. If this logic is valid, the nexus between past harm (or discrimination) and the charitable trust has to be tight. It has to be limited in time (until healing takes place); it must be limited to those groups which in fact were harmed and are still suffering from such harms; and it must be directly linked to subject matters where historic evidence of harm exists and to instances where such harm has left a tangible mark in the present.

[114] (1940) 2 WWR 545. But see the dissent of O'Halloran JA, resting his opinion on an "elementary principle of the common law", that ". . . All British subjects have the same rights and privileges under the common law—it makes no difference whether whites or coloured; or what class, race or religion" (at 550). See criticism in D.A. Schmeiser, *Civil Liberties in Canada* (London, Oxford University Press, 1964), 272.

[115] (1961) 25 WWR (NS) 240.

[116] *Langstaff* v. *The Bar of the Province of Quebec* (1915) 47 SC 131, 137.

[117] (1899) 15 Que. SC 104. The Quebec Court of Appeal (1899) 8 QB 379, rejected the analogy the court below had made between theatres and inns, but nevertheless left the question of racial exclusion open (at 383, translation from French original):

"I did not find that the question arose as to whether blacks, or a particular class of individuals, could be excluded. The statute of 1780 had indeed declared that liveried servants could not be admitted to a theatre, but the ruling soon fell into disuse, and I have not uncovered any other trace of the question. In the United States, certain states have passed special laws permitting the

Wren,[118] and, more recently, the Quebec Superior Court in *Gooding*[119] and the Ontario Court of Appeal in *Canada Trust*, found to the contrary, rejecting discrimination as being contrary to public policy. None of these decisions has presented a robust analysis of the idea of public policy as a legal concept.[120]

This section has tried to demonstrate through the analysis of *Franklin* and *Canada Trust* that the common law must take issue with the exercise of property rights so as to exclude would-be patrons from land used for commercial, non-individual purposes. The argument advanced here is that public policy considerations echo the *in rem* aspect of property rights, as claims against the public as such. Therefore, integral to the use of such property rights, and to the application of public policy considerations governing the disposition of property, is the concept of a public, or a community.

It is submitted that excluding gays, lesbians, blacks, Jews or, for that matter, freckled people is difficult to reconcile with a principled approach to the concept of a community organised around the idea of human dignity. It is not clear that a coherent approach to *in rem* property rights, as mirrored in the concept of public policy, would automatically uphold the prejudicial use of one's commercial property to exclude members of groups or classes organised around nearly immutable characteristics. Such use is in tension with the concept of a community of equal moral agents deserving respect for their dignity and, further, allowing such use places the community in a self-contradiction of sorts.

The analysis above suggests that the common law regime should not be viewed as subsumed by the adjacent human rights code, nor should the presence of the code be ignored in common law adjudication. While consistency with the statutory regime is not an imperative for the common law, taking account of statutory developments in order to evaluate the internal consistency of the common law is. Leaving political choices of policy to the statutory arena requires that the common law not automatically accept a political choice contained in a statute; at the same time, the common law must take note of the rationale behind the choice the community has made, and examine whether the argument embedded in the statute requires elucidation of the common law rule on point.

---

exclusion of blacks, but the debate continues as to whether these laws are or are not constitutional, because they would be contrary to equality among persons. One nevertheless acknowledges the right of theatre managers to sell or give admission tickets only to particular classes of individuals and to exclude others. However this question may be resolved, it does not bear on the present case, and we uphold the decision, because we believe that there was a contract between the parties and that the defendant violated this contract without a legitimate reason".

[118] *Supra* n.29.

[119] *Gooding, supra* n.31, at 442: "[w]hereas, all racial discrimination is illegal, being contrary to public order and standards of good behaviour" (translation from French original).

[120] Neither, for that matter, did *Bhadauria, supra* n.88, where the court refused to engage with the public policy expressed in the Ontario Human Rights Code. At least one scholar wondered whether, after *Bhadauria*, public policy considerations were still part of the common law. See H. Kopyto, "The Bhadauria Case: The Denial of the Right to Sue for Discrimination" (1981) 7 *Queen's L J* 144, 150.

IV. A FINAL NOTE

This chapter attempted to articulate several approaches towards a conceptualisation of the limits of the exercise of property rights. By no means do these articulations represent the final or exhaustive word on the subject; other avenues
could be pursued and further engagement with theory and case law would certainly yield better understanding. In any event, our search for coherence and
consistency under the common law demands that we try to articulate our best
understanding of the co-existence of property rights and public policy, of the
liberty to dispose of one's property as one sees fit and the duty not to harm
another, or the community. Thus, it seems that common law lawyers, judges
and scholars should further examine the relationship between discrimination
and property rights in the context of general commerce. This chapter, therefore,
could be seen as an invitation for further discourse.

Part IV

Labour Law

12

Enforcement of Employment Contracts and the Anti-Slavery Norm

TODD D. RAKOFF

I. INTRODUCTION

T HE RIGHT NOT to be a slave is the most basic of all human rights. In this
chapter, I explore the connection between this anti-slavery norm and the
treatment of employment contracts in the law of the United States. Many of the
other chapters in this book on human rights in private law focus on human
rights which are well established as public law norms, but which have only
uncertain, or indirect, application to private law. By contrast, I deal with one
whose application to both public and private law matters, at least in the United
States, is absolutely clear. What follows, then, can be seen as an inquiry into the
further work that needs to be done, after the question of applicability is settled,
to bring a human rights norm down to private cases.

II. THE PROHIBITION ON SLAVERY

International efforts to suppress slavery and the slave trade have a long history,
and present what is probably the archetype of international cooperation to protect a human right. There are two fundamental statements of the international
right. The Slavery Convention of 25 September 1926 binds the contracting
States "[t]o prevent and suppress the slave trade" and "[t]o bring about, pro-
gressively and as soon as possible, the complete abolition of slavery in all its
forms".[1] A bit more expansively, the Universal Declaration of Human Rights
proclaims: "[n]o one shall be held in slavery or servitude; slavery and the slave
trade shall be prohibited in all their forms".[2] And of course there are numerous

---

[1] Slavery Convention, Art. 2. Originally promulgated under the aegis of the League of Nations,
this Convention now resides under the umbrella of the UN Protocol Amending the Slavery
Convention, 23 Oct. 1953. The Convention's scope was broadened to cover debt bondage, and some
other practices, in 1956, in the Supplementary Convention on the Abolition of Slavery, the Slave
Trade, and Institutions and Practices Similar to Slavery.

[2] Universal Declaration of Human Rights, Art. 4.

constitutions, statutes and court decisions throughout the world proclaiming the internal law of individual countries to be in accord with the same sentiments.

Unfortunately, "slavery or servitude" has not, by force of these words, been eliminated from the human condition. Rights, even rights enforceable in the ordinary domestic courts, are not enough. In India, for example, the Bonded Labour System (Abolition) Act of 1976 outlaws debt bondage; yet, at least by the estimate of the organisation Human Rights Watch, more than 15 million children in India work in servitude in order to pay off a debt.[3] For problems of this scale, public action and the organised force of governments must provide the basic cure.

We in the United States, of course, know full well the need to bring public force to bear to eliminate slavery. Whatever the causes of our mid-nineteenth century Civil War, which historians debate, it became a crusade against this evil institution. In his articulation of the war's purposes, President Lincoln went behind the legalities of our Constitution—which had tolerated slavery—and relied instead on the grand statement of "unalienable rights", including liberty, set forth in our Declaration of Independence.[4] And in the most immediate upshot of the war, the Constitution was rewritten to provide, in its Thirteenth Amendment:

Section 1. Neither slavery nor involuntary servitude, except as a punishment for crime whereof the party shall have been duly convicted, shall exist within the United States, or any place subject to their jurisdiction.

Section 2. Congress shall have power to enforce this Article by appropriate legislation.

For the purpose of relating this text to private law issues, three features are especially important. First, the Thirteenth Amendment prohibits not only "slavery", but "involuntary servitude" as well. From a drafting point of view, this represented merely the adoption of a customary phrase.[5] But that phrase encompassed an understanding that the evil to be addressed could not be fully described as slavery—could not, in other words, be seen as merely the problem of one person owning another. The institution might be cloaked most commonly in the legal garb of property, but it could also be created through other legal forms having similar effects. In early colonial America, the line between being a "slave" and being a contractually "indentured servant" had at times been very hazy; in nineteenth century America, conditions which seemed to those who promulgated the Amendment to be similar to slavery existed in the debt-peonage systems of territories that had been acquired from Mexico. Whatever the outer boundaries of the text, it was meant to be expansive, and in particular was meant to reach forms of domination based on contract as well as on property.

---

[3] Human Rights Watch, "The Small Hands of Slavery: Bonded Child Labor in India" (1996), as summarised on the Human Rights Watch web site, www.hrw.org.

[4] See G. Wills, *Lincoln at Gettysburg* (New York, Simon & Schuster, 1992).

[5] The same terms had been famously used in the Northwest Ordinance of 1787.

Second, the Amendment states a purely negative norm. What is prohibited is, as just suggested, prohibited in all its guises; but it remains true that the Amendment contains only a prohibition. By contrast, the Universal Declaration of Human Rights not only prohibits slavery or servitude; it also states positively that "[e]veryone has the right to work, to free choice of employment, to just and favorable conditions of work and to protection against unemployment".[6] Nothing in the Thirteenth Amendment or anywhere in the US Constitution says anything like the same.

Finally, this anti-slavery norm is powerfully established by the Thirteenth Amendment—almost uniquely powerfully. Virtually everything else in the US Constitution helps constitute the government, authorises action by the government, or limits what the government can do; indeed, the second section of this Amendment, adding to the powers delegated to Congress, falls within this tradition. But the first section is not so limited. Of course it outlaws governmental maintenance of an institution of slavery, such as existed in the southern states before the Civil War. But the first section of the Amendment, by its terms and as construed by the courts, also makes the anti-slavery norm operative private law—makes it directly applicable to the interactions of non-governmental persons and entities.[7] And since it is part of a Constitution which itself is the supreme law of the land, that norm is as powerfully established as anything can be in the American legal system.

III. THE MULTIPLE FACES OF LEGAL NORMS

It is, however, easier to state a norm applicable absolutely to all kinds and classes of cases than it is to put it into practice in such a comprehensive way. Whether there is any principled distinction between public and private law and, if so, what it is, are matters much disputed in jurisprudence; and it is not the purpose of this Article to address the issue in any systematic way. What does need to be pointed out, however—since it forms the basis for what follows—is that nominally similar legal norms often assume different forms when used to test the validity of social institutions, from the forms they have when applied to dyadic disputes.

Perhaps two American examples related to the regulatory and common law of contractual relations—far away from the usual concerns of "human rights"—will help illustrate the general point. The first concerns what we may call the anti-deception norm. In its traditional formulation in the United States, conceived by the common law on the model of A directly negotiating with B, B must have actually relied on A's falsehood to justify an action for fraud.

---

[6] Universal Declaration of Human Rights, Art. 23.

[7] The only comparable provision that comes easily to mind is the 18th Amendment, which directly prohibited "the manufacture, sale or transportation of intoxicating liquors"; it, however, was repealed by the 21st Amendment.

However, when the norm was restated in statutory form as part of the regulation of general commercial marketing practices, A's advertising was outlawed merely for having the tendency or capacity to deceive.[8] Individual reliance was no longer relevant, given the broad, institutional reform purposes of the law. Again, there is also within American contract law a broad anti-unconscionability norm. When applied to individual transactions in ordinary lawsuits, however, judges are chary of its use, and usually require considerable proof of both substantive unfairness and interactional irregularity in the particular situation before upsetting a transaction.[9] By contrast, state and federal legislatures set, and regularly revise, precise minimum wages—in effect the stipulation of the point below which the rate of pay would be unconscionable—applicable quite without regard to the interaction of the employer and employee.[10] The general judgements as to the state of the market (in this case, the labour market) that the judges feel unable to make are just those the legislatures enact into law. Whatever the precise features of the legal landscape that justify the distinctions made in these two examples, the general point is plain: the application of broad norms like the anti-deception norm or the anti-unconscionability norm is inherently contextual to some degree, and the institutional scale in question is a large part of the relevant context.

If we return now to the anti-slavery norm as stated in the Thirteenth Amendment (or indeed in human rights texts generally), we must take it as outlawing first and foremost a broad social institution. Slavery is a condition of society, with, indeed, somewhat different attributes in different places; in the United States slavery, both legally and practically, put some people at the disposition of others for their entire lifetimes; kept them in a state of social and personal degradation; and maintained its sway through a socially organised and governmentally supported system of coercion. But the Amendment, although passed to ratify in law the fruits of a war against this institution, abolished slavery and involuntary servitude even when they were only indirectly dependent, or not dependent at all, on governmental action. We thus must face the question how the translation between contexts, as regards this norm, is to be made.

IV.   THE FIRST DOCTRINAL POSSIBILITY: DURESS

The case to start with—because it is at an extreme—is *Bailey* v. *State of Alabama*.[11] As the name suggests, Bailey was appealing his conviction for a crime. He had been tried, found guilty, fined, and sentenced to 136 days in lieu of the fine he could not pay. But what was his crime? He had agreed to work for

---

[8] Federal Trade Commission Act, 15 USC § 45, as interpreted in *Charles of the Ritz Distributors Corp* v. *FTC* (1944) 143 F 2d 676 (2d Cir.).
[9] *Williams* v. *Walker-Thomas Furniture Co* (1965) 350 F 2d 445 (DC Cir.).
[10] For example, Fair Labor Standards Act, 29 USC § 206(a).
[11] 219 US 219 (1911) (hereinafter *Bailey*).

a year as a farm hand for $12 a month (this was 1907); had accepted a $15 advance on his wages which was to be worked out by deduction from his wages at the rate of $1.25 a month; and had then left his employer after a little over one month, without repaying the as-yet-unearned part of the advance.

While Alabama's statutory pattern was complicated, the Supreme Court understood it to say that "the mere breach of a contract for personal service, coupled with the mere failure to pay a debt which was to be liquidated in the course of such service, is made sufficient to warrant a conviction".[12] Was this consistent with the Thirteenth Amendment and the statutes Congress had passed to implement it? It was held that it was not. "The plain intention" of the Thirteenth Amendment, wrote Justice Hughes, "was to abolish slavery of what-ever name and form and all its badges and incidents; to render impossible any state of bondage; to make labour free, by prohibiting that control by which the personal service of one man is disposed of or coerced for another's benefit which is the essence of involuntary servitude".[13] "The fact that the debtor contracted to perform the labor" did not change the matter; "the compulsion of the service" was the same even though the obligation originated in an agreement.[14] "The contract exposes the debtor to liability for the loss due to the breach, but not to enforced labor".[15]

This seems straightforward; but the easy plausibility of the argument was punctured by Justice Holmes' dissent:

> The Thirteenth Amendment does not outlaw contracts for labor. That would be at least as great a misfortune for the laborer as for the man that employed him. For it cer-tainly would affect the terms of the bargain unfavorably for the laboring man if it were understood that the employer could do nothing in case the laborer saw fit to break his word. But any legal liability for breach of a contract is a disagreeable consequence which tends to make the contractor do as he said he would. Liability to an action for damages has that tendency as well as a fine. If the mere imposition of such con-sequences as tend to make a man keep to his promise is the creation of peonage when the contract happens to be for labor, I do not see why the allowance of a civil action is not, as well as an indictment ending in a fine. Peonage is service to a private master at which a man is kept by bodily compulsion against his will. But the creation of the ordinary legal motives for right conduct does not produce it. Breach of a legal contract without excuse is wrong conduct, even if the contract is for labor, and if a State adds to civil liability a criminal liability to fine, it simply intensifies the legal motive for doing right, it does not make the laborer a slave.[16]

Any remedy for breach of a labour contract, says Holmes, provides an incentive not to breach which runs counter to the desires of the party wishing to breach; how much of an incentive is desirable is merely a policy question. One implica-tion of this analysis is that the issue of remedies for breach of contract is best left

---

12 *Ibid.*, at 234.
13 *Ibid.*, at 241.
14 *Ibid.*, at 242.
15 *Ibid.*
16 *Ibid.*, at 246.

to the legislative judgement, and part of Holmes' motives for making this argument was surely his desire to allow state legislatures freedom in adjusting the law of employment to twentieth-century industrial conditions; as such it belongs alongside his famous dissent in the *Lochner* case.[17] But taken on its own terms—as a construction of the anti-slavery norm—the argument clearly presents a serious (and one might add very modern-sounding) challenge to the majority's assertions.

Holmes' argument rests on making all remedies for breach of contract merely points on a continuum; they are all the same, just a bit more or less. What on his view, then, does constitute slavery or involuntary servitude? The drift of his argument seems to be that contractual labour becomes "involuntary servitude" only if the contract itself is the product of duress. The hallmark of slavery, on this view, is that it is a regime of violence; the anti-slavery norm is applicable to private as well as public law because violence can be private as well as public.

For the doctrine of duress to bear this weight, it would have to be considerably reconceived, but neither the majority nor the dissent does (or seems to want to do) the necessary work. How are we to know whether or not Bailey's contract was entered into under duress? Both the majority and the dissent seem to assume that his contract of labour was entered into voluntarily; accordingly, we can surmise that no facts were introduced at trial indicating specific coercive acts on the part of his employer. But both judgments also explicitly refuse to consider as relevant the fact that Bailey was a black man living in the deep south of the United States at the beginning of the twentieth century.[18] In this, they follow the approach of the common law of contracts in refusing to consider background circumstances as by themselves productive of duress.

Now, it would be possible to reject this common-law approach to duress and in the name of the anti-slavery norm develop a different conception of duress applicable to employment contracts. But at least if we are developing doctrine for judges (rather than legislatures) to use, there is much to be said for avoiding answering in an ordinary piece of litigation the very large question whether societies as a whole, or market circumstances as a whole, are duressful for some (or all) of the contracting parties.

However, if we stick with the ordinary conception of duress, and make it the operative test for application of the anti-slavery norm, then we are in effect giving no force to the norm at all in private law situations. If servitude is involuntary only if entered into under duress, and duress is determined as the common law of contracts determines it, then the prohibition on involuntary servitude simply makes unenforceable a set of contracts that are already unenforceable.

---

[17] *Lochner* v. *New York* 198 US 45 (1905).

[18] I put to one side the possibility that the majority was in fact making a judgment as to the inherent coerciveness to a black labourer of conditions in Alabama in 1907; even if this were true as a matter of the motive for the judgement (on the theory that the more the Justices protested it was not true, the more they revealed their true psyches), the Court clearly proposed to enunciate a different sort of doctrine.

Given that the use of the phrase "slavery or involuntary servitude" was meant to go beyond property-based conceptions of the evil and to reach more broadly into the very possibility of (and historical reality of) servitude by contract, this approach seems to substantially underread the reach of the Amendment.

A way to elide this problem is to take the "involuntary" of "involuntary servitude" to refer, not to the time of making the contract, but rather to the time of its performance. Indeed, case law prior to passage of the Amendment had so construed the very phrase as it appeared in state constitutions,[19] and prior Supreme Court precedent had so treated the phrase, too.[20] But if this is the majority's implicit response to Holmes, it, too, faces difficulties. For if the involuntariness lies in the having to do even what one has agreed to do, then how can the majority so blithely accept the existence of a damages remedy for breach of an employment contract even as it outlaws the use of criminal sanctions?

Perhaps the majority assumed that there was an inherent difference between "criminal sanctions" and "contractual remedies" such that Alabama had made, in effect, a categorical mistake. Although one who understands the traditions of the law can understand judges taking this attitude, on analysis an assertion of a hard-and-fast distinction will not hold up. For one thing, there have long been intermediate or mixed cases, one of which, debtors' prison, was rather close to Bailey's own situation. (Historically, sending people to prison for failing to pay a debt was partly a civil matter—there was no fixed term of incarceration and a debtor could get out by paying, or having his friends pay, what was due—but it was also penal in the straightforward sense that the debtor was incarcerated). More importantly, Holmes is surely right that the award of damages, just like the levying of a criminal fine or incarceration, depends on the judgment of the legal system backed up by the force of the state. However cumbersome the actual process of enforcing it might be, a damages remedy is coercive and meant to be so.

In short, our problem comes to this. We want to know how to apply the prohibition on "slavery or involuntary servitude" to individual lawsuits rather than overall states of society. One possibility would be to use a public law, society-wide vision of duress to test the private transaction, but for reasons of judicial competency and legitimacy we do not do so. Another possibility is to use a private law vision of duress, but then we find the anti-slavery norm to be nugatory as applied to private transactions. The law in fact seems to differentiate the cases according to the remedy used, but at least in the most famous Supreme Court case applying the Thirteenth Amendment to the matter, we find no satisfactory reason for doing so.

---

[19] *The Case of Mary Clark*, 1 Blackf. 122 (Ind, 1821) (construing the Constitution of Indiana, a successor state in the Northwest Territory).

[20] *Clyatt* v. *United States* 197 US 207 (1905).

V. THE SECOND DOCTRINAL POSSIBILITY: COERCED PERFORMANCE

Essentially the same structural problem arises in another, rather more plentiful, line of cases. The issue of *Bailey*[21] is continuous with, if more extreme than, the issue of how far the equity powers of courts will be used to enforce, by an order of specific performance or by an injunction, contracts of employment. While these cases are often discussed without reference to the anti-slavery norm, perhaps it is by looking at them that we will find the rationale that has so far eluded us.

Will courts order the specific performance of contracts of employment? The answer, for jurisdictions within the United States at least, is that they will not.[22] This refusal is most commonly rationalised, especially in the secondary literature, in terms of two ordinary policies of the law that do not rely on the presence of the human right encapsulated in the anti-slavery norm. On analysis, however, neither of the proffered rationales seems adequate to the task.[23]

First, it has traditionally been said that the proper performance of service contracts is too hard for courts to superintend: how can the courts know whether the ball player and the opera singer they have ordered to perform are living up to their obligations or instead, even if physically present, are just malingering? But today, when courts in appropriate cases superintend the construction of buildings and the reconstruction of a broad range of complex institutions, this argument falls a bit short. It seems that rather than having a flat rule in labour cases, the courts ought to balance the difficulty of enforcement with the need for relief, just as they do in these other complicated, continuous performance situations. And in any event the courts could always throw the risk of bad performance on the party seeking relief, and issue a decree limited to what could be easily overseen, such as physically turning up for the job.

Alternatively, the rule against specific performance has been justified as an extension of a general policy against coercing personal relationships, rationalised on the basis that the very fact of coercion will undermine the relationship sought to be bolstered. But as regards the ordinary employment case, this notion has been undermined by the quite common use of the remedy of reinstatement to rectify violations of labour or anti-discrimination statutes on the part of employers. If the relationship can be coerced on one side—if the employer can be forced to take the employee back—then the fact that it cannot be coerced

---

[21] *Supra* n.11.

[22] Restatement of Contracts 2d, § 367 (1)(1979); E.A. Farnsworth, *Contracts* (3rd edn., Boston, Mass., Little Brown, 1999), § 12.7.

[23] This point is carefully developed in R.S. Stevens, "Involuntary Servitude by Injunction" (1921) 6 *Cornell L Q* 235.

on the other side cannot be justified in terms of not wanting to force relationships by judicial decree.[24]

Especially in light of modern developments which have generally liberalised the scope of equitable relief, the continuing strength of the rule against specifically enforcing an employee's promise to work bears witness to the presence of another policy targeted directly at this type of case; bears witness, that is, to the presence of the anti-slavery norm. Some cases flatly so state. "An unwilling employee cannot be compelled to continue to provide services to his employer either by ordering specific performance of his contract, or by injunction. To do so runs afoul of the Thirteenth Amendment's prohibition against involuntary servitude".[25] But there is little in the case law that works out how the connection is to be made.

We can try to get a purchase on this problem by looking at the doctrinal pattern in a bit more detail. As already said, courts will not order employees, even if they have agreed to work for a definite length of time, specifically to perform their promises to work. But a damages remedy can be recovered if damage can be shown. In addition, equitable relief will sometimes issue to prevent the breaching employee from working for someone else. (This rule is probably best known in Anglo-American jurisprudence as "the doctrine of *Lumley* v. *Wagner*".[26]) Putting to one side various technical questions—such as whether the promise not to work for another must be explicit, or can be implied; or how "unique" the employee must be to warrant saying that a damage remedy is inadequate—the broad point is that such relief will be granted in the USA, if at all, only to prevent the employee from working for a competitor of the employer.[27] An injunction against an employee's working for any and all other employers, including those not in competition with the employer who has been left, will not be issued. Even if the employee has specifically covenanted not to work for others, the covenant will be enforced only in so far as it is shown to be "reasonable", and reasonableness must be established by the need to protect the employer from some injury beyond the mere loss of the employee.[28]

---

[24] For discussion of the point see *Hopkins* v. *Price Waterhouse* (1990) 920 F 2d 967, 980 and note 12 (DC Cir.) (ordering the defendant to accept the plaintiff into partnership by force of an anti-discrimination statute).

As I understand the English authorities, the refusal to order employment there still runs in both directions; accordingly, the "no forced relationship" rule perhaps does more work in English law, and the "no slavery" rule less work, than in the United States. See *Chitty on Contracts* (28th edn., London, Sweet & Maxwell, 1999) section 28–018. This does not mean that the anti-slavery norm has no impact on English employment law: see J. Beatson, *Anson's Law of Contract* (27th edn., Oxford, Oxford University Press, 1998) at 598–9. But perhaps, lacking constitutional dimension, it has less. The fact that such a norm may be directly imbedded in the common law rather than in a written constitution does not, in my view, change the intellectual terrain very much, so long as the norm is understood to refer, in the first instance, to a prohibited general state of society.

[25] *Beverly Glen Music, Inc.* v. *Warner Communications, Inc.* (1986) 178 Cal. App. 3d 1142, 1144, 224 Cal. Rptr. 260, 261.

[26] (1852) 1 De G M & G 604, 42 ER 687.

[27] See Restatement of Contracts 2d, § 367, Illustration 4 (1979); Farnsworth, *supra* n.22.

[28] I.K.H. Decker, *Covenants Not to Compete* (2nd edn., New York, J. Wiley, 1993) section 3.1; D.J. Aspelund and C.S. Baker, *Employee Noncompetition Law* (New York, C. Boardman Co., 1999) section 1.01.

Yet this pattern is not easily explained. Especially instructive is the inability of the employer to obtain an injunction prohibiting the defaulting employee from working for all other employers during the remainder of the promised period of employment. Certainly this is not because such a decree would command the maintenance of a personal relationship; that is exactly what it would not do. Nor, since it is so flatly negative, would it be hard to superintend. But it is not so easy to see how this rule rests on the anti-slavery norm, either. Surely the outlawed institutions of slavery or involuntary servitude did not consist of people being ordered to sit at home in idleness.

VI. CONSTRUCTING THE BROADER NARRATIVES

We may construct the requisite connection between the anti-slavery norm and the pattern of the law in these private disputes in either of two ways.

The first approach views the essence of the anti-slavery norm as embodying a freedom against one very important kind of human domination: as embodying the right of one human being not to have his labour controlled by another. But in the ordinary case of employment we are not talking about directly abusive control such as existed between an overseer and a slave; or at least the doctrines we are discussing are not limited to such abrasive situations. We must, then, imagine control taking place more as a matter of institutional organisation than personal domination; and if we imagine that, it is the daily experience of almost all workers in the modern, organised workplace that in fact their labour is controlled in large part by others. Indeed, since the question of remedy arises only if we suppose an employee whose leaving constitutes a breach, we must also suppose that these ordinary methods of control have not been abused, for then they may well amount to a constructive discharge by the employer. We are, in short, a good way along the road to embracing the position that in a market society the usual conditions of work, at least for the ordinary worker, do not represent freedom; or, to put the matter more in terms of the actual doctrinal pattern, these conditions do represent freedom only if the employee is always able to refuse an order and leave. In short, work ceases to be "involuntary servitude" only if the employee can always quit.

Of course, a worker's ability to quit has both juridical and social aspects. The possibility of an employer securing an injunction against the employee's working for other employers would not, juridically speaking, prevent an employee from quitting. But presumably in such a case the employee would not be paid for not working, since the employer would receive no tangible benefit; and few workers can afford to live without a paycheck. As a practical matter, then, the routine availability of such an injunction would make it impossible to exercise the underlying right.[29] Or at least this is sufficiently often true that it is not worth the effort to separate out those cases in which the employee could afford to sit idle.

[29] See, for example, Restatement of Contracts 2d, § 367, Comment c (1979).

On this view, the connection between the right to quit and the rule of not being enjoined from working for others is only contingent; the negative injunction does not *per se* represent involuntary servitude in the same way that a positive order of specific performance would. Hence, when the balance of injury shifts—when the employer can show additional injury arising from the employee's going beyond just quitting to also working for a competitor—an injunction can properly issue. As to the availability of the damage remedy, it is not very restrictive. In the ordinary case, as the law measures damages they will come to very little; ordinarily a substitute worker can be found in the market at much the same rate of pay. When, for unusual reasons, the damages measure would be great, that is simply another example of a case in which the law, by awarding a large sum, appropriately recognises that the balance of injury between employer and employee has changed.

An alternative account can be built starting with a view of the anti-slavery norm as embodying a more positive freedom, as encapsulating a human power to start life afresh. What is essentially wrong with slavery, on this view, is its immutable categorisation of people and its concomitant denial of opportunity. Or, to bring the matter closer to the modern workplace, on this view the point of quitting is not just to get out from under bad circumstances. The point is to begin something new, to make something more of oneself. Quitting one's job, rightly seen, is not a negative act; it is the first step in pursuing an affirmative and culturally valued course of conduct.

On this view, the rationalisation of the no-general-injunction rule would be just as direct as that of the no-specific-enforcement rule. The reason courts will not issue an order which would allow an employee to quit but not to work for anyone else is quite simply that such an order does not allow for the idea that quitting is a positive act, that the very best reason to quit is precisely to go to work in a different situation. The allowance of a damage remedy can also be accounted for. While it—if it amounts to anything—does inhibit quitting, it does so only to the extent of the costs to the employer; by making the employee bear those costs, we increase the probable social rationality of the employee's decision to do something new. What is harder to rationalise, on this view, is the willingness to issue an injunction against the employee's going to work for the employer's competitor; that willingness appears to constitute a direct denial of the worker's right. Perhaps that is so; in at least one American jurisdiction even an explicit covenant against working for a competitor cannot, generally speaking, be enforced.[30] More broadly, even where such a covenant can be enforced, the courts limit enforcement not only by looking at the scope of the potential injury but also at the employee's potential prospects. For instance, they generally want to be satisfied that the geographical scope of the proposed injunction is limited—an almost tangible recognition, in a mobile society, of the notion that when one leaves a job, it is for the purpose of moving on and starting over.

[30] See Ann. Cal. Bus. and Prof. Code § 16600 and annotations thereto.

Which of these analyses is better is a debatable point. One can imagine human situations in which the ability just to get out from an oppressive working situation is the essence of the matter, and others in which the ability to start afresh is the main thing. As a matter of social imagery, the first approach, with its emphasis on the potential oppressiveness of workplaces even in a regime of formally free labour, fits rather easily with the European tradition of social thought and its emphasis on class conflict. It may be that the second line of reasoning should have greater appeal in the United States, where class-conflict has been downplayed, but leaving one's situation in order to get a better deal is part of the folklore of a nation of immigrants. Jurisprudentially, both analyses explain some of the actually enforced rules very easily, while the explanations for other rules come out rather creakily. Under the first approach, the rule that employees will not ordinarily be enjoined from working for others, even though such work is in breach of their contracts, rests on an over-generalisation or formalisation of the underlying purpose of making the ability to quit a realistic possibility; the real life possibilities of the defendants are not inquired into. Under the second approach, the willingness to issue such an injunction even in a case of harmful competition represents a crude compromise of rights with harms. As to answering Holmes' critique, perhaps the second explanation has a bit of an edge; at least the first one, with its emphasis on the practical incentives set up by different remedies, seems more open to his complaint that it is all a sliding scale, and therefore not susceptible to drawing a clear dividing line between involuntary servitude and free labour. By contrast, if we have in mind not simply quitting, but quitting to move on and start something new, the possible remedies are indeed different in kind: the injunction (or, on the actual facts of *Bailey*,[31] making a crime of the breach) flatly prohibits the new venture, while assessing damages simply puts a price on it.

If we now turn our attention from rationalisations to outcomes, we see that in a great many cases the two approaches will yield similar results. Both, for example, seem to be opposed to permitting punitive damages to be awarded even for an intentional breach of an employment contract. On the first analysis, such a remedy would make the pressure not to quit too great; on the second, such a remedy would exceed the only permissible purpose for damages, to make the defaulter take into account the social costs of starting anew. In the American legal system, this rule might even be said (as a proper extension of *Bailey*) to have constitutional status. But we can also imagine cases in which the approaches would not specify congruent results. For example, especially in the "new economy" in which commerce is less and less tied to a locale, there may be a case in which all of an employee's possible future employers are direct competitors with his present one, to whom he has committed himself for a period of years. It seems that a judge following the second approach would be less likely to enforce the covenant to the full extent of the employer's harm than one following the first approach would be.

[31] *Supra* n.11.

For present purposes we need not decide which approach is preferable. As stated at the start, the purpose of this chapter (and of the symposium of which it is part) is to exhibit and discuss problems of method. From this more abstract point of view, the two apparently divergent accounts in fact share a great many features. Each requires some understanding of the purposes and structures of the legal institution of contract. Each requires some view of the role of labour in a market economy. Most importantly for present purposes, each requires some theory of what there is, in the ordinary employment relationship, that threatens to replicate a central feature of the social institution of slavery or servitude. Or, if it is too grand to say that these asserted resemblances amount to a theory, let us say there needs to be some account of what constitutes a reasonable analogy.

VII. CONCLUSION

For some people the work I have just described will be considered "private law" work, and for some people it will not. Whatever the label, any application of the anti-slavery norm to the contracts that individual workers make will require a repositioning of that norm from its ordinary starting point. Policies and images surrounding the norm as applied to states and conditions of society have to be translated into policies and images applicable to individual interactions in an otherwise accepted social order. As can be seen from our exploration of two rival accounts of the application of this particular human rights norm to a particular class of private law matters, the needed work is not merely technical and free from doubt. It is debatable and a matter of social vision as much as of technique.

All this work has to be done even though these competing analyses concern a norm whose application to private transactions is as certain as anything in a legal system—at least in the legal system of the United States—can be. If this example is at all representative, it seems that deciding that a human rights norm is directly applicable to the regime of private law is only the beginning of the matter.

13

Human Rights and the Employment Relationship: A Look Through the Prism of Juridification

GUY MUNDLAK

I. HUMAN RIGHTS AND THE EMPLOYMENT RELATIONSHIP— DEFINING THE PROBLEM

THE EMPLOYMENT RELATIONSHIP is intractably linked to human rights issues. To ask today whether human rights apply to the employment relationship may seem a huge step backwards in time.[1] After years of legislation and court rulings on the right of workers to associate in trade unions and on equality in the workplace, the road has been cleared for more innovative explorations on the intersection of human rights and employment. Today, the relationship between the contractual (private) nature of employment and the human rights (public) dimension extends numerous intellectual and policy frontiers. Freedom of association in trade unions is acknowledged as a human right, recognised by both the International Covenant on Civil and Political Rights and the Covenant on International Economic, Social and Cultural Rights.[2] The right to work, which is institutionalised and formalised in the employment contract, is itself a human right, together with the associated rights that deal with working conditions and the principle of anti-discrimination in employment.[3] Similarly, there is growing recognition, somewhat paradoxically in tandem with the forces of globalisation, that some work-related rights represent not only fair labour

---

[1] This is not to say that there are no voices calling for reversing what they view as an unfortunate trend. The most lucid argument in this respect is made by Richard Epstein. See, for example, R.A. Epstein, "In Defense of the Contract at Will" (1984) 51 *U Chi. L Rev*. 947; R.A. Epstein, *Forbidden Grounds* (Cambridge, Mass., Harvard University Press, 1992).

[2] International Covenant on Social, Economic and Cultural Rights (ICESCR) (1966); International Covenant on Political and Civil Rights (ICCPR) (1966); Also see International Labour Organisation, Convention No 87 on the Freedom of Association and Protection of the Right to Organise (1948), and Convention No 98 on the Right to Organise and Collective Bargaining (1949); ILO Declaration on Fundamental Principles and Rights at Work (1998); See generally, S. Leader, *Freedom of Association* (New Haven, Conn., Yale University Press, 1992).

[3] Arts. 6–8 of the ICESCR. A. Sen, "Work and Rights" (2000) 139(2) *Intl. Lab. Rev*. 119–28.

standards, but also fundamental human rights in themselves.[4] Finally, there is an acceptance, although uneven and still controversial, that civil rights also apply to the contractual sphere, and place obligations on the contracting parties.[5] In this chapter I would like to focus for the most part on this last issue.

Traditionally human rights were considered to govern only the relationship between individuals and the State, and their objective was to constrain the power-hungry nation state.[6] More recently legislatures and courts have started to consider the application of human rights to the private sphere as well. When questioning the desirability of this development in the context of the employment relationship there are two different avenues of inquiry that can be pursued. The first seeks to demonstrate the justification for the diffusion of human rights from the public to the private sphere. Drawing on analytical jurisprudence and political theory, the debate draws on the differences between the two spheres, and on the nature of human rights.[7] On this path of inquiry, no particular reason exists to focus on employment contracts. The nature of inquiry is not based on issues of power relations, or on any other special attribute usually singled out to exemplify the employment relationship.[8] I will bracket this debate which takes up the larger share of this volume, and assume that human rights can be applied to the private sphere and hence can surely be applied to the employment relationship.

A second path of inquiry observes the diffusion of human rights into the employment relationship as part of a broader trend of intense juridification of the employment sphere. In this process, the legislature and the courts develop public limitations on the private sphere arrangement. As will be demonstrated, juridification of the employment sphere should not be regarded as a monolithic phenomenon. It is a result of multiple objectives and its strategy resorts to public limitations of various kinds. The study of juridification is more sociological in nature than the analytical methodology described earlier. It seeks to explore the effects of legal intervention on social interactions. Along this avenue, the inquiry addresses the difference between public limitations that are based on human rights and other forms of public limitations imposed on the employment relationship.

    [4] B.A. Langille, "The ILO and the New Economy: Recent Developments" (1999) 15(3) *Intl. J Comp. Lab. Law & Indus. Relations* 229–58; G. Kelly, "Employment and Concepts of Work in the New Global Economy" (2000) 139(1) *Intl. Lab. Rev.* 1–28; L. Compa and S. Diamond (eds.), *Human Rights, Labor Rights and International Trade* (Philadelphia, Penn., University of Pennsylvania Press, 1996).

    [5] Cf C. Summers, "The Privatization of Personal Freedoms and Enrichment of Democracy: Some Lessons from Labour Law" [1986] *U Ill. L Rev.* 689; P. Weiler, "The Charter at Work: Reflections on the Constitutionalizing of Labour and Employment Law" (1990) 40 *U Toronto L J* 117; F. Raday, "The Constitutionalization of Labour Law" in R. Blanpain and M. Weiss (eds.), *The Changing Face of Labour Law and Industrial Relations, Liber Amicorum for Clyde W. Summers* (Baden Baden, Nomos 1993), 83; D. Oliver, *Common Values and the Public-Private Divide* (London, Butterworths, 1999) 123–46; F. Raday, "Privatizing Human Rights and the Abuse of Power" (2000) 13(1) *Can. J of Law & Juris.* 103 (hereinafter Raday, "Privatizing Human Rights").

    [6] L. Henkin, *The Rights of Man Today* (London, Steven and Sons, 1979), 2.

    [7] See, for example, P. Benson, chap. 10 this vol; A. Fagan, chap. 4 this vol.

    [8] For a thorough exploration and critique of the absence of power relations from the analysis of the "Privatization of Human Rights", see Raday, "Privatizing Human Rights", *supra* n.5.

I argue that the process of juridification of the employment relationship holds a dialectic quality and therefore should be observed critically. It is rooted in social and economic failures to achieve satisfactory solutions to problems that characterise the employment relationship. This failure leads to the development of legal constraints, public in nature, on the private contractual arrangement. Observing the objectives of imposing these legal constraints, it appears that public limitations also carry a negative effect on the employment relationship. However, I will argue that public limitations seeking to protect human rights in the context of the employment relationship fare relatively well in the overall balance and are therefore, generally, justified. They correct market imperfections and can therefore lead to more efficient outcomes. They have a positive distributive effect. They introduce values that are otherwise marginalised in the private sphere and that are difficult to incorporate into the parties' contract by other means. This does not imply that the mere recognition of human rights in the employment context is always effective. Yet, as I will argue, the advantages outweigh the disadvantages, and in the absence of other social and economic institutions that can promote the protection of human rights for individuals *qua* workers, this form of juridification is justified.

In the following (second) section I elaborate on the meaning of juridification and demonstrate its development. Given the sociological nature of the discussion, it is difficult to account for it in the abstract, so in the third section I introduce its nuts and bolts in Israel. I will however provide indications that the social processes underlying juridification in Israel are common to most developed countries. In the fourth section of this chapter I discuss various justifications for the process of juridification and demonstrate the potential mismatch between the objectives and the outcomes. In the final section I demonstrate the dialectic nature of juridification, and highlight the reason why the component of juridification that deals with the core of human rights protection is nevertheless of particular strength.

II. JURIDIFICATION: CAUSES AND CHARACTERISTICS

1. The three phases of juridification

Juridification is the process of establishing mandatory legal norms that replace extra-legal regulation of social or economic relationships. In this process, legal norms replace extra-legal norms and legal sanctions replace social or economic sanctions, such as shame, loss of authority, decline in stock value and diminishing reputation.[9]

---

[9] There is no clear consensus regarding the definition of juridification, and what distinguishes it merely from more general terms such as "regulation". Cf A. Gladstone, Rapporteur's Report, in *Legal Perspectives—The Juridification of the Employment Relationship* (Proceedings of the Vth International Industrial Relations Association (IIRA), European Regional Industrial Relations Congress, 1997); J. Clarke, "The Juridification of Industrial Relations" (1985) 14 *Indus. Relations J* 69 (juridification is the process in which the State steers social and economic life); Spiros Simitis

Three stages of juridification may be distinguished. The first is of lesser importance in the present context: it relates to the question whether a social relationship or a given interaction is justiciable. The answer is generally affirmative with regard to many realms of life. This is certainly true with regard to the employment relationship. However, justiciability merely indicates that a particular issue *can* be addressed by legal principles. It does not necessarily suggest that legal principles are *in fact* being applied, or that they provide the *most appropriate* response.

The second stage of juridification deals with individuals' decisions to lobby the legislature or file a petition in court, asking for a legal remedy in situations where legal intervention was uncommon in the past. This stage stems from individual and group efforts of turning a justiciable issue into a *de facto* legal question. Why some issues are advanced by legislation, others by litigation, and others remain outside the legal discourse despite their justiciability is part of the juridification puzzle. The answers to these questions are sociological rather than jurisprudential. They require a grasp of how law is used strategically in social reform processes.

The third stage of juridification deals with the legal norm that is enacted by the legislature or decided by the court, once the issue has been brought to their attention. While from an analytical perspective there is considerable difference between incremental judicial incorporation of human rights into the contractual sphere and statutory intervention,[10] the study of juridification can view them as two components of the same social process. Legislatures impose limitations on the employment relationship by means of statutory provisions that override contractual agreements. Similarly, when a claim related to the contractual sphere is brought to court, the court can decide that the solution lies in the parties' mutual intent as established in the contract, but it can also decide, for various reasons, to adopt a regulatory solution which is anti-contractarian in nature. Whether in statute or in case law, these are the public limitations on the contractual sphere.

A complete process of juridification in the contractual sphere therefore consists of three elements: justiciability, the framing of a legal claim, and the formation of a norm which rests on public values that constrain the freedom of contract. My main interest in this chapter is to assess the third and final stage of juridification, namely the legal norm that is being developed in the new juridification of the employment relationship. This will be done in greater detail in the following sections. But to understand the objectives of

emphasises that juridification is a by-product of industrialisation whereby there is a gradual replacement of a society based on contractual agreements by regulatory law. See S. Simitis, "Juridification of Labor Relations" in G. Teubner (ed.), *Juridification of Social Spheres* (Berlin, Walter de Gruyter & Co, 1987) 62–113. Following Simitis and Teubner, Mitchell emphasises that the term juridification connotes more than the proliferation of legal norms, but also dysfunctional problems associated with it. See R. Mitchell, "Juridification and Labour Law: A Legal Response to the Flexibility Debate in Australia" (1998) 14 *Intl. J Comp.Lab. Law & Indus. Relations* 113.

[10]   This point is made by Raday, "Privatising Human Rights", *supra* n.5.

juridification, we must resort to the second phase as well, and understand the reasons for the rapid juridification of the employment relationship that has taken place during recent decades. The second stage takes place when individuals or groups begin to approach the court or the legislature and make a legal claim.

2. Juridification and the breakdown of the post-Second World War paradigm of labour law

The labour market, and hence the employment relationship, is governed predominantly by three competing bodies of law.[11] At the basis of the employment relationship is the employment contract. Like other contracts it is governed by the fundamental rules of contract law and the freedom of contract. However, no other archetype of contracts is as heavily regulated as employment contracts.[12] One source of limitations is to be found in statutory labour standards. Typically these deal *inter alia* with issues such as minimum labour standards (for example, minimum wage and working hours), health and safety regulation, and anti-discrimination law. These provisions can be classified together with regulatory measures used in other contractual areas such as consumer contracts, insurance and agency law. A second source of constraints on the contractual sphere is unique to the labour context and is often designated as autonomous labour law. These are the norms rooted in collective bargaining. Although the norms negotiated in collective bargaining constrain the individual contracting parties' sphere of bargaining in the same manner as the statutory provisions, they are strikingly different in both content and scope, in that they are a result of detailed bargaining between the organised groups.

The three forms of labour market regulation exist in all developed countries, and almost generally worldwide. But they are configured differently depending on the legal and social culture of each country. For example, France is known for its strong inclination towards statutory regulation, while the Nordic countries often opt for negotiated collective regulation. By comparison, in the United States the unconstrained contractual sphere is relatively broader than in the European countries. These admittedly very crude examples are presented only to demonstrate that the depth and scope of public limitations on the employment contract are not a result of purely analytical structures, but must be understood as reflections of societal values and institutions.

---

[11] See generally P. Weiler, *Governing the Workplace* (Cambridge, Mass., Harvard University Press, 1990).

[12] C. Summers, "Similarities and Differences Between Labour Contracts and Civil and Commercial Contracts" in *General Reports of the XVI World Congress of Labour Law and Social Security* (2000), 47.

The post-Second World War paradigm of employment contracts in developed countries was based on a strong preference for collective bargaining.[13] The extent and nature of autonomous regulation differed considerably from one country to another. Some European countries, such as Sweden, Belgium and Israel, developed legal and social structures that ensured extensive coverage of collective agreements over the labour market. In others, such as the North American countries, coverage was less comprehensive, although still significant. Given the competing nature of the regulatory options described earlier, the preference for collective bargaining reduced the need for explicit restrictions on the parties' freedom of contract by means of statutory legal norms. The role of law was confined to the maintenance of the institutional infrastructure that was needed to support autonomous collective bargaining. This paradigm of employment contract was based on a number of premises: the importance of national economies that make extensive use of Keynesian measures; an industrial stronghold, based on strong internal labour markets and an expansive public sector, which are more accommodating to traditional forms of collective bargaining; a homogeneous workforce (predominantly male workers who worked full-time for an indefinite period); and a strong sense of class identity.

The post-Second World War paradigm gradually eroded as each of these underlying premises was transformed. Globalisation processes have made national-based organisation of labour more difficult, while at the same time the mobility of capital has reduced employers' willingness to negotiate with unions. A shift from traditional industries, coupled with increasing processes of privatisation and the growth of the service sector, have also made the organisation of workers more difficult. As a result there is a growing disparity in the working conditions of workers in the various sectors. The entry of women into the labour force has effectively demonstrated the male bias that prevailed in collective bargaining, and introduced new interests of workers who must juggle work and family commitments, combat prevailing discriminatory attitudes, and cope with a market modelled on the interests of the sole-breadwinner (male) worker. These changes have all contributed to the gradual decline in class politics and class identity. Following the civil rights movements of the 1960s, class identity was gradually replaced by multicultural framing of individual identities and social interaction. The militant male blue-collar (and workers in the public sector) class ceased to exist as such, and workers ceased to identify themselves first and foremost as members of a class. They were now working men and women in an ever more fragmented society, giving voice to their complex interests that were legitimated by the civil rights movement. They were organised along lines of occupation, gender, race, sexual orientation, age and religion. They had to

---

[13] See generally S. Deakin, "Legal Origins of Wage Labour: The Evolution of the Contract of Employment From Industrialization to the Welfare State" in L. Clarke, P. de Gujsel and J. Jansenn (eds.), *The Dynamics of Wage Relations in the New Europe* (Dordrecht, Kluwer, 2000) 32–44; K. Van Wezel Stone, "The Postwar Paradigm in American Labour Law" (1981) 90 *Yale L J* 1509, 1524–5.

cope with a constantly changing labour market that shifted from rewards on the basis of tenure and job classification to rewards for merit and mobility, and the ongoing accumulation of human capital. Class politics gave way to market competition.

The process of juridification stems from the post-Second World War paradigm's fragility. Two complementary, yet distinct, forces exacerbated this process: the decline of the autonomous collective bargaining regime and the rise of the individual-rights regime. Collective (autonomous) regulation of the labour market is characterised by the combination of the dense web of mandatory standards it provides and a dispute resolution arrangement that does not rely on adjudication (for example, arbitration, bipartite and tripartite committees, and labour-management consultation). Consequently, the decline of the collective bargaining regime has brought about two gaps in the social organisation of work. The weakening power and reduced coverage of collective agreements have resulted in many workers having no social and economic protection in the labour market, aside from the public limitations in statutory law, the scope of which is limited. Workers who no longer enjoy the protection of collective agreements include those who have moved to lucrative positions in well-paying industries (for example, high-tech engineers and symbolic analysts), but for the most part it consists of the low waged workers, peripheral workers employed on the basis of atypical employment contracts (also referred to as contingent or precarious work arrangements), workers in the growing services sector and the like. These workers have only their slim market power, which is effected by their low levels of skill, a mismatch between available skills and employers' demands, a growing structural unemployment, or segregated labour markets based on low wages and atypical employment contracts. Moreover, some issues that were negotiated in detail in collective agreements are rare, or non-existent, in individual contracts. For example, occupational jurisdictions, promotions, and shopfloor grievance procedures are no longer negotiated because workplaces have changed their organisational structures, and no longer rely on a strong and stable internal labour market. Yet other issues do not surface at the individual bargaining table because some aspects of the employment contract, especially the non-monetary ones (i.e., those that are not reflected in the wage, such as protection against dismissals, employees' privacy, organisational culture and the like), are particularly difficult to negotiate and the contractual outcomes are potentially ridden with market failures.

In the absence of collective backing, employees turn to courts, seeking public assistance to compensate for their alleged weakness in individual bargaining. The growing demand for judicial protection reflects the employees' sense that they are being treated unfairly.[14] The juridification of contractual relations also seeks to redress the discrepancy between employees' perception of the rights

---

[14] On the importance of fairness in the present context see R. Solow, *The Labor Market as a Social Institution* (Cambridge, Mass., Blackwell, 1990).

they have and those that they have in fact.[15] In addition, the decline of the collective paradigm has led to the weakening of alternative dispute resolution systems that were rooted in collective agreements. Consequently, even workers who have individually negotiated rights must resort to fully-fledged adjudication to claim their right. The decline of collective negotiations has therefore resulted in increased reliance on adjudication, which became the dominant method for both rights-making and rights-claiming.

In addition to the gap that was opened by the erosion of the collective bargaining regime, the process of juridification can also be explained as an outcome of a growing rights discourse that started with the civil rights movement in the 1960s in many developed countries. Drawing on a constitutional rights-based litigation, individuals and groups began to advance legal claims that promoted interests related to group recognition and individual identity. These claims were different from those negotiated in the past by trade unions, and at times highlighted the tension between class-based claims and polycentric recognition claims. The evolving rights discourse affected the juridification process in a number of interrelated ways. It provided legitimacy for adjudication of rights, it increased the importance of the equality principle in both the public and the private spheres, and it significantly weakened the priority of class over other individual and group attributes. The intensified rights-discourse also increased the legalisation of economic organisations, which responded by rationalising organisational structures as a means of defence against litigation.[16] This process has led to an intra-organisational juridification, with the adoption of due-process structures and rhetoric. The assumption underlying these intra-organisational structures was that form (rationalisation) would affect substance (the legal justification of employers' decisions).

In sum, increased juridification has been a result of a hollowing out of the post-Second World War paradigm, with its emphasis on collective and autonomous making of norms. Although law was strongly present in that paradigm, its role was limited to the institutional infrastructure for negotiations. The law did not determine the substantive norms governing the employment relationship, as these were the "game's outcomes" and the law was concerned mostly with the "rules of the game". Once this model weakened, various objectives appeared: correcting market failures, aiding the weaker segments of the workforce who had lost (or never had) organised power, encouraging a competitive high-trust work environment, rationalising intra-organisational decision-making, and forging a new partnership between labour and capital in a dynamic yet fragmented environment. What cannot be done through markets

---

[15] For an indication of the extent of this discrepancy and its nature see P. Kim, "Bargaining With Imperfect Information: A study of Worker Perception and At-Will World" (1997) 83 *Cornell L Rev.* 105; P. Kim, "Norms, Learning, And Law: Exploring The Influences On Workers' Legal Knowledge" [1999] *U Ill. L Rev.* 447.

[16] Cf L. Edelman, "Legal Environments and Organizational Governance: The Expansion of Due Process in the American Workplace" (1990) 95(6) *Am. J Soc.* 1401–40; J. Sutton, F. Dobbin, K. Meyer and R. Scott, "The Legalization of the Workplace" (1994) 99 *Am. J Soc.* 944–71.

is done through law, hence juridification. More individuals, groups and organisations were bringing claims to court for the purpose of advancing one of these objectives. The judicial and legislative responses to this process have often been by way of advancing new rules that regulate the employment relationship. Ironically, while the 1980s brought about a growing process of privatisation and deregulation of markets to advance a neo-liberal socio-economic agenda, the labour market experienced a boost of new regulations. The myth of individualisation of employment contracts could be justified only as representing a shift from collective (autonomous) ordering of the labour market to a more individual rights-based discourse.[17] However, the individualisation of the labour market should certainly not be translated into a descriptive statement about deregulation and the expansion of the negotiable sphere. If we take a non-union establishment and compare the legal environment it faced 20 years ago with that which it faces today, we will find the current environment more regulated, and public intervention into the contractual sphere greater and more complex.

The account of juridification has thus far been detached from a particular social system. I claim that most of its components are typical of industrialised and developed countries in general. It is however difficult to paint in broad strokes the contours of a phenomenon that is so heavily rooted in micro-societal transformations. Furthermore, the legal means by which juridification takes place differ from one country to another and thus make broad generalisations difficult. I would therefore draw on the Israeli example in order to analyse the third stage of juridification (i.e., the new public limitations that are being imposed on the private contractual relationship).

III. JURIDIFICATION: THE ISRAELI CASE—FORM AND SUBSTANCE, LAW AND SOCIETY

The three phases of juridification are clearly discernible in Israel, and are a product of legal and social transformations. As in the previous section, the first phase of juridification—the holding of justiciability—can be put aside. The current approach in Israeli law holds all realms of life to be justiciable, and the employment relationship does not even touch on the difficult periphery of this ruling.[18] It is therefore the second and third phases of juridification which are of more interest.

The second phase of juridification is reflected in the myriad issues which are currently reaching the courts and the legislature and which have not been a subject to judicial scrutiny in the past. The main reason for the intensive juridification of the employment relationship in Israel (as elsewhere) is attributed to the decline of

---

[17] W. Brown, S. Deakin, M. Hudson, C. Praten and P. Ryan, *The Individualisation of Employment Contracts in Britain* (Cambridge, Centre for Business Research, 1998).

[18] A. Bendor, "Are There Any Limits to Justiciability? The Jurisprudential and Constitutional Controversy in Light of the Israeli and American Experience" (1997) 7 *Ind. Intl. & Comp. L Rev.* 311.

collective bargaining. The collapse of the previous industrial relations system in Israel has been quite dramatic, and processes that have taken decades elsewhere have occurred in Israel within a relatively short period of time.[19] The factors described in the previous chapter account for this transformation, leading to a shift of the Israeli industrial relations system from a corporatist regime to an Anglo-American one. Whereas the whole labour market was previously governed by peak-level bargaining between the social partners, the role of collective bargaining has been narrowed in several respects. First, the major bargaining arena today is no longer national, as was the typical case in the heyday of the corporatist regime. Instead, bargaining has shifted to the branch and enterprise level. Secondly, union membership has dropped from approximately 85 per cent in the 1980s to an estimated 40 per cent today. Coverage of collective agreements has also dropped from almost universal coverage to approximately 60 per cent of the workforce. Moreover, some collective agreements no longer provide the same detailed web of rules and procedures which were considered essential for the bargaining partners in the past. Some agreements do not even provide seniority and tenure arrangements that were considered to be the pillars of organised labour in the past.[20]

The changes in the industrial relations system were complemented by changes in social values. The intense, occasionally suffocating, collective bargaining regime of the past, in which minority groups and weak employees were marginalised in favour of broad class interests, has produced a whiplash effect. Individuals seek to distance themselves from the allegedly common good interest that was established in peak-level bargaining between employers and the Histadrut (The Israeli general federation of trade unions). Moreover, the growing polarisation of Israeli society introduces many workers at the higher echelons of the labour market, who are less concerned about the bread and butter issues, and therefore pursue innovative claims in non-traditional areas, such as privacy and free speech. The evolving high-tech sector has introduced numerous problems at an intensity which was unknown before, such as issues of competition and the transfer of human capital and knowledge across the boundaries of the firm. Finally, an additional reason for the intensive juridification of the employment relationship can be traced to the spillover effect of the juridification trend that prevails in other areas of Israeli society. This is partly a result of a growing number of lawyers seeking to make innovative claims.[21] But it is also a result of the general social

---

[19] On changes in the Israeli industrial relations see G. Harel, S. Tzafrir and P. Bamberger, "Institutional Change and Union Membership: A Longitudinal Analysis of Union Membership Determinants in Israel" (2000) 39 *Indus. Relations* 460. On the implications of these changes on the legal regime in general see G. Mundlak, "The New Labor Law as a Social Text: Reflections on Social Values in Flux" (1998) 3 *Israel Studies* 119–58.

[20] F. Raday, "The Insider-Outsider Politics of Labor-Only Contracting" (1999) 20 *Comp. Lab. Law & Policy J* 413, 436–8.

[21] In 1999 there were approximately 10,000 students studying law, which is approximately 5 times the number of law students a decade ago. The figures are taken from the Israeli Statistical Bureau, *Annual Statistical Abstract of Israel*, 2000, 1990.

environment, characterised by growing scepticism of authority, expertise and national interests, which are no longer deemed to override individual concerns. Thus, when the family, the military rank-and-command hierarchy, and medical treatment are all becoming a subject to claims and litigation for ongoing rights, it would almost seem odd if the employment relationship remained immune.

Although the explanation for the second phase of juridification is for the most part external to the legal rule, it could not have materialised into fully-fledged juridification in the absence of important changes in jurisprudence. Three significant complementary legal processes evolved throughout the last two decades. The first is the blurring of the public and the private, by means of indirect application of public values and human rights to the private contractual relationship.[22] While this was held to be a controversial thesis in the past, the case law has currently settled down, favouring the accommodation of public values within private law. Although this first component of the trio serves as the focus of this volume, it would be wrong to detach it from the other components. Secondly, the courts have turned away from a rule-based approach, and shifted the weight of adjudication towards broad standards, such as "good faith" and "public policy", which appear in the law.[23] There is currently an equilibrium, albeit a controversial one, in which the legislature provides the courts with valves of discretion, intentionally defined in very vague terms, and the court makes use of these instruments, which are highly effective for the piecemeal development of the law. Thirdly, the Supreme Court signalled a change towards "jurisprudence of values", which is result-oriented and seems to define the content of rights according to a view of the desired common good.[24] This anti-liberal paradigm is not fully developed but its implementation has proved especially useful for the diffusion of public values and human rights into the employment relationship.

The three changes in jurisprudence nurture the third phase of juridification, which in turn encourages the increased reliance of individuals and groups on legal strategies to advance their interests. Otherwise phrased, the legal system's high rate of responsiveness to rights claims, and the development of legal infrastructure that accommodates these claims, makes the legal strategy, for better or for worse, the major tool for social transformation in the hands of individuals and groups.

The third phase of juridification is being developed on both the legislative and adjudicative fronts. As for the former, a pivotal shift from autonomous collective

---

[22] See A. Barak, "Constitutional Human Rights and Private Law" (1996) 3 *Rev. Const. Stud.* 218; see also A. Barak, chap. 2 this vol.; CA 294/91, *Jerusalem Community Burial Society GHSE v. Kestenbaum* 46 (2) PD 464 (Hebrew).

[23] M. Mautner, "The Law and Culture in Israel: The 1950s and the 1980s" in P. Lahav, R. Harris, S. Kedar and A. Likhovski (eds.), *The History of Law in a Multi-Cultural Society: Israel, 1917–1967* (Aldershot, Ashgate Publishing, forthcoming 2001).

[24] FH HC 4601/95 *Sarusi v. The National Labour Court* 52(4) PD 817 (Hebrew).

bargaining to State sponsored juridification took place in 1988, when the regulation of the minimum wage was legislated and therefore removed from its traditional venue of corporatist, peak-level, bargaining. However, the generous crop of legislation following it for the most part avoided the regulation of fair wages and benefits, and focused instead on anti-discrimination law. During the last decade the legislature has passed and amended numerous laws that responded to pressures of human rights groups and other interest-groups' lobbying efforts. Although the courts have been favourable to anti-discrimination arguments in the past, even in the absence of explicit statutory provisions, the enactment of the new laws has created a qualitative difference by pushing the limits of an equality-based perception of human rights into the private relationship. These limits have extended beyond the mere prohibition against discrimination, and into the more controversial areas of affirmative action and equal pay for equal *value* of work (comparable worth). The coverage of employment anti-discrimination law is also a reflection of the evolution of organised interest groups in Israel, outside the labour-dominated civil society that prevailed in the past. While the first legislation dealt only with a prohibition on discrimination on the basis of gender, in 1991 the emerging gay and lesbian movement in Israel succeeded in lobbying for a prohibition against discrimination on the basis of sexual preference.[25] A strong human rights lobby compiled a lengthy list of groups in a later 1995 amendment, and an active non-governmental organisation (NGO) representing people with disabilities succeeded in lobbying for the new law on equal opportunities for people with disabilities (1998).[26] To the list of anti-discrimination laws it is possible to add the Law on Prevention of Sexual Harassment at Work enacted in 1998, which was also based on a constitutional discourse of human dignity.

While the legislature was mounting new laws in the law books, based on a discourse of equality and human rights, the courts were not sitting idle. New legal challenges that resulted from the breakdown of the corporatist paradigm of labour law, and of the growing expectation that law should fill the vacuum that was associated with it, generated a new body of law. The courts have relied primarily on two legal instruments for this development. The first is the requirement of good faith in both bargaining and performance of contractual obligations, and the second is the prohibition against contracts that violate public policy. Both principles are found in the Law of Contracts (General Part). They have been interpreted by the Supreme Court, in contexts other than labour, as providing a valve through which public values of a normative calibre are introduced into the contractual relationship, thus constraining, or constructing, the

---

[25] A. Harel, "The Rise and Fall of the Israeli Gay Legal Revolution" (2000) 31 *Colum. Hum. Rts. L Rev.* 443–71; A. Kama, "From Terra Incognita to Terra Firma: The Logbook of the Voyage of Gay Men's Community into the Israeli Public Sphere" (2000) 38 *J Homosexuality* 133.

[26] N. Ziv, "Disability Law in Israel and the United States—A Comparative Perspective" (1999) 28 *Israel Yearbook on Human Rights* 171–202.

parties' freedom of contract.[27] In the employment context, the use of these two valves has been extensive.

On the basis of good faith, the courts have developed traditional good-faith requirements, such as increased levels of disclosure during the bargaining process, and the development of a residual prohibition on the abuse of contractual rights.[28] However, it is particularly in the employment context that the courts have introduced the requirement that management should act rationally. Thus it has been suggested that management must use only tests that have been found reliable and valid.[29] On the basis of the good-faith doctrine the courts have also gradually eroded the principle of "employment-at-will", according to which an employee can be discharged for any reason.[30] Recently, the court started to sum up the incremental change, and noted that the current case law already required that employees could be dismissed only for a just cause.[31] These new limitations on the managerial prerogative, which in the past were a matter for professional, but not legal, concern, may alter the way human resource managers have to design selection, promotion and dismissal decisions. Their need to comply, on the basis of good faith, with due process requirements, transparency, reliability and validity of their testing procedures, and what amounts to a basic sense of fairness, may become a matter for a comprehensive managerial manual.

Complementing the good-faith requirements, on the basis of the public-policy doctrine, the courts introduced civil rights as workers' rights that must be balanced against the employers' property rights. Chronologically, the first balancing act was applied with regard to contractual covenants not to compete. The National Labour Court decided that some contractual limitations on employees after the termination of the employment contract were unreasonable, and therefore void.[32] The court did not strike out these covenants altogether, but substituted for the unreasonable contractual arrangement that which the court deemed reasonable under the circumstances.

---

[27] The difference between "constraining" and "constructing" the parties' freedom of contract is aptly demonstrated by two competing judicial positions. One view holds public limitations as necessary to the creation of a market-place, and therefore compatible with the idea of the freedom of contract. The other poses public limitations as a constraint on the freedom of contract, albeit a necessary one under a theory of balancing competing rights. Although the two views may lead to similar outcomes, they represent a different understanding of markets and the freedom of contract. For a demonstration of the debate, see FH 22/82, *Beit Ules* v. *Raviv*, 43(1) PD 441 (Hebrew).

[28] Cf National Labour Court 97/3–68 *Shaked* v. *The Jewish Agency* (unpublished, 1998) (Hebrew); National Labour Court 97/3–7 *Lavon* v. *MTM Constructions For Industry and Craft Inc.* 32 PDA 584 (Hebrew); National Labour Court 93/3–40 *Easteronix Inc.* v. *Grafunkel* 25 PDA 456 (Hebrew).

[29] National Labour Court 97/4–70 *Tel-Aviv University* v. *The Histadrut* 30 PDA 385.

[30] G. Mundlak, "Information-Forcing and Cooperation-Inducing Rules: Rethinking the Building Blocks of Labour Law" in G. De Geest *et al.* (eds.), *Law and Economics and the Labour Market* (Cheltenham, Elgar, 1999) 55–91.

[31] National Labour Court 375/99 *The Economic Corporation to the Development of Kfar Mandah (1997) Inc.* v. *Muhamad Zaidan* (unpublished, 2000) (Hebrew).

[32] Cf National Labour Court 91/3–148 *Gissler Inc.* v. *Cohen* 23 PDA 115 (Hebrew).

Recently, the court shifted the balance between the various rights involved, and held that where there was no substantiated fear that the employee would transfer the employer's trade secrets, such covenants would be totally void.[33] In a case involving the transfer of ownership of a newspaper, in which the new owner restricted the editor's freedom of expression, the Jerusalem district labour court balanced the editor's freedom of speech with the owner's property right, holding that the limitations imposed on the editor must be voided. On appeal, the National Labour Court acknowledged the propriety of the balancing act, although it reached an opposite conclusion on the appropriate balance, favouring the employer's right of ownership.[34] Similarly, the court held that in the use of employment tests, the managerial prerogative must be balanced against the employees' constitutional right to privacy, and where the invasion of privacy is not merited by the employer's proprietary interest, the tests will be voided.[35] The balancing of privacy and property rights is likely to be clarified in the future, especially with regard to the use of monitoring devices. Digital technology, with its capacity to gather, store and process personal data, also increases individuals' attention to their privacy interests.

A different type of development in Israeli labour law is also of significance for the diffusion of human rights into the employment relationship. It is reflected in a series of recent cases which, for the first time, prescribes the rights and obligations of the parties to the collective bargaining agreement. Ironically, prescribing legal rights for unions is an indication of their weakness rather than their strength. In the past the collective bargaining process was based for the most part on principles of voluntarism. Given the extensive coverage of the Israeli industrial relations system, the process was rarely contested by employers. With the growing weakness of labour, employers have started to resist their employees' efforts to organise, refusing to negotiate with the union, and seeking to terminate existing collective agreements. Juridification in these cases translated into claims about the parties' legal rights, substituting the social norms that accommodated agreements at the bargaining table. In the new case law on collective bargaining, the courts rely heavily on the discourse of property rights, freedom of association, and freedom of occupation, all of which are expressly recognised, or widely acknowledged within the new constitutional discourse in Israel. Especially peculiar is the fate of the right to property, which was considered in the past to exceed other rights and to entrench the managerial prerogative. To balance its seemingly one-sided tilt, the courts have developed the employee's property, or quasi-property, right, and have used it simply as a means of strengthening the employees' rights.[36] Consequently, the court has

---

[33] National Labour Court 164/99 *Dan Frumer and Checkpoint Software Technologies* v. *Redguard* 23 PDA 294 (Hebrew).

[34] Jerusalem District Labour Court 90/3–1000 *Joanna Yechiel* v. *Palestine Post* (unpublished, 1993) (Hebrew); National Labour Court 93/3–223 *Palestine Post* v. *Joanna Yechiel* 27 PDA 436 (Hebrew).

[35] *Supra* n.29.

[36] National Labour Court 400024/98 *The Histadrut* v. *Zim* (unpublished, 2000) (Hebrew).

determined that employers may not dismiss employees in response to their interest in organising and pursuing collective bargaining.[37] Employers must consult with unions, on demand, with regard to a broad range of issues.[38] Employers may also encounter some limitations imposed on them before they withdraw from a collective agreement, even if the collective agreement expressly allows such withdrawal.[39]

To conclude this section, social changes that have led to the decline of extra-legal norms that stabilised society in the past have given way to a juridified discourse of legal rights. Although this change stems from society and not from law, it was encouraged and accommodated by general changes in jurisprudence. Together, these changes have brought into existence new chunks of law, including anti-discrimination legislation, good faith requirements for rational management, public-policy requirements that add up to a workers' bill of rights, and quasi-constitutional support for the collective bargaining regime. In the process of making the new labour law, the public constraint is sometimes framed explicitly in terms of protecting human rights. At other times other public values are drawn upon, such as rationality and fairness. However, within the judicial and legislative rhetoric human rights cannot always be neatly distinguished from public values in general. Given the current debate on the view of core labour rights as human rights, it may be possible to address some of the traditional interventions in the contractual sphere as a human rights issue. Freedom of association and organised labour's rights, prohibition of child labour, and anti-discrimination law are considered to extend beyond mere labour standards, and must be regarded as human rights issues.

The blurring between human rights and other public values can be viewed from another perspective. Some human rights justifications are framed in a broad manner, for example, by reference to the right to human dignity, and thus serve as a flexible valve for broad public intervention. Whether this public intervention always addresses human rights issues, or merely draws on human rights rhetoric to justify public intervention of a lower calibre is a matter that should be scrutinised carefully on a case-by-case basis. Similarly, it was demonstrated that the human rights rhetoric of property rights that are currently being ascribed to workers may be used as a general term to empower workers. Property rights are therefore applied as a device to correct what the court deems to be a general inequality of bargaining power which results from the weakening of the corporatist collective bargaining regime. The following discussion must therefore cluster the new cases and laws together, for they are inseparable.

[37] National Labour Court 1008/00 *Horn & Leibobitz Inc.* v. *The Histadrut* (unpublished, 2000) (Hebrew).
[38] National Labour Court 4000005/98 *The Histadrut* v. *The State of Israel* (unpublished, 2000) (Hebrew).
[39] National Labour Court 97/4–44 *Haifa Chemicals Inc.* v. *The Histadrut* 30 PDA 216 (Hebrew).

IV. THE DIALECTICS OF JURIDIFICATION

Given the growing number of cases in which employees are asking courts and legislatures to provide mandatory standards that curtail the managerial prerogative, it is necessary to assess this third stage of juridification and the legal agents' high rate of responsiveness to the new types of legal claims. In doing so, it is important to distinguish between the multiple causes and purposes underlying the new juridification. The analysis of the second phase of juridification indicates that it would be wrong to regard the diffusion of human rights jurisprudence into the employment relationship as a project focused solely on the actual protection of human rights. Human rights are currently being used as an instrument to devise a new employment contract in which there is a division of labour between private negotiations and public values. Whereas sometimes a particular intervention seeks to address one purpose, at other times it seeks to provide multiple purposes simultaneously. The substitution effect between the traditional means of collective bargaining and the new reliance on constitutional rights in litigation indicates that the emerging strategy is aimed at promoting all the objectives of the traditional body of labour law. These include, first and foremost, the issue of distribution of power and outcomes between labour and capital, as well as efficiency, co-operation, and trust.

Yet the constantly spreading process of juridification, based on constitutional and quasi-constitutional rhetoric, holds a dialectical quality. Not only does the new law suffer from various faults that diminish its capacity to address the overly ambitious objectives of the lawmakers, it can sometimes lead to perverse results which undermine the original objectives it sought to achieve. Some have observed these outcomes of juridification in terms of paradoxes.[40] A more critical view may hold juridification's creeping expansion to be a Pyrrhic victory. This view may lean too heavily in favour of determinism and pessimism. A dialectic view implies that the new juridification must be understood critically. It displays both the advantages and the shortcomings. On some issues the advantages outweigh the shortcomings, while on others the analysis indicates the opposite outcome. To observe this dialectic quality, it is worth looking at each objective ascribed to the new juridification separately.

1. Objective 1: the diffusion of human rights into the employment relationship is intended to empower workers *vis-à-vis* their employers

It is possible to paraphrase this objective by viewing the new juridification as the post-industrial emancipation of workers. In the words of Spiros Simitis,

---

[40] S. Sitkin and R. Bies, "The Legalization of Organizations: A Multi-Theory Perspective" in S. Sitkin and R. Bies (eds.), *The Legalistic Organization* (Thousand Oaks, Cal., Sage, 1994) 19–49.

"[t]he employee finally steps out of the shadow of the bourgeois individual".[41] The assumption according to which human rights apply only to the public sphere, and are not affected by inequalities in the private sphere, has been replaced by the acknowledgement that civil liberties in the public sphere are not equally accessible to all individuals.[42] The effects of social stratification, which renders human rights an unfulfilled promise for some, can be remedied by two intertwining human rights strategies. The first is to expand the list of human rights, most notably by recognising the social, economic and cultural rights.[43] The second is to diffuse human rights into the private sphere, thus increasing the number of agents whose autonomy and freedom is restricted by others' rights. The two strategies are non-exclusive and could be developed together.

However, drawing on human rights rhetoric is not a panacea, and the promise for workers may remain unfulfilled.[44] Even when rooted in deontological reasoning, which is commonly not the case when human rights are diffused into the private sphere, two interrelated obstacles arise before a transformative workers' bill of rights. First, the employment relationship has two parties, and employers can frame their claims in constitutional and human rights terms as well. As long as the nexus of contracts (i.e., the firm; the employer) can claim a human right, the new constitutional discourse that caters to the process of juridification is two-sided and can be viewed, from the workers' perspective, as a double-edged sword.[45] Secondly, rights are generally not absolute, and must be balanced with competing rights and public interests. Consequently, the human rights discourse seeks to draw a balance between the employers' and the workers' constitutional claims. Assuming that there is no predefined balance that can serve as a benchmark for assessing judicial or legislative outcomes, the constitutional discourse may provide very different outcomes, contingent on the time and place in which the constitutional balance was made. A human rights discourse can therefore structure a workers' bill of rights, but it can also potentially entrench managerial power as a trump card which overrides all other human rights. The mere reliance on the discourse of human rights is ideologically open-ended and can be used both to break and to entrench power relations in the private sphere.

Furthermore, a critique of rights has been launched by both the left and the right. It has been argued that rights are alienating and atomising, and defeat

---

[41] S. Simitis, "The Rediscovery of the Individual in Labour Law" in R. Rogowski and T. Wilthagen (eds.), *Reflexive Labour Law* (Deventer, Kluwer, 1994) 183–206.

[42] This line of analysis can be traced back to K. Marx, "On the Jewish Question" in *Karl Marx, Early Writings* (R. Livingstone and G. Benton trans., New York, Vintage Books, 1975) 16–211.

[43] "Proclamation of Teheran" in Final Act of the International Conference on Human Rights, Teheran, 22 April to 13 May 1968, UN Doc A/CONF 32/41 (1968); Vienna Declaration and Programme of Action, World Conference on Human Rights, Vienna, 14–25 June 1993, UN Doc A/CONF 157/23 (1993).

[44] For a similar argument, see Raday, "Privatising Human Rights", *supra* n.5.

[45] Compare M. Horowitz, "Rights" (1988) 23 *Harv. CR CL L Rev.* 393.

the formation of communities.[46] Rights have been argued to silence debates on the common good. They shift the focus from political and social change to an excessive use of legal strategies that are of limited impact. Ironically rights can inhibit social change rather than mobilise it. Much of this critique has been recently developed in the United States and reflects a particular type of rights talk, which has a strong liberal tilt and a pro-markets flavour. Diffusing rights into the private sphere of the employment relationship can be conducted in various ways and must not necessarily fall into some of the individualising schemes of the American sort. However, the criticism aptly portrays the strong individual orientation of rights discourse, and thus demonstrates that the new rights-based juridification cannot serve as a substitute for the post-Second World War paradigm which was based on collective organisations.

There is nothing intrinsic in the human rights discourse that ensures its usefulness as a substitute for the autonomous collective regime, or as a measure for the protection of workers. The divide between the human rights movement and the labour movement in the past suggests that the two movements need not be considered natural allies.[47] Labour has not been a universal advocate of human rights, although in some countries labour has taken an active role in the battle for human rights, South Africa being a useful example from the recent past.[48] In other countries labour was not at the forefront of human rights activism, and often viewed the individual rights-based discourse as a threat to labour solidarity, which is necessarily collectively-based. The effects of human rights as a new form of labour market regulation is therefore dependent on the list of rights that are being recognised, and the way rights are being applied, interpreted and balanced.

2. Objective 2: juridification seeks to aid workers who are least well off in terms of market power, on the assumption that they cannot negotiate a safety net by themselves

This objective is the core of labour law's vocation.[49] Workers who have strong market leverage can negotiate their own safety net and do not need the legal rule, assuming of course the absence of market failures, which will be discussed later. Workers with weak bargaining power need the mandatory rule to protect them, in the sense of ensuring minimum standards, above and beyond prevailing

---

[46] Demonstrating different points of view to substantiate this claim see M. Tushnet, "An Essay on Rights" (1984) 62 *Tex. L Rev.* 1363; M.A. Glendon, *Rights Talk: The Impoverishment of Political Discourse* (New York, Free Press, 1993); M. Sandel, *Democracy's Discontent: America in Search of a Public Philosophy* (Cambridge, Mass., Belknap Press, 1996).

[47] V.A. Leary, "The Paradox of Workers' Rights as Human Rights" in L. Compa and S. Diamond (eds.), *Human Rights, Labor Rights and International Trade* (Philadelphia, Penn., University of Pennsylvania Press, 1996) 22–47.

[48] Cf H. Ebrahim, *The Birth of a Constitution* (Cape Town, Oxford University Press, 1998).

[49] H. Collins, "Labour Law as Vocation" (1989) 105 *LQR* 469.

market standards. The new juridification seeks to reinforce the safety net for workers by offering universal protection on the basis of public values. It therefore reflects community standards of fairness that serve as a minimum threshold for all employment contracts, regardless of any individual worker's bargaining power.

There are however two difficulties with the fulfilment of the distributive objective. Both highlight the tension between individuals and class. First, while certain rights may aid individuals in particular cases, they may not always have the desirable distributive consequences for workers as a group. Raising labour costs carries implications, the extent of which is debated, for unemployment. This debate has been aptly illustrated in the context of minimum wage regulation which is occasionally argued in terms of the right to dignity or the right to adequate income.[50] Yet while measurement issues are somewhat controversial with regard to the pecuniary benefits such as wage, they become wholly uncertain in issues such as reference letters, privacy and the law of dismissals.[51] While the empirical studies must be read carefully with regard to each and every rule, it is quite evident that the insiders-outsiders problem is acute in the distribution of goods in the labour market. The pervasiveness of the problem is a result of the unique nature of the "commodity" being traded in the employment relationship.[52]

The second problem with the distributive objective is that the creation of new rights provides the substantive norms, but does not in itself ensure their enforcement. Enforcement of the new web of norms relies on the actual adjudication of rights claims. Litigation is initiated by the individual worker, who must take into account the high expense involved, the length of time, the risk of losing his or her job as a result, and the burden of proof, which is usually placed on the plaintiff. To the extent that the new human rights discourse is used to provide an extensive redistributive safety net that replaces the old regime of collective bargaining, the substitution is only partial. As noted, autonomous labour law had the advantage of creating rights that were always coupled by an autonomous enforcement mechanism, which was based on the collective power of workers. There was a sense of coherence between the substance of the norm and the means of its enforcement. This coherence disappears in the new juridification because there is a mismatch between the norms which reflect public values and the means of enforcement which remain a private matter.

---

[50] On the minimum wage debate see D. Card and A. Krueger, *Myth and Measurement: The New Economics of the Minimum Wage* (Princeton, NJ, Princeton University Press, 1995); "Review Symposium" (1995) 48(4) *Indus. & Lab. Relations Rev.* 49–827.

[51] See, for example, J.H. Verkerke, "Employment Contract Law" in P. Newman (ed.), *The New Palgrave Dictionary of Economics and the Law* (New York, Palgrave Press, 1998), ii, 47–52 (arguing that we lack empirical understanding of how legal rules affect employees); J.H. Verkerke, "Legal Regulation of Employment Reference Practices" (1998) 65 *U Chi. L Rev.* 115 (discussing the effects of mandating reference letters).

[52] C. Offe, "Two Logics of Collective Action" in C. Offe (ed.), *Disorganized Capitalism* (Cambridge, Mass., MIT Press, 1986).

The problem of enforcement renders many of the new rules available only to those workers who have a stronger market power. They have the funds and liquidity that are needed to conduct litigation over rights. Workers with strong market power, given a high demand for their skills, can take the risk of losing their jobs. Workers with low levels of skills, especially at times of structural unemployment, are often unable to claim their new legal rights. Consequently, the distributive impact of the new juridification may increase market inequality. Just like the old regime of autonomous labour law, where core workers who were covered by collective bargaining were sometimes privileged at the expense of peripheral workers, the new regime provides universal rights that are difficult to enforce and therefore privilege the stronger segment of the workforce.

3. Objective 3: juridification is intended to correct market failures and promote efficiency

A different kind of objective that is attributed to the new juridification is based on premises of efficiency. This objective may appear to be in tension with the common vocabulary of human rights, the justification of which often rests on anti-utilitarian considerations. The strong reliance of the new juridification on human rights and public values could be justified in an economic analysis in two alternative ways. First, it is arguable, as John Stewart Mill tried to demonstrate, that the protection of human rights increases general utility.[53] A more modern type of argument is premised on the assumption that in the negotiation over employment rights (all or some), the labour market functions imperfectly, and various market failures justify regulatory intervention. The first argument is often overlooked, especially because it is based on utility, and it is calculated for society as a whole. Modern economic analyses of the labour market tend to prefer a narrower view of utility, one which is calculable in monetary units, and the analysis of labour markets tends to focus on the participants in the labour market itself rather than on general social concerns. By contrast, the second argument has received much attention.

The difficulty with the efficiency justification of the new juridification, with its strong public and constitutional thrusts, is that the discourse of market failures is precariously illusive. Market failures can be found everywhere or nowhere, depending on the result that one seeks to justify.[54] A careful analysis however reveals that there are some potential market failures that are typical to negotiations over non-wage components of the employment relationship.[55]

---

[53] J.S. Mill, *Utilitarianism* (London, Logmans Green, 1907) 41–61.

[54] D. Kennedy, "Distributive and Paternalist Motives in Contract Law and Tort Law, With Special Reference to Compulsory Terms and Unequal Bargaining Power" (1982) 441 *Maryland L Rev.* 563.

[55] See generally C.R. Sunstein, *Human Behavior and the Law of Work* (University of Chicago, J.M. Olin Working Paper No 100, 2nd series, 2000).

Problems of information asymmetry are acute when the employer's policy is not measurable in quantifiable terms. Thus, while wages are more readily negotiable, a human resource policy requires a thorough reading and an assessment of the policy's implementation in practice. The employee, or potential candidate, is rarely informed to the extent required by such scrutiny. The problem is augmented by barriers to efficient negotiations, as employees are not always inclined to reveal their preferences, considering the risk that those may be interpreted as an adverse signal. Similarly, employers may hesitate to reveal practices that are favourable to employees, because of the risk of adverse selection of employees. Thus, much is not said, and cannot be said, during the negotiations over the employment contract. Moreover, non-wage issues are commonly a local public good that cannot be negotiated individually. Promotion schemes, monitoring devices and organisational culture are often developed with the intention of uniform applicability to all workers, and their strength draws on the economy of scale, whereby these components are uniformly applied to a large group of workers. Employment contracts, even in non-unionised settings, tend to resemble contracts of adhesion, at least with regard to the non-wage components of the contract. An analysis that more readily deviates from the assumptions of rationality in bargaining is likely to highlight even further complications that question whether market ordering of employment contracts is efficient.[56]

However, even for those who are aware of market failures, the solution of juridification is not self-evident. The new regulation, endorsed in public terms and human rights, often replaces market imperfections with governmental imperfections.[57] From the efficiency point of view, tailoring the most efficient rule for dismissals, use of a monitoring device or organisational culture is a highly complex task. Replacing the intersubjective process of learning the norms as they are created with objective legal tests that distinguish right from wrong is error-prone. Creating one norm that fits all workplaces, despite their variations and the diverse interests of the workforce and employers, cannot replicate more complex patterns that evolve in the market-place. Information asymmetry between the negotiating parties is substituted by informational barriers that deny third parties (such as judges and legislatures) the necessary understanding of shopfloor level processes and intra-firm dynamics. In the new juridification, the choice therefore is between two faulty systems, and policy-makers ought to settle for the second best, which may not always be the regulatory solution.

---

[56] See *ibid.*; C. Jolls, C. Sunstein and R. Thaler, "A Behavioral Approach to Law and Economics" in C. Sunstein (ed.), *Behavioral Law and Economics* (Cambridge, Cambridge University Press, 2000) 13–58.

[57] R. Cooter, *The Strategic Constitution* (Princeton, NJ, Princeton University Press, 2000) 72–149.

4. Objective 4: juridification is intended to promote managerial rationality

While in the past human resource managers studied a host of courses designed to evaluate the quality of different methods of human resource management, they must now take a rigorous course on judicial discretion. Legal rhetoric is important and instructive, but it is not the single most important way to think and talk about things.[58] The use of a few basic standards such as good faith, public policy, balancing of interests and reasonableness that are flexible enough to fit commercial relationships, as well as family, work and professional and political relationships, conflates differences in the various spheres in which our daily lives are lived. Moreover, not only is the legal rhetoric occasionally vague because of its use of general standards that are broadly applied, but it also delivers nuanced decisions that can be easily misread. Thus, there is a risk that if we say that a managerial practice stands up to judicial scrutiny, we also tend to think that it is good. The impact of legal rhetoric tends to be imperialistic. Holding that a certain practice conforms, for example, with the margins of discretion permissible in the balancing of managerial property rights and the employees' privacy rights, becomes a stamp of approval for the practice. Yet the real stamp of approval, which should be judged in other terms, such as its impact on motivation, efficiency, satisfaction, or even morality, often can be ignored once the legal statement has been made.

The growing domination of legal rhetoric over alternative discourses is not "good" or "bad". Sometimes it is absolutely necessary. There are voices that are being silenced in alternative discourses. Such for example were the voices of sexually harassed women in the workplace who were required to remain silent because their claim could affect profits and motivation (male motivation that is). When an identifiable group of voices is being silenced, or when market norms or managerial norms disregard certain types of interests, legal rhetoric can complement or even substitute existing norms. At other times it is necessary to provide leeway for alternative discourses to flourish. As pointed out, the prominence of the legal discourse is not always necessary, and it can also be harmful. Most notably, in a business environment it can inhibit experimentation and adversely affect industrial pluralism. Consequently, juridification fares better when it sounds concerns that are foreign to alternative frames of thought and discourses, and it is less justified when it tries to replicate the interests that reside naturally within the market rhetoric, such as rationality and efficiency.

---

[58] R. Stutman and L. Putnam, "The Consequences of Language: A Metaphorical Look at the Legalization of Organizations" in S. Sitkin and R. Bies (eds.), *The Legalistic Organization* (Thousand Oaks, Cal., Sage Publications, 1994) 281–302.

5. Objective 5: juridification seeks to promote a sense of justice (substantive or procedural) in the workplace and to advance mutual trust between the employer and the employees

The employment relationship requires a high level of trust. When trust does not develop, we observe what has been designated as internal inefficiency.[59] The intra-organisational state of distrust leads the parties to the employment contract to a limited formal compliance with basic obligations of the employment contract. Strategic behaviour of the parties who seek to capture quasi-rents at the expense of the other party inhibits a more productive relationship, where the employee contributes ingenuity and motivation, and the employer seeks to enhance the employee's welfare.

Some regulatory measures do not try to probe the corporate culture. The asserted objective of minimum wage legislation, for example, is to establish a just wage, but there is no assumption that in itself it improves relationships on the shopfloor. Other arrangements however seek to affect corporate culture and aid the parties to forgo their efforts to capture quasi-rents and realise the mutual advantages of co-operation and trust. In this category of rules we can list some of the anti-discrimination norms, legislation on the prevention of sexual harassment, just-cause dismissals policy and the establishment of works councils (mandatory labour-management committees that have the statutory power to co-manage various issues, such as health and safety). Similarly, the use of law's mandatory power to prevent the parties to the collective bargaining agreement from defecting from the collective pact, seeks to encourage labour-management co-operation.

The abovementioned rules try to induce a change in the internal corporate culture. The problem however is that corporate culture consists of an amorphous body of norms that are difficult to define, and compliance with which is difficult to ascertain by a third party.[60] The law therefore adheres only to the visible attributes of culture. The law can hold that a committee must meet once a month, but it cannot seriously require the committee's members to co-operate. The law can require that an employee will have a chance to explain her behaviour before she is dismissed, but it cannot ensure that the employer will be open minded and consider the explanation. Because there is a mismatch between what the law tries to do and what it does in fact, there are endless ways in which

---

[59] There are various accounts of this problem, including A. Fox, *Beyond Contract: Work, Power and Trust Relationships* (London, Allen & Unwin, 1974) (discussing the low-trust syndrome); H. Leibenstein, *Inside the Firm* (Cambridge, Mass., Harvard University Press, 1987) (designating the problem as X-inefficiency); S. Deakin and F. Wilkinson, "Labour Law and Economic Theory: a Reappraisal" in G. de Geest, J. Siegers and R. van den Bergh (eds.) *Law and Economics and the Labour Market* (Cheltenham, Elgar Publishing, 1999) 1, 23–28 (highlighting the need to assess the effects of legal regulation on trust dynamics within the firm).

[60] E.B. Rock and M.L. Wachter, "The Enforceability of Norms and the Employment Relationship" (1996) 144 *Pa. L Rev.* 1.

a rigid corporate culture can disregard the law's instructions. The employer will write down every minor mistake the employee makes, "just in case there is a lawsuit". The employer will demonstrate in writing that the employee was given a fair chance to fight her dismissal—"fair chance" being a few minutes' hearing before the manager and two witnesses. Similarly, the employee will make sure that every dirty word or differential treatment she received is written down, and preferably witnessed. Rather than seeking to overcome the day-to-day problems, the two sides are engaged in recording, remembering and preparing the inevitable lawsuit.

Conceptually, juridification and trust can be considered an oxymoron. If I comply with the legal rule only because I have to, I am not taking part in the development of trust, which evolves from a voluntary disposition.[61] I signal trust if I am willing to do something *I do not have to do*, indicating that I am giving up my power or authority or legal advantage because I trust the other party will reciprocate. If I surrender my power advantage because the law requires me to do so, I am not signalling trust. In this sense, juridification may even be a vice.

Again, there is the flip-side of juridification. Cultural change is not spontaneous. Respect for employees' dignity, and the learning of co-operation and trust, do not happen merely because the invisible hand demonstrates their efficiency.[62] The legal rule also has an expressive function that should not be understated.[63] Some employers will manufacture a corporate culture based on trust because they see its advantages. They consider the legal rule to be redundant. Others will resist a co-operative, high-trust environment, regardless of the legal rule. They do not care about the legal rule either. They will find ways to bypass any piece of regulation that is being imposed on them. For that purpose they have their lawyers who are generously paid. There is also a group of employers, the size of which is difficult to measure, who are affected by the expressive content of the legal rule. They will learn the importance of due process or substantive justice at the workplace because they tried it and it actually paid off. If this group is very small, perhaps we can do without the most intrusive legal rules that try to affect corporate culture. If the size of the group is more significant, then the legal effort may be more worthwhile.

---

[61] On trust see generally D. Gambetta, "Can We Trust Trust?" in D. Gambetta (ed.), *Trust: Making and Breaking Cooperative Relationships* (Oxford, Blackwell, 1980) 213–37; C. Snow, "Building Trust in the Workplace" (1997) 14 *Hofstra Lab. L J* 465; L. Mitchell, "Trust and Team-Production in Post-Capitalist Society" (1999) 24 *Iowa J of Corporate Law* 869.

[62] An evolutionary analysis actually indicates that an unregulated environment may promote relationships that are not structured on trust, despite the fact that there are more, or equally efficient outcomes: A. Levine and L.D. Tyson, "Participation, Productivity and the Firm's Environment" in A. Blinder (ed.), *Paying for Productivity* (Washington, DC, Brookings Inst, 1990) 183–243.

[63] On the analysis of expressive law see E. Anderson and R. Pildes, "Expressive Theories of Law: A General Restatement" (2000) 148 *U Pa. L Rev.* 1503.

Thinking about the diffusion of human rights and public values into the traditionally private sphere of the employment relationship has been described here as a combination of sociological and juristic trends. The growing application of a constitutional discourse to the employment relationship is not merely the outcome of analytical progress in the study of human rights. It is rooted in the vacuum that has developed as a result of the post-Second World War paradigm of employment contracts, and in the usefulness of the constitutional discourse as a flexible and adaptable source for public values. The familiar phrase, "labour is not a commodity" seeks representation and recognition in a legal niche. The intuition, according to which there must be something more to the employment contract beyond the mere exchange facilitated by the law of contract, is no longer being responded to by traditional legal means. In the absence of the power of traditional labour-law niches, the constitutional discourse provides a rack from which a new type of law is being dynamically created. Whether on the basis of human rights, or on the basis of public values such as fairness and justice, this development rejects the divide between the public and the private. Looking at the diffusion of human rights and public values into the employment relationship is not intended only to protect human rights. The use of human rights and public values is a heuristic device for advancing several objectives.

However, as I argued in the previous section, the limits of this new strategy must be acknowledged. The designation of the new juridification as a "human rights discourse" provides the necessary legitimacy. Yet, it was demonstrated that the various objectives of the new juridification are not easily attainable. On the basis of two examples the concluding section will demonstrate that the stronger the nexus between the new juridification and the traditional objectives of human rights, the more favourable is the result of the new juridification. However, when human rights and public values are used for purposes that are more difficult to link to traditional human rights issues, the analysis indicates a more precarious balance.

To choose the two examples, I return to the new juridification in Israel, as described in previous sections. One type of public intervention is based on the diffusion of civil liberties into the sphere of the employment relationship traditionally thought of as private. Freedom of occupation, freedom of speech, privacy and equality have all been balanced by the managerial right of ownership and freedom of contract. A second type of public intervention is based on general public interests, such as fairness, justice and equality. On the basis of this intervention, the courts and the legislature have, for example, limited the right to dismiss workers at will, required due process justice in the workplace, and ruled that testing procedures must be valid and reliable. The difference between the two categories cannot be likened to the difference between interests and rights. The abovementioned interests are often rooted in human rights, most notably in the right to dignity, and more recently in the balancing of the employers' and employees' rights of property. Moreover, equality appears in both categories and its affiliation to one group rather than another is a controversial question in itself. Given my inclination to stay away from purely analytical distinctions, what I suggest is that there is a core to the human rights discourse, and a penumbra. The farther away we move from the core, the more ambivalent the effects of juridification are; and the potential for a mismatch between intended effects and actual effects is likely to be greater.

The two examples chosen to illustrate the differences are the constraint of privacy in the workplace and the requirement for validity and reliability of testing methods. The two limitations imposed on the employment relationship are different. Imagine that a human resource manager's catalogue of products offers a thought-reading machine. Assuming the machine works perfectly, it could serve as a highly useful device in the hands of management. It would be both valid and reliable in identifying important features such as employees' loyalty, and its use would therefore be rational from a managerial point of view. However it would severely infringe the employee's right to privacy. On the other hand, if the machine is not accurate, its results could not be indicative of the worker's intimate thoughts, and thus the infringement of privacy would be attenuated. At the same time, the machine would fail to comply with the legal test of validity and reliability, and reliance on its results would be irrational. This hypothetical machine is not wholly detached from reality. A similar analysis can be suggested for handwriting experts (graphologists), or for the use of lie detectors (polygraphs), and even to some psychological tests.[64] Both limitations on managerial power, one rooted in the right to privacy, the other in dignity and fairness, are part of the new juridification. Yet the dialectics of juridification presented in the previous section indicate that they should be treated differently.

1. Privacy

The limitation imposed on the managerial prerogative to use tests on the basis of the right to privacy is closer to the right's core than the requirement to use tests rationally (i.e., only those tests that are valid and reliable), where the connection with human dignity and equality is somewhat tenuous. The right to privacy, a relative latecomer on the human rights map, has developed with a strong

---

[64] The use of these measures is often regulated even in regimes that tend to sustain a strong public-private distinction. For a comparative overview, see J. Craig, *Privacy and Employment Law* (Oxford, Hart Publishing, 1999). See, for example, in the USA, Employee Polygraph Act 29 USC §§ 2001–2009, as well as an abundance of state-level regulations.

affinity to the regulation of private interactions.[65] The threat to individual privacy is not limited to governmental intrusion into a private sphere. It expands into private relationships where the gathering of data on individuals in a market regime can be used to infer the individual's profile of interests and preferences.[66] Given the growing commodification of information in a market society, this profile has a high commercial value and can be of much use to suppliers of goods, as well as to employers. Technological advances allow the storage of information for a long period time, as well as the use of previously stored information with newly gathered data, to create new information that was not anticipated at first. It is therefore difficult to consent to an infringement of privacy, as the consent is limited to the individual's perception of the infringement at a given point of time and place. Yet consent to reveal one's preferences to another for one purpose alone may be followed by storage of this information in the semi-public domain. It could later be checked against other bits of data collected for other purposes, the whole accumulating to a more comprehensive exposure of the individual than she ever consented to.

Moreover, while the right to privacy has been interpreted in the past as the "right to be left alone", it also encompasses a deeper meaning, namely the right to control the way one's identity is perceived by others.[67] The growing use of monitoring devices and intrusive psychological screening in the workplace limits the employee's sense of self-control over her self and her identity. The panoptic design of the new workplace, with low-walled cubicles that expose workers to their peers and managers, the collection of personal and intimate information for screening purposes, and easy monitoring made possible by digital technology can render the worker fully exposed to a hierarchical organisation.

The right to privacy has not been properly protected by the old regime governing the employment relationship. For employers, information on their workers and potential candidates is highly valuable. The employment relationship is characterised by a strong information asymmetry, where the employer lacks access to even the most basic information necessary to predict a worker's productivity *ex ante*, and even calculate it *ex post*. From the design of technology (for example, the assembly line), to compensation schemes (for example, piecemeal compensation) and to the use of monitoring devices, many managerial

---

[65] The legal right to privacy is often traced back to Warren and Brandeis' seminal article in the late 19th century: S. Warren and L. Brandeis, "The Right to Privacy" (1890) 4 *Harv. L Rev.* 193. On the evolution of the right in political theory, see A. Westin, "The Origins of the Modern Claims to Privacy" in F. Schoeman (ed.), *Philosophical Dimensions of Privacy: An Anthology* (Cambridge, Cambridge University Press, 1984) 56–74.

[66] The protection of data has been stronger in Europe than in North America, although both regions have abandoned the traditional public-private distinction and its implications for justification of regulation. See generally F. Cate, *Privacy in the Information Age* (Washington, DC, Brookings Institute, 1997).

[67] Cf. J. Inness, *Privacy, Intimacy and Isolation* (New York, Oxford University Press, 1992). Also see the development of privacy's broader meaning in a different context: J. Cohen, "Examined Lives: Informational Policy and the Subject as an Object" (2000) 52 *Stan. L Rev.* 1373.

choices are motivated by the need to collect better information on the workers' capacities and preferences. Unions, just as much as the employer, have an interest in gathering information on their membership. Unions are eager to know how much each worker earns and what fringe benefits she receives. Full information regarding these issues is a key to the negotiation and enforcement of rights in the workplace. Diffusing the right of privacy into the employment relationship is therefore a result of both the weakening of the autonomous collective regime and of individuals' vulnerability in a collective bargaining regime. It can also be explained by a growing awareness of, and sensitivity to, privacy concerns that did not exist at the heyday of the post-Second World War regime.[68] This is part of the individual-based rights-talk that has been said to serve as a catalyst for the new juridification.

Given the commercial value of personal information, it also cannot be expected that a market regime will provide adequate protection of privacy.[69] Arguably, workers who are concerned about their privacy will negotiate their interests with a potential employer, and employers will have to assure employees' privacy interests in order to attract the best and most qualified workers. However, employees cannot seriously negotiate protection for their privacy interests. An employee who demands protection of her privacy in a job interview signals she has something to hide. That is the problem of adverse signalling. An employer that provides its workers the protection of privacy, while other employers do not, may attract workers who have something to hide. That is the problem of adverse selection. Privacy in the workplace is also a public good and therefore difficult to negotiate on an individual basis. Violations of privacy are also sometimes difficult to detect. Monitoring devices are often positioned in secret places. Information collected on workers may be sold or combined with information from other sources, and the employee, even if she has consented to the collection of information, may not be aware of the diverse purposes for which this information may be used.

Thus, the regulation of privacy in the workplace is justified on the basis of market failures. It provides a layer of protection that both market ordering and collective ordering do not supply. In the process of juridifying managerial discretion, the law on privacy indeed substitutes professional considerations with legal ones. Yet this is necessary because alternative regulatory regimes (markets or autonomous collective bargaining) are not likely to voice the concerns of privacy.

At the same time there are limits to what we can expect from this regulatory intervention. First, the distributional impact of protecting privacy is ambiguous. Litigation costs are high, and intimate information may be revealed in the

---

[68] On the development of the right to privacy and social attitudes to the threat of privacy invasion see P. Regan, *Legislating Privacy: Technology, Social Values and Public Policy* (Chapel Hill, NC, University of North Carolina Press, 1995) 42–68.

[69] P. Kim, "Privacy Rights, Public Policy and the Employment Relationship" (1996) 57 *Ohio St. L J* 671.

process, thus raising high barriers that can seriously limit the litigation options. Secondly, the privacy limitation does not seriously induce trust between the parties. Invasion of privacy, for example, when intrusive monitoring devices are used, signals distrust in the employees. The mere regulatory prohibition does not, in itself, spark a more trusting environment. The case law on privacy maintains the individual right of privacy, but it does little to promote a healthier relationship between the employer and the employee.[70]

2. Rationality as a human right

The link between managerial rationality and human rights is more tenuous. The inflationary development of the right to human dignity as an umbrella over all that is to be desired and hoped for runs the risk of trivialising the issues which compose its core. The use of constitutional rhetoric to promote managerial rationality may therefore dilute the impact of the newly branching constitutional protection, rather than aid in its development.

The good faith rule that seeks to induce managerial rationality is also difficult to justify in terms of market failures. Whether a testing device is beneficial to the company is something for which the market provides a good signal. If a test selects bad workers, the company makes less profit. The market provides both a signal and a sanction. On the other hand, judges have no special competence in assessing validity and reliability of tests. In fact, if we move beyond the first class in statistics, we also learn that it is difficult, or perhaps even incoherent, to find out if a test is valid and reliable. At most we can identify when it is not. Making managerial rationality a mandatory legal norm is perhaps consistent with market assumptions, but it is difficult to justify exactly on these grounds. What is intentionally consistent with market norms can, and should, remain in the market realm.

The requirement for managerial rationality therefore does not fare very well with regard to either the efficiency or the human rights objective. However, imposing rationality by law may seem to be a mild infringement of the managerial

---

[70] The Italian rule on this issue is interesting. According to Art. 4 of the Italian Act 300/1970, if an employer wants to use monitoring devices it must first negotiate with the trade union or works council and assess alternative measures to solve the problem it wants to address. The law in a sense suggests that before an employer takes a step that demonstrates distrust (use of monitoring devices), it must go through a trust-building process. If this does not work, the law will not bar the employer. The Italian law is therefore more sensitive to the limits of the legal rule, and does not pretend to create trust where trust is impossible. However, it also uses deliberative processes to push the parties towards a higher level of trust, rather then merely avoiding the use of monitoring devices. Despite the fact that this arrangement fares better with regard to the objective of trust building, it remains weak in terms of enforcement with respect to informatic systems of control (badges, data collections, etc.), which can be used simultaneously for safety, organisational reasons and for personal control of individuals. This problem also indicates the difficulty of regulation to cope with the totality of corporate culture, and the limitations of regulation that is directed at very particular practices. I thank Marco Biagi for the information on enforcement.

prerogative, and one that is consistent, to an extent, with both efficiency and human rights concerns. Even if the rule cannot be justified on these grounds, it does not seriously conflict with them either. However, the list of vices highlighted by the analysis of juridification has not been exhausted. Given the complexity of litigating rationality, it is likely to be qualitatively more expensive then making a legal claim for receiving a forfeited wage. A plaintiff must bring expert witnesses, and respond to those brought by the employer. Given that the rule for dismissals in Israel is still that of employment at will, there is no guarantee (to say the least) that after initiating such litigation, the employee will be able to keep her job. Most litigation results in compromises, and therefore the workers face high costs of lit-igation, a slow process, and only a very partial compensation for any injury they may succeed in proving. On top of this is the risk of judicial error. Thus, the good-faith rule in this context is aimed mostly at those workers who have the money, the liquidity, and a high opportunity wage which can help them to recover from liti-gation. However, these do not qualify as the least well-off workers. True, there may be individual victims of market ordering who are not compensated for being rejected on the basis of an invalid examination they were required to take. But if they have market power they will find another job. If they do not have market power litigation is unlikely to be their optimal solution. As a class it is difficult to characterise those workers who pay the price of market ordering, and, as the pre-vious analysis demonstrates, only the strongest workers will be able to rely on this rule. The distributive objective of this rule is therefore questionable.

Furthermore, the juridification of managerial rationality channels profes-sional discretion to legal concerns. It is no longer permissible for managers to conduct a cost-benefit consideration, in which the employer may decide to dis-count the costs and forgo a certain level of validity, at the price of potentially obtaining employees who are just mediocre. Validity has become a mandatory requirement. It is now more risky to try out new tests that have not yet been val-idated, because it is legally impermissible. Thus, managerial experimentation and risk-taking which are conducive to the corporate environment have become an act in bad faith. It may be argued that what is good for the business envir-onment is bad for the employees, who serve as the guinea pigs of experimenta-tion. However unlike systemic discrimination against women or minorities, it is hard to pinpoint why there is a problem when firms compete among themselves, *inter alia*, on the basis of their testing methods. Substituting market rhetoric with a mandatory legal discourse that merely seems to replicate the final output of a competitive market takes away the importance of the *process*, in which multiple firms try out different testing methods. At the final stage of this process they learn by themselves what are the best practices. By contrast, the legal norm presents a "know-it-all" rhetoric which cannot seriously substitute the "learn-ing-by-doing" process that characterises markets.

Finally, regulating the use of tests is an intrusive law that enters the depth of corporate culture. Rational management can promote trust, but choosing tests out of the spectrum permitted by law does not induce a higher level of trust. If the employer desires rationality and succeeds in demonstrating its rational management to the workers, it may win their positive attitude. The employees know that "what they see is what they get". They know that if they work harder they will be promoted quicker. If the employer prefers to adopt an erratic managerial attitude, then rational tests, as mandated by law, are not likely to improve the general quality of the corporate culture. The law deals in an anecdotal fashion with one visible aspect of a complex culture, and the employer's compliance with the law on this particular point will not, in itself, lead to a greater level of co-operation.

VI. CONCLUSIONS

For those concerned with the justification for diffusing human rights into the private sphere of the employment relationship, the analysis here suggests various objectives that could justify this process. When considering the diffusion of the human rights' core, the analysis demonstrates that, as in the case of discrimination, markets do not necessarily weed out practices that infringe individual human rights. It is noteworthy that the economic analysis of the labour market and the deontological analysis of human rights cannot be neatly separated. Even those who believe that human rights should be protected in the private sphere as well must assess the virtues of juridification in comparison with market (private) ordering. The outcome of analysis must rely on the relative advantages of the regulatory regimes. The case made here in favour of diffusing the right to privacy into the employment relationship draws on such a comparative analysis. The argument made here is of course tentative and requires further elaboration. The present analysis merely attempts to list the necessary questions, based on the potential objectives that may be attributed to this process.

On the other hand, for those who endorse the constitutionalisation of the private sphere, on the assumption that human rights can, and should, empower individuals in their relationship with others, and not only in their relationship with the state, the analysis provided here suggests that the emerging human rights rhetoric is not a panacea. Even with regard to the argument favouring the protection of employees' right to privacy, there are indications that the constitutional guarantee is riven with potential flaws. The regulation of managerial rationality was more strongly contested, on the basis of the various rationales that may be claimed to justify the rule. Taking an agnostic approach that accepts the various objectives as legitimate, even *en arguendo*, the discussion here demonstrates that there is a potential mismatch between the objectives for juridification, whatever these maybe, and the power of law to fulfil these objectives.

The move from the post-Second World War paradigm to the new juridified version of labour law, on the basis of broad constitutional and quasi-constitutional values, can be portrayed as the only possible legal response, albeit a limited one.

However, the analysis here suggests that despite the value-laden rhetoric of the human rights discourse, and the importance associated with constitutional values, the substitution is far from being perfect. Drawing solely on the development of a new rights discourse cannot substitute the associational and deliberative features of the post-Second World War paradigm. It often corresponds to the highly individualistic nature of the labour market at present, and therefore mostly aids workers who are self-reliant. It does not address the fundamental legal and social structures that give rise to a growing inequality in society. Despite the universal nature of human rights, the new juridification is not enjoyed universally by all workers, and therefore it does not overcome the insiders-outsiders dilemma of labour markets.

The critical analysis suggested here indicates that human rights and public values inserted into the employment relationship as a means for compensating the decline of the post-Second World War order does not, and cannot, offer a comprehensive solution. It is impossible to substitute the system of collective bargaining, as imperfect and fragile as it was, with an individual-based conception of legal rights. The developing discourse of human rights in the workplace must therefore be viewed not only as progress, but also as a failure. The regulatory solution risks the marginalisation of further efforts to reconsider a collective-based system that is better adjusted to the new labour market. It is better to consider the new juridification as a limited response that must be complemented by other forms of reflexive regulation, rather than the conclusive source for workplace related norms.

Part V

The Law of Torts

14

Negligence and Human Rights: *Re-Considering* Osman

EWAN McKENDRICK

I. INTRODUCTION

THE TASK OF predicting the likely impact of the enactment of the Human Rights Act 1998 on English private law is an extremely difficult one. The problem is caused in large part by the lack of case law and the relative dearth of academic writing on the issue from an English private law perspective. In time both of these shortcomings will be remedied but it will inevitably take time for this to happen. In the meantime the law is in an uncertain state[1] and, in many ways, we can only speculate as to the future shape of the law. The Act may turn out to be something of a damp squib or it may have a transforming effect on English private law. The truth is likely to lie somewhere in between these two extremes. The Act will have a major impact on certain areas of private law, but other parts will remain relatively unaffected.

One way of seeking to ascertain the likely impact of the Human Rights Act is to apply it to concrete fact situations. For example, one can apply it to the facts of well-known cases decided by the courts prior to the enactment of the Act and then apply the Act to that fact situation. A comparison of the outcome before and after the enactment of the Act will give us some insight into its likely impact on private law. This approach is not without its problems. The case chosen may not be representative. It can also be difficult to predict exactly how a court would have decided a case had it been required to apply a different set of rules. But the approach does have its advantages in that it requires us to face up to some of the difficult questions which will confront the judges, namely the application of rather broad standards to the facts and circumstances of an individual case.

---

[1] This uncertainty was heightened by the fact that, at the time of writing, the cases of *Z* v. *United Kingdom* app. no. 29392/95 and *TP and KM* v. *United Kingdom* app. no. 28945/95 had been argued before the European Court of Human Rights and judgments were pending. Both cases were appeals from the decision of the House of Lords in *X* v. *Bedfordshire County Council* [1995] 2 AC 633 (hereinafter *X* v. *Bedfordshire*). Judgement was given in both cases on 10th May 2001, after the completion of this essay, but it has been possible to provide a brief account of the decisions and their likely impact upon English tort law in a postscript to this essay.

A case which provides a useful vehicle for these purposes is the decision of the Court of Appeal in *Osman* v. *Ferguson*,[2] which was later considered by the Grand Chamber of the European Court of Human Rights in *Osman* v. *United Kingdom*.[3] It may seem rather unusual to take *Osman* as an example, given that the European Court of Human Rights held that the applicants' human rights had in fact been violated. But the human right which the Court held had been violated was the right contained in Article 6(1) of the Convention, namely that "in the determination of his civil rights and obligations . . ., everyone is entitled to a fair and public hearing within a reasonable time by an independent and impartial tribunal established by law". It therefore follows that, were the facts of *Osman* to recur, an English court could not dismiss the claim in the same way as the Court of Appeal dismissed it. But it does not follow from this that the claim would necessarily succeed. It may fail for other reasons. It is therefore necessary to set out the facts of *Osman* with some care before seeking to examine how the case would be resolved now that the Human Rights Act 1998 is in force.

II.   OSMAN: THE FACTS

The facts of *Osman* v. *Ferguson*[4] are simple but tragic. The claimants were Mrs Mulkiye Yousof Osman and her son Ahmet Osman. Mrs Osman was born in Cyprus in 1948 and her son was born in England in 1972.[5] At the relevant time Ahmet Osman was a pupil at Homerton House School. One of the teachers at the school was Mr Paul Paget-Lewis.[6] Mr Paget-Lewis formed a close attachment to Ahmet Osman. The school was aware of this attachment from as early as 1986. Over time the attachment grew and assumed an increasingly sinister form. In January 1987 Mr Paget-Lewis began to harass Ahmet Osman's friend, Leslie Green, accusing him of "deviant sexual practices".[7] His aim in making these accusations was to dissuade Ahmet Osman from being friendly with Leslie Green. By this stage Mr Paget-Lewis had formed what McCowan LJ in the Court of Appeal termed "a strong and unhealthy attachment"[8] to Ahmet Osman. This "attachment" manifested itself in different ways. In March 1987 graffiti appeared in the school in which it was alleged that a sexual relationship existed between Leslie Green and Ahmet Osman and the school discovered that

---

[2] [1993] 4 All ER 344.

[3] [1999] FLR 193.

[4] *Supra* n.2.

[5] No reference is made in the Court of Appeal to the ethnic origin of the claimants but it is referred to in the judgment of the ECtHR. Their ethnic origins may not be without significance given the well-publicised allegations, which have been made against the Metropolitan Police in relation to the conduct of investigations into crimes committed against members of racial minorities.

[6] It appears that his real name was, in fact, Ronald Stephen Potter. He had previously changed his name by deed-poll to Paget-Lewis, the name of a pupil at a school at which he was then teaching: see *supra* n.3, at 202.

[7] *Supra* n.2, at 346.

[8] *Ibid.*

files relating to Ahmet Osman and Leslie Green had been stolen from the school office. Mr Paget-Lewis was suspected of being responsible for both of these events, although he denied any involvement when interviewed by the deputy head teacher of the school. In April[9] or May[10] of 1987 Mr Paget-Lewis changed his name by deed poll to Paul Ahmet Yildrim Osman. After Mr Paget-Lewis had so changed his name the headmaster of the school wrote to the local education authority, informing them of Mr Paget Lewis' change of name and expressing his fears for the safety of Ahmet Osman. By now the local police had become involved. The headmaster's diary showed that there were four meetings between him and a police constable between 3 March 1987 and 17 March 1987. There was at least one further meeting with the police in May 1987.

On 19 May 1987 Mr Paget-Lewis was seen by a local education authority psychiatrist. The psychiatrist stated that, in his opinion, Mr Paget-Lewis did not seem to be sexually deviant but that he did have "personality problems" and he noted that his judgement in relation to his relationship with Ahmet Osman was "reprehensibly suspect".[11] He recommended that Mr Paget-Lewis should be allowed to remain as a teacher at the school but that he should receive "some form of counselling and psychotherapy".[12] Unfortunately, things did not improve: on the contrary, they got worse. On or about 21 May 1987 a brick was thrown through the window of the Osman family home. In June and July of 1987 the tyres of Mr Osman's car were slashed on two occasions. All of these events were reported by Mr Osman to the police. Mr Paget-Lewis was suspected of being responsible for all of these events.

Mr Paget-Lewis was seen again by the local education authority psychiatrist in June 1987. He concluded that Mr Paget-Lewis was temporarily unfit for work and, at the second meeting in June, he recommended that Mr Paget-Lewis should no longer teach at the school and a "transfer on medical grounds was strongly and urgently recommended".[13] On 18 June 1987 Mr Paget-Lewis was suspended from his duties, pending an investigation by the local education authority.

The suspension did not bring an end to the incidents involving the Osman family. In August or September 1987 a mixture of engine oil and paraffin was poured on an area outside the Osman family home. In October 1987 the windscreen of Mr Osman's car was smashed, probably with a hammer. In November 1987 the lock of the Osman family home was jammed with superglue, dog excrement was smeared over the door-step and the light bulb was stolen from the light in the outside porch on more than one occasion. Once again these incidents were reported to the police and Mr Paget-Lewis was suspected of being responsible for them all.

[9] The European Court of Human Rights stated that Mr Paget-Lewis changed his name on 14 April 1987: see *supra* n.3, at 201.
[10] The date given by the Court of Appeal: see *supra* n.2, at 346.
[11] *Supra* n.3, at 202. This meeting is not referred to by the Court of Appeal.
[12] *Ibid.*, at 203.
[13] *Ibid.*

In November 1987 Mr Paget-Lewis suddenly overtook a car in which Mr Osman and others were travelling and cut in front of them.[14] Mr Paget-Lewis took matters further on 7 December 1987 when he drove the wrong way up a one-way street and deliberately rammed a car in which Leslie Green was travelling. Mr Paget-Lewis was cautioned by the police. In an interview with the local education officer on 15 December 1987 it was alleged that Mr Paget-Lewis had said that he was going to do a "sort of Hungerford"[15] but not at the school. On 22 December the driver of the van which had been rammed by Mr Paget-Lewis gave a statement to the police in which he stated that Mr Paget-Lewis had told him "I am not worried about all this because in a few months I will be doing life".[16] The Osmans alleged that they were visited by a police officer after the incident on 7 December and that in the course of that meeting the police officer told them that he knew that Mr Paget-Lewis was responsible for the acts of vandalism and he "gave them assurances that he would cause the incidents to stop".[17] The government denied that any such assurance had been given.

In January 1988 the police began the process of laying an information before the magistrates' court with a view to prosecuting Mr Paget-Lewis for driving without due care and attention. Between January and March of 1988 Mr Paget-Lewis spent some time travelling around England. He hired a number of cars in the name of Osman. On 17 January 1988 he broke into cars at a clay-pigeon shoot in Yorkshire and stole a shotgun from one of the cars. The incident was reported to the local police but not to the Metropolitan Police. Finally, at 11pm on 7 March 1988 Mr Paget-Lewis followed Mr Osman and Ahmet Osman to their home. He held the family at gunpoint. He compelled Mr Osman and Ahmet Osman to kneel on the kitchen floor. He then turned out the light and shot them both, killing Mr Osman and severely wounding Ahmet Osman. He then drove to the home of the deputy headmaster of the school where he had worked. There he shot both the deputy headmaster and his son, killing the latter and wounding the former. Mr Paget-Lewis was arrested in the early hours of 8 March. When interviewed by the police he admitted that he had been planning the attacks for some time, but he denied responsibility for some of the events which took place between March and June 1987. On 28 October 1988 Mr Paget-Lewis was convicted of two charges of manslaughter and was "sentenced to be detained in a secure mental hospital without limit of time pursuant to Section 41 of the Mental Health Act 1983".[18]

On 28 September 1989 Mrs Osman and Ahmet Osman commenced proceedings against the consultant psychiatrist who had examined Mr Paget-Lewis and the Commissioner of Police of the Metropolis in which they alleged that both

---

[14] This incident is referred to by the Court of Appeal, *supra* n.2, at 347, but not by the ECtHR.

[15] In 1987 a gunman in the town of Hungerford shot and killed 16 people before committing suicide. It should be noted that the government denied that any reference had been made to Hungerford in the course of the interview.

[16] *Supra* n.2, at 347–8.

[17] *Supra* n.3, at 205.

[18] *Ibid.*, at 207.

parties had been negligent and that, as a result, they had both suffered loss and damage. They alleged that the police had been negligent in various respects. In particular they alleged that the police had been negligent in failing to apprehend Mr Paget-Lewis prior to the shootings on 7 March 1988. Further they alleged that the police had failed to interview him, search his home, or charge him with any offence more serious than not possessing an MOT certificate for his car and/or driving without due care and attention. On 19 August 1991 the Commissioner of Police of the Metropolis applied under RSC Order 18 rule 19 to strike out the statement of claim as disclosing no reasonable cause of action.[19] Sir Peter Pain dismissed the application.[20] The Commissioner of Police of the Metropolis appealed to the Court of Appeal. The appeal was heard on 6 October 1992 and judgment was given the following day. The Court of Appeal allowed the appeal and struck out the claim against the Commissioner.

The principal judgment was given by McCowan LJ. Beldam LJ and Simon Brown LJ gave short concurring judgments. After giving a brief account of the facts as alleged[21] by the claimants, McCowan LJ turned to consider the decisions of the House of Lords in *Home Office* v. *Dorset Yacht Co Ltd*[22] and *Hill* v. *Chief Constable of West Yorkshire*[23] together with the decision of the Court of Appeal in *Alexandrou* v. *Oxford*.[24] The principal issue before the court was whether, on the basis that all the material facts in the statement of claim were true, they were capable of establishing that the defendants owed a duty of care towards the claimants. The answer to this question was held to turn upon whether there was a relationship of proximity between the parties and whether or not it was fair, just and reasonable to impose a duty of care on the defendants. The first issue, that of proximity, was treated lightly by the Court of Appeal.[25] McCowan LJ stated that it could well be said that the Osman family were exposed to a risk from Mr Paget-Lewis "over and above that of the public at large".[26] In his judgment the claimants had an "arguable case that as between [Ahmet Osman] and his family on the one hand, and the investigating officers, on the other, there existed a very close degree of proximity amounting to a special relationship".[27] Simon Brown LJ agreed with McCowan LJ but Beldam LJ was more circumspect. He preferred "not to express in an interlocutory appeal an opinion whether the facts set out in the statement of claim are, if proved,

---

[19] The first defendant, namely the consultant psychiatrist, was not involved in the striking out application.

[20] His judgment is not reported.

[21] There was no investigation into the facts of the case. The court assumed for the purposes of the appeal that the facts were as alleged by the claimants. The court's approach to the facts is discussed in more detail *infra*, text accompanying nn. 85–89.

[22] [1970] AC 1004 (hereinafter *Dorset Yacht*).

[23] [1989] AC 53 (hereinafter *Hill*).

[24] [1993] 4 All ER 328.

[25] The reason for this was doubtless that counsel for the police advanced the argument as "his subsidiary point": *supra* n.2, at 351.

[26] *Ibid.*, at 350.

[27] *Ibid.*

sufficient to establish a relationship of sufficient proximity to found a duty of care owed to the plaintiffs by the officers of the second defendant's force".[28] Having concluded that there was, arguably, a relationship of proximity between the parties, the court then turned to the question whether it was fair, just and reasonable to impose a duty of care on the police. Counsel for the police argued that it was contrary to public policy to impose a duty of care on the police and placed considerable reliance upon the decision of the House of Lords in *Hill* which he claimed was "indistinguishable".[29] McCowan LJ accepted the submission, stating that in his judgment "the House of Lords decision on public policy in *Hill's* case dooms this action to failure as against the second defendant".[30] It was a "plain and obvious case falling squarely within a House of Lords decision".[31] The reasons of public policy which negated the duty of care were, essentially, that the imposition of a duty of care would not promote the observance of a higher standard of care by the police but would in fact result in the significant diversion of police resources from the investigation and suppression of crime.

The claimants applied for leave to appeal to the House of Lords but their application was refused on 10 May 1993. The claimants had therefore exhausted their domestic right of appeal and so they turned to Europe and the European Convention on Human Rights which, at that time, had not been incorporated into English law. The claimants alleged that there had been a violation of Articles 2, 6, 8 and 13 of the Convention. The European Commission of Human Rights declared the application to be admissible on 17 May 1996. In its report of 1 July 1997 the Commission expressed the view that there had been a violation of Article 6(1) of the Convention but that there had been no violation of Articles 2 and 8 and that no separate issue arose under Article 13. The case was then referred to the European Court of Human Rights on 22 September 1997.

The Court gave its judgement on 28 October 1998. The Court concluded that there had been no violation of Article 2 of the Convention which provides that "everyone's right to life shall be protected by law".[32] Equally there had been no violation of Article 8 which states that "everyone has the right to respect for his

---

[28] *supra* n.2, at 354.

[29] *Ibid.*, at 353.

[30] *Ibid.*, at 354.

[31] *Ibid.*

[32] While the court stated that it was sufficient for the applicants to show that the authorities had not done all that could be reasonably expected of them to avoid a real and immediate risk to life of which they had or ought to have had knowledge, on the facts the court concluded that the applicants had "failed to point to any decisive stage in the sequence of the events leading up the tragic shooting when, it could be said that the police knew or ought to have known that the lives of the Osman family were at real and immediate risk from Paget-Lewis": see *supra* n.3, at 225. All that the applicants could do was to point to a series of "missed opportunities" by the police but nothing that would have "enabled the police to neutralise the threat posed by Paget-Lewis". Three judges dissented (Judges De Meyer, Lopes Rocha and Casadevall) on this particular issue and found that there had in fact been a violation of Art. 2.

private and family life".[33] The Court also concluded that there was no separate issue under Article 13 of the Convention.[34] But it did find that Article 6(1) was applicable and that it had been violated. The Court was unanimous in reaching this conclusion. On the applicability of Article 6 the Court concluded that:

> the applicants must be taken to have had a right, derived from the law of negligence, to seek an adjudication on the admissibility and merits of an arguable claim that they were in a relationship of proximity to the police, that the harm caused was foreseeable and that in the circumstances it was fair, just and reasonable not to apply the exclusionary rule outlined in the *Hill* case. In the view of the Court the assertion of that right by the applicants is in itself sufficient to ensure the applicability of Art 6(1) of the Convention.[35]

Having found that Article 6(1) was applicable the Court turned to consider whether it had been violated. While the Court recognised that the right contained in Article 6(1) may be subject to limitations, it concluded that "a limitation will not be compatible with Art 6(1) if it does not pursue a legitimate aim and if there is not a reasonable relationship of proportionality between the means employed and the aim sought to be achieved".[36] The Court concluded that there was not such a relationship of proportionality. This was so for a number of reasons: (i) the applicants' claim "never fully proceeded to trial in that there was never any determination on its merits nor on the facts on which it was based",[37] (ii) no consideration was given to "competing public interest considerations" which pointed in the direction of the imposition of liability upon the police,[38] (iii) the applicants' claim involved the alleged failure to protect the life of a child so that the harm sustained was of "the most serious nature",[39] (iv) the allegations made by the applicants were of "grave negligence as opposed to minor acts of incompetence"[40] on the part of the police, (v) an action against Mr Paget-Lewis or against the local education psychiatrist would not have enabled the applicants to ascertain why the police did not take action sooner against Mr Paget-Lewis and (vi) the applicants were "entitled to have the police account for their actions and omissions in adversarial proceedings".[41] The Court therefore concluded that there had been a violation of Article 6(1) and it awarded the applicants damages of £10,000 each together with a sum of £30,000 in respect of their costs.

---

[33] The reasons given for the conclusion that there had been no breach of Art. 8 were very similar to those given in relation to Art. 2, namely that the applicants had not established that the police knew or ought to have known at the time that Paget-Lewis represented a real and immediate risk to the physical integrity of Ahmet Osman. Three judges (Judges De Meyer, Lopes Rocha and Casadevall) dissented on this particular issue and found that there had in fact been a violation of Art. 8.

[34] However one judge did consider it necessary to examine the applicants' complaints under Art. 13.

[35] *Supra* n.3, at 229.

[36] *Ibid.*, at 231.

[37] *Ibid.*, at 232.

[38] *Ibid.*

[39] *Ibid.*

[40] *Ibid.*

[41] *Ibid.*

III. THE REACTION TO *OSMAN*

The decision of the European Court of Human Rights in *Osman* has been the subject of a considerable amount of discussion and analysis, much of it hostile. The hostility has not been confined to academic commentators. It has extended to the judiciary. Thus Lord Browne-Wilkinson has stated that he found the decision in *Osman* "extremely difficult to understand"[42] while Lord Hoffmann, writing extra-judicially, stated that "this decision fills me with apprehension".[43] Lord Cooke has been rather more restrained, simply noting that the decision in *Osman* "seems to be somewhat controversial in England".[44] Academic commentary has been more mixed.[45] Some have been supportive[46] while others have been distinctly hostile.[47] When seeking to evaluate *Osman* there are two dangers which we must avoid. The first is to minimise or trivialise the decision. To do so would be to make a profound mistake because it is not possible to ring-fence private law and to pretend that human rights law will not intrude into it. The *extent* of the intrusion is presently a matter of debate; the fact that it has occurred is not. The second danger is to exaggerate the significance and scope of *Osman*. This is a particular danger for tort lawyers. The fear of opening the floodgates is an ever-present one for many tort lawyers and this can lead to unwarranted prophecies of doom and destruction. Indeed, the prophets of doom have been quick to seize upon the decision in *Osman* and to subject it to criticism. However, it is not my purpose here to rehearse the arguments which have been advanced either in support of *Osman* or by way of criticism of it. Rather I wish to ascertain the options which are open to a court which is faced with an *Osman*-type fact situation.

---

[42] *Barrett* v. *Enfield London Borough Council* [1999] 3 WLR 79 (hereinafter *Barrett*), 84. In *Palmer* v. *Tees Health Authority* [1999] Lloyd's Rep. Med. 351 (hereinafter *Palmer*), Stuart-Smith LJ (at 354) and Pill LJ (at 362) expressed their agreement with the opinion of Lord Browne-Wilkinson.

[43] Lord Hoffmann, "Human Rights and the House of Lords" (1999) 62 *MLR* 159, 164.

[44] *Darker* v. *Chief Constable of the West Midlands Police* [2000] 3 WLR 747 (hereinafter *Darker*), 759.

[45] See L. Hoyano, "Policing Flawed Police Investigations: Unravelling the Blanket" (1999) 62 *MLR* 912; T. Weir, "Down Hill—All The Way?" [1999] *CLJ* 4; M. Lunney, "A Tort Lawyer's View of *Osman* v. *United Kingdom*" (1999) 10 *King's College L J* 238; M. Vranken, "Duty of Care, Public Policy, and the European Convention on Human Rights: *Osman* v. *United Kingdom*" (1999) 7 *Torts L J* 40; G Monti, "*Osman* v. *UK*—Transforming English Negligence Law into French Administrative Law" (1999) 48 *Intl. & Comp. L Q* 757; B. Markesinis, J.B. Auby, D. Coester-Waltjen and S. Deakin, *Tortious Liability of Statutory Bodies: A Comparative and Economic Analysis of Five English Cases* (Oxford, Hart Publishing, 1999), especially at 96–104; P. Gilliker, "*Osman* and Police Immunity in the English Law of Torts" (2000) 20 *Legal Stud.* 372 and C. Gearty 'Unravelling *Osman*' (2001) 64 *MLR* 159.

[46] See, for example, Markesinis, Auby, Coester-Waltjen and Deakin, *supra* n.45 and Gilliker, *supra* n.45.

[47] See, for example, Weir, *supra* n.45 and Lunney, *supra* n.45.

IV. *OSMAN* REPLAYED

There are a number of options open to a judge faced by a replay of the facts in *Osman*. It is important to explore the range of options with some care because it is only by doing so that one can explore the potential scope of *Osman*. The options are: (i) follow the decision of the Court of Appeal in *Osman* v. *Ferguson* and effectively ignore the decision of the European Court of Human Rights; (ii) strike out the claim on public policy grounds, but after giving fuller consideration to the range of competing public policy issues; (iii) strike out the claim on the ground that there was a lack of proximity between the claimants and the Metropolitan police; (iv) strike out the claim after a fuller consideration of the facts of the case; (v) strike out the claim after making findings of fact on the evidence, (vi) allow the case to proceed to full trial, where it may or may not succeed. Given that this is not an essay on English tort law, these options will not be explored in great detail. If suffices to explore the options before offering some concluding remarks upon the possible impact of *Osman* on the tort of negligence in English law.

1. Ignoring *Osman* v. *UK*

The first option is to follow the decision of the Court of Appeal in *Osman* v. *Ferguson* and effectively ignore the decision of the European Court of Human Rights in *Osman* v. *UK*. This option is not one which is open to the English courts, however much they may dislike the reasoning of the European Court. Section 2(1) of the Human Rights Act 1998 provides that the courts when "determining a question which has arisen in connection with a Convention right must take into account any . . . judgment . . . of the European Court of Human Rights". To ignore *Osman* v. *UK* would be to act inconsistently with section 2(1).[48] Of course the picture would change completely if the European Court of Human Rights were itself to depart from *Osman*. But in *Z* v. *United Kingdom*[49] the European Court chose to distinguish *Osman* rather than depart from it and so it is extremely unlikely that the court will elect to depart from *Osman*.

So the judges cannot stick their heads in the sand and pretend that *Osman* never happened. Nevertheless it is interesting to note that there has been a marked reluctance, especially on the part of some of the judges in the House of Lords, to mention *Osman*, never mind place any emphasis upon it. In recent months the House of Lords seems to have become more reluctant to strike out

---

[48] The fact that the courts are obliged to take *Osman* into account once the Human Rights Act comes into force was expressly recognised by Lord Cooke in *Darker, supra* n.44, at 759.

[49] *Supra* n.1. The likely implications of this decision are noted briefly in a postscript to this essay.

negligence claims[50] but it has not invoked *Osman* as a justification for its more liberal approach. On the contrary, their Lordships appear at times to have gone out of their way to state that it was not necessary for them to place any reliance upon *Osman* in reaching their decision not to strike out the claim.[51] The influence of *Osman* thus appears to be covert rather than overt but there can be little doubt that it is there[52] and it is not an option for the English courts effectively to ignore *Osman*.

2. A fuller consideration of the policy issues

The second option is to give fuller consideration to the competing public policy issues before striking out the claim on the ground that it was not fair, just and reasonable to impose a duty of care on the police in the investigation and suppression of crime. One of the criticisms levelled by the European Court of Human Rights against the decision of the Court of Appeal in *Osman* v. *Ferguson* was that the judges had failed to give consideration to "competing public interest considerations" which pointed in the direction of the imposition

---

[50] See, for example, *Waters* v. *Commissioner of Police of the Metropolis* [2000] 1 WLR 1607; *Phelps* v. *Hillingdon London Borough Council* [2000] 3 WLR 776 (hereinafter *Phelps*); *Arthur J.S. Hall & Co (a firm)* v. *Simon* [2000] 3 WLR 543 (hereinafter *Arthur*); *W* v. *Essex County Council* [2000] 1 WLR 601 and *Barrett, supra* n.42.

[51] Thus in *Barrett, supra* n.42, only Lord Browne-Wilkinson referred to *Osman* (at 84–6) and then in critical terms. The majority reached their decision without the need to rely on *Osman* (Lord Hutton expressly stated, at 115, that it was unnecessary for him to "discuss the implications" of *Osman*). A similar reluctance can be found in other cases. Thus in *W* v. *Essex, supra* n.50, *Osman* v. *UK* was cited to the House of Lords but was not mentioned in the speeches. In *Phelps, supra* n.50, Lord Slynn found it unnecessary to consider *Osman* (at 802), while Lord Clyde made only passing reference to the case (at 808–9). The speeches in *Arthur, supra* n.50, are more equivocal. Only Lord Hobhouse (at 607) made express reference to the decision in *Osman* v. *UK* but the other speeches did display a greater willingness to consider the implications of Art. 6. As one might expect Lord Hoffmann found it unnecessary to consider Art. 6 (at 578) but Lord Hope (at 581–3 and 589), Lord Hutton (at 605) and, to a lesser extent, Lord Millett (at 624) all gave consideration to the impact of Art. 6 upon the negligence claim. *Osman* was distinguished by Lord Hope in *Holland* v. *Lampen-Wolfe* [2000] 1 WLR 1573 (hereinafter *Holland*), 1578 and by Lord Cooke in *Darker, supra* n.44, at 759. A further passing reference to *Osman* can be found in the speech of Lord Clyde in *Horvath* v. *Secretary of State for the Home Department* [2000] 3 WLR 379, 398.

[52] Thus in *Palmer, supra* n.42, Pill LJ stated (at 360) that the decision in *Osman* v. *UK* "weighed heavily" upon the decision of the House of Lords in *Barrett, supra* n.42. He so concluded notwithstanding the fact that the majority did not find it necessary to consider *Osman* (see *supra* n.51). Nevertheless his inference seems correct. The Court of Appeal seems to be much more willing than the House of Lords to give consideration to *Osman* and to assess its impact on the English law of tort: see, for example *L and P* v. *Reading Borough Council*, unreported, CA, 12 March 2001; *Wilson* v. *First County Trust* [2001] 2 WLR 302, 313 (Sir Andrew Morritt V.-C.); *S* v. *Gloucestershire County Council* [2000] 3 All ER 346 370–3 (May LJ); *Kent* v. *Griffiths* [2000] 2 All ER 474 (hereinafter *Kent*), 484–5 (Lord Woolf MR); *Jarvis* v. *Hampshire County Council* [2000] 2 FCR 310 (hereinafter *Jarvis*), 333–6 (Morritt LJ) and 342–4 (Chadwick LJ) and *Gower* v. *London Borough of Bromley* [1999] ELR 356 (hereinafter *Gower*), 361–2 (Auld LJ). The discussion in *Jarvis* is, perhaps, particularly noteworthy on the ground that the House of Lords in *Phelps, supra* n.50, reversed the decision in *Jarvis* but did not find it necessary to consider the decision in *Osman* (see *supra* n.51).

of liability upon the police.[53] In defence of the Court of Appeal it should be pointed out that that balancing exercise had already been carried out by the House of Lords in *Hill*[54] which was binding upon the Court of Appeal. The principal issue for the Court of Appeal was whether or not the facts of *Osman* fell within the scope of the principle laid down in *Hill* and, as has been noted,[55] the Court of Appeal concluded that it fell squarely within the scope of that decision.[56] The decision of the Court of Appeal to follow the "public policy" reasoning in *Hill* seems entirely reasonable; indeed, no other course of action was open to it. Not only would it be unreasonable to expect the courts to engage in a fresh balancing exercise in every case, it would also be contrary to the requirements of the doctrine of precedent.

So does *Osman* make it impossible to strike out a claim on the ground that it is contrary to public policy or not fair, just and reasonable to impose a duty of care? The answer appears to be that it is not impossible, but it is certainly very difficult. A blanket immunity for a particular defendant or class of defendant is now unlikely[57] to survive judicial scrutiny.[58] The reason for this appears to be that the Court must always have regard to the facts and circumstances of the individual case and consider whether or not the defendant is entitled to claim the immunity on the facts of the case.

But it does not follow from this that it is impossible for a court to strike out a claim on public policy grounds. A distinction can be drawn between a blanket immunity and a general immunity, to which there are, or may be, exceptions.

---

[53] *Supra* n.3, at 232. It should also be noted that the court expressly approved of the decision of the Court of Appeal in *Swinney* v. *Chief Constable of the Northumbria Police Force* [1997] QB 464 (hereinafter *Swinney*) where such a balancing exercise was in fact carried out.

[54] *Supra* n.23.

[55] See *supra*, text accompanying nn. 25–31.

[56] The Court of Appeal might have concluded that the ground of decision in *Hill* was that there was no relationship of proximity between the parties so that the analysis of the policy issues in *Hill* was all obiter. This would have been a very narrow reading of the case. The applicant's claim was struck out on two grounds (lack of proximity and reasons of policy) and not just one.

[57] It is not impossible. Thus, a witness has an immunity from suit in negligence in respect of anything said in the witness box: *Taylor* v. *Director of the Serious Fraud Office* [1999] 2 AC 177; *Darker*, *supra* n.44. Similarly, in *Holland*, *supra* n.51, the claimant alleged that she had been defamed by the defendant, who at the time was acting as an education services officer at a US military base in England. The defendant claimed sovereign immunity and it was held by the House of Lords that he was entitled to such immunity and that the conferral of immunity upon the defendant did not violate Art. 6 of the European Convention on Human Rights. Lord Hope (at 1578) distinguished *Osman* on the ground that it was concerned with the grant of an immunity under domestic law and it did not involve any international law obligation, whereas Lord Millett stated (at 1588) that Art. 6 did not extend the scope of a court's power of adjudication so that it could not confer on a national court a power which it did not have as a matter of international law. The fact that sovereign immunity confers a form of blanket immunity did not of itself involve a violation of Art. 6.

[58] See, for example, *Arthur*, *supra* n.50, in which the House of Lords held that an advocate no longer had an immunity from suit in negligence in respect of the conduct of litigation or work intimately connected with litigation. The outcome of the case was not particularly surprising but the reasoning of the court may have occasioned some surprise. Rather than go down the Art. 6 route (as many had predicted: see, for example, R. Money-Kyrle, "Advocates' Immunity after *Osman*" (1999) 149 *New LJ* 945, 981), the House of Lords chose to re-examine the question as a matter of common law and made limited use of Art. 6 (on which see *supra* n.57).

While the former is unlikely to be acceptable, the latter may be consistent with Article 6. Thus in *Kinsella* v. *Chief Constable of Nottinghamshire*[59] Tucker J stated that *Osman*[60] demonstrates:

> that the general rule does not provide a blanket immunity in all cases. In each case, a balancing exercise may have to be carried out. It may be necessary to weigh the public policy considerations of ensuring that police forces are able to carry out their public duties and functions in the investigation and suppression of crime without being exposed to potential liability for negligence on the one hand, against other matters of public interest, such as the protection of informers, on the other. Where after such an exercise has been performed, it is apparent to the Court that the general rule is not outweighed by any other considerations, then the immunity continues to exist and an allegation of negligence cannot survive.

The Court must therefore have regard to the facts and circumstances of the individual case, in particular to those facts and circumstances which suggest that liability should be imposed upon the defendant. It is likely that the courts will now be reluctant to strike out a claim on the ground that it is not fair, just and reasonable to impose a duty of care, but a court which does so, having regard to the facts and circumstances of the individual case, may not be acting inconsistently with *Osman*.[61]

3. No proximity

The third option open to a court is to strike out the claim on the ground that there was no relationship of proximity between the parties. There is at least one obvious obstacle in the way of such a conclusion, namely that the Court of Appeal in *Osman* v. *Ferguson* held that there was arguably a relationship of proximity between the police and the claimants. It is, however, important to note that the argument based on a lack of proximity between the parties was a subsidiary argument of the defendants. The principal argument was based on public policy. Today that order would undoubtedly be reversed. For the reasons which have already been given, a defendant would be very reluctant to go into court relying exclusively or principally upon public policy. So the defendant would lead with the argument that there was no proximity between the parties. There are two issues which arise here. The first is whether, consistently with *Osman* v. *UK*, a lack of

---

[59] *The Times*, 5 May 1999. On the facts the claim in negligence was in fact struck out. Tucker J stated that he had reached the "firm conclusion" that there was nothing on the facts of the case which was capable of "giving rise to such countervailing considerations as would outweigh the general public policy of preserving the well-established rule of immunity for police forces against suits of negligence". See also *Donnelly* v. *Chief Constable of Lincolnshire*, unreported, QBD, 26 July 2000, Gray J.

[60] *The Times*, 5 May 1999. He also made reference at this point to the decision of the Court of Appeal in *Swinney*, *supra* n.53, a case that is discussed in more detail *infra*, text accompanying n.65.

[61] This seems to emerge from the decisions of the European Court of Human Rights in *Z* v. *United Kingdom* and *TP and KM* v. *United Kingdom* which are discussed in the postscript to this essay.

proximity between the parties can act as a justification for striking out a claim in negligence and the second is whether or not it is open to a court in a case such as *Osman* to find that there was no relationship of proximity between the parties.

As to the first of these issues, the judges in the European Court in *Osman* v. *UK* did not suggest that proximity was an illegitimate filter; on the contrary, they appeared to accept that a court was entitled to strike out a claim on the basis that there was no relationship of proximity between the parties,[62] a point subsequently accepted by the Court of Appeal in *Palmer*.[63] Yet the proposition that lack of proximity is a legitimate ground on which a court can strike out a claim in negligence is not without its difficulties. In particular, "proximity" has proved to be a particularly elusive concept in the tort of negligence[64] and it is not always easy to disentangle it from the factors which are taken into account when deciding whether or not it is fair, just and reasonable to impose a duty of care.[65] But one consequence of *Osman* is to make it necessary to draw a sharper line of demarcation because of the recognition of the fact that proximity is a legitimate filter, whereas public policy is at best a filter of a very dubious kind.

This leads on to the second issue, namely whether or not a court faced with a replay of the facts of *Osman* could legitimately conclude that there was no relationship of proximity between the parties and strike out the claim on that ground. While McCowan LJ did conclude in the Court of Appeal that there was arguably a relationship of proximity between the parties his analysis of the issue was very brief and, further, Beldam LJ expressly reserved his opinion on the point. So the issue may yet be open to argument. The resolution of the issue is not entirely easy, largely because of the uncertainties which surround the meaning of the word "proximity". It can be argued that there was a relationship of proximity between the parties because the police knew of Mr Paget-Lewis' obsession with Ahmet Osman, knew that acts of violence had taken place and that Mr Paget-Lewis was in all likelihood the person responsible for some, if not all, of these acts and they also knew that members of the Osman family, and Ahmet Osman in particular, were in some danger. Support for the proposition that there was a relationship of proximity between the parties can be gleaned from the case of *Swinney*[66] where it was held that there was arguably a relationship of proximity between the police and a police informer. But *Swinney* is not decisive because it is easier to demonstrate that the police have assumed a responsibility towards a police informer than it is to show that they have assumed a responsibility towards a member of

---

[62] *Supra* n.3, at 230 ("the combined effect of the strict tests of proximity and foreseeability provided limitation enough to prevent untenable cases ever reaching a hearing and to confine liability to those cases where the police have caused serious loss through truly negligent actions").

[63] *Supra* n.42, at 356 (Stuart-Smith LJ) and at 362 (Pill LJ).

[64] There are numerous judicial dicta to this effect: see, for example, *Caparo Industries plc* v. *Dickman* [1990] 2 AC 605 (hereinafter *Caparo Industries plc*), 618 (Lord Bridge); *Alcock* v. *Chief Constable of South Yorkshire* [1992] 1 AC 310, 410 and *Stovin* v. *Wise* [1996] AC 923, 932 (Lord Nicholls).

[65] See the cases cited *supra* at n.63 and the discussion of this issue by the Court of Appeal in *Palmer*, *supra* n.42.

[66] *Supra* n.53. See also *L and P* v. *Reading Borough Council*, unreported, CA, 12 March 2001.

the public who is known to them to be a possible, even a likely, victim of crime. *Osman* falls somewhere in between *Swinney* and *Hill*.[67] It is probably in a grey area, and as such it would be very difficult, if not impossible, for a court to strike out the claim on the ground of lack of proximity because it would be necessary to examine the facts in greater detail in order to ascertain what the police actually knew and whether or not they assumed, or could be held to have assumed, a responsibility towards the Osman family.[68]

The current position is less than satisfactory in that it encourages defendants to argue that there was no relationship of proximity between the parties in order to escape from *Osman* and strike out the claim. The somewhat elastic nature of the concept of "proximity" has the further consequence that it can be used by the courts as a means by which the decision in *Osman* can be evaded. In this sense "proximity" can act as a smokescreen behind which a judge can consider factors which otherwise would be considered openly under the rubric of "policy" or "fair, just and reasonable". It is unlikely that the European Court of Human Rights will permit a judge to use proximity in this way and so nullify or confine the decision in *Osman*. A court which attempted to evade *Osman* in this way would in all probability confer on the European Court a "new invitation . . . to intervene in our law".[69] Thus far the English courts have not attempted to evade *Osman* in this way. While there has been recognition of the fact that a lack of proximity can justify a decision to strike out, at the same time the courts have acknowledged that a lack of proximity should not be used as a passport to strike out a claim in negligence but that regard must always be had to all the facts and circumstances of the case.[70]

4. Give greater consideration to the facts and circumstances of the individual case

The fourth option is to strike out the claim after giving fuller consideration to the facts and circumstances of the individual case. It can be argued that this is not in fact an additional option but that it is merely a variant of the second and third options. This may well be true but it is nevertheless important to note that one

[67] *Supra* n.23, where the victim was a member of the public who was not known by name to the police and the assailant had been interviewed by the police in conmnection with the investigation but had not been identified by the police as the likely perpetrator of the series of crimes in question. It is interesting to speculate how *Hill* would be decided under the *Osman* standard. At no time did the European Court suggest that the result in *Hill* was wrong. But at the same time it disapproved of the policy factors relied upon by the House of Lords in *Hill*. So if *Hill* remains correct it must be on the basis that there was no relationship of proximity between the parties.

[68] There remains some uncertainty about the actual facts of *Osman*. For example, the government denied that Mr Paget-Lewis had told the police some of the things which he was alleged to have said (for example, the reference to the Hungerford incident) and it also denied that the police had given the Osman family assurances about their safety.

[69] Markesinis, Auby, Coester-Waltjen & Deakin, *supra* n.45, at 120. Although the European Court of Human Rights in *Z* v. *United Kingdom* and *K P* and *T M* v. *United Kingdom* did not in fact accept a new invitation to intervene in English law. On the contrary, it interpreted its own decision in *Osman* narrowly. See further the postscript to this essay.

[70] See in particular, *Gower*, *supra* n.52, at 362, *per* Auld LJ.

feature of the decision of the European Court in *Osman* is that it gave much fuller consideration to the facts of the case than did the Court of Appeal.[71] At the time at which *Osman* was decided no evidence was admissible on an application to strike out a claim on the ground that it disclosed no reasonable cause of action. The court simply proceeded on the assumption that the facts were as they were pleaded by the plaintiff. In consequence the factual basis upon which the court proceeded was very limited. In theory this should not have caused plaintiffs any hardship because the assumptions of fact were all made in their favour. On the other hand such an apparently casual approach to the facts might have left plaintiffs with a sense of injustice in that no one in court was apparently willing to take more than a cursory interest in what was alleged to have taken place.

Since *Osman* v. *Ferguson* was decided the Civil Procedure Rules 1998 have come into force. These Rules have made far-reaching changes to the conduct of litigation in England and Wales and have given to the courts much greater powers of case management. One change which must be noted in the present context is that there is no longer an embargo on the court receiving evidence in an application to strike out a claim.[72] Further, under Rule 24.2 of the CPR the court has power to give summary judgment against a claimant where the court considers that the claimant has no real prospect of succeeding on the claim and there is no other reason why the case should be disposed of at a trial. Once again there is no embargo on the court considering evidence so that the court need no longer proceed on the basis of an assumed state of affairs. It can have regard to the evidence and to actual facts. Some indication of the likely consequences of these changes can be gleaned from the following passage from the judgment of May LJ in *S* v. *Gloucestershire*[73]:

> For a summary judgment application to succeed in a case such as these where a strike out application would not succeed, the Court will first need to be satisfied that all sub-stantial facts relevant to the allegations of negligence, which are reasonably capable of being before the Court, are before the Court; that these facts are undisputed or that there is no real prospect of successfully disputing them; and that there is no real prospect of oral evidence affecting the Court's assessment of the facts. There may be cases where there are gaps in the evidence but where the Court concludes, for instance from the passage of time, that there is no real prospect of the gaps being filled . . . Secondly, the Court will need to be satisfied that, upon these facts, there is no real prospect of the claim in negligence succeeding and that there is no other reason why the case should be disposed of at a trial. If by this process the Court does so conclude and gives summary judgment, there will, in my view, have been proper judicial scrutiny of the detailed facts of the particular case such as to constitute a fair hearing in accordance with art 6 of the convention.[74]

---

[71] A point developed in more detail *infra*, text accompanying nn. 83–6.

[72] The power of the court to strike a claim is contained in Rule 3.4(2) of the Civil Procedure Rules. The fact that there is no longer an embargo on the court receiving evidence was judicially acknowledged by May LJ in *S* v. *Gloucestershire, supra* n.52, at 372.

[73] *Supra* n.52.

[74] *Supra* n.52, at 373.

These procedural changes may go some way towards meeting the objections expressed by the European Court in *Osman*, especially when taken alongside the new-found reluctance of the English courts to strike out a claim on the ground that it is not just and reasonable to impose a duty of care on the defendant. But they might not go all the way. Two of the factors relied upon by the European Court in *Osman* were that the court should have regard to the nature of the harm suffered by the claimant and the extent of the negligence which has been alleged against the defendant. In other words, the greater the loss suffered by the claimant and the greater the extent of the negligence of the defendant, the less willing the judge should be to strike out the claim at a preliminary stage. The first of these issues does not present an enormous challenge to the English courts because they have in practice been more willing to find the existence of a duty of care where the harm which the claimant has suffered is physical damage rather than economic loss or psychological harm.[75] But the second does present more of a challenge on the ground that English law has not traditionally distinguished between different degrees of negligence.[76] A change made to the tort of negligence to take account of the extent of the defendant's negligence cannot be implemented by making some procedural changes and a greater judicial reluctance to strike out claims. Nor can it be done by placing more emphasis on proximity in deciding whether or not to strike out a claim because proximity focuses on the nature of the relationship between the parties and not on the conduct of the defendant. The obligation to have regard to the facts and circumstances of the case in deciding whether or not to strike out a claim may therefore require the English courts to give attention to matters (such as the extent of the defendant's negligence) which were previously the subject of little or no attention.[77] If this is the case, the change should be recognised openly and not hidden away as simply another factor to be taken into account when deciding whether or not there is a relationship of proximity between the parties.

5. Make findings of fact

The fifth option open to the judge is to strike out the claim after making some findings of fact. This option differs from the previous one only in that in this version it is not enough for the judge simply to read through the evidence which has been adduced by the parties; he or she must actually make some findings of fact as to what caused the loss in respect of which the claimant has

---

[75] See, for example, *Murphy* v. *Brentwood District Council* [1991] 1 AC 398, 498 (Lord Oliver) and *Caparo Industries plc, supra* n.64, at 618 (Lord Bridge). This difference of treatment has sometimes been hidden by judicial insistence that the same tests be applied by the court whether the harm suffered is physical damage or economic loss: see *Marc Rich & Co AG* v. *Bishop Rock Marine Co Ltd* (*The Nicholas H*) [1996] AC 211.

[76] *Palmer, supra* n.42.

[77] See further *infra*, text accompanying n.98.

brought the action. In some cases claimants simply want to find out what happened to their loved ones. They do not wish to be met by a defendant who says that he is prepared to assume that the facts are as alleged by the claimant. The claimant wants to be given an explanation for what happened. He or she wants to see the defendant admit that the harm was caused by the fault of the defendant. There are indications in the judgment of the European Court in *Osman* that this point was recognised by the Court. Thus the Court stated that:

> Neither an action against Paget-Lewis nor against Dr Ferguson, the ILEA psychiatrist, would have enabled [the claimants] to secure answers to the basic question which underpinned their civil action, namely why did the police not take action sooner to prevent Paget-Lewis from exacting a deadly retribution against Ali and Ahmet Osman. They may or may not have failed to convince the domestic Court that the police were negligent in the circumstances. However, they were entitled to have the police account for their actions and omissions in adversarial proceedings.[78]

It is not entirely clear what it means to say that the claimants were entitled to "have the police account for their actions and omissions in adversarial proceedings". Does it mean that the claimants were entitled to cross-examine the police in order to discover what the police had done and why they had done it? Or would it suffice for a judge to explain to them that, having read the papers, there was simply no basis in law for the claim which they wished to bring? Article 6 does not confer on the claimant the right to cross-examine a potential defendant so it would be going too far to conclude that the claimants were entitled to cross-examine the police involved in the investigation of the various incidents which preceded the attack on Ahmet Osman and the death of Mr Osman. But the claimants were entitled to their day in court and that involved more than a dismissal of the claim on the basis of the facts as alleged in the pleadings. While a court may not be required by Article 6 to make findings of fact in every case, it should at the very least consider the evidence in greater detail than the Court of Appeal appeared to do in *Osman* v. *Ferguson* and it should not approach the legal issues on the basis of an assumed state of facts.

6. Proceed to trial

The final option is to refuse to strike out the claim and allow it to proceed to trial where the judge can decide on the evidence whether or not there has been a breach of duty and a sufficient causal connection between the breach and the loss. At this stage the court may conclude either that there has been a breach of duty or that there has not; but that will depend upon a careful evaluation of all the evidence. There are some signs that the English courts are now more reluctant to strike out claims at the duty stage and that they will leave it to the breach

---

[78] *Supra* n.3, at 232.

stage to weed out unmeritorious claims.[79] It is, however, important to stress that *Osman* does not stand for the proposition that it is now impossible to strike out a claim prior to the trial of the action. It does make it more difficult for a court to strike out a claim but, for reasons which have already been given,[80] a court which has considered the competing public policy issues and which has examined the facts and circumstances of the case with sufficient care can strike out a claim which is clearly and obviously unmeritorious.

It is suggested that this option is in fact the most likely option to be chosen by a judge faced with a replay of the facts of *Osman*. It would be a bold judge who struck out the claim on the ground of a lack of proximity between the parties[81] and it is not easy to conceive of competing public policy issues which would have justified the court in striking out the claim on the ground of public policy at a preliminary stage.[82] The fourth option is the other serious contender. It may be possible for a judge to conclude, consistently with the approach set out by May LJ in his judgment in *S* v. *Gloucestershire*,[83] that the claim is obviously unmeritorious and either strike it out or give summary judgment against the claimants. A judge who is not prepared to take such a step is likely to allow the case to proceed to trial.

V.   *OSMAN*: A BRIEF EVALUATION

The decision in *Osman* has been the subject of considerable critical comment.[84] Here it will suffice to make three brief observations. The first is that, to some extent, *Osman* seems to rest on a perception of the tort system as some kind of public inquiry rather than a system of compensation for wrongfully inflicted harm. This can be seen most clearly in the Court's description of the "basic question which underpinned the civil action" in terms of ascertaining the reasons "why did the police not take action sooner to prevent Paget-Lewis from exacting a deadly retribution against Ali and Ahmet Osman".[85] This view of the function of the tort system is not one which is universally shared by tort lawyers and it may be that it over-states the point which the European Court was endeavouring to make.[86] It may be that the European Court was simply trying

---

[79] See, for example, *Barrett, supra* n.42; *W* v. *Essex, supra* n.50 and *Phelps, supra* n.50.

[80] See *supra*, text accompanying nn.57–61.

[81] See *supra*, text accompanying nn.62–70.

[82] That said, the European Court of Human Rights in *Z* v. *United Kingdom* and *K P* and *T M* v. *United Kingdom* did acknowledge that a judge can strike out a negligence claim after a "careful balancing of the policy reasons for and against the imposition of liability". The difficulty in a case such as *Osman* may lie in locating policy factors of sufficient weight to counter the policy reasons which point in the direction of the imposition of liability.

[83] *Supra* n.73.

[84] See generally *supra* n.45.

[85] *Supra* n.3, at 232.

[86] A point which emerges from the decisions in *Z* v. *United Kingdom* and *TP* and *KM* v. *United Kingdom*, which are discussed in a postscript to this essay.

to tell the English courts that they must work harder at ascertaining the facts of a case before deciding to strike out a claim as unarguable. Indeed, a notable feature of the decision of the Court in *Osman* and of the Commission in *TP and KM* v. *United Kingdom*[87] and *Z* v. *UK*[88] is the emphasis placed on the facts of the case. The account of the facts in *Z* is a particularly shocking account of children living in the most appalling conditions. In contrast the account of the facts given by the Court of Appeal in *Osman* v. *Ferguson* and by the House of Lords in *X* v. *Bedfordshire County Council*[89] is brief and, in the case of *X*, a sanitised version of the horrors set out in *Z*. However when we turn to the discussion of legal principle, the position may be said to be reversed. It can be said with some justification that the legal reasoning in *Osman*, *TP and KM* and *Z* is not of the highest legal order, whereas the quality of the legal reasoning in *X* (but not *Osman* v. *Ferguson*) is far more impressive. What may be required is an adjustment in the practice of the English appellate courts. Instead of engaging in an elaborate analysis of legal principle based on a partial or even shaky grasp of the facts, appellate courts must ensure that they have a firm grasp of the facts before striking out a claim as unarguable. In particular the practice of taking hypothetical fact situations and basing legal argument on these hypotheticals may require modification. Courts may have to learn to take the facts more seriously.

Secondly, *Osman* attaches significance to the idea that the claimant should have his day in court, apparently irrespective of the outcome of the case. In response to this the point can be made: what is the point of permitting a claim to proceed to trial if ultimately the claim is likely to fail? Is this not a waste of time and money? But it may be that what *Osman* is trying to tell us is that claimants should be entitled to ventilate their grievances in court even if they are ultimately doomed to fail. In other words, what was wrong in *Osman* was not the result (that the police were not liable) but that the claimants were not given an appropriate opportunity to bring the matter before the court. But the arguments are not all one way on this point. The cost of litigation in England is very high and this is likely to remain so over the short to medium term. A defendant who is faced with a trial which may last anywhere between one week and two months may well be inclined to settle because, even if he wins the litigation, he may be unable to recover all of his costs from the claimant. In this sense *Osman* may well lead to "the reluctant settlement of an unmeritorious claim".[90] If a defendant cannot find a reasonably quick way of striking out an unmeritorious claim, the likelihood is that the defendant will be persuaded by its insurers or its legal advisors to settle the claim even if the claim is largely devoid of merit. It could be argued that the European Court in *Osman* has failed to pay sufficient attention of the right of the defendant to obtain a fair trial.

[87] *Supra* n.1.
[88] *Supra* n.1.
[89] *Supra* n.1.
[90] Weir, *supra* n.45. However the European Court in *Z* v. *United Kingdom* and *TP* and *KM* v. *United Kingdom* drew back from this wider interpretation of *Osman* and it acknowledged that there is little point in embarking upon the "expensive and time-consuming process" of hearing evidence if the end-result will be the dismissal of the applicants' claim.

Thirdly, in so far as the decision in *Osman* appears to make it more difficult for a court to strike out a claim at an early stage, it can be said to run counter to the central thrust of the recent civil procedure reforms in England and Wales. Of course, much here depends on the scope of *Osman* itself. This point was recognised by Lord Woolf MR in *Kent* v. *Griffiths*[91] when he stated that:

> it would be wrong for the Osman decision to be taken as a signal that, even when the legal position is clear and an investigation of the facts would provide no assistance, the Courts should be reluctant to dismiss cases which have no real prospect of success. Courts are now encouraged, where an issue or issues can be identified which will resolve or help to resolve litigation, to take that issue or those issues at an early stage of the proceedings so as to achieve expedition and save expense. There is no question of any contravention of art 6 of the ECHR in so doing. Defendants as well as claimants are entitled to a fair trial and it is an important part of the case management function to bring proceedings to an end as expeditiously as possible.[92]

It is important to bear in mind here that Lord Woolf is the architect of the new Civil Procedure Rules in England. Part 1 of the Civil Procedure Rules sets out the overriding objective of the new rules in the following terms:

(1) These Rules are a new procedural code with the overriding objective of enabling the Court to deal with cases justly.
(2) Dealing with a case justly includes, so far as is practicable—
    (a) ensuring that the parties are on an equal footing;
    (b) saving expense;
    (c) dealing with the case in ways which are proportionate—
        (i) to the amount of money involved;
        (ii) to the importance of the case;
        (iii) to the complexity of the issues; and
        (iv) to the financial position of each party;
    (d) ensuring that it is dealt with expeditiously and fairly; and
    (e) allotting to it an appropriate share of the Court's resources, while taking into account the need to allot resources to other cases.[93]

To the extent that the decision of the European Court in *Osman* has made it more difficult for courts to strike out cases at an early stage it can be said that it runs counter to the thrust of the civil procedure reforms in England, at least in terms of their emphasis on speed and economy. It may also be that the European Court has failed to take account of the cost of civil litigation in England. Thus Tony Weir has stated that:

> One wonders if the judges in Strasbourg were fully aware of quite how expensive in time and trouble litigation in England actually is, involving, as it does, discovery of

---

[91] *Supra* n.52.
[92] *Ibid.*, at 485.
[93] CPR Part 1 Rule 1.1. The court must seek to give effect to the overriding objective when it exercises any power given to it by the Rules or interprets any rule. To this extent, the overriding objective can be said to permeate the rules as a whole.

documents, oral testimony of witnesses and the use of one of a small number of judges
. . . or, indeed, of how effective the threat or provoking such a waste of time and trouble can be in eliciting the reluctant settlement of an unmeritorious claim.[94]

Of course the point can be made that the new Civil Procedure Rules may themselves contain a partial answer to the problems highlighted in *Osman*. In so far as the rules succeed in bringing down the cost of litigation the need to make frequent use of the strike-out procedure may be reduced. Allied to this are the case management powers given to the judges.[95] So it may be that the new rules can be operated consistently with the decision in *Osman* but there does appear to be a difference in philosophy between the two. The emphasis in *Osman* is upon the importance to the claimant of his or her day in court, while in the Civil Procedure Rules the emphasis is upon the need to resolve disputes quickly and efficiently, which in turns place less emphasis on the importance of formal court hearings.

VI. THE IMPACT OF *OSMAN* ON THE TORT OF NEGLIGENCE

The final issue relates to the impact which *Osman* may have on the development of the tort of negligence in England. Four brief observations can be made. The first relates to the scope of the decision in *Osman* and its impact on the future of the duty of care concept in English law. Is *Osman* to be seen purely in procedural terms (that is to say, in terms of the right of access to the court) or also in substantive terms (that is to say, the impact which it has on the tort of negligence itself)? It can be argued that *Osman* itself has no impact on substantive law because it does not dictate a particular outcome to the court hearing; the court hearing the case could have concluded that on the facts there was no negligence on the part of the defendants. While it is true that *Osman* does not dictate a particular finding on the question whether or not the police were negligent, it does have an impact on the substantive law of negligence in that it removes or reduces the defendants' ability to argue that, even if they had been negligent, they were still not liable to the claimants. And this is one of the major functions of the duty of care concept as it currently operates in English tort law. It enables a defendant to argue that, even if he or she has been negligent, still he or she is not liable to the defendant. Some authors have seen in *Osman* the demise of the duty of care concept itself. Thus it has been stated that the duty of care concept:

> has no real parallel in any of the modern civil law systems, is exceptionally vague and blunt. Its vagueness can either be used to conceal all meaningful discussion of the policy arguments that underlie these disputes or, conversely, turn the judicial process into an open-ended and unsubstantiated debate over value judgments. Either way, it seems

---

[94] Weir, *supra* n.45, at 6. Once again the European Court in *Z* v. *United Kingdom* and *K P and T M* v. *United Kingdom* recognised this point in adopting a narrow interpretation of *Osman*.

[95] On which see further *supra*, text accompanying n.72.

to be encouraging our Courts to impose, in practice if not in theory, blanket immunities, effectively preventing future litigants from asserting that the facts of their dispute justify a different legal outcome. For a long time English law has tolerated this essentially "unjust" result in the interests of what one could broadly describe as "administrative convenience". The growing constitutionalisation of private law, especially through the medium of human rights legislation, and the need for growing accountability, may, however, be about to defeat this peculiarity of English law. Not everyone will weep for the possible demise of a notion of a duty of care . . .[96]

It is perhaps too early to write the obituary of the duty of care concept in English law but it may be that it will pay a less prominent role in English tort law[97] in the future. To the extent that *Osman* has reduced the ability of defendants to strike out claims in negligence on the ground that no duty of care was owed to the claimant, the substantive law of tort has been changed.

Secondly, the decision appears to introduce new terminology into the law of tort. While administrative lawyers are familiar with the idea of proportionality, it may take tort lawyers some time to come to grips with the idea of proportionality as a tool for regulating the imposition of liability.[98] Both the European Court in *Osman* and the Commission in *KP and TM* and *Z* refer to "gross negligence" or "grave negligence", but as Stuart-Smith LJ observed in *Palmer* "in establishing liability in tort there are no gradations of negligence and the notion of gross negligence is not recognised".[99] But this view may not last. *Osman* may prove in the long run to have admitted gross negligence into English tort law by the back door.

The third point is whether or not *Osman* can be confined to cases of physical injury so that it has no impact on the recovery of economic loss. This is an important point in that English law has consistently adopted a restrictive approach to the recovery of pure economic loss in the tort of negligence.[100] There are references in *Osman* to the fact that the life of a child was at stake and this obviously weighs more in the scales than economic loss. This may be taken to suggest that the economic loss cases should not be open to review. On the other hand, if we return to the procedural focus of Article 6 and the right of access to the court, it can be maintained that these procedural considerations apply as much to claims to recover economic loss as they do to claims based on physical injury.

Finally the effect of *Osman* may be able to expose public authorities to greater liability in tort and this may have a significant impact on the role of public authorities in England. English law accepts that I am not my brother's keeper

---

[96] Markesinis, Auby, Coester-Waltjen and Deakin, *supra* n.45, at 3.

[97] Particularly in the light of the decision of the European Court in *Z* v. *United Kingdom* and *K P* and *T M* v. *United Kingdom*, discussed in a post-script to this essay.

[98] See, for example, *Palmer*, *supra* n.42, where counsel for the claimant argued (at 354) that "the requirement of proportionality must . . . be considered". The Court of Appeal, however, refused to extend the scope of liability "by some notion of proportionality based on the gravity of the negligence alleged or proved" (at 356).

[99] *Supra* n.42, at 356.

[100] See, for example, *Murphy* v. *Brentwood District Council* [1991] 1 AC 398 and *Caparo Industries plc*, *supra* n.64.

and so I am not as a general rule liable should I fail to intervene to save him from danger [101] but public authorities who stand back and allow harm to be inflicted on a third party may now stand in a different position.[102] Parents may not be liable in negligence for the way in which they bring up their children but the State as parent may be liable for failure to take reasonable care in bringing up children committed to its care.[103] This obviously raises a question why public authorities should be liable where private citizens would not be so liable. But it also raises a question about the consequences of imposing liability on public authorities. Most local authorities in England and Wales are strapped for cash and have to make difficult decisions about the allocation of scarce resources. They now face the prospect of having even fewer resources as a result of being ordered to pay damages to the victims of past misfortunes. In other words the courts must face up to the distributive consequences of their decisions.[104] Given the plight of local authorities and the National Health Service in the UK it is possible to argue that local authorities should be shielded to some extent from liability in negligence. Not everyone will agree with this. It can be argued that local authorities should not be shielded from liability in any way but rather should be exposed to the possibility of a claim in tort in order to give them an incentive to carry out their tasks with greater skill and care. The arguments on this point are obviously not all one way. Reasonable minds can differ on this issue. But, if this is the case, what is the justification to seeking to impose a particular solution to this problem in the name of human rights? As Tony Weir has put it:

> Nations should decide for themselves whether public funds should be directed to victims of past malfunction in public services or used to reduce the number of such malfunctions in the future.[105]

VII. POSTSCRIPT

On 10 May 2001 the Grand Chamber of the European Court of Human Rights gave judgment in the cases of *Z* v. *United Kingdom*[106] and *TP and KM* v. *United Kingdom*[107] in which the court distinguished *Osman* on grounds that are likely to limit considerably the impact of *Osman* on English tort law. The aim of this short postscript is not to engage in an extensive analysis of these important decisions but rather to highlight briefly their implications for *Osman* itself.

---

[101] *Dorset Yacht, supra* n.22, at 1060.

[102] Much here turns on the decision of the European Court of Human Rights in *Z* v. *UK, supra* n.1 and the postscript below.

[103] See, for example, *Barrett, supra* n.42, and *Phelps, supra* n.50.

[104] A rare, albeit controversial, example of this is provided by the speech of Lord Steyn in *McFarlane* v. *Tayside Health Board* [1999] 3 WLR 1301, especially 1318–20.

[105] Weir, *supra* n.45, at 7.

[106] *Supra* n.1.

[107] *Supra* n.1.

In *Z* v. *United Kingdom* the European Court held that there had been a violation of Articles 3 and 13[108] of the European Convention but, by a majority,[109] that there had been no violation of Article 6. In *TP and KM* v. *United Kingdom* it held that there had been a violation of Articles 8 and 13 but no violation of Article 6. The crucial point for present purposes lies in the finding in both cases that, while Article 6 was applicable to the applicants' case,[110] there had been no violation of the Article. This conclusion was rather unexpected given that it required the Court to adopt a narrow reading of its own decision in *Osman*.[111]

In many ways the decisions represent an uneasy settlement of the vigorous debate triggered by *Osman*. Without referring explicitly to the criticisms levelled against *Osman* by senior members of the English judiciary, the Court has adopted a restrained interpretation of *Osman* that takes account of many of the concerns expressed by its critics. At the same time the Court was careful to point out that the tort of negligence in England has moved on in cases such as *Barrett*[112] and *W* v. *Essex CC*[113] where, as has been noted,[114] the House of Lords declined to strike out the claimants' negligence claim. The Court can therefore claim, with some justification, that English law has moved in a direction that has brought it substantially into line with the requirements of Article 6. The European Court and the English judiciary can therefore both take something from this decision. The European Court can point to the changes made to English tort law as a result of the influence of *Osman,* while the English judiciary can in turn note that their expressions of concern have in all probability contributed to the restrained interpretation of *Osman*.

In terms of the different possible interpretations of *Osman* explored in this essay, the decisions in *Z* v. *United Kingdom* and *TP and KM* v. *United Kingdom* probably come closest to the second option, namely that a court can strike out

---

[108] The reasoning of the Court in relation to Article 13 is certain to generate much discussion. Art. 13 has not been incorporated into the Human Rights Act 1998. The Act contains its own remedial provisions in sections 7–9 but this does not of itself render Article 13 redundant. It will still be applied by the European Court and, where relevant, an English court must have regard to the case-law under Art. 13 in the interpretation of the Act. The effect of reliance on Art.13 was to outflank the Art. 6 argument by giving the applicants a financial remedy under Art. 13. In essence, the majority judges held that the applicants' complaint was of a violation of Art. 13, not Art. 6. Some of the minority judges, who found that there had been a violation of Art. 6 did not find it necessary to consider Art. 13. Art. 13 was similarly held to be irrelevant in *Osman* itself.

[109] Lady Justice Arden, sitting as an *ad hoc* judge, filed a concurring opinion in relation to Art. 6. As far as the minority is concerned, five judges were party to two partially dissenting opinions. The ground of dissent was essentially the same in each case, namely that the majority had erred in concluding that there had been no violation of Art. 6. The dissentients were of the view that the present case was governed by *Osman* and they could see no reason not to apply it on the present facts. The gulf between the minority and the majority evidences the narrowness of the interpretation of *Osman* by the majority.

[110] On the ground that, at the outset of the proceedings, there was a serious and genuine dispute about the existence of the right asserted by the applicants under domestic law: see para. 89 of the judgment in *Z* v. *United Kingdom* and para. 94 of the judgment in *K P and T M* v. *United Kingdom*.

[111] It also runs counter to the approach adopted by the Commission.

[112] *Supra* n.42.

[113] *Supra* n.50.

[114] See *supra* n.50-52.

a negligence claim on the ground that it was not fair, just and reasonable to impose a duty of care provided that it engages in a fuller consideration of the competing policy issues. It is now clear that a striking out procedure does not of itself violate Article 6[115] and the Court acknowledged that there is little point in a court embarking on the 'expensive and time-consuming'[116] process of hearing evidence if it cannot provide the applicants with any remedy.[117] The Court also confirmed that 'Article 6 does not in itself guarantee any particular content for civil rights and obligations in national law'.[118] The crucial passage in the judgement of the European Court is to be found in the following statement:

> The Court considers that its reasoning in the *Osman* judgement was based on an understanding of the law of negligence (see, in particular, paragraphs 128 and 139 of the *Osman* judgment) which has to be reviewed in the light of the clarifications subsequently made by the domestic courts and notably the House of Lords. The Court is satisfied that the law of negligence as developed in the domestic courts since the case of *Caparo*. . . and as recently analysed in the case of *Barrett* v. *Enfield LBC* includes the fair, just and reasonable criterion as an intrinsic element of the duty of care and that the ruling of law concerning that element in this case does not disclose the operation of an immunity. In the present case, the Court is led to the conclusion that the inability of the applicants to sue the local authority flowed not from an immunity but from the applicable principles governing the substantive right of action in domestic law.[119]

The Court noted that the House of Lords in *X* v. *Bedfordshire*[120] had engaged in a 'careful balancing of the policy reasons for and against the imposition of liability on the local authority in the circumstances of the applicants' case'[121] so that it could not be said that their Lordships had applied an exclusionary rule or an immunity which deprived the applicants of access to court. In the light of the decisions in *Z* v. *United Kingdom* and *T P and K M* v. *United Kingdom* it would appear that the flaw in *Osman* v. *Ferguson*[122] was its limited analysis of the competing public policy issues. A court which engages in a careful evaluation of the competing public policy issues and which then concludes that the applicant's claim should be struck out on the ground that it is not fair, just and reasonable to impose a duty of care should have little to fear from Article 6. The impact of *Osman* has been confined, the duty of care concept has survived[123] and tort

---

[115] See *Z* v. *United Kingdom, supra* n.1, para. 97 and *K P and T M* v. *United Kingdom, supra* n.1, para. 102.

[116] See *K P and T M, ibid.*

[117] In so concluding the Court must be taken to have rejected the proposition that the claimant should have his day in court, irrespective of the outcome of the case. See *supra* text accompanying n. 87.

[118] See *Z* v. *United Kingdom, supra* n.1, para. 87 and 98.

[119] See *Z* para. 100.

[120] *Supra* n.1.

[121] See *Z* para. 99

[122] *Supra* n.2.

lawyers need no longer fear the opening of the floodgates. In retrospect the decision may even be seen as a welcome reminder to the judiciary of the need to demonstrate that they have carefully considered all aspects of a claim before reaching a decision to strike it out.

[123] Thus denting the hopes of some commentators. See *supra* n.96.

15

Horizontal Equality and the Law of Torts

OFER GROSSKOPF*

I. INTRODUCTION

THIS CHAPTER SEEKS to explore the relationship between tort law and equality. In its core, tort law clearly reflects a notion of equality: no man is allowed to cause damage to his fellow since no one is superior to another.[1] Yet many of those who argued for the replacement of the tort system in the last four decades had done so under the flag of equality.[2] My aim in the chapter is not to resolve this tension but to suggest that it is intrinsic to the existence of the law of torts.

In its essence, the tension between the conflicting views on the relationship between tort law and equality represents a struggle between two distinct concepts of equality: "vertical equality", which concerns the balance between the wrongdoer and her victim; and "horizontal equality", which concerns the fair allocation of scarce resources among victims. Vertical equality is at the heart of tort law. Horizontal equality is considered antagonistic to the law of torts. But why exactly are the horizontal concept of equality and the tort system in conflict? Why can we not view both concepts of equality as fundamental and strive to accomplish both, the first through tort law and the second through State benefits (for example, social security or national health insurance)?

Two possible theories may explain this puzzle. The conventional view among social reformists seem to be that "any compensation scheme which gives preference to accident victims is likely to impede the ultimate goal of providing for all

* I would like to thank Barak Medina for his indispensable help and comments.

[1] See, for example, T. Honoré, "The Morality of Tort Law—Questions and Answers" in D. Owen (ed.), *Philosophical Foundations of Tort Law* (Oxford, Clarendon, 1995) 73, 78–9 ("On a wide view [corrective justice] requires those who have without justification harmed others by their conduct to put the matter right. This they must do on the basis that harm-doer and harm-sufferer are to be treated as equals, neither more deserving than the other").

[2] Two notable examples are M. Franklin "Replacing the Negligence Lottery: Compensation and Selective Reimbursement" (1967) 53 *Va. L Rev.* 774 ("I do not see why, as an initial proposition, today's law should care *how* a limb was broken, whether by an intentional wrongdoer, a negligent automobile driver, a nonnegligent driver, a wall toppled by an earthquake or a fall in the bathtub"); S. Sugarman, "Doing Away with Tort Law" (1985) 73 *Cal. L Rev.* 555.

injured, ill and disabled people, irrespective of the cause of their condition, but based on their relative need for support".[3] According to this theory, tort law is an obstacle that prevents us from achieving horizontal equality.

The first part of this chapter deals with four different claims that may support this theory. Though I do not dispose of those claims altogether, I do argue that they are either unconvincing or highly debatable. At present, at least, they do not provide strong support for the "tort impede horizontal equality" theory.

The second theory, which is presented in the second section of the chapter, is based on opposite premises. It utilises the fact that tort law, at least in its compensative form, can operate only within an environment that rejects horizontal equality, in order to argue that greater horizontal equality will either suppress the need or diminish the effectiveness of the tort system as a mechanism for achieving vertical equality. According to this theory, which at present seems to me much more promising, horizontal equality decreases the justification for having a tort system, but not the other way around. The incompatibility is therefore not between the theoretical concepts of horizontal and vertical equality, but between greater horizontal equality on the one hand and the continuing use of the tort system as a mechanism for achieving vertical equality on the other.[4]

II. THE VERTICAL AND HORIZONTAL CONCEPTS OF EQUALITY

Though the concepts of vertical and horizontal equality are quite intuitive, a brief exposition may still be useful. Despite its absolute appearance, "equality" is a relative concept. If we have two subjects, X and Y, and we wish to treat them equally with respect to the allocation of a given scarce resource, say R, we are committed to the idea that the same allocation process, let us call it "equal treatment", must be applied to both subjects. However, we are not committed to the idea that they will receive the same things, or that they will end up having the same things. The abstract principle of "equality" means only that "like should be treated alike"; it does not tell us which persons are "like" and what constitutes treating them "alike". Therefore the abstract principle of "equality" is too

---

[3] I. Englard, *The Philosophy of Tort Law* (Dartmouth, Aldershot, 1993), 114.

[4] A few words on my methodology are in order. My starting point, which I take as given, is that, at least in modern legal systems, achieving greater horizontal equality and greater vertical equality are desirable policy goals. Building on this assumption I try to evaluate whether, and on which grounds, these goals are incompatible.

For the purpose of elaborating my starting point I utilise existing definitions of equality concepts (basically those of Ernest Weinrib) which I find intuitively appealing. I do not, however, attempt to defend those concepts, nor to explain their historical origin. Those issues, though crucial, are exogenous to my project. Please note, however, that, as opposed to Weinrib, my usage of these concepts (horizontal equality and vertical equality) is not strictly explanatory. I treat these concepts as normative guidelines for my inquiry (i.e., as desirable social goals) and not solely as unifying principles for explaining the structure of legal institutions.

vague; some have even taken the next logical step and described it as an "empty idea".[5]

For the principle of "equality" to have a more definite meaning we must specify who are the subjects we consider "like" and in what sense are we to treat them "alike". The concepts of vertical and horizontal equality offer two diverged ways to fill in the blanks left by the abstract principle of "equality".

Vertical equality concentrates on the relationship between actors whose actions may influence each other: close parties who may find themselves in the positions of "doer" and "sufferer". It specifies that treating them "alike" means that each is allowed to influence the other only in a limited set of legitimate ways, and is therefore forbidden from affecting him by means of a class of illegitimate acts that can be described as "wrongs".

Consider the claim that the tort system represents a mechanism for achieving vertical equality. The tort system is based on the following allocation process:

(1) If no wrong was committed between X and Y then any allocation of R between X and Y is fair (including the allocation R_{NWR} (X), R_{NWR} (Y)).

(2) If a wrong was committed by X against Y then it is fair to reallocate R between X and Y according to the principle that R(Y) = Max (R_{NWR} (Y), R_{WR} (Y)) and vice versa.[6]

This allocation process is designed to allow the courts to take into account only one basic variable, namely whether a wrong was committed between the parties, and by default to reject all other possible variables, such as the parties' identity, needs or wealth, as irrelevant, and hence illegitimate.[7]

The tort system therefore achieves "equal treatment" between X and Y in the sense that it symmetrically protects each of them against the commission of a wrong by the other party. In other words, though it does not make X and Y equal in their possessions, it makes them equal in the protection that the law provides them as regards whatever they do have. This is the essence of the Aristotelian notion of "corrective justice": equality as equal protection against illegitimate deviation from the existing normative baseline.[8]

The concept of horizontal equality, by contrast, concentrates on the relationships between parties that find themselves in the same position. It asserts that members who are similarly situated should receive the same social means,

---

[5] The best known statement of this assertion is P. Westen, "The Empty Idea of Equality" (1982) 95 *Harv. L Rev.* 537.

[6] The symbol "$_{NWR}$" represents the state of the world in which no wrong was committed, while the symbol "$_{WR}$" represents the state of the world in which a wrong was committed.

[7] Courts may examine such issues in order to decide whether a wrong was committed (for example, professional experts may be held negligent for omissions that will not expose a layperson to liability), but only as far as they are relevant to the evaluation of the defendant's conduct toward the plaintiff.

[8] See E. Weinrib, "The Care One Owes Ones Neighbors: Corrective Justice" (1992) 77 *Iowa L Rev.* 403, 407–9. ("The parties do not have the same quantity of holdings, but they are equal as the owners of whatever they do have".)

regardless of the way they fell victim to their misfortune.[9] The relative merits established by one's condition are the relevant criterion for applying this concept of equality. "distributive justice", a form of equal treatment that compares what we have, not the way we were able to achieve it, stands at the heart of horizontal equality.

In the present context the question of horizontal equality is most often presented by comparing tort victims to other disabled or handicapped people, such as persons who were born with a disability or who became disabled as a result of illness. Why, it is often asked, should society care about the way one was injured? Are we to care more about babies who were injured as a result of medical negligence then about those who suffer from "natural" birth defects? Does equal treatment not require that the same resources be supplied to all victims according to their needs, regardless of the process that harmed them?

Those who find it hard to answer any of these questions may believe that the State cannot be content with ensuring the transactional fairness of the allocation process (i.e., ensuring that the allocation process was not affected by illegitimate transfers). They argue that it must also accept the duty to review and, if necessary, amend the allocation process according to its outcomes. In their view, the State needs to advance not only vertical equality, but horizontal equality as well.

III.   ARE HORIZONTAL EQUALITY AND THE TORT SYSTEM COMPATIBLE?

At first sight no contradiction seems to exist between having a tort system as a mechanism for achieving vertical equality and advancing horizontal equality through state actions such as social security legislation and national health insurance. Why can the same legal system not strive for both equality between wrongdoers and victims and equality among victims? Nevertheless, in both tort and anti-tort literature the prevailing opinion seems to be that there is a conflict between tort law and the horizontal notion of equality, at least with regard to

---

[9] We may, of course, conceive of different definitions of "horizontal equality" which take into account not only one's present condition, but also the way it came to be. For example, one may argue that birth defects are "acts of God", and therefore those who suffer from them should be treated differently from those who were harmed by "acts of men". Nevertheless, in the present context such competing definitions seem to me implausible. As mentioned in *supra* n.4, the term "horizontal equality" is used in this chap. to designate certain policy goals that are common to modern legal system. As opposed to "vertical equality", which supplies the legal system with reasons to compel a certain person to make amends to the victim, "horizontal equality" is pointed toward the State, and provides it with arguments about the way it should allocate common resources in order to mitigate private losses. While it is clearly equitable for the State to consider how the harm was caused in order to decide whether or not to impose it on any given person, I find it quite hard to think of acceptable justifications that will allow the modern State to consider such issues when it allocates public resources to mitigate private losses, except in relatively rare circumstances (for example, intentionally self-inflicted damage, or natural disaster crisis). I am indebted to Prof. Todd D. Radkoff for raising this point.

personal injury cases.[10] My purpose is critically to examine two possible theories that may explain this opposition. The first is that the existence of a tort system obstructs the achievement of horizontal equality, and the second is that advancing horizontal equality diminishes the justification for having a tort system.[11]

1. First theory: the existence of a tort system obstructs the achievement of horizontal equality

Let me examine four different arguments that may support the theory that having a tort system damages the struggle for horizontal equality.

(a) *Claim No. 1: Tort Law Creates a Class of Privileged Victims*

Horizontal equality requires that all victims be dealt with according to their relative merits: one's condition, and not the way it was caused, ought to determine one's entitlement to relief. Tort law, by definition, deviates from this requirement, by allowing a certain class of victims to receive preferential treatment on account of the specific cause of their misfortune. While non-tort victims must satisfy themselves with the benefits the State provides, tort victims can recover their losses from the wrongdoer as well.[12] The incompatibility of tort and horizontal equality, according to this claim, is the inequality between tort and non-tort victims created by the tort system.[13]

Though the argument is sound, I doubt if it adds much support to the theory that the tort system impedes the efforts to achieve greater horizontal equality. Of all the disabled and handicapped people in our society, only a tiny minority obtain tort compensations.[14] Furthermore, even those 'lucky' few receive a

---

[10] As early as 1913 Jeremiah Smith had argued that the "modern common law" (i.e., the fault-based tort system that evolved in the 19th century in the USA and England) was "absolutely incongruous" with comprehensive compensation plans (i.e., workmen's compensation plans which may bring about "State Insurance, not confined to harm suffered by hired laborers") and predicted that "the public are not likely to be 'content for long under these contradictory systems'. In the end, one or the other of the two conflicting theories is likely to prevail". See J. Smith, "Sequel to Workmen's Compensation Acts" (1914) 27 *Harv. L Rev.* 352, 363–4.

[11] Since I take most scholars, as well as myself, to be instrumentalists these days, I examine the relationship between torts and horizontal equality based on the effect each of them may have on the prospect of implementing the other.

[12] Compare Franklin, *supra* n.2, at 777–8 (arguing that even if there was no "poverty" problem—for example, every victim had adequate accident insurance—the tort system would still be problematic since it clashes with the "social value of treating like injuries alike").

[13] Ernest Weinrib had argued that "[b]ecause corrective and distributive are the categorically different and mutually irreducible patterns of justificatory coherence, it follows that a single external relationship cannot coherently partake of both": Weinrib, *supra* n.8, at 417–18. I take his argument to be the general formalist explanation of the observation I make in the text.

[14] The Pearson Royal Commission had estimated in 1978 that only 1.5% of all the disabled and handicapped people in the UK receive tort compensation. Even if we allow for differences among legal systems, and across time, this datum is unlikely to change in any significant way. See P.S. Atiyah, *The Damages Lottery* (Oxford, Hart Publishing, 1997) 99–101.

lump sum with which they are free to do whatever they like. The tort system simply makes very few of the victims a lot richer than they would have been without it. Obviously, in a society that allows money to have a great deal of influence, this is a considerable advantage. Nevertheless, it does not seem to affront horizontal equality in a different way from any other mechanism that creates wealth inequality (for example, differential wages). In a society that tolerates a great deal of wealth inequality, it is therefore implausible to view the meagre wealth effect of the tort system as a main source of incompatibility between it and horizontal equality.

(b) *Claim No. 2: The Tort System Diminishes the Amount of Resources Available for Non-Tort Victims*

A much stronger argument against the compatibility of the tort system and horizontal equality is that there is simply not enough money to support them both. Consider, for example, the way in which Professor Atiyah chose to illustrate the shortcomings of the British tort system: "[i]t is rather as though faced with a hundred homeless people living on the street, we picked out one or two and lodged them in the Ritz at our expense".[15]

Obviously, Professor Atiyah's basic assumption is that tort compensation is paid from the same pool that provides for disabled people as a whole. This assumption is by no means trivial. On the face of it, the money needed to compensate tort victims comes from wrongdoers (or at least potential wrongdoers), namely specific individuals who are responsible for the wrong, while the money needed to advance horizontal equality comes from the State, namely from the general public via taxes. Why is it then that Professor Atiyah believes that those seemingly divergent streams actually derive from the same source?

Professor Atiyah's claim is based on the evident reality that tort compensation for physical injuries is paid mainly by insurance companies or public authorities, which ultimately pass them on to the general public through insurance premiums and taxes.[16] Since it is the general public, and not only the wrongdoers, who pay tort damages, and hence it is the same general public who finance social benefits via taxes, we allegedly have a trade-off between funds assigned to compensate tort victims and resources allocated to social benefits. Therefore, charging the public more in order to compensate tort victims leaves less public money for advancing horizontal equality.

Attractive as it may seem, this line of argument is highly debatable on empirical grounds. Its core assumption is that the tort system is inefficient, that is, its contribution to the general welfare of society is less than its costs. Conversely, if the claim that the tort system enhances efficiency by deterring undesirable

---

[15] See P.S. Atiyah, *The Damages Lottery* (Oxford, Hart Publishing, 1997) 99–101, at 32.
[16] *Ibid.*, at 21–2, 108–37.

behaviour is correct, its existence need not burden the general public.[17] Therefore, for those who believe that a tort system can be efficient, Atiyah's descriptive assertion is reduced to a normative claim: if we do not consider it fair that
vertical equality be achieved at the cost of horizontal equality, we must require,
as a point of justice, that our tort system comply with efficiency standards.[18]

The only way to sustain Atiyah's argument as a descriptive matter is to make
the empirical claim that the tort system is inefficient, and that it cannot be made
efficient by any conceivable reform.[19] This claim is highly debatable,[20] and at
present it seems that it can be established only by those who are willing to adopt
what Judge Posner has termed "the misconception . . . that definite costs always
outweigh indefinite benefits".[21]

(c) *Claim No. 3: Tort Law Discredits the Political Claims of Non-Tort Victims*

A third argument for the incompatibility of horizontal equality and the tort system is based on "the familiar problem of the good being the enemy of the best".
In the present context this problem translates into the fear that "the need for a
better approach to compensation becomes less urgent because at least some victims are helped. More important, vested interests entrench and multiply. As the
system grows, the stakes increase, and these interests find more reasons to fight
the displacement of tort. At the same time liberalizing tort law takes time talent,
and attention away from work on superior compensation plans".[22] This line of
argument shares with the preceding one the assumption that horizontal equality

---

[17] Some have suggested that we could achieve the major efficiency gains of the tort system by
other legal schemes, such as administrative sanctions, and then use the profits from this operation
in order to compensate all the victims on equal basis. Compare Franklin, *supra* n.2, at 802–12. Be
that as it may, this is just another way of saying that any tort system is doomed to be inefficient: the
argument implicitly presumes that all tort systems decrease the size of the social pie once alternative
legal schemes are taken into account.

[18] Please notice that my argument is not grounded on the highly contestable "first maximize then
divide" method, which became the hallmark of many economic analysis of law. In fact, it is Atiyah's
assumption, not mine, that only distributive issues are at stake. My claim is only that if the tort
system helps in creating a bigger pie, and horizontal equality is simply a matter of redistributing the
pie, we need not accept the argument that the tort system cuts down on the economic resources
available for achieving horizontal equality.

[19] As a supplement to his main argument about the unfairness of the tort system as a compensatory mechanism, Atiyah argues that the tort system contributes only marginally to the advancement of other social goals, such as deterrence and public accountability: Atiyah, *supra* n.14, at chap.
7. In light of this assertion there can be no doubt that Atiyah himself does not believe that the tort
system enlarges the social pie.

[20] Pointing out that many tort systems are subsidised by the State via the financial budget given
to the courts will not do. It is certainly possible (and practicable) to devise an autarkic court system
for resolving tort disputes, so those who believe that state funds are better allocated for other purposes than settling tort claims (for example, advancing horizontal equality), should simply argue for
court reforms.

[21] R. Posner, "Can Lawyers Solve the Problem of the Tort System?" (1985) 73 *Cal. L Rev.* 747,
752.

[22] Sugarman, *supra* n.2, at 592.

and the tort system draw on common resources; this time, however, it is not the tangible resources needed for their administration but the political power needed for their adoption.[23]

Thus presented, the argument seems to be both obscure and anti-democratic. Indeed, the political struggle over resource allocation is fierce, and bigger and broader coalitions may have greater chance of success in it, but this is usually not the sort of reasoning we allow against legitimate political campaigns. If tort victims have unique moral and political claims against those who have harmed them (as the notion of vertical equality suggests), it seems inappropriate to discredit their demands for State protection simply because doing so may force them (and their supporters) to join other legitimate political campaigns.

One way to rescue this claim from illegitimacy is to assimilate the goals of tort law and horizontal equality. Indeed, as Glanville Williams observed 50 years ago, "if all notions of deterrence and ethical retribution are dropped from the law of tort, and the purpose is regarded as merely one of compensating the victim, the question arises whether this compensation cannot be better secured through a system of insurance".[24] The obvious problem with this argument is similar to that noted earlier with regard to claim no. 2: most of us are not ready (yet) to adopt its basic premise. We do not view the tort system merely as an inefficient compensation mechanism. We are willing to ascribe to it some notions of vertical equality.

(d) *Claim No. 4: Tort Law Discredits the Moral Claims of Non-Tort Victims*

The fourth and final claim for the "tort impedes horizontal equality" theory can be summarised as follows: tort law sends the implicit message that only those who have been injured by others are entitled, as a matter of justice, to redress.[25] Hence, its mere subsistence reflects disbelief in the moral rights of other victims. Furthermore, the legal decision not to allow a tort claim can be understood not only as a negative moral judgement (i.e., the alleged wrongdoer should not be liable for the victim's loss) but also as a positive moral judgement (i.e., the victim should be liable for his loss).[26]

Even if we accept the controversial underlying assumptions of this claim about the interdependence of law and morality, we must still reject it on its merits. At most, the subsistence of tort law reflects the conviction that tort victims have a unique and distinguishable moral claim for redress against those who caused their losses, a moral claim not shared by non-tort victims. Yet it does not add to or detract anything from the moral force of claims made by other groups

---

[23] Compare also J. Fleming, "Is There a Future for Tort?" (1984) 44 *La. L Rev.* 1193, 1207 ("there are those who strenuously criticize special plans . . . for diverting efforts from enacting a system of comprehensive social insurance").

[24] G. Williams, "The Aims of the Law of Tort" (1951) 4 *Current Legal Probs.* 137, 172.

[25] Compare J. Coleman, *Risks and Wrongs* (Cambridge, Cambridge University Press, 1992), 262–3.

[26] *Ibid.*, at 230–3, 261–5.

of victims, or by victims in general, against society as a whole. To give one simple example, the fact that no single person can be sued for the injury suffered by an army veteran as a result of his service does not, in any way, impair his moral right to repair against the State. Such rights to repair, whether specific or general, must stand or fall on their own merits, and therefore lose nothing from the subsistence of tort law.[27]

The claims presented so far strive to establish the proposition that the mere subsistence of the tort system has negative effects on the struggle for greater horizontal equality. My responses to them are meant to show that they are either unconvincing as a major source of incompatibility or based on certain controversial premises. Hence, at best, the theory they intend to support is highly debatable.

2. Second theory: advancing horizontal equality diminishes the justification for having a tort system

The second theory, which I believe is better founded, explains the incompatibility of the tort system and horizontal equality by the opposite argument to the one presented by the first theory. It is not that the tort system undermines the struggle for horizontal equality, but that horizontal inequality is a precondition for the existence of the tort system. According to this view, greater horizontal equality means less room for the law of torts.

The assertion that horizontal equality cuts back on the role played by the tort system as a mechanism for achieving vertical equality can be made on two different levels, depending on one's understanding of the term "vertical equality". If we view vertical equality as aimed at the outcomes ("the wrongful loss") we will argue that by achieving horizontal equality public law suppress the need to create private law duties in order to achieve vertical equality. On the other hand, if we understand vertical equality as action ("wrong") oriented, we will agree that under horizontal equality tort law is no longer an effective device to achieve vertical equality, but we will strongly disagree with the claim that vertical equality, as such, has been attained.

Allow me first to clarify the difference between those two interpretations of the "vertical equality" concept, and then to examine the implications of each for the compatibility of horizontal equality and the tort system.

(a) The "Loss Oriented" and "Wrong Oriented" Interpretations of Vertical Equality

One way to understand the demands of vertical equality is that it constitutes a requirement that the wrongdoer ought not to be allowed to cause unjustified

[27] Close reading of Coleman's statements will lead to the same conclusion. The gist of Coleman's argument is that non-tort victims cannot base their claims on the moral principle of corrective justice. Therefore, we should read him as saying that they have no claim in justice, as far as corrective justice is concerned, and not as a general matter.

losses to the victim. Vertical equality, according to this view, reflects the desire to attain a balance between the wrongdoer and her victim in light of the actual harm caused to the victim.[28] I refer to this notion of vertical equality as "loss oriented".

A competing understanding of the vertical equality concept is that the wrongdoer should not be allowed to act towards her victim in a way that will cause him wrongful losses. The wrongdoer's actions, and not the mere loss that they create, disturb the balance between the parties, and therefore it is the wrong, not the loss, that needs to be corrected.[29] I use the term "wrong oriented" in relation to this interpretation of vertical equality.

The loss oriented and wrong oriented interpretations of vertical equality are closely associated with, though not reducible to, the "compensation" and "deterrence" approaches to tort law. The loss oriented notion of vertical equality stresses the need to preserve the victim's wellbeing, and in that respect creates the impression that the main goal of the tort system is to compensate the victim. Conversely, the wrong oriented notion of vertical equality emphasises our obligation to the victim's rights, and therefore makes us think that the aim of the tort system is to deter the wrongdoer.

Assimilating the loss oriented notion of vertical equality to "wellbeing" or "wealth" preservation, and the wrong oriented notion of vertical equality to "right" or "interests" protection,[30] allows us to see that although each of them claim universality, neither deserves it. The same tort system can support both views in different contexts. For example, it can be argued that the common law wrong of "assault and battery" preserves the victim's body integrity, while the

---

[28] Jules Coleman, for example, founded his conception of "corrective justice" on the basic perception that "the point of corrective justice is to eliminate, rectify, or annul wrongful (or unjust) losses" (Coleman, *supra* n.25, at 306). In his book Coleman retracts from his strong "annulment conception" of corrective justice, in favour of what he terms "a mixed conception of corrective justice". Nevertheless, as he himself emphasises, his "mixed conception of corrective justice" is still "loss oriented", and not "wrong oriented": *ibid.*, at 324–6. Another tort theory that Coleman classifies as "loss oriented" is Epstein's theory of "strict casual liability": *ibid.*, at 315.

[29] Ernest Weinrib, for example, rejects the notion that corrective justice can "be merely a reassertion of the distributive equality disturbed by the defendant's action" and bases it instead on the idea that "in natural right theory, the embodiment of the abstract will in one's body and property, creates rights that other agents are under a duty to respect. The duty is owed specifically to the holder of the right, and the violation of the duty entitles the holder of the right to a legal remedy" (Weinrib, *supra* n.8, at 419–20, 424). A second example of "wrong oriented" tort theory is Fletcher's theory of "risk reciprocity": see G Fletcher, "Fairness and Utility in Tort Theory" (1972) 85 *Harv. L Rev.* 537.

[30] Compare J. Coleman, "The Practice of Corrective Justice" in D. Owen (ed.), *Philosophical Foundations of Tort Law* (Oxford, Clarendon, 1995) 53, 66 ("One way in which Ernest Weinrib's theory and mine differ is that in his account the object of rectification is the 'wrong', whereas in my account it is the 'wrongful loss'. The difference between us reflects differences in our overall political and metaphysical commitments. For me, corrective justice is to be understood as a practice within a liberal political morality that emphasizes autonomy and well being: thus the emphasis on loss, which I think of in terms of diminishing welfare. For Weinrib, the Hegelian, the important normative objects are abstract and only indirectly connected to human welfare or interests: thus the emphasis on wrongs—understood as strongly objective metaphysical objects"). It is only fair to add that Ernest Weinrib does not accept Coleman's characterisation of his position.

common law wrong of "negligence" protects only the victim's wellbeing.[31] If so, the wrong of "assault and battery" represents the notion of wrong oriented vertical equality while the wrong of "negligence" stands for the notion of loss oriented vertical equality.

Given that both notions of vertical equality can coexist in the same legal system, we must now examine the implications of advancing horizontal equality for the ability to achieve each of them by the tort system. The first and crucial step toward this goal is to grasp fully the implications of horizontal equality for the loss suffered by tort-victims.

(b) *The Effects of Horizontal Equality on the Loss Suffered by Tort Victims*

The victim's loss must be evaluated in light of the relevant social and legal contexts. Consider the following example. A boy aged 14 is hit by a car, and due to the injury can never walk again. His loss consists of numerous kinds of hardships and inconveniences that he will have to suffer as a result of his disability. However the magnitude of his loss is not *a priori* fixed by the medical diagnosis, but depends to a very large extent on the social arrangements that exist in his society. Do schools and universities have the proper facilities for handicapped students? Will he be able to enter public buildings such as restaurants, cinemas and sports arenas? Can he use public transportation? Will he be able to drive a car? Is there a law prohibiting employers to discriminate on the basis of physical disabilities? Is this law effective? The degree of our commitment to the wellbeing of handicapped people affects the loss one suffers from becoming handicapped. The more social resources are invested into advancing horizontal equality the smaller is the loss one suffers from one's physical disabilities.

Since the victim's loss is measured against the social and legal background, and since the degree of our commitment to the idea of horizontal equality is partly responsible for this background, there is a negative correlation between advancing horizontal equality and the extent of the victim's loss. In other words, there is a trade-off between the private loss and the public efforts to advance horizontal equality.

Israel's National Health Insurance Act (NHI) can serve as another example of the trade-off between private loss and horizontal equality. The NHI was enacted in 1994 to provide every resident of the State of Israel with basic medical care on a just and equal basis. The Act defines a "basic health plan" that each resident is entitled to receive, almost free of charge,[32] from a "health service provider" of his or her choice.[33] The State is responsible for financing the

---

[31] Compare J. Coleman and J. Kraus, "Rethinking the Theory of Legal Rights" (1986) 95 *Yale L J* 1335, 1364–5 ("As a matter of logic or necessity, legal rights are neither protected domains of autonomy or levels of protected welfare. Their content is a contingent matter depending on the foundational theory").

[32] Some small and regulated fees can be charged for medicines, doctor's visits, etc.

[33] A health service provider cannot refuse to accept any resident who wishes to join it, and, as a general matter, must treat all of its members on an equal basis.

basic health plan, and it does so mainly through a general income tax, the revenues of which are divided among the health service providers according to the number of their members.

The NHI clearly reflects the notion of horizontal equality among residents with regard to basic health care. The NHI does not encompass every aspect of medical care (for example, dental care), nor does it prevent patients from seeking presumably better, and definitely much more expensive, private medical treatment. Nevertheless it is an unmistakable recognition of governmental responsibility to ensure equal treatment in the sphere of health care, at least as regards basic medical care.[34]

Does the NHI, which is basically part of Israeli public law, have any effect on its private law? Can a wrongdoer, or his insurer, claim that since any resident is entitled to basic medical care from the State, the cost of such treatments can no longer be a part of the tort-victim loss? After great confusion, and conflicting decisions in the lower courts, these issues finally came before the Supreme Court in a case called *Sahar Insurance* v. *Elhadad*.[35]

Mr and Mrs Elhadad were seriously injured in a car accident. According to Israeli law they were entitled to tort-like compensation against their insurance company.[36] The insurance company admitted liability, but claimed that since the plaintiffs, like any other residents of the State of Israel, held rights to free medical care under the NHI, their "loss" as a result of the accident did not include the traditional damage item of "medical expenses". The plaintiffs responded to this assertion by making the following allegations. (a) The NHI does not cover accident victims, who have a right to sue in tort; (b) in any case, plaintiffs' rights to receive medical care according to the NHI should not derogate from their private law right to be fully compensated by the wrongdoer.

---

[34] Michael Walzer has argued that in modern western States, including the USA, medical care is socially perceived as a "human want" and hence must be supplied equally, on the basis of medical needs, to all members of the community: M. Walzer, *Spheres of Justice—A Defense of Pluralism and Equality* (New York, Basic Books, 1983), 86–91. This claim is, of course, highly debatable in the USA. See, for example, R. Nozick, *Anarchy, State and Utopia* (Oxford, Blackwell, 1974), 233–5 (arguing that the claim that society "should make provision for the important needs of all its members . . . ignores the question of where the things or actions to be allocated and distributed come from"). Yet it certainly captures the spirit of the NHI.

[35] CA 5557/95, 51(2) PD 724 (Hebrew).

[36] Israel has no-fault traffic legislation that covers all the victims of motor vehicle accidents, including the driver himself. See D. Kretzmer, "No-Fault Comes to Israel" (1976) 11 *Israel L Rev.* 288; I. Englard, "Traffic Accident Victim Compensation in Israel—A Decade of Experience with No-fault" in C. Oldertz and E. Tidefelt (eds.) *Compensation for Personal Injury in Sweden and Other Countries* (Stockholm, Juristforlaget, 1988), 155. It is important to note that the particular context of the case (i.e. traffic accidents that are dealt with according to a statuary no-fault compensation plan) in no way affects the generality of the ruling. In fact, later cases applied this ruling, as a matter of course, in other areas of tort law, such as medical malpractice and work accidents.

As absurd as the first allegation may sound, it does have some support both in the drafters' intent[37] and in the NHI itself.[38] Nevertheless, the court flatly rejected it. The judges viewed the NHI as welfare legislation intended to apply equally to all residents of Israel, regardless of the cause of their misfortune. Therefore they were unwilling to adopt any interpretation that conflicted with this notion of horizontal equality, unless it was unambiguously supported by the Act itself.

The plaintiffs' second allegation directly referred to the "loss" issue. Basically what they asked the court to do was to disregard their public law entitlements when it came to deciding on their private law rights.[39] The court, however, was unwilling to do so. Once the State provides the victim with the right to basic medical care, the fact that he may need such treatments can no longer be considered his "loss".[40] Therefore, only necessary medical treatments outside the scope of the Basic Health Plan could still be claimed in tort after the enactment of the NHI.

The lesson to be learned is quite simple: since horizontal equality set the threshold against which the victim's loss is to be evaluated, advancing horizontal equality reduces the loss tort-victims suffer.[41] What we must consider next is how this lesson affects our subject of inquiry: the effectiveness of the tort system as a mechanism for achieving vertical equality. My conclusions on this issue are summarised by the two following claims:

(c) *Claim No. 1: Greater Horizontal Equality Diminishes the Need to Achieve Loss Oriented Vertical Equality by the Tort System*

It is quite clear that if governmental efforts to advance horizontal equality remedy the "loss" suffered by tort-victims, we no longer need to allow tort claims in order to achieve loss oriented vertical equality. The purpose of vertical equality,

---

[37] The initial scope of the basic health plan was set according to the services offered on voluntary insurance grounds by the largest health service provider in Israel prior to the enactment of the NHI. See s. 7(a)(1) of the NHI. Those services, as the drafters knew, did not include the provision of medical care in case of an accident covered by the law of torts.

[38] S. 3(a) of the NHI declares that "any resident is entitled to health care according to this statute, unless he is entitled to them according to some other statute".

[39] This result may be achieved under the "collateral source rule" in the USA: see J. Fleming, "The Collateral Source Rule and Loss Allocation in Tort Law" (1966) 54 *Cal. L Rev.* 1478 and *infra* n.45.

[40] The "loss" is transferred to the victim's health service provider who can directly sue the wrong-doer, or his insurer, for reimbursement according to s. 22 of the NHI. In fact, protecting the wrong-doer or her insurer from "double liability" was another reason given by the court for blocking the victim's claim for "medical expenses".

[41] Private actions may also set the appropriate baseline for loss evaluation in some cases. Consider for example the case of "sick pay". If an employee seeks compensation in tort for "lost earnings" then she must show that the wrong deprived her of her right to receive her salary. Therefore "if the employers is bound by contract or statute to pay the employee wages while away from work through sickness, then the employee has not 'lost' any income and cannot recover it in damages": P. Cane, *Atiyah's Accidents, Compensation and the Law* (6th edn., London, Butterworths, 1999), 324.

according to the loss oriented view, is only to allocate losses. "If there is a comprehensive plan put into effect for dealing with those losses by imposing them on everyone . . . then corrective justice itself imposes no duties within that community".[42] Consequently, pushing forward the goal of horizontal equality inevitably diminishes the need to employ the tort system as a mechanism for achieving loss oriented vertical equality.

(d) Claim No. 2: Greater Horizontal Equality Decreases the Effectiveness of the Tort System as a Mechanism for Achieving Wrong Oriented Vertical Equality

The wrong oriented view of vertical equality rejects the notion that equality between the wrongdoer and her victim is purely a matter of loss distribution. Therefore it cannot accept the assertion that once the victim's loss is removed, there is no longer a need to correct the imbalance between the wrongdoer and her victim. This imbalance was created due to the wrong (i.e., the wrongdoer's actions or omissions), not the loss, and it is hardly creditable that spreading the loss by the State corrects this imbalance in any way.

Since the requirements of "wrong oriented" vertical equality are not synonymous with loss spreading, the need to achieve it does not diminish once horizontal equality is advanced. Yet, as we saw, horizontal equality affects the size of the victim's loss, and consequently also the operation of the tort system. Lesser compensation means both that tort-victims have less incentive to sue, and that wrongdoers have fewer incentives to respect victim's rights. If we assume that the tort system effectively served the goal of wrong oriented vertical equality under horizontal inequality, we have good reason to believe that it will not be able to do so under horizontal equality.[43]

Can we reform the legal system in order to protect wrong oriented vertical equality under conditions of horizontal equality? One possibility is to allow the State to sue wrongdoers for the benefits they received in the form of reduced liability.[44] Another solution is to allow tort victims to receive compensation that exceeds their actual loss, a money award that is calculated as if there were no State action.[45] These solutions are not flawless, but their merits need not be

---

[42] Coleman, *supra* n.25, at 403–4.

[43] In the extreme case, were the State to extinguish the victim's loss entirely, tort law is totally ineffective in achieving wrong oriented vertical equality. In less extreme cases, tort law retains part of its effectiveness.

[44] See H. Dagan and J. White, "Governments, Citizens and Injurious Industries" (2000) 75 *NYU L Rev.* 354; the NHI adopts a somewhat different solution by allowing health service providers to sue tortfeasors and insurance companies for reimbursement according to their actual expenses. See s. 22 of the NHI.

[45] This is the prevalent solution in the USA on account of the "collateral source rule". According to this rule, which applies "across the board to all benefits from any source other than the defendant or co-defendant", no deduction whatsoever is allowed for collateral benefits. See J. Fleming, *The American Tort Process* (Oxford, Clarendon Press, 1988), 206–11. Israel's Social Security Act goes part way in this direction by providing that tort-victims receive at least 25% of the damages award

examined here.[46] Suffice it to say that they deviate from the classical features of the tort system—if they are private law solutions they allow the plaintiff to receive a windfall,[47] and if they try to work round this problem their alliance with the private law becomes obscure.[48]

IV. SOME TENTATIVE CONCLUSIONS

What are the lessons to be learned from the above discussion? I suggest the following tentative conclusions.

First, supporters of horizontal equality are better advised to concentrate on the merits of their claims, rather than on the shortcomings of the tort system. Indeed, if the tort system can operate only in an unequal environment, there is good reason to believe that those who run it will resist any "environmental" change.[49] By contrast, for the great majority who do not suffer from this predisposition, compensating tort victims need not be at the expense of greater horizontal equality. Tort law is not a major enemy of horizontal equality, though horizontal equality is a major enemy of the law of torts.

Secondly, it is predictable that if the trend toward greater horizontal equality with respect to physical wellbeing continues, we will witness the demise of tort

---

against the wrongdoer, regardless of the social security benefits they are entitled to. See s. 330 of the Social Security Act, 1995. The majority of the Supreme Court had recently portrayed this rule as "an anomaly within the law of torts". See CA 686/97 *Menorah* v. *The Estate of Mosh Tamar* (dec.) (unpublished) (Hebrew). It is interesting to note that a similar solution was introduced in England, as a political compromise, by s. 2 of the Law Reform (Personal Injuries) Act 1948 (only half the value of certain social security benefits is deductible from tort damages). This arrangement was strongly criticised, and was eventually abolished by the Social Security (Recovery of Benefits) Act 1997. See Cane, *supra* n.41, at 327–9.

[46] One obvious setback, shared by both solutions mentioned in the text, is that they require us to isolate and quantify the benefits received from the State. In some cases, such as social security benefits, this burden may be trivial. In others, such as facilitating public services for the use of disabled people, this difficulty seems formidable.

[47] I.e., they allow the victim to receive an award that exceeds his loss. Admittedly, at least within common law jurisdictions, this will not be such a revolutionary shift, since other recognised private law remedies, such as restitution and punitive damages, already allow the plaintiff to receive a windfall in that sense. Compare the Law Commission's Report on Aggravated, Exemplary and Restitutionary Damages, Law Com No 247. From this perspective, the American "collateral source rule" is in harmony with the American tendency to support private enforcement through punitive damages. See Fleming, *supra* n.45, at 214–24.

[48] The NHI's solution, allowing health service providers to sue tortfeasors directly, is, strictly speaking, still part of the private law. This solution also has some common features with the doctrine of subrogation and with restitutionary rights for the discharge of the defendant's legal liability. Nevertheless, it is unique since the tortfeasor was discharged from liability by the mere enactment of the NHI, and not by the health service provider's actual treatment. Therefore, and in light of the semi-public character of the health service providers, it is not clear whether we should view s. 22 as a private law right to reimbursement, or as a revenue clause based on merits.

[49] See *supra*, text accompanying nn.22–4. Compare England, *supra* n.3, at 115.

law in the realm of personal injuries.[50] In its place we are likely to develop new and creative ways to secure wrong oriented vertical equality; private and public causes of action that are directed at controlling tortfeasors' behaviour, including restitution and punitive damages,[51] are likely to flourish.

Thirdly, those who wish to sustain the tort system despite the advancement of horizontal equality (for example, by supporting the American "collateral source rule") must argue their case on non-compensatory grounds. Though it is unlikely that horizontal equality will ever cover the full terrain of tort law, there seems to be no point in keeping a tort system in order to compensate for items such as "pain and suffering" or loss of high income.[52]

Hence, the justification for the survival of the tort system in a world that respects horizontal equality must shift. In fact, the function of private law as a whole must switch from loss spreading to behaviour control.[53]

---

[50] Compare Fleming, *supra* n.45, at 25–31 ("in most other developed countries insurance plans have made considerable advance in replacing tort liability as a source of accident compensation . . . Since tort damages would be reduced by these benefits, resort to tort recovery by the victim is largely discouraged . . ."). In the context of horizontal equality, much as in other contexts, the "trend" depends not only on one's community but on one's time-framework as well. When I indicate that the general "trend" in this realm is toward expansion, I adopt a relatively broad time frame. Others, of course, may prefer to concentrate on a much more limited time frame, and could therefore see things differently. See, for example, England, *supra* n.3, at 116 ("[in light of the more recent political and economic realities] the present prognosis is that, even in the field of personal injuries, tort law will, in most countries, continue to play a role, in addition to, or in conjunction with, insurance schemes").

[51] American courts rejected the assertion that the "collateral source rule" amounts to punitive damages, and argued that it "partially serves to compensate for the attorney's share and does not actually render 'double recovery' for the plaintiff": *Helfend* v. *Southern California Rapid Transit District* (1970) 465 P 2d 61 (Cal.). This is surely an odd explanation. Even if the "American rule" on attorney fee recovery makes tort awards under-compensatory, allowing victims to sue for losses they have not suffered is still a "windfall", albeit one that might be justified on incentive, rather than compensatory, grounds.

[52] "Pain and suffering" and loss of high income are unlikely to be compensated by social insurance plans, and therefore represent the terrain that is unlikely to be covered by horizontal equality. Compare Fleming, *supra* n.45, at 27.

[53] At present the move toward horizontal equality exists mainly in the realm of body integrity, and not in the sphere of individual wealth. Compare England, *supra* n.3, at 110. Therefore the observations presented in the text are relevant primarily to personal injury cases.

16

Privacy in the Digital Age: Vanishing into Cyberspace?

GEBHARD M. REHM

I. INTRODUCTION

THE TECHNOLOGICAL DEVELOPMENTS of the past decades, particularly the rapid progress in computer technology, the almost revolutionary changes triggered by the Internet[1] in our private and professional lives, and the quantity of information that can easily and cheaply be retrieved from and processed in electronic databases have not only enormously facilitated data processing mechanisms, but also have permitted the compilation, storage and amalgamation of large amounts of information in a matter of seconds. On average, adults in the developed world are now registered in 200 computer databases.[2] This development has obvious implications for our privacy. In this context, I understand privacy as the right to decide on the disclosure of personal information to others or to the government and to control the flux of information relating to oneself (the "informational aspect").[3] The German Federal Constitutional Court has termed this entitlement the right to informational self-determination.[4] Admittedly, it is not obvious what type of matters the term personal information encompasses. Many items of information do not relate to only one individual, but to many people. For the purposes of this chapter, the term will refer to all data that allow reliable conclusions with respect to a particular person. A

---

[1] The Internet is a worldwide network that connects smaller groups of linked computers. It allows users to communicate with computers from other groups. The computers and networks forming the Internet are owned by government institutions, corporations, educational organisations, and private individuals. For a technical description of the Internet see *Reno* v. *ACLU* 117 S Ct 2329, 2334 (1997).

[2] See www.oneworld.org/index_oc/issue697/davies.html.

[3] Under US constitutional law, the right to privacy also protects the individual's autonomy in making certain important decisions such as regarding abortion. See *Whalen* v. *Roe* 429 US 589, 599–601 (1973). This aspect of the right is not relevant to my subject.

[4] In its landmark *Census* decision, the Bundesverfassungsgericht (Federal Constitutional Court) (hereinafter BVerfG), 15 Dec. 1983, 65 Entscheidungen des BVerfG (Reports of the Federal Constitutional Court) (hereinafter BVerfGE) 1, 42 (hereinafter *Census*). For an analysis of the scope and limitations of this right in comparison with the right to privacy under US constitutional law see G.M. Rehm, " 'Just Judicial Activism'? Privacy and Informational Self-Determination in US and German Constitutional Law" (2001) 32 *U West L A L Rev*. 275, 277 *et seq.*

few examples will suffice to illustrate the potentially adverse effects of the digital revolution on privacy: credit card and bank records unambiguously reveal our spending and consumption habits; telephone bills reflect communication patterns and partners; Internet service providers can analyse their clients' preferences by counting the number and duration of clicks on particular webpages; and companies offering cellular telephone services can locate their customers carrying their telephones at any given time with a margin of error of 100 metres. Beyond this, health maintenance organisations and credit risk agencies can compile profiles on their clients, and detailed information previously unknown even to the individual himself can be unearthed through genetic engineering. Taken together, these mechanisms provide genuinely personal information in an amount, intensity and density unimaginable in a world without computers. The Orwellian nightmare of perfect categorisation of human beings, complete personal profiles and surveillance suddenly seems frighteningly real.[5]

And this fear is not completely unfounded. The use of personal data is not merely a theoretical possibility. The British weekly, *The Economist*, a paper that certainly cannot be suspected of being overly business-hostile but nonetheless known for closely guarding its journalists' anonymity, recently conducted an experiment.[6] A staff journalist hired a private investigator to find out as much as possible about the journalist, beginning only with his name. He asked the private investigator to conduct the search from the confines of his office as much as possible. The results shocked the hard-baked journalists at *The Economist*. Within one week, the private investigator had unearthed "quite a bit" about the journalist: his salary, the value of his house, his address and telephone number, his partner's name, a former partner's name (information that the journalist, not surprisingly, considered to be the most sensitive and dangerous), his mother's name and address, his employer, and the names and addresses of people who had been directors of a company with him.[7] At first glance, one might classify this type of information as innocuous, but that could be a grave misjudgement. Apart from the fact that these data allow the compilation of a not so innocuous personal profile, it is this kind of information that typically serves as the basis for test questions that businesses ask their customers for purposes of identification when communicating with them on the telephone or electronically. Its availability opens the door to further investigations, information and abuse. Consequently, the *New York Times*, in a recent article, warned about a crime that has mushroomed in the wake of the digital revolution: identity theft.[8] Identity thieves obtain loans and credit cards and sometimes are even bold enough to secure residences in someone else's name. The accessibility of

---

[5] I am referring to G. Orwell, *Nineteen Eighty-Four* (Paris, Gallimard Publishing, 1950).

[6] See the report in "Living in the Global Goldfish Bowl", *The Economist*, 16 Dec. 1999, 58.

[7] The availability of similar information is also reported in T. Kelley, "An Expert in Computer Security Finds his Life is a Wide-Open Book", *NY Times*, 13 Dec. 1999, 17.

[8] See T. O'Brien, "Officials Worried Over a Sharp Rise in Identity Theft", *NY Times*, 3 Apr. 2000, 1.

personal information such as social security number, date of birth, credit card numbers, maiden name, the names of spouses, etc.—i.e., information that *The Economist*'s private investigator retrieved from databases—places these criminals in a position to compose a complete identity without any difficulty. Apart from the emotional distress, the victims whose identity has been abused often have to face fake credit card charges or wrong credit reports, which are not always easy to settle. Financial losses can go unnoticed if the victims fail to check their bank or credit card statements carefully, not to mention the considerable losses that the business partners of identity thieves may sustain.

II. THE CONCEPT OF PRIVACY

Should this development be a cause for concern from a human rights perspective? Most legal systems that follow the philosophical tradition of the Enlightenment guarantee the individual a constitutional right to privacy in some way, though in different intensities. But in order to answer the questions whether and how privacy should be protected in a private law relationship, we should first examine the main rationales for protecting privacy in general.

1. The case for protection of privacy

(a) *Philosophical and Legal Arguments*

An Orwellian society that reduces human beings to mere objects of surveillance and control would be inconsistent with Kant's conception of man as a rational, autonomous and responsible being.[9] Kant's conception is the philosophical basis of any democratic society based on the rule of law. If we did not conceive of ourselves as having the capacity to act responsibly and rationally, our participation in the political process would be a travesty and the democratic system would be doomed to failure. The invasion of privacy gnaws at this conception because it leads to more heteronomy in the individual's decision-making process. The more others know about a certain person, particularly those who wield power over her, such as the government or her employer, the more this person will be induced to subordinate her own judgement to their will. To be sure, everybody tries to anticipate the repercussions of his actions and is thus never completely autonomous in his decisions in the strictest sense. But while our existence as social beings mandates attention to the consequences of our actions for others, there are nonetheless instances in which respect for the opinion of another is unwarranted in the circumstances. Even though this distinction requires a value judgement for which I am unable to provide an easy catch-all

---

[9] See I. Kant, *Kritik der Praktischen Vernunft* (Darmstadt, Wissenschaftliche Buchgesellschaft, 1998) 225.

definition, respect for the opinion of another person seems generally justified when the latter's interest has a rational (legal, economic, social, etc.) nexus with the decision in question. Where this nexus is lacking, there is no need for taking another's opinion into account. For example, let us imagine a worker who considers participating in a political demonstration. His employer objects to this demonstration for some reason, even though it would not affect her business: should the employee take this attitude into account? If the demonstration were to be held during working hours, he certainly should and this heteronomy would be justified, because his participation would affect the employer's legitimate interests. There is, however, no reason for the employee to pay heed to the employer's attitude if he is not going to participate in the demonstration during working hours. The employee should not have to fear any reprisals from his employer for his political activity. Unfortunately, some employers still may sanction their employees in a situation where there is no effect on their job performance or other legitimate employer interests. In order to avoid any chilling effects[10] on the employee's right to political activity by way of unjustified sanctions, we should grant the employee the right to keep this activity to himself. Hence, a right to privacy can contribute to more autonomous individual decision-making while still respecting the legitimate interests of others.

Unlimited collection and availability of data not only conflict with the philosophical values that constitute the core tenets of democratic societies, but they also violate the spirit, if not the letter, of the liberties that human beings enjoy in democratic societies and that transform the aforementioned philosophical values into law. For example, Article 8 of the European Convention on Human Rights protects the right to a private sphere;[11] the due process clause of the Fourteenth Amendment to the US Constitution[12] and several other constitutional

---

[10] These chilling effects are generally a cause for concern from a human rights perspective. See, for example, the German *Census* decision, *supra* n.4, at 43; or the US decision in *Laird* v. *Tatum* 408 US 1 (1972), 11, citing *Baird* v. *State Bar of Arizona* 401 US 1 (1971), *Keyishian* v. *Board of Regents* 385 US 589 (1967), *Lamont* v. *Postmaster General* 381 US 301 (1965); *Baggett* v. *Bullitt* 377 US 360 (1964).

[11] The text of this provision reads:

"Article 8—Right to respect for private and family life
1. Everyone has the right to respect for his private and family life, his home and his correspondence.
2. There shall be no interference by a public authority with the exercise of this right except such as is in accordance with the law and is necessary in a democratic society in the interests of national security, public safety or the economic well-being of the country, for the prevention of disorder or crime, for the protection of health or morals, or for the protection of the rights and freedoms of others".

[12] The text of the 14th Amendment to the US Constitution reads: "Section 1 . . . No State shall make or enforce any law which shall abridge the privileges or immunities of citizens of the United States; nor shall any State deprive any person of life, liberty, or property, without due process of law; nor deny to any person within its jurisdiction the equal protection of the laws". The US Supreme Court in *Roe* v. *Wade* 410 US 113 (1973), held the due process clause of the 14th Amendment to be the central pillar of privacy protection (though with respect to the decision-making aspect).

provisions[13] guarantee the right to privacy under certain circumstances; and Article 2(1) in conjunction with Article 1(1) of the German Constitution, the Basic Law, guarantees the right to informational self-determination.[14] Surveillance, or even only the fear of being controlled, not only has the potential to infringe upon these privacy rights, but also tends to have a chilling effect on the exercise of other freedoms such as freedom of speech or freedom of association. People fear or actually have to face rebukes and sanctions from the government, their employers, their neighbours or anybody hostile to a certain type of behaviour, even if they are only exercising such fundamental rights as freedom of speech. They are less inclined to abstain from this kind of behaviour if it goes largely unnoticed. American gynecologists performing abortions could tell a thing or two about the risks they face in practising their profession and, therefore, most probably prefer to keep it secret. Having the right to control the flux of information relating to oneself and to be left alone thus is an important and necessary element of and supplement to constitutional rights such as freedom of speech that are enshrined in many democratic constitutions.

(b) *The Growing Threat to Individual Privacy by Other Individuals*

Traditionally, government has been perceived as the main threat to individual privacy, even though Warren and Brandeis' classic article on the subject[15] deplored, first and foremost, the lack of respect for the individual's privacy by another individual. In private law relationships, the right to privacy almost exclusively used to gain significance in cases in which the media had overstepped its boundaries and reported intimate details of the lives of prominent people,[16] but governmental invasion of privacy also affected the average person. The need to protect the individual from an overly curious government arose mainly due to the latter's superior methods of obtaining personal information. All governments devote considerable resources to maintaining a secret service that uses state of the art technology to spy on its citizens and third parties. The governmental monopoly on the criminal law system and the virtual impossibility for a citizen to evade the taxation system, the social security system or other government agencies that permit, or even require, the extensive collection of data have

[13] For a discussion of these provisions, which include the 1st, 3rd, 4th, and 5th Amendments to the US Constitution, and their importance for privacy protection: see *Griswold* v. *Connecticut* 381 US 479 (1965).

[14] *Supra* n.4. The text of Arts. 1(1) and 2(1) of the Basic Law reads as follows: "Article 1 (1) Human dignity is inviolable. To respect and protect it is the duty of all State authority. Article 2 (1) Everyone has the right to free development of his personality insofar as he does not violate the rights of others or offend against the constitutional order or against morality". An English translation of the Basic Law can be found at www.uni-wuerzburg.de/law/gm00000_.html.

[15] S.D. Warren and L.D. Brandeis, "The Right to Privacy" (1890) 4 *Harv. L Rev.* 193.

[16] For a discussion on the implications of this conflict under German law, see, for example, A. Heldrich, "Privates Glück in der Medienwelt" in A. Heldrich, P. Schlechtriem and E. Schmidt (eds.), *Festschrift für H Heinrichs* (Munich, C.H. Beck, 1998) 319; G.M. Rehm, "Persönlichkeitsschutz Prominenter und Pressefreiheit der Unterhaltungsmedien" [1999] *Archiv für Presserecht* 416.

granted the government better access to data and, hence, more power than any private individual or institution could ever wield.

This predominant focus on the relationship between government and the individual is, however, no longer warranted. Computer technology and extensive databases put private companies and individuals on almost equal footing with the government.[17] Knowledge is power. This is particularly true with regard to intimate personal information, but it also applies to seemingly innocuous data that reveal a great deal about a person if combined with other items of information.

2. A case against the right to privacy?

But protection of privacy also has its downsides. Richard Posner has argued that a greater availability of personal information allows individuals to organise their relations more efficiently. It relieves them from having to invest in obtaining information that the concerned person could easily, and cheaply, provide and permits them to structure their transaction more efficiently.[18] Companies are in a position to generate cost-efficient advertisements and to formulate their offers closely to the needs of their potential customers without having to pay for expensive market research if they know what their clients are looking for. A creditor who is well informed about her debtor's default risk can save herself a great deal of expense in risk control. These gains enlarge the cake, allowing all parties involved to receive a bigger piece.

Furthermore, privacy is not the only value that deserves protection in the Internet-business context. Media companies and other businesses enjoy the constitutional rights of freedom of speech and freedom of the press and can invoke their rights freely to exercise their professions. Since they are dependent on a certain amount of information about their transaction partners in order to organise their businesses properly and efficiently, these rights protect to a certain degree the collection of this information. These rights cannot simply be ignored or discounted against a countervailing right to privacy. The efficient organisation of private transactions and the respect for countervailing rights of third parties are incompatible with an individual's exclusive control over information relating to himself. Thus the legislature and judiciary not only have to consider the protection of privacy, but must also formulate principles that respect all the interests involved instead of ignoring, or even snuffing, them.

---

[17] There is no reason, however, to underestimate the continuing—and ever-growing—capacity of governments to invade their citizens' privacy. The Echelon surveillance system run by the USA, the UK, Canada, Australia and New Zealand and recent movement in the UK and Germany towards installing cameras at inner city squares are merely aspects of this growing threat. But the relationship between the government and individuals is not my subject here. For a discussion of this issue, see, for example, Rehm, *supra* n.4.

[18] See R. Posner, "The Right of Privacy" (1978) 12 *Ga. L Rev.* 393, 399 *et seq.*

1. Self-regulation versus government rules

But how should this balancing process work in practice? The European Union and the United States apparently follow two different methodical concepts. While the European Data Protection Directive, not yet incorporated into the law of all Member States,[19] will establish stringent governmental regulation of privacy protection[20]; American proposals, on the other hand, rely mainly on the concept of self-regulation, i.e., voluntary submission to certain privacy rules. Recent initiatives in the US Congress suggest, however, that some decision-makers on the other side of the Atlantic regard as necessary certain governmental rules for the protection of privacy.[21]

Is one of these approaches superior to the other? The two solutions can be distinguished on the basis of three main criteria: the incentive for market participants to accept the rules; the capability of these rules to eliminate undesirable privacy policies; and the effectiveness of their enforcement.

(a) *Acceptance of Rules by the Market Participants*

At first glance, self-regulation seems—as always—a good idea because according to conventional wisdom, "the invisible hand" of the perfectly competitive market should lead to the most efficient solution.[22] If we click on a website, we can usually—already today—review the privacy policy of the person or company running that website. If we do not like this policy, we are not bound to submit any further information. In the long run, the theory goes, websites with privacy policies that do not match the expectations of the market-place will disappear because they will not attract a sufficient number of visitors.[23] This scenario, however, seems hardly realistic. Many website hosts have a strong interest in obtaining as much information about their visitors as possible. What reason could an information broker or identity thief have to agree to rules that would destroy her "business" idea? From a less extreme perspective, many companies simply have a legitimate interest in finding out as much as possible about their clients' consumption tendencies. These market participants have hardly any

[19] Under European law, directives are binding as directly applicable law only on the Member States, and not the citizens of those States. The Members States are obligated to transform directives into national law. They also are bound with regard to the result of directives, but do have a choice with regard to form and methods. See Art. 249(3) (ex Art. 189(3)) of the Treaty Establishing the European Community [1997] OJ C340/173.

[20] Directive 95/46/EC [1995] OJ L281/31.

[21] See W. Safire, *International Herald Tribune*, 2 May 2000, 9.

[22] See, for example, P.A. Samuelson and W.D. Nordhaus, *Economics* (16th edn., Boston, Mass., Irwin & McGraw-Hill, 1998) 148.

[23] For an analysis of standard contracts in the insurance business along these lines see R. Posner, *Economic Analysis of Law* (4th edn., Boston, Mass., Little, Brown & Co, 1992) 114.

reason to agree to overly strict rules that protect privacy. Those who pose the greatest threat to privacy will be the hardest to persuade in favor of its protection.

(b) The "Lemon" Problem

The large and fragmented Internet market presumably will not be able to eliminate overly lenient privacy policies if self-regulation governs. These policies are basically similar to general conditions in any standard contract. Competition rarely leads to the elimination of undesirable general conditions, because that would require a person looking for a particular product or service to incur high transaction costs in comparing the general conditions that the various providers offer.[24] The meaning and monetary consequences of particular conditions are rarely easily or cheaply ascertainable, and the identification of the most advantageous set of general conditions is a difficult task even for seasoned lawyers. To review a particular privacy policy and evaluate its consequences is a great deal more difficult and costly than simply shopping for the best price for a particular product. The market for general conditions thus lacks sufficient transparency to permit perfect competition. "Lemons", i.e., "bad" general conditions, can thus survive in the market, and it may pay to have them.[25]

Rather than eliminating websites with deficient privacy policies, the very contrary is likely to occur under a system of self-regulation: a race to the bottom in terms of privacy protection. People or institutions with stricter initial privacy policies would be at a disadvantage because their competitors could take advantage of their superior information. Without competitors, the companies might prefer to follow the rules of self-regulation. But since they do not know, and do not have a safe method of finding out, whether and to what degree their competitors are going to respect these rules, they are likely not to respect the rules either. A few black sheep are thus sufficient to indirectly force the white sheep to abuse personal information as well.

Governmental regulation can generally solve this transparency problem because it allows consumers to place trust in the application of similar standards of privacy protection without having to perform costly searches themselves. It is more efficient than leaving the elimination of undesirable clauses to the market forces.

(c) Ease of Enforcement

Governmental regulation also makes the actual enforcement of a certain privacy policy more likely. The government can impose a wider variety of

---

[24] See H.B. Schäfer and C. Ott, *Lehrbuch der Ökonomischen Analyse des Zivilrechts* (2nd edn., Berlin, Springer, 1995) 421.

[25] This is just another example of how high information costs allow products with deficient qualities to survive even though the market mechanism should generally eliminate them. See G. Akerlof, "The Market for 'Lemons': Quality Uncertainty and the Market Mechanism" (1970) 84 *Q J Econ*. 488.

sanctions on market participants that do not comply with the required standards than individuals can. The government is also more likely to enforce these standards than a private individual, who often lacks the resources to go after a market participant who has violated his own privacy policy. Enforcing a self-regulatory rule is generally more cumbersome and therefore less likely to happen. First, the victim would have to learn of the violation. Acquiring this information is more difficult for individuals than for the government because the latter has many more sources and resources for this purpose. Secondly, the victim would bear the burden of proof for establishing a market participant's particular privacy policy at the relevant time. Meeting this requirement can be quite cumbersome. After all, the website host can easily change his privacy policy on his webpage without leaving any trace, whereas it is not hard to prove whether a law was in force or not. Furthermore, enforcement would require the victim physically to locate the violator. Locating the responsible managers of a company that consists mainly of a computer and suddenly disappears from the Internet can be very difficult and costly. In international cases, the problem is even more acute. Would a resident of Rome really invest in enforcing his privacy interests against a company operating its business from Shanghai? Most likely he would consider it neither promising nor worthwhile. The enforcement of a governmental rule admittedly also would be problematic in international contexts. But governments generally tend to enforce their laws internationally with greater zeal and resources than private parties are willing and able to do in defending their rights. Moreover, countries seeking to provide safe harbours for companies with dubious business practices can easily resist attempts to enforce self-regulation provisions. Ignoring domestic laws, however, will trigger much more political pressure from the respective countries, particularly if these laws conform to internationally homogeneous standards.

Finally, self-regulation can work only if the suppliers of goods and services are relatively homogeneous, because this would facilitate the enforcement of rules and would make the participants more likely to adhere to them. But this is hardly the case with the World Wide Web, a system that is far too complex to allow for mutual checks and balances. The participants operate in too many different countries, legal systems, languages and changing circumstances to permit transparent competition.

In sum, governmental—preferably international—regulation would be superior to a system of self-regulation on all three counts. Competition among websites for an appropriate level of privacy protection does not work because of the lack of transparency of the market for privacy policies and due to the fact that those who pose the greatest threat to privacy will not respect strict rules and will thus virtually compel others to ignore them as well.

2. Governmental regulation versus controlled self-regulation

The superiority of governmental regulation derives primarily from the greater transparency of its rules. But binding governmental regulation typically suffers from being relatively static, and it frequently eliminates competition that would allow for improvement through the development of new solutions and could adapt more easily to changing circumstances. International treaties in particular are very hard to change, although such agreements would generally be desirable in order to establish similar conditions for all participants in a genuinely international and rapidly changing environment. The advantages of both concepts could, however, be combined. The transparency problem could be solved if a certain body with high credibility, possibly a governmental or government-supervised institution or some kind of industry association, were to signal acceptable privacy standards of particular hosts. The examples of the International Organisation for Standardisation (ISO)[26] and the German government-sponsored Warentest Foundation[27] are quite encouraging as to the service that such bodies can provide for market transparency by testing the quality of products and services and grading them accordingly. The Warentest Foundation, for example, has already published a survey on the protection of customer data by large companies doing business on the Internet.[28] The US Senate Committee on the Judiciary provides a handbook on tools for protecting one's privacy on the Internet.[29] The German Ministry of Economy and Technology maintains a website with similar guidelines.[30] All these measures can contribute greatly to reducing the information costs for individuals and thus reinstate the market selection process.

A lenient standard for standing to bring suit could supplement these tools and mitigate the enforcement problem. If certain associations, such as consumer protection organisations, are granted a broad right to claim against the unacceptability of certain privacy policies, abuses could be rooted out more efficiently. In Germany, comparable broad definitions of standing to bring an action in section 13 of the Statute on General Conditions ("AGBG") and section 13 of the Statute Against Unfair Competition ("UWG") are considered a necessary supplement to the prohibitions on unfair general conditions[31] and competition practices, although there are certain undeniable negative side-effects, such as over-zealous consumer protection organisations. In sum, the most promising methods of protecting privacy are governmental regulation and, as much as possible, controlled self-regulation.

---

[26] For information on ISO, see www.iso.ch.
[27] For further information, see www.stiftung-warentest.de.
[28] See FINANZtest, No. 5/2000.
[29] See http://judiciary.senate.gov/privacy.htm.
[30] See www.sicherheit-im-internet.de.
[31] See, for example, P. Schlosser, "Introduction to the AGBG" in J. Staudinger (ed.), *Kommentar zum Bürgerlichen Gesetzbuch*, *AGBG* (13th edn., Berlin, Sellier, 1998) n.15.

IV. THE PRINCIPLES OF PROTECTION OF PRIVACY

If we assume that governmental regulation is superior to self-regulation and controlled self-regulation the best alternative, how should the applicable rules be structured and what should their guiding principles be? I have argued that the government and private individuals increasingly pose similar threats to individual privacy. If this assumption is correct, traditional criteria and mechanisms of privacy protection against the government may provide relief also against private individuals. The German Federal Constitutional Court's *Census* decision, which concerned the relationship between government and the individual, established two main principles, which, in my opinion, also warrant attention in the context of private legal relations.

1. Self-determination

(a) *General Justification*

The first principle relates to self-determination. One important danger of unlimited collection of data arises from the fact that the individual is unaware of the scope of knowledge others have about her. This uncertainty has the potential to cause the chilling effect that I have already mentioned.[32] An individual's right to control the flux of information about oneself could attenuate this effect. If the individual has to agree expressly to the collection or transfer of her personal data, she is less likely to be uncertain about other people's knowledge about her. This is particularly true if the other party has no right to sell or otherwise transfer the collected information to third parties without her express consent. The German Federal Constitutional Court has invoked self-determination as a guiding principle in privacy protection cases.[33] The German Federal Government is also currently drafting a statute that grants the right to genetic information to the individual concerned in order to prevent employers or insurance companies from compelling the other party to the contract to provide this information.[34] Only recently, the US Supreme Court upheld the Drivers Privacy Protection Act[35] as constitutional.[36] This statute, in response to a deal concluded by the State of South Carolina, prevents states from selling information and photographs from driver's licence applications to private investigators.

[32] See *supra*, text accompanying n.10.
[33] See *Census, supra* n.4, at 41.
[34] See *Frankfurter Allgemeine Zeitung*, 29 Apr. 2000, 1.
[35] 18 USC §§ 2721–2725 (1994).
[36] *Reno* v. *Condon* 528 US 141, 120 S Ct 666 (2000).

The principle of self-determination, however, entails granting a property right to personal information[37] to the person concerned. Does such an allocation of this right make sense? Does it really protect anybody if the Coase theorem is correct? Under this theorem, every property right will end up in the hands of the person who values it most no matter to whom it is allocated initially.[38] All things being equal, whether we follow the principle of self-determination or let other people take advantage of personal information will make no difference.

The answer is less difficult than it seems at first. Coase had to make a few, but quite rigorous, assumptions under which his theorem would hold.[39] It requires that there be no transaction costs, particularly no information costs, or that at least the gain from rearranging the rights is greater than these costs.[40] We would thus need a transparent market in which the right could be traded without incurring great expenses. That is, however, not necessarily the case in our constellation. The party possessing a particular piece of information would have to incur considerable costs in finding out how the person interested in this information will use it. Setting aside all problems involved in calculating the value of a given right, if she values her right at $25, while it is worth $23 to the market participant, the right will end up in her hands. Regardless of whether she initially holds that right, she should eventually acquire it. This would not be the case, however, if she were to incur transaction costs of $6. In that case, the final arrangement would be influenced by the initial allocation. Assuming that the market participant holds the right initially, he would keep it, because it would cost the other person $31 to acquire her right, which she would not consider worthwhile. On the other hand, if she is the initial holder of the right, it will remain in her hands because the market participant would not value it highly enough. In the opposite situation, in which the other person values the right less highly ($23) than she does ($25), the efficient[41] arrangement (allocation to her) might not be made because of the transaction costs for her in the amount of $6. Transaction costs, therefore, render the initial allocation of the right highly relevant. And they cannot be overlooked, despite the relative ease with which electronic communications and the Internet provide communication.

But even if we ignore transaction costs, if the initial allocation of the property right in the information does not matter according to the Coase theorem, we might just allocate it to the private party as well. The market participant does

---

[37] I use the term property right here in its economic sense, which is broader than its legal connotation. For an elaboration of this concept, see, for example, H. Demsetz, "Toward a Theory of Property Rights" (1967) 57 *Am. Econ. Rev.* 347. According to Demsetz, an owner of property rights possesses the consent of his fellows to allow him to act in particular ways. "These rights convey the right to benefit or harm oneself or others": *ibid.*, at 347.

[38] See R. Coase, "The Problem of Social Cost" (1960) 3 *J L & Econ.* 1.

[39] *Ibid.*, at 15.

[40] Coase was, of course, aware of this caveat. See *ibid.*, at 15.

[41] I understand the term efficiency here in the sense of the Kaldor-Hicks concept, according to which the winners of the transaction could compensate the loser, whether or not they actually do so. See, for example, Posner, *supra* n.23, at 14.

not have to worry, because he will acquire the right in the end anyway. And with respect to private information, I have an intuition (well, moralism), which, for economists, might possibly be irrational, that the right to make use of personal information is more closely related to the person concerned by it than to the person trying to exploit it, and we should therefore allocate the right to this information to the former before others can make harmful use of that information. I consider this person to be typically in the best position to balance her interests in disclosing or keeping certain pieces of information to herself.

(b) *Application in Practice*

What does the principle of self-determination mean in concrete terms? First of all, individuals should have the right to receive detailed information about the exact purposes for which data on them are being collected. The data—absent the individual's express consent—may then be used only for these purposes. Data storage has to conform to certain minimum technical standards in order to prevent it from being too easily accessible to third parties. Recent events, such as the spreading of the infamous "I LOVE YOU" virus have proven that it is next to impossible to achieve 100 per cent safety against the ingenuity of canny hackers. But compliance with certain minimum requirements does not seem too demanding a standard. These standards could be developed under the auspices of international organisations such as the International Organisation for Standardisation.[42]

Self-determination also requires the customer's express consent to the disclosure and sale of data, not merely an opting-out model. If the individual is to bear the burden of demanding that data collection and transfers be limited, privacy will often suffer from oversight and inertia. Thus, in an opt-out model, self-determination would often be a legal fiction. The principle of self-determination leaves it in the hands of the person concerned to protect his privacy. In order to permit a rational balancing process, an opt-in model is preferable.

2. The principle of proportionality

The second pillar of regulation of privacy protection would be a criterion that one could describe as a principle of proportionality. It would be central to allowing the balancing of the information needs of the market participant and the individual's interest in privacy. Under German constitutional law, the principle of proportionality requires that the infringement of a right be appropriate for achieving the purpose of the act in question, that it not infringe upon the right more than necessary for achieving this purpose, and that the infringement not be completely disproportionate to the advantage obtained by the infringing party.[43] Unless the parties expressly agree to different rules, the following could be an outline for concrete rules.

[42] See *supra* n.26.
[43] See, for example, the *Census* decision, *supra* n.4, at 46.

The first criterion would require that the collection of data be justified from a business perspective in the context of the particular legal transaction and not be motivated only by the desire to sell that information to third parties.

Secondly, the invasion of privacy should be as minimal as possible. Take as an example a bank that is interested in estimating the default risk of a customer who has incurred a current account deficit in the event of his death. The bank has two possible means of conducting this estimation. It could require the customer to disclose his medical history in a detailed manner. It could, however, also require him to insure against this risk. Usually this type of insurance is available for a nominal amount. The requirement of insurance would most likely be the lesser invasion of the debtor's privacy and would thus be the preferable alternative.

The degree of invasion of privacy can also be reduced by collecting and storing data in an anonymous manner, provided that this solution serves the business purpose equally well, is feasible, and does not jeopardise the goal of ascertaining this information in the first place. Anonymous collection and storing of data can also reduce the risk of third parties illegally obtaining those data. This criterion also has a time factor. Often, data do not serve a particular purpose after the passage of a certain amount of time. Therefore, an obligation to delete this type of information after its storage has lost its business justification would also serve the principle of proportionality. There is, for example, no need for telephone companies to keep records of telephone connections if the telephone bill has been fully paid and if there is nothing to indicate any future dispute between the parties.

Thirdly, the invasion of privacy would be disproportionate if the company were to require disclosure of very intimate data in order to reach a relatively unimportant goal. In the abovementioned example of the bank, the requirement to disclose one's medical records in order to permit a better estimate of the default risk would probably be disproportionate if those medical records could contribute only very little to evaluating the size of the risk. That is likely to be the case with respect to a current account deficit, but not in the case of life insurance, where much larger amounts are usually at stake.

These comments are intended only to provide examples of how the principles of self-determination and proportionality could be translated into concrete criteria and measures that could contribute to solving the clash between privacy and countervailing interests in a way that gives due consideration to all values involved. They obviously do not exhaust the problem.

V. CONCLUSION

Over the last few years, we have witnessed a digital revolution that has fundamentally changed data processing mechanisms and the availability of vast amounts of information about every individual. This is cause for grave concern for anyone who considers privacy a value worthy of protection, which, I think, those who adhere to the philosophical and legal tradition of democracies usually do. Self-regulation does not provide sufficient means for coping with this development. To be sure, there is no perfect means of protecting privacy on the Internet. But in order to avoid massive violations of privacy rights and to allow further expansion of the Internet, certain legal minimum standards in privacy protection, complemented by controlled self-regulation, should guarantee that people can continue to make use of the Internet without fear of massive violations of their rights. Self-determination and proportionality should be the guiding principles in structuring a comprehensive system of privacy protection, while at the same time, allowing consideration for countervailing interests such as freedom of speech and the right to free exercise of one's profession.

Index